HISTORY OF
CLASSICAL SCHOLARSHIP

HISTORY OF
CLASSICAL
SCHOLARSHIP

FROM THE BEGINNINGS TO
THE END OF
THE HELLENISTIC AGE

RUDOLF PFEIFFER

OXFORD
AT THE CLARENDON PRESS

Oxford University Press, Great Clarendon Street, Oxford OX2 6DP

Oxford New York

Athens Auckland Bangkok Bogota Bombay
Buenos Aires Calcutta Cape Town Dar es Salaam
Delhi Florence Hong Kong Istanbul Karachi
Kuala Lumpur Madras Madrid Melbourne
Mexico City Nairobi Paris Singapore
Taipei Tokyo Toronto Warsaw
and associated companies in
Berlin Ibadan

Oxford is a trade mark of Oxford University Press

Published in the United States by
Oxford University Press Inc., New York

British Library Cataloguing in Publication Data
Data available

ISBN 0-19-814342-7

1 3 5 7 9 10 8 6 4 2

Printed in Great Britain
on acid-free paper by
Bookcraft (Bath) Ltd.,
Midsomer Norton

VXORI CARISSIMAE SACRVM

PREFACE

An enterprise like this *History* though adventurous and lengthy needs only a brief and modest prologue. For the undertaking as a whole must justify itself without introductory recommendations and preparatory arguments; apologies for its deficiencies would have no end.

Nobody will deny to scholarship, whether in its highest or in its humblest form, its own right, and as long as one carries on the daily work of interpretation, of textual criticism, of historical reconstruction one may expect approval; but to turn from that activity to reflection upon the past of scholarship and upon the scholars of bygone days may be deemed inopportune and unnecessary. Yet, if such scepticism is by any means to be converted, it will surely be by confrontation with the very facts of history; and to make the important facts visible in their historical perspective is precisely our purpose. For it was in the course of time and the succession of peoples and generations that the full nature and the many forms of scholarship were revealed. The history of classical scholarship, therefore, is classical scholarship in the making. And a book reconstructing its history under this aspect can claim to be regarded as an integral part of scholarship itself. We say 'important facts', because it is obvious that we do not want to know what is obsolete and past for ever, but what is still enduring; we want to explore the continuity of knowledge, the *philologia perennis*.

This continuity was maintained not only by the intellectual power of great scholars, but equally by their moral principles of absolute honesty and unremitting patience in the pursuit of truth. In deference to these principles I have made it my task to collect and interpret as far as possible all the primary evidence from the original sources; the most relevant passages will be found in the text, not in the notes. For that and other reasons this is hardly a bedside book about the lives and works of scholars, enlivened with anecdotes and jokes. Biographical data, though by no means disregarded, are confined within proper limits. I have inevitably been able to give only a small selection of modern secondary literature, and I may often have been at fault in selecting the wrong references; but I am not quite ignorant of all the books which I have not quoted. Furthermore, I have not attempted in every case to picture what dons call the 'background', but only when the general ideas and events of the time exercised a strong influence on scholars or even changed the course of scholarship.

A history of scholarship should draw attention to what was new and fruitful, distinguish error from truth, and the opinion of the passing day from that true knowledge which lasts for ever, that is, as we said, 'perennial'. But the dearth of preparatory studies of single problems, based on full documentary evidence, is an obstacle to the achievement of such an ambitious goal. I shall sound a warning whenever I feel completely incompetent; and as I used the epithet 'adventurous' in the first sentence of this preface, I sincerely hope the book will be understood and accepted in this light.

There have, of course, been earlier attempts in this field since the days of Henri Étienne who wrote in 1587 *De criticis veteribus Graecis et Latinis*. But only *one* really comprehensive book exists: J. E. Sandys, *A History of Classical Scholarship*, in three volumes of 1,629 pages. Admiration is mixed with envy when one learns from Sandys's biographer[1] that he started to write the *History* on 1 January 1900, had the first volume published by the Cambridge University Press in 1903 (second edition 1906, third edition 1921) and the second and third volumes in 1908; the three volumes were reprinted in Boston in 1958. Even though out of date in many respects, this standard work will always remain an indispensable reference book, and no subsequent writer on the same subject can fail to be grateful for the range and thoroughness of its material. But, as a whole, Sandys's work is rather a catalogue of classical scholars, century by century, nation by nation, and book by book than a real history of scholarship itself; there is no leading idea, no coherent structure, no sober discrimination between the transient and the perennial. G. Funaioli, 'Lineamenti d'una storia della filologia attraverso i secoli',[2] is much more compressed even than Sandys's *Short History*, but the material is presented in a lively personal style. A. Gudeman's *Outlines of the History of Classical Scholarship* (last edition Boston 1902), much enlarged in the German edition *Grundriss der Geschichte der klassischen Philologie* (1909 2nd edition) is only bibliographical; brought up to date and pruned of its inaccuracies, it could be a useful tool for further research.

Besides these factual surveys there are a few sketches by great scholars which are strong just where we found Sandys wanting: they convey general ideas, are discriminating, suggestive, stimulating. A. Böckh,

[1] N. G. L. Hammond, *Sir John E. Sandys (1844–1922)* Cambridge 1935, pp. 80 ff. Sandys compressed the subject-matter of his monumental work into one volume for the classical student and the general reader in his *Short History of Classical Scholarship*, 1915.
[2] *Studi di Letteratura antica* I (1948) 185–364.

who was a classical scholar, a profound philosopher, and a far-sighted historian as well, gave a very noble sketch in a few pages of his *Enzyklopädie und Methodologie der philologischen Wissenschaften* (published after his death, second edition 1886, pp. 300–9). A quite individual and brilliant survey was contributed by Wilamowitz in 1921 to the *Einleitung in die Altertumswissenschaft*, 'Geschichte der Philologie' (third edition 1927, reprinted 1960); it is a very subjective review of classical scholars made by a great master who calls up the dead heroes of the past from the other world and praises or blames them. Wilamowitz acknowledged a debt to the lectures of Otto Jahn; but he seems to have written a good deal of his *History* from memory, a stupendous but not unfailing memory. So still more weight should be given to the sections devoted to ancient and modern scholars in his many books on Greek authors than to this brief general account of eighty pages.

I cannot refrain—*pace* Wilamowitz—from mentioning Friedrich Nietzsche, Ritschl's favourite pupil, in this connexion; at the age of twenty-four he seriously considered writing 'Eine Geschichte der literarischen Studien im Altertum und in der Neuzeit'. He wanted to find out the general ideas that had influenced the study of antiquity and to demonstrate the links between classical scholarship and the dominant philosophy of every age. There are some remarkable notes on this subject[1] in his letters and papers between 1867 and 1871, but, of course, he did not work it out, but made his way towards his own fatal philosophy. About the same time an English classical scholar who had his own ideas about scholarship and the functions of a university, Mark Pattison, conceived the plan of writing the history of learning from the Renaissance onwards.[2] In the end he completed only fragments; but, in spite of his well-known religious bias, these fragments, especially on the great French scholars of the sixteenth and seventeenth centuries, are exemplary, because his studies in detail are always informed by an awareness of the history of scholarship as a whole. In our own days no one has devoted and is devoting more thought and labour to historical problems of classical studies than Arnaldo Momigliano. Though his emphasis is, of course, on the study of ancient history and most of his contributions deal with scholars and writings of modern times, the universal range of the author's ideas and knowledge justifies the title of his collected essays: *Contributo alla storia degli studi classici*.[3]

[1] F. Nietzsche, *Werke und Briefe, Historisch-kritische Gesamtausgabe; Werke* 1 (1934) pp. cxx f., 3 (1935) 319 ff., 440 with references to manuscripts and earlier editions.

[2] *Memoirs* (1885) 319 ff. *Essays* (1889) on the Stephani, Scaliger, etc.

[3] 1 (1955), 11 (1960); see esp. 11 463–80 'L'eredità della filologia antica e il metodo storico'

This is a personal selection of books which I have found not only instructive, but inspiring; lectures, speeches, and papers are excluded.

The present volume is concerned with the foundations laid by Greek poets and scholars in the last three centuries B.C. for the whole future of classical scholarship. It starts with a brief survey of the pre-Hellenistic ages in Greece and a few hints at the oriental background. But then full use is made of the available evidence, especially that of the papyri, to demonstrate the fresh start made by Hellenistic poets after 300 B.C. and to describe the essential achievements of five generations of creative scholars in Alexandria and of their epigoni down to the age of Augustus. By the singular courtesy of Mr. P. M. Fraser I was allowed to read parts of his forthcoming comprehensive work on *Ptolemaic Alexandria* in typescript; I thank him most warmly for this privilege which has saved me from a variety of errors.

The Alexandrian scholar poets are our ancestors, and we should at least try not to be unworthy of this noble ancestry. 'The historian must become old in order to develop his art to the full' is one of Ranke's maxims; this is particularly true of the historian of scholarship. Only one who has practised scholarship all his life should dare to write about its history. As soon as the second volume of Callimachus was published in 1953 by the Clarendon Press, I submitted to the Delegates a proposal for a *History of Classical Scholarship*.

'De non interrumpendo per aetatem studio' is the subject of one of Petrarch's latest and most sympathetic 'Lettere senili'.[1] Boccaccio was worried about Petrarch's continuously working too much for his age; but his old friend and master replied that there is no reason to abandon study because of old age, and reminded him of the saying of Ecclesiasticus 18. 6: 'Cum consummaverit homo tunc incipiet.' I have at least attempted to take this advice and shall always be deeply grateful that the Delegates immediately and graciously responded to my appeal. But I advanced only 'testudineo gradu', until I could retire to work in a sort of *clausura* and obtained the necessary secretarial help. I was very fortunate to find the assistance of a young classical scholar, Mr. S. E. Arnold, who is now, while preparing his doctorate, in the service of the Bavarian State Library; indefatigable and efficient, he helped me in many ways: arranging the vast amount of material collected through decades, making a careful typescript, and checking the innumerable

(with bibliography). A third volume of the *Contributi* and the publication of the *Sather Classical Lectures* of 1961 are in prospect.

[1] *Rer. sen. libr.* XVII 2; reprinted in Petrarca 'Prose', *La Letteratura Italiana, Storia e Testi* 7 (1955) 1156.

references. The Bayerische Akademie der Wissenschaften and the British Academy were kind enough to vote me annual grants towards the considerable expenses arising from this permanent assistance. Three Munich libraries, the Bavarian State Library, the University Library, and the Library of the Seminar für klassische Philologie, as well as the Bodleian Library during my annual visits to Oxford, were liberal in granting me every facility. It is impossible to mention by name the many Oxford and Munich friends from whose discussions I have profited through all these years; but there is one to whom I owe more than can be expressed by words, Eduard Fraenkel. Everyone who is familiar with his books and reviews knows how intimately he is acquainted with the scholarly tradition; generous with advice whenever asked for it, he was also a constant driving force behind the scenes.

The draft of every chapter was read by Mr. J. K. Cordy of the Clarendon Press. With unfailing patience and courtesy he smoothed out or, more often, reshaped my English; for this competent and generous help he deserves the profound gratitude of the author and of the reader. I am indebted to the skill and vigilance of the Printers, especially of the Reader, and in the reading of the proofs I enjoyed the help of an experienced scholar, my colleague Professor Max Treu, and, during his absence in Greece, of my pupil Dr. Rudolf Führer. I started this section of the preface with my thanks to the Delegates of the Clarendon Press; I finish it with my particular thanks to the Secretary to the Delegates, Mr. C. H. Roberts, for his encouraging interest and persistent support.

My first publication in 1914 bears the dedication 'Uxori carissimae sacrum'. I renew the words of the dedication with still deeper feeling for all that she has done for me in the course of more than half a century.

CONTENTS

PART ONE
PREHISTORY OF GREEK SCHOLARSHIP

Contents

PART TWO

THE HELLENISTIC AGE

colometry and strophic structure. Hypotheses to his text of tragedies and
comedies. Great lexicographical studies, based on his own editions, and
formal grammatical inquiries, ancillary to his editorial work. Selective
list of the foremost authors.

Callistratus and other Ἀριστοφάνειοι. Aristarchus, the Ptolemies, the great
crisis of 145/4 B.C. Running commentaries and monographs on Greek poetry
from Homer to Aristophanes, also critical editions of the Homeric and
other poems; critical signs the link between text and commentary. The
first commentary on prose writers, Herodotus and possibly Thucydides.
No authentic maxim of Aristarchus on the principle of interpretation.
General grammatical and metrical observations in the course of the
exegetical work. Literary criticism.

The Attalids and the cultural life of Pergamum; library, parchment.
Crates of Mallos, Stoic allegorist and cosmologist; two monographs on
Homer; opposition to Aristarchus. The definite place of linguistic
studies in the system of Stoic philosophy; grammatical rules and terms
strictly fixed. Crates' mission to Rome in 168 B.C. Writers on antiquities:
Antigonus of Carystus, Polemo of Ilium, called στηλοκόπας, Demetrius of Scepsis.

Dissemination and renewal of scholarship in the whole Greek world after
the Alexandrian crisis of 145/4 B.C. Apollodorus of Athens: Chronicle in
iambic verse, new system of dating; monograph on the Homeric Catalogue
of Ships a description of heroic Greece with explication of local names;
books 'On Gods' a study of Homeric religion with analysis of proper
names; minor works on Attic and Doric comedy and on mimes.
   Dionysius Thrax, teacher at Rhodes; influence on Rome. Interpretation
of Homer, other commentaries and treatises. The problem of the Τέχνη
γραμματική under his name: its authenticity and its arrangement in the
Byzantine manuscripts. Technical grammar the latest achievement of
Hellenistic scholarship. Tyrannion of Amisos, Asclepiades of Myrlea,
Philoxenus of Alexandria; their grammatical writings, their relations to
Rome. Didymus of Alexandria compiler of commentaries on Greek poets,
historians, and orators and of comic and tragic lexica; moved by love of
learning to preserve the scholarly heritage of the Hellenistic age.

ABBREVIATIONS

AG	*Anecdota Graeca* (Bachmann, Bekker, Boissonade).
AGGW	*Abhandlungen der Göttinger Gesellschaft der Wissenschaften.*
AJA	*American Journal of Archaeology.*
AJP	*American Journal of Philology.*
AL(G)	*Anthologia Lyrica (Graeca)*, ed. E. Diehl, 1925 ff.
APF	*Archiv für Papyrusforschung.*
Barwick, *Stoische Sprachlehre*	K. Barwick, 'Probleme der stoischen Sprachlehre und Rhetorik', *Abh. d. Sächs. Akad. d. Wissenschaften zu Leipzig, Phil.-hist. Kl.* 49. 3 (1957).
BCH	*Bulletin de Correspondance Hellénique.*
Bursian	*Bursians Jahresbericht über die Fortschritte der klass. Altertumswissenschaft.*
Call.	Callimachus I, II, ed. R. Pfeiffer, 1949–53 (repr. 1965/6).
CGF	*Comicorum Graecorum Fragmenta* I, ed. G. Kaibel, 1899.
Cl. Phil.	*Classical Philology.*
Cl. Qu.	*Classical Quarterly.*
Cl.R.	*Classical Review.*
CMG	*Corpus medicorum Graecorum.*
DLZ	*Deutsche Literaturzeitung.*
DMG	*Deutsche Morgenländische Gesellschaft.*
Düring, 'Aristotle'	I. Düring, 'Aristotle in the ancient biographical tradition', *Studia Graeca et Latina Gothoburgensia* v (1957).
FGrHist.	*Die Fragmente der griechischen Historiker*, von F. Jacoby, 1923 ff.
FHG	*Fragmenta Historicorum Graecorum*, ed. C. Müller, 1841 ff.
GGA	*Göttingische Gelehrte Anzeigen.*
GGM	*Geographi Graeci minores*, ed. C. Müller, 1855 ff.
GGN	*Nachrichten der Gesellschaft der Wissenschaften zu Göttingen.*
GL	*Grammatici Latini*, ed. H. Keil, 1855 ff.
GRF	*Grammaticae Romanae Fragmenta*, rec. H. Funaioli, I (1907, repr. 1964).
Gr. Gr.	*Grammatici Graeci*, 1878–1910 (repr. 1965).
JHS	*Journal of Hellenic Studies.*
Kenyon, *Books and Readers*	F. G. Kenyon, *Books and Readers in ancient Greece and Rome*, 2nd ed. (1951).
L-S	H. G. Liddell and R. Scott, *Greek–English Lexicon.* New edition by H. Stuart Jones, 1925–40.
Marrou	H.-I. Marrou, *A History of Education*, translated by G. R. Lamb (1956).
NJb.	*Neue Jahrbücher für das klass. Altertum.*
Pack[2]	R. A. Pack, *The Greek and Latin literary texts from Greco-Roman Egypt*, second revised and enlarged edition 1965.
Pasquali, *Storia*	G. Pasquali, *Storia della tradizione e critica del testo* (1934, repr. 1952).
PLG[4]	*Poetae Lyrici Graeci*, quartum ed. Th. Bergk, 1882.
PMG	*Poetae Melici Graeci*, ed. D. L. Page, 1962.
P.Oxy.	*Oxyrhynchus Papyri.*

PRIMI	*Papiri della R. Università di Milano*, vol. I, ed. A. Vogliano, 1937.
PSI	*Papiri della Società Italiana.*
RE	Paulys *Real-Enzyklopädie der klassischen Altertumswissenschaft*, hg. v. Wissowa–Kroll–Mittelhaus, 1894 ff.
Rh.M.	*Rheinisches Museum für Philologie.*
Rutherford, 'Annotation'	W. G. Rutherford, 'A Chapter in the History of Annotation', *Scholia Aristophanica*, III (1905).
Sandys i³	J. E. Sandys, *A History of Classical Scholarship*, I. 3, ed. 1921.
SB	*Sitzungsberichte (Berl. Akad., Bayer. Akad.*, etc.).
Schmidt, 'Pinakes'	F. Schmidt, 'Die Pinakes des Kallimachos', *Klass.-philol. Studien* I (1922).
SIG³	*Sylloge Inscriptionum Graecarum*, ed. W. Dittenberger, ed. tertia, 1915–24.
Steinthal	H. Steinthal, *Geschichte der Sprachwissenschaft bei den Griechen und Römern mit besonderer Rücksicht auf die Logik*, 2 vols. 2. Aufl. 1890 (repr. 1961).
Susemihl	F. Susemihl, *Geschichte der griechischen Literatur in der Alexandrinerzeit*, 2 vols., 1891/2.
SVF	*Stoicorum Veterum Fragmenta*, ed. I. de Arnim, 1905 ff.
TAPA	*Transactions of the American Philological Association.*
TGF²	*Tragicorum Graecorum Fragmenta*, ed. A. Nauck, 2. ed., 1889.
Vors.	*Die Fragmente der Vorsokratiker*, von H. Diels. 6. Aufl. hg. v. W. Kranz, 1951–2.
Wendel, 'Buchbeschreibung'	C. Wendel, 'Die griechisch-römische Buchbeschreibung verglichen mit der des vorderen Orients', *Hallische Monographien* 3 (1949).
W.St.	*Wiener Studien.*

PART ONE

PREHISTORY OF
GREEK
SCHOLARSHIP

I

POETS, RHAPSODES, PHILOSOPHERS
FROM THE EIGHTH
TO THE FIFTH CENTURIES

SCHOLARSHIP is the art of understanding, explaining, and restoring the literary tradition. It originated as a separate intellectual discipline in the third century before Christ through the efforts of poets to preserve and to use their literary heritage, the 'classics'. So scholarship actually arose as 'classical' scholarship.

At least three centuries had prepared the way, and their contribution should not be minimized. On the contrary, there had been very important attempts at studying the language, collecting learned material, and applying some form of literary criticism. But all these efforts belong to the history of poetry, historiography, philosophy, or pedagogy. It was only when the new Hellenistic civilization changed the whole perspective in this field as in others that these various activities, formerly disconnected, were united into one selfconscious discipline. In this sense the history of classical scholarship does not start before the third century.[1] The particular point I am attempting to make is this: a novel conception of poetry held by the poets themselves led the way to the scholarly treatment of the ancient texts; devotion to pure learning came later.

Nevertheless, a short survey of the preliminary stages is indispensable; the early Greek forerunners of the Hellenistic scholars must be carefully considered.

The epic poets were inspired by the Muses, and the poet who created the main part of our *Iliad* is the greatest poet of all time. It has often been said that Homer must be his own interpreter; this is true also in a quite specific sense. He not only created but again and again 'interpreted' his own powerful language in the course of his poem. Thus the earliest Greek poetry that we know included a sort of 'philological element'; poetry itself paved the way to its understanding. This is of signal importance for the origin and development of scholarship (as we shall see later on).[2] On

---

[1] See below, pp. 88 ff.   [2] See below, pp. 140 and 149.

the other hand, one should not speak of 'Homer as a philologist'.[1] When epic poets themselves add elucidating words, half-lines, lines to ambiguous expressions, or to proper names, this may be due to a desire to make themselves clear, but no less to pleasure in playing on words, to delight in similarity of sound. It is certainly a genuine part of their traditional poetical technique, not a combination of learning and poetry.

The poet of our *Odyssey* asked the Muse: 'Of the man tell me, Muse, of the man much turned that roved very many ways' ἄνδρα μοι ἔννεπε, Μοῦσα, πολύτροπον ὃς μάλα πολλά / πλάγχθη. The attribute to ἄνδρα is so to speak 'explained' by the following relative sentence:[2] it does not mean the man of versatile mind (versutum, πολύμητιν, πολυμήχανον), but one of many moves, πολλὰς τροπὰς ἔχοντα (versatum, πολύπλαγκτον). The ambiguous sense of πολύτροπος (cf. *K* 330) is much discussed in ancient and modern times.[3] The proem of the *Odyssey* is dependent on the opening lines of the *Iliad*; there μῆνιν... οὐλομένην is followed by ἣ μυρί᾽ Ἀχαιοῖς ἄλγε᾽ ἔθηκε 'the accursed wrath that set countless woes on the Achaeans', and the exact parallel of the whole structure shows that the relative sentence is meant to be a defining one in the *Odyssey* as well.[4]

The sound of the ancient names of gods and heroes not only delighted the ear of the epic poet, but also reminded him of similar sounds in familiar words: many assonances and even 'etymologies' were the result.[5] The most famous example is 'Odysseus' in which one could hear ὀδύρομαι (α 55, etc.) as well as ὀδύσσομαι (α 62, cf. τ 407–9 and Soph. fr. 965 P.); so the very name hinted at the lamentable fate of the πολύτλας or at the 'man of wrath'. Later epic poets took the same line: Hesiod[6] in the proem of his *Works and Days* praised Zeus, δεῦτε Δία ἐννέπετε ... ὅν τε διὰ βροτοὶ ἄνδρες (*Op.* 2 f.), where the repeated ΔΙΑ in the same place of the hexameter sounded apparently not playful, but solemn. Hesiod was followed by Aeschylus in a hieratic lyric passage, *Ag.* 1485 ff.: ἰὼ ἰή, διαὶ Διὸς παναιτίου πανεργέτα· τί γὰρ βροτοῖς ἄνευ Διὸς τελεῖται; Aeschylus also

---

[1] L. Ph. Rank, *Etymologiseerung en verwante Verschijnselen bij Homerus* (Diss. Utrecht 1951) 74–100 'Homerus als philoloog'. (With bibliography; cf. esp. the very useful collection of evidence.)

[2] See also Rank pp. 78 f.

[3] From Antisthenes on (Schol. α 1, p. 9. 16 Dind.); see below, p. 37.

[4] Similar 'epexegetical' clauses α 299 f., γ 383, λ 490 and in the *Iliad, passim*. On other 'explanatory lines' see J. Forsdyke, *Greece before Homer* (1956) 26.

[5] About fifty names in *Iliad* and *Odyssey*, see Rank 35 ff. A list of etymologies and puns from Homer to Aeschylus in O. Lendle, *Die Pandorasage bei Hesiod* (Diss. Marburg 1953, publ. Würzburg 1957) 117–21.

[6] E. Risch, 'Namensdeutungen und Worterklärungen bei den ältesten griechischen Dichtern', *Eumusia, Festgabe für E. Howald* (Zürich 1947) 72 ff.: in Hesiod such 'etymologies' are not later additions, but genuine; p. 89, differences between 'Homer' and Hesiod.

derived another form of Zeus' name from ζῆν¹: φυσιζόου γένος τόδε /
Ζηνός ἐστιν ἀληθῶς 'this (Epaphus) is the offspring of the life-producing
Zeus in truth' (*Suppl.* 584), anticipating a learned 'etymology' wide-
spread in the fourth and third centuries.²

Besides such epexegetical and etymological elements there seems to be
also a very old 'allegorical' element in epic poetry. This occurs in the
unique Λιταί-passage in *Iliad I* 502 ff.;³ here we have no simple personi-
fication of the 'Prayers', the daughters of Zeus, as the epithets in *I* 503
clearly show: Λιταί . . . Διὸς κοῦραι μεγάλοιο / χωλαί τε ῥυσαί τε παρα-
βλῶπές τ' ὀφθαλμώ. Ancient and modern interpreters have rightly seen
that these epithets, actually picturing the attitude of the penitent,⁴ are
transferred to the 'Prayers'. The Λιταί-passage should not be termed an
αἶνος;⁵ this always means a fictitious *story* which has its special significance
in the present circumstances, as in *Odyssey* o 508. But no story is told
about the Λιταί. One can hardly deny that it is a genuine allegory;
Archilochus and Alcaeus followed in this line. When rhapsodes of the
sixth century started to detect 'hidden meanings' in many parts of the
Homeric poems,⁶ they were only developing, in this as in other fields,
something which the imagination of a great poet had once created.

By the end of the eighth century B.C. the *Iliad* and *Odyssey* were substantially complete. They were composed in a common Greek language;
and on the basis, so to speak, of this epic poetry as a priceless popular
possession the whole Greek people, the Πανέλληνες, began to feel its
unity in spite of all the differences of race and class and in spite of the
changing political and social conditions. So we may understand how
the rhapsodes were able to continue their successful activity throughout
the Greek world also beyond the 'epic age'. They had, as before, some
difficulty with old and rare single words or strange combinations of them;
they, therefore, sometimes altered their original form and even gave
them a new meaning. This reshaping may appear to the modern mind
quite arbitrary or even mistaken; yet it can be regarded as an early

---

¹ *Sitz. Ber. Bay. Akad.* 1938, H. 2, p. 9. 2; cf. E. Fraenkel, Aesch. Ag. (1950) on l. 1485,
and in general on l. 687.
² Plat. *Crat.* 396 B δι' ὃν ζῆν . . . ὑπάρχει.—The Platonic Socrates seems to have been the
first to get away from the traditional playing with similarities of sound; see C. J. Classen,
'Sprachliche Deutung als Triebkraft platonischen und sokratischen Philosophierens', *Zetemata* 22 (1959) esp. 127 ff., cf. below, pp. 61 f.
³ On the structure of *Iliad* 9 and its position in the whole of our *Iliad* see *DLZ* 1935, 2129 ff.
On its allegorical character see Leaf ad loc. and E. R. Dodds, *The Greeks and the Irrational*
(1951), 6; K. Reinhardt, 'Personifikation und Allegorie' in *Vermächtnis der Antike* (1960) 37 f.
⁴ [Heraclit.] *Quaest. Homer.* c. 37, ed. Bonn., p. 54. 7 = ed. Buffière (1962) p. 44.
⁵ As Reinhardt is inclined to do, loc. cit.
⁶ See below, pp. 10 f.

attempt at interpreting the traditional text.¹ But there must have been a limit beyond which the rhapsodes were no longer free to make their own additions or to reshape the epic texts.

We may assume that Greeks living in the first half of the sixth century, if not earlier, regarded the creative period of epic poetry as concluded. But there is no reliable tradition, let alone conclusive evidence,² of a collection of epic poems, or about a constitution of the text of the *Iliad* and *Odyssey* at that time in any particular place. The endless discussion of possibilities and probabilities belongs to the history of scholarship in post-classical antiquity and still more in our modern age. We shall have the opportunity of dealing with these questions, when we come to those periods.

Here we have only to state the well-known fact that the story that Peisistratus 'assembled' the formerly 'scattered' songs of Homer cannot be traced back beyond the first century B.C.³ Not only in the later embroideries, but in the whole conception of a powerful statesman as a collector of literary texts, as the earliest founder of a Greek 'library', as head of a committee of scholars, we seem to have a projection of events of the Ptolemaic age into the sixth century. Yet in modern times, from d'Aubignac⁴ and Bentley to Lachmann, that late ancient tradition was regarded as trustworthy. In 1838 Ritschl⁵ even went so far as to interpolate into the obviously defective text of the Megarian historian Dieuchidas (quoted by Diog. L. 1 57) a phrase describing Peisistratus as 'compiler of the Homeric poems' ⟨ὅσπερ συλλέξας τὰ ʿΟμήρου κτλ.⟩. But the Megarian historians, Dieuchidas⁶ as well as Hereas,⁷ spoke only

---

¹ M. Leumann, 'Homerische Wörter', *Schweizerische Beiträge zur Altertumswissenschaft* 3 (1950) *passim*, esp. 157–261 and 323; see below, pp. 12 and 79.

² See below, p. 25.

³ Cic. *de or.* III 137 'qui primus Homeri libros confusos antea sic disposuisse dicitur, ut nunc habemus'; Cicero's source was possibly Asclepiades of Myrlea Περὶ γραμματικῶν, see G. Kaibel, 'Die Prolegomena Περὶ κωμῳδίας, *AGGW* Phil.-hist. Kl. N.F. II 4 (1898) 26 and on Asclepiades see below, p. 273. *Adesp. AP* XI 442 Πεισίστρατον ὃς τὸν ʿΟμηρον / ἤθροισα σποράδην τὸ πρὶν ἀειδόμενον. The testimonia again printed by R. Merkelbach, *Rh.M.* 95 (1952) 23 ff., and J. A. Davison, *TAPA* 86 (1955) 1 ff. Cf. Dorothea Gray in John L. Myres, *Homer and his Critics* (1958) 290 ff.

⁴ *Dissertation sur l'Iliade*, ed. V. Magnien (Paris 1925) 46 f. 'La composition de Pisistrate: elle est reçue parmi les savants comme certaine, et donne un grand poids à l'opinion que j'ai mise en avant.' W. Schmid, *Geschichte der griechischen Literatur* 1 1 (1929) 161, gives a wrong reference to d'Aubignac.

⁵ *Die Alexandrinischen Bibliotheken unter den ersten Ptolemaeern und die Sammlung der homerischen Gedichte durch Pisistratus nach Anleitung eines Plautinischen Scholions* (reprinted in *Opusc. Philol.* 1 (1866) 54); on the so-called 'Scholion Plautinum' see below, p. 100. Leaf's supplement is equally misleading (Homer, *Iliad* I² (1900) xviii, taken over with a slight alteration by Merkelbach p. 29).

⁶ *FGrHist* 485 F 6, vol. III B p. 450, *Kommentar* I 392, II 232.

⁷ Ibid. 486.

about some lines of Homer which they regarded as interpolations inserted against Megarian interests by Athenians, either Solon or Peisistratus. There is no reference to Peisistratus as a 'collector' in Dieuchidas, nor would the insertion of a few lines in the catalogue parts of *B* (546) and λ (631) be sufficient to prove the existence of an authoritative sixth-century Attic text of Homer. Nevertheless, Ritschl's arbitrary supplement of 1838 and its doubtful consequences were gladly accepted by many scholars,[1] as if it were new evidence from the fourth century, the time of the Megarian chronicle. Soon afterwards (1846), however, George Grote published the first volumes of his *History of Greece* which he had begun to write in the twenties; they contained the first penetrating criticism[2] of the traditional belief in the Peisistratus legend (Part I, ch. 21). Karl Lehrs, one of the earliest German admirers of the eminent historian,[3] continued in this line,[4] using new arguments, and others followed; but towards the end of the nineteenth century a reaction set in,[5] and the controversy is still going on.

It is hardly surprising that Peisistratus, together with Polycrates of Samos, headed the list of Greek book collectors which ends with Ptolemy II; for the excerpt in the epitome of Athenaeus I 3a looks to me rather like such lists of famous founders and inventors as the so called *Laterculi Alexandrini*[6] or the catalogues in *P.Oxy.* x 1241. If Gellius, *N.A.* VII 17, goes back to Varro, *de bibliothecis*,[7] and Isidor. *etym.* VI 3, 3–5 to Suetonius,[8] respectable grammarians credited Peisistratus with being the first founder of a public library in Athens: '*bibliothecam . . . deinceps ab Atheniensibus auctam Xerxes . . . evexit . . . , Seleucus Nicanor* (*sic*; v. *RE* II A 1233) *rursus in Graeciam rettulit. Ptolemaeus . . . cum studio bibliothecarum Pisistratum aemularetur*' etc. (Isidor. loc. cit.). It has recently been argued[9] that the discovery of oriental libraries which included extensive literary texts from the second millennium B.C., and our knowledge of the general cultural policy

---

[1] Still by W. Schmid, *Geschichte der griech. Lit.* I 1 (1929) 160. 6.
[2] See L. Friedländer, *Die homerische Kritik von Wolf bis Grote* (Berlin 1853) 12 ff.; the importance of Grote's attack had been rightly stressed by G. Finsler, *Homer* I 1³ (1924) 109.
[3] *Grote's Geschichte von Griechenland* (1852) = *Populäre Aufsätze*² (1875) 447 ff.
[4] 'Zur homer. Interpolation' *Rh.M.* 17 (1862) 481 ff. = *De Aristarchi studiis Homericis* (2. ed. 1865) 442 ff. (3. ed. 1882, 438 ff.); reference to Grote 440, n. 275.
[5] O. Seeck, *Die Quellen der Odyssee*, 1887 (see Finsler, I 117 f.).
[6] H. Diels, *Abh. Berl. Akad.*, 1904, Abh. 2.
[7] H. Dahlmann, 'Terentius Varro', *RE* Suppl. VI (1935) 1172 ff., esp. 1221.
[8] Sueton. *de vir. ill.* fr. 102, p. 130 R. Cf. Tertull. *apol.* 18. 5, and Hieronym. *ep.* 34. 1.
[9] C. Wendel, 'Buchbeschreibung' 19 f.; G. Zuntz, *The Text of the Epistles, Corpus Paulinum* (London 1953) 270 and *Zeitschrift d. DMG* 101 (1951) 193 ff. considered the possibility that 'Babylonian methods, required to ensure the preservation of works of literature' had early connexions with archaic Greece as well as later influence on Alexandria; cf. below, pp. 103 and 126.

of mighty Greek rulers support this slender tradition. But there is not yet any pre-Alexandrian evidence, and we may still suspect that those early book collectors[1] were inventions modelled on the Hellenistic kings.[2] Considering the whole attitude of early Greeks to the book,[3] the existence of public libraries in the sixth century is unlikely.

However, from all these various and doubtful passages one certain fact seems to emerge: the lively activity of so-called ῥαψῳδοί as reciters of epic poems in the sixth century, often at competitive performances. Some scattered and contradictory references[4] agree in one point: those contests were instituted for the festival of the Panathenaea; and there was a rule that a rhapsode should begin his recitation where the preceding reciter had left off (ἐξ ὑπολήψεως ἐφεξῆς [Plat.] *Hipparch.* 228 B, ἐξ ὑποβολῆς Diog. L. 1 57). For our purpose, it does not matter who laid down such a rule; where the Homeric poems are concerned, the evidence points to the time of the Peisistratids, while a Periclean[5] decree of 442 (Plut. *Per.* 13. 4) seems to refer to a much wider μουσικῆς ἀγών, a contest for all sorts of poetical and musical performances. In the sixth century, therefore, a traditional text must have been available to which the rhapsodes were compelled to keep; they now became the professional reciters of established literary works ascribed to 'Homer'. In the new, the lyric, age these epic poems were acknowledged as 'classical'; and the persons known to have not only recited but also explained and criticized them from their own point of view were again rhapsodes. This fact, though often overlooked, is particularly significant. For it shows that it was poetically gifted or at least poetically minded people, who made the first attempt at interpreting the heritage of the epic age; one may even regard it as a continuation of the earlier self-interpretation of the poets.[6]

It was as a highly estimated rhapsode that Xenophanes of Colophon (born in 565?)[7] wandered through the Greek world from the east to

---

[1] See below, p. 25.

[2] All the evidence is most carefully collected by F. Schmidt, 'Pinakes' 4 ff.: 'Zeugnisse über griechische Bibliotheken', cf. pp. 30 f.—'May be little more than mythical' is the verdict of Kenyon, *Books and Readers* 2nd edition (Oxford 1951) 24.—On Greek and Roman libraries see C. Wendel and W. Göber, 'Das griechisch-römische Altertum' in *Handbuch der Bibliothekswissenschaft*, 2. ed. III 1 (1955) 51–145; cf. Wendel's shorter article 'Bibliothek' in *RAC* II (1954) 231–74, esp. 238–46.

[3] See below, p. 17.

[4] See J. A. Davison, *TAPA* 86 (1955) 7 and *JHS* 78 (1958) 38 f.

[5] H. T. Wade-Gery, *The Poet of the Iliad* (Cambridge 1952) 77, n. 77 to p. 30.

[6] See above, pp. 3 f.

[7] *Vors.* 21 B 8, 4 n.; for Xenophanes as a rhapsode see K. Reinhardt, *Parmenides* (1916) 132 ff. H. Thesleff, *On Dating Xenophanes*, Helsinki 1957, tried to prove that Xenophanes was born about 540 or still later and left Colophon about 515; if this is correct, it lowers the date of Theagenes and others. But it will not be easy to accept Thesleff's arguments.

southern Italy and Sicily. Reciting his own poems (ἀλλὰ καὶ αὐτὸς ἐρραψῴδει τὰ ἑαυτοῦ, *Vors.* 21 A 1), he attacked Homer and Hesiod because they 'had imputed to the gods all that is shame and blame for men' (*Vors.* 21 B 11), '. . . unlawful things: stealing, adultery, deceiving each other' (B 12, cf. 10; 13–16). There is no clear evidence that Xenophanes recited 'Homer', but the possibility can hardly be denied that he began his long career as an itinerant poet and philosopher by reciting 'Homeric' poems; in the course of time he may have recognized that their whole conception of the gods—the pluralism, the anthropomorphism, the morality—was a dangerous error. Every line of Xenophanes' own poems shows how deeply he had been in love with the great poetry of the past and how well he was acquainted with its style and thought.[1] As his older contemporary, the lyric poet Stesichorus of Himera, had 'recanted' his 'Homeric' error about Helen,[2] so Xenophanes, reversing his attitude, vigorously attacked his former idol.[3] It is somewhat paradoxical that the protest of a self-conscious,[4] religious rhapsode should be the starting-point of Homeric criticism in antiquity; it remained the privilege of philosophers[5] to follow his lead and to criticize the way in which Homer presented the gods, until Plato, for this and other reasons expelled him from his ideal city.[6]

On the other hand, the very fact that Homer, 'from whom all men have learned since the beginning' (Xenophan. B 10 ἐξ ἀρχῆς καθ᾽ Ὅμηρον ἐπεὶ μεμαθήκασι πάντες), had been rejected in the sixth century must have induced other rhapsodes to defend him and to find means to maintain his old authority. It is expressly stated that the first of these defenders was Theagenes of Rhegium,[7] during the lifetime of Xenophanes himself.

---

[1] See *Anth. Lyr. Gr.* fasc. 1³ (1949) pp. 63 ff. annotation.

[2] *PMG* fr. 192 ff. = Stesich. 15 f. (two palinodes).

[3] Timon fr. 60. 1 D. called Xenophanes Ὁμηροπάτης 'trampler on Homer', cf. Zoilus Ὁμηρομάστιξ below, p. 70; this parallel seems to support the variant reading Ὁμηροπάτης in Diog. L. IX 18 (-απάτης v.l.), though E. Vogt, *Rh.M.* N.F. 107 (1964) 295 ff., strongly pleads for the genitive Ὁμηραπάτης ἐπικόπτην 'censor of the Homeric deceit' (cf. *Vors.* 21 A 35). Timon, in his parodic style, exaggerated and disfigured Xenophanes' attacks on Homer.

[4] 21 B 2. 12: ἡμετέρη σοφίη, that is, 'our knowledge and practice of poetry'.

[5] Heraclit. *Vors.* 22 A 22, B 42, etc.; on Pythagoras' so-called criticism see H. Schrader's references in Porphyr. *Quaest. Hom. ad Il.* (1880) 383 and *in Od.* (1890) 2. 6. W. Burkert, 'Weisheit und Wissenschaft, Studien zu Pythagoras, Philolaos und Platon', *Erlanger Beiträge zur Sprach- und Kunstwissenschaft* 10 (1962), is perfectly right when he does not refer to any Pythagorean 'interpretation' of Homer, see also p. 258. 13 on the *Odyssey*.

[6] See below, p. 58.

[7] *Vors.* 8 A 1 κατὰ Καμβύσην 529–522 B.C.; 8 A 2 πρῶτος. Cf. F. Buffière, *Les Mythes d'Homère et la pensée grecque* (1956) 103 f., and H. J. Rose, *JHS* 78 (1958) 164 f. P. Lévêque, 'Aurea catena Homeri, Une étude de l'allégorie grecque', *Annales littér. de l'Université de Besançon* 27 (1959).

Porphyry's explanation of the 'Battle of the Gods' quoted in the Scholion to *Iliad* Y 67[1] is obviously derived from a Stoic source and is to be used with the greatest caution; terms like τὸ ἀπρεπές, meaning 'myths about the gods which do not befit their divine nature' (οὐ πρέποντας τοὺς ὑπὲρ τῶν θεῶν μύθους), or ἀλληγορία, the 'hidden meanings' (ὑπόνοιαι) of such myths, are probably Hellenistic; but even so there may be some kernel of truth in the tradition that this kind of 'apology' is very old and began with Theagenes 'who first wrote on Homer' (ἀπὸ Θεαγένους τοῦ Ῥηγίνου, ὃς πρῶτος ἔγραψε περὶ Ὁμήρου). At least in the fourth century, long before allegorism as a method was fully developed by Stoic philosophers, interpretations of the Homeric 'Battle of the Gods' by 'hidden meanings' were known to Plato, who rejected θεομαχίας altogether either ἐν ὑπονοίαις πεποιημένας or ἄνευ ὑπονοιῶν (*Rep.* II 378 D). The philosophical source of the long Scholion to *Iliad* Y 67 sees in the pairing of the gods by the poet the antagonism of three pairs of natural elements, τὸ ξηρὸν τῷ ὑγρῷ καὶ τὸ θερμὸν τῷ ψυχρῷ μάχεσθαι καὶ τὸ κοῦφον τῷ βαρεῖ; furthermore it identifies the divinities with human faculties: Athena with φρόνησις, Ares with ἀφροσύνη, Aphrodite with ἐπιθυμία, and Hermes with λόγος. Such physical allegories would not have been without parallel in the sixth century; in the few fragments of Pherecydes of Syros and in the records about him the divinities represent cosmic forces, and there is a trend to conscious 'allegory' (*Vors.* A 8. 9; B 4 a sort of battle of gods). There is no agreement about the exact date of Pherecydes either among ancient chronographers[2] or among modern scholars. If it is correct that 'he can hardly have lived much before the *end* of the sixth century'[3] allegory may have been initiated by rhapsodes like Theagenes in order to defend offensive passages of Homer against moralists, and it may have been used afterwards by philosophical and theological writers like Pherecydes for their own purposes,[4] irrespective of offensive or inoffensive passages. But if he lived about or before the middle of the century it may well have been the other way round; only new evidence could bring a final decision.[5]

There is no doubt that in the Homeric field Theagenes always headed

[1] Schol. B Y 67, H. Schrader, Porphyr. *Quaest. Hom. ad Il.* 240, 14 = *Vors.* 8 A 2.
[2] Wilamowitz, 'Pherekydes', *Sitz. Ber. d. Preuss. Akad.* (1926) 126 f. = *Kleine Schriften* v 2 (1937) 128 f.; K. v. Fritz, *RE* XIX (1938) 2025 ff.
[3] So emphatically W. Jaeger, *The Theology of the Early Greek Philosophers* (Oxford 1947) 67.
[4] This seems to be the opinion of F. Wehrli, *Zur Geschichte der allegorischen Deutung Homers im Altertum* (Diss. Basel 1928) 89.
[5] Diels-Kranz, *Vors.* 8, were probably right in placing Theagenes immediately after Pherecydes; the case for the priority of Pherecydes is put by J. Tate, *Cl.R.* 41 (1927) 214; cf. *Cl. Qu.* 28 (1934) 105–14 'On the history of allegorism'.

the list of the interpreters; as it continued to be the duty of the rhapsodes
in later times also (see Plat. *Ion, passim*; Xenoph. *Symp.* III 6) not only to
recite, but also to explain Homer, one can hardly avoid the conclusion
that he was a prominent member of that ancient guild.[1] Besides his
'allegorical' interpretation of the Battle of the Gods, <u>Theagenes'</u> interest
in the text itself is attested by a variant reading in *A* 381 for which he[2] is
cited; and grammatical writing about Homer's correct usage of the
Greek language is said to have started with him (ἡ γραμματική . . . ἡ περὶ
τὸν ἑλληνισμόν[3] . . . ἀρξαμένη . . . ἀπὸ Θεαγένους *Vors.* 8. 1a). Finally he is
placed at the head of the writers 'who first searched out Homer's poetry
and life and date' (περὶ τῆς ῾Ομήρου ποιήσεως γένους τε αὐτοῦ καὶ χρόνου
καθ᾽ ὃν ἤκμασεν προηρεύνησαν πρεσβύτατοι μὲν Θεαγένης τε ὁ ῾Ρηγῖνος,
followed by Stesimbrotus and Antimachus, *Vors.* 8. 1). It is hard to say
what is meant by γένος and ἀκμή; but this may well have been the first
attempt at giving a short sketch of Homer's life, by collecting traditions
about his descent, birthplace, family, and lifetime. This testimonium,
usually neglected, is in accordance with the result of modern investigations about the date of the βίοι ῾Ομήρου and the Ἀγὼν ῾Ομήρου καὶ
῾Ησιόδου. As preserved to us,[4] they are products of late antiquity; but the
earliest forms of those books, narrating the life of Homer and his contest
with Hesiod, go back to the sixth century,[5] that is, to the time of
Theagenes. They contain a collection of rather amusing stories of
the adventures of an itinerant poet; in this respect they differ widely
from the merely genealogical and chronological statements of a dry
γένος.

Both γένος and βίοι are documents of the comprehensive activity of the
rhapsodes in the Homeric field. A group of them were called ῾Ομηρίδαι[6]
and were believed by some to be descendants of Homer himself;[7] for our
purpose it is important to note that they were not only performers, but

---

[1] Wilamowitz, *Der Glaube der Hellenen* II (1932) 215. 2; cf. F. Wehrli 91.

[2] *Vors.* 8. 3 καὶ Θεαγένης οὕτως προφέρεται; cf. A. Ludwich, *Aristarchs homerische Textkritik* I
113 n. 128, about προφέρεται.

[3] See R. Laqueur, *Hellenismus* (1925) 25; cf. below, p. 158.

[4] Homerus, ed. T. W. Allen, vol. v, and Wilamowitz, *Vitae Homeri et Hesiodi*, 1916.

[5] Wilamowitz, *Ilias und Homer* (1916) 367, 439; cf. E. Vogt, *Rh.M.* 102 (1959) 220 f. (see
below, p. 50, n. 5 on Alcidamas). *Βίοι* of early lyric poets, Alcaeus and Sappho, also originated
in the course of the sixth century B.C.

[6] W. Schadewaldt, *Von Homers Welt und Werk*[3] (1959) 55 f.; see also *Die Legende von Homer,
dem fahrenden Sänger* (1942) 101. 72; H. T. Wade-Gery, *The Poet of the Iliad* (1952) 19 ff., tried
to argue that the Homeridai, members of a Chiot family, were the only performers of Homer's
works in early times, until in the fifth century 'star' performers arose beside them.

[7] Acusilaus *FGrHist* 2 F 2, Hellanic. 4 F 20 and Jacoby's Commentary. About *families* of
poets in India see Steinthal, *Geschichte der Sprachwissenschaft bei den Griechen und Römern* I[2]
(1890) 30 (but they were priests too).

also interpreters of the poems.[1] How far they also produced poems of their own,[2] or whether, for instance, the original form of the so-called Homeric βίοι was poetical,[3] remain open questions; it is by no means unlikely that some of them were minor poets. In India the reciters of old poetry gradually ceased to write new poems; they presented and explained the old ones. It is at any rate clear that what Pherecydes and Theagenes wrote was in prose.

We are not told whether the rhapsodes of the sixth century had any technical resources for understanding the old epic poems; they may have used written collections of rare and obsolete epic words, γλῶσσαι as they were called from the fifth century onwards;[4] Aristotle in his *Poetics* (1459 a 9 f.) expressly recognizes glosses as a feature peculiar to epic poetry. One is tempted to assume that the explanations of Homeric proper names and obscure words by 'etymology' were further developed, collected, and transmitted by rhapsodes, perhaps together with the glosses. It is therefore not surprising to find among the few prose fragments of the sixth century that Pherecydes explained the Κρόνος of the old theogonies in etymological terms as Χρόνος (*Vors.* 7 A 9). Only by taking account of such forerunners can we understand how it was that in the fifth century etymology prospered so vigorously: Hecataeus of Miletus tried to infer historical facts from the 'true meanings' of names of persons and places, and philosophers from Heraclitus onwards thought hard about names (ὀνόματα) in order to discover the nature or essence of things.

But it is a great mistake of some modern linguists to credit the Ionians of the sixth century with a grammatical system of 'cases'. It would hardly be worth while to take notice of this strange view if it had not been accepted without qualification by E. Schwyzer in his *Greek Grammar*.[5] In a rhetorical book *Περὶ σχημάτων* (under the name of Herodian)[6] three lines of Anacreon (fr. 3 D.[2] = fr. 14 *PMG*) are quoted as an example of the πολύπτωτον, 'the employment of the same word in various cases':

$$\text{Κλευβούλου μὲν ἔγωγ' ἐρέω,}$$
$$\text{Κλευβούλῳ δ' ἐπιμαίνομαι,}$$
$$\text{Κλεύβουλον δὲ διοσκέω.}$$

---

[1] Evidence for their 'learning' in the article 'Homeridai' by Rzach, *RE* VIII 2147 f.—The word ῥαψῳδός itself (which does not concern us here), its composition and meaning, is again discussed by H. Patzer, *Herm.* 80 (1952) 314–25 (ῥαψῳδός = 'Reihsänger').

[2] Kynaithos, Schol. Pind. *N.* II 1c, and Wade-Gery, loc. cit. (above, p. 11, n. 6).

[3] See Th. Bergk, *Griechische Literaturgeschichte* I (1872) 930 f.; E. Rohde, *Rh.M.* 36 (1881) 220 = *Kleine Schriften* I 104; W. Schmid, *Griechische Literaturgeschichte* I 1 (1929) 85. 2.

[4] *JHS* 75 (1955) 72 = *Ausgewählte Schriften* (1960) 154. See above, p. 5 and below, pp. 78 f.; cf. K. Latte, *Philol.* 80 (1925) 147 ff.

[5] *Griechische Grammatik* I (1939) 6. 2.

[6] *Rhet. Gr.* VIII 599 f. Walz = III 97. 20 Spengel.

Here there is not only an absolute parallelism of three sentences, there is also a threefold variation of the same theme, and a sequence of the name Cleobulus first in the genitive, then in the dative, and finally in the accusative. This has been taken as clear evidence of a three-case system,[1] recognized by Ionian grammarians of the sixth century and applied by the poet.

The interesting passage in Περὶ σχημάτων starts from a definition of πολύπτωτον: ὅταν ἤτοι τὰς ⟨ἀντ⟩ονομασίας[2] ἢ τὰ ὀνόματα εἰς πάσας τὰς πτώσεις μεταβάλλοντες διατιθώμεθα τὸν λόγον ὡς παρὰ Κλεοχάρει; Cleochares is then quoted as having used the name of Demosthenes in the usual order of the five cases of Greek nouns, and two further examples are added. ἔστι δὲ τοιοῦτον σχῆμα καὶ παρά τισι τῶν ποιητῶν ὡς παρ' Ἀρχιλόχῳ καὶ Ἀνακρέοντι. παρὰ μὲν οὖν Ἀρχιλόχῳ . . . (fr. 70 D.[3]); in two trochaic tetrameters of Archilochus the name of a Leophilus is four times repeated; in spite of the corruptions and variant readings in the manuscripts[3] the most reasonable assumption is that the name appeared in four different cases, possibly in the order -ος, -ον (sc. -εω), -ῳ, -ον. The lines of Anacreon already quoted are introduced by the words: παρὰ δὲ Ἀνακρέοντι ἐπὶ τριῶν. The author of Περὶ σχημάτων was obviously very proud of having found these two rare examples.

It may be that the rhetorician Cleochares in the first half of the third century B.C. knew of a *theoretical* order of five cases of the Greek noun

[1] E. Sittig, 'Das Alter der Anordnung unserer Kasus', *Tübinger Beiträge zur Altertumswissenschaft* 13 (1931) 26. Against Sittig see K. Barwick, *Gnomon* 9 (1933) 587 f., 'Stoische Sprachlehre' 46; Schwyzer did not take account of these important objections which were repeated and augmented by M. Pohlenz, *NGGW*, Phil.-hist. Kl., N.F. III 6 (1939) = *Kleine Schriften* I (1965) 87 ff., and by R. Hiersche, 'Entstehung und Entwicklung des Terminus πτῶσις "Fall" ', *Sitz. Ber. d. Deutschen Akad. d. Wiss. Berl.* 1955, Nr. 3, 5 ff. and finally by Barwick himself; without taking notice of these articles H. Koller, 'Die Anfänge der griechischen Grammatik', *Glotta* 37 (1958) 5. 2 and 34 ff., against Sittig. Still worse than Sittig G. H. Mahlow, *Neue Wege durch die griechische Sprache und Dichtung* (1926) 212: 'Die Grundlagen der Grammatik waren längst Allgemeinbesitz. . . . Anakreon . . . macht sich den Scherz zu deklinieren; der erste Vers mit dem Nominativ ist leider nicht erhalten.' No proof is given for this rather sweeping statement; the assumption that a line is missing before Κλευβούλου μὲν ἔγωγ' ἐρέω is obviously wrong: the beginning of the stanza is quoted.

[2] Wilamowitz, *Antigonos von Karystos* (1881) 52. 12, changed the 'senseless ὀνομασίας' of the manuscripts into ἀντωνυμίας, referring to Spengel III 34. 23; he could have referred also to III 139. 1; but perhaps ἀντονομασίας should be restored, which means 'pronoun' in Dionys. Hal. *de comp. verb.* 2 p. 7. 7 Us.–Rad. (ἀντωνυμίας only in cod. v), in Ap. Dysc. *de pron.* 4. 18, 5. 10 Schn., where the grammarian rejects this form used by another grammarian, and in Pap. Yale 446, first century A.D. (no. 2138 Pack²) ed. Hubbell, *Cl. Phil.* 28 (1933) 189 ff.

[3] E. Lobel, 'Questions without answers', *Cl. Qu.* 22 (1928) 115 f., gives the exact readings of the manuscripts; these are correctly repeated in the critical apparatus by F. Lasserre, *Archiloque* (Paris 1958) fr. 122, p. 40 (only partly in Diehl, *Anth. Lyr. Gr.³*, fasc. 3 [1952] to fr. 70), but no editor so far seems to have accepted Lobel's suggestions as regards the text of the poet.

fixed by Stoic grammarians and philosophers,[1] but this is by no means certain. However, if one is bold enough to attribute to Anacreon the knowledge of a case-system in the second half of the sixth century, it would be inconsistent not to assume a similar knowledge for Archilochus in the first half of the seventh century; for according to the writer Περὶ σχημάτων both these poets employed a proper name in various cases, Archilochus four and Anacreon three times. Yet nobody has gone as far as that. And nobody seems to have spotted in Archilochus another possible example of a 'polyptoton', not of the noun, but of the pronoun.[2] This occurs in the hymnic style of predication in the prayer to Zeus.[3] So we see that it is a poetical figure in Ionic poetry; the earliest evidence, so far, is in the two fragments of Archilochus, followed by Anacreon's Cleobulus poem. Such figures arise from the spontaneous pleasure of the poet in playing on the various forms of the same word; the best-known example is the proem of Hesiod's *Works and Days*, and it has sometimes been thought because of its anaphoras and antitheses that the passage of Hesiod was influenced by 'rhetoric'.

But this misunderstanding has vanished with the recognition that the literary prose-style from the fifth century on took up forms and figures of speech from early poetry. It is a similar mistake to assume a sort of grammatical theory behind the artistry of Ionic verse.[4] The fact is that creative poetry foreshadowed the technical devices of future centuries[5] and may well have influenced the development of later theories.

Poets continued throughout the ages to 'interpret' in a certain way expressions and ideas of their own or of their predecessors. Homer always remained the principal subject,[6] and we may assume that his poems were

[1] See below, p. 244; J. Wackernagel, *Vorlesungen über Syntax* I² (1926) 312, speaks only of the possibility; F. Blass in Kühner–Blass, *Griechische Grammatik* I 2. 363, K. Barwick, *Gnomon* 9 (1933) 594, are too confident.

[2] In the various late excerpts Περὶ σχημάτων the so-called Herodian speaks about the 'polyptoton' of pronouns and nouns like Alexander Numenii fil. (III 34. 23 Sp.) and the Anonymous (III 139. 1 Sp.), but refers only to the three passages with proper names already quoted; the two other writers quote only examples of pronouns. Wilamowitz, *Antigonos*, 52, n. 12, is disposed to identify 'Herodian' with Alexander; see also *RE* I 1456 Alexandros no. 96.

[3] Archilochus fr. 94 D.³ ὦ Ζεῦ, πάτερ Ζεῦ, σὸν μέν . . ., σὺ δ' . . ., σοὶ δέ . . . is the reading of all the manuscripts; I am inclined to suspect that Archilochus wrote in the first line the genitive of the personal pronoun σέο (σεῦ), followed by the nominative σύ and the dative σοί (for the predicative use of the genitive of the personal pronoun compare [Hom.] *hy. Ap. Pyth.* 89); but even the possessive pronoun would be sufficient for the form of a polyptoton. Archilochus also played upon the etymology of the name of Apollo, see below, p. 62, n. 1.

[4] No 'canon' of selected writers did exist in the sixth century, see below, p. 15, n. 1.

[5] One may compare what has been said about 'etymologies' or allegory in epic poetry, above pp. 4 f.

[6] No details will be given here about lyric and tragic poetry (but see, for instance, E. Fraenkel in Aesch. *Ag.* 358 f., where Aeschylus apparently gives his interpretation of *E* 487 ff.).

extremely important in education. We know of no tradition about the 'selected authors to be read in school' at Athens or anywhere else in the sixth and fifth centuries.[1] But quite exceptionally, in the fragments of Aristophanes' earliest comedy, the Δαιταλῆς (427 B.C.), the examination of the bad boy in Homeric glosses is preserved (fr. 222 K.): λέξον Ὁμήρου γλώττας· τί καλοῦσι κορύμβα; (*I* 241) . . . τί καλοῦσ' ἀμενηνὰ κάρηνα; (κ 521). The boy, interested in modern rubbish, has no idea of the ἀρχαία παιδεία, delightfully pictured in Aristophanes' *Clouds* 961 ff. by the δίκαιος λόγος (first produced in 423 B.C.). It was the so-called Sophistic movement which—in Aristophanes' opinion—endangered the whole structure of the traditional Greek education.

[1] W. Schmid, *Geschichte der griechischen Literatur* I 4 (1946) 212: 'der Kanon der Schul-schriftsteller in der Grammatikerschule des 6. und 5. Jahrhunderts'; this remark without any further reference must be a slip of the pen.—The very scanty evidence for the early fifth century is discussed by Marrou 42 f. Literary education.—On Aristoph. fr. 222 see also the remarks of J. D. Beazley, *AJA* 54 (1950) 319 and H. Erbse, *Herm.* 81 (1953) 170, 178. 2.

II

THE SOPHISTS, THEIR
CONTEMPORARIES, AND PUPILS
IN THE FIFTH AND FOURTH CENTURIES

THE Sophistic movement of the fifth century holds a unique position in the history of the ancient world; it never repeated itself, and, in a historical sense, one should not speak of a 'second Sophistic' in Roman times. The part it played in the early history (or prehistory) of classical scholarship was an intermediary one. The Sophists were linked with the past in so far as they developed their ideas out of hints in earlier literature; so we have always to look back to poetry as well as to philosophy and history. On the other hand, they were the first to influence by their theories not only prose writing, rhetoric, and dialectic above all, but also contemporary and later poetry; so they force us to look ahead.

The Sophists can be regarded, in a sense, as the heirs of the rhapsodes. They also came from every part of the Hellenic world and wandered through all the Greek-speaking lands; but in the age after the expulsion of the tyrants and the defeat of the Persian invader their ways quite naturally converged on Athens, the leading democratic city-state, where they could gather their best pupils around them. The Sophists explained epic and archaic poetry, combining their interpretations with linguistic observations, definitions, and classifications on the lines laid down by previous philosophers; but their interest in Homeric or lyric poetry as well as in language always had a practical purpose, 'to educate men', as Protagoras himself said in Plat. *Prot.* 317 B (= *Vors.* 80 A 5): ὁμολογῶ σοφιστὴς[1] εἶναι καὶ παιδεύειν ἀνθρώπους. Their aim was not to interpret poetry for its own sake or to find out grammatical rules in order to understand the structure of language. They aimed at correctness of diction and at the correct pronunciation of the right form of the right word; the great writers of the past were to be the models from which one had to

---

[1] The word σοφιστής (see *Vors.* 79) is not used here in the general sense of a skilled or wise man (Aesch. *Pr.* 944. Hdt. 1 29, IV 95); Protagoras apparently is claiming to be a member of that modern professional group of teachers and educators called σοφισταί.

learn. In that way they became the ancestors of the virtuosi in the literary field. If scholarship were a mere artifice, they would indeed have been its pioneers;[1] for they invented and taught a number of very useful tricks and believed that such technical devices could do everything. But for this very reason they do not deserve the name of 'scholars'—they would not even have liked it. Still less should they be termed 'humanists';[2] Sophists concerned themselves not with the values that imbue man's conduct with 'humanitas', but with the usefulness of their doctrine or technique for the individual man, especially in political life.

Some examples, drawn from individual aspects of their activity, will be given later; we shall look at the Sophistic practice of interpretation, analysis of language, literary criticism, antiquarian lore, and polymathy.

However, there is one of their services to future scholarship on which we have to dwell a little longer; and for that reason we take it first. The very existence of scholarship depends on the book,[3] and books seem to have come into common use in the course of the fifth century, particularly as the medium for Sophistic writings. Early Greek literature had to rely on oral tradition, it had to be recited and to be heard; even in the fifth and fourth centuries there was a strong reaction against the inevitable transition from the spoken to the written word; only the civilization of the third century can be called—and not without exaggeration— a 'bookish' one.[4]

This may be the right moment for having a look at 'the oriental background' against which the whole of Greek culture had arisen, in so far as it is relevant for Greek scholarship. While aware of this historical process, I am, naturally enough, rather reluctant to speak of it as I have not the slightest acquaintance with the languages concerned; so I am forced to rely on the reports and interpretations of specialists and to draw conclusions from them with due reserve.

Excavations in Mesopotamia[5] revealed the early existence not only of

[1] P. B. R. Forbes, 'Greek Pioneers in Philology and Grammar', *Cl.R.* 47 (1933) 105 ff., gives a useful short survey of some achievements of the Sophists; but they were not 'pioneers' in scholarship in the strict sense of the word, as it is used here.
[2] W. Jaeger, *Paideia* I (1934) 377, 380 f.
[3] The elder Pliny went even further, when he said (*h.n.* XIII 68): 'cum chartae usu maxime humanitas vitae constet, certe memoria'; hardly any Greek would have gone as far as that (see below, p. 32).
[4] See below, p. 102.
[5] Eduard Meyer, *Geschichte des Altertums* I 2⁵ (1926) 334 ff. (§§ 312 ff.) (in particular pp. 335 f., 340, 342 f.). A more recent survey with a new chronology and extensive bibliography is given by A. Moortgat, 'Geschichte Vorderasiens bis zum Hellenismus', in A. Scharff und A. Moortgat, *Ägypten und Vorderasien im Altertum* (München 1950) 93–535, esp. 315 ff., 471 ff.— *Handbuch der Bibliothekswissenschaft*², hg. von G. Leyh, III 1 (1955) 1–50; F. Milkau u. F. Schawe, 'Der alte Vorderorient' on libraries in Egypt and in the Near East; on writing see

archives with documents on clay tablets, but also of 'libraries' with
literary texts. From about 2800 B.C., so we are told, the Sumerian-
speaking inhabitants maintained record offices as well as libraries and
schools in connexion with the temples of their gods. The keepers of the
clay tablets who had to preserve the precious texts attached importance
to the exact wording of the originals and tried to correct mistakes of the
copyists; for that reason they even compiled 'glossaries' of a sort. Towards
the end of the third millennium Semitic invaders from the north (the
Babylonians, as they were afterwards called) adopted the Sumerian
methods of preservation and also made lists containing the Sumerian
words and their Accadian equivalents. In the course of the second millennium the Hittites conquered large parts of Anatolia; there are cuneiform tablets found in their capital Boğasköy showing in three parallel
columns equivalent words in Hittite, Sumerian, and Accadian.[1] Similar
discoveries, dating from the second half of the second millennium, were
made during the excavations of Ugarit (Ras-Shamra) in northern Syria.
In the seventh century B.C. much of the earlier, especially the 'Babylonian', tradition was copied for the palace-library of the great Assyrian
king Assurbanipal, who was no less proud of his writing abilities than of
his conquests; there are more than 20,000 tablets and fragments in the
British Museum.

His learned scribes had inherited a truly refined technique and they
developed it further in the descriptive notes at the end of each tablet.[2]
Without romantic exaggeration we can say that these scribes felt a
'religious' responsibility for the correct preservation of the texts, because
all of them had to be regarded as sacred in a certain sense.[3] Their complicated method of 'cataloguing' was invented for the particular writing
material, the clay tablets, and the lists of words from different languages
were a product of the singular historical conditions of Mesopotamia and
the surrounding countries. But no 'scholarship' emerged from those
descriptive notes and parallel glossaries, which served only the practical
needs of the archives, libraries, and schools of temples. We find much the
same in other fields: the extensive oriental 'annals' did not lead to

also vol. I[2] (1952) 1–105. For the use of writing in Mesopotamia see Kenyon *Books and
Readers* 6 f.—On the early stimulating influence of Mesopotamian writing on Egypt see H.
Frankfort, *The Birth of Civilisation in the Near East* (London 1951) 106 f.

[1] For recent excavations of clay tablets with important texts in Accadian and translation
into Hittite see K. Bittel, 'Ausgrabungen in Boğazköy' (1952–7) in *Neue deutsche Ausgrabungen
im Mittelmeergebiet und im vorderen Orient* (Berlin 1959) 108.

[2] Full details are given by C. Wendel, 'Buchbeschreibung', 2 ff.

[3] Cf. E. Meyer, loc. cit. 462 f., 583 ff., 597 f. (religion and literature); C. Wendel 11 (but
the kings were not gods as in Egypt).

a methodical writing of history. George Sarton[1] in his *History of Science* rightly emphasizes the importance of a controlled language for the rise of 'Babylonian science', which needed 'linguistic tools of sufficient exactitude'. But it seems to be rather misleading to speak of 'the birth of philology'[2] at about 3000 B.C. Sarton, however, did not try to trace a line of descent from this oriental 'philology' (by which he apparently meant some sort of linguistic studies) to early Greece. On the other hand C. Wendel, in considering how technical devices for writing and for preserving the written tradition may have reached the Ionians in Asia Minor, argues convincingly that they had come from the east, not from Egypt;[3] but, in the present state of knowledge, one can do no more than hint at possibilities of contact. It is not unlikely that the Greek inhabitants of the west coast of Asia Minor and of the islands had been writing on animal skins before they used the Egyptian papyrus and continued to do so occasionally. Although there was literary evidence for the use of leather-rolls by oriental, especially Aramaic, scribes not only in Persia, but also in Mesopotamia, Phoenicia, and Palestine,[4] actual specimens were very rare, until the Aramaic parchments of the fifth century B.C. (now in the Bodleian library) were published in 1954.[5] The statement of Herodotus (v 58) in his much-discussed 'excursus' (regarded sometimes even as an 'interpolation') is thus fully confirmed in so far as it implied that leather-rolls had been in common use in 'barbarian' countries; consequently we are not entitled to doubt the other part of his remark about the Ionians (v 58. 3): καὶ τὰς βύβλους διφθέρας καλέουσι ἀπὸ τοῦ παλαιοῦ οἱ "Ιωνες, ὅτι κοτὲ ἐν σπάνι βύβλων ἐχρέωντο διφθέρῃσι αἰγέῃσί τε καὶ οἰέῃσι· ἔτι δὲ καὶ τὸ κατ' ἐμὲ πολλοὶ τῶν βαρβάρων[6] ἐς τοιαύτας διφθέρας γράφουσι.

In the famous paragraph which precedes, Herodotus speaks about the

[1] G. Sarton, *A History of Science* (1952) I. Ancient science through the golden age of Greece 67, with numerous references to texts and modern books on Mesopotamic excavations; see also S. N. Kramer, *From the Tablets of Sumer* (Indian Hills, Colorado 1956), ch. 24, describing a 'library catalogue' (about 50,000 Sumerian tablets in the museum in Philadelphia).

[2] W. von Soden, 'Leistung und Grenze sumerischer und babylonischer Wissenschaft', *Welt als Geschichte* 2 (1936) 411 ff., 509 ff., stresses the limits of that Sumerian and Accadian 'Listenphilologie' in a very learned article; but in conformity with the fashion of the thirties he can see 'true scholarship' inaugurated only by 'the nordic race'; cf. *Sitz. Ber. d. Österr. Akad.* 235 (1960) 1.

[3] C. Wendel, loc. cit. 85 ff.—Kenyon 44 f.

[4] See below, p. 20, n. 4.

[5] Abridged and revised edition by G. R. Driver, *Aramaic Documents* (1957) 1 ff.; cf. C. H. Roberts, 'The Codex', *Proc. Brit. Acad.* 40 (1954) 172, n. 1, 182.

[6] Cf. Ctesias, 688 *FGrHist* 5 (vol. III c, 450. 17 Jacoby, 1958) ἐκ τῶν βασιλικῶν διφθερῶν, ἐν αἷς οἱ Πέρσαι τὰς παλαιὰς πράξεις . . . εἶχον συντεταγμένας; however little credit Ctesias of Cnidos may deserve as a writer of Persian history, his reference to the διφθέραι can no longer be disregarded; see also Driver, loc. cit. and H. Hunger in *Geschichte der Textüberlieferung* 1 (1961) 30 (and 34 on the preparation of parchment, cf. below, pp. 235 f.).

'alphabet' which the Ionians received from the Phoenicians and adapted to the Greek language (v 58. 1, 2): οἱ δὲ Φοίνικες οὗτοι οἱ σὺν Κάδμῳ ἀπικόμενοι . . . ἐσήγαγον . . . καὶ γράμματα, οὐκ ἐόντα πρὶν Ἕλλησι ὡς ἐμοὶ δοκέειν . . . Ἴωνες, οἳ παραλαβόντες διδαχῇ παρὰ τῶν Φοινίκων τὰ γράμματα, μεταρρυθμίσαντές σφεων ὀλίγα ἐχρέωντο, χρεώμενοι δὲ ἐφάτισαν, ὥσπερ καὶ τὸ δίκαιον ἔφερε ἐσαγαγόντων Φοινίκων ἐς τὴν Ἑλλάδα, Φοινικήια κεκλῆσθαι. Greeks, therefore, were 'illiterate' in earlier times, as it seemed to Herodotus. But he must have known another tradition from one of his main sources, Hecataeus[1] of Miletus, with whom two other Milesian writers, Anaximander[2] and Dionysius,[3] agreed: namely that 'before Cadmus, Danaus brought letters over' πρὸ Κάδμου Δαναὸν μετακομίσαι αὐτά (τὰ στοιχεῖα). Danaus had sailed from Egypt (not from Phoenicia) to the Argolid: the rivalry between Egypt and the Near East in this field is apparent from the beginning and persistent up to today.[4] Since hundreds of clay tablets, covered with writing in the so-called Linear B Script (which had been known before only from Knossos) were found near Pylos by C. W. Blegen (1939) and in other places of the Greek mainland (Mycenae, 1950, by Alan J. B. Wace), it has been obvious that Herodotus was wrong when he expressed his opinion, although very cautiously (ὡς ἐμοὶ δοκέειν), that Greece was illiterate before the introduction of the Phoenician alphabet. The tablets are said to have been written between the fifteenth and the twelfth centuries B.C., in the late Helladic or, as Furtwängler had termed it, the Mycenaean epoch (the fullest records for Pylos are from the thirteenth century).[5] We may call it the 'Heroic age', supposing that it was the world of the heroes whose stories we read in the Homeric poems. The surviving examples of that Mycenaean writing (at the moment more than 1,000 tablets) do not go beyond 'lists of commodities and personnel'; there are no names of scribes, no check or alterations by a corrector as on the Accadian or Ugarit tablets we mentioned. The contents as well as the method are very primitive compared

[1] 1 *FGrHist* 20; see also Jacoby's notes 11–13 to the commentary on 489 *FGrHist* (1955).
[2] 9 *FGrHist* 3.
[3] 687 *FGrHist* 1; the testimony of these three historians was put together by Apollodorus 244 *FGrHist* 165.
[4] See above, p. 19, and about Egypt Siegfried Schott, 'Hieroglyphen, Untersuchungen zum Ursprung der Schrift', *Akademie der Wissenschaften und der Literatur in Mainz, Abhandlungen der geistes- und sozialwissenschaftlichen Klasse*, 1950, Nr. 24, pp. 63, 86, on the probable relation between hieroglyphs, Semitic scripts, and Greek alphabet; cf. p. 9.
[5] I have not much confidence in the later dating of the Knossos Tablets by L. R. Palmer, *Mycenaeans and Minoans* (London 1961) and 'The Find-Places of the Knossos Tablets' in the book *On the Knossos Tablets* (Oxford 1963); my doubts are strengthened by the convincing arguments put forward by J. Boardman in his part of the same book 'The Date of the Knossos Tablets', where he maintains against Palmer the correctness of the earlier dating by Evans (about 250 years).

with those of the earlier and the contemporary oriental 'libraries'. If Michael Ventris's ingenious theory of the decipherment of this syllabic script is correct,[1] we are confronted with a strange and primitive pre-Homeric 'Greek' language in a script that entails countless ambiguities. It is hardly conceivable that this clumsy script could have been used for a literary text.[2] However that may turn out, we know now that there is some truth in the statement of Herodotus' Milesian predecessors that Danaus anticipated Cadmus. Local writers of Κρητικά[3] voiced the claim of the island of Crete (against Cadmus) as the place where letters had been most anciently invented, and antiquarian authors περὶ εὑρημάτων[4] registered other claimants; but all these various stories point in *one* direction: they dispute the priority of the 'Phoenician' alphabet and hint at another earlier Greek script; and in this respect they are only now surprisingly confirmed.

The Phoenician origin of the 'alphabet', however, as it was used in historical Greek times, has never been seriously called in question. Herodotus is by no means the earliest authority for this;[5] some of the Milesian writers already quoted are half a century earlier, the oldest inscription of Teos (ὃς ἄν . . . Φοινικήια ἐκκόψει) was written soon after Mycale (479 B.C.),[6] and even Sophocles' Ποιμένες can now be dated with probability to the sixties of the fifth century (463 B.C.?):[7] 'Φοινικίοις γράμμασι'.[8] The truth of this literary tradition, which was, as we see, not limited to Herodotus, but quite common in the first half of the fifth

---

[1] *JHS* 73 (1953) 84–103, 'Evidence for Greek Dialect in the Mycenaean archives'.

[2] Even John Chadwick, Ventris's faithful collaborator, was rather reserved (*The Decipherment of Linear B* [Cambridge 1959] 130) in contrast to Alan Wace's overwhelming optimism (see *Documents in Mycenaean Greek* [Cambridge 1956], Foreword xxix).

[3] Dosiades, 458 *FGrHist* 6 and Diod. v 74. 1 = 468 *FGrHist* 1 (III B 411. 13 ff.).

[4] Scamon of Mytilene (probably early fourth century) 476 *FGrHist* 3. Fuller testimonia are given by H. Erbse, *Attizistische Lexica* (1950) 218. 28; cf. Andron of Halicarnassus, 10 *FGrHist* 9; Ephorus 70 *FGrHist* 105 and 106 called Cadmus the actual inventor, not merely the importer as Herodotus v 58, Aristotle fr. 501 R. or Zenon of Rhodes 523 *FGrHist* 1 vol. III B p. 498. 20 ff. (= Diod. v 58. 3).

[5] As Pearson says in his note to Soph. fr. 514.

[6] *SIG*³ 38. 38 (W. Ruge, *RE* v A [1934] 545. 60 ff.).

[7] *P.Oxy.* xx (1952) 2256, fr. 3. 4, hypothesis of Aeschylus' *Supplices*; Sophocles had been second, and amongst the rather confused series of titles Ποι]μέσιν is fairly certain.

[8] Hesych. v. 'Φοινικίοις γράμμασι'. Σοφοκλῆς Ποιμέσιν (fr. 514 P.). ἐπεὶ δοκεῖ Κάδμος αὐτὰ ἐκ Φοινίκης (ἐν φοίνικος cod.) κεκομικέναι. From the same source (Diogenian) Ael. Dionys. (fr. 318 Schw. = p. 148. 8 Erbse) in Eust. p. 1757. 58 Φοινίκια γράμματα, ἐπεὶ φασι δοκεῖ Κάδμος ἀπὸ Φοινίκης αὐτὰ κομίσαι; although the names of poet and play are omitted, the passage should be quoted in the apparatus to the Sophocles-Fragment. Mythical chronology puts Cadmus 300 years before the Trojan war; the subject of the play was events subsequent to the landing of the Greeks on the coast of the Troad. The inhabitants as well as the invaders could well have been acquainted with Phoenician letters according to that chronology (it is remarkable that epic heroes in tragedy use writing or at least speak about it).

century, can be established by a comparison of Greek inscriptions of the
late eighth century B.C. with Semitic writing of this and the preceding
century: similarities of letter forms show that the Phoenician model
had been followed and was modified about that time.[1] From the same
regions of the Near East the Ionians seem to have learned to prepare
skins for writing material, and, as the Egyptian papyrus was called
βύβλος in Greek,[2] after the city of Byblos, we may assume that it was first
imported from the Phoenicians, before the foundation of Naukratis
established direct contact between Egypt and Greece in the seventh
century. So everything leads up to the conclusion—in the present state
of our knowledge—that the introduction of letters and of papyrus dates
from the early eighth or the late ninth century;[3] the route[4] may have
been along the south coast of Asia Minor to Rhodes.[5]

At the very end of antiquity, Nonnus was loud in his praise of Cadmus' gifts (4. 259 ff.): ὁ πάσῃ / Ἑλλάδι φωνήεντα καὶ ἔμφρονα δῶρα
κομίζων / γλώσσης ὄργανα τεῦξεν ὁμόθροα, συμφυέος δέ / ἁρμονίης στοιχηδὸν
ἐς ἄζυγα (vowels) σύζυγα (consonants) μείξας / γραπτὸν ἀσιγήτοιο τύπον
τορνώσατο σιγῆς. But this so-called 'gift' deserves the gratitude not only
of the ancient world but of a great part of mankind in all ages. The
Phoenician script was neither cuneiform nor strictly syllabic; it consisted
of single characters, but only for the consonants. When the Greeks
adopted those letter forms they took the decisive step of using them for *all*

[1] G. R. Driver, *Semitic Writing* (1948) 178; J. Forsdyke, *Greece before Homer* (1956) 20 f.;
T. J. Dunbabin, 'The Greeks and their Eastern Neighbours', *Society for the Promotion of Hellen.
Studies, Suppl. Paper No.* 8 (1957) 59 ff.; Dorothea Gray in John L. Myres, *Homer and his
Critics* (1958) 266 ff.; A. G. Woodhead, *The Study of Greek Inscriptions* (1959) 13 f. 'Criterion
of close approach' between early Greek and Phoenician letter forms; G. Klaffenbach,
Griechische Epigraphik (Göttingen 1957) 34 f. The complete evidence up to 1960 is presented
by L. H. Jeffery, 'The Local Scripts of Archaic Greece. A Study of the Origin of the Greek
Alphabet and its Development from the Eighth to the Fifth Centuries B.C.', *Oxford Monographs on Classical Archaeology* (1961) 12 ff., date of introduction of the alphabet, and Addenda,
p. 374.
[2] Hdt. v 58. 3 (above, p. 19), cf. Aesch. *Suppl.* 946 f., see below, p. 26, n. 4.
[3] Wilamowitz in 1884 put the introduction of the new alphabet 'spätestens in das 10.
Jahrhundert' (*Homerische Untersuchungen* 287) and he never changed his mind, see *Geschichte
der griechischen Sprache* (1928) 9; A. Rehm, *Handbuch der Archäologie* i (1939) 197, says even
'the eleventh century cannot be excluded'; cf. Schwyzer, *Griechische Grammatik* i (1939)
141.
[4] Historians, archaeologists, and epigraphists are inclined to accept this hypothesis, see
especially Miss Jeffery pp. 5 ff. (place of introduction), and Addenda p. 374. Perhaps the
formidable God 'Kumarbi' of a Hurrian epic came the same way to influence Hesiod's
Kronos story: see U. Hölscher, *Hermes* 81 (1953) 405 f.; Dunbabin 56 f.
[5] One should not overlook the ancient local tradition in Ῥοδιακά that Cadmus sailed from
Phoenicia via the island of Rhodes to Greece: Zenon of Rhodes 523 *FGrHist* 1 (= Diod. v 58.
2, 3) Κάδμος ὁ Ἀγήνορος . . . κατέπλευσεν εἰς τὴν Ῥοδίαν . . . καὶ τὴν Λινδίαν Ἀθηνᾶν ἐτίμησεν
ἀναθήμασιν, ἐν οἷς ἦν χαλκοῦς λέβης . . . οὗτος δ' εἶχεν ἐπιγραφὴν Φοινικικοῖς γράμμασιν, ἅ φασιν
πρῶτον ἐκ Φοινίκης εἰς τὴν Ἑλλάδα κομισθῆναι· cf. Polyzelus of Rhodes 521 *FGrHist* 1.

the 'elements' of their language, which they called στοιχεῖα,[1] vowels as well as consonants. Now for the first time the quantity of the syllables and especially the structure of the quantitive verse could be displayed. A true alphabet[2] had come into being. It was one of the great creations of the Greek genius; as it can now be dated to the ninth or eighth century B.C., it belongs to the *epic age*. For these two centuries the epic poems were representative; the *Iliad* and the *Odyssey* still reveal to us how the Greek genius became conscious of itself and found its own nature in that particular moment of its history. A new aspect of the world arose, the true Greek aspect. I used to emphasize in my lectures on Homer the important fact that the adaptation of the Phoenician characters and the final form of the great epic poems belong to the same age. That the alphabet 'might have been invented as a notation for Greek verse' is a rather attractive idea,[3] and one wishes it could be proved; our earliest alphabetic inscriptions of the eighth century which are *not* all in verse,[4] can hardly help. But no doubt there was a new beginning, not a simple continuity from the heroic to the epic age. It is paradoxical to use a historical evaluation of the recently discovered Mycenaean writing as a basis for conclusions about a gradual inner development of Greek civilization from the thirteenth to the ninth century.[5] For, on the contrary, a comparison of that syllabic script on the tablets with the earliest alphabetic writing illustrates more than anything else a 'revolutionary' change, a completely new start. From this new start τὸ τέλος, the goal of

[1] H. Diels, *Elementum* (Leipzig 1899); ibid. p. 58. 3, the prophetic note that we shall find one day the 'old system' of writing. A. Evans had made the first announcement of its discovery in Oxford 1894.—On the term στοιχεῖα see below, p. 60 and Excursus.

[2] Plat. *Crat.* 431 E τό τε ἄλφα καὶ τὸ βῆτα καὶ ἕκαστον τῶν στοιχείων; cf. Diels, loc. cit. 18 ff., 58 ff.; Suet. *Div. Iul.* 56. 6 *quarta elementorum littera* 'the fourth letter of the alphabet'.

[3] Wade-Gery, *The Poet of the Iliad* (1952) 11–14; a different view on the date of a 'written copy' in D. L. Page, *History and the Homeric Iliad* (Berkeley 1959) 260.

[4] *Epigrammata, Greek Inscriptions in Verse from the Beginnings to the Persian War*, by P. Friedländer and H. B. Hoffleit (Berkeley 1948) p. 7. Two important verse inscriptions of about 700 B.C. were published later: fragmentary hexameters painted on an oinochoe in Ithake, *BSA* 43 (1948) 80 ff., pl. 34, Jeffery pp. 230, 233, pl. 45. 1. 2; the unique verse graffito, three lines written in the Phoenician retrograde style, found in Ischia, *Rend. Linc.* 1955, 215 ff., pls. 1–4, Jeffery pp. 45, 235 f., 239, pl. 47. 1.

[5] Alan J. B. Wace, *Documents in Mycenaean Greek* xxvii ff., strongly pleads for a slow evolution and speaks with scorn of the opposite 'classicistic' prejudice.—I totally disagree with the picture given by M. P. Nilsson, *Homer and Mycenae* (London 1933) 206–11, who believes in the origin of Greek epics in the 'glorious Mycenaean age' and a renascence of epics in Ionic times.—The new tablets, so far, do not contain any literary text or any hint at poetry; nevertheless, they have provoked Professor T. B. L. Webster (with whom I agree in some details), into writing *From Mycenae to Homer* (London 1958), in which he tries—unsuccessfully, but with immense erudition and bold imagination—to reconstruct songs of Mycenaean palaces. On the other hand, J. A. Notopoulos, 'Homer, Hesiod and the Achaean Heritage of oral Poetry', *Hesperia* 29 (1960) 177 ff., argues for the existence of an 'Achaean' oral *epic* poetry which survived in the mainland ('Hesiod', etc.) as well as in Ionia ('Homer', etc.).

a definitive alphabetic system, must have been reached in a fairly short time. There were minor alterations and slight improvements, but there was no 'pro-gress' any more either in Greek or in post-Greek times.[1] The alphabet was 'perfect', it had found its own nature, ἔσχε τὴν ἑαυτοῦ φύσιν, in the epic age. The same happened in other provinces of Greek civilization, in literature and art.

A new instrument had been created, which was, on the one hand, important for the expression of exact nuances of language in poetry and philosophy and, on the other hand, indispensable for scholarly interpretation and analysis. In this sense the adapted Phoenician characters were called 'helpers towards the λόγος' by Critias in the second half of the fifth century in an elegiac poem about various inventions of peoples and cities: Φοίνικες δ' εὗρον γράμματ' ἀλεξίλογα[2] (*Vors.* 88 в 2. 10), 'the Phoenicians invented letters which help men to think and to speak' (βοηθοῦντα εἰς λόγον Eust. p. 1771. 44). In the archaic period which followed the epic age the Greeks' first aim was at beauty of script; for evidence we have only to look at the early inscriptions on stone still preserved. This tendency towards harmony and even 'geometric' norms was observed by later writers: Πυθαγόρας αὐτῶν (sc. τῶν γραμμάτων) τοῦ κάλλους ἐπεμελήθη, ἐκ τῆς κατὰ γεωμετρίαν γραμμῆς ῥυθμίσας . . . αὐτὰ γωνίαις καὶ περιφερείαις καὶ εὐθείαις[3] (Schol. Dionys. Thr. *Gr. Gr.* III 183. 32). Archaic Greece took a pride in writing as a work of art, there is a striving for τὸ καλόν, as inscriptions show, and it can hardly be doubted that literacy was fairly widespread; but the important questions are how far first poetry and then philosophy were written down and at what time some form of commercial publication finally came into being.

The pattern of development in prehistoric Greece becomes visible only against the oriental background; so we were forced to go out of our way for a little while. Now in Greece we find no guild of scribes, no caste of priests to which knowledge of writing was restricted, no sacred books[4] of which the transmission was their special privilege. The Greek alphabetic

---

[1] The best expert on 'grammatology' I. J. Gelb, *A Study of Writing* (London 1952) 239 (cf. 184) made the statement: 'In spite of the tremendous achievements of the Western civilization in so many fields of human endeavour, writing has not progressed at all since the Greek period. . . . The complex causes for this conservative attitude may very well be beyond our capacity to comprehend.' But under the aspect of τέλος and φύσις we may well be able to comprehend it (see below, p. 68).

[2] This ἅπαξ λεγόμενον is not only attested and explained by Eustathius, who gives a choice of three different meanings, but already quoted in the Συναγωγὴ λέξεων χρησίμων p. 74. 7 Bachm. and in Phot. Berol. p. 73. 3 Reitzenstein; L–S should not list it as 'dubious'.

[3] A. Rehm, 'Inschriften als Kunstwerke', *Handbuch* 216. 3; Jeffery, photographs of archaic inscriptions on 72 plates.

[4] Except perhaps for small sects of mystics.

script was accessible to everyone, and in the course of time it became the common heritage of all citizens who were able to use a pen (or a brush) and to read; the availability of writing materials in early times has been mentioned already, and especially the import of papyrus from Egypt, where it had been used as far back as the third millennium in the form of smaller or larger rolls for ritual and literary purposes. So all the necessary conditions for producing Greek books were in existence from the eighth or seventh century onwards, it seems. If we try to answer the two questions in the last paragraph, we are led to distinguish four periods. There probably was first a time of merely oral composition and oral tradition of poetry. The second stage, we assume without further proof, began with the introduction of alphabetic writing. Epic poets, heirs of an ancient oral tradition, began to put down their great compositions in this new script:[1] we still possess as the product of that creative epic age the two 'Homeric' poems. The transmission remained oral: the poets themselves and the rhapsodes that followed them recited their works to an audience; and this oral tradition was secured by the script which must have been to a certain degree under proper control. There is, so far, no evidence for book production on a large scale, for the circulation of copies, or for a reading public in the lyric age. The power of memory was unchallenged, and the tradition of poetry and early philosophy remained oral. From the history of script and book we get no support either for the legend of the Peisistratean recension of the Homeric poems or for the belief that Peisistratus and Polycrates were book collectors and founders of public libraries.

No further change is noticeable until the fifth century,[2] when the third period began, one in which not only oral composition, but also oral tradition, began to lose its importance. The first sign of this is the sudden appearance of frequent references to writing and reading in poetry and art from the seventies of the fifth century onwards; the image of scribe

---

[1] The opposite view is taken by E. R. Dodds in the very lucid chapter 'Homer as Oral Poetry' in *Fifty Years of Classical Scholarship* (Oxford 1954) 13–17; he has been completely convinced by Milman Parry's collection of formulaic material. But this only proves that Greek epic poems were the result of a long oral tradition and were destined for further oral transmission; there is no decisive argument against the composition of *Iliad* and *Odyssey* in writing. Parry's so-called 'negative check' is entirely misleading: Apollonius Rhodius followed the Hellenistic theory of variation and consciously avoided formulae, repetitions, and the like. An important part of M. Parry's priceless collection of *Serbocroatian Songs* has been published (1953–4); but I wonder what help they may be for Homer, however contemptuously A. B. Lord, 'The Singer of Tales', *Harvard Studies in Comparative Literature* 24 (1960), may dismiss those Homeric scholars who do not yet give full credit to Parry's revelations.

[2] E. G. Turner, *Athenian Books in the Fifth and Fourth Centuries B.C.* (Inaugural Lecture, London 1952).

and reader had apparently caught poetic imagination as well as the imagination of the vase painters for the first time. It can hardly be by chance that all the great poets began to use the new symbol of the *written* word for the mental activity of 'recollection', of μνήμη; this is particularly remarkable, if we remember the part which physical memory had played in the past. In Aeschylus' *Prometheus* 460 f. the god who took a pride in having invented γραμμάτων τε συνθέσεις / μνήμην ἁπάντων, μουσομήτορ' ἐργάνην told Io: πλάνην φράσω / ἣν ἐγγράφου σὺ μνήμοσιν δέλτοις φρενῶν (ibid. 788 f.);[1] Sophocles expressly repeated this image in his earliest play *Triptolemus* (about 466 B.C.?).[2] Aeschylus was bold enough to attribute even to a god like Hades a δελτογράφος φρήν, *Eum.* 273–5 μέγας γὰρ Ἅιδης ἐστὶν εὔθυνος βροτῶν . . ., δελτογράφῳ δὲ πάντ' ἐπωπᾷ φρενί. We find in Aeschylus not only this conception of divine 'tablets of the mind', but also the idea of Zeus' tablets on which men's crimes have been noted. This image reminds one of the great deities of oriental religions writing their sacred books, but Aeschylus followed the Hesiodic tradition that made Δίκη a πάρεδρος of Zeus, and entrusted her with the office of his δελτογράφος, as we have learned quite recently: (Δίκη) . . . [γράφουσα] τἀπλακήματ' ἐν δέλτῳ Διός (Aesch. *Aitnai* [?] about 470 B.C.).[3] About half a century later Euripides also referred to those records: τἀδικήματ' . . . κἄπειτ' ἐν Διὸς δέλτου πτυχαῖς / γράφειν τιν' αὐτά (*Melanippe*, probably ἡ σοφή, fr. 506 N.[2]). The traditional expression for writing material in tragedy remained δέλτος,[4] even when one might suppose that the poet was actually speaking about literary texts written on papyrus-rolls.[5]

---

[1] Cf. Aesch. *Suppl.* 179 αἰνῶ φυλάξαι τἄμ' ἔπη δελτουμένας (sc. filias). Pind. *O.* x. 2 (about 474) ἀνάγνωτε . . . πόθι φρενὸς ἐμᾶς γέγραπται.

[2] Soph. fr. 597 P. θοῦ δ' ἐν (Pf.: οὐδ' αὖ A, σὲ δ' ἐν V) φρενὸς δέλτοισι τοὺς ἐμοὺς λόγους (θοῦ δ' ἐν δέλτοισι, cf. Call. fr. 75. 66 ἐνεθήκατο δέλτοις); cf. Aesch. *Cho.* 450, Soph. *Phil.* 1325; Eur. *Tro.* 663 ἀναπτύξω φρένα 'unroll my mind' (like a book).

[3] *P.Oxy.* xx (1952) 2256, fr. 9a 21 ed. E. Lobel = Aesch. fr. 530 Mette; recognized by E. Fraenkel, *Eranos* 52 (1954) 64 ff., as a fragment of the festival play for Hieron's foundation of the city Aetna; cf. F. Solmsen, *The Tablets of Zeus, Cl. Qu.* 38 (1944) 27–30.

[4] The only exception, so far, seems to be Aesch. *Suppl.* 946 f. ταῦτ' οὐ πίναξίν ἐστιν ἐγγεγραμμένα / οὐδ' ἐν πτυχαῖς βίβλων κατεσφραγισμένα, a folded papyrus sheet of a sealed contract. For δέλτος see the references and notes above; see also Soph. *Tr.* 683, fr. 144 P., Eur. *IT* 760, [*IA*] 112. *Batrachomyomachia* 1. 3 is not our earliest evidence, but one of the many late additions, see *Herm.* 63 (1928) 319 (= *Ausgewählte Schriften*, 113). Gods were supposed to continue using the old δέλτοι, διφθέραι, ὄστρακα, see Babr. 127 and the many proverbs collected by O. Crusius, *De Babrii aetate* (1876) 219; cf. F. Marx, *Ind. lect. Greifswald* (1892/3) vi. No conclusions about the actual use of writing material at certain times can be drawn from such passages.

[5] Eur. *Erechth.* fr. 369. 6 f. N.[2] δέλτων ἀναπτύσσοιμι γῆρυν, ἂν σοφοὶ κλέονται; one may compare Socrates unrolling the treasures of the sages of old time in Xenoph. *Mem.* 1 6, 14: τοὺς θησαυροὺς τῶν πάλαι σοφῶν ἀνδρῶν . . . ἀνελίττων; see below, p. 28, n. 2.

If we turn from the literary field to the Attic vase painters, we do not find any pictures of 'books' on black-figured vases; scenes of the simple life of the βάναυσοι were their favourite subjects. Scenes of the cultivated life, in which representations of inscribed rolls find a place, appear first in the red-figured style, the work of the contemporaries of the tragic poets, from about 490 to 425 B.C. At least three of these paintings seem to be slightly earlier than the dated plays of Aeschylus.[1] On half a dozen vases, letters or words of epic or lyric poems, written across the open papyrus roll, can still be deciphered.[2] We see youths and schoolmasters reading the text; in the second half of the fifth century famous names like those of Sappho, Linos, Musaios are added to these figures. On a Carneol-Scarabaeus even a Sphinx is represented as reciting the famous riddle from an open book in her paws (about 460 B.C.).[3] We are justified, I believe, in taking the coincidence of the literary passages and the vase-paintings as evidence of a change in the common use of books; no doubt it was a slow change, leading gradually to the fourth and final period, when a conscious method of παράδοσις, of literary tradition by books, became established.

We are not able to follow out the development in this period of transition step by step. There seems to be no new evidence, only a few casual allusions in Old Comedy and in Platonic dialogues, which are well known but need to be carefully reconsidered. Eupolis, Aristophanes' contemporary, mentioned, probably in the twenties of the fifth century, the place οὗ τὰ βιβλί᾿ ὤνια, 'where the books are on sale'.[4] Socrates was able to get hold of the books of Anaxagoras very quickly, when he had heard someone reading an interesting passage from one of his writings, though he was much disappointed by them.[5] When Plato represented him in the *Apology*[6] as referring to Ἀναξαγόρου βιβλία τοῦ Κλαζομενίου, Socrates mentioned the very cheap price of a drachma, at which copies could be bought by anyone in the market-place,[7] with irony, if not with contempt.

[1] F. Winter, 'Schulunterricht auf griechischen Vasenbildern', *Bonner Jahrbücher* 123 (1916) 275–85, esp. 281 f.

[2] J. D. Beazley, 'Hymn to Hermes', *AJA* 52 (1948) 336 ff., discusses in detail an unpublished vase in the manner of Duris and eight other representations of inscribed rolls; the earliest one, the schoolmaster of the Panaitios-Painter, is confidently dated about 490 B.C. Three items of Beazley's list are fully treated again by Turner, *Athenian Books* (1952) 13–16, who further discusses an Athenian pyxis (no. 1241). Against the assumption of E. Pöhlmann, *Griechische Musikfragmente* (Nürnberg 1960) 83 f., that some of the signs on the open scrolls were noted melodies, see R. P. Winnington-Ingram, *Gnomon* 33 (1961) 693, who correctly takes them for poetic texts and gives three more references in note 2 (cf. ibid. 1962, 112).

[3] R. Lullies, 'Die lesende Sphinx', *Festschrift f. B. Schweitzer* (Stuttgart 1954) 140 ff.

[4] Fr. 304 K., but see the exact wording of the whole passage. On βιβλιοθῆκαι, Poll. IX 47.

[5] Plat. *Phaed.* 97 B (= *Vors.* 59 A 47).　　　　[6] Plat. *Apol.* 26 D (= *Vors.* 59 A 35).

[7] Loc. cit. ἃ ἔξεστιν ἐνίοτε, εἰ πάνυ πολλοῦ, δραχμῆς ἐκ τῆς ὀρχήστρας πριαμένοις (-ους Diels–

Therefore the figure should not be taken too seriously;[1] but the fact that books of Anaxagoras were available to the general public in Athens[2] is fairly certain. There is no certainty, on the other hand, about the tradition, reported by Clement of Alexandria in his lists of 'first inventors', and often repeated, that Anaxagoras was 'the first to publish a written book'.[3] The plague of bad βιβλία in Aristophanes' Cloud-cuckoo-town[4] is a satiric counterpart to conditions in Athens towards the end of the century; at about 400 B.C. books were even exported to countries on the Black Sea.[5] Something must have happened to stimulate book production to such a degree; the influence of the Ionian Anaxagoras, even though settled in Athens before the Peloponnesian war and enjoying Pericles' friendship, can hardly have been sufficient.

In the course of the fifth century the tragic poets, the historians, and the Sophists became the predominant figures in the literary life of Athens. Tragedies were composed for performance in the theatre of Dionysus, but were also available as 'books' afterwards. The only unmistakable evidence, however, is Dionysus' confession in Aristophanes' *Frogs* 52 f. (produced in January 405 B.C.): ἐπὶ τῆς νεὼς ἀναγιγνώσκοντί μοι / τὴν Ἀνδρομέδαν πρὸς ἐμαυτόν 'when I was reading (Euripides') *Andromeda* (produced in 413 B.C.) to myself on board'.[6]

We may reasonably assume that the Athenians could not have taken the point of parody in the many paratragedic passages of Attic Comedy unless they had *read* the tragedies, as we find the god of the theatre reading the *Andromeda*. In the fourth century Aristotle even distinguished

Kranz) κτλ.; ὀρχήστρα does not refer to the theatre of Dionysus, but to a part of the ἀγορά, see W. Judeich, *Topographie von Athen*[2] (1931) 342. 2; A. W. Pickard-Cambridge, *The Dramatic Festivals of Athens* (1953) 36. 4.

[1] As Anaxagoras had been dead for nearly thirty years, the copies may have been 'second hand'. N. Lewis, *L'Industrie du papyrus* (Thèse Paris 1914) 62 f., and Turner, *Athenian Books* 21, were puzzled when they compared the real cost of papyrus and of copying at that time with Socrates' statement.

[2] Athenian βιβλιοπῶλαι mentioned in old comedy: Aristomenes fr. 9 K., Theopomp. fr. 77 K., Nicoph. fr. 19. 4 K.; see also above, p. 26, n. 5.

[3] Clem. Al. *Stromat.* 1 78 (II pp. 50 f. St.) = *Vors.* 59 A 36 ναὶ μὴν ὀψέ ποτε εἰς Ἕλληνας ἡ τῶν λόγων παρῆλθε διδασκαλία τε καὶ γραφή . . . οἱ δὲ Ἀναξαγόραν . . . πρῶτον διὰ γραφῆς ἐκδοῦναι βιβλίον ἱστοροῦσιν. Clement seems to have understood γραφή as 'writing', but the sense may have been 'drawing', if one compares *Vors.* II 6. 23 and II 11. 2 ⟨μετὰ⟩ διαγραφῆς Diels; the fact of the ἔκδοσις is emphasized by Th. Birt, *Die Buchrolle in der Kunst* (1907) 213, and by Stählin in *Vors.* loc. cit.; cf. E. Derenne, 'Les procès d'impiété' (below, p. 31, n. 5) 25. 3.

[4] Aristoph. *Av.* 974 ff., 1024 ff., 1288.

[5] Xenoph. *Anab.* VII 5. 14, in the cargoes of vessels wrecked near Salmydessos ηὑρίσκοντο . . . πολλαὶ βίβλοι γεγραμμέναι.

[6] Cf. Aristoph. *Ran.* 1114 βιβλίον τ' ἔχων ἕκαστος μανθάνει τὰ δεξιά. From the whole context of the often discussed lines 1109–18 it is obvious to me that Aristophanes meant to say there is no danger of ἀμαθία, of inexperience, or ignorance on the side of the Athenian audience; the theatre-goers are military servicemen and enlightened (σοφοί) 'readers of books, able to understand the right points'.

certain plays, which were particularly suitable for reading, from those
with a purely ἀγωνιστική and ὑποκριτικὴ λέξις, and described their poets
as ἀναγνωστικοί. But it is a mistake to think that there were poets who
wrote their plays only for reading.[1] There have never been such writers;
plays were always composed for acting in the first place. Euripides'
book-knowledge is ridiculed by Aristophanes,[2] and he is said to have been
the owner of a whole library.[3] Wilamowitz[4] once tried to demonstrate
that the texts of the tragedies were the first proper Greek 'books', βιβλία;
for earlier writings he used the term ὑπομνήματα. But ὑπόμνημα never
meant an independent finished writing; it may refer to notes reminding
one of facts heard or seen in the past, or to notes jotted down and collected as a rough copy for a future book, or to explanatory notes to some
other writing, that is, a commentary.[5] It is quite arbitrary to call the early
Ionic prose-writings, such as those of Heraclitus and Hecataeus, 're-
minders'; they were more or less finished works, copied by pupils and
friends, or deposited in a temple, as in the case of Heraclitus.[6] We
should not underrate the influence of tragedy on the development of the
book; but so far it is not proved that the tragedians were the first writers
to have their works made available as βιβλία to a wider public.

Herodotus seems to have lectured publicly, reciting here and there
a single λόγος,[7] an ἀγώνισμα ἐς τὸ παραχρῆμα ἀκούειν in Thucydides'
phrase, and he certainly was open to Sophistic ideas and stylistic devices.[8] His 'history' as a whole, the first great work of Greek prose
literature, was finally written down in Italy about 430 B.C. and published
only posthumously. It can hardly have had any influence on the growth
of the book. But when in the following generation Thucydides hoped that
his historical ξυγγραφή would be a κτῆμα ἐς ἀεί (I 22. 4), he was already
thinking of his future readers. So great an increase in the spreading
abroad of the written word had apparently taken place between the two
generations. It is no surprise to find that in the last decade of the fifth
century the local Attic tradition also, which had hitherto been oral, was
fixed for the first time in a book, the Ἀττικὴ ξυγγραφή (Thuc. I 97. 2) of

---

[1] The correct interpretation of Aristot. *Rhet.* III 12 p. 1413 b 12 is given by O. Crusius,
Festschrift für Th. Gomperz (1902) 381 ff., but the wrong interpretation is repeated everywhere.   [2] Aristoph. *Ran.* 943, 1409.   [3] Athen. 13 A.
[4] *Einleitung in die Tragödie* (1889) 121 ff.
[5] References in the article of F. Bömer, 'Der Commentarius', *Herm.* 81 (1953) 215 ff., but
he did not mention Wilamowitz's theory.
[6] I fully agree in this point with Turner, *Athenian Books* 17.
[7] Marcellin. *Vita Thuc.* 54; Paroemiogr. cod. Coisl. 157 = Append. II 35, ed. Gotting.,
vol. I 400 εἰς τὴν Ἡροδότου σκιάν. This late tradition, often rejected, was rightly accepted by
F. Jacoby, *RE*, Suppl. II 330, and John L. Myres, *Herodotus, Father of History* (1953) 5.
[8] F. Jacoby, *RE*, Suppl. II 500 f.

Hellanicus of Lesbos;[1] his connexion with contemporary Sophists is clearly perceptible.

It is a notable coincidence that under the archonship of Euclides (403/2 B.C.) the Ionic alphabet was officially adopted for public documents in Athens instead of the local Attic script.[2] If the written tradition started in Ionia, as we assumed, it is natural that Ionic characters were predominantly in use for literary purposes in other parts of Greece as well.[3] In Athens their increased popularity in the second half of the fifth century may have been brought about by the itinerant Sophists who mostly came from Ionic cities; the letters described in Euripides' *Theseus* (fr. 382 N.[2], produced before 422 B.C.) are apparently Ionic. Occasional transcriptions of texts were necessary (and, no doubt, some mistakes were made in the process); but no general μεταχαρακτηρισμός[4] of earlier literature took place. Quite naturally, the Ionic script became, in the course of time, the universally accepted hand both for literary texts[5] and for documents.

There remains the question whether the Sophists[6] can really claim to have played the decisive part in this change. One of the leading Sophists, Prodicus himself, is put on a par with a 'book' by Aristophanes, *Tagenistas* (fr. 490 K.) 'either a book or Prodicus has ruined the man', τοῦτον τὸν ἄνδρ᾽ ἢ βιβλίον διέφθορεν / ἢ Πρόδικος. The alternative at least shows that pure literariness was regarded as characteristic of a Sophist; at the same time it points to the danger of Sophistic books, perhaps of books in general. From Plato's *Symposium* (117 B), of which the whole scene is staged in 416 B.C., one can infer[7] that Prodicus' *Horai* were in circulation as a 'book' at that time; later on from a copy of this book Xenophon took the famous parable of Hercules at the crossroads (*Mem.*

---

[1] F. Jacoby, *Atthis* (Oxford 1949) 216 f., Index p. 431 oral tradition and *RE* VIII (1913) 107, 111, 138, Hellanicus and the Sophists.

[2] Theopomp. 115 *FGrHist* 155.

[3] Cf. Schol. Dionys. Thr., *Gr. Gr.* III p. 183. 20 ff. Hilg.

[4] The theory of a universal and systematical transliteration is maintained by R. Herzog, 'Die Umschrift der älteren griechischen Literatur in das jonische Alphabet', *Programm zur Rektoratsfeier der Universität Basel* (1912), but he is not able to prove his point either by the valuable collection of so-called evidence or by his arguments. J. Irigoin, *L'histoire du texte de Pindare* (1952) 22–28 still tried to maintain the theory of μεταγραμματισμός.

[5] Our earliest specimen seems to have been written in the third quarter of the fourth century B.C. See below, p. 102; cf. C. H. Roberts, *Greek Literary Hands 350 B.C.–A.D. 400* (1955) I.

[6] E. Curtius, *Wort und Schrift* (1859; reprinted in 'Alterthum und Gegenwart' I, 1875) 262: 'Sophistik . . . da begann in Athen die Lese- und Bücherwut'. R. Harder, 'Bemerkungen zur griechischen Schriftlichkeit', *Antike* 19 (1943) 107 = *Kleine Schriften* (1960) 79 'Thukydides und die Sophisten führen das Schreibwesen zum endgültigen Sieg'; Turner, *Athenian Books* 16–23.

[7] K. v. Fritz, *RE* XXIII 86 (rightly against H. Diels's note to *Vors.* 84 B 1).

II 1. 21–34 = *Vors.* 84 B 2). Xenophon also records an interview of Socrates with a certain Euthydemus, called ὁ καλός (*Mem.* IV 2. 1 ff.), who had a remarkable collection of books of poets as well as of 'Sophists' (ποιητῶν τε καὶ σοφιστῶν τῶν εὐδοκιμωτάτων).[1] As professional teachers, the Sophists had to give book texts of the great poets (Plat. *Protag.* 325 E) to their pupils, but they started also to distribute copies of their own writings as παραδείγματα, models,[2] and to write practical textbooks.[3] Oral instruction, though still most important,[4] was no longer sufficient for their special purpose (Plat. *Phaedr.* 228 A). If there is any truth in the tradition[5] that Protagoras' books were collected from their owners and burned on the agora when he was accused of atheism (about 416/15 B.C.?), an established trade and distribution of books among the Athenian public at that time must be assumed. This may still have been on a small scale; the discussions about the problem, even about the danger, of this new habit were mainly concerned with Sophistic writings. We find an example of this in Aristophanes' sneer at Prodicus; his point of view was merely ethical. A more general philosophical opposition arose from the side of Socrates[6] and Plato; it is voiced again and again from the early dialogue *Protagoras* to the late *Phaedrus*.[7] Two points in these much discussed passages[8] are relevant to our purpose. In the first place the immediate target for the attacks was the Sophists, their exaggerated respect

[1] Cf. Isocr. 2 (ad Nicocl.) 13 μήτε τῶν ποιητῶν τῶν εὐδοκιμούντων μήτε τῶν σοφιστῶν μηδενὸς οἴου δεῖν ἀπείρως ἔχειν; both Xenophon and Isocrates refer to contemporary writers, not to the σοφοί of old.

[2] Cf. Marrou 54. For references to such sample speeches put into writing see W. Steidle, 'Redekunst und Bildung bei Isokrates', *Herm.* 80 (1952) 271. 5. On the preference for the written word by Isocrates in the line of the Sophists, ibid. 279, 292, 296.

[3] Plat. *Phaedr.* 266 D καὶ μάλα που συχνά . . . τά γ' ἐν τοῖς βιβλίοις τοῖς περὶ λόγων τέχνης γεγραμμένοις; cf. M. Fuhrmann, *Das systematische Lehrbuch* (1960) 123 f.; see also below, p. 76, n. 5.

[4] Protagoras and Prodicus used to read manuscripts to their pupils (Diog. L. IX 50, cf. 54 = *Vors.* 80 A 1). Hippias repeatedly read his Τρωικός to the Spartans and Athenians (Plat. *Hipp. mai.* 286 BC = *Vors.* 86 A 9). See also Diels, *NJb* 25 (1910) 11: 'Da die Sophistik . . . den mündlichen Unterricht durch eine *Unzahl* praktischer Handbücher und Broschüren eindringlicher und nachhaltiger gestaltete' (italics are mine); this may be a little exaggerated.

[5] *Vors.* 80 A 1 τὰ βιβλία αὐτοῦ κατέκαυσαν ἐν τῇ ἀγορᾷ ὑπὸ κήρυκι ἀναλεξάμενοι παρ' ἑκάστου τῶν κεκτημένων, ibid. A 3, 4, 23; cf. E. Derenne, 'Les Procès d'impiété', *Bibliothèque de la Fac. de Philos. et des Lettres, Univ. de Liège*, 45 (1930) 55; against J. Burnet, *Greek Philosophy* I (1924) 112, and his followers see E. R. Dodds, *The Greeks and the Irrational* (Berkeley 1951) 189 and n. 66, p. 201, who gives a correct interpretation of Plat. *Men.* 91 E about Protagoras and the whole background for 'prosecutions of intellectuals on religious grounds'.

[6] Cf. Xenoph. *Mem.* IV 2. 9.

[7] Plat. *Prot.* 329 A, esp. *Phaedr.* 274 B ff.; cf. *Epist.* II 314 C, VII 341 B ff.

[8] On the attitude to books and on the problem of the spoken and the written word there is a lucid chapter in P. Friedländer, *Platon*, I² (1954) 114 ff. with bibliography p. 334 (English translation, New York 1958, bibliography pp. 356 f.); III² (1960) 220 f. on the passage in *Phaedr.* with n. 33, p. 469. See also the general remarks by E. R. Curtius, *Europäische Kultur und lateinisches Mittelalter* (Bern 1948) 304 ff., esp. 306 f. 'Das Buch als Symbol'.

for the written word, and their own preference for the use of books. Such an attitude, it was argued, propagated by influential teachers, was bound to weaken or even to destroy physical memory (μνήμη), on which the oral tradition of the past was based, and in the end would be a threat to true philosophy, which needs the personal intercourse of the dialectician to plant the living word in the soul of the listener. The second point may have been still more important for the future. The Socratic and Platonic arguments are the expression of a general, deeply rooted Greek aversion against the written word; they strengthened this instinctive mistrust in later 'literary' ages also and thus helped to promote sober 'criticism'. The Greek spirit never became inclined to accept a tradition simply because it was written down in books. The question was asked whether it was genuine or false, and the desire remained alive to restore the original 'spoken' word of the ancient author when it was obscured or corrupted by a long literary transmission. If books were a danger to the human mind, the threat was at least diminished by Plato's struggle against them; no real 'tyranny' of the book[1] ever established itself among the Greeks, as it did in the oriental or in the medieval world.

It remains true that their contribution to the development of the book was one general service the Sophists did for Greek civilization as a whole and for future scholarship in particular. We now turn to their individual achievements in the field of learning, and discuss a few representative specimens. For our purpose, the most important part of their activity was the 'interpretation' of early poetry. But was this really a true ἑρμηνεία τῶν ποιητῶν? The only substantial specimen which still survives is the explanation of a monostrophic lyric poem of Simonides by Protagoras in Plato's dialogue (*Prot.* 339 A ff. = *Vors.* 80 A 25).[2] There can hardly be any doubt that the choice of this particular poem to Scopas on the idea of the ἀνὴρ ἀγαθός[3] was intentional, and it is often said that there existed

---

[1] When Turner, *Athenian Books* 23, finishes his excellent lecture with the flourish: 'By the first thirty years of the fourth century books have established themselves, and their *tyranny* lies ahead', I part company with him. E. Curtius was right when he stated in his festival speech *Wort und Schrift* (1859) (= *Alterthum und Gegenwart* I 255) '*immer* blieb . . . eine Stimmung zurück, welche sich gegen die *Herrschaft* des Buchstabens sträubte'. The custom of reciting poetry and artistic prose remained alive up to the end of antiquity, see E. Rohde, *Der griechische Roman*[3] (1914) 327 ff.; see also Wilamowitz, *Die hellenistische Dichtung* I (1924) 98. 118, about 'Buchpoesie', and 'Rezitationspoesie'.

[2] Cf. Themist. *or.* 23, p. 350. 20 Dind. Πρωταγόρας . . . τὰ Σιμωνίδου τε καὶ ἄλλων ποιήματα ἐξηγούμενος; a reference to this passage of Themistius (which Schneidewin, *Simonidis Cei fragmenta* (1835) 16, rightly regards as derived from Plato's dialogue) is missing in *Vors.* 80 A and in M. Untersteiner, *Sofisti, Testimonianze e Frammenti* I (1949) 2 A.

[3] We are concerned only with Protagoras' way of expounding the Simonidean text, not with the problems of this text itself; E. Diehl, *Anth. lyr. Gr.* II² (1942) 77 ff. Simonid. fr. 4 (= fr. 5 Bergk) with bibliography; D. L. Page, *Poetae Melici Graeci* (Oxford 1962) 282 f.,

a sort of spiritual relationship between Simonides and the early Sophists. I was rather sceptical about this conception of Simonides as a 'proto-Sophist', as this fragment seemed to be unique; but there is now a close parallel to the Scopas poem in a recently published Simonidean fragment dealing with καλόν, αἰσχρόν, ἀρετά, ἐσθλός.[1] The whole Platonic passage would be of little or no value, if it contained a mere caricature[2] of the Sophist's teaching. As a matter of fact, there is no lack of the usual Socratic irony, but at the same time Plato, who always felt a genuine respect for Protagoras, draws an essentially adequate picture of his procedure. Protagoras is scrutinizing a well-known work of probably the most famous poet of his generation (Simonides died in about 468 B.C., Protagoras was born in about 490 B.C.); how clever to discover just there an obvious contradiction (339 B ἐναντία λέγει αὐτὸς αὑτῷ ὁ ποιητής). This kind of critical examination of the poet's single words and their proper meaning (for example ἔμμεναι and γενέσθαι) is in the Sophist's view the most important mental training; it is necessary for a young man to be trained in this way because it helps him to become himself περὶ ἐπῶν δεινόν.

In a similar way Protagoras discovered an incorrect use of the form of the command (μῆνιν ἄειδε, θεά) instead of the wish in the first line of the *Iliad* (*Vors.* 80 A 29; also 80 A 30 on Homer Φ 240);[3] the straightforward quotation of this by Aristotle (*Poet.* 19. 1456 b 15) confirms in a way the assumption that Plato in the passage about the Simonidean poem does not ridicule Protagoras as long as the great Sophist himself is speaking. On the other hand, when Socrates in his extensive refutation of Protagoras' arguments gives a series of interpretations in detail and an explanation of the whole (341 E διανοεῖσθαι, 344 B τὸν τύπον αὐτοῦ τὸν ὅλον καὶ τὴν βούλησιν), Plato indulges in a sort of sparkling parody of the

---

[1] Simonid. fr. 37 (an improved text). Further discussions are referred to by P. Friedländer, *Platon* II² (1957) 18–21; 279, n. 18. The only paper which concentrates on the *interpretation* of the poem in the Platonic dialogue by Protagoras and Socrates is that of H. Gundert, 'Die Simonides-Interpretation in Platons Protagoras', *Festschrift O. Regenbogen* (Heidelberg 1952) 71–93; and only Gundert came to the astonishing conclusion that Plato seems to have been unable to grasp the 'archaic' style of the poem, and to have been unaware of the mistakes he made in its interpretation (p. 92. 34 'Die zentralen Mißverständnisse blieben ihm selbst verborgen', cf. p. 82).

[1] Simonid. fr. 36 Page (= *P.Oxy.* 2432). I am tempted to conjecture that the lost subject to l. 1 τό τ]ε καλὸν κρίνει τό τ' αἰσχρόν was καιρός; καιρός very often occurs in discussions of such ethical notions in Sophistic writing and in later tragedy; see Fr. trag. adesp. 26, p. 844 N.² in Δισσοὶ λόγοι (*Vors.* 90. 2. 19) and Wilamowitz, *Sappho und Simonides* (1913) 178. 1; M. Untersteiner, *The Sophists* (1954) 367, Index v. καιρός.

[2] This expression is still used by J. W. H. Atkins, *Literary criticism in Antiquity* I (1952) 42.

[3] On Homeric studies in the fifth century B.C. see the useful collection of evidence in H. Sengebusch, *Dissertatio Homerica*, first printed in *Homeri carmina*, ed. Dindorf (1855/6) 111 ff.

Sophistic 'method'. Socrates (*Prot.* 340 A ff.) is represented as borrowing from another prominent member of that circle, Prodicus, who was a fellow countryman of the Cean poet Simonides and the first authority on 'synonyms'; Prodicus is appealed to for a sharp distinction between the senses of ἔμμεναι and γενέσθαι which Protagoras had denied, and for the absurd identity of χαλεπόν and κακόν (341 A). In order to save a wise man like Simonides from sinning against reason, Socrates finally has recourse to the most violent transpositions of an adverb (ὑπερβατὸν δεῖ θεῖναι ἐν τῷ ᾄσματι τὸ ἀλαθέως, 343 E) and of an adjective (ἑκών, 345 E, 346 E); later grammarians and rhetoricians derived the name of the figure 'hyperbaton' from this passage.

It will hardly be possible to discern the real image of Sophistic interpretation through these malicious and amusing Socratic distortions; but if we catch a likeness of the 'historic' Protagoras at the beginning of his own discussion (339 A ff.), that passage is quite sufficient to show that he was not aiming at the true reading and meaning of the Simonidean text; the criticism of wording and sense in which he displays his own superiority is regarded as useful for the discipline of the mind of his pupils. It is this educational value which the Platonic Socrates most emphatically denies at the end (347 C ff.). One cannot question the ancient poet himself and discuss his poems with him (cf. also *Hipp. min.* 365 D), but only talk about a given literary text; such attempts do not lead to the truth, but result in arbitrary opinions. Behind this sceptical attitude to the Sophistic interpreters of the written word, there is in this early dialogue the first sign of Plato's distrust of poetry itself as a source of true wisdom of which we shall hear more later on.[1]

It is very likely that Protagoras' contemporaries and followers in the next generation practised a similar kind of interpretation;[2] there are hints in Plato's *Protagoras* as regards Prodicus and Hippias,[3] but no clear evidence. When Callicles (Plat. *Gorg.* 484 B)[4] in his speech about 'the law of nature' (νόμον . . . τὸν τῆς φύσεως 483 E) refers to a passage of a Pindaric poem (fr. 169 Sn.) he is by no means interested in explaining the text. On the contrary, he quotes the saying about the νόμος βασιλεύς[5]

---

[1] See below, pp. 58 f.
[2] Basilios Tsirimbas, *Die Stellung der Sophistik zur Poesie im V. und IV. Jahrhundert bis zu Isokrates* (Diss. München 1936) 53 ff.
[3] Cf. *Vors.* 86 B dub. about 'prosody' in B 15, Ψ 328.
[4] See E. R. Dodds, *Plato: Gorgias* (Oxford 1959) 270 ff.—*P.Oxy.* 2450 (published 1961) fr. 1, col. II starts with l. 6 of the Platonic quotation, but it may still be of some help; the numerous references to Pindar's lines are given in extenso by A. Turyn, *Pindari Carm.* (1948) fr. 187.
[5] M. Gigante, *Νόμος βασιλεύς* (1956) 146 ff. 'Ippia e Callicle, interpreti di Pindaro'.

to show that Pindar's νόμος is the same 'right of the stronger' which he,
Callicles himself, championed in his long ῥῆσις; and whatever Pindar's
view was, he could never have agreed with Callicles. Hippias (Plat.
Protag. 337 D), in a short reference to Pindar's line, apparently took
νόμος in a quite different way as 'convention'.[1] Critias (Plat. *Charm.*
163 B) used a half-line of Hesiod *Op.* 311 ἔργον δ' οὐδὲν ὄνειδος to support
his argument, when he wanted to work out the difference between
ἐργάζεσθαι, πράττειν, and ποιεῖν in the manner of Prodicus.[2]

One might suspect that in explaining Homer the Sophists, as educa-
tionalists, would have been inclined to follow the 'allegorical' line, which
began with Theagenes in the later sixth century. But there seems to have
been only one philosopher in the middle of the fifth century whom we
may label with confidence an allegorist, a pupil of Anaxagoras,[3] not
a Sophist, Metrodorus of Lampsacus (*Vors.* 61). He extended 'physical'
explanation from the gods to the heroes Ἀγαμέμνονα . . . αἰθέρα, Ἀχιλλέα
ἥλιον . . . Ἕκτορα σελήνην κτλ. (61 A 4,[4] cf. 2 and 3 πάντα εἰς ἀλληγορίαν
μετάγων); there is also one reference to a grammatical question (61 A 5
τὸ 'πλεῖον' δύο σημαίνειν φησί), exactly as in the case of Theagenes. In
Plato's *Ion* 530 C Metrodorus is associated with Stesimbrotus of Thasos
and a certain Glaucon, otherwise not known; the 'rhapsode' Ion claims
'to speak so beautifully about Homer, as neither Metrodorus nor Stesimbrotus nor Glaucon nor anyone else could do' (*FGrHist* 107 T 3). As
nothing is said about allegory, we must not infer from this passage that
Stesimbrotus used the same method as Metrodorus;[5] in the fragments of
his book on Homer (F 21–25) there is not the slightest trace of allegorical
interpretation. He is quoted in our Scholia to the *Iliad* about Nestor's
cup and about the division of the universe between the three sons of
Kronos; furthermore, he is mentioned as one who wrote, later than
Theagenes and before Antimachus of Colophon, who is attested to have

---

[1] See also Hdt. III 38.

[2] *Vors.* 84 A 18, registered under the *name* of Prodicus; it should be said that Critias is the
speaker. Cf. *Charm.* 163 D; Xenoph. *Mem.* I 2. 56.

[3] Diog. L. II 11 (*Vors.* 59 A I and 61 A 2). Even if we could trust Favorinus' statement
about Anaxagoras (δοκεῖ δὲ πρῶτος τὴν Ὁμήρου ποίησιν ἀποφήνασθαι εἶναι περὶ ἀρετῆς καὶ
δικαιοσύνης), it would not mean that he explained Homeric poetry as moral *allegory* (as many
people seem to believe including Sandys, *Hist.* I³ 30), but that he first made known its ethical
tendency; in that respect he would have been a predecessor of Aristophanes, see below,
pp. 47 f.

[4] On new combinations and readings of Pap. Herculan. 1081 and 1676 see J. Heidmann,
Der Pap. 1676 *der Herculan. Bibliothek* (Diss. Bonn 1937) 6 f. and F. Sbordone, 'Un nuovo libro
della Poetica di Filodemo', *Atti dell'Accad. Pontaniana*, N.S. IX (1960) 252 f.

[5] This traditional mistake is particularly stressed by W. Schmid, *Geschichte der griechischen
Literatur* I 2 (1934) 678, and worked out by F. Buffière, *Les Mythes d'Homère et la pensée grecque*
(Paris 1956) 132–6 'L'exégèse allégorique avant les Stoiciens'.

been his pupil, not only on Homer's poetry but also on his life and date. If this is correct, Stesimbrotus leads us to a very remarkable figure in the history of poetry and learning, of whom we shall hear later on, Antimachus of Colophon.[1]

At the moment, however, we have to look back to the Sophists. If it were true that Antisthenes had taken over the allegorical interpretation of Homer from Metrodorus,[2] we should at last have found a Sophistic allegorist. Antisthenes[3] was a pupil of Gorgias and influenced also by Prodicus, before he joined the circle of Socrates. We have a long list of titles of books by him on Homeric subjects (Diog. L. vi 17. 18), especially on the *Odyssey*, of which some quotations are preserved in our Scholia; there seems to have been even one book Περὶ 'Ομήρου ἐξηγητῶν.[4] So he was apparently much concerned with Homer and his interpretation; if we can trust Dio Chrysostom (*or.* 53. 5 Περὶ 'Ομήρου), Antisthenes was the first to make the distinction between 'seeming' and 'truth' in the Homeric poems (ὅτι τὰ μὲν δόξῃ, τὰ δ' ἀληθείᾳ εἴρηται τῷ ποιητῇ) which was later so often employed to explain contradictions. Such an explanation was necessary, because Homer was to Antisthenes an authority for moral doctrines; he paid no attention either to hidden meanings[5] or to the

---

[1] See below, pp. 93 f. Antimach. ed. B. Wyss (1936) test. 9 and fr. 129; cf. Callim. fr. 452. F. Jacoby in his commentary on Stesimbrotus, ii D p. 343. 22, rightly accepts Suidas' testimony about Antimachus (rejected by Wyss, loc. cit., p. iv), and says about Stesimbrotus: 'Von Beruf Rhapsode und im Sinne der Zeit auch Homerphilologe' and p. 349. 17 'verwendet alle Mittel der damaligen Philologie'. We had better avoid the term 'Philologie' for this period.

[2] W. Schmid *Geschichte d. griech. Lit.* i 1 (1929) 131, i 2 (1934) 679; Konrad Müller, 'Allegorische Dichtererklärung', *RE*, Suppl. iv (1924) 17; J. Geffcken, 'Entwicklung und Wesen des griechischen Kommentars', *Herm.* 67 (1932) 399 'unerfreuliche Allegoristik'; he even attributes to Antisthenes 'the first real commentary on a writer', namely on Heraclitus, but the Antisthenes who commented on Heraclitus (Diog. L. ix 15 = *Vors.* 22 A 1. 15) has been identified long ago as one of the other three Ἀντισθένεις mentioned by Diog. L. vi 19, the 'Ηρακλείτειος: Wissowa, *RE* i 2537. 36; cf. F. Dümmler, *Antisthenica* (1882) 16 ff.; his acute observations in Ch. 2, 'De Homeri sapientia', are partly misleading, esp. p. 24. The right line was taken by D. B. Monro, *Homer's Odyssey* xiii–xxiv (1901) 412 in his survey of ancient Homeric criticism; J. Tate in two articles on allegorism (see above, p. 10, n. 5) and finally in his vigorous polemics against R. Höistadt corroborated the statement that 'Antisthenes was not an allegorist' *Eranos* 51 (1953) 14–22 with detailed arguments. So F. Buffière (1956) did not repeat the old mistake, as he did in the case of Stesimbrotus (above, p. 35, n. 5).

[3] There is no recent collection of testimonia and fragmenta: Antisthenis *Fragmenta*, ed. Aug. Guil. Winckelmann, Zürich 1842, reprinted in Mullach's *F. Philos. Gr.* ii (1881), 261 ff.; rhetorical fragments in *Art. script.* ed. L. Radermacher (1951) b xix; see also H. Sengebusch, *Diss. Hom.* (1855/6) 115 ff. about his Homeric studies. See Addenda.

[4] Schol. a 1, ε 211 = η 257, ι 106, 525 (critical text in Schrader, Porphyr. *Quaest. Hom. in Od.* 1890); Diog. L. vi 17 περὶ ἐξηγητῶν, περὶ 'Ομήρου codd., corr. Krische, see Schrader, Porphyr. *Quaest. Hom. ad Il.* (1880) Proleg. p. 386.

[5] The *ironical* remark about ὑπόνοιαι in the conversation of Antisthenes, Niceratus, and Socrates (Xenoph. *Symp.* iii 6) is not made by Antisthenes, but by Socrates when he comments on the ignorance and folly of the rhapsodes who do not know the 'undersenses'.

literal sense. When he discussed πολύτροπος (α 1)[1] at some length, he was
not attempting to understand the proem of the *Odyssey* but to define the
general ethical meaning of the compound by which the figure of Odysseus
is characterized; Odysseus' experience in all manner (τρόποι) of words is
to him much superior to the brutal strength of Ajax (see also his fictitious
orations Αἴας and 'Οδυσσεύς).[2] The main point, however, is this: 'the
investigation of words is the beginning of education', ἀρχὴ παιδεύσεως ἡ
τῶν ὀνομάτων ἐπίσκεψις.[3] As far as we know the leading Sophists and their
immediate descendants like Antisthenes, none of them may be counted as
an allegorist. This is significant for the whole movement and not unimportant for the future. Furthermore, the answer to our question at the
beginning of this section must be in the negative: no true ἑρμηνεία τῶν
ποιητῶν did exist. The Sophistic explanations of poetry foreshadow the
growth of a special field of inquiry, the analysis of language; the final
object is rhetorical or educational, not literary.

No wonder, therefore, that the Sophists became more efficient in this
sphere than in any other one. Protagoras seems to have led the way with
his concept of ὀρθοέπεια;[4] he possibly dealt with 'correctness of diction' in
his famous book called Ἀλήθεια 'Truth'. Homer was criticized for com-
manding the Muse instead of praying to her, as we have seen in the
remarks about 'interpretation'. For Protagoras had established the rule
that four classes of sentences are to be distinguished: 'Wish (prayer),
question, answer, command', διεῖλέ τε τὸν λόγον πρῶτος εἰς τέτταρα·
εὐχωλήν, ἐρώτησιν, ἀπόκρισιν, ἐντολήν . . . οὓς καὶ πυθμένας εἶπε λόγων,
'which he called also bases ('fundamental principles' L–S) of speeches'.[5]

---

[1] See above, p. 4; cf. Hippias in Plat. *Hipp. min.* 364 c, 365 b?
[2] *Art. script.* b xix 11. 12 Raderm. Antisthenes followed the vulgate version of the epic
cycle (Bethe, *Homer* ii pp. 165 f. and 170 f.) that Ajax carried the body of Achilles. But there
seems to have been another early version, preserved by Ov. *met.* xiii 284 ff. and Schol. ε 310,
in which Odysseus carried the body; this is not an 'error' of the scholiast, *pace* Bethe who
omitted Ovid's testimony. The existence of a different version is confirmed by a fragment of
early epic hexameters *P.Oxy.* xxx ed. E. Lobel (1964) 2510. 13 and 21 in which Odysseus
does the carrying of the corpse.
[3] *Art. script.* b xix 6; cf. C. J. Classen, 'Sprachliche Deutung' *Zetemata* 22 (1959) 173–6, on
Antisthenes' interpretation of ὀνόματα (with bibliography 173. 6); see also F. Mehmel,
Antike und Abendland iv (1954) 34 f.
[4] See *Excursus*.
[5] Diog. L. ix 53 f. = *Vors.* 80 a 1 = *Art. script.* b iii 10. 11. This division into *four* 'bases' is
confirmed by Quintil. *inst.* iii 4. 10: Protagoran . . . qui interrogandi, respondendi, mandandi,
precandi . . . partes solas putat (= *Art. script.* b iii 12; not in *Vors.*). οἱ δὲ εἰς ἑπτά in our text of
Diog. L. ix 54 (*Vors.* ii⁵ p. 254, 14 f.) does not mean that others *said* that Protagoras made
a division into seven classes; it means that others *made* an alternative division, and we know
from the passage in Quintilian just quoted that Anaximenes did so (*Art. script.* b iii 12 and
xxxvi 9). It is a rather disturbing 'Parenthesis' in the text of Diog. L.—Alcidamas (see
below, pp. 50 f.) divided sentences into four classes, using other names (b xxii 8 and 9).

When a poet is thinking of a prayer to the Muse, he ought to employ the appropriate expression, and not the expression for the command: Μῆνιν ἄειδε, θεά. In the proem of the *Iliad* the poet is guilty also of an incorrect use of gender. The sense of words like μῆνις 'wrath' or πήληξ 'helmet' is clearly masculine; Μῆνιν . . . οὐλομένην, instead of οὐλόμενον, therefore was regarded by Protagoras as an incorrectness of construction;[1] he was apparently the first to divide τὰ γένη τῶν ὀνομάτων into Males, Females, and Things, ἄρρενα καὶ θήλεα καὶ σκεύη,[2] and to demand a strict observance of this division in the use of gender and ending of words. The comic poets readily made fun of such a novel doctrine of the correctness of gender. There is no doubt that Socrates in Aristophanes' *Clouds* (658 ff.)[3] reproduces the essence of Protagoras' teaching, when he starts with the characteristic words: δεῖ σε . . . μανθάνειν . . . ἅττ' ἐστὶν ὀρθῶς ἄρρενα. The perplexed pupil is instructed not to use ἀλεκτρυών for the 'hen', but ἀλεκτρύαινα (666), because this would be the correct feminine form for a female animal, and not to say τὴν κάρδοπον, but τὴν καρδόπην (678), as a word cannot have a masculine termination, if it is feminine. Ἀλεκτρύαινα as well as καρδόπη are inventions of the comic poet (cf. also *Clouds* 681 ff. and 847 ff.), but there are important new observations and discussions behind these playful lines.

We cannot go any further. The assumption that Protagoras was also the first to draw a distinction between the tenses of the verb is a rather unfortunate one; we have no special reference or quotation as we had in all the previous cases, beyond the short remark in Diog. L. ix 52 καὶ πρῶτος μέρη χρόνου[4] διώρισε καὶ καιροῦ δύναμιν ἐξέθετο, 'he first distinguished and defined(?) parts of time and set forth the importance of καιρός'. Whatever these mysterious words mean, they do not speak either of the 'verb' (never mentioned in the tradition about Protagoras) or the 'tenses'. Even in Plato χρόνος never means 'tense', but always 'time'.[5] The context in which the remark appears is more or less concerned with rhetoric,[6] and καιρός seems to point in the same direction. But another possibility is suggested by a few passages in later philosophical and

[1] Aristot. *Soph. El.* 14 p. 173 b 17 σολοικισμός (= *Vors.* 80 A 28 = *Art. script.* B III 7).
[2] Aristot. *Rhet.* III 5 p. 1407 b 6 (= *Vors.* 80 A 27 = *Art. script.* B 6).
[3] *Vors.* 80 C 3 = *Art. script.* B III 8 with Radermacher's notes.—Aristoph. *Nub.* 658 ff. are delightfully explained in every detail by J. Wackernagel, *Vorlesungen über Syntax* II (1924) 1–5.
[4] *Vors.* 80 A 1. M. Untersteiner, *I sofisti* I (1949) 19 'tempi del verbo'; W. Schmid, *Gr. Lit. Gesch.* I 3 (1940), 23. 11 'Tempora', etc.; C. P. Gunning, *De Sophistis Graeciae praeceptoribus* (Diss. Utrecht 1915) 112. 3, gives more bibliographical references; he himself proposes a rather trivial interpretation (a fixed time-table for his lectures) which is, strangely enough, mentioned by Diels–Kranz in their note ad loc.
[5] See below, p. 77.
[6] See Radermacher's note to *Art. script.* B III 24.

grammatical literature, such as Sextus Empiricus, *P.H.* III 144 (I, p. 173.
2 Mutschmann–Mau) ὅ τε χρόνος λέγεται τριμερὴς εἶναι, 'time is said
to be divided into three parts', past, present, future.[1] If Protagoras[2]
actually reflected on such a division of χρόνος in general, this might have
led to the later distinction of the (seven) so-called tenses, just as he possibly paved the way for the later doctrine of four moods by his four
species of sentences.

From the few incoherent fragments,[3] some of them perhaps not even
genuine, no plausible reconstruction of a true 'theory' of ὀρθοέπεια is
possible. We had better look back to Plato, *Prot.* 339 A, from which we
started; there we are told the real aim of all these endeavours which are
comprehensively termed εὐέπεια. If one has learned to distinguish which
words and sentences are correctly (ὀρθῶς) formed and which not, one
will be able to acquire eloquence, which is the chief part of education
(παιδεύσεως μέγιστον μέρος).

Nearly all the better-known Sophists after Protagoras made their own
contributions in the linguistic field. The representative figure became
Prodicus of Ceos; he was the coeval of Socrates (born 469 B.C.) and about
twenty years younger than Protagoras.[4] Apparently using the formula of
his great predecessor, Prodicus declared πρῶτον γάρ, ὥς φησι Πρόδικος,
περὶ ὀνομάτων ὀρθότητος μαθεῖν δεῖ (Plat. *Euthyd.* 277 E),[5] and Socrates
said παρὰ Προδίκου εἰδέναι τὴν ἀλήθειαν περὶ ὀνομάτων ὀρθότητος (*Crat.*
384 B); it was for this declamation on 'the correctness of words' that he
charged his listeners the unusual fee of fifty drachmai (ἡ πεντηκοντά-
δραχμος ἐπίδειξις).[6] The same rare expression ὀρθότης is used only once and

---

[1] Cf. the passage about τὰ χρονικὰ ἐπιρρήματα Ap. Dysc. *de adv.* p. 123. 21 Schn. τὰ μέντοι
οὐ διορίζοντα τὸν χρόνον, κοινὴν δὲ παράτασιν δηλοῦντα τοῦ παντὸς χρόνου (sc. νῦν, ἤδη); Schol.
Dionys. Thr., *Gr. Gr.* III 59 and 97 Hilg. (to § 19 Uhlig), esp. 97. 12 ff. τὰ χρονικὰ ἐπιρρήματα
ἢ καθολικὸν χρόνον δηλοῖ ἢ μερικόν . . . 19 f. τὰ καιροῦ παραστατικά, τουτέστι τὰ ὑποτομὴν
χρόνου δηλοῦντα (σήμερον, χθές, αὔριον).

[2] Diog. L. very liberally credited Protagoras with 'first inventions'; he or his source clearly
changed Plato's *Euthydem.* 286 C, οἱ ἀμφὶ Πρωταγόραν . . . καὶ οἱ ἔτι παλαιότεροι, into οὗτος
πρῶτος διείλεκται. So we should not take πρῶτος διώρισε too seriously.

[3] It is of no use to apply a much later term (see below, p. 202) to his efforts and call him
an 'analogist' or to say that, in the universal dispute between φύσις and νόμος, language was
to Protagoras a product of human convention (Burnet), or of nature (Gunning); the clear
antithesis does not seem to have been fixed before Hippias (below, pp. 53, 63) in the next
generation (see also *Excursus* to p. 37).—There is a charmingly written paper by G. Murray,
The Beginnings of Grammar (1931), repr. in *Greek Studies* (1946) 171–91, but not quite reliable
in all its details.

[4] K. v. Fritz, 'Prodikos', *RE* XXIII (1957) 85 ff. The beautiful and enthusiastic paper of
F. G. Welcker, 'Prodikos von Keos, Vorgänger von Sokrates', first published in *Rh.M.* 1832
and 1836, reprinted with Addenda in *Kleine Schriften* II (1845) 393–541 is still worth reading;
on Prodicus' study of language see esp. 452 ff.

[5] *Vors.* 84 A 16 = *Art. script.* B VIII 10 with Radermacher's note.

[6] *Vors.* 84 A 11 (cf. 12) = *Art. script.* B VIII 6; cf. below, p. 62.

with some emphasis by Aristophanes, when the language of Euripides' prologues is being tested τῶν σῶν προλόγων τῆς ὀρθότητος τῶν ἐπῶν (*Ran.* 1181).[1] In the two lines of the prologue of Euripides' *Antigone* (fr. 157 sq. N.[2]) two words are rejected by Aeschylus in the *Frogs* (1182 ff.) as not properly describing Oedipus' fate ἦν . . . εὐτυχής[2] and εἶτ' ἐγένετο ἀθλιώτατος, on the ground that he was unfortunate from the very beginning. The criticism here is not of the *form* of words (as in the 'Protagorean' passage of the *Clouds* 658 ff.), but of their meaning. So it is very likely that we get a glimpse of Prodicus[3] in these lines of the *Frogs*; the remark about ἦν–ἐγένετο even reminds us of the heated debate about the distinction of εἶναι and γίγνεσθαι in Plato's *Protagoras* (340 B ff.), where Socrates finally appeals to Prodicus. He was the acknowledged authority on the differentiation of kindred terms; all the direct references in Plato and Aristotle (*Vors.* 84 A 13–19) are in complete harmony with Aristophanes' hint in the *Frogs*. Even if there is a slight ironical exaggeration in Plato's picture of Prodicus' teaching, there can be no doubt that he in particular liked to deal with two or three different words which seemed to have the same sense (not called 'synonyms' before Aristotle, below, p. 78); his aim was to show the error in this assumption. The precise meaning of ἀμφισβητεῖν and ἐρίζειν, of εὐφραίνεσθαι and ἥδεσθαι, of βούλεσθαι and ἐπιθυμεῖν, of ποιεῖν, πράττειν, ἐργάζεσθαι was by no means the same to Prodicus; by a subtle discrimination between them, called διαίρεσις,[4] he instructed his pupils 'about the correct use of the words', περὶ ὀνομάτων ὀρθότητος (which should not be confused with Protagoras' purely 'formal' ὀρθοέπεια).

It has been said[5] that Prodicus intentionally neglected etymological arguments for his task of διαίρεσις. But in his book Περὶ φύσεως ἀνθρώπου, quoted by Galen,[6] he objected to the use of φλέγμα for 'mucus' (phlegm) in medical literature precisely from the etymological point of view; as it is derived from φλέγω 'burn, inflame', it must mean 'inflammation' and the

---

[1] For metrical reasons he said ἐπῶν instead of ὀνομάτων, which would hardly fit into the iambic trimeter together with the decisive term ὀρθότητος and with προλόγων.

[2] Modern editors keep the wrong variant reading, εὐδαίμων, in spite of the protest of Nauck, *TGF* (1889), Add. p. xxv, and Wilamowitz, *Aischylos-Interpretationen* (1914) 81. 1.

[3] L. Spengel, Συναγωγὴ τεχνῶν (1828) 41, first compared *Ran.* 1181 with the references by Plato to Prodicus; but he confused the issue in so far as he identified the ὀρθότης ὀνομάτων of Prodicus with Protagoras' ὀρθοέπεια and was followed by others.

[4] *Vors.* 84 A 17–19; see also Plat. *Prot.* 358 A τὴν δὲ Προδίκου τοῦδε διαίρεσιν τῶν ὀνομάτων παραιτοῦμαι, ibid. 341 C, and Radermacher's notes on *Art. script.* B VIII 10 and 11.—A complete list of Prodicus' synonyms is given by Hermann Mayer, *Prodikos von Keos und die Anfänge der Synonymik* (Diss. München 1913) 22 ff.

[5] W. Schmid, *Gr. Lit. Gesch.* I 3 (1940), 46. 8.

[6] *Vors.* 84 B 4; Galen himself wrote three books Περὶ ὀνομάτων ὀρθότητος.

like; for a humour (mucus, 'phlegm' still, in spite of Prodicus' protest, current in English) one should say βλέννα. Even if one finds such considerations rather pedantic, one has to admit that they have no longer the playful character of previous centuries; they are not philosophical[1] speculations either, but sober and new reflections on problems of language. By dwelling on precise distinctions of meaning, Prodicus was led to an awareness of the different usage in different parts of the country; in the course of the explanation of Simonides' poem, he utters the curious opinion that Pittacus was not able τὰ ὀνόματα . . . ὀρθῶς διαιρεῖν ἅτε Λέσβιος ὢν καὶ ἐν φωνῇ βαρβάρῳ τεθραμμένος (Plat. *Prot.* 341 C, cf. 346 D), 'as a Lesbian and grown up in a foreign idiom he could not correctly differentiate the words'. In his *Cratylus* Plato seems to be reproducing similar Sophistic discussions from a source of the fifth century about ξενικὰ ὀνόματα,[2] when he refers to Aeolic or Doric words as 'alien', that is, different from the familiar Attic form.[3] Herodotus,[4] whether influenced by his contemporaries like Prodicus or not, was able to observe acutely subtle differences between the languages of four Ionic cities (1 142), and travelling through so many foreign countries he made use of such observations on language for his historical conclusions. But he aimed at ἱστορίη, not at formal knowledge and rhetorical practice, as the Sophists did. It was their work, and especially that of Prodicus, which apparently stimulated future studies[5] in the field of γλῶσσαι, as the first glossaries were called in the third century. It is hardly surprising that in Aristophanes'[6] gibes it is Prodicus' name that turns up as the alternative to a book: ἢ βιβλίον . . . ἢ Πρόδικος. He was an essentially literary man, even if we can trust the tradition about his political mission from his native island to Athens; it was a lucky hit of Plutarch's to combine this amiable Sophist and the leading scholar-poet of about 300 B.C., Philitas, as typical valetudinarians from their early years: Πρόδικον τὸν σοφιστὴν ἢ Φιλίταν τὸν ποιητήν . . . νέους μέν, ἰσχνοὺς δὲ καὶ νοσώδεις καὶ τὰ πολλὰ

---

[1] There were also rather wild 'etymological' speculations current in the circle of the so-called Heracliteans, see K. Reinhardt, *Parmenides* (1916) 241 f.

[2] In pre-Hellenistic times διαλεκτικά means 'dialectics', not 'dialect'; ξενικά is the usual term for non-Attic, see below, pp. 62, 79.

[3] *Cratyl.* 401 C Attic οὐσίαν, others ἐσσίαν, ὠσίαν; 409 A Doric ἅλιον, Attic ἥλιον; 434 C ἡμεῖς μέν φαμεν 'σκληρότης', Ἐρετριεῖς δὲ 'σκληροτήρ'. More examples are given by K. Latte, 'Glossographika', *Philol.* 80 (1925) 158 ff., who thinks of an Ionic Heraclitean as Plato's source.

[4] On Herodotus and Hecataeus see H. Diels, 'Die Anfänge der Philologie bei den Griechen' *NJb* 25 (1910) 14 ff.; cf. below, p. 45, n. 1.

[5] On the immediate influence on Antisthenes' concept of ὀνομάτων ἐπίσκεψις see above, p. 36; cf. also Democritus' γλῶσσαι and ὀνομαστικῶν [sic] *Vors.* 68 B 26 (below, p. 42).—For later writers περὶ συνωνύμων see Schmid–Stählin, *Gr. Lit. Gesch.* II 2⁶ (1924) 1080.

[6] Fr. 490 K. and for his *Ὧραι* as a circulating 'book' see above, p. 30.

κλινοπετεῖς δι᾽ ἀρρωστίαν ὄντας (*an seni* 15, p. 791 E).[1] The picture of Prodicus as a weakling seems to be taken over from Plato (*Prot.* 315 D), but it might have been originally derived from a contemporary comic poet, as it was certainly the new comedy that made fun of Philitas' frailty.

One of the foremost Ionic philosophers in the second half of the fifth century, Democritus, was a native of Abdera like Protagoras and a coeval of Prodicus and Socrates (about 465–about 370 B.C.); a great traveller, he said of himself: 'I came to Athens—and no one recognized me.'[2] Plato never mentions Democritus, though he tells us so much about his contemporaries. Amongst his writings, which covered nearly every field of knowledge, there was a small section called Μουσικά in Thrasyllus' catalogue,[3] after ἠθικά, φυσικά, etc. Aristotle again and again refers to Democritus' views on physics or ethics, but never to this literary section. Its title and those of the individual works, Περὶ ῥυθμῶν καὶ ἁρμονίης, Περὶ ποιήσιος, κτλ., are derived from the Πίνακες[4] of the Alexandrian library and preserved only in Diogenes Laertius; none of the few later writers who quoted a Democritean saying on poetry, language, or criticism attributed it to one of these books; the attributions of the respective fragments in our modern collections are made according to the subjects of the sayings and are therefore quite arbitrary. We cannot even be certain that genuine Democritean expressions were used for the headings. Democritus' knowledge of the 'philosophy' of his fellow townsman Protagoras is attested by his polemics against it (68 A 114, B 156); so we should very much like to know if Democritus borrowed from him the important term ὀρθοέπεια:[5] Περὶ Ὁμήρου ἢ ὀρθοεπείης καὶ γλωσσέων (68 A 33, XI 1 = B 20 a). The wording of this title suggests a distinction between a 'straight' epic diction and the obsolete words needing explanation; this would be no startling novelty, as the correctness of Homer's use of the Greek language and the difficulty of his rare vocables were discussed at least from the sixth century on.[6] In his admiration of Homer's divine genius and inspired poetry he is on the side of Theagenes and the rhapsodes against Xenophanes and Heraclitus; but in conformity with his Sophistic contemporaries he seems to have abstained from allegorical

---

[1] Not mentioned in *Vors.* or in *Art. script.*; cf. *Philetae Coi reliquiae*, ed. G. Kuchenmüller (Diss. Berlin 1927) test. 14, cf. test. 15 *a–b*, 16 and p. 22; see below, p. 91.

[2] *Vors.* 68 B 116; Demetr. Phal. fr. 93, Wehrli, *Die Schule des Aristoteles* 4 (1949) 64, on Democritus and Athens.

[3] *Vors.* 68 A 33, X and XI; B 15 c–26 a. ('Philologische Schriften.')

[4] O. Regenbogen, v. Πίναξ, *RE* XX (1950) 1441 f.

[5] See above, p. 37, and *Excursus* on ὀρθοέπεια.

[6] See above, pp. 11 f.

explanations.[1] Democritus was an ingenious innovator[2] of philosophical language himself; he must have had an intimate knowledge of earlier poetry and prose and an open mind also for general questions of language. To judge from our scanty evidence, he hardly went beyond the steps made by the great Sophists, and I am inclined to suspect that in this field the impulse came from their side. But while the Sophists used to concentrate on individual problems,[3] Democritus' universal spirit apparently considered all of them[4] in turn. He was not really concerned with either the interpretation of Homer or rhetorical training in the service of education, but with his own philosophical doctrines. So he was pleased to detect an epic line in which his own identification of νοῦς and ψυχή was anticipated, as Aristotle reported (68 A 101); his general linguistic[5] theory (68 B 26, a badly corrupted passage of Proclus) may well have been connected with his concept of the origin and development of civilization as expressed in his principal work on Physics, the Μικρὸς διάκοσμος.[6] Surely there is no reason to say that Democritus foreshadowed Alexandrian scholarship or even to proclaim him as the 'Altmeister unserer Wissenschaft', as his most fervent admirer did.[7]

When we now turn to questions of literary criticism, we should expect to discover in the Sophists a new attitude to epic poetry. In the sixth century the activity of the rhapsodes was very lively, and it continued into the fifth century.[8] It looks as if all or most of the narrative epics were regarded as the works of *one* poet, called Homer. The earliest writer of elegiacs that we know, Callinus of Ephesus, in the first half of the seventh century ascribed to him even the epics on the Theban wars;[9] in the popular story-books of the sixth century about the life of Homer and about his contest with Hesiod he is the maker of a remarkable number of poems, mainly on the Trojan war, but also on *The Afterborn*, the Ἐπίγονοι in the Theban wars, and on the *Taking of Oechalia*. At the same time

[1] In this point I agree with R. Philippson, Democritea I. 'D. als Homerausleger', *Herm.* 64 (1929) 166 ff.

[2] K. v. Fritz, *Philosophie und sprachlicher Ausdruck bei Demokrit, Plato und Aristoteles* (New York 1938) 24 ff.

[3] On Protagoras see above, p. 42, on Prodicus p. 41, n. 5, on Hippias p. 53, n. 5.

[4] Cf. Aristot. *de gen. et corr.* 315 a 34 ἔοικε . . . περὶ ἁπάντων φροντίσαι (68 A 35).

[5] Cf. below, p. 59, n. 2 (Plat. *Crat.*) and p. 79, n. 2 (Aristotle).

[6] 68 B 4 c ff.; Diels should not have followed K. Reinhardt in printing the whole of Diod. I 7 and I 8 as excerpts from Democritus; but we cannot go into the details of the endless dispute. On the objections to Reinhardt, 'Hekataios von Abdera und Demokritos', *Herm.* 47 (1912) 492 ff. = *Vermächtnis der Antike* (1960) 114 ff., see G. Pfligersdorffer, 'Studien zu Poseidonios', *Sitz. Ber. Österr. Akad.*, Phil.-hist. Kl. 232 (1959) 5. Abh., 100 ff.

[7] H. Diels, first in the year 1880, repeated in 1899 and 1910, see *NJb* 25 (1910) 9.

[8] See above, pp. 11 ff. and 35.

[9] Callin. fr. 6 B.[4] (= Paus. IX 9. 5), see E. Bethe, *Thebanische Heldenlieder* (1891) 147.

Theagenes wrote about Homer's life and poetry,[1] but we do not know how far he connected all these epics with him. In the great competitions at the Panathenaic festival not only our two preserved epic poems were recited, but many others in proper order. Similarly, in the fifth century Aeschylus' famous saying that his tragedies are 'slices from the great banquets of Homer'[2] refers to the mass of epic narrative poems, and the same is meant by the writer who described[3] Sophocles, the φιλόμηρος, as 'delighting in the epic cycle', from which he derived most of his plots, as Euripides did after him. Who finally started to examine that enormously rich epic production and to differentiate between the single poems and their respective poets?

If we consult Wilamowitz, who made the most penetrating inquiries into this problem as a whole,[4] we meet a number of highflown concepts: 'Das fünfte Jahrhundert beschränkt wesentlich *aus künstlerischem Urteil* (the italics are mine) seinen [Homer's] Nachlass auf Ilias, Odyssee und Margites.' But, in fact, there is no evidence to be found of the 'higher criticism' to which he refers, or the 'examination of poetical value', or the 'essentially artistic judgement'.[5] The only author whose critical observations we can still read is Herodotus, who simply noticed (II 116) the discrepancy between the account of Paris' and Helen's route from Sparta to Troy in the *Cypria* (fr. 12 Allen = fr. 10 Bethe) and that in the *Iliad* (Z 289 ff.) and consequently denied Homer's authorship of the *Cypria*; speaking of the Hyperboreans in Homer's *Epigonoi* (IV 32) he cautiously added 'if Homer[6] really made this epic poem' (*Epig.* fr. 3 Allen). The historian asks if the tradition of epic poetry is trustworthy; a strictly logical discussion of Helen's story (II 113–20) discovers contradictions and leads to the conclusion that the Iliadic tale about Helen in Troy was wrong and that the Egyptians knew better. There is no comparison of the literary qualities of different epics in order to separate the best poems

---

[1] See above, p. 11.

[2] Athen. VIII 347 E = test. 47, Aesch. ed. Wilamowitz 1914, p. 16 τεμάχη τῶν Ὁμήρου μεγάλων δείπνων.

[3] Athen. VII 277 E = test. ad l. 94 *Vitae*, Soph. *El.* ed. Iahn–Michaelis³ (1882) 20 ἔχαιρε... τῷ ἐπικῷ κύκλῳ. The term κύκλος was obviously still being applied to the complete cycle of epic, that is Homeric, poems by the 'Eristics' whom Aristotle refuted (see below, p. 73).

[4] U. v. Wilamowitz, *Homerische Untersuchungen* (1884), ch. II 4, pp. 328 ff. 'Der epische Cyclus', esp. pp. 352 f., 366 f. Cf. E. Schwartz, *Die Odyssee* (1924) 154, and T. W. Allen, *Homer, Origins and Transmission* (1924) 51, 75.

[5] *Die Ilias und Homer* (1916) 365; cf. *Platon* I (1919) 71 (about the fifth century): 'Auch die höhere Kritik, *die Prüfung der Gedichte auf ihren Wert* [italics are mine] und ihr Alter wagt sich hervor und hat den Erfolg, daß dem Homer alle heroischen Epen außer Ilias und Odyssee abgesprochen werden.' Cf. H. Diels, *NJb* 1910, 13.

[6] Cf. *Certamen Homeri et Hesiodi* 15 p. 43. 1 Wil. *Vitae Hom.* = Allen, Hom. v p. 235, l. 260 Ἐπιγόνους ... φασὶ γάρ τινες καὶ ταῦτα Ὁμήρου εἶναι.

from the rest.[1] In vain we look round for more. Wilamowitz's reference[2] to Stesimbrotus and Hippias of Thasos, not repeated in this connexion in his later books, does not help. We had occasion to mention the fragments of Stesimbrotus' book on Homer when we spoke of allegorism; he did not deal with 'formal offences' in different epic poems, but only with the contents of some passages of the *Iliad*. Hippias[3] proposed two readings in *B* 15 and in *Ψ* 328 as solutions (λύσεις) of rather odd textual problems quoted only by Aristotle;[4] there is no reason why he should be assigned to the fifth century, and he obviously did not concern himself with relations of epic poems to each other.

At first it may be unexpected and somehow disappointing that in the age of the Sophists no distinct traces can be found of that κρίσις ποιημάτων, which was to be regarded as 'the finest flower of scholarship'[5] in the best Hellenistic times. On second thoughts, however, we may find this result in harmony with the general line we took that the Sophists should not be regarded as 'pioneers of scholarship'. The study of epic poetry only subserved their rhetorical and educational aspirations.

The foremost stylist was the Sicilian Gorgias from Leontini, and he had also an inclination to theorize on stylistic problems.[6] Born at the beginning of the fifth century and thus coeval of Protagoras, he is said to have reached the age of 105 or even 109 years; but his first visit to Athens was paid only in 427 B.C., after Protagoras and Prodicus had started their activity there. The final object of their teaching was, as we have pointed out, to educate (παιδεύειν) each pupil by making him περὶ ἐπῶν δεινόν (*Prot.* 338 D); if Gorgias shifted the *whole* emphasis on to the rhetorical training, according to Plato's statement (*Meno* 95 C δεινοὺς λέγειν, *Gorg.*

[1] H. Diels, *NJb.* 25 (1910) 13, considerably over-estimated the merits of Herodotus ('der zuerst . . . mit Glück den echten und den unechten Homer abzugrenzen suchte . . . die höchste Stufe der philologischen Kritik . . . im V. Jahrhundert', etc.).

[2] *Hom. Untersuch.* 366; after mentioning Herodotus' passage on the disagreement of *Iliad* and *Cypria* in a point of subject-matter he continues: 'Formelle Anstöße muß selbst die kindliche Philologie der Thasier Stesimbrotus und Hippias genommen haben.' On Stesimbrotus see above, p. 35.

[3] F. A. Wolf, *Prolegomena ad Homerum* (1795) CLXVIII. 'Hippias, acumine artibus Loyolae digno' owes his modern fame to the whole page which F. A. Wolf dedicated to him in his small volume.

[4] Aristot. *Poet.* 25 p. 1461 a 22 and *Soph. El.* 4 p. 166 b 1 ff.; on the details of these two passages see the commentaries on the *Poetics*; on λύσεις and λυτικοί see below, pp. 69 ff.

[5] Dionys. Thr. 1 p. 6. 2 Uhl. κρίσις ποιημάτων, ὃ δὴ κάλλιστόν ἐστι πάντων τῶν ἐν τῇ τέχνῃ.

[6] *Vors.* 82 AB; *Art. script.* B VII. One would not expect to find a book of his entitled 'Ονομαστικόν, though it is ascribed to Γοργίᾳ τῷ σοφιστῇ by Poll. IX praef. and quoted I 145 (ἐπίβολος = ἔμβολος 'peg', not in L–S under ἐπίβολος); cf. C. Wendel, *RE* XVIII (1939) 507. There is no reference to this 'Ονομαστικόν by Diels–Kranz or Radermacher; it should have been mentioned under *Dubia* or *Falsa*. Gorgias the Athenian *FGrHist* 351 who wrote Περὶ ἑταίρων might be the author; see below, p. 208, n. 6.

459 c ff.), and did not expressly claim to be an educationalist, we may still regard him as belonging to the wider circle of the Sophistic movement.[1]

The two rhetorical παίγνια of Gorgias preserved to us, the *Praise of Helen* (*Vors.* 82 b 11[2] = *Art. script.* b vii 39) and the *Defence of Palamedes* (b 11 a = b vii 44), reveal his eagerness to create a new prose-style, rivalling the poetry of the past, and thus show himself a worthy disciple of his fellow countryman, the poet Empedocles.[3] The Homeric Scholia contain at least *one* example showing how he took over one antithesis from a line of the *Iliad* and amplified it by a second one: Δ 450 ἔνθα δ' ἅμ' οἰμωγή τε καὶ εὐχωλὴ πέλεν ἀνδρῶν; Schol. T Γοργίας· ἀνεμίσγοντο δὲ λιταῖς ἀπειλαὶ καὶ εὐχαῖς οἰμωγαί (b 27 = b vii 43), quoted perhaps from one of his lost model-speeches.[4] Somewhere he referred to Homer as a descendant of Musaeus (b 25), not of Orpheus. The themes of his declamations, originally epic subjects, had been recently treated by all the Attic tragedians, and Gorgias' artistic prose is much more indebted to them than to earlier poetry. But beyond stylistic devices Gorgias seems to have had a quite new and personal interest in the tragic drama. No pronouncements either of the other Sophists or of Herodotus or Democritus are extant about the great contemporary Attic poetry; only Gorgias, speaking about Aeschylus, called one of his plays, the *Seven against Thebes* 'full of Ares', μεστὸν Ἄρεως (b 24).[5] The same phrase occurs in Aristophanes' *Frogs* 1021 δρᾶμα ποιήσας Ἄρεως μεστόν.—ποῖον; —τοὺς "Επτ' ἐπὶ Θήβας, where it is spoken by Aeschylus himself to Dionysus. Chronologically, it is just possible that Gorgias, who survived the end of the fifth century by about ten years, took the words out of the comedy, produced in 405.[6] But apparently in Plutarch's Peripatetic source of the fourth century Gorgias was said to have coined the felicitous phrase; if we accept this tradition (as we are bound to do in such cases), Aristophanes must have borrowed the expression from Gorgias. It is also much more plausible that the Aristophanic Aeschylus used a famous phrase favourable to himself than that Gorgias quoted Aristophanes verbatim. It is quite legitimate to raise the further question whether Aristophanes owes anything else in his literary statements or judgements

---

[1] On this question and the position of Gorgias see E. R. Dodds, *Plato: Gorgias* 6–10.

[2] Cf. Gorgiae *Helena*, recogn. et interpretatus est O. Immisch (*Kleine Texte für Vorlesungen und Übungen* 158 [1927]), with a very useful commentary.

[3] *Vors.* 31 A 1 § 58; see also above, p. 14.

[4] b 17 = B vii 19 and b 14 = b vii 1.

[5] See *Excursus*.

[6] This view was vigorously championed by O. Immisch, 29 f.; but see Radermacher's review, *Philol. Wochenschrift* 1928, 5 ff.

to Gorgias or to other contemporary Sophists. But the result of learned investigations[1] and clever combinations does not amount to more than the probability that the words and ideas in the gigantic contest between Aeschylus and Euripides are not entirely Aristophanes' own inventions. We have noticed *one* point of contact with Gorgias in *Frogs* 1021. Apart from this characterization of a single tragedy, some casual statements of Gorgias on tragic art and on poetic art in general and its relation to artistic prose are preserved, but they have no manifest parallels in Aristophanes' comedies. In Plutarch (*de glor. Ath.* 5, p. 348 C, cf. *de aud. poet.* p. 15 D) Gorgias is quoted as saying: ἡ τραγῳδία ... παρασχοῦσα τοῖς μύθοις καὶ τοῖς πάθεσιν ἀπάτην, ὡς Γοργίας (*Vors.* 82 B 23) φησίν, ἣν (ἣν 15 D: ἦν 348 C) ὅ τ' ἀπατήσας δικαιότερος τοῦ μὴ ἀπατήσαντος (cf. Δισσοὶ λόγοι 3. 10, *Vors.* 90, II, p. 411. 1) καὶ ὁ ἀπατηθεὶς σοφώτερος τοῦ μὴ ἀπατηθέντος, 'tragedy ... by (the display of) myths and passions has caused a deceit such that he who deceives is juster than he who does not and the deceived is wiser than the one who is not deceived'. This may be a serious, not an ironical, remark on art producing 'illusions'. When Euripides charges Aeschylus, ὡς ἦν ἀλαζὼν καὶ φέναξ οἵοις τε τοὺς θεατάς / ἐξηπάτα (Aristoph. *Ran.* 909), he simply means that his adversary is an impostor and liar who cheats his audience; such a reproach (of ψεῦδος) is characteristic of literary polemics and parodies from early times, not a comic distortion of a supposed Sophistic 'doctrine' of illusionism. In this case, there is no relation between Gorgias and Aristophanes.

We have observed that poetry itself paved the way to its understanding, and poets naturally were the competent critics of poetry; this particularly applies to dramatic criticism.[2] It is one of the important topics of Old Comedy from its beginning,[3] and Aristophanes is to be regarded as the greatest heir of this tradition. We have been able to use some single lines of Aristophanes in order to find out with their help how the Sophists started to interpret early poetry or to reflect on language; it is likely that

[1] M. Pohlenz, 'Die Anfänge der griechischen Poetik', *NGG* 1920, Phil.-hist. Klasse, 142–78 = *Kleine Schriften* II (1965) 436 ff., tried to prove that Aristophanes used a theoretical book of Gorgias, which contained a syncrisis of Aeschylus and Euripides. Even if this conclusion cannot be accepted, the article offers a valuable collection of relevant passages from the fourth and fifth centuries and started a very lively discussion. Wilamowitz, Radermacher, W. Kranz, M. Untersteiner (*The Sophists*, Engl. transl. 1954, with a useful bibliography 192 f.), W. Schadewaldt, E. Fraenkel, and others took part in it; Pohlenz, *Herm.* 84 (1956) 72 f. = *Kl. Schr.* II 585 f., quite amiably retracted a good deal of his own overstatements.

[2] Regarding the judges who made the decision in dramatic contests, A. Pickard-Cambridge, *The Dramatic Festivals of Athens* (1953) 98, dryly remarks: 'That there was any demand for critical capacity seems unlikely.' So these κριταί do not concern us.

[3] A. E. Roggwiller, *Dichter und Dichtung in der attischen Komödie* (Diss. Zürich 1926), collected the material rather inadequately (see E. Wüst, *Philol. Wochenschr.* 1927, 1137 ff.); W. Schmid, *Gesch. d. griech. Lit.* I 4 (1946) 11, 13, 21, 209, etc.

Aristophanes adopted more topics from contemporary discussions than the single phrase of Gorgias on Aeschylus, but we should not take the risk of transferring his literary judgements by mere conjecture back to one or other of the Sophists. He had his own ideas and his own creative language; and it is just in this aesthetic field that expressions apparently coined by Aristophanes were taken up by the poets of the third century.[1] Fundamentally, his attitude to poetry was opposed to that of the Sophists; he regarded the earlier poetry as the most important part of the ἀρχαία παιδεία. Greek poetry was quite naturally 'ethical' from epic times onwards; it was only in the great crisis towards the end of the fifth century that a consciousness arose of this innate ethical tendency as a problem.[2] The documentary evidence for the new reflection on it is given by Aristophanes, especially in the *Frogs*, where the great poets of the past, represented by Aeschylus, are approved as the moral leaders of their people, while contemporary poets, represented by Euripides, or 'philosophers', like Socrates and the Sophists, are condemned as destroyers of morals.

In the course of his declamation on Helen Gorgias stresses again the importance of the ἀπάτη, the 'deception', which every λόγος (speech), whether in verse or prose, is able to produce (*Hel.* 8. 10 and probably 11). Then he calls poetry in general a 'speech in verse', τὴν ποίησιν ἅπασαν καὶ νομίζω καὶ ὀνομάζω λόγον ἔχοντα μέτρον (*Hel.* 9), which sounds like depreciating it in the interest of rhetoric; but, on the other hand, he goes on to describe the extremely powerful effect of this 'metrical composition' on the listeners, ἧς τοὺς ἀκούοντας εἰσῆλθε καὶ φρίκη περίφοβος καὶ ἔλεος πολύδακρυς καὶ πόθος φιλοπενθής κτλ., 'shuddering in great fear and tearful wailing and yearning for grief'. One is, of course, inclined to confine these words to tragedy, as Aristotle did in the *Poetics*,[3] but Gorgias certainly meant to include epic and lyric poetry as well, if we can trust the text of our two manuscripts. I am not sure that it is not even implied for the first time that oratory, the pure and simple word without music or metre, can be equally effective. For Gorgias started this part of his

---

[1] See below, pp. 137 f.

[2] Cf. *DLZ* 1935, 2134 and my whole review of W. Jaeger, *Paideia* I (1934); see also *Die griechische Dichtung und die griechische Kultur* (1932) 18.

[3] See Pohlenz, loc. cit. 167 ff., and especially W. Schadewaldt, 'Furcht und Mitleid?' *Herm.* 83 (1955) 129 ff., 144, 158, 165 = *Hellas und Hesperien* (1960) 346 ff., who provides the most detailed and convincing interpretation of the relevant terms φόβος (φρίκη) and ἔλεος; cf. also H. Flashar, 'Die Lehre von der Wirkung der Dichtung in der griechischen Poetik', *Herm.* 84 (1956) 18 ff.: he scrutinized the Corpus Hippocraticum in order to show that φόβος and ἔλεος with all the somatic symptoms mentioned by Gorgias have their origin in the literature on medical science. On Aristotle see below, p. 75.

declamation with the solemn proposition (*Hel.* 8) λόγος δυνάστης¹ μέγας
ἐστίν, 'logos is a mighty ruler . . . it has the power to stop fear and to
remove grief and to effect joy and to increase lamenting', δύναται γὰρ καὶ
φόβον παῦσαι καὶ λύπην ἀφελεῖν καὶ χαρὰν ἐνεργάσασθαι καὶ ἔλεον ἐπαυξῆσαι.
This sounds like a hymn in prose² on a divine power; indeed the logos is
said to 'accomplish works most divine', θειότατα ἔργα ἀποτελεῖ. Such
sentences are a true specimen of Gorgias' style, but they can hardly be
regarded as traces of a doctrine on poetics. Single striking formulae, like
that of φρίκη and ἔλεος, were adapted to later theories, as Aristophanes
selected that on the *Seven*. It was Gorgias' main ambition to teach his
pupils the technical devices of his grand new style; but the formal perfection ought to have the emotional effects on the hearers which he
described. Gorgias' efforts have often been subjected to ridicule in
ancient³ and modern⁴ times; this is easier than to try to reach a balanced
judgement on them. The artificialities and empty phrases of the virtuoso
may be boring or even repellent, particularly to the philosophic mind;
but we still feel a genuine φιλία, a love for the λόγος, as the moving power
behind them. This seems to have 'enchanted' his contemporaries and to
have exerted a lasting influence.⁵ Such a stimulus cannot be entirely
disregarded in a history of φιλολογία.

Of Gorgias' many pupils the most distinguished were Isocrates and
Alcidamas, two different, even contrasting figures. Like his master,
Isocrates⁶ (436–338 B.C.) has not been a favourite either with philosophers
or scholars; but nobody can deny him his true love and mastery of
language. He brought his own oratorical skill to perfection and succeeded
in teaching the following generations of the fourth century; as a pedagogical genius he may be compared with Melanchthon. In spite of his
polemical speech 'against the Sophists', κατὰ τῶν σοφιστῶν (*or.* 13), in
which he attacks the false claims of his rivals, he represents the 'literariness' of the whole movement at its height. Following Gorgias, he too
wrote a 'hymn' to the λόγος.⁷ In contrast to Gorgias, however, his λόγος

¹ Pohlenz, loc. cit. 174 ff., M. Untersteiner, *The Sophists* (1954), pp. 107, 114. J. W. H.
Atkins, *Literary Criticism in Antiquity* I (1934, reprinted 1952) 18.
² About 2,000 years later in 1444 Lorenzo Valla opened his *Elegantiae Latini Sermonis* with
a similar fervent hymn on the Latin language.
³ *Auctor Περὶ ὕψους* 3. 2 τὸ οἰδοῦν, μειρακιῶδες, ψυχρόν, κακόζηλον κτλ.
⁴ J. D. Denniston, *Greek Prose Style* (1952) 10 ff., 'the influence was, I believe, wholly bad'.
⁵ E. Norden, *Die antike Kunstprosa* I (1898) 63–79, 'Gorgias und seine Schule'; pp. 15 ff.
'Die Begründung der attischen Kunstprosa'.
⁶ *Art. script.* B XXIV Radermacher (1951). Marrou 79–91 ; I have always found W. Jaeger's
judgement on Isocrates (*Paideia* III 199–225, esp. 222 f.) well balanced, and disagree with
Marrou on this point. W. Steidle, *Herm.* 80 (1952), 257 ff., esp. 274 ff., 296.
⁷ Isocr. *or.* 3, Nicocl. 5–9 = *Art. script.* B XXIV 41. 3, repeated almost verbatim in *or.* 15,
Antidos. 253–7.

did not aim at the emotional effects of φρίκη and ἔλεος, of 'shuddering and wailing', but at rational persuasion by sober arguments (πείθειν, πίστεις); he is said to have called rhetoric πειθοῦς δημιουργόν, 'persuadendi opificem' (*Art. script.* B XXIV 18, cf. 19 ἐπιστήμην πειθοῦς). Some Sophists unfortunately confused this creative reasoning, the λόγος, with sterile learning, γράμματα, as Isocrates complained (*or.* 13 κ. σοφ. 10 ff.); for his part no doubt, he highly valued the comprehensive knowledge of literature, poetry as well as artistic prose (*or.* 2 *in Nicocl.* 13, etc.), but only in so far as it led to the final ideal, to εὖ λέγειν 'good speaking'.[1] This is not meant in a purely formal sense. 'To use the λόγος well', λόγῳ καλῶς χρῆσθαι, is the best guarantee of παίδευσις, of 'culture' (*or.* 4, *Panegyr.* 49); and 'those are called Greeks rather who share in our [i.e. Athenian] culture than those who share in our common race' καὶ μᾶλλον Ἕλληνας καλεῖσθαι τοὺς τῆς παιδεύσεως τῆς ἡμετέρας ἢ τοὺς τῆς κοινῆς φύσεως μετέχοντας (ibid. 50, cf. 15. 293). For the first time the cultural unity of the 'Greeks' is quite consciously proclaimed in this most famous sentence of Isocrates; it points far into the future.[2] For these general reasons he deserves his place in the history of scholarship.

Alcidamas,[3] perhaps slightly older than Isocrates, was in favour of the improvisation of speeches in practice and theory. He regarded the epic rhapsodes as improvisators and himself as continuing the rhapsodic tradition in oratory; it may have been in the same tradition that he took up and retold the old popular story of the 'Contest of Homer and Hesiod' in αὐτοσχεδιάζειν, 'improvising', of which we found the first traces in the sixth century.[4] This treatise of Alcidamas[5] was probably a part of a larger book with the title Μουσεῖον (which originally means 'shrine of the Muses'); it is tempting to attribute to the same book the other fragments of Alcidamas dealing with poetry.[6] Epic poetry is mainly represented by

[1] Cf. Marrou 81.

[2] See 'Humanitas Erasmiana', *Studien der Bibl. Warburg* 22 (1931) 2, n. 2.

[3] *Art. script.* B XXII; other fragments in *Orat. Att.* rec. Baiter–Sauppe II (1850) 154–6; see above, p. 37, n. 5.

[4] See above, pp. 11 and 43 f.; F. Nietzsche, 'Der Florentinische Traktat über Homer und Hesiod, ihr Geschlecht und ihren Wettkampf', *Rh.M.* 25 (1870) 528 ff. and 28 (1873) 211 ff. =*Philologica* I (1910) 215–76; he was only wrong in the assumption that the 'Contest' was an 'invention' of Alcidamas; otherwise his reconstruction of Alcidamas' *Museum* was confirmed by two recent papyri, see the following note.

[5] On the Michigan Papyrus (first publ. 1925) and the Flinders Petrie Pap. (first publ. 1891) see E. Vogt, 'Die Schrift vom Wettkampf Homers und Hesiods', *Rh.M.* 102 (1959) 193 ff., *Gnom.* 33 (1961) 697, with bibliographical additions, and *Antike und Abendland* XI (1962) 103 ff. (The Flind. Petr. Pap. is now P. Lit. Lond. 191, revised by H. J. M. Milne, *Catal. of the Lit. Pap. of the Brit. Mus.* (1927) 157.) On the *subscriptio* Περὶ Ὁμήρου in the Michigan Pap. see E. R. Dodds, *Cl. Qu.* 46 (1952) 188.

[6] F. Solmsen, 'Drei Rekonstruktionen zur antiken Rhetorik und Poetik', *Herm.* 67 (1932) 133 ff.

references to the *Odyssey*; he called it a 'fair mirror of human life' καλὸν
ἀνθρωπίνου βίου κάτοπτρον, at that time a startling metaphor, which met
with Aristotle's sharp disapproval (*Rhet.* III 3 p. 1406 b 12).[1] Other short
sentences may point to his definition of tragic pathos, which perhaps
owed something to that of his master Gorgias.[2] Alcidamas also mentioned
lyric poets (Archilochus, Sappho) and philosophers (Pythagoras, Anaxagoras) honoured by certain Greek cities.[3] So it is clear that his book was
a compilation of varied learned material, and this links him with the
group of Sophists to whom we now finally come, those who mainly or
exclusively collected and described 'antiquities'. Ἀρχαιολογία was the
Greek term for 'antiquarian lore' as distinguished from the great political
and military 'history'; *antiquitates*, Varro's Latin translation of ἀρχαιολογία,
became the familiar expression for this branch of indispensable knowledge,
depreciated or overestimated with equal injustice at later times.

It was Hippias of Elis[4] as represented in Plato's dialogue (*Hipp. mai.*
285 D = *Vors.* 86 A 11) who used the word ἀρχαιολογία for the first and
only time in pre-Hellenistic literature; 'people like to hear about the
genealogies of heroes and men, about the early foundations of cities, καὶ
συλλήβδην πάσης τῆς ἀρχαιολογίας,[5] and so he had 'to learn and to teach
all these things most carefully'. Plato represents him as boasting of his
universal knowledge as well as of his practical skill in everything (*Hipp.
min.* 368 B = *Vors.* 86 A 12). Malicious though this picture may be,
Hippias deserves positive credit for investigating some special 'antiquities'.
His register of Olympic winners, Ὀλυμπιονικῶν ἀναγραφή (B 3) is probably the first attempt[6] at establishing a basis for Greek chronology.[7] The
title of a book on Ἐθνῶν ὀνομασίαι (B 2) points to ethnographical
antiquities for which the explanation of names was important;[8] from
another book simply called Συναγωγή, 'Collection', (B 4) comes the story

---

[1] E. Fraenkel, Aesch. *Ag.* II 385 f. On the great success of the metaphor (*speculum vitae*,
etc.) in ancient and medieval Latin literature see E. R. Curtius, *Europäische Literatur und
Lateinisches Mittelalter* (Bern 1948) 339. 1.

[2] F. Solmsen (above, p. 50, n. 6) 140 ff.

[3] *Art. script.* B XXII 14; cf. Radermacher's note on 13. The title *Museum* was taken up by
Callimachus, I 339.

[4] *Vors.* 86; selection of fragments with commentary *FGrHist* 6 (reprinted 1957 with Addenda) and *Art. script.* B XI.

[5] E. Norden, *Agnostos Theos* (1913) 372 f. ἀρχαιολογία in der älteren Sophistik.

[6] On its reliability as a historical source see L. Ziehen, *RE* XVII (1937) 2527 ff. On similar
publications of the last decades of the fifth century see F. Jacoby, *Atthis* (1949) 59.

[7] The fundamental importance of the chronological system for co-ordinating the traditions
about facts of the past was recognized by Hecataeus (about 500 B.C.), but he was completely
misled by the fictitious lists of Spartan kings of which he actually tried to make use for that
purpose.

[8] Cf. Hellanicus 4 *FGrHist* 67 and Damastes of Sigeion, 5 *FGrHist*.

of a celebrated beauty who was married to fourteen men. There must have been the utmost variety in subject-matter if we take into account all the other surviving short references to mythology, geography, history, and especially to early poets and philosophers. Hippias (b 8) observed that the word τύραννος was not introduced into the Greek language before the time of Archilochus; Homer called even the worst despot βασιλεύς.

Hippias made parallel excerpts from the poets of old (b 6), Orpheus, Musaeus, Hesiod, Homer; it is noteworthy that we find exactly the same sequence in Aristophanes (*Ran.* 1030 ff.), in Plato (*Apol.* 41 A; without Hesiod *Ion* 536 B), and even in Hermesianax (fr. 7. 16 ff. Powell). It is quite likely that he added a similar collection of parallel passages from the earliest philosophers, in which Thales[1] continued the line of the four poets just mentioned. The 'Ολυμπιονικῶν ἀναγραφή was not a chronicle but a list of names with only a few necessary remarks; so, I think, it is hardly correct to call his literary collections the beginning of a 'history' of literature and philosophy.[2] Instead, the proper form of all the antiquarian writings of Hippias and his contemporaries seems to have been the catalogue, the list, the πίναξ.[3] The Sophist was in need of this knowledge as orator and teacher; as in other fields, it was not a scholarly interest in the customs of life in former ages or even in the 'history of culture', but the practical requirements of his calling, that inspired his efforts.[4]

We have put the study of antiquities first, because it was particularly characteristic of Hippias; but as a genuine polymath[5] he incorporated into his educational programme not only all literary knowledge, but also elementary scientific subjects. Independently, it seems, of any Pythagorean tradition, he listed together astronomy, geometry, arithmetic, and 'music',[6] a combination of sciences that had a long and varied history until finally Boëthius[7] gave it the name *quadrivium*, nearly a thousand years after Hippias.[8] Hippias' own interests were by no means limited to

---

[1] See b 7 and B. Snell, 'Die Nachrichten über die Lehren des Thales und die Anfänge der griechischen Philosophie- und Literaturgeschichte', *Philol.* 96 (1944) 170 ff.; cf. F. Jacoby, *FGrHist* I² (1957) p. 542 Nachträge zum Kommentar 6 F 4 and G. B. Kerferd, 'Plato and Hippias', *Proceed. Class. Association* 60 (1963) 35 f.

[2] See above, n. 1.

[3] O. Regenbogen, Πίναξ *RE* xx (1950) 1412 f.   [4] See above, pp. 17, 45.

[5] Xenoph. *Mem.* IV 4. 6 = *Vors.* 86 A 14 διὰ τὸ πολυμαθὴς εἶναι; Cic. *de or.* III 127 (not in *Vors.* 86). On the changing reputation of the πολυμαθής see below, p. 138, n. 1.

[6] Plat. *Hipp. mai.* 285 BC (= *Vors.* 86 A 11) and *Prot.* 318 E with reference to Hippias. H. I. Marrou, 371, n. 12, believes that μουσική means 'acoustics' in this passage.

[7] Boëth. *Instit. arithm.* p. 5. 6 Friedlein.

[8] P. Merlan, *From Platonism to Neoplatonism* (1953; 2nd ed. 1961) 78 ff. 'The origin of the Quadrivium'; see also A. Cornel. Celsus ed. F. Marx, *Corp. Medic. Lat.* 1 (1915), VIII–XIII, on names, number, order of the *artes* from the Sophists to Boëthius. Cf. below, p. 253.

four or to seven subjects, and he was not the inventor of the seven
liberal arts. He was not a serious philosopher or political theorist, but as
he was always eager to startle his audience by some novelty, he managed
to give a new turn to the contemporary discussion of 'physis and nomos';
at least, in Plato's *Protagoras*[1] it was Hippias who first used the antithetic
formula φύσει—νόμῳ in the sense 'by nature'—'by convention', a formula
which became almost classical. In his studies of language he accepted,
like others, Protagoras' concept of ὀρθοέπεια; he took part in the lively
debates[2] on the epic poems (B 9), on Homeric Heroes (A 9, B 5), on the
life of the poet Homer (B 18). One field, so far avoided by other Sophists,
was entered by Hippias alone. Questions of rhythmics and metrics had
been the concern of the musicians, possibly of Lasus of Hermione[3]
towards the end of the sixth century, certainly of the Athenian Damon,[4]
the teacher of Pericles; Hippias seems to have been the first 'literary'
man, not a musician, to treat language together with music, distinguishing
'the value of letters and syllables and rhythms and scales' περί τε γραμμάτων δυνάμεως καὶ συλλαβῶν καὶ ῥυθμῶν καὶ ἁρμονιῶν.[5] From single
sounds he went on to several letters taken together, that is to syllables[6]
and their quantities, then to certain sequences of long and short syllables,
to rhythms, and finally to 'harmonics'.[7] The traditional Greek unity of
word and 'music' was still maintained, but the emphasis may have been
shifted from 'music' to language;[8] the end of this important development
came in the second half of the fourth century, when we find poetical
diction and metre[9] treated in complete isolation from rhythmics. The
part played by Hippias and perhaps other Sophists in the period of
transition is hardly noticed by modern scholars. A versatile Sophist like

[1] Plat. *Prot.* 337 C (= *Vors.* 86 C 1), see above, pp. 35, 39, n. 3.

[2] See above, pp. 36, 43 ff.

[3] W. Schmid, *Geschichte der griechischen Literatur*, I 1 (1929) 544 ff. Lasus is said to have
caught Onomacritus at the court of the Pisistratides forging oracles of Musaeus (Hdt. VII
6 = *Vors.* 2 B 20a).

[4] *Vors.* 37 esp. B 9; Aristoph. *Nub.* 638 ff.; Wilamowitz, *Griechische Verskunst* (1921) 59 ff.,
and *Platon* I (1919) 71; W. Schmid op. cit. I 2 (1934) 731 ff.

[5] Plat. *Hipp. mai.* 285 D = *Vors.* 86 A 11, cf. above, p. 52, n. 6. See also Plat. *Hipp. min.*
368 D = *Vors.* 86 A 12 καὶ περὶ ῥυθμῶν καὶ ἁρμονιῶν καὶ γραμμάτων ὀρθότητος; *Cratyl.* 424 C,
Phileb. 18 B ff. Cf. Democr. above, pp. 42 f.

[6] Cf. Aesch. *Sept.* 468 γραμμάτων ἐν ξυλλαβαῖς.

[7] ἁρμονία usually means the different 'tunings' (Plat. *Rep.* III 398 D ff., and on this passage
Isobel Henderson, 'Ancient Greek Music', *New Oxford History of Music* I (1957) 384 f.); I can
see no reason why it should be understood in the passage on Hippias as 'melodic line',
'pitch-accents' (as it apparently has to be taken in Δισσοὶ λόγοι 5. 11 = *Vors.* II 413. 14, see
H. Gomperz, *Sophistik und Rhetorik* (1912) 71, 148).

[8] It was about the same time towards the end of the fifth century that Glaucus of Rhegium
wrote Περὶ τῶν ἀρχαίων ποιητῶν καὶ μουσικῶν (see F. Jacoby, *RE* VII 1417 ff.) without separat-
ing 'musicians' and 'poets' of old times, as it seems.

[9] See below, p. 76 (Aristotle).

Hippias was almost bound to write verses of his own also: epics, tragedies, dithyrambs (A 12); a lament in elegiacs on the drowned Messenian boy choir (B 1 ἐλεγεῖα ... ἐποίησεν) may remind us of Archilochus' elegy on the drowned Parians.[1]

As Hippias claimed competence in so many fields, so do the Satyrs in a play which Sophocles[2] apparently produced late in his life; in the well-preserved fragment[3] they recommend themselves to a king (Oineus?) as suitors of his daughter because they have not only all the desirable abilities in games and contests in poetry, music, and dancing,[4] but also the most useful knowledge in various branches of science and scholarship. It is a charming and humorous picture, not a malicious travesty, of exactly that universalism which Sophists like Hippias used to display.

We find the same combination of antiquarian lore with poetry in Critias (about 460–403 B.C.),[5] so that we may group him with Hippias. He is said to have been a pupil of Gorgias (*Vors.* 88 A 17) and certainly was for some time an associate of Socrates (ibid. A 4); but when he finally tried to put Sophistic ideas on the 'right of the stronger'[6] into practice, he met an early death as 'tyrannorum dux' at the battle of Munichia (A 12). Strong aristocratic prejudices are patent in his writings on literature. In an unknown work in prose (B 44) he utterly condemned the self-revelations of the lowborn Archilochus, but he celebrated in an epic poem the 'sweet' Anacreon, once a friend of one of Critias' own noble ancestors[7] and a 'weaver of songs' for the pleasures of high society; the ten hexameters (B 1 = fr. 8 D.[3]) may be a part of a longer poem on the lives and works of a number of poets, starting perhaps from Homer as the son of a rivergod (B 50). So we rightly place Critias beside Alcidamas and

---

[1] Fr. 7 D.[3] and *P.Oxy.* 2356.

[2] I confidently attribute *P.Oxy.* 1083, fr. 1 (reprinted in D. L. Page, *Greek Literary Papyri* 1 [1942], no. 31 and in *Satyrographorum Graec. fragmenta*, ed. V. Steffen (2nd ed. 1952) 258) to Sophocles. v. 13 ἐψευσμένα occurs twice in Sophocles, *O.R.* 461 and fr. 577 P., but there is no perfect passive either in Aeschylus or Euripides. This is the decisive passage. Furthermore, the future ἐξερῶ is found twelve times in Sophocles (nine times perfect and aorist) not in Aeschylus, and only twice in Euripides, but in different phrases. The anaphora v. 9 ff. was noticed as possibly Sophoclean by Hunt in *P.Oxy.* VIII p. 61; cf. also P. Maas, *Berlin. Philol. Wochenschrift* 32 (1912) 1427–9. A number of new fragments, written by the same hand and published in *P.Oxy.* XXVII (1962) as no. 2453 by E. G. Turner, strengthen the case for Sophocles.

[3] The other more than thirty small fragments written by the same scribe may belong to other plays (and even to other poets).

[4] Cf. Soph. *Amphiaraus* fr. 121 P. satyrs dancing the letters.

[5] *Vors.* 88; poetical fragments also in *Anth. Lyr. Gr.* ed. Diehl fasc. 1[3] (1949) 94 ff.; new complete edition with commentary by A. Battegazzore in *Sofisti*, ed. M. Untersteiner IV (1962) 214–363.

[6] See above p. 35.

[7] See A. E. Taylor, *A Commentary on Plato's Timaeus* (1928) 23 ff.

Hippias. In his elegiacs he produced a catalogue of inventors (B 2 = fr. 1 D.[3]), Greek as well as foreign, from which we have already quoted[1] the invention of the alphabet by the Phoenicians, an epoch-making event in the history of mankind and particularly in the history of scholarship. Other elegiacs deal with customs, inventions, or even constitutions in different parts of Greece and show his open preference of Sparta as a model (B 6 = fr. 4 D.[3]) His special interest in inventions and his taste for collecting learned material are completely in the tradition of the Sophists; so is his educational aim (see also B 9 = fr. 7 D.[3]). As we know his considerable poetical faculties from the fragments of his tragedies and satyr-plays (B 10–29), we are not surprised that he was the only Sophist who also put some of his learned material into verse, in order to make it perhaps more attractive for the reader. Critias, as writer of 'antiquarian' elegiacs and 'literary' epics, holds an important position in the middle between the *poetae philosophi* of the past and the *poetae docti* of the future, being himself neither a philosopher nor a scholar. Some contemporary writers, Euenus (*Art. script.* B xx), Licymnius (ibid. B xvi), Agathon (*TGF* p. 763 N.[2]), more familiar to us as poets of elegiacs, dithyrambs, tragedies, were in close relation to the Sophistic movement. What is left to us of Greek literature confirms that it went through a time of uneasiness and crisis at about 400 B.C.[2]

We said above (p. 16) that in a certain sense the Sophists can be regarded as heirs of the early rhapsodes. Now the rhapsodes, still reciting and interpreting[3] the traditional poetry at the end of the fifth century, survived the crisis. They had quite naturally become pupils of the Sophists. Socrates in Plato's *Ion*[4] complained that the clever, 'divinely inspired' rhapsode had neither τέχνη nor ἐπιστήμη, neither 'art' nor 'knowledge' (536 C οὐ γὰρ τέχνη οὐδ' ἐπιστήμη περὶ Ὁμήρου λέγεις ἃ λέγεις, cf. ibid. 532 C). The same reproach was made against the Sophists in general, although for a quite different reason. Their various activities in the literary field were based only on observation and practical experience. There can be no doubt about their own efficiency and their kindling of sparks in other minds. They made a decisive contribution to the development of the book on which the rise and further existence of

---

[1] See above, p. 24; cf. A. Kleingünther, Πρῶτος Εὑρετής, *Philol.* Suppl. Bd. 26. 1 (1933) 145.

[2] See also the new relation of λόγος to μουσική above, p. 53.

[3] Plat. *Ion* 530 C (τὸν γὰρ ῥαψῳδὸν ἑρμηνέα δεῖ τοῦ ποιητοῦ τῆς διανοίας γίγνεσθαι τοῖς ἀκούουσι); see also above, p. 35.

[4] If I say 'Plato's *Ion*', I mean that the ideas and arguments of this much disputed dialogue are genuinely Platonic; a critical review of the dispute is given by H. Flashar, *Der Dialog Ion als Zeugnis platonischer Philosophie* (Berlin 1958) 1–16.

scholarship depended. They awakened and maintained a new interest in early poetry, even if interpretation meant no more to them than mental training. Rhetorical virtuosity was the immediate result of their analysis of language and their 'critical' study of literature. Nevertheless, their genuine love of language was not without stimulating influence on generations who started more serious researches. Finally, if they had to accumulate wide erudition for their own performances and the instruction of pupils, such collections turned out sometimes to be suggestive for later studies. But all their endeavours, considerable as they were, had a more or less casual and arbitrary character; even the mathematics they taught apparently remained on an empirical level.

III

THE MASTERS OF PHILOSOPHY IN ATHENS: SOCRATES, PLATO, ARISTOTLE

THE Sophists did not proceed from the way of ἐμπειρία to a conscious method, to a τέχνη, an 'art' which combined practical skill and theoretical knowledge. Scholarship, as we stated at the very beginning, is such a τέχνη. The failure of the Sophists to achieve this aroused the Socratic–Platonic criticism and opposition.[1] But it was not the general polemics, the various arguments against the Sophists, or minor readjustments by Plato that were decisive; what did matter was the completely new approach, namely the eager desire to acquire τέχνη, 'art', to gain 'genuine knowledge based on reason' (ἐπιστήμη), to try to reach the Truth (τῆς ἀληθείας ... πεῖραν Prot. 348 A, cf. Phaedr. 270 A f., Meno passim). This went far beyond Protagoras' vague doctrine of 'correctness', which was characteristic of the Sophistic mind. The rigorous Platonic demand for full mastery of the subject, for clear definitions and sober proofs, made it possible for the first time to lay a truly scientific foundation in every field of intellectual activity; it determined the whole future of scholarship as well as of science. We do not have to deal with science, and, as in the strict Platonic sense ἐπιστήμη refers to exact sciences, especially mathematics, and then to ethics (the knowledge of the ἀγαθόν),[2] we confine ourselves to

[1] Plat. Phaedr. 270 B μὴ τριβῇ μόνον καὶ ἐμπειρίᾳ, ἀλλὰ τέχνῃ, cf. Gorg. 463 B, 465 A. An exact definition is given by Aristot. Metaphys. A 1 p. 981 a 5 γίγνεται δὲ τέχνη, ὅταν ἐκ πολλῶν τῆς ἐμπειρίας ἐννοημάτων μία καθ᾽ ὅλου γένηται περὶ τῶν ὁμοίων ὑπόληψις 'Art arises when from many notions of experience there comes a single universal judgement', W. D. Ross, Arist. Metaph. 1 (1924) 114, translation. On the Platonic character of this chapter and its relation to the treatment in the Protrepticus see W. Jaeger, Aristoteles (1923) 68 ff. = Engl. translat. by R. Robinson (2nd ed. 1948) 68 ff. (τέχνη and ἐπιστήμη are not distinguished by Aristotle in this chapter, but see Anal. post. 100 a 9). I. Düring, Aristotle's Protrepticus (1961) 242 agrees with Jaeger and Ross. It cannot be proved and it is not likely that Plato used a sort of 'formula' coined in Hippocratic circles, see K. Deichgräber, Die griechische Empirikerschule (1930) 273. 1. This negative statement is confirmed by F. Heinimann, 'Eine vorplatonische Theorie der τέχνη', Mus. Helv. 18 (1961) 105 ff., who thoroughly scrutinized early Sophistic and medical writings; the novelty of the Socratic–Platonic differentiation between ἐμπειρία and τέχνη becomes quite evident.

[2] K. v. Fritz, 'Der Beginn universalwissenschaftlicher Bestrebungen und der Primat der Griechen', Studium Generale xiv (1961) 618 f., on this particular problem; on the meaning of ἐπιστήμη 610 ff.

τέχνη.[1] There is no need to go into the vexed question whether it is possible to distinguish between the original Socratic contribution and the Platonic representation of it; but it is almost certain that the character who indefatigably asks questions about τέχνη in the *Apology* and in many dialogues is meant to be the historical Socrates himself.

When we described the results of the Sophistic movement in our province of learning, we noted Plato's reaction in some cases, and we shall not repeat what was said then. Socrates never wrote a book, and Plato had great doubts about the value of the written word so much favoured by the Sophists. He believed their task of interpreting the old poets to be useless or even impossible. Behind this sceptical attitude to the interpreters, whether rhapsodes or Sophists, there lies Plato's deep distrust of the poets themselves.[2] Poetry was to him something ἄλογον, 'not reasonable' or even 'contrary to reason'. He regarded it from the beginning as 'inspired' (*Apol.* 22 A–C, *Ion* 533 E etc.),[3] and later on, according to the doctrine developed in *Rep.* x, also as 'mimetic' (esp. 595 ff.). This was not in contradiction to his general view, which he never gave up, but an additional explanation, based on the following metaphysical argument: 'Imitation (μίμησις) takes only the third place after the prototypes and the world of objects (ibid. 597 E) and so Homer's poetry as imitation is play, not seriousness' (εἶναι παιδιάν τινα καὶ οὐ σπουδὴν τὴν μίμησιν ibid. 602 B); still worse, there are others, like the tragedians, 'who produce an evil political order in the soul of the individual' (ibid. 605 B). In Plato's ideal city as the realm of reason the citizens would be endangered by the poets; therefore they have to be expelled (with very few exceptions, ibid. 607 A; cf. *Leg.* 817 BC). The 'ancient quarrel' between philosophy and poetry (παλαιὰ . . . διαφορὰ φιλοσοφίᾳ τε καὶ ποιητικῇ ibid. 607 B 5), started by Xenophanes, was renewed on a higher level (see also *Rep.* II, esp. 379 ff. on poets and gods). Consequently there could be no place for literary criticism; an 'inspired' poetry is inaccessible to it, and a 'playful' mimetic art seemed to be hardly a worth while subject for serious criticism. As for the polymathy, including the antiquarian studies, of people like Hippias, nobody would expect Plato to have particularly valued that, even if he had not expressed his opinion unmistakably in the Hippias dialogues.

[1] On τέχνη, ἐμπειρία, and ἐπιστήμη see H. Steinthal II² 162–79; see also below on Dionys. Thr. pp. 268 and 272.

[2] E. R. Dodds, *Plato: Gorgias* (1959) 322; H. Flashar, *Der Dialog Ion* (1958) 106 ff.: 'Platon und die Dichter' with bibliography.

[3] ἐνθουσιασμός must imply 'divine' origin (θείᾳ μοίρᾳ καὶ κατοκωχῇ *Ion* 536 C); but this poetical unconscious 'enthusiasm' is fundamentally different from the ἐνθουσίασις of the philosopher (*Phaedr.* 249 CE) who is led by reasoning to knowledge and truth πρὸς τῷ θείῳ γιγνόμενος.

This cursory survey again emphasizes the divergencies of approach and sounds rather discouraging; but did Plato at least appreciate the efficiency of the Sophists in the linguistic sphere where they seemed to be at their best? The Sophistic analysis of language was haphazard and often pretentious; Socrates developed it in a most constructive and methodical way and created a new refined instrument for dialectic. Plato in his *Cratylus* was the first to put problems of language in the centre of a comprehensive philosophical debate; they remained present to his mind, as they turned up again and again in later dialogues (*Sophistes* 252 A ff., *Philebus* 18 B ff., occasionally also in *Symp.* 198 B f., *Rep.* 462 C ff., *Theaet.* 206 D, *Tim.* 49 E, cf. *Ep.* VII 342 B ff.). Sophistic debates and the discoveries of contemporaries were, no doubt, a sort of stimulus for Plato; but he went back also to the Homeric studies and to the serious 'linguistic' studies of earlier philosophers. Cratylus[1] himself, a so-called Heraclitean, naturally represents the ideas of Heraclitus, but there are Eleatic elements admixed by the other interlocutor Hermogenes, and possibly also Democritean elements;[2] a philosophy of language in general emerges. The Platonic dialogue deals exclusively with 'words' and their relation to 'things', and Plato's whole interest is concentrated on the possibility of the knowledge of τὰ ὄντα, of the 'world of things'. It is only if we keep this main tendency in our mind that we may be able to grasp the meaning of some of his individual statements on language, particularly on etymology, which otherwise sound rather startling to the modern mind, and are easily misunderstood.[3]

Protagoras, it seems, used but *one* expression for words, ὀνόματα; so apparently did Antisthenes.[4] Plato in his *Cratylus* used two, ὀνόματα and ῥήματα (399 AB, 425 A, 431 B); they were more clearly distinguished and defined in the *Sophistes* (262 A): ὀνόματα are understood as 'names of things' and ῥήματα as 'things said about them'.[5] This was neither a technical distinction in the sense of the later grammar ('noun' and 'verb') nor a logical one ('subject' and 'predicate' in the Aristotelian

---

[1] *Vors.* 65 (only testimonies, no fragments); J. Stenzel, *RE* XI 1660 ff.

[2] See above, p. 42, and below, *Excursus* to p. 60.

[3] Steinthal I[2] 79 ff. The *complete* title of this great work deserves attention; it was first published in 1863, dedicated to A. Böckh, and its chapters on *philosophy* of language are not yet superseded. On Steinthal's own theories see J. Wach, *Das Verstehen* III (1933) 206–50.— P. Friedländer, *Platon* II[2] (1957) 181 ff. Kratylos; bibliography in notes 1, 7, 8, 20, pp. 310 ff.; cf. also Sandys I[3] 92–96; G. Murray, *Greek Studies* 176–9 in a paper quoted above, p. 39, n. 3, on *Cratylus* not very sympathetic and partly mistaken; R. H. Robins, *Ancient and Mediaeval Grammatical Theory in Europe* (1951) 12 ff.; Barwick, 'Stoische Sprachlehre' 70–79 (Platons Kratylos).

[4] Protagoras: above, pp. 37 ff., Antisthenes pp. 36 f.

[5] I borrow my translation from G. Murray's paper, loc. cit.

sense of ὑποκείμενον and κατηγορούμενον); it was proposed and explained in the course of the discussion on the value of words for the knowledge of things (τὰ ὄντα), which was Plato's main concern, as we have just said.[1] If someone is called Διὶ φίλος (*Crat.* 399 B), φίλος is a ῥῆμα, because it is said about him; Δίφιλος, as the name of someone, is an ὄνομα. Both are δηλώματα, 'means of making something known', as Plato said in the *Sophistes* (261 E), where ὄνομα refers to the πράττοντες (doing the action) and ῥῆμα to the πρᾶξις (the action); but they do not make anything known until they are 'twined together' and produce a λόγος, a sentence: ἄνθρωπος μανθάνει (262 C).

If words really are δηλώματα, it is worth while to inquire into the 'elements' out of which they are made. Hippias the Sophist may have entered this province before Plato, dealing with letters and syllables and rhythms in a different way, perhaps following Democritus.[2] Plato called the elements of sound (which he apparently identified with 'letters' γράμματα, as the first components of the syllable) στοιχεῖα (*Crat.* 393 D, 424 C, 426 D); in the *Sophistes* (252 B) he used the same term for the first principles of the physical world.[3] A few decades later Aristotle's favourite pupil, Eudemus of Rhodes, was not able to find any earlier evidence of this usage; so he acknowledged Plato's priority, στοιχεῖα πρῶτος αὐτὸς ὠνόμασε τὰς τοιαύτας ἀρχάς (fr. 31 Wehrli).[4] This may well be correct. Eudemus would only be refuted, if a passage of the Peripatetic philosopher Adrastus of Aphrodisias (second century A.D.) could be dated back into the fifth century B.C.;[5] then Plato as well as Aristotle would be deprived of the claim to the introduction of several important scientific terms, such as ὀνόματα and ῥήματα, φωναὶ πρῶται ... στοιχειώδεις ... ἀδιαίρετοι. So far, there has not been the slightest proof, nor has any clear pre-Platonic evidence been detected; but, of course, it may turn up one

---

[1] Plato speaks about the δύναμις of ὀνόματα *Crat.* 394 BC. The source of Diog. L. III 25 (Favorinus as in III 24, F. Leo, *Die griech.-röm. Biographie* (1901) 55; cf. ibid. 46 ff., about εὑρήματα) refers, I should think, to this passage or to similar ones when it calls attention to some εὑρήματα of Plato's: καὶ πρῶτος ἐθεώρησε τῆς γραμματικῆς τὴν δύναμιν. Whatever Diog. L. meant by δύναμις, Plato never pretended to speculate on 'grammar', which did not yet exist in the later technical sense. The translations of the often-quoted remark of Diog. L. differ widely and are misleading: Sandys I³ 92 'the first to speculate on the nature of grammar', or R. H. Robins, loc. cit. 17 'first considered the potentialities of grammar'. In Strato's line σκοπεῖν ἕκαστον τί δύναται τῶν ῥημάτων (below, p. 91) δύναται simply refers to the proper 'meaning' of the rare vocables.

[2] See above, p. 53.

[3] Cf. *Theaet.* 201 E, 202 E, 203 B, *Phileb.* 18 C στοιχεῖα, as letters; as first principles cf. *Tim.* 48 B, 54 D.

[4] Cf. Diog. L. III 24; in this case we can trace the statement of Diog. L to a reliable source (via Favorinus?); on the other hand, see the sceptical remarks to p. 35, n. 3 and above, n. 1.

[5] See *Excursus*.

day, as Plato freely adopted expressions coined by others. As he himself seems to have used στοιχεῖα at first, in the *Cratylus*, in a literary sense (φωνῆς στοιχεῖα), one is tempted to assume that the term originally meant the letters to be drawn up in a row (στοιχέω, στοῖχος), the alphabet,[1] and was then transferred to science, to physics, and mathematics. Objections have been raised against this hypothesis and strong arguments advanced for the priority of mathematics,[2] on the ground that a younger contemporary of Plato's, a pupil of Eudoxus, Menaechmus,[3] applied στοιχεῖα to elementary mathematical demonstrations. Whatever may be the outcome of this controversy, for our purpose Plato's statements in the *Cratylus* are decisive, as they alone influenced later terminology. So did the names of the groups into which he divided the στοιχεῖα (*Crat.* 424 c); the first group are τὰ φωνήεντα 'the vowels', the second group (τὰ ἕτερα) are τά τε ἄφωνα καὶ ἄφθογγα, 'the consonants and the mutes', to use the modern terms; the consonants which are not ἄφθογγα are called ἡμίφωνα by Aristotle.[4] For his division Plato expressly refers to the experts on στοιχεῖα: οὑτωσὶ γάρ που λέγουσιν οἱ δεινοὶ περὶ τούτων, by whom he may have meant Hippias or other Sophists.[5] Plato's own new question was whether a correspondence between sound and meaning in these primary elements could be found; he considers that ῥῶ may suggest rapid motion (*Crat.* 426 c, 434 c) and may be an 'imitative sound' as in ῥεῖν and ῥοή, or that λάβδα suggests something smooth and soft (λεῖον, μαλακόν), and so on.

In the course of the dialogue several similar questions are raised, of which we can mention only one or two. When some στοιχεῖα, significant in themselves, are put together and formed into words, should it not be possible to find out their 'true' meaning (τὰ ἔτυμα) and so finally reach the essence of things? Now, this looks like the old task of ἐτυμολογία, familiar from Homeric times as an innate striving of the Greek mind to understand and explain the ὀνόματα, particularly the ancient proper names of gods and men; the poets were followed by the philosophers (Heraclitus, Democritus), historians (Hecataeus, Herodotus), and Sophists (Prodicus, Hippias?), who occasionally and arbitrarily tried their hand

[1] On the origin of the Greek alphabet see above, pp. 20 ff.

[2] The masterly pamphlet of H. Diels, *Elementum* (Leipzig 1899), opened the debate on the origin of στοιχεῖον; the complete history of the controversy is given by W. Burkert, '*Στοιχεῖον*. Eine semasiologische Studie' (see *Excursus* to p. 60) who himself strongly pleads for the mathematical origin; see also above, p. 23, n. 1 and Jeffery, *The Local Scripts* 40.

[3] Eudem. fr. 133, Wehrli, *Die Schule des Aristoteles* 8 (1955) 55. 2; cf. Plat. *Tim.* (above, p. 60, n. 3).

[4] On 'semi-vowels' see Aristotle below, p. 76.

[5] Plat. *Crat.* 424 c and e, *Hipp. min.* 368 d, *Phileb.* 18 bc; Hippias, see above, pp. 53, 60; cf. Eur. *Palamed.* fr. 578. 2 N.² (415 b.c.).

at this traditional game. The Platonic Socrates, on the other hand, started a methodical and consistent inquiry into the fundamental problem 'whether the names themselves will bear witness that they are not at all given at haphazard, but have a certain correctness': εἰ ἄρα ἡμῖν ἐπιμαρτυρήσει αὐτὰ τὰ ὀνόματα μὴ πάνυ ἀπὸ τοῦ αὐτομάτου οὕτως ἕκαστα κεῖσθαι, ἀλλ᾽ ἔχειν τινὰ ὀρθότητα (Crat. 397 A). A word has 'correctness', if it expresses the essence of the thing: ὀνόματος, φαμέν, ὀρθότης ἐστὶν αὕτη ἥτις ἐνδείξεται οἷόν ἐστι τὸ πρᾶγμα (428 E), cf. δηλοῦν οἷον ἕκαστόν ἐστι τῶν ὄντων (422 D).

For Prodicus the Sophist ἡ τῶν ὀνομάτων ὀρθότης had meant the proper distinction of kindred terms and their correct use in oratory; Socrates gave the same expression a totally different and purely philosophical meaning. He let a torrent of examples rush at his partners in the debate, partly ingeniously contrived ones, partly wild fancies. Not content with the old etymology of Ἀπόλλων as the 'destroyer' (404 E and 405 E),[1] he offers no less than four new ἔτυμα revealing the god's four powers, as the ἁπλοῦ, ἀεὶ βάλλοντος, ἀπολούοντος, ὁμοπολοῦντος (406 A). It is characteristic of the Platonic Socrates that he no longer relied on mere similarities of sound (Ἀπόλλων = ἀπολλύων κτλ.).[2] When he derived the name of the Muses (Μοῦσα, Doric Μῶσα) from μῶσθαι 'to seek after, to meditate', he did no worse than modern linguists.[3] Going on to Apollo's mother Λητώ, he referred to many ξένοι who call her Ληθώ because of her 'smooth character', her λεῖον ἦθος; so he seriously looked to non-Attic forms in Greek dialects or obsolete forms used by the early Greeks (οἱ παλαιοί 407 A on Athena, cf. 418 BC) for help in tracing etymologies. Finally when there was no help from any Greek source, Socrates suspected 'foreign' origin (409 D ff. ὅτι πολλὰ οἱ Ἕλληνες ὀνόματα . . . παρὰ τῶν βαρβάρων εἰλήφασιν, cf. 416 A): πῦρ, ὕδωρ, and some others might have been borrowed from the Phrygians, although slightly modified (410 A).[4] But in his best ironical mood, he regarded such assumptions of borrowing from the barbarians as 'evasions': αὗται γὰρ ἂν πᾶσαι ἐκδύσεις εἶεν καὶ μάλα κομψαὶ τῷ μὴ ἐθέλοντι λόγον διδόναι περὶ τῶν πρώτων ὀνομάτων ὡς ὀρθῶς κεῖται (426 A), 'all these may be evasions and very clever

---

[1] The etymology (from ἀπόλλυμι) is at least as early as Archilochus fr. 30 D.³, who played upon the name of the god as he played on the various forms of a single word, above, p. 14. Wilamowitz, Glaube der Hellenen II 114. 4, was not right in rejecting the idea of an etymological play by Archilochus, proposed already by Apollod. 244 FGrHist 95. 10, cf. Aesch. Ag. 1081, Eur. fr. 781. 12 N.².

[2] See above, p. 5, n. 2.

[3] O. Gruppe, Griechische Mythologie und Religionsgeschichte II (1906) 1076. 1; J. B. Hofmann, Etymologisches Wörterbuch des Griechischen (1949) 206.

[4] Cf. pp. 41 and 79.

ones on the part of those who are not willing to give account of how the primary words are correctly given'. Not only here but in nearly every case, Socrates immediately raised doubts and objections to the arguments which he himself had just advanced at length.[1]

From the so-called primary words there is but a step to the general question of the <u>origin of words</u>: do words exist as a product of nature (φύσει) or as the result of convention (νόμῳ)?[2] As far as I am aware the dialogue does not say 'language' (λέξις, λόγος), but always ὀνόματα; the question is who first gave names to things. This controversy in the *Cratylus* is only part of the whole great dispute between φύσις and νόμος which began in the second half of the fifth century B.C.[3] One of Socrates' interlocutors pleaded for 'nature' itself as the giver of names, the other for 'convention'; Socrates argued against both of them, as he argued in other cases even against himself, pitilessly exposing every obscurity in the arguments. Therefore, all these negative parts of the *Cratylus* have their special importance; at the end, when the claims of two kinds of names to be 'like the truth' conflicted with each other, Socrates reached the final negative conclusion: 'It is plain that we must look for something else, not names, that will show us without names which of these two kinds are the true ones, which of them, that is to say, show the truth of things', δηλονότι ἄλλ' ἄττα ζητητέα πλὴν ὀνομάτων, ἃ ἡμῖν ἐμφανιεῖ ἄνευ ὀνομάτων ὁπότερα τούτων ἐστὶ τἀληθῆ, δείξαντα δηλονότι τὴν ἀλήθειαν τῶν ὄντων (438 D). A little further on, a short positive statement is added about τὰ ὄντα: 'that they are to be learned and sought for not from names, but much better through themselves than from names', ὅτι οὐκ ἐξ ὀνομάτων ἀλλὰ πολὺ μᾶλλον αὐτὰ ἐξ αὑτῶν καὶ μαθητέον καὶ ζητητέον ἢ ἐξ ὀνομάτων (439 B; cf. 438 E τὰ ὄντα . . . αὐτὰ δι' αὑτῶν). The phrases ἄλλ' ἄττα . . . πλὴν ὀνομάτων and τὰ ὄντα . . . αὐτὰ ἐξ or δι' αὑτῶν seem to indicate another stage of Platonic philosophy, which is reached in the Seventh Letter (*Ep.* VII pp. 342 A ff.) where word and image (ὄνομα and εἴδωλον) have their proper place assigned in the dialectical process. Meanwhile the verdict on the ὀνόματα in the *Cratylus* may be another disappointment to us; but this is not the whole story.

On the way to his final conclusion Socrates expressed some new ideas; these discoveries were more important for the future than those of the

---

[1] John Ruskin's 'etymologies' of Shakespeare's names are at least as bizarre as many in the *Cratylus*; the difference is that Ruskin seems to have been quite in earnest when he derived Desdemona from δυσδαιμονία or Ophelia from ὠφέλεια, etc. 'Munera Pulveris', 5th essay § 134, *Works*, II (1872) 143.

[2] See above, p. 53 (Hippias), below, p. 79 (Aristotle).

[3] F. Heinimann, 'Nomos und Physis', *Schweizerische Beiträge zur Altertumswissenschaft* I (1945); on language 46 ff.

Sophists and can be regarded as 'rudiments' of linguistic knowledge.[1]
'Changes of sound' in some names are explained by the desire for
εὐστομία, 'goodness of sound' (euphony): Φερέπαφα, the original form
according to the etymology, was changed into Φερρέφαττα (404 D), Φίξ
into Σφίγξ (414 CD), or even bolder still, 'Ηθονόη into Ἀθηνάα (407 B
παραγαγὼν . . . ἐπὶ τὸ κάλλιον; cf. 408 B, 409 C, 414 C, 417 E). These individual examples must not be taken too seriously; but the same phonetic
principle, avoidance of cacophony, is still used by modern linguists[2] to
explain the origin of striking Greek word-forms. We have already mentioned that Socrates, in working out etymologies, referred also to earlier
forms no longer used in his time; these references are based on the
general observation that formal changes happen in the course of time for
various reasons; the sense of a word may have been obscured by these
changes, and we must try to discover the original form (410 C; cf. 418 C,
420 B). 'Chronological' (not yet 'historical') considerations of this kind
were supplemented by comparison of Greek with foreign words (409 D
ff.), the first very slight hint at a comparative study of languages. Socrates'
suggestion that the rudimentary sounds of the primary words possibly
have a particular significance may give him a claim to be the ancestor
of a theory called 'sound-symbolism',[3] which is still alive in our own days.

The interpretation of the *Cratylus* leaves no doubt that from the Platonic
point of view the study of language can never be regarded as ἐπιστήμη;
there is not a word even about a γραμματικὴ τέχνη in the sense of 'grammar'.[4] A classical scholar like Wilamowitz[5] could not quite suppress his
indignation about Plato's attitude; he regretted that Plato 'für die
Grammatik nichts übrig hatte'; otherwise he would have understood
that for logical training it could do the same as the mathematics on which
he exclusively insisted, or sometimes even better. But, as we have seen,
'grammar' as a methodical τέχνη did not yet exist and could not have
been applied to logical training; mathematics, on the other hand, had
been developed for centuries and was regarded by Plato as true ἐπιστήμη.

This leads us back to the general remarks with which we began this
short chapter. The distinction of ἐμπειρία and τέχνη made by Plato in his

[1] See Friedländer, *Platon* II² 190 f.; Barwick 76 ff. influence on the Stoics and on the
Alexandrians; cf. also below, p. 243.
[2] W. Schulze, *KZ* 43 (1910) 185–9 = *Kleine Schriften* (1933) 304–8 'Kakophonie'.
[3] E. Cassirer, *Philosophie der symbolischen Formen* I Die Sprache (1923) 139 ff., refers to
Leibniz, W. v. Humboldt, Jacob Grimm, Hermann Paul; E. Schwyzer, *Griechische Grammatik* I (1939) 37, mentions the revival of this theory by A. Meillet and his school.
[4] On ἐπιστήμη see above, p. 57; γραμματικὴ τ. means no more than the fitting or non fitting
together of γράμματα single letters (*Soph.* 253 A). See also below, p. 76 on Aristotle.
[5] Wilamowitz, *Platon* I (1919) 561. 3 (a very characteristic note with reference to his own
schooldays).

polemics against the Sophists was to become fundamental for grammatical theory, as we shall see. This is more important than the effect of the individual discoveries we found in his *Cratylus*. It was not the rhetorical enthusiasm, the passionate love of language shown by teachers from Protagoras to Isocrates, that were decisive, but Plato's rigorous criticism of language and his sober proofs of its limitations. The unique compound of his spirit, at once creative, critical, and artistic, gave the strongest impulse to future generations.

The first decades of the fourth century were a period full of danger; after the political catastrophe of Athens in 404 B.C., the crisis of the city-state and the inevitable change in social conditions heralded the approach of a new age. In these years, before the final turning-point was reached with Alexander's empire, two philosophical schools of the utmost importance were founded in Athens. Plato succeeded in setting up his school (after 388 B.C.) in a grove sacred to the Muses and to the hero Akademos; this organization, a religious guild called the Academia,[1] lasted for more than 900 years. As Plato had paved the way for scholarship, so also in later revivals of what we call 'humanism' Platonism played its part, whether we think of Origen or the Florentine Academy or Erasmus or Winckelmann and Humboldt.

The greatest pupil of the Platonic Academy from the year 368 B.C. until Plato's death in 348 B.C. was a foreigner of Ionian stock, Aristotle, who finally established his own school at the other end of Athens (335–323 B.C.); this school bore the name Peripatos,[2] at least from the time of Theophrastus, who apparently was able to occupy a large grove of the Muses near the temple of Apollo Lyceus. The Peripatos was destined to remain in productive rivalry with Plato's foundation until the middle of the fourth century A.D. It is mainly due to these two firmly established Athenian organizations that relatively many works of their founders are well preserved; they were better able to collect, copy, distribute, and hand them on to posterity than any previous philosophical circles in the east or west. There is no evidence about the early fortunes of Plato's dialogues; but it is a fair guess that the first generation of his pupils tried to collect, to arrange, and to copy the autographs of the master,[3] and that this

[1] H. Herter, *Platons Akademie* 2nd ed. (1952) with bibliography 25 ff.; P. Boyancé, *Le Culte des Muses chez les philosophes grecs* (1937) 262 ff. The first to try to reconstruct a history of the Academy as the model of scientific organization was H. Usener, 'Organisation der wissenschaftlichen Arbeit', *Preuss. Jahrb.* 53 (1884) 1 ff. = *Vorträge u. Aufsätze* (1907) 67 ff.

[2] K. O. Brink, 'Peripatos', *RE*, Suppl. 7 (1940) 899 ff. (offprint 1936); cf. the testimonia for Περίπατος, etc., in Düring *Aristotle* 404–11.

[3] Wilamowitz, *Platon* II (1920) 324; against the assumption of a fundamental edition made by the Academy after Plato's death G. Jachmann, 'Der Platontext', *Nachr. der Göttinger*

'Academy Edition' became the basis of all the later ones. On the other hand, we have no certain knowledge of any oral 'esoteric' instruction (in the line of Pythagoras) being given by Plato himself to a selected inner circle of disciples.[1] In Aristotle, however, we have to make a distinction between those of his books called *Dialogues*, written down probably in his earlier 'Academic' period for a wider reading public,[2] and the works produced in connexion with his teaching, not only as the head of his own school in his second Athenian period, but also earlier between 348 and 335 B.C., when he was staying in the Troas, in Lesbos, and in Macedonia at the royal court. These seem to have originated from lectures and earlier smaller essays; but they were genuine 'writings', γράμματα, read to the audience in his school. Later on they may have been sometimes rearranged and finally made public by members of the Peripatos; they form the bulk of the extant works and are often called Πραγματεῖαι, 'Treatises'.[3] Between these two groups there is a third one, 'Memoranda and Collections', put down for lectures and books, and published post-humously, but lost to us as a whole, like the *Dialogues*; only fragments are preserved, and many titles in the amazing lists of Aristotelian writings.[4]

We have watched the slow progress of the 'written' word from the fifth to the fourth century and the part the early Sophists and their younger pupils played in it.[5] It may appear rather paradoxical that Academy and Peripatos, the schools of their opponents, should have made a decisive new step towards the end of our third period in the

Akademie (1941) Nr. 7. 334, who argues for the first edition's having been made by Aristophanes of Byzantium (see below, pp. 196 f.). Against Jachmann H. Erbse, 'Überlieferungsgeschichte der griechischen klassischen und hellenistischen Literatur' in *Geschichte der Textüberlieferung* 1 (Zürich 1961) 219 ff.

[1] F. Wehrli, 'Aristoteles in der Sicht seiner Schule, Platonisches und Vorplatonisches' in *Aristote et les problèmes de Méthode* (Louvain 1960) 336, with reference to H. J. Krämer, 'Arete bei Platon und Aristoteles', *Abhandlungen d. Heidelberger Akad. d. Wiss., Phil.-hist. Kl.* (1959) 6, pp. 380–486; in an impressive but not very convincing manner Krämer revived the idea of an 'esoteric' Plato who revealed the essence of his philosophy not in his written dialogues, but only in the oral instruction of the inner circle of his pupils.

[2] *Fragm.* ed. V. Rose (1886) no. 1–111; *Fragm. selecta* ed. W. D. Ross (1955) pp. 1–99; testimonia for the term ἐξωτερικοὶ λόγοι Düring, *Aristotle* 426–43.

[3] W. Jaeger, *Studien zur Entwicklungsgeschichte der Metaphysik des Aristoteles* (1912) 131–48, first explained the complicated process of 'publication'. F. Dirlmeier, 'Merkwürdige Zitate in der eudem. Ethik des Ar.', *Sitz. Ber. Heidelberger Akad.*, Philos.-hist. kl., 78. 1962, 2. Abh., collecting the evidence for cross-references in Aristotle's books, stresses the λόγος-character also of the written work more strongly. There are many improvements on Jaeger's theory; as regards Plato, Dirlmeier unfortunately agrees with Krämer.

[4] Text of the ancient lists in V. Rose (above, n. 2), pp. 3–22; cf. P. Moraux, *Les Listes anciennes des ouvrages d'Aristote* (Louvain 1951). New critical edition and commentary by Düring, *Aristotle*; cf. M. Plezia, *Gnom.* 34 (1962) 126 ff.

[5] See above, pp. 25–32, 58.

history of the 'book'; they used books,[1] so often maligned, especially by
Plato, in order to save the fundamental work of their own masters.
Aristotle and his followers could not have achieved their immensely
learned compilations if they had not accumulated as many writings of the
past[2] as they could get hold of; after the occasional allusions to modest
earlier collections[3] it is well attested that the first large private library
was founded by Aristotle and passed on to his successors,[4] who probably
transferred it to the Lyceum.

Dio Chrysostom says in his speech on Homer (Περὶ ʿΟμήρου or. 36. 1,
vol. II, p. 110 Arn. = or. 53 II 274 Reiske): Ἀριστοτέλης ἀφ' οὗ φασι τὴν
κριτικήν τε καὶ γραμματικὴν ἀρχὴν λαβεῖν, 'Aristotle, from whom, as they
say, criticism and grammar made a beginning'. This view of Dio's
anonymous source[5] is shared by many modern scholars, for instance
L. Urlichs[6] ('Zu einer Wissenschaft der Philologie hat Aristoteles den
Grund gelegt'), or W. Jaeger[7] ('Aristoteles . . . Schöpfer der Philologie')
or F. Mehmel[8] ('Aristoteles . . . der eigentliche Ahnherr . . . der Philologie
überhaupt'). Writers, whether on the history of classical scholarship, on
Aristotle, or on Homeric criticism, agree in regarding Aristotle as 'founder', 'creator', or at least 'ancestor', unconsciously, as it seems, reviving
an opinion of late antiquity. If this common conviction were correct, one
would have to suppose that the earliest Hellenistic poets and scholars
after 300 B.C., Philitas and his followers, simply continued the work of
Aristotle and his Peripatetic school. We have put forward a quite different
view,[9] and we shall have to deal with this question thoroughly later on,
when we trace the line from the fourth to the third century and examine
the relation of the Alexandrians to the Peripatos in detail.

As the mistaken views on Aristotle's position which we have cited were
derived from his work on Homer, it will be convenient to look first at his
book on *Homeric problems* and to consider his interpretations. We shall go
on to the literary criticism on Homer and on tragedy in his *Poetics*, then
to his studies of language, and finally to his antiquarian collections, continued in the grand style by his pupils. This division into four groups is

---

[1] Reading of plays became quite common, see Aristot. *Poet.* 1462 a 12, 17.

[2] Aristot. *Top.* 105 b 12 ἐκλέγειν δὲ χρὴ καὶ ἐκ τῶν γεγραμμένων λόγων.

[3] See above, pp. 7 f.

[4] Strab. XIII 608 Ἀριστοτέλης . . . πρῶτος ὧν ἴσμεν συναγαγὼν βιβλία, Schmidt, *Pinakes* 7 and
31 (Voralexandrinische Bibliotheken). Düring, 'Aristotle' 337 f. 'Aristotle's library'.

[5] Possibly Asclepiades of Myrlea, see below, p. 158.

[6] 'Grundlegung und Geschichte der Klassischen Altertumswissenschaft', *Handbuch der
Klassischen Altertumswissenschaft* I (2nd ed. 1890) 33 ff. 'Geschichte der Philologie'.

[7] Jaeger, *Aristoteles* 350 = Engl. transl. 328 'the creator of philology'.

[8] 'Homer und die Griechen', *Antike und Abendland* 4 (1954) 37.

[9] See above, pp. 1 ff., and below, pp. 88 ff.

precisely the same as in the chapters on the Sophists and on Plato, except that the order varies in each case; a scheme of this sort may look rather pedantic, but it is perhaps justified, if it makes access to large and scattered material a little easier.

Aristotle accepted the Platonic notions of ἐμπειρία and τέχνη, 'experience' and 'art', defining them at the beginning of his *Metaphysics*; he did not remain on the old empirical level of the Sophists, but tried, like Plato, to find a new methodical approach to theoretical knowledge.[1] On the other hand, he took up many literary subjects treated by the Sophists or Ionian philosophers and other questions raised by them which had no interest for Plato. Some years ago in a festival speech on philhellenism[2] I hinted at a new and central idea of Aristotle's whole philosophy[3] and its importance for the understanding of the great literary tradition. According to Aristotle all living organisms—plants, animals, men—move and change in order to approach their final 'form' (τέλος 'end') and so to attain their own 'nature' (φύσις); so he could expressly say that 'the nature is the end', *Pol.* 1 2, p. 1252 b 32 ἡ δὲ φύσις τέλος ἐστίν.[4] Between a living organism and a literary whole there is an analogy, as Aristotle emphasized in his *Poetics* (1458 a 20). The stories in narrative poetry 'should be based on a single action, one that is a complete whole in itself (ὅλην καὶ τελείαν), with a beginning, middle, and end, so as to enable it, like a living creature of complete unity (ὥσπερ ζῷον ἓν ὅλον) to produce its own proper pleasure (τὴν οἰκείαν ἡδονήν)'.[5] We must, of course, keep in our mind an essential difference. The living organisms have their τέλος ('end'), so to speak, inside them from the very beginning, but the literary formations (and all the other artificial ones) are originated from outside, by a 'maker', a ποιητής; their development thereafter is supposed to be 'analogous' to that of a ζῷον.[6] The greatest Greek poets of the past had indeed created works of perfection, works which had found their own 'nature' (φύσις). They actually had reached their 'end' beyond

---

[1] Aristot. *Metaphys.* A 1, see above, p. 57, n. 1; Aristot. *Soph. El.* 33 p. 184 a 2–8 against the ταχεῖα . . . ἄτεχνος . . . διδασκαλία 'the rapid unscientific teaching' of the Sophists; οὐ γὰρ τέχνην, ἀλλὰ τὰ ἀπὸ τῆς τέχνης διδόντες παιδεύειν ὑπέλαβον 'they fancied they were educating when they were imparting not the art itself but only the results'.

[2] 'Von der Liebe zu den Griechen', *Münchener Universitätsreden*, N.F. 20 (1958) 14 = *Ausgewählte Schriften* (1960) 282.

[3] K. v. Fritz, *Studium generale* XIV (1961) 620 ff.

[4] p. 1252 b 32 οἷον γὰρ ἕκαστόν ἐστι τῆς γενέσεως τελεσθείσης, ταύτην φαμὲν τὴν φύσιν εἶναι ἑκάστου ὥσπερ ἀνθρώπου, ἵππου, οἰκίας; cf. *Phys.* III 6 p. 207 a 8, v 4 p. 228 b 13.

[5] Bywater's translation (Aristotle, *On the Art of Poetry*, 1909), except for ὥσπερ–ὅλον; on ἡδονή see below, p. 75; cf. ibid. 1450 b 34 ζῷον.

[6] The conception of an analogy between a λόγος and a ζῷον is Platonic, *Phaedr.* 264 D; but Aristotle draws quite new consequences.

which there was no progress any more. Therefore, it was not too difficult for Aristotle to apply his novel conception of teleology to this unique achievement. His various tasks of interpretation, poetical theory, linguistic and antiquarian study were guided by this general philosophical conception.

Nevertheless, the empirical research was done with great care; Aristotle seems to have taken immense trouble to solve numerous problems of the Homeric poems, some of which had been discussed for two centuries. Since Xenophanes had started his attacks on moral grounds and Theagenes had replied with allegorical explanations, the Homeric battle had hardly ever stopped.[1] Aristotle joined the company of the defenders of Homer. Without ever mentioning Plato's name in this connexion, he made the first effort to restore the full authority of the epic poet against Plato as well as against minor detractors.

Probably over a long period of time Aristotle had drawn up for his lectures a list of 'difficulties' of interpretation in Homer with their respective 'solutions'; this custom of ζητήματα προβάλλειν may have prospered at the symposia of intellectual circles. Aristotle's collection was afterwards published, as it seems, in six books, Ἀπορήματα Ὁμηρικά[2] or τὰ Ὁμήρου προβλήματα[3] of which thirty-eight quotations are preserved, mostly in Porphyry's *Homeric Questions*.[4] In addition to that, nearly the whole of chapter 25 of the *Poetics*,[5] written Περὶ προβλημάτων καὶ λύσεων, deals with censures (ἐπιτιμήματα) of Homer and with answers to them (λύσεις). Plato, amongst his many complaints about Homer's representation of gods and heroes, had declared that it cannot be true that Achilles dragged Hector's body around the tomb of Patroclus (*Rep.* 319 B ταῦτα οὐ φήσομεν ἀληθῆ εἰρῆσθαι); but Aristotle justified it by referring to the Thessalian custom (which still existed in his own time) of dragging men's bodies around the tombs of those they had murdered (fr. 166 Rose).[6]

[1] See above, pp. 9 ff., 36, 38, 44, 50, 58 ff.

[2] Diog. L. v 21 = Aristot. *fragm.* p. 7, no. 118 Rose = Düring p. 48, no. 118; only fr. 179 R. is quoted with this title.

[3] *Vita vulg.* 3 p. 76. 22 Rose = Düring p. 132; *Vita Hesych.* 106 Ἀπορ. Ὁμηρ. six books p. 14 R. = Düring p. 86, *Vita Hesych.* 147 Προβλ. Ὁμ. ten books p. 16 R. = Düring p. 87; Ptolemy el-Garib, Catalogue 98 'On recondite problems in Homer, in ten parts', Düring p. 230, cf. p. 22 Rose, *Vita Marciana* 4 p. 76. 16 Rose = Düring p. 97 Ὁμηρικὰ ζητήματα. If these three different titles refer to the same writing of Aristotle, the title Ἀπορήματα quoted by Phrynichus and the Antiatticista fr. 179 R. may be 'original', and the figure six in Diog. L. and Hesych. 106 may be correct.

[4] Fr. 142–79 Rose pp. 120 ff. Porphyrius *Quaest. Homer. ad Iliadem*, coll. H. Schrader (1880) 415 ff. and id. *ad Odysseam* (1890) 180 ff. on Aristotle's *Homeric Problems*.

[5] See Bywater's Commentary (above, p. 68, n. 5) p. 323.

[6] Schol. B Ω 15 = Porphyr. pp. 267 f. Schrader διὰ τί ὁ Ἀχιλλεὺς τὸν Ἕκτορα εἷλκε περὶ τὸν τάφον τοῦ Πατρόκλου . . . ἔστι δὲ λύσις, φησὶν Ἀριστοτέλης, καὶ εἰς τὰ ὑπάρχοντα ἀνάγων ἔθη, ὅτι τοιαῦτα ἦν, ἐπεὶ καὶ νῦν ἐν τῇ Θετταλίᾳ περιέλκουσι περὶ τοὺς τάφους (sc. τῶν φονευθέντων τοὺς

The form of the quotation διὰ τί . . . ἔστι δὲ λύσις leaves no doubt that it is taken out of the work on *Homeric Problems*; but Aristotle may have mentioned the Thessalian custom also in his Θεσσαλῶν πολιτεία (fr. 495–500 Rose). In any case, it is an example of the way he used the stupendous treasures of his collections for the correct interpretation of the epic poet against less learned predecessors who had raised subjective moral arguments without being aware of historical facts. A similar difficulty (K 152) was solved by reference to a primitive custom still surviving among the Illyrians (fr. 160 Rose and *Poetics* c. 25 p. 1461 a 3). 'Others one must solve (διαλύειν) by considering the diction (λέξις)', as for instance by the assumption of an obsolete word (γλώττη) :[1] by οὐρῆας μὲν πρῶτον (A 50), for example, 'perhaps he does not mean mules, but guards' (οὐ τοὺς ἡμιόνους λέγει, ἀλλὰ τοὺς φύλακας p. 1461 a 10). We do not know whether the much-discussed question why Apollo in this passage of the *Iliad* strikes first the mules and dogs[2] was also in the list of Aristotle's *Homeric Problems*, but we do know by chance that the most infamous and malicious detractor of Homer, Zoilus of Amphipolis, had included it in his nine books κατὰ τῆς Ὁμήρου ποιήσεως (fr. 6 Friedlaender). So Aristotle's interpretation in this case (as also immediately afterwards, *Poet.* 1461 a 14) may have been directed against that spiteful contemporary, the 'Ὁμηρο-μάστιξ, 'Scourge of Homer'.[3] At the same time Heraclides Ponticus, one of Plato's favourite pupils, who later was closely related with Aristotle,[4] wrote two books on 'Homeric Solutions' (Λύσεων Ὁμηρικῶν α΄β΄),[5] apparently with the same apologetic character. Although certain circles of the Alexandrine Museum seem to have adopted this 'method' of ζητήματα, which amused Ptolemaic kings and Roman emperors, as it had amused Athenian symposiasts, the great and serious grammarians disliked it as a more or less frivolous game.[6] It was mainly continued by the philosophic schools, Peripatetics, Stoics, Neoplatonists, and by amateurs, until Porphyry (who died about A.D. 305) arranged his final collection of Ὁμηρικὰ ζητήματα[7]

φονέας vel sim.) ; detailed references are given in my note on Callimachus fr. 588, who may have used Aristotle as a source for his Aetia.

[1] See below, p. 78.

[2] Schol. A ad loc. διὰ τί . . . λύοντες ; see *Excursus.*

[3] Suid. s.v. Ζωῖλος ; cf. above, p. 9, n. 3 ; U. Friedlaender, *De Zoilo aliisque Homeri obtrectatoribus*, Diss. Königsberg 1895. On Hippias of Thasos (*Poet.* 1461 a 22) see above, p. 45, and n. 4. *Soph. El.* 4.

[4] F. Wehrli, *Die Schule des Aristoteles* 7 (1953) 59 f. καὶ ὕστερον ἤκουσεν Ἀριστοτέλους on fr. 3.

[5] Fr. 171–5 Wehrli ; cf. Dicaearch. Wehrli, *Schule des Arist.* 1 (1944) fr. 90–93 and Demetr. Phaler. ibid. 4 (1949) fr. 190–3.

[6] Lehrs, *De Aristarchi Studiis Homericis*[3] (1882) 206.

[7] I have always felt rather uneasy about H. Schrader's bold reconstruction (see above, p. 69, n. 4 and *Excursus* to p. 70) ; it is a relief to learn from a thorough re-examination of the attested fragments of Porphyry and of the 'exegetic' Scholia (*b*) to the *Iliad* that the bulk of

in the grand style, in which he very probably still used Aristotle's original work.¹

Of the various Neoplatonic lives of Aristotle² only one mentions an 'edition of the Iliad'; after the *Homeric Questions* in the list of works come the words: καὶ ἡ τῆς 'Ιλιάδος ἔκδοσις ἣν δέδωκε τῷ Ἀλεξάνδρῳ. This refers to the famous story of the so-called 'Iliad of the Casket', by some dismissed 'as a picturesque legend',³ by others accepted as a historical fact.⁴ So it may be worth while to reconsider the whole evidence. According to Plutarch, Onesicritus,⁵ the steersman of the royal ship and a not always unreliable historian, reported: 'Alexander always kept with his dagger under his pillow a copy of the *Iliad* Ἀριστοτέλους διορθώσαντος ἣν ἐκ τοῦ νάρθηκος καλοῦσιν.'⁶ While the late *Life* of Aristotle speaks of an ἔκδοσις, an 'edition' of the *Iliad*, Plutarch (Onesicritus?) calls it a διόρθωσις, a text 'revised' or 'emended' by Aristotle.⁷ Alexander's copy of Homer is mentioned by Strabo (XIII 594),⁸ not as edited or revised by Aristotle, but φέρεται γοῦν τις διόρθωσις τῆς 'Ομήρου ποιήσεως, ἡ ἐκ τοῦ νάρθηκος λεγομένη, τοῦ Ἀλεξάνδρου μετὰ τῶν περὶ Καλλισθένη καὶ Ἀνάξαρχον ἐπελθόντος καὶ σημειωσαμένου τινά: 'there is a rumour about some revised text of the Homeric poems . . . when Alexander with Callisthenes and Anaxarchus went over it and made some marks on it.'⁹ Our sources agree about the fact that Alexander used to have a text of Homer or at least of the *Iliad* with him in a precious box; this is quite credible, as he was a true φιλόμηρος and honoured his ancestral hero Achilles as his lifelong model. It is also possible that he was given that copy by Aristotle,

these Scholia with ζητήματα cannot be regarded as excerpted from Porphyry, see H. Erbse, 'Beiträge zur Überlieferung der Iliasscholien', *Zetemata* 24 (1960) 17–77.

¹ The assumption that Porphyry had Aristotle's Ἀπορήματα in its original form at hand is confirmed by Erbse, loc. cit. pp. 61 ff.

² 'Vita Marciana' in Aristot. *fragm.* p. 427. 5 Rose; cf. 'Vita Latina' ibid. p. 443. 6 'Yliadis dictamen quod dedit Alexandro' = Düring, 'Aristotle' 97 (4) and 151 (4). A sceptical 'non liquet' was the result of the acute re-examination of the tradition by O. Gigon in his commentary on the 'Vita Marciana', *Kleine Texte für Vorlesungen und Übungen* 181 (1962) 36 f.

³ D. B. Monro, *Homer's Odyssey* Books XIII–XXIV (1901) 418; see also W. Leaf, *Strabo on the Troad* (1923) 150.

⁴ W. Schmid, *Geschichte der griech. Lit.* I 1 (1929) 163. 4; W. D. Ross, *Aristotle* (5th ed. 1949) 4; W. W. Tarn, *Alexander the Great* I (1948) 2.

⁵ 38 *FGrHist* 134 in Plut. *Alex.* 8; it is not a verbatim quotation.

⁶ Plut. *Alex.* 26 tells of this valuable box (κιβώτιον) of Darius, in which Alexander put the *Iliad*, adding that 'not a few of the trustworthy attest it' οὐκ ὀλίγοι τῶν ἀξιοπίστων μεμαρτυρήκασιν; cf. Plut. *de Alex. fort.* I 4 p. 327 F; Plin. *n.h.* VII 29 (30).

⁷ On ἔκδοσις and διόρθωσις see H. Erbse, *Herm.* 87 (1959) 286 ff. and A. Ludwich, *Aristarchs Homerische Textkritik* II (1885) 431 f. and below, p. 94.

⁸ At the beginning of this chapter XIII 1. 27 Demetrius of Skepsis is quoted, but he cannot be the source of the later part.

⁹ Callisthenes, *FGrHist* 124 T 10. On Anaxarchus see F. Wehrli, *Schule des Aristoteles* 3 (1948) 67 on Clearchus fr. 60; cf. W. Leaf, *Strabo on the Troad* (1923) 150.

his tutor for three years, who certainly read Homer with him.[1] But our sources by no means agree about Aristotle's having made a recension of the text for his pupil. In fact, it is very improbable that he did. If such an Aristotelian ἔκδοσις had ever existed, why is it never mentioned[2] by the Alexandrian grammarians in our Scholia, which otherwise refer to ἀρχαῖα ἀντίγραφα or ἐκδόσεις κατ᾽ ἄνδρα and κατὰ πόλεις? They drew their quotations from his *Homeric Problems*. There is a second even stronger argument against this very doubtful tradition. We are well informed on the titles of Aristotle's lost works,[3] but not a single edition of a text appears in these lists. The only[4] pre-Hellenistic editor of Homer was the poet Antimachus.[5]

Aristotle, we conclude, made no recension of the Homeric or any other text; neither was he an 'interpreter' of the Homeric poems. What he actually did was to answer a long series of attacks by censorious critics; according to his theory, these poems were above such censure, and he had to prove their absolute superiority. This point is stressed by Dio Chrysostom at the beginning of his praise of Homer, already quoted:[6] καὶ αὐτὸς Ἀριστοτέλης . . . ἐν πολλοῖς διαλόγοις περὶ ποιητοῦ διέξεισι θαυμάζων αὐτὸν ὡς τὸ πολὺ καὶ τιμῶν. Of the 'many dialogues' (if this is not a rhetorical exaggeration) in which 'he goes through Homer in detail (?)', we possess only a few fragments of the dialogue Περὶ ποιητῶν,[7] where he displays his particular interest in the ancient Ionian traditions on the 'Life' of Homer.[8] The quotations[9] of single Homeric lines or passages, drawn from

[1] Dio Chrys. *or.* 11 79 εἰ τοιαῦτά σε (Alexandrum) διδάσκει (Aristoteles) περί τε ἀρχῆς καὶ βασιλείας εἴτε Ὅμηρον ἐξηγούμενος εἴτε ἄλλον τρόπον.

[2] F. A. Wolf, *Prolegomena ad Homerum* (1795) CLXXXIII, had already noticed that, but did not draw the consequences; A. Ludwich, *Aristarchs Homerische Textkritik* 11 (1885) 432 f. was on the right lines.

[3] See above, p. 66, n. 4.

[4] At least as long as the edition of one Euripides remains a shadow. Suid. 3694 Adler s.v. Εὐριπίδης, τραγικός, τοῦ προτέρου ἀδελφιδοῦς (a nephew of an Euripides who was older than the famous tragedian) ὡς Διονύσιος ἐν τοῖς Χρονικοῖς (= Dionys. Hal. 4 *FGrHist* 251, but Jacoby says it might be a confusion with Dionys. ὁ μουσικός). ἔγραψε δὲ Ὁμηρικὴν ἔκδοσιν εἰ μὴ ἄρα ἑτέρου ἐστίν. In *P.Oxy.* 221, col. VI 17 (Schol. Φ 155 f.) F. Blass suppl. ἐν τῇ κατ᾽ Ε[ὑρι-/πίδην καὶ] ἔν τισιν ἄλλαις referring to Eust. p. 366. 13 (ad B 865) ἡ δὲ κατ᾽ Εὐριπίδην (sc. ἔκδοσις) μετὰ τὸν τρίτον στίχον (B 866) . . . γράφει τέταρτον τοῦτον . . . Τμώλῳ ὑπὸ νιφόεντι . . . (= Υ 385), οὖ δὴ στίχου καὶ ὁ γεωγράφος μνησθείς φησιν (Strab. XIII 626).

[5] See below pp. 94 f.

[6] Above, p. 67; Aristot. *Fragm.* ed. Ross pp. 4 and 67.

[7] Aristot. fr. 70–77 Rose; pp. 67–72 Ross. An imaginative reconstruction of the Dialogue is given by A. Rostagni, 'Il dialogo Aristotelico Περὶ ποιητῶν', *Riv. fil. cl.* 4 (1926) 433–70 and 5 (1927) 145–73, reprinted in *Scritti minori* I (1955) 255–326 with bibliographical additions; see especially F. Sbordone, 'Il primo libro di Ar. intorno ai poeti', *Atti Accad. Pontaniana*, N.S. 4 (1954) 217–25.

[8] Fr. 76 Rose = Περὶ ποιητ. 8 Ross. Homer mentioned also in fr. 70, 75; see also Alcidamas, above, p. 50.

[9] A. Römer, 'Die Homercitate und die homerischen Fragen des Aristoteles', *Sitz. Ber. der*

memory in the usual way and scattered through his various writings, show that he was not meticulous about the accuracy of the text.

'Homer' now meant definitively *Iliad* and *Odyssey*, with the addition of the *Margites*.[1] It looks as if *all* Plato's epic quotations were taken from *Iliad* and *Odyssey*[2] and we may guess that he regarded only these two poems as Homeric; but Aristotle seems to have been the first who expressly said that they surpassed all the other epic poems and gave his reasons. *Iliad* and *Odyssey* alone were 'like a living organism', satisfying his preconception of perfect poetry; after characterizing the exemplary structure of each poem (τῶν ποιημάτων ἑκάτερον) he makes the final statement: πρὸς γὰρ τούτοις λέξει καὶ διανοίᾳ πάντα[3] ὑπερβέβληκε, in addition, they (sc. these two poems) surpass all (sc. other poems) in diction and thought. There is no evidence of such a clear aesthetic evaluation of *Iliad* and *Odyssey* in earlier times, as we saw;[4] even in the fourth century the 'Eristics' still regarded the complete 'cycle' of epics as Homer's poetry, as we have to conclude from Aristotle's own references in his logical writings. 'In the syllogism Homer's poetry is a figure because of its being a circle', ὅτι ἡ Ὁμήρου ποίησις σχῆμα διὰ τοῦ κύκλου ἐν τῷ συλλογισμῷ (*Soph. El.* 1 10 p. 171 a 10), is an example of the Sophistic fallacies to be refuted in Aristotle's appendix to his *Topics*; he quoted a slight variation later on in the *Analyt. Post.* (A 12 p. 77 b 32) ἆρα πᾶς κύκλος σχῆμα; ἂν δὲ γράψῃ, δῆλον. τί δέ; τὰ ἔπη κύκλος; φανερὸν ὅτι οὔκ ἐστιν.[5] This fallacy (κύκλος = 'circle' and = epic cycle = Homeric poems) is understandable only if the old vulgate opinion was still alive that Homer was the maker of the whole of epic poetry.

After Aristotle there is no trace of this vulgate any more; his differentiation between Homer, the poet of *Iliad* and *Odyssey*, and the rest of the early epic poets, of whom he displays intimate knowledge in chapter 23 of

philos.-philolog. und hist. Classe der Bayer. Akad. (1884) 264–314; G. E. Howes, 'Homeric Quotations in Plato and Aristotle', *Harvard Studies in Classical Philology* 6 (1895) 210–37.

  [1] See below, p. 74.

  [2] J. Labarbe, 'L'Homère de Platon'' *Bibliothèque de la Faculté de Philos. et Lettres de l'Université de Liège*, Fasc. 117 (1949), 410; cf. below, p. 74, n. 5.

  [3] *Poetics* 1459 b 16 πάντα is the reading of the Parisinus A (saec. x fin.) and of most of its apographa, also of the copy (saec. vi) used by the Arabic translator, according to Gudeman–Tkatsch; πάντας Riccardianus 46, called B or R (saec. xiii/xiv) and apographa (e.g. the copy used by Aldus). Not only the manuscript-tradition, but the text of the whole passage which deals with the two ποιήματα, proves that πάντα is the correct reading; πάντας would mean that he, Ὅμηρος, surpasses all the other poets. This was, at least in later times, often stated, but it does not fit into the context of chapter 24 of the *Poetics*.

  [4] Above, pp. 43 ff.

  [5] Cf. Philopon. ad loc., *Commentaria in Aristot. Graeca* xiii 3 ed. Wallies (1909) 156 f., see E. Kapp in E. Schwartz, *Die Odyssee* (1924) 154 and Wilamowitz, 'Lesefrüchte', *Hermes* 60 (1925) 280 = *Kleine Schriften* iv (1962) 368 (where the text of *Soph. El.* has to be corrected: ἡ Ὁμήρου ποίησις, not τὰ Ὁ. ἔπη); E. Schwartz, *Herm.* 75 (1940) 5 f.

the *Poetics*, seems to have been final. The arguments he used were identical with those in the analysis of tragedy which forms the centre of the whole treatise. This is not surprising, when we remember that his method is to subsume every single phenomenon under his general doctrine, in poetry as everywhere else. As in Attic tragedy, there is unity, completeness, and greatness (ἕν, ὅλον, μέγεθος) in Homer's two genuine poems (1450 b 27 ff.–1459 a 24 ff.). This 'inner' unity was not attained in any of the other epics (1451 a 19 ff.); tragedy, on the other hand, had a still higher degree of unity and was to that extent even 'better' than epic (ch. 26). The exemplary tragedy was the *Oedipus Tyrannus* of Sophocles. Plato had denied the 'seriousness' of epic poetry, denouncing it as 'play' (παιδιά); but Aristotle not only defined tragedy as an 'imitation of serious action' (μίμησις πράξεως σπουδαίας 1449 b 14), but also said of Homer 'as regards serious subjects, in the highest degree a poet' (τὰ σπουδαῖα μάλιστα ποιητής 1448 b 34). Homer even anticipated the 'dramatic' imitations (μιμήσεις δραματικάς ibid. b 35), and as *Iliad* and *Odyssey* were regarded as analogous to tragedy, so was his *Margites* to Attic comedy.[1] This poem[2] ridiculing one of the famous ninnies of old must have been very popular in the fourth century, as orators and philosophers quite surprisingly referred to it or quoted it several times. But the second book of the *Poetics*, in which comedy was discussed, is missing, and the twenty half-lines of a recently published papyrus[3] do not reveal the poetic quality of the *Margites*;[4] we are still at a loss to see how the poem fitted into the theory of the philosopher and why it was deemed worthy to be placed close to the *Iliad* and *Odyssey*[5] and later on admired even by an aesthetic subtilist like Callimachus.[6]

The term ὀρθότης, 'correctness', quite frequently occurred in the Sophistic and Platonic treatment of literary matter.[7] Plato in his old age admitted at least the practice of choral lyric,[8] which included singing and dancing, into the second best ideal city of the *Laws*. The ὀρθότης he demanded for this poetry had a strictly ethical meaning. The 'correct'

---

[1] καὶ τὰ τῆς κωμῳδίας σχήματα πρῶτος ὑπέδειξεν οὐ ψόγον, ἀλλὰ τὸ γελοῖον δραματοποιήσας 1448 b 36.

[2] Homeri *Opera* ed. T. W. Allen, vol. v (1912) 152 ff. testimonia and fragmenta.

[3] *P.Oxy.* XXII (1954) 2309 ed. E. Lobel.

[4] The bold combinations of H. Langerbeck, 'Margites', *Harvard Studies in Classical Philology* 63 (1958) 33–63, are hardly helpful. M. Forderer, *Zum homerischen Margites* (Amsterdam 1960) 5 ff. argues against the attribution of the papyrus to the Homeric *Margites*.

[5] The Ps.-Platonic *Alc.* II 147 B quotes the *Margites* as Homeric (fr. 3 Allen), cf. above, p. 73, n. 2; Aristotle might have learnt to appreciate the poem as a member of the Academy.

[6] Callim. fr. 397.

[7] See above, p. 39, and *passim*.

[8] See *Excursus*.

poetry was to promote moral discipline, not to effect 'pleasure' (ἡδονή) ; 'modern' art of the fourth century with its tendency to disrupt or to mix up the traditional forms, aiming only at pleasure, encouraged lawlessness and became therefore a political danger.[1] Aristotle, in his sober way, although subordinating all the other arts to πολιτική in his *Nicomachean Ethics*, made a distinction in the *Poetics* (1460 b 13) as regards ὀρθότης : 'there is not the same kind of correctness in poetry as in politics, or indeed any other art.' He had also no objection to its producing pleasure ; on the contrary, pleasure should be required of poetry, that is of every species— epic, comedy, tragedy—its proper pleasure, ἡ οἰκεία ἡδονή (1453 b 11).[2] The emotional effect of tragedy had been discussed before by Gorgias and by Plato ;[3] accepting, as it seems, Gorgias' formula of 'horror and wailing', Aristotle came to a conclusion opposed to that of Plato. He concluded that it did not have an evil influence on the soul of the individual, but produced pleasure by the catharsis of those emotions just mentioned (1453 b 11 on tragic pleasure) ; tragedy, superior in other respects, attains that poetic kind of pleasure better than the epics and is to that extent also the higher form of art (1462 b 12 ff.).[4]

After the occasional literary criticism of early poets and Sophists, after Plato's pertinent questions and demands, the *Poetics* of Aristotle was the first attempt at discovering a rational order in the province of literary art, as was his object in all the other branches of knowledge. We started from the general concept of his 'teleology'; but we saw that this speculative concept is regularly controlled by the analysis of reality and 'the many notions of experience'. So the *Poetics* is a τέχνη in the true sense of that term which Aristotle took over from Plato.

If we look at his studies of language and antiquities, we find this statement fully confirmed. From the final lines of the first chapter of his little book Περὶ ἑρμηνείας, 'On the expression of thoughts in speech', we might expect that Aristotle is going to treat Plato's distinction (διαίρεσις) between ὄνομα and ῥῆμα and his definition of sentence (λόγος) more fully in this logical treatise : πρῶτον δεῖ θέσθαι τί ὄνομα καὶ τί ῥῆμα, ἔπειτα τί ἐστιν ἀπόφασις καὶ κατάφασις καὶ ἀπόφανσις καὶ λόγος (de interpr. 1 p. 16 a 1), 'first we must define the terms "noun" and "verb", then the

---

[1] Plat. *Leg.* 655 ff., 668 B, 700 BD about ὀρθότης and ἡδονή. J. Stroux, 'Die Anschauungen vom Klassischen im Altertum' in : *Das Problem des Klassischen und die Antike*, ed. by W. Jaeger (1931) 2 ff., derived from these passages the idea of classicism (Klassik), but he apparently misunderstood the Platonic ὀρθότης. On κρίσις ποιημάτων and *classicus* see below, pp. 204 ff.
[2] Cf. 1453 a 35, 1462 b 13 and above, p. 68.
[3] Gorgias, above, p. 48, Plato, p. 58.
[4] Cf. above p. 74 ; Bywater's translation freely used.

terms "denial" and "affirmation" and "proposition" and "sentence".[1]
But he confines his detailed inquiries to the terms belonging to the subject
of syllogistic, especially to 'apophansis'; in three very short chapters he
says only a few words on ὄνομα (ch. 2), on ῥῆμα (ch. 3), and on λόγος (ch.
4). Their relation to Plato's *Sophistes* (quoted above, p. 59) is obvious,
but there is a new Aristotelian psychological element (ch. 1) in that he
assumes 'likenesses of real things in the soul; words and sentences are
symbols of these likenesses and through them symbols of the things'.[2]
There is no need for us to go into these psychological and logical subtleties,
as Aristotle himself continues by saying that the investigation of words and
sentences 'belongs rather to the study of rhetoric or of poetics' (ῥητορικῆς
γὰρ ἢ ποιητικῆς οἰκειοτέρα ἡ σκέψις ibid. 4 p. 17 a 6). So we realize again,
as in our observation on Plato, that even in Aristotle's time, in the later
fourth century, no separate branch of 'grammar' was yet established;
questions of language, as far as they were not of a mere logical nature,
had to be relegated to rhetoric or poetics. And it was indeed in his books
on these two subjects that Aristotle undertook to improve upon his
predecessors.

In his *Poetics*, chapter 20,[3] he first gave a complete list of the parts of
'diction' (τῆς λέξεως ἁπάσης ... τὰ μέρη 1456 b 20 ff.) from the 'primary
elements' (στοιχεῖα) up to the 'sentence' (λόγος). For the single 'in-
divisible sounds' he used Plato's term and his differentiation, but between
the 'vowels' and 'consonants' he brought in the 'semi-vowels Σ and Ρ'
(ἡμίφωνα). Probably following Hippias the Sophist, he only slightly
touched on the formation of the syllables, their quantity and prosody,
and left all the theoretical details to the metricians[4] and their metrics;
as a special branch of learning, separated from rhythmics and 'music',
it appears for the first time in Aristotle. In the third book of the *Rhetoric*,
also dealing with diction, he calls all other words which are neither
ὀνόματα nor ῥήματα 'ligaments', σύνδεσμοι[5] (1407 a 20, cf. 1413 b 33);

---

[1] E. Kapp, 'Greek Foundations of Traditional Logic', *Columbia Studies in Philosophy* 5
(1942) 47; I use his translation.

[2] My paraphrase, which gives the essence of the difficult text 16 a 3-8, is based on Kapp's
translation (loc. cit. p. 49).

[3] I take this chapter as genuinely Aristotelian in substance; on the heated dispute see the
commentaries on the *Poetics*; see also recently A. Pagliaro, 'Il capitolo linguistico della
Poetica' in *Nuovi saggi di critica semantica* (1956) 77-151.

[4] *Poet.* 1456 b 34 I read with Bernhardy and Spengel τοῖς μετρικοῖς (not ἐν τ. μ.), cf. *Part.
an.* 660 a 8 παρὰ τῶν μετρικῶν; *Poet.* ibid. b 38 τῆς μετρικῆς (sc. τέχνης).—On the former
unity of word and 'music' see above, p. 53.

[5] This may be in the line of an earlier Sophistic tradition, cf. Isocr. (*Art. script.* в XXIV 22)
τοὺς συνδέσμους τοὺς αὐτοὺς μὴ σύνεγγυς τιθέναι κτλ. (see also Radermacher's note on fr. 24);
as soon as we enter the field of rhetoric, the priority of Sophistic textbooks (above, p. 31, n. 3)
completely lost to us, is always possible.

this sounds rather anatomical (cf. Eur. *Hipp.* 199 μελέων σύνδεσμα, 'sinews'), and so does the other term, ἄρθρον, 'joint' (cf. Soph. *Tr.* 769 ἅπαν κατ' ἄρθρον), which he introduces in chapter 20 of the *Poetics* (1457 a 6). They both have a function only in connexion with ὀνόματα or ῥήματα; as terms they have a wider and less distinct sense than the so-called 'conjunctions' and the 'article' in later strictly grammatical writings. The idea of the λόγος as an 'organism' suggested, I should think, the use of such expressions.

On ὀνόματα and ῥήματα Aristotle now had much more to say than in his logical writings. In the same chapter of his *Rhetoric* (1407 b 7) he quoted Protagoras' three genders word for word, but in his *Poetics* (1458 a 8), while still accepting the categories of males and females, he dropped the third term (names of 'things') as inadequate and substituted τὰ μεταξύ 'the intermediaries'.[1] As he began to classify the ὀνόματα by their respective 'terminations', this third group actually occupies a position 'between' the two others, in so far as in their 'terminations' (that means in their concluding letter) some of these words resemble the masculine and others the feminine nouns. This rough division[2] according to gender and termination had to be refined, but its principle was kept for all times. As the wide sense of ῥήματα, 'things said about ὀνόματα', was taken over from Plato, Aristotle treated a 'predicative adjective' also as a ῥῆμα: ἔστιν ἄνθρωπος λευκός (*De interpr.* 20 b 1, cf. Plat. *Cratyl.* 399 B, above p. 60). There was some difficulty when he tried to define the 'verb'; ῥῆμα is that which 'also indicates time', τὸ προσσημαῖνον χρόνον (*De interpr.* 16 b 6 ff.). In Protagoras χρόνος could never have meant 'tense'[3] and Plato did not mention it; so in this case Aristotle seems to have been the first to point out that different forms of the ῥῆμα express different temporal relations. Again he enlarges upon this notable conception in the *Poetics*, ch. 20, when he recognizes as verbs proper the present and perfect tenses (1457 a 18); in *De interpretatione* (16 b 16) he called the future and imperfect tenses πτώσεις ῥήματος, 'modifications of the verb', using the same term which covers the 'oblique cases' of a noun and all sorts of derivations from it, such as adjectives or adverbs (*De interpr.* 16 b 1 and *Poetics* 1457 a 19 πτῶσις ὀνόματος ἢ ῥήματος). We cannot go into the very complicated details; the few words said may be sufficient to show that

---

[1] Cf. *Soph. El.* 14 p. 173 b 28 ff., ibid. b 40 τῶν λεγομένων . . . σκευῶν, after referring to Protagoras' criticism of Homer's 'incorrect' use of the gender, Aristotle, of course, proved that Protagoras, not Homer, was wrong; on Protagoras see above, p. 38.

[2] Cf. D. Fehling, 'Varro und die grammatische Lehre von der Analogie und der Flexion', *Glotta* 35 (1956) 261 f.

[3] See above, pp. 38 f.

78 *The Masters of Philosophy in Athens*

πτῶσις (the Latin *casus* of the *nomen*), applied to noun and verb alike by
Aristotle, was coined as a *logical* term; it was to cause many headaches to
ancient and modern grammarians and linguists.[1] The last item in the list
is the λόγος, which certainly means 'sentence'. The definition (1457 a
23) partly repeats what was said in *De interpretatione* ch. 4 (λόγος . . .
φωνὴ σημαντικὴ κατὰ συνθήκην κτλ. 16 b 26); but now, referring to the
parts of the sentence defined before, it runs like this: λόγος δὲ φωνὴ
συνθετὴ σημαντικὴ ἧς ἔνια μέρη καθ᾽ αὐτὰ σημαίνει τι, 'a sentence is a composite indicative sound, some of the parts of which indicate something
by themselves.' This, of course, means that not only composite sentences,
but also nouns or verbs in isolation can indicate something, whereas
'ligaments' and 'joints' cannot. We remember Plato's words in his *Sophistes*
262 A–C, that nouns and verbs cannot make anything known, unless they
are twined together and produce a sentence.[2] Aristotle's criticism is again
based on his formal logic.

The list of the eight constituents of 'diction' was never meant to be
anything like a linguistic *system*, but it still was a fairly coherent analysis of
some fundamental terms. There are some other remarks on language,
scattered through various writings, where Aristotle coined the terms or
took them from sources unknown to us; we select only a few as relevant to
our purpose. Prodicus had taught his pupils the proper use of words
having different forms but more or less the same sense; Aristotle called
such words 'synonyms' συνώνυμα, probably first in his logical writings
(*Top.* 158 b 38, 163 a 24, cf. *Cat.* 1 a 6), then in the lost part of his
Poetics (fr. 1 Bywater,[3] cf. *Rhet.* III 2 p. 1404 b 39 ff.), where he recommended the use of synonyms to the poet. He treated also as essentially
poetical the 'compounds', the διπλᾶ, which in his subdivision of ὀνόματα
he had already separated from the ἁπλᾶ, the 'simple' words (*De interpr.*
16 a 23, 16 b 32); they were considered as the highlights of the dithyrambic style (*Poet.* 1459 a 9, *Rhet.* 1406 b 1, cf. 1405 b 35). Much more
important than compounds and synonyms was another group, the rare
and obsolete words, the glosses, γλῶσσαι. Aristotle expressly stated that
such words are most in place in heroic poetry (*Poet.* 1459 a 9 f., cf. 1461 a
10, where by assuming a gloss, οὐρῆας is taken to mean 'guards', see above,

---

[1] A 'case'-system of Ionian grammarians in the sixth century is a very poor modern invention; see above, pp. 12 ff. with notes and bibliography on πτῶσις.
[2] See above, p. 60, cf. 77.
[3] Simplic. in Aristot. *Cat.* (Comment. in Ar. Gr. VIII ed. Kalbfleisch) 36. 13 ἐν τῷ Περὶ
ποιητικῆς συνώνυμα εἶπεν εἶναι ὧν πλείω μὲν τὰ ὀνόματα, λόγος δὲ ὁ αὐτός; on Prodicus see
above, pp. 39 f. Fragments of a treatise, possibly Theophr. Περὶ λέξεως, dealing with συνώνυμα, διπλᾶ, etc. in the manner of Aristot. *Poet.* c. 20–22, were published by B. Snell in
Griechische Papyri der Hamburger Staats- u. Universitätsbibliothek (1954) no. 128, pp. 36 ff.

p. 70); the statement was repeated in his *Rhetoric* (1406 b 3 γλῶτται τοῖς ἐποποιοῖς, cf. 1404 b 23 with reference to the *Poetics*). As glosses are contrasted with the 'current' words (κύρια), there are dialectical as well as foreign words, τὰ ξενικά[1] (*Poet.* 1457 b 3), included in this group; in prose they should be used sparingly. Aristotle's remarks on glosses continue an earlier tradition, certainly of the fifth century: Aristophanes used the expression 'Ομήρου γλώττας and possibly Democritus wrote a book Περὶ 'Ομήρου . . . γλωσσέων.[2] But long before that epic poets and rhapsodes had favoured such obscure expressions and may have made collections for their own professional use.[3] After Aristotle, at about 300 B.C., a completely new impulse was given to these studies, when two poets made the first comprehensive learned collections of epic and dialectical glosses, Philitas of Cos and Simias of Rhodes.[4] We cannot tell at what time the so-called γλωσσογράφοι, often quoted in our Scholia to Homer,[5] started their work, but it was surely not before the later third century.

In the old dispute on the origin of words Aristotle was quite definite: 'no word is by nature', φύσει τῶν ὀνομάτων οὐδέν ἐστιν (*De interpr.* 2 p. 16 a 27); his answer to the question of the relation of words to things (which worried Plato so much) has already been quoted.[6]

The combination of Platonic and earlier Ionian–Sophistic elements was characteristic of Aristotle's studies of language. There could not be anything Platonic in his antiquarian research; it had to be in the other tradition. There we found Hippias of Elis as the leading 'archaeologist' or 'antiquarian', using his learned collections for epideictic purposes. Aristotle[7] surpassed all his predecessors in universality of knowledge; in contrast to the Sophists he was able to put a vast quantity of material in order according to his own philosophical principles and by organizing the co-operation of his pupils. As a consequence of his basic teleological point of view the different stages through which things reached their 'end' had to be investigated; so chronology, as a help towards recognizing their development in the past, acquired a new importance. We can understand the reason why he took so much pains to establish reliable

---

[1] Cf. above, p. 41 and p. 62.

[2] On Aristophanes see above, p. 15, on Democritus pp. 42 f.

[3] See above, p. 12; on their occasional mistakes and the consequences of their wrong explanations see above, pp. 5 f. and p. 6, n. 1.

[4] See below, pp. 90 f.

[5] K. Lehrs, *De Aristarchi studiis Homericis*, 3rd ed. (1882) 37 f., collected the evidence, but he was wrong in assuming that those γλωσσογράφοι were schoolmasters of the fourth century; see K. Latte, 'Glossographika', *Philol.* 80 (1925) 148. 26.

[6] See p. 63 on the origin of words, p. 76 on their relation to things.

[7] W. Jaeger, *Aristoteles* 346 ff. 'Die Organisation der Forschung' (= Engl. transl. 324 ff.).

lists of the victors in the great national games. The catalogues of Aristotle's writings mention a series of titles[1] referring not only to the Olympian games,[2] which had been previously treated by Hippias, but also in particular to the Pythian games.[3] This work, undertaken in the archives of the Delphic priests together with his relative Callisthenes, who wrote a history of the Sacred War,[4] met with enormous success; according to an inscription found in 1896 the authors were 'praised and crowned' by the Delphians;[5] and the payment of public money to a well known stone-cutter, for the laborious carving on to stone of the complete Πυθιονικῶν ἀναγραφή, is registered in an inscription of the year 331 B.C.[6] Even if it had only the form of a πίναξ (see l. 10), like earlier Sophistic antiquarian writings, with an introduction on the foundation of the Pythian games and a refutation of legendary reports, an engraved prose work of such a considerable length,[7] dedicated no doubt to the god himself, has few parallels; it might be regarded as another testimony of Aristotle's personal attachment to Apollinism[8] that he was granted this exceptional honour. It is a fair guess that the later registers of victors in the Panhellenic contests[9] were ultimately based upon this work of Aristotle.

---

[1] Diog. L. v 21, no. 130–4; Fragm. ed. Rose p. 8. See Moraux, *Les listes anciennes des ouvrages d'Aristote* (1951) 123–6 and 199; Düring, *Aristotle* 49. 339 f.; see also Jacoby in *FGrHist* iii B 415, Kommentar (1955) p. 215 and n. 24.

[2] It is possible that Aristotle mentioned in *this* list of Olympian victors the victory of Empedocles in 496 B.C. and that Eratosthenes took it over from this book, not from the dialogue Περὶ ποιητῶν to which the passage (fr. 71 Rose) is generally attributed; so we would gain at least one short fragment, see A. Rostagni, *Scritti minori* i (1955) 257 f.

[3] Fr. 615–17 Rose.   [4] *FGrHist* 124 T 23 and F 1.

[5] Published by T. Homolle, *BCH* 22 (1898) 260 ff. and 632; reprinted with supplements and notes in *Syll.*³ (1915) no. 275. The final edition by E. Bourguet in *Fouilles de Delphes* iii 1 (1929) no. 400 (unfortunately often overlooked) is reprinted with commentary and bibliography by M. N. Tod, *A selection of Greek historical inscriptions* ii (1948) no. 187.

[6] Published by E. Bourguet, *BCH* 24 (1900) 464 ff., and *Fouilles de Delphes* iii 5, no. 58. 42; cf. *Syll.*³ 252. 42. It gives the only certain date. In spring 334 Callisthenes went with Alexander to Asia Minor; this is the *terminus ante quem* for the composition of the list.

[7] We should, of course, very much like to learn the exact length of the lost work of Aristotle; but Bourguet loc. cit. iii 1, p. 240 has conclusively demonstrated that this is impossible. The cost of 'two minas' in 331 may be only an instalment for the work done in this year, and the prices paid in the fourth century were quite different from those paid in the third century on which the calculations of Homolle and others were based. The figure of '60,000 words' given by W. Jaeger, *Aristoteles* (1923) 348 with particular emphasis and repeated in all the later editions and translations is a slip of the pen; Homolle's estimate to which Jaeger refers was 60,000 *letters*, Pomtow, *Syll.*³ 275 and 252 calculated only about 20,000 letters. O. Regenbogen, 'Πίναξ', *RE* xx (1950) 1414, 20 ff. followed Pomtow (21,000 letters), but we had better not accept any of these figures.

[8] See 'The Image of the Delian Apollo and Apolline Ethics', *Ausgewählte Schriften* (1960) 70.

[9] The most important is the list of Olympian victors, *P.Oxy.* 222 (vol. ii, 1899, with the commentary of Grenfell and Hunt); it is reprinted in *FGrHist* iii b (1950) no. 415 in the chapter xviii 'Elis und Olympia' pp. 301–14, with introduction, commentary and notes in separate volumes to all the historical fragments referring to this part of Greece and to the Olympian games. Chapter xvii deals with Delphi pp. 297 ff. and the Pythian games p. 301.

When Aristotle returned to Athens after Alexander's and Callisthenes' departure, he began to search the official records kept by the archons for the performances of plays and dithyrambs.[1] Three relevant titles are mentioned in the lists of his writings.[2] Nothing further is known of a book entitled Περὶ τραγῳδιῶν; the Νῖκαι Διονυσιακαί (or Νικῶν Διονυσιακῶν ἀστικῶν καὶ Ληναίων in Hesychius) were possibly used by the author of the record of victors inscribed on the Ionic epistyles of a building early in the third century B.C. (now *I.G.* II² 2325).[3] Verbal quotations remain only from the third work, the surpassingly important Διδασκαλίαι (fr. 618–30 Rose), and there is some likelihood that the inscription engraved on the wall of the building just mentioned was based on it (*I.G.* II² 2319–23).[4] The poets were the 'producers', the διδάσκαλοι, of their dramas, and the catalogues of the productions were called διδασκαλίαι: on stone there were entered first the archon's name, then the names of the competing poets with the titles of their respective plays in order of success and the names of the protagonists with the victorious actor at the end. Aristotle's book[5] was based on the archon's archives and may have contained more literary material than the inscriptions, which were based on excerpts from the book and were kept up to date afterwards in the same style. The parallel to the procedure in Delphi is obvious. The great Alexandrine scholars, who had no access to the Athenian archives or inscriptions, had to use Aristotle's compilations; in that way a few relics of the original work are still preserved in the Byzantine Scholia to the Attic dramatists, but it is questionable whether every reference to διδασκαλίαι without his name should be counted as a genuine Aristotelian fragment (as by Rose). In Aristotle's philosophical theory the highest place of poetical perfection was assigned to Attic tragedy; no wonder therefore that to him the dates and details of every single play were relevant for his purpose of recognizing the actual historical process of the development of tragic art.

---

[1] A. Pickard-Cambridge, *The Dramatic Festivals of Athens* (1953) 68 ff.—A. Wilhelm, 'Urkunden dramatischer Aufführungen in Athen', *Sonderschriften des Österr. Archaeolog. Instituts in Wien* VI (Wien 1906, reprinted 1965) remains the classic work on this subject.

[2] Ar. fragm. pp. 8 and 15 Rose; cf. Regenbogen, 'Πίναξ' *RE* xx 1415 ff.

[3] Reprinted by Pickard-Cambridge, op. cit. 114–18, cf. p. 105. 2 and Moraux, *Les listes anciennes* 127.—The inscription of νῖκαι *IG.* II² 2318, which was given the name *Fasti* by Wilamowitz (*GGA* 1906 614 = *Kleine Schriften* VI [1937] 378) seems to have no relation to Aristotle, Pickard-Cambridge 69 f., 105 (106 ff. text), Moraux, loc. cit. 127. 24.

[4] Reprinted by Pickard-Cambridge, op. cit. 110—13, cf. 71 and Moraux, loc. cit. 127 f.

[5] G. Jachmann's reconstruction in his dissertation *De Aristotelis didascaliis* (Göttingen 1909) is not yet superseded; but see above, n. 3 on the *Fasti*, which he was inclined to use for his reconstruction.

At about the same time (after 334 B.C.) as Aristotle was compiling the records of performances of plays from the Athenian archives, his friend and fellow student Lycurgus, who was in charge of the public finances from 338 to 326 B.C., had an official copy made of the works of the three great tragedians; this was deposited in the public archives, and the actors were compelled by law to keep to this authorized text.[1] The growing corruption of the tragic texts by actors' interpolations since the beginning of the fourth century was thus to be checked; but it is uncertain whether this regulation had any practical effect. We are told that Ptolemy III (247–221 B.C.) borrowed this official copy from the Athenians, but never returned it;[2] so it may have been of some use in the Alexandrian library, although we should not overestimate its critical value.

Aristotle's writings on politics offer a close analogy. On the one hand we have his philosophical work Πολιτικά, on the other his extensive collection of Πολιτεῖαι (fr. 381–603 Rose),[3] which brought together the histories of the constitutions of 158 cities and tribes, most of them Greek. It was one of the great days in the history of scholarship when the British Museum acquired in 1889 four papyrus rolls[4] containing thirty columns of a nearly complete text of Aristotle's Ἀθηναίων πολιτεία which was first published by F. G. Kenyon at the beginning of 1891. The wealth of new information and many new problems were immediately set forth by Wilamowitz with incomparable courage and quickness of mind in his two volumes entitled *Aristoteles und Athen* (1893, about 800 pages). The controversies on questions of Aristotle's sources, of his relations to the Attic historians, the so-called Atthidographers,[5] of the literary type of the *Constitution* are still in full swing.[6] Two points may be mentioned here. We must be very grateful that Aristotle quoted Solon's own verses for the history of the Solonian reform, thus presenting us with precious new lines

[1] [Plut.] *Decem oratorum vitae* VII p. 841 F = Schmidt, *Pinakes* test. 6 a; cf. Pickard-Cambridge, op. cit. 101, 153.

[2] Galen, *comment.* II 4 in Hippocr. *Epidem.* III, *CMG* v 10. 2. 1 (1936) p. 79. 8; see below, p. 192.

[3] A new fragment of the Αἰνίων πολιτεία to which we had no reference, will have to be added between fr. 472 (Αἰγινητῶν) and 473 (Αἰτωλῶν) from *P.Oxy.* xxx ed. E. Lobel (1964) 2527. 5.

[4] P. Lit. Lond. 108 (Pack[2] no. 163); H. J. M. Milne, *Catalogue of the Literary Papyri in the British Museum* (1927) 84, with bibliography of editions.—Fragments of two small leaves of a papyrus codex (Pack[2] no. 164) acquired in 1880 by the Egyptian Museum of Berlin and identified by the singular acumen of Th. Bergk in the last month of his life 1881, *Rh.M.* 36 (1881) 87 ff. = Opuscula II (1886) 505–33.

[5] F. Jacoby, *Atthis* (1949) *passim*; cf. *FGrHist* III b II (1954) 459 ff.

[6] See the survey and balanced judgement in the Introduction to Aristotle's *Constitution of Athens and Related Texts*, translated with an Introduction and Notes by K. v. Fritz and E. Kapp (New York 1950).

of his elegiac and iambic poetry.[1] He was, of course, far from interpreting the poems, but selected those passages which seemed to contain actual evidence for Solon's struggle and failure and success, and could be used as a historical source for his particular purpose. Thanks to the papyrus we are able to see the purpose and the structure of the *Politeiai* and their relation to the *Politics* more clearly. In the *Constitution of Athens* two parts can be distinguished (and it may have been the same in others of Aristotle's many *Constitutions*). In the second part the democratic constitution as it existed in his own days is described; the first, introductory, part shows how the Athenian state arrived at this final form describing the different stages, in this case eleven, through which it reached its 'nature'. In this development the Solonian reform gave the decisive turn to radical democracy. Aristotle in writing 'history' too remained the political philosopher, true to his general teleological concept.

The latest date mentioned in the papyrus is the year 329/8 B.C. (ch. 54. 7); but there remain several open questions, namely at what time Aristotle started to collect the vast material for the *Politeiai*, who may have co-operated with him, and whether he ever intended to publish it. The same applies to the Δικαιώματα,[2] which include a passage on the death of Alexander Molossus in the year 331/30 B.C.; but if they were used by Philip of Macedon for his policy of κοινὴ εἰρήνη, a great deal of the collection must have been available between 338 and 336 B.C. To Aristotle's antiquarian studies belong also the Νόμιμα βαρβαρικά, *Non-Greek Customs* (fr. 604–10 Rose); in collecting such ethnographical material he again had a predecessor in Hippias, and many followers in Hellenistic times. There is no doubt about his lively interest in proverbs, but the existence of a monograph on Παροιμίαι has been subject to discussion—mistakenly, I believe—since Παροιμίαι appear in the list of Aristotle's works,[3] and he is expressly blamed by Isocrates' pupil Cephisodorus for having collected proverbs (Ath. 11 60 D παροιμίας ἀθροῖσαι), which is sound evidence. In his first anti-Platonic dialogue, Περὶ φιλοσοφίας, he regarded proverbs as 'survivals of a pre-literary philosophy'[4] and treated them in a survey of early wisdom, together with the 'Orphics', the Delphic maxims (γνῶθι σαυτόν, etc.) and the precepts of the Seven Wise

---

[1] One should not disregard Wilamowitz's commentary in *Griechisches Lesebuch* 11 1. Halbband (1902) 20 ff.

[2] Fr. 612–14 Rose. Perhaps 'Pleas of right' or 'Legal decisions between different Greek States', as the (not very reliable) *Vita Marciana* 4 p. 97 Düring, says: Δικα]ιώματα Ἑλληνίδων πόλεων ἐξ ὧν Φίλιππος τὰς φιλονεικίας τῶν Ἑλλήνων διέλυσεν; cf. Gigon's commentary p. 39. Two new references, see Moraux, *Les listes anciennes* 122 f. and Düring 140 f.

[3] Diog. L. v 22 no. 137, Hesychius no. 127 (προοιμίων cod.).

[4] W. Jaeger, *Aristoteles* 131 f. = Engl. translat. 130; cf. fr. 13 Rose = fr. 8 Ross (p. 75).

Men. He liked to embellish his later writings on rhetoric and politics[1] with proverbial quotations. One of his pupils, Clearchus of Soloi, enlarged his master's collection by writing two books of Παροιμίαι[2] which for the amusement of his readers he cast in a literary narrative form; many others followed,[3] who were content to arrange dry lists. But it was Aristotle who first from his philosophical point of view called attention to those traditional sayings and their peculiar form of 'brevity and pregnancy' (συντομία καὶ δεξιότης).

Finally, there is another type of collection at least as consequential as Didaskaliai or Politeiai, to which Aristotle led the way, the collection of doctrines of philosophers according to special topics, called δόξαι. We have mentioned a previous collection made by Hippias of parallel passages, not only from the oldest poets, but also from the earliest philosophers. Now Aristotle opened his great systematic works, for instance the *Metaphysics*, with a review of his predecessors and guided his listeners and readers through those earlier views to the final doctrine of his own, which presented itself as the end, the τέλος, of a natural development.[4] But it was only by the combined efforts of his school that the monumental work could be continued and accomplished. Theophrastus was commissioned to make a collection of the *Opinions of the Physicists*, Φυσικῶν δόξαι,[5] from Thales down to his own age in sixteen (or eighteen) books; other pupils like Eudemus did the same for special sciences. In modern times all these writers have come to be called 'Doxographers'.[6] Their 'ancestor', Aristotle himself, could not but see the earlier doctrines in the light of his own teleological philosophy.

---

[1] Bonitz, *Index* s.v. παροιμία.

[2] Fr. 63–83, F. Wehrli, *Die Schule des Aristoteles* 3 (1948) with commentary; see also Theophrastus, Dicaearchus.

[3] K. Rupprecht, 'Paroimiographoi', *RE* xviii (1949) 1735 ff., with reference to the fundamental researches of O. Crusius.

[4] Cf. Jaeger *Aristoteles* 358 ff. = Engl. translat. 334 ff.

[5] O. Regenbogen, *RE*, Suppl. 7 (1940) 1535 ff.

[6] *Doxographi Graeci*, ed. H. Diels (1879); I do not know whether Diels coined the new term or his great teacher in Bonn, Hermann Usener; E. Schwartz, *Rede auf H. Usener* (1906) 11 = *Gesammelte Schriften* 1 (1938) 311 'Usener hat den Begriff der doxographischen Überlieferung geschaffen'. The compound παραδοξογράφος is to be found in Tzetz. *Hist.* 11 151.

PART TWO

THE HELLENISTIC AGE

I

THE RISE OF SCHOLARSHIP
IN ALEXANDRIA

IN the stupendous work of Aristotle the τέλος of the classical age was reached, the end of the intellectual development of the Attic as well as of the Ionian period. Aristotle died in 322 B.C., one year after his pupil Alexander, who had opened the doors to a new world. He himself belonged to the world of the old Greek city-state with its cultural unity; it was with the great writers of the past that he was intimately connected. The 'retrospective' character of his writings on literature is a quite natural result of his philosophy.

The former unity of the Greek world, threatened by political and social changes throughout the fourth century,[1] rapidly disintegrated in its concluding decades. Alexander's empire, short-lived as it was and apparently of no deeper influence on Aristotle's thought, split up after the death of the conqueror; the turmoil of the wars of succession was followed by a sort of stability once new states had been firmly established about the beginning of the third century.[2] The members of these states were subject to the rule of a sovereign and his officials. The free political life, once in perpetual motion in the old city-state, was brought to a standstill. This, no doubt, had its disadvantages, but not in every respect, as we shall see presently. Now for the first time the Greeks were convinced that the old order of things in the political as well as in the intellectual field, in their whole way of life indeed, was gone for ever. They became conscious of a definitive break between the mighty past and a still uncertain present. Of this dividing line Aristotle and his personal pupils were yet unaware.

The new generation of about 300 B.C. living under a new monarchy

---

[1] See above, p. 65.

[2] *The Cambridge Ancient History* VII (1928); M. Rostovtzeff, *Social and economic history of the Hellenistic world*, 3 vols. (Oxford 1941); H. Bengtson, 'Griechische Geschichte' 2. Aufl., *Handbuch der Altertumswissenschaft* III 4 (1960) 285 ff. Zeitalter des Hellenismus; 354 ff. and 415 ff. Quellen und Darstellungen. W. W. Tarn, *Hellenistic Civilisation*, 3rd ed. (1952). The historical background and the transition from the fourth to the third century is described also by U. von Wilamowitz, *Die hellenistische Dichtung in der Zeit des Kallimachos*, vol. 1 (1924), cf. *DLZ* 1925, 2134 ff.

realized that the great old poetical forms also belonged to ages gone for ever.[1] Poetry had shown signs of exhaustion and even dissolution throughout the fourth century. But there was still something left of the creative resourcefulness of the Greek genius; it manifested itself again under the changed conditions. A strong desire to rebuild was slowly growing up in the field of poetry as in others too. Poetry had to be rescued from the dangerous situation in which it lay, and the writing of poetry had to become a particularly serious work of discipline and wide knowledge, τέχνη and σοφίη. The new writers had to look back to the old masters, especially of Ionic poetry, not to imitate them—this was regarded as impossible or at least as undesirable—but in order to be trained by them in their own new poetical technique. Their incomparably precious heritage had to be saved and studied. This was felt to be, first of all, a necessity for the rebirth and future life of poetry, and secondly an obligation to the achievements of past ages which had given birth to the masterpieces of Hellenic literature. The relation of the new generation to the past was entirely different from that of Aristotle, the whole perspective of literary criticism was changed.[2]

Thus a novel conception of poetry, held by the poets themselves, led the way to the revival of poetry as well as to a new treatment of the ancient poetical texts and then of all the other literary monuments.[3] I am here repeating the general statement with which I started this book, and I shall now try to reconstruct the historical process from the scanty evidence still available to us; it is just sufficient to give us a glimpse of classical scholarship in the making.

The first of these new poets was Philitas[4] from the island of Cos, who

---

[1] In this whole chapter I make free use of my paper 'The Future of Studies in the Field of Hellenistic Poetry', *JHS* 75 (1955) 71 ff. = *Ausgewählte Schriften* (1960) 154 ff. I had tentatively stated the same opinion on the relation of poetry and scholarship in a sketch 'Von den geschichtlichen Begegnungen der kritischen Philologie mit dem Humanismus', *Archiv für Kulturgeschichte* 28 (1938) 192 ff. = *Ausgewählte Schriften* 160 ff. See also *Philologia Perennis*, Festrede (München 1961, Bayer. Akademie der Wissenschaften) 4 ff. The agreement expressed by H. Haffter in his lecture 'Geschichte der klassischen Philologie', *Das Erbe der Antike* (Erasmus-Bibliothek, Zürich 1963) 13–30, was gratifying and encouraging to me.

[2] I have made this point in various papers just quoted and in my lectures; see also below, pp. 135 f. I was highly pleased to find the same view expressed by H. W. Garrod in his stimulating Gray Lectures, *Scholarship, its Meaning and Value* (Cambridge 1946) 16 f.

[3] F. Susemihl, *Geschichte der griechischen Literatur in der Alexandrinerzeit*, is still an invaluable storehouse of information on the whole literature of the age; see also W. Schmid–O. Stählin in W. von Christ, *Geschichte d. griech. Lit.* II 1[6] (1920); A. Lesky, *Geschichte d. griech. Lit.* (2. Aufl. 1963) 690 ff., esp. 744 ff. A competent survey of research in the first half of the twentieth century is given by E. A. Barber, 'Hellenistic Poetry' in *Fifty Years of Classical Scholarship* (Oxford 1954) 214–32.

[4] J. U. Powell, *Collectanea Alexandrina* (1925) 90–96 and *Anth. Lyr. Graeca* ed. E. Diehl II[2] (1942), fasc. 6. 49–55, contain the poetical fragments only; complete edition, including the

lived in the last third of the fourth century and probably in the first two decades of the third.[1] There could have been no better designation applied to him than that preserved by Strabo xiv 657 (= test. 13 K.) in his list of famous Coans : ποιητὴς ἅμα καὶ κριτικός, 'poet as well as scholar'.[2] The combination of these two words, never applied to anyone before, exactly describes the key position of Philitas at the beginning of a new era. The stress is laid on ποιητής; he was, first of all, a writer of subtle verse: elegiacs, short epics, epigrams. The two greatest poets of the next generation, Theocritus and Callimachus, praised him in prominent passages of their chief poems: Theocritus in the *Thalysia*, a harvest festival in Philitas' native island of Cos (vii 40), and Callimachus in the programmatic elegy against his adversaries with which he opened the first book of the *Aitia* (fr. 1. 9–12); the beginnings of the lines are missing in the papyrus, but from the Florentine Scholia we conclude that the shorter poems of Philitas and Mimnermus were compared with their longer ones and preference was given to the ὀλιγοστιχίη, the pieces of a few lines.[3] The main point was, of course, not the length, but the exquisite workmanship, the τέχνη; no doubt Philitas was regarded as the first of the new poets to aim at artistic perfection in a limited space. Callimachus' praise is frequently echoed by Roman poets, especially by Propertius and Ovid.

Hermesianax of Colophon, himself a minor poet, is said to have been a pupil and friend of Philitas;[4] he praised his master in his elegiac catalogue of love-affairs of poets and philosophers[5] as having been honoured by a statue in his native island. He was the only post-classical poet found worthy by Hermesianax of being added to the series of illustrious earlier poets starting with Orpheus. So in the later lists[6] of the foremost Greek elegists he alone figures together with Callimachus after the great Ionian elegiac poets.

Little is known about Philitas' contemporaries. Simias of Rhodes may have had similar aims, as he wrote various poems as well as *glosses* under

prose fragments, with prolegomena and commentary, by G. Kuchenmüller, *Philetae Coi reliquiae*, Diss. Berlin (1928).

[1] The problems of dates are discussed by A. von Blumenthal, *RE* xix (1938) 2165 f.
[2] On κριτικός and γραμματικός see below, pp. 157 ff.
[3] See my explanatory notes to the passage, Call. 1 (1949) 2; the lively discussion on it is going on, see for instance W. Wimmel, 'Kallimachos in Rom', *Hermes-Einzelschriften* 16 (1960) 87 ff. with bibliography 87. 1; his own supplement on l. 9 is not convincing, see also G. Luck, *Gnomon* 33 (1961) 370.—Other references of Callimachus to Philitas see Call. ii (1953) Index p. 137.
[4] Schol. Nic. *Ther.* 3 (= test. 20 Kuch.).
[5] Fr. 7. 77 Powell.
[6] Test. 8 a. b. 12 Kuch.

the reign of Ptolemy I.[1] Besides some fragments of epics and lyrics, a few epigrams are preserved and three *carmina figurata*;[2] these poetical artifices were intended to reproduce by the differing lengths of their lines the shapes of certain objects. The *Egg*, the *Axe*, and the *Wings* were Simias' creations, and he may be regarded as the 'inventor' of this genre; he was immediately followed by no lesser a poet than Theocritus in the *Syrinx* and by Dosiades of Crete[3] in the *Altar*, who both in contrast to Simias[4] composed real riddles (γρῖφοι) in that playful form. In the course of time these poems aroused curiosity and admiration or anger and contempt in the minds of their readers; they show us that from the very beginning the combination of poetical talent and wide learning could easily lead to deliberate and provocative obscurity. But no such tendency is visible in the writings of Philitas, and there is no reason to trace the origin of the *Technopaegnia* to his 'school'.[5]

The work of Philitas the poet was inseparably allied to the work of Philitas the scholar, the κριτικός. For the new poetical technique could not be successfully practised without the constant help of the old masters. Glossaries, invaluable in the first place for the choice of words, helped also to give an understanding of the great poetry of the past. The Greek interest in rare words was very old: we have seen how occasional collections were made and how Aristotle paid particular attention to glosses.[6] But it was a new thing for a leading poet to write an extensive work on the subject. Philitas' book, since it was referred to as Ἄτακτοι γλῶσσαι, Ἄτακτα, or Γλῶσσαι (fr. 29–59 Kuchenmüller), was apparently not systematically arranged like the later collections made by grammarians; we may compare the name *Miscellanea* given by the poet Politian to his various learned writings put together without proper arrangement.

---

[1] H. Fränkel, *De Simia Rhodio*, Diss. Göttingen (1915); cf. P. Maas, *RE* III A (1927) 155 ff. It may be significant that he is never called ποιητής, but only γραμματικός: see Strab. XIV 655 (among the famous Rhodians) and Suid. s.v. Σιμ[μ]ίας; but we have from his three books of γλῶσσαι only four words quoted by Athenaeus and from his four books of ποιήματα about thirty quotations, some of them complete poems.

[2] See Theocritus, ed. A. S. F. Gow II (1950) 552 ff. with references. Ausonius, *Opusc.* XII ed. Peiper (1886) 155 ff., coined the word *Technopaegnion* for his verse playing with monosyllables or single letters of the alphabet; I have not been able to find out who transferred the name to the entirely different Greek poems for which no ancient comprehensive term exists.

[3] A. Hecker's identification of the poet with the writer of Κρητικά (*Comment. crit. de Anth. Gr.* I [1852] 127) has not yet been refuted, see *FGrHist* 458 (1955) Commentary 331.

[4] The result of Merkelbach's conjectures on the text of the 'Egg' (*Mus. Helv.* 10 [1953] 68 f.) is in so far improbable as the poem would be a rather hard riddle.

[5] W. Schmid, *Geschichte der griechischen Literatur* II 1[6] 125, unfortunately did so, and Kuchenmüller (p. 21) agreed; but he rightly rejected (p. 24) the incredible fancies of R. Herzog, *Philol.* 79 (1924) 426 ff., who detected in Philitas the central and celebrated figure in Herondas' *Dream*.

[6] See above, p. 78. On Antimachus see below, p. 94.

Philitas' compilation of rare dialectical expressions, technical terms, and Homeric vocables immediately became famous all over the Greek world. In an Attic comedy of the third century, the *Phoenicides* of Strato, the cook uses archaic Homeric words for commonplace things, and his desperate master is obliged 'to take the books of Philitas and look each word up to find its meaning', ὥστ' ἔδει / τὰ τοῦ Φιλίτα λαμβάνοντα βυβλία / σκοπεῖν ἕκαστον τί δύναται τῶν ῥημάτων; this passage figures already in a verse anthology for schools written as early as the later third century B.C.[1] Attic comedy did more than quote Philitas' well-known books; it joked at his frailty as a valetudinarian, so that his person must somehow have been familiar to the Athenian audience.[2]

How much Philitas' glosses were used by the great Alexandrian poets we cannot tell, as too few verbal excerpts are preserved; but nearly one and a half centuries later Aristarchus found it necessary to write against Philitas, πρὸς Φιλίταν,[3] as his Homeric interpretations were still authoritative. A marginal note to Strabo III 168, which later crept into Strabo's text, quotes the title Φιλίτας ἐν Ἑρμηνείᾳ, the sense of which is uncertain;[4] but in this book he is said to have explained the gloss μελαγκράνινον as 'plaited of black rushes', citing an anonymous distichon;[5] by a startling coincidence a recently published poetical onomasticon (*P.Hibeh* 172) begins with colour-compounds formed from the same prefix μελα-.[6] It would be an enormous increase of Philitas' scanty fragments, if we were entitled to attribute this list of about 125 words to his γλῶσσαι; it is very tempting to do so, and it was quite natural that the first editor raised this question very seriously. On the other hand, he did not suppress the obvious objection to this hypothesis, namely the fact that the words in the papyrus are listed without explanation, while according to the passage in Strato's comedy the meaning of the rare words could be found in Philitas' 'dictionary'; most of the thirty attested quotations from the Ἄτακτα show the same arrangement. There is nothing indeed in the

[1] Strato in Athen. IX 382 c = *CAF* III 361 f. Kock. O. Guéraud–P. Jouguet, *Un Livre d'Écolier du IIIe Siècle avant J.-C.* (Le Caire 1938) 34, reprinted in D. L. Page, *Greek Literary Papyri* I (1942) no. 57. 42–44, p. 266. I quote the papyrus text together with Page's translation; see also above, p. 60, n. 1.
[2] See above, pp. 41 f.   [3] Fr. 54, 55 K.
[4] Ἑρμηνεία is a quite unusual title whether it means 'expression' (cf. above, p. 75) or 'interpretation'; three variant readings in the text of the *Iliad* may have been discussed in such a book (fr. 56–58 K.).
[5] Fr. 53 K.; cf. fr. 17 Pow.
[6] *The Hibeh Papyri* II ed. E. G. Turner (1955) 1–7, written between 270 and 230 B.C. I should guess that in *P.Hib.* 172 l. 5 it was not the Homeric [κελαι]νεφής that followed the four rare compounds with μέλας, but that a new compound [μελαν]νεφής or [μελαι]νεφής (= μελαινονεφής as κελαινεφής for κελαινονεφής) concluded this series, cf. below, p. 118, n. 5; then the κυανο- compounds start with κυανοχαίτης.

new Ὀνομαστικόν of compound adjectives which clearly points to Philitas
as its author;[1] but it may be due to his influence that such comprehensive
lists as that in *P.Hibeh* 172 were compiled in the course of the third
century B.C.[2]

The Coan poet and scholar was chosen by Ptolemy I as tutor to his
son born in the spring of 308 B.C. in the island of Cos.[3] Ptolemy, the son of
Berenice, was crowned as co-regent with his father in 285 and followed
him as king of Egypt from 28 3to 247 B.C., being married in the seventies
to his sister Arsinoe.[4] They showed themselves most liberal in promoting
that poetry and scholarship of which Philitas had been the first representative. The young Ptolemy's literary education was completed by his second
tutor, Zenodotus of Ephesus, himself a pupil of Philitas;[5] for instruction
in science Strato ὁ φυσικός[6] was called by the wise father to Alexandria
from Aristotle's school, to which he returned as Theophrastus' successor
in 287 B.C. Whether Philitas taught the son in Cos or in Alexandria we
cannot tell, nor where or when Zenodotus took over the tutorship of the
children; Zenodotus and Strato may have been teachers of Arsinoe too.
But one fact emerges quite clearly from the reliable tradition. Zenodotus,
who is said to have written epic verse himself of which nothing is known,[7]
initiated Homeric studies on a grand scale and in a methodical way both
as editor and lexicographer. So, we see, it was only *after* Philitas, the

[1] The new text does not contain γλῶσσαι in the proper sense of the word, dialectical or rare
poetical vocables, but only such 'compounds' as Aristotle had called διπλᾶ ὀνόματα and
treated as essentially poetical and as characteristic of the dithyrambic style, quite separate
from the glosses (above, p. 78). The editor has observed that 'the author of this list . . . was
drawing on the whole body of choral and tragic lyric as well as the epic . . . more than
thirty are unknown to our lexica'. I have tried to supply an 'unknown' compound in *P.Hib.*
172. 5. The best suggestion for the corrupt αλιτεσγης in l. 56 seems to be ἀλιτεγγής cf. ἀτεγγής
(= ἄτεγκτος) in the epigram published in *Mnemosynon*, Th. Wiegand dargebracht (1938)
32 = *Griechische Versinschriften* I, hg. von W. Peek (1955), no. 1913. 7.

[2] In Philitas' own lifetime a fellow countryman of his, Xenocritus of Cos, was the first to
write a Hippocratic glossary (Deichgräber p. 221. 24); among his many followers another
Coan in the next generation, Philinus, the founder of the Empirical School of Medicine,
became the most influential medical glossographer, see Susemihl 1 (1891) 346 and 818; *RE*
VIII 1851, XIX 2193. Testimonies and fragments in K. Deichgräber, *Die griechische Empirikerschule* (1930) 221 f. 'Zur empirischen Lexikographie', cf. 254 ff.

[3] Suid. v. Φιλίτας . . . διδάσκαλος τοῦ δευτέρου Πτολεμαίου. On chronological and biographical details of the Ptolemies see *RE* XXIII (1959) 1603 ff. 'Ptolemaios' and cf. A. E.
Samuel, 'Ptolemaic Chronology', *Münchener Beiträge zur Papyrusforschung* 43 (1962); on the
date of the birth of Ptolemy II cf. T. C. Skeat, 'The Reigns of the Ptolemies', *Mizraim* 6
(1937) 7 ff.; on Cos see Call. *hy.* IV 165 ff. and Scholia; cf. Theocr. XVII 58 and Scholia.

[4] The year of the marriage is still uncertain, see on Call. fr. 392 and Add. I and II.

[5] Suid. v. Ζηνόδοτος (test. 22 K.) . . . μαθητὴς τοῦ Φιλίτα . . . καὶ τοὺς παῖδας Πτολεμαίου
ἐπαίδευσεν.

[6] F. Wehrli, 'Straton von Lampsakos', *Die Schule des Aristoteles* 5 (1950) fr. 2, with commentary.

[7] Only in Suid. (above, n. 5) is Zenodotus called ἐποποιὸς καὶ γραμματικός.

poet and scholar, that the true scholar came into being, and this scholar was the personal pupil of the poet. Alexandria, perhaps since about 320 B.C. Ptolemy's capital in Egypt,[1] by attracting the leading spirits from the islands and from the great eastern cities, became the cultural centre too.

The impetus to the new movement apparently came from the south-eastern corner of the Greek world; we should also remember that the foremost epigrammatist of the time, Asclepiades, was a native of the island of Samos, and that Hedylus was his fellow countryman. Two poets of the same generation were born in Colophon, Hermesianax, mentioned as a friend of Philitas, and Phoenix, who wrote a dirge on his native city after its destruction by Lysimachus and perhaps followed his compatriots to Ephesus to compose choliambic poems. From still further to the south-east, from Soloi in Cilicia, came Aratus, the poet of the *Phaenomena*, to whom—as to Philitas and Asclepiades—Callimachus (*Ep.* 27, fr. 460) devoted verses full of love and praise. Aratus became a pupil of the poet and scholar Menecrates at Ephesus, the home of Zenodotus.[2]

If anyone can be regarded as a precursor of the poets and scholars of the years of transition to the Alexandrian age, it is Antimachus of Colophon.[3] An Ionian from the same eastern region, he was a sort of link between earlier and Hellenistic literature (living at the end of the fifth century he has been mentioned above more than once).[4] The quality of his poems, the epic *Thebaid* and the elegiac *Lyde*, was open to controversy throughout the fourth and the third centuries. In a poetical contest at the festival of the Lysandreia in Samos[5] Antimachus was defeated by an obscure epic poet Niceratus;[6] on the other hand, the young Plato took a fancy to him—possibly because of the moral and educational tendency of his poems, of which we are told[7] but have no evidence in the fragments. Plato, of all people, could stand a complete recital of Antimachus' verses from which the rest of the audience fled in despair.[8] Whatever truth there

---

[1] P. M. Fraser (see p. 102, n. 1) 2 f. n. 1; objections were raised by C. Bradford Welles, 'The Discovery of Sarapis and the Foundation of Alexandria', *Historia* 11 (1962) 273 f.

[2] On Menecrates of Ephesus and his pupil Aratus see below, p. 120.

[3] Antimachi Colophonii *reliquiae*. Collegit B. Wyss 1936. A number of new small hexametric fragments published by E. Lobel in *P.Oxy.* xxx (1964) 2516, 2518, and 2519, can be attributed to Antimachus.

[4] See pp. 36, 72; cf. p. 58, Antimachus belonged to the 'very few exceptions'.

[5] Test. 2 W. The Samians called their ancient Ἡραῖα at that time Λυσάνδρεια, in honour of Lysander, Duris 76 *FGrHist* 71. Konrat Ziegler, *Das hellenistische Epos* (1934) 13, eager to find as many 'historical' epic poems as possible, made the mistake of regarding Λυσάνδρεια as the title of an Antimachean epic: 'Antimachos mit seinen Λυσάνδρεια'; cf. Antim. fr. [171] W. p. 75.

[6] As ἐποποιός mentioned by Praxiphanes fr. 18, Wehrli, *Die Schule des Aristoteles* 9 (1957) 98, together with a number of more famous contemporaries.

[7] Test. 16 W.; cf. p. XLI. [8] Test. 3 W. = Cic. *Brut.* 191.

may be in this anecdote, it is well attested that Plato sent his pupil Heraclides Ponticus to Colophon on purpose to collect Antimachus' poems.[1] Plato's partiality roused the anger of Callimachus, who detested Antimachus' verses as 'fat and inelegant' and denied Plato any critical faculty in the field of poetry.[2] In contrast to him, Asclepiades and Posidippus appreciated the 'sentimental' elegy on *Lyde*, and so apparently did Hermesianax;[3] it is hardly surprising that Callimachus' stoutest opponent, Apollonius Rhodius, admired the *Thebaid* as well as the *Lyde*, imitated them in his epic poem on the Argonauts, and also quoted a line with a gloss.[4] The heated controversy reveals the novelty and importance of Antimachus' poetry.

This poet is also the only pre-Hellenistic author of an 'edition' of Homer of which we can be certain,[5] as it is frequently referred to in our Scholia: ἡ Ἀντιμάχου, ἡ Ἀντιμάχειος, ἡ κατὰ Ἀντίμαχον, sc. ἔκδοσις. Later in the second century, Aristarchus had before him a number of earlier editions; two classes were distinguished, one of which the name of the editor was handed down, αἱ κατ᾽ ἄνδρα, and one of which only the place of origin was known, αἱ κατὰ τὰς πόλεις (or αἱ ἀπὸ τῶν πόλεων) sc. ἐκδόσεις. Antimachus is the earliest of the first group, followed by Zenodotus, a full century later. We have no reason to assume that Antimachus made a 'recension' of the Homeric poems, collating manuscripts and emending the text; his work is never called a 'διόρθωσις'.[6] On the other hand, Zenodotus is expressly and rightly, as we shall see, described as πρῶτος τῶν Ὁμήρου διορθωτής (Suid. s.v. Ζηνόδοτος). This is the decisive difference between Antimachus and Zenodotus. Following the early Ionian tradition, Antimachus wrote on Homer's life, and regarded him quite naturally as a Colophonian,[7] perhaps in a sort of introduction to the text. His intensive study of Homeric language is shown by the many glosses[8] with which he adorned his own verses.

[1] Test. 1 W. = Heraclid. Pont. fr. 6, Wehrli, *Die Schule des Aristoteles* 7 (1953) 9; on Heraclides see above, p. 70.

[2] Call. fr. 398 and 589. Even if we can trust Proclus and if Callimachus' harsh criticism was anticipated by the historian Duris, a pupil of Theophrastus (76 *FGrHist* 83), it is by no means likely that a *general* Peripatetic opinion was uttered by Duris and taken up by Callimachus, as E. Schwartz, *RE* v (1905) 1854 assumed; in that case a Peripatetic of the second century B.C., Agatharchides of Cnidus, would hardly have composed an Epitome of the *Lyde* (test. 21 W. cf. praefationem p. XLII).

[3] See above, p. 89.

[4] Antimach. ed. Wyss pp. XLVIII ff. and below, p. 146, n. 4.

[5] See above, p. 72. Fr. 131-48, 178, 190 and pp. XXIX f. W.

[6] On the terminus see above, p. 71, n. 7; see also A. Ludwich, *Die Homervulgata als voralexandrinisch erwiesen* (1898) 155 f. on Antimachus. H.-I. Marrou, *Saint Augustin et la fin de la Culture antique* (Paris 1938) 20-23.   [7] Fr. 129 f. W.

[8] Lists of 'glosses' Wyss p. 101, cf. pp. 67 f. The most remarkable example is his reading

Antimachus as a poet and 'scholar' remained a solitary figure in his time (about 400 B.C.). It was nearly a century—an eventful century in philosophy and oratory—before what we called a 'new movement' started with Philitas; this then continued from generation to generation without a serious break. It reached its climax shortly after Philitas in Alexandria, where the great masters of poetry and the initiators of scholarship were *his* followers, as we have tried to demonstrate. They were not Peripatetics. When Callimachus in the programmatic introduction to his *Aitia*,[1] in which he praised Philitas, pictured himself as a young poet receiving the advice of Apollo, there was nothing Peripatetic in the god's gracious counsel.[2] In the Scholia to this elegy[3] the famous Peripatetic Praxiphanes was counted among the poet's adversaries, and it was *against* him that Callimachus published a pamphlet.[4] The line Philitas—Zenodotus—Callimachus, of which we have stressed the non-Aristotelian character, met in Alexandria with a genuine Peripatetic line from Athens; this was the second stage of the whole process, not its beginning.[5] The pupils of Aristotle were able to bring priceless help to the ποιηταὶ καὶ κριτικοί who already existed in Alexandria; they transferred collections of learned material from their Athenian home to them, they instigated further antiquarian research, they stimulated new literary criticism, often opposed to their master's views, and they taught them to organize institutions for the promotion of scholarship. We shall find not a few Aristotelian elements even in Callimachus' prose-writings.[6]

Ptolemy, the son of Lagus, now the first king in Alexander's city, Alexandria, had been one of his ablest generals and truest friends; turning

οὖσον νεός 'cable of a ship' in *Od.* 21. 390 which he used in his *Lyde*, fr. 57 W. It is preserved only on an ostracon of the third century B.C., while our manuscripts have ὅπλον νεός, the usual epic and Ionic expression for 'rope', which recent editors of the *Odyssey* unfortunately are anxious to keep in the text.
[1] See above, p. 89.
[2] Call. fr. 1. 21–28. I emphasized this point in *Herm.* 63 (1928) 520 f. against Rostagni (= *Ausgew. Schriften* 114); cf. *Archiv für Kulturgeschichte* 28 (1938) 192 = *Ausgew. Schriften* 160.
[3] Schol. Flor. 7 to Call. fr. 1.
[4] Fr. 460 with annotations. See also below, p. 125 n. 1 and p. 136. The problem was thoroughly and eloquently treated by K. O. Brink, 'Callimachus and Aristotle: an inquiry into Callimachus Πρὸς Πραξιφάνην, *Cl. Qu.* 40 (1946) 11–26; but Rostagni was not to be persuaded to change his mind, see his review of Callimachus I, *Riv. fil. cl.* N.S. 28 (1950) 72 f.; cf. also *Scritti minori* II (1956) 278 f., 319 and I (1955) 321, where, unfortunately, old mistakes are still repeated ('Callimaco fu certamente ad Atene alla scuola di Prassifane'). The correct view is taken by Wehrli, *Die Schule des Aristoteles* 9 (1957) in his commentary on Praxiphanes fr. 15–17; ibid. on fr. 8–10 about his disputed claim to have been the first γραμματικός see below, p. 158.
[5] As far as I can see, only E. Schwartz, *Charakterköpfe aus der antiken Literatur* II³ (1919) 48, has laid the necessary stress on this historical sequence.
[6] Fr. 403–66; see below, pp. 127 ff.

historian[1] in the later years of his reign, he was to give the most reliable
account of Alexander's deeds. He well knew what Aristotle had meant to
Alexander and was anxious to get one of his pupils and successors over to
Egypt. But Theophrastus refused to leave Athens; Strato came, but returned soon to the Lyceum as its head. Only Demetrius of Phaleron,[2]
one of Theophrastus' prominent pupils, stayed; having fled after 297
B.C. to Alexandria, he had to remain there as a political refugee, highly
esteemed by his royal host.[3] He was a prolific writer on various subjects,[4]
and a statesman, under whose ten years of 'strategia' Athens had enjoyed
a peaceful and prosperous breathing-space. Having been an active
politician for so long, he could not help meddling in high politics even in
Egypt. In his counsels to the king he favoured the son of Antipater's
daughter Eurydice, Ptolemy's third wife, as successor to the throne; but
by the king's decision, the son of his fourth wife, Berenice, followed him
in 283 B.C. as Ptolemy II, whereupon Demetrius fell into disfavour and
met his doom. This, at least, is the story told by the much-maligned
Hermippus, who is expressly quoted by the source or sources of Diogenes
Laertius for his lives of the Peripatetics.[5] There is not one word about
Demetrius' assistance to Ptolemy I in cultural matters either in this or
in the other ample biographical literature. In addition to this, there is
complete silence about Demetrius in the scanty, but apparently reliable,
tradition on the king's greatest foundations for scholarship. We shall
speak first of the Museum and then of the library (or libraries).

The 'Museum' was instituted by Ptolemy I, Πτολεμαῖος ὁ πρῶτος
συναγαγὼν τὸ μουσεῖον,[6] 'who brought together the Museum'; it is called
a σύνοδος,[7] an 'assembly', a 'community', and its religious character is
shown by the fact that its head was a priest nominated by the king,
ἱερεὺς τοῦ Μουσείου.[8] The members, devoted to the service of the Muses,
had their seat in the precincts of the royal palace,[9] and were given every

---

[1] *FGrHist* 138 with Jacoby's commentary (1930), cf. H. Strasburger, *Ptolemaios und Alexander*,
Leipzig 1934 and *RE* XXIII (1959) 2471 ff.

[2] F. Wehrli, *Die Schule des Aristoteles* 4 (1949); selection in *FGrHist* 228.

[3] Plut. *de exil.* 7 p. 601 F = fr. 61 W. πρῶτος ὢν τῶν Πτολεμαίου φίλων; this may mean that
he belonged to the so-called πρῶτοι φίλοι of the king. H. Kortenbeutel, *RE* XX (1941) 95 ff.
'Philos' missed this testimony in his list of φίλοι and πρῶτοι φίλοι of the Hellenistic kings; as it
refers to the years between 297 and 283 B.C., it is earlier than all the others he collected.

[4] On Homer, on Aesop, etc., in the spirit of Aristotle see fr. 112, 188–93 W.; Περὶ τῆς
δεκαετίας Diog. L. v 81.

[5] Diog. L. v 78 = fr. 69 W.

[6] Plut. *Non posse suaviter vivi secundum Epicurum* 13, p. 1095 D.

[7] Strab. XVII 794, who visited the place in Augustan times and gave a detailed description.

[8] W. Otto, *Priester und Tempel im hellenistischen Ägypten* I (1905) Griechische Kultvereine
166 ff. and 197 ff., list of the ἱερεῖς and Addenda = II 321, 326.

[9] Strab. XVII 793 τῶν βασιλείων μέρος (sc. τὸ Μουσεῖον); cf. Tzetz. below, p. 101.

facility by the sovereigns for fulfilling their duties to the Muses. Once the
epic poet had been inspired by the goddess, and poetry itself began to
open the way to its own understanding;[1] in the fourth century the two
great philosophical schools, Academy and Peripatos, had their proper
places in groves sacred to the Muses.[2] Now the rebirth of poetry and the
recovery of the old masterpieces were protected by the daughters of
Memory. The new Museum[3] was a very peculiar metamorphosis of the
Μουσεῖα of the mother country, not a branch of the Athenian institutions transferred to Egypt by some Peripatetics. The community[4] did not
include philosophers, but men of letters and a great many scientists, and
we shall have to consider the possibility of a mutual influence later on.[5]
They had a carefree life: free meals, high salaries, no taxes to pay, very
pleasant surroundings, good lodgings and servants. There was plenty of
opportunity for quarrelling with each other. Recently a new witness has
turned up, a trustworthy one in so far as he was a member of the Museum
himself. Callimachus in his first Iambus, putting on the guise of the old
Hipponax coming from the dead, admonished the φιλόλογοι[6] not to be
so jealous of one another, but to follow the example given by the Seven
Sages in the story of the cup of Bathycles, which he tells in all its amusing
details. We already had the evidence of another, very malicious witness
from abroad, the devoted pupil of Pyrrhon the sceptic, Timon of Phlius
(about 320–230 B.C.), who in his hexametric lampoons, his *Silloi*, attacked
not only contemporary Stoic and Epicurean philosophers, but also the
inmates of the Museum (fr. 12 Diels = 60 Wachsmuth): 'Many are
feeding in populous Egypt, scribblers on papyrus, ceaselessly wrangling
in the bird-cage of the Muses', βιβλιακοὶ χαρακῖται[7] ἀπείριτα δηριόωντες

---

[1] See above, pp. 1 f.   [2] See above, p. 65.

[3] Was *Ashmole's Museum* in Oxford (opened in 1683 and mentioned in the same year as
'Mr. Ashmole's Musaeum' [*sic*]) the first to be called 'Museum' in the modern sense? Cf.
H. M. Vernon, *A History of the Oxford Museum* (1909) 15 and *Handbook to the University of
Oxford* (1948) 231.

[4] In Plutarch's sentence μουσεῖον, dependent on the verb συνάγειν, can only mean the
assembly of all the members; and this fits also the whole context of Plutarch's chapter. C.
Wendel (above p. 8, n. 2), in *Handbuch der Bibliothekswissenschaft* III 1² (1955) 65, tried to
interpret it as 'having gathered the books into the Museum' and used it as evidence for the
foundation of the library; he was misled by expressions which quite clearly state the fact of
book-collecting: συναγαγὼν βιβλία Strab. XIII 608 (see above, p. 67, n. 4 and below, p. 99,
n. 2), or Ath. V 203 E περὶ δὲ βίβλων πλήθους . . . καὶ τῆς εἰς τὸ Μουσεῖον συναγωγῆς. Arist. *ep.*
9, below, p. 100. Wendel missed the unique evidence given by Irenaeus–Eusebius, see below,
p. 98.

[5] See below, p. 156.

[6] Fr. 191. Dieg. VI 2 ff. συγκαλοῦντα τοὺς φιλολόγους (corrected from -σοφους) . . . αὐτοῖς
. . . ἀπαγορεύει φθονεῖν.

[7] χαρακῖται seems to be an arbitrary new formation by Timon; from the context and from
the attribute βιβλιακοί one should guess that he meant 'writers' and formed it from the verb
χαράσσειν. I know that linguists regard the nouns of -ιτης as denominatives and understand

Μουσέων ἐν ταλάρῳ. The image of the birdcage stuck: scholars as beings, like rare birds, cut off from life. Timon's contempt for the new scholarship is illustrated by the anecdote[1] that he told his 'pupil', the poet Aratus, he should use the 'old copies' of Homer (τὰ ἀρχαῖα ἀντίγραφα) not those ἤδη διωρθωμένα 'already corrected', alluding no doubt to the editorial work of Zenodotus. Satire and anecdotes accompany the whole history of classical scholarship from its very beginning; we need only remember Philitas[2] or think of Scaliger, Bentley, Mommsen, or Housman. But it has never disturbed scholars either to be compared in antiquity with rare birds in a cage or to be called 'mummies' in our own day.[3] I once mildly protested[4] against the attempt[5] to regard the Hellenistic scholar poets as confined to an 'Ivory Tower',[6] which has become so strangely fashionable in recent years. Certainly they had to write their books for small circles of well-educated connoisseurs, but even such a leading figure as Callimachus was deeply attached to his native country Cyrene, to the worship of the Cyrenean Apollo, and to one of the strong forces of the age, ruler-worship; first Philitas and then the successive heads of the library acted as tutors of the heirs to the throne and were exposed to the hazards of political strife.[7]

The king, as we have heard, brought together the members of the Museum. We do not hear of their obligation to lecture; but in nearly all the *Lives* of the poets and scholars 'teachers' as well as 'pupils' are mentioned. Even if we have to be careful in accepting the details of this biographical tradition, ultimately preserved in Suidas' *Lexicon*, we may assume the gradual growth of a free fellowship of masters and disciples. Of the many institutions inside the Museum the library was the most memorable one: Euseb. *hist. eccl.* v 8, 11 (an excerpt from Iren. *adv. haer.* III 21. 2 Massuet):[8] Πτολεμαῖος ὁ Λάγου φιλοτιμούμενος τὴν ὑπ' αὐτοῦ κατεσκευασμένην βιβλιοθήκην ἐν Ἀλεξανδρείᾳ κοσμῆσαι τοῖς πάντων ἀνθρώπων συγγράμμασιν ὅσα γε σπουδαῖα ὑπῆρχεν, κτλ., 'Ptolemy the son of

χαρακῖται (from χάραξ 'pale') as 'cloisterlings' (so also L–S s.v.), see E. Redard, 'Les Noms grecs en -της, -τις, princip. -ιτης, -ῖτις', *Études et Commentaires* v (1949) 27; but the invention of a satirist may not be subject to this grammatical rule. Casaubon on Athen. I 22 D was probably right, although Wachsmuth appealed against him to the 'leges grammaticae' (*Corpusc. poes. epicae Gr. ludibundae* II² 183).

[1] Diog. L. IX 113; cf. Wilamowitz, 'Antigonos von Karystos', *Philol. Untersuch.* 4 (1881) 43. On Timon and Aratus see below, p. 121.

[2] See above, p. 91.　　　　　　　　　　　　　　　　[3] *Philologia Perennis* (1961) 22.

[4] *JHS* 75 (1955) 73 = *Ausgewählte Schriften* 158.

[5] E. A. Barber in *Fifty Years of Classical Scholarship* (1954) 230.

[6] See Excursus.

[7] See below, p. 211, Ptolemy VIII and Aristarchus, possibly also Ptolemy III and Apollonius Rhodius, p. 141.

[8] Cf. W. W. Harvey's edition III 24, vol. II pp. 111 ff. with Grabe's note.

Lagus having the ambition to equip the library, established by him in Alexandria, with the writings of all men as far as they were worth serious attention', etc.; then the story of the translation of the Pentateuch into Greek for the new library is told. Curiously enough, this is our only evidence for the establishment of the library by Ptolemy I.[1] We have already quoted[2] half a sentence from Strabo's report on the fate of Aristotle's library, πρῶτος (sc. Ἀριστοτέλης) ὧν ἴσμεν συναγαγὼν βιβλία, to which we have now to add the second half (XIII 608) : καὶ διδάξας τοὺς ἐν Αἰγύπτῳ βασιλέας βιβλιοθήκης σύνταξιν, 'and taught the kings of Egypt the arrangement of a library'. This points to Peripatetic influence on the organization of the library.

Immediately the name of Demetrius of Phaleron comes to mind, because this Peripatetic[3] of the most varied erudition belonged after 297 B.C. to the entourage of the king. He must have been a sort of link between Athens and Alexandria; but how far can we prove that the king carried out the ideas of his distinguished guest? Demetrius was always a great favourite with Wilamowitz, who represented him as having 'das universale Museion in Alexandria gestiftet'[4] and even as the first head of the library.[5] The sources which we have examined so far are silent about Demetrius.

We have only two rather strange references to the part Demetrius is said to have played in organizing the library or libraries (not the Museum). One is contained in the so-called *Letter of Aristeas*,[6] a fictitious[7]

---

[1] Schmidt, *Pinakes*, did not print the text of Eusebius in his collection of testimonia 4–28; so it escaped Wendel also, see above, p. 97, n. 4. Clem. Al. *Strom.* I 22. 1 vol. II p. 92 St. combines Iren. loc. cit. (ἐπὶ βασιλέως Πτολεμαίου τοῦ Λάγου) with Aristeas below, p. 100 (ἢ ὥς τινες ἐπὶ τοῦ Φιλαδέλφου ἐπικληθέντος).

[2] Strab. XIII 608 and above, p. 67, n. 4; on the whole chapter see Düring, 'Aristotle', pp. 382 and 393 f. [3] See above, pp. 96 f.

[4] 'Antigonos von Karystos' 291. This statement was taken over by Susemihl I 7 f. ('ohne Zweifel . . . das gelehrte Studium der Peripatetiker, hinübergetragen durch Demetrios und Straton'). It was repeated word for word by Müller-Graupa in his very useful and comprehensive article 'Museion', *RE* XVI (1933) 801 f. and became a commonplace in almost every modern book. The very reserved and critical judgement of E. Martini, 'Demetrios', *RE* IV (1901) 2837 f., was hardly noticed or rejected; see E. Bayer, 'Demetrius Phalereus', *Tübinger Beiträge zur Altertumswissenschaft* 36 (1942) 105 ff.

[5] *Die hellenistische Dichtung* I 22, 'erster Vorstand' in contradiction to his own correct remark p. 165 on Zenodotus; pp. 160 f. Museum.

[6] Aristeae *ad Philocratem epistula*, ed. P. Wendland (Leipzig 1900) 9; revised edition of H. St. J. Thackeray (Cambridge 1900) as appendix to H. B. Swete's *Introduction to the Old Testament in Greek*. Later editions and translations are based on this text of Thackeray's, who used Wendland's edition. Amongst them the edition by M. Hadas (New York 1951) is useful because of its introduction, short commentary, and especially its bibliography; he only missed Jacoby's pertinent remarks on Hecataeus Abd. 264 *FGrHist* 21–24 = III a (1943) 61–75, esp. 65 f. New Edition in *Sources Chrétiennes* vol. 89 (1962) by A. Pelletier.

[7] Ludovicus Vives, the Spanish humanist, seems to have been the first to challenge the authenticity of the *Epistle* in his notes to Augustin. *De Civ. D.* XVIII 4 which he edited in 1522 with Erasmus, 'Letter to the Reader' (*ep.* 1309 Allen).

narrative of the origin of the Greek translation of the Pentateuch, to be dated probably into the later second century B.C.; the other is preserved in Tzetzes' *Prolegomena to Aristophanes*,[1] compiled in the twelfth century A.D. and partly translated into Latin by an unknown Italian humanist of the fifteenth century A.D. in an annotation to Plautus.[2]

The relevant passages must be quoted verbatim; paraphrases are of no use. Aristeae *ep.* 9–10 (= Euseb. *p.e.* VIII 2. 1–4) κατασταθεὶς ἐπὶ τῆς τοῦ βασιλέως βιβλιοθήκης Δημήτριος ὁ Φαληρεὺς ἐχρηματίσθη πολλὰ διάφορα πρὸς τὸ συναγαγεῖν, εἰ δυνατόν, ἅπαντα τὰ κατὰ τὴν οἰκουμένην βιβλία, καὶ ποιούμενος ἀγορασμοὺς καὶ μεταγραφὰς ἐπὶ τέλος ἤγαγεν, ὅσον ἐφ᾿ ἑαυτῷ, τὴν τοῦ βασιλέως πρόθεσιν. Παρόντων οὖν ἡμῶν ἐρωτηθεὶς πόσαι τινὲς μυριάδες τυγχάνουσι βιβλίων, εἶπεν· ὑπὲρ τὰς εἴκοσι, βασιλεῦ· σπουδάσω δ᾿ ἐν ὀλίγῳ χρόνῳ πρὸς τὸ πληρωθῆναι πεντήκοντα μυριάδας τὰ λοιπά. Προσήγγελται δέ μοι καὶ τὰ τῶν Ἰουδαίων νόμιμα μεταγραφῆς ἄξια καὶ τῆς παρὰ σοὶ βιβλιοθήκης εἶναι. Then Aristeas went on to tell the story of the Septuagint, with particular emphasis on the association of Demetrius with the great enterprise. This association was the only reason why the author mentioned Demetrius and the king's library. The king is Ptolemy II,[3] as Arist. *ep.* 35 refers to a well known deed of Ptolemy I as one of 'my father's' and *ep.* 41 to the 'queen Arsinoe, the sister', and Demetrius is in charge of the royal library. These two surprising statements flatly contradict the traditions[4] on Demetrius' lifetime as well as on the

---

[1] I say Tzetzes' *Prolegomena*, because I follow G. Kaibel who (after Consbruch) attributed also the anonymous treatises to Tzetzes: 'Die Prolegomena Περὶ κωμῳδίας', *AGGW*, philos.-hist. Kl., N.F. II 4 (1898) 4; cf. the detailed arguments in Wendel's masterly article 'Tzetzes', *RE* VII A (1948) 1973 ff. Against the attribution R. Cantarella, Aristophanis *comoediae* I (1949) Prolegomena p. 38 and A. Plebe, 'La teoria del comico da Aristotele a Plutarco', *Università di Torino, Pubblicazioni della Facoltà di Lettere e Filosofia* IV 1 (1952) 115–21, written without taking regard of Wendel's article. I always refer to Kaibel's edition in *CGF* I (1899), see below, p. 101, n. 1.—A new edition of Tzetzes' *Prolegomena* will be published together with all the *Prolegomena de comoedia* in a volume of the *Scholia in Aristophanem*, ed. edendave curavit W. J. W. Koster, see vol. IV 1 (Tzetz. in Aristoph. *Plut.*) Groningen 1960, p. xx.

[2] It was called 'Scholium Plautinum' by F. Osann, who discovered it in a Plautine codex of the Collegio Romano in 1819 but left the piecemeal publication to others. They bear very illustrious names: Meineke (1830), Welcker (1835) who was terribly misled by it, Ritschl (1838), cf. above p. 6; it should not be forgotten that it was W. Dindorf who told Welcker the identification of the mysterious 'Caecius' as Tzetzes, *Rh.M.* 4 (1836) 232. The manuscript itself was rediscovered by E. Breccia as Vat. Lat. 11469 for E. A. Parsons, *The Alexandrian Library. Glory of the Hellenic World* (London 1952). This American bibliophile treated his subject with moving enthusiasm and even added two facsimiles of the relevant page to his long chapter on the Plautine Scholium. W. J. W. Koster, 'Scholium Plautinum plene editum', *Mnemosyne*, ser. IV, vol. XIV (1961) 23 ff.

[3] The king is never called Φιλάδελφος; this might be used as a further argument for dating the composition of the *Epistula* into the second century B.C., not later. For towards the end of the century the title 'Philadelphos', applied before only to his wife Arsinoe, became quite common for the king himself (see H. Volkmann, *RE* XXIII 1645, 50 ff.).

[4] See above, p. 96, and below, p. 154.

sequence of the librarians. Tzetzes, compiling the *Prolegomena* to his commentary on three comedies of Aristophanes, mentioned first the scholar poets who had to deal with the scenic poets under the reign of Ptolemy II (ὑπὸ Πτολεμαίου τοῦ Φιλαδέλφου) and then went on:[1] ὁ γὰρ Πτολεμαῖος φιλολογώτατος ὢν διὰ Δημητρίου τοῦ Φαληρέως καὶ ἑτέρων ἐλλογίμων (γερουσίων Mb 8) ἀνδρῶν δαπάναις βασιλικαῖς ἁπανταχόθεν τὰς βίβλους εἰς Ἀλεξάνδρειαν συνήθροισεν καὶ δυσὶ βιβλιοθήκαις ταύτας ἀπέθετο· ὧν τῆς ἐκτὸς μὲν ἀριθμὸς τετρακισμύριαι δισχίλιαι ὀκτακόσιαι, τῆς δὲ τῶν ἀνακτόρων ἐντὸς συμμιγῶν μὲν βίβλων ἀριθμὸς τεσσαράκοντα μυριάδες, ἀμιγῶν δὲ καὶ ἁπλῶν μυριάδες ἐννέα . . . τὰ δὲ συνηθροισμένα βιβλία οὐχ Ἑλλήνων μόνον, ἀλλὰ καὶ τῶν ἄλλων ἁπάντων ἐθνῶν ἦσαν καὶ δὴ καὶ Ἑβραίων αὐτῶν . . . ὅτε δὴ καὶ τὰς τῶν Ἑβραίων διὰ τῶν ἑβδομήκοντα (ἑβδομήκοντα δύο Mb 24) ἑρμηνευθῆναι πεποίηκεν. The Italian humanist left out the references to the Hebrews and the Septuagint, but kept the passage on Demetrius' assistance to Philadelphus and on the two libraries, and, by a particularly bad slip in translating, Callimachus became 'aulicus regius bibliothecarius'. If we consider the enormous success Aristeas' letter had in the Christian era,[2] we are not surprised to find traces of it still in Tzetzes,[3] mixed up with grammatical excerpts from Scholia to Aristophanes and to Dionysius Thrax.[4] We notice two points in which Tzetzes differs from Aristeas: Demetrius is not called 'head' of the royal library, and—more important for our purpose—two libraries are mentioned as existing under Ptolemy II, with the number of books in each. A second library 'outside the palace' was, as we learn from other sources, connected with a Serapeum and became famous in Roman times. Ptolemy I had introduced the god Serapis into Alexandria[5] and built a temple for his worship[6] in the district of Rhakotis. Tzetzes' words had always been unreservedly accepted as a testimony for the foundation of a second library by Ptolemy II; as that library was said to have been built ἐν τῷ Σεραπείῳ later than the Museum library,[7] Ptolemy II was also

---

[1] *CGF* I (1899) ed. G. Kaibel p. 19. Pb 4 ff.; cf. p. 31, Mb 8 ff., the later version with variations, additions, corrections which do not concern us here.

[2] See the testimonia collected by Wendland, loc. cit. pp. 87–166.

[3] Possibly via Epiphanius; Wendland pp. 89 f. and 139 ff.

[4] C. Wendel, *RE* VII A 1975 f.

[5] Tac. *hist.* IV 83 f. in his well-informed digression on the god Serapis.

[6] Demetrius of Phaleron is said to have been inspired to write poetry, at least once in his life, *paeans* on the new god: fr. 200 Wehrli and his very sceptical comments p. 87. As a 'hymnographe inspiré et dévôt de Sarapis' Demetrius had his statue erected next to Pindar in Memphis according to J.-Ph. Lauer et Ch. Picard, 'Les Statues Ptolémaïques du Sarapieion de Memphis', *Publications de l'Institut d'Art et d'Archéologie de l'Université de Paris* III (1955) 69 ff.

[7] Epiphan. Περὶ μέτρων καὶ σταθμῶν 168 c 15. 16 ff. Dind. = test. 27 b Schmidt pp. 11 f. ἐν τῇ πρώτῃ βιβλιοθήκῃ τῇ ἐν Βρουχείῳ οἰκοδομηθείσῃ· ἔτι δὲ ὕστερον καὶ ἑτέρα ἐγένετο βιβλιοθήκη ἐν τῷ Σεραπείῳ μικροτέρα τῆς πρώτης, ἥτις καὶ θυγάτηρ ὠνομάσθη αὐτῆς.

regarded as the founder of a new temple of Serapis. But the foundation tablets of the Serapeum, excavated[1] in 1945 on the very hill of Rhakotis where Ptolemy I had built a sanctuary before, bear the name of his grandson, Ptolemy III (246–221 B.C.); Tzetzes' report thus becomes questionable.[2] The person, the wealth, and the activity of Ptolemy II so much fascinated posterity that he was easily credited with some of the merits of his father as well as of his son. This son, called Euergetes, the pupil of the poet of the *Argonautica* and very keen on acquiring ancient texts,[3] is now attested as founder of the new temple; this does not imply that he added a library to its precincts, but it does not exclude it either. The question which of the Ptolemies set up the 'smaller' or 'daughter' library and at which place it was situated, looks to be insoluble at the moment. Figures in our manuscript tradition are very often unreliable; as regards the number of books in the Alexandrian libraries, there are also contradictions between Aristeas and Tzetzes,[4] mistakes made by the Latin translation, and different figures in the other sources. They agree, however, in one point, that hundreds of thousands of papyrus rolls were stored there during the first half of the third century B.C.

It is obvious that we have reached the age which we called—hesitatingly—a 'bookish' one; the book is one of the characteristic signs of the new, the Hellenistic, world. The whole literary past, the heritage of centuries, was in danger of slipping away in spite of the learned labours of Aristotle's pupils; the imaginative enthusiasm of the generation living towards the end of the fourth and the beginning of the third century did everything to keep it alive. The first task was to collect and to store the literary treasures in order to save them for ever. It is precisely to this period, the later decades of the fourth century B.C., that we can assign the earliest of the papyri which have come to light in Egypt and provide us

---

[1] Callimachus II (1953) xxxix. 6 with references to A. Wace, *JHS* 65 (1945) 106 ff., and A. Rowe, 'The Discovery of the famous Temple and Enclosure of Sarapis at Alexandria', Suppl. aux *Annales du Service des Antiquités de l'Égypte*, Cahier No. 2 (1946). On later discoveries and discussions see P. M. Fraser, 'Two Studies on the Cult of Sarapis in the Hellenistic World', *Opuscula Atheniensia* III (Lund 1960) 11. 6, *Skrifter utgivna av Svenska Institutet i Athen*, ser. i in 4°, vol. VII. Welles, *Historia* 1962, 271–98 (see above, p. 93, n. 1) tries to persuade us that the cult of Serapis in Rhakotis was instituted by Alexander himself, when he founded Alexandria on his return from Siwah in 331 B.C.; but as far as he prefers the stories of Callisthenes and Ps.-Callisth. to the report of Ptolemy–Arrian, it is very hard to believe in his reconstruction.

[2] Not only Parsons, *The Alexandrian Library* 347 ff., but also serious works like the *Handbuch der Bibliothekswissenschaft* III 1 (2nd ed. 1953) 55 or the *Geschichte der Textüberlieferung* I (1961) 63 failed to take notice of the excavations.

[3] Schmidt, *Pinakes*, test. 6 b.

[4] See above, pp. 100 f.; cf. test. 24 a, Schmidt, *Pinakes* pp. 9 f., and the explanation of the figures p. 37.

with actual specimens of Greek books.[1] We can even guess that the significant change in the nature of Greek writing[2] which took place in the first half of the third century B.C. may have been due to the aesthetic sense of the great scholar poets. These books were the necessary means for the regeneration of poetry as well as for the birth and growth of scholarship. We see how very important the gradual progress of book production in earlier centuries was.[3]

Starting from the oriental background, we have followed its development by the Greeks themselves, which now appears as the preparation for the new era. If there was a revival of oriental or Egyptian influence, probably in some technical devices,[4] it should not be over-estimated.[5] The alphabet was one of the decisive creations of the Greek genius which opened a new era of cultural life; in contrast to the Orient and to Egypt, with their guilds of scribes and castes of priests, the Greek alphabetic script was accessible to everyone.[6] It was also a revolutionary change that free public access was had to the immense written treasures of the Alexandrian libraries; they were not temple- or palace-libraries to which a privileged minority was admitted, but they were open to everyone who was able and willing to read and to learn. There was a free world of the spirit even in the new monarchies, and the preconditions for such a development existed only where Greek civilization prevailed. The unprecedented interest in books was kindled by the new scholar poets, who were in desperate need of texts; by a notable coincidence the royal patrons and their advisers immediately fulfilled these imperative demands in a princely way. We shall find a similar sequence of events when in the Italian renaissance the ardent zeal of the poets and humanists from Petrarch to Politian led to the recovery of the Classics and the setting-up of great libraries.

In the course of this chapter the question of Demetrius' contribution to scholarship in Alexandria has been discussed. Of the only two sources,

[1] On the recent find of a papyrus (Commentary on the Orphic *Theogony*) near Salonica see S. G. Kapsomenos, 'Der Papyrus von Dervéni', *Gnom.* 35 (1963) 222 f., and Ἀρχαιολογικὸν Δελτίον 19 (1964, published 1965) 17–25 (with plates 12–15), who is inclined to assign the handwriting to the middle of the fourth century B.C. (C. H. Roberts thinks of about 300 B.C. and P. M. Fraser of 280 B.C.). Cf. below, p. 139, n. 7 and p. 237.

[2] See C. H. Roberts, *Greek Literary Hands* 350 B.C.–A.D. 400 (Oxford 1956) xv and plates 1–5 with commentary.

[3] See above, pp. 19, 25–27, 29, 66 f.

[4] Cf. above, p. 18 and especially the references to Wendel and Zuntz, p. 7, n. 9.

[5] A. Thibaudet, *La Campagne avec Thucydide* (7th ed. 1922) 58 ff., and K. Kerényi, *Apollon. Studien über antike Religion und Humanität* (Wien 1937) 186, may be quoted as typical examples of exaggerating the influence of the ancient Egyptian tradition on the new course in Alexandria.

[6] See above, pp. 24 ff.

Aristeas and Tzetzes, Tzetzes turned out to be partly, although indirectly, dependent on Aristeas, and chronological confusions in both of them were obvious. The necessary conclusion is that the vulgate version of Demetrius' key position rests on very poor evidence. Nevertheless, on general grounds we may believe in the probability that, by his advice to the king, he furthered the new scholarship and brought to it the influence of his great master Aristotle. We have argued[1] that this new scholarship originated from the ideas of Philitas and Zenodotus in Alexandria; we must now try to get away from those uncertain modern reconstructions and grapple with a serious new historical problem: the relation[2] between this new scholarship and the Peripatetic tradition, not only at the beginning of the third century but throughout the Hellenistic age.

[1] See above, pp. 95 f.
[2] In my earlier short papers (above, p. 88, n. 1) there was no space for working out this relation; the Aristotelian line, therefore, remained too much in the dark.

II

ZENODOTUS AND HIS
CONTEMPORARIES

IN the previous chapter on the rise of scholarship in Alexandria one name occurred again and again, that of Zenodotus of Ephesus.[1] He was the first of a series of great personalities in an age in which the supremacy of the individual was being everywhere asserted. The individual, conscious of having entered a new sphere of intellectual activity, easily inclined to a slightly exaggerated subjectiveness. There was no tradition of scholarship yet that Zenodotus could have inherited. He had to find his own way. We should therefore not be surprised if sometimes he stumbled. It is unjust to measure him by the standard of his followers in the third and second centuries, who tried in the course of time to build up a regular technique of editing and expounding texts; compared with them he is bound to appear somewhat unequal or arbitrary in his textual criticism. Radically opposed theories are held by modern scholars concerning Zenodotus' Homeric criticism, because our so-called evidence, coming from the polemics of his adversaries, has often been misunderstood.

We have mentioned the collecting and storing of books in Alexandria; Zenodotus presumably took part in this formidable enterprise, as the king chose him to be his first librarian.[2] Tzetzes' late excerpts from Scholia on Aristophanes and Dionysius Thrax are our only source for those parts of the early history of the Museum library on which the *Letter of Aristeas* is silent. The first sentence of Tzetzes' *Prolegomena* contains one of these unique pieces of information: Ἰστέον ὅτι Ἀλέξανδρος ὁ Αἰτωλὸς καὶ Λυκόφρων ὁ Χαλκιδεὺς ὑπὸ Πτολεμαίου τοῦ Φιλαδέλφου προτραπέντες τὰς σκηνικὰς διώρθωσαν βίβλους, Λυκόφρων μὲν τὰς τῆς κωμῳδίας, Ἀλέξανδρος δὲ τὰς τῆς τραγῳδίας, ἀλλὰ δὴ καὶ τὰς σατυρικάς. Then comes the passage on Demetrius of Phaleron and on the translation of the Hebrew books quoted in the last chapter,[3] before Tzetzes takes up his first sentence and

---

[1] See especially above, pp. 92, 94, 104. He, if anyone, would deserve a new monograph. Meanwhile see H. Düntzer, *De Zenodoti studiis Homericis*, Göttingen 1848, and A. Römer, 'Über die Homerrecension des Zenodot', *Abhandlungen der Bayer. Akad. der Wissenschaften*, I. Classe, 17. Bd., 3. Abh. 1885. See Addenda. [2] Suid. v. Ζηνόδοτος.
[3] Cf. pp. 101 ff.; *CGF* I 1 (1899) ed. G. Kaibel pp. 19 f., Pb 1 ff. and 20 ff. The beginning of version Ma pp. 24 f. is almost identical with Pb; but Mb pp. 31 f. has a slightly different

goes on: τὰς δὲ σκηνικὰς Ἀλέξανδρός τε, ὡς ἔφθην εἰπών, καὶ Λυκόφρων διωρθώσαντο, τὰς δὲ ποιητικὰς Ζηνόδοτος πρῶτον καὶ ὕστερον Ἀρίσταρχος διωρθώσαντο.

The stumbling-block in this remarkable paragraph[1] is the expression διορθοῦν, repeated again and again. As regards Zenodotus, it is in conformity with the wording of all the other grammatical sources and the references in our Scholia on Homer; he was indeed the first διορθωτής[2] of the Homeric and other poems, revising and emending the text, and διορθοῦν was the proper technical term. The reference to Aristarchus proves conclusively that this is what the *Prolegomena* mean; they do not refer to the collecting or arranging of books in the library. No distinction is made between Zenodotus' work and that of Alexander Aetolus and Lycophron; they are said to have done the same for the scenic poets as he had done for the epic (and lyric) poets, διώρθωσαν (or διωρθώσαντο), that is, they made critical editions.[3] Modern scholars have been generally startled by this remark, and that is quite understandable; the 'logical' procedure would have been to put the mass of collected books in order, to sort them out, classify and catalogue them, and then to compare the manuscripts and revise the text, not to start immediately with a treatment of the difficult tragic and comic texts. A stronger objection is the lack of any reference to Alexander and Lycophron in our Scholia on the tragedians and on Aristophanes, in contrast to the many references to Zenodotus in our Homeric Scholia. For such reasons some have tried to give διορθοῦν a non-committal sense[4] ('to make straight', that is, 'to put in the right order') or to charge the not always trustworthy[5] Tzetzes with a mistake. The Italian humanist who translated part of the *Prolegomena* on the margin of a Plautine manuscript boldly changed διώρθωσαν into the

---

wording: Ἀλέξανδρος ὁ Αἰτωλὸς καὶ Λυκόφρων ὁ Χαλκιδεὺς ἀλλὰ καὶ Ζηνόδοτος ὁ ᾽Εφέσιος τῷ Φιλαδέλφῳ Πτολεμαίῳ συνωθηθέντες (i.e. compulsi, cf. Tzetz. in Hes. *Op.* p. 12. 4 Gaisf. συνώθησαν = compulerunt and Tzetz. *epist.* ed. Pressel p. 56 θεῷ συνωθηθείς) βασιλικῶς ὁ μὲν τὰς τῆς τραγῳδίας, Λυκόφρων δὲ τὰς τῆς κωμῳδίας βίβλους διώρθωσαν, Ζηνόδοτος δὲ τὰς ῾Ομηρείους καὶ τῶν λοιπῶν ποιητῶν and pp. 32. 1 ff. τῶν ῾Ελληνίδων δὲ βίβλων ... τὰς τραγικὰς μὲν διώρθωσε (sc. Ptolemaeus rex) δι᾽ Ἀλεξάνδρου τοῦ Αἰτωλοῦ κτλ. on Lycophron, Zenodotus, Aristarchus, etc.

[1] It is reprinted by Schmidt, *Pinakes* test. 24 a, b, c, and fully discussed pp. 39 f., but I cannot accept his conclusions. The text of Tzetzes and the *Schol. Plautin.* was much better dealt with thirty years earlier by H. Pusch, 'Quaestiones Zenodoteae', *Dissertationes Philologicae Halenses* xi (1890) 203–7.

[2] See above, p. 94.

[3] On Lycophron see also below, p. 119; it is unlikely that no one attempted an edition of the scenic poets before Aristophanes of Byzantium about 200 B.C.; but his work, of course, cast every earlier effort into the shade.

[4] Cf. Sandys I[3] 121 'responsible for the classification'; 'preliminary sorting out' E. A. Barber, *Oxf. Class. Dict.* s.v. Alexander Aetolus and Lycophron, and so many others.

[5] See above, p. 102.

phrase 'poeticos libros in unum collegerunt et in ordinem redegerunt', and he has even been praised for being the only one to find the correct meaning.[1] But this is an arbitrary assumption, based on a modern prejudice. If we replace our meagre evidence by a fictitious story, the picture of the decisive first decades of the third century B.C. and of their poets and scholars is in danger of being falsified. This is the reason why we have taken some trouble to re-examine the tradition. It does not tell us anything about the administrative work in the royal library and the handling of its books, as we might expect from other passages of the *Prolegomena*, but about the three earliest διορθωταί, the revisers of the most important poetical texts in the possession of the king. Scholarly co-operation of this kind between two distinguished poets and the pupil of Philitas is quite characteristic of these years.

The king in whose reign this happened, or even to whose 'impulse' it was due, is said to have been Ptolemy II (288–247 B.C.); there is no reason so far to reject this tradition, as in some other cases, in which there has been a confusion with Ptolemy I or Ptolemy III.[2] With the chronology of Hellenistic poets and scholars we are on particularly treacherous ground, but we must not let overscepticism deprive us of the few more or less reliable dates. Zenodotus may have started to prepare his principal work on the Homeric poems before his royal pupil came to the throne; his ἀκμή was put in the time of Ptolemy I, that is, before 288 B.C., by ancient chronographers.[3] But it is quite likely that he finished and published his edition and his glossary under the young king in the first decade of his reign. The two experts in scenic poetry seem to have arrived in Alexandria some time after 285 B.C.; but how much later we are not able to guess.[4] It is fairly certain that Lycophron was no longer in Eretria after 273 B.C., but that does not help very much. Alexander Aetolus belonged to the literary circle of Antigonus Gonatas at Pella (after 276 B.C.?), so did Aratus. Aratus went to Syria for a few years and then returned to Macedonia.[5] In the same way Alexander may have interrupted

[1] See Schmidt, *Pinakes* 40. On the so-called *Scholium Plautinum* see above, pp. 100 ff.; its author hardly knew that 'in ordinem redigere' did not mean 'put into the right order', but that it was the Latin equivalent of the Greek ἐγκρίνειν, cf. Quintil. *inst. or.* I 4. 3 'auctores alios in ordinem redegerint, alios omnino exemerint numero', that is 'to put them on the list of the classics'. On διορθοῦν ∼ dirigere in the Schol. Arat. see below, p. 121, n. 4.
[2] See above, p. 102.
[3] Suid. v. Ζηνόδοτος Ἐφέσιος . . . ἐπὶ Πτολεμαίου γεγονὼς τοῦ πρώτου; E. Rohde, Γέγονε, *Kleine Schriften* I (1901) 127 f., believed that Philitas as well as his pupils Zenodotus and Theocritus were all dated too early. The real difficulty lies only in the tradition that Aristophanes of Byzantium was his 'pupil'. This is hardly compatible with such an early date for Zenodotus, but see below, p. 172.
[4] See below, pp. 119 ff. [5] See below, p. 120.

his stay at Pella for several years in order to work for Ptolemy II in Alexandria and then gone back afterwards. I have scanned the chronological combinations of ancient and modern times anew; but I shall not trouble the reader with the separate items. The negative result as a whole is of some importance to us: there is no reliable tradition or convincing argument to be found against the priority of Zenodotus.

The principal 'Zenodotean question' is, of course, another one: what was the character and value of his critical work? We shall see that Zenodotus published a new text of epic and lyric poetry and a glossary, but he did not publish any commentary or monograph. So his successors had no opportunity of learning at first hand the reasons for his decisions. We must assume, though no evidence exists, that they could use an oral tradition of Zenodotus' viva voce exegesis,[1] noted down by his pupils and handed on to later generations, or, failing this, that they hazarded their own opinions about the ground of his constitution of the Homeric text. In our Scholia which are only excerpts from the ancient Hypomnemata some cautious remarks of Aristarchus or of the Aristarcheans are occasionally preserved: $\mu\acute{\eta}\pi o\tau\epsilon \ldots \acute{v}\pi\epsilon\acute{\iota}\lambda\eta\phi\epsilon\nu$ 'perhaps . . . he took . . . to mean';[2] but we may be sure that they are omitted in most cases. Later ancient and modern scholars accepted pure guesses and dubious oral tradition as evidence of Zenodotus' scholarship; no wonder a bewildering divergence of modern opinions on Zenodotus has arisen out of such mistakes. We should be conscious of the fact that we are on treacherous ground whenever Zenodotus' reasons are praised or blamed. In a case like $\varDelta$ 88 he was blamed for having altered the text 'because he believed it is out of character for a goddess to *endeavour* to find the object of her search'. But this is mere guesswork; an early Ptolemaic papyrus, published in 1906,[3] agrees with the text Zenodotus had accepted (not invented) for reasons we do not know.

There was no authentic written tradition of Zenodotus' arguments for his alterations or omissions of Homeric lines; but his successors were in a position to compare Zenodotus' text with that of other manuscripts, as they had even more copies at their disposal than Zenodotus himself, and so they could see the differences in the number of lines and in the readings. In this respect their statements deserve credit.[4] There is even

---

[1] The term in later grammatical literature was $\mathring{a}\pi\grave{o}$ $\phi\omega\nu\mathring{\eta}s$, Choerob. in Theodos. *Gr. Gr.* IV 1. 103. 3 and IV 2. 1. 3 Hilg.; cf. Rutherford, 'Annotation' 31 ff. and the references given by Diels–Schubart and Zuntz, p. 212, n. 7, below.

[2] Schol. A *A* 63, *B* 553, cf. $\emph{\emph{ἴσως}}$ *B* 641. *Λ* 548. *P* 134 (see below, p. 118, n. 2).

[3] See below, p. 114.

[4] G. M. Bolling in his careful and valuable studies *The External Evidence for Interpolation in*

a chance of inquiring into the nature of the earlier and contemporary copies of the Homeric text that Zenodotus might have been able to use. We have had to touch on the history of this text several times. It is very likely that from the sixth century B.C. onwards a traditional text of the epic poems existed to which the professional reciters, the rhapsodes, had to keep; but that it was a sixth-century Attic text which became authoritative everywhere cannot be proved.[1] The poet Antimachus of Colophon, who regarded Homer as a Colophonian, produced the earliest edition of which we know at the end of the fifth century.[2] The frequent quotations by writers of the fourth century, especially Plato and Aristotle,[3] show considerable variants. It is difficult to use them for conclusions about a fourth-century text of Homer, as philosophers, orators, and historians often quote from memory, but it can happen that their readings agree with early papyri.[4]

Actual fragments of ancient books with Homeric lines are extant from the beginning of the Ptolemaic era onwards. Since J. P. Mahaffy started to publish the *Flinders Petrie Papyri* in 1891,[5] fragments of such early copies have continued to turn up from time to time. Compared with the enormous quantity of Homeric papyri from the third century B.C. to the seventh century A.D. known to us at present, their number (about twenty) is very small,[6] but their importance for our purpose is relatively great. They surprisingly differ not only from our medieval manuscript tradition, but also from the papyri later than 150 B.C.; quite a number of new lines ('plus verses') and of new readings occur besides a few omissions.[7] It would be too much to say that these early Ptolemaic texts give

Homer (1925), *The Athetized Lines of the Iliad* (1944), *Ilias Atheniensium* (1950), did not give any credit to the various utterances of the later grammarians, and did not admit internal reasons for athetizing, but oversimplified the case, in so far as he assumed that *every* line suspected or omitted by Zenodotus (and his great successors) was unattested or very badly attested in early copies (cf. below, p. 114); nevertheless, his *Ilias* of 1950 gives a complete and useful survey of Zenodotus' atheteses and omissions.

[1] See above, pp. 5–7; Ritschl's arguments in which he made some good points are spoiled by his general theory of the 'Peisistratus-recension', which is wrong.

[2] See above, p. 94.

[3] See above, pp. 73 f.; on the so-called λυτικοί see pp. 69 ff. and Excursus.

[4] See Aeschin. 1 149 = Pap. Heidelberg p. 46, 87 Gerhard, 'Ptolemäische Homerfragmente', below, n. 7.

[5] Royal Irish Academy: *Cunningham Memoirs*, no. 8 ff. (Dublin); this publication provoked A. Ludwich to write his controversial book *Die Homervulgata als voralexandrinisch erwiesen* (1898).

[6] Pack[2] lists 680 Homeric papyri in a total of 3026 literary papyri. See Addenda.

[7] Grenfell and Hunt, *The Hibeh Papyri* I (1906) 67–75, opened the discussion of the problem in the introduction to *P.Hib.* 19–23 (Pap. of *Iliad* and *Odyssey* about 285–250 B.C.); these few outstanding pages are fundamental and not yet superseded. G. A. Gerhard, 'Ptolemäische Homerfragmente', *Veröffentlichungen aus der Heidelberger Papyrussammlung* IV (1911), with important new texts and useful explanations. Cf. Homeri *Ilias* ed. T. W. Allen 1 (1931)

the impression of a 'chaos'; but we can appreciate Zenodotus' problem when we realize that he was confronted with such a great number of more or less differing copies. We may assume that he ignored carelessly written private copies circulating in Egypt, of which a few specimens are extant, and was eager to look for better ones.

There is a temptation to think in this connexion of the official Athenian copy of the tragic poets which was 'acquired' for the Alexandrian library and helped to constitute the text of the tragedies.[1] Indeed I should guess that it is the recollection of this attested fact that lies behind the modern inventions of an 'Attic' more or less official copy of Homer for the Panathenaic festivals. There is no hint of the existence of such a copy anywhere in ancient literature; it has even been argued that the Alexandrian scholars kept silence just because they used it as the main source of their editions. But it must be emphasized that there is not the slightest evidence so far to show either that there was an authoritative sixth-century Attic text or that a fourth-century one arrived in Alexandria; it remains one of several vague possibilities. Many copies from cities[2] all over the Greek world were assembled in the royal library, even from the periphery, from Massilia in the west and Sinope in the north-east. It is not improbable that Zenodotus, examining manuscripts in the library, selected *one* text of Homer, which seemed to him to be superior to any other one, as his main guide; its deficiencies he may have corrected from better readings in other manuscripts as well as by his own conjectures. Διόρθωσις can be the term for either kind of correction. It is hard to imagine any other way. The Italian humanists had to face a similar situation when numerous manuscripts of Latin classics were recovered and they had to prepare their editions; they used to pick out one 'codex pervetustus' which they followed and occasionally emended by comparison with other codices as well as by their own conjectures. But there was no 'central' library like that in Alexandria in the Renaissance; and in any case, of course, an analogy can do no more than indicate what may or perhaps was likely to have happened.

This is the result, a meagre result, we have to confess, of our preliminary inquiry into the nature of the texts of the Homeric poems accessible to Zenodotus for his διόρθωσις. Let us now turn to that 'principal

---

Prolegomena 57 ff., 194 ff., P. Collart, 'Les Papyrus de l'Iliade' in P. Mazon, *Introduction à l'Iliade* (1942, repr. 1948) 37–74, chronological table pp. 63 ff.—G. Pasquali, *Storia della tradizione e critica del testo* (1934, reprinted 1952) 220 ff., and H. Erbse, 'Über Aristarchs Iliasausgaben', *Herm.* 87 (1959) 275 ff., are most helpful and also give further bibliographical references. On Bolling's book, see p. 108, n. 4.

[1] See above, p. 82.
[2] See the ἐκδόσεις κατὰ πόλεις above, p. 94.

question'¹ which we put above: what use did he make of those copies?
Did he carefully consider their lines and variant readings and constitute
his text on this 'documentary' evidence, or did he suspect or even delete
lines and change the wording according to his own arbitrary judgement?
The best way will be to select a few typical examples and to examine
them as thoroughly as possible. We can start with the text of two lines
(*A* 4–5) of the proem of the *Iliad*; the interpretation of this one short
Homeric sentence will reveal nearly all the difficulties of Zenodotus' new
enterprise,² which he undertook with the boldness of a well equipped
pioneer. It is a lucky chance that the fifth-century reading of *A* 5 is quite
certain from a rare concord of the three tragedians: Aesch. *Suppl.* 800 f.
κυσὶν δ᾽ ἔπειθ᾽ ἕλωρα κἀπιχωρίοις / ὄρνισι δεῖπνον, Soph. *Ant.* 29–30 (νέκυν
. . .) ἐᾶν δ᾽ ἄκλαυτον, ἄταφον, οἰωνοῖς βοράν,³ Eur. *Ion* 504 f. πτανοῖς . . .
θοίναν θηρσί τε φοινίαν δαῖτα, *Hec.* 1078 κυσίν τε φοινίαν δαῖτα. They all
must have had before them a text αὐτοὺς δὲ ἑλώρια τεῦχε κύνεσσιν / οἰωνοῖσί
τε δαῖτα, not the vulgate text οἰωνοῖσί τε πᾶσι. And δαῖτα is exactly what
Zenodotus wrote in his edition, though it is attested only by Athenaeus
(*epit.* 1 12 F).⁴ This line is not preserved in any extant Ptolemaic papyrus,
and there is no trace of this variant left in our manuscripts and Scholia,
where only the reading οἰωνοῖσί τε πᾶσι is preserved without further com-
ment.⁵ What we still read there is the remark of Aristonicus in Schol.
Ven. A, that Zenodotus athetized the two lines 4 and 5. He kept them in
his text, as we have seen, but he must have marked them with a marginal
'obelus'.⁶ The reason for obelizing *A* 4–5 may have been that they were
omitted in a copy of his or that the context of the poem in the opinion
of the editor runs more smoothly when ἐξ οὗ δή immediately follows upon
μῆνιν . . . ἥ . . . προΐαψε, not upon Διὸς δ᾽ ἐτελείετο βουλή. Thanks to

---

¹ Cf. the most valuable discussion by Pasquali, *Storia* 224–30.

² For that reason I dare to choose it in spite of its text having been subjected to vehement
discussion for ages. I should like to refer to A. Nauck, *Mélanges Gréco-Romains* III (1874) 9–14
and IV (1880) 463; E. Schwartz, *Adversaria* (Index Gottingae 1908) 7 f., Pasquali, *Storia* 236 f.;
cf. Leaf, Bolling, Von der Mühll ad loc. A. Pagliaro, 'Nuovi saggi di critica semantica',
Biblioteca di cultura contemporanea 51 (1956) 8, 21, 35 ff. On Apollonius Rhodius' reading of *A* 3
see below, p. 147.

³ Restored by E. Fraenkel, *Mus. Helv.* 17 (1960) 238; the interpolation of the Sophoclean
line into [Eur.] *Phoe.* 1634 was recognized by Valckenaer. Soph. *Ai.* 830, *Phil.* 957 are not to
the point.

⁴ ἐπὶ μόνων τῶν ἀνθρώπων δαῖτα (Eust. p. 19. 45: δαῖτας Ath.) λέγει ὁ ποιητής, ἐπὶ δὲ
θηρίων οὐκ ἔτι. ἀγνοῶν δὲ ταύτης τῆς φωνῆς τὴν δύναμιν Ζηνόδοτος ἐν τῇ κατ᾽ αὐτὸν ἐκδόσει
γράφει· 'αὐτοὺς–δαῖτα', τὴν τῶν γυπῶν καὶ τῶν ἄλλων οἰωνῶν τροφὴν οὕτω καλῶν, μόνου ἀνθρώπου χωροῦντος ⟨εἰς⟩ τὸ ἴσον ἐκ τῆς πρόσθεν βίας, διὸ καὶ μόνου τούτου ἡ τροφὴ δαὶς καὶ μοῖρα τὸ
ἑκάστῳ διδόμενον (Suid. v. δαιτὸς ἐίσης II p. 14. 5 Adler ex Athenaeo). The author of the
Epitome, Eustathius, quoted this passage twice in his commentary on the *Iliad* p. 19. 45
(*A* 5) and 256. 8 (*B* 467).

⁵ But see Eust. below, p. 113. ⁶ On the critical σημεῖα see below, p. 115.

Athenaeus' testimony we know in this case that Zenodotus read a peculiar text of the two lines in ancient copies; on the other hand, his predilection for a clear syntactical structure and for as concise a text as possible may have made him suspicious of their genuineness.[1]

The arguments of his critics also can teach us yet a little more about Zenodotus. The critical sign (⪖ διπλῆ περιεστιγμένη) on the margin of the codex Ven. A at line *A* 5 indicates that Aristarchus disapproved of the reading of Zenodotus. Furthermore, it is Aristarchean to observe the poet's usage, to reject δαῖτα in the sense of animal food as non-Homeric,[2] and to charge Zenodotus with ἄγνοια (as in Schol. A to *Δ* 88, *Σ* 247, *Ω* 528); in another case where again the epitome of Athenaeus is our only source, this time for a much-disputed passage on the use of lamps in the Homeric age, it has been proved that it goes back to Aristarchus' opinion on Homer's λύχνος.[3] But if we look at the whole chapter in Athenaeus (*epit.* 1 12 C–F), of which we have quoted only the end, the polemics against Zenodotus' reading in *A* 5, it will take us still further. Its main subject is a detailed explanation of the Homeric δαιτὸς ἐΐσης (*θ* 98 and *I* 225 are quoted), also directed against Zenodotus, who understood it (apparently in his glossary) as δαιτὸς ἀγαθῆς.[4] The objection made is that the true sense must be 'a meal in equal portions'.[5] Civilized men, in contrast to primitive people, cared for equally shared meals, and even the noun δαίς itself, to be derived from δατεῖσθαι, points to a deliberate 'distribution'; therefore it cannot be used either for uncivilized men or for animals. These sentences on early civilization have a Peripatetic ring; they echo the spirit in which Dicaearchus traced the 'Life of Greece'[6] from the dawn of history to later ages. The passage from Athenaeus is only a part of a long excerpt Περὶ τοῦ τῶν ἡρώων καθ' Ὅμηρον βίου[7] where we meet Peripatetic

---

[1] It seems to be a strange mistake for G. M. Bolling to deprive his *Ilias Atheniensium* of the sixth century B.C. (1950) of these two lines for the sake of his mechanical theory; in this case γίνεται δὲ τὸ προοίμιον κόλον, as the Schol. A warned. I fully agree with P. Von der Mühll, *Kritisches Hypomnema zur Ilias* (1952) 14 n. 5 in this point and I very much regret that we disagree on δαῖτα. If Apollonius' copies read κεφαλάς in l. 3, ll. 4–5 must have been left out, see below, p. 147.

[2] See above, p. 111, n. 4. What he thought of *Ω* 43, where δαίς is the meal of the lion, we do not know, as the Scholia on *Ω* are very poor; he may not have had the simile in his text or he may have constructed βροτῶν ἵνα δαῖτα.

[3] *Stud. It.* 27–28 (1956) 427 = *Ausgewählte Schriften* 2 f.

[4] See below, p. 115; cf. Hesych. εἶσον· ἀγαθόν, Schol. T *Ω* 69 ἐΐσης] . . . ἢ τῆς ἀγαθῆς, ὡς 'καί σφιν δαῖτ' ἀγαθήν' (*Ψ* 810). See also Eust. 1401. 56 ff. (a 138) who quotes Athenaeus.

[5] Apollon. Soph. p. 64. 31 ἐΐσης· πρὸς ἴσον ἑκάστῳ διδομένης, giving Aristarchus' interpretation.

[6] Fr. 59 Wehrli (*Die Schule des Aristoteles* I, 1944) in Zenob. Ath. III 62 Miller, *Mélanges* p. 372 and [Plut.] *proverb.* cod. Laur. no. 18 Crusius (Wehrli quotes only the vulgate tradition).

[7] Athen. 1 8 E ff. = chapters 15–24 and later.

antiquarian lore together with interpretations by Alexandrian gram-
marians.¹ In our case, the grammarian who disapproved of a reading in
the text (δαῖτα), and of the explanation of another word in a Homeric
glossary (εἴσης), used a Peripatetic doctrine for his arguments; this is
a very welcome example² of the relation of the new scholarship, which
was eager to restore the correct wording and to find out its true meaning,
to the Aristotelian tradition of interest in the antiquarian lore of ancient
customs and their evolution.

I hesitate to go any further. Aristarchus, no doubt, is responsible for
οἰωνοῖσί τε πᾶσι having replaced in all our manuscripts the fifth-century
and Zenodotean reading δαῖτα. But there is, as we said,³ no comment in
our Scholia. Only Eustathius expressly mentioned the variant πᾶσι:
δαῖτα;⁴ he even defended πᾶσι and rejected δαῖτα. Zenodotus had not
understood, so he argued, that πᾶσι was said καθ' ὑπερβολήν (like μύριοι
in B 468); therefore he 'ejected (ἐξῶσε)' πᾶσι and 'wrote instead of it
(ἀντέγραψε)' δαῖτα. It is worth mentioning this mistake of Eustathius or of
his source, because it was typical to invent some reason for Zenodotus'
'conjectures' and to charge him with arbitrarily changing the traditional
correct text. For Eustathius πᾶσι was the original reading. We, however,
do not know anything about its origin: whether it is an old variant, or an
alteration of the fourth century B.C. due to a Peripatetic doctrine and
etymology,⁵ or a later conjecture.⁶ But even if this last question is left
unanswered, we should be satisfied with the wealth of information on
Zenodotus we have gained from the discussion of two lines of the *Iliad*.

In *A* 5 Zenodotus followed a fifth-century reading still preserved in the
text of three tragedies. When he athetized *A* 225–33 (Schol. A ἠθέτηκε),
he was influenced by a fourth-century copy which had omitted these lines
because of Plato's criticism (*Rep.* 389 E); *Π* 432–58,⁷ severely reprehended

---

¹ Cf. Robert Weber, 'De Dioscuridis Περὶ τῶν παρ' Ὁμήρῳ νόμων libello', *Leipziger
Studien zur class. Philologie* XI (1888) 87 ff., esp. 112 f. = Dioscor. fr. 34, 130 f. on Aristarchus,
131 f. on Peripatetics. E. Schwartz, *Adversaria* (1908) 8.

² See above, p. 104.

³ See above, p. 111.

⁴ Eust. p. 256. 8 on *B* 467, not on *A* 5 p. 19. 45; the unique passage seems to have been
overlooked in the extensive literature on *A* 5, because it was not connected with this line, but
with *B* 467. Even if it is a personal remark of the archbishop, it is in the line of the ancient
polemics against Zenodotus.

⁵ E. Schwartz, *Adversaria* 8, believed in such recensions 'in quibus propter illud veri-
loquium δαῖτα in πᾶσι mutatum erat' and was followed by Pasquali, *Storia* 237.

⁶ As a matter of fact, πᾶσι is a rather suspect expletive, as πᾶς and 'omnis' are in many
places, see G. Jachmann, 'Vom frühalexandrinischen Homertext', *NGG* 1949, Phil.-hist.
Kl. N. 7, pp. 173 f., with further references. In Catullus' translation of Call. fr. 110. 77 the
'suspectum' word 'omnibus' may be an expletive of the translator, not a corruption.

⁷ Schol. A *Π* 432 Z. καθόλου περιγράφει τὴν ὁμιλίαν τοῦ Διὸς καὶ τῆς Ἥρας. Schol. T παρὰ
Z. οὐκ ἦν ὁ διάλογος τῆς Ἥρας καὶ τοῦ Διός. On περιγράφειν see G. N. Bolling, *The External*

by Plato (*Rep.* 388 CD), had probably been left out in several of Zenodotus' copies, and so he cancelled them altogether. At least, it is more likely[1] that there was such an intermediary source than that Plato's moral criticism had this immediate effect on Zenodotus. Finally, he has been found to agree with the early third-century Hibeh-papyrus 20 in the omission of *Δ* 89. In our Schol. A to *Δ* 88 a deliberate reason was invented for Zenodotus' alteration of 88 and omission of 89, and he was blamed for his ἄγνοια;[2] but we now realize that there were copies of the *Iliad* in his time without this line.[3]

These three examples from the fifth to the third centuries, in which Zenodotus' text is shown to be based on documentary evidence, show how unjustly he was charged by ancient critics, and by those modern scholars who followed them, with making arbitrary changes for wrong internal reasons. On the other hand, the fact that such examples could be multiplied should not tempt us into the dangerous generalization that he *never* altered the traditional text without external evidence. Indeed we have already assumed that two lines of the proem of the *Iliad* which must have been in earlier copies were athetized by Zenodotus for internal reasons;[4] there are a number of other cases, in which a similar ground is equally probable. I refer to *Λ* 78–83,[5] *M* 175–81, *P* 134–6.[6] My impression is that changes of this sort are incomparably less frequent than the others; but beyond a certain probability we cannot go.

It would be an intolerable contradiction of the spirit of the new scholarship, if Zenodotus, 'himself an epic poet, had occasionally inserted verses of his own to complete the sense'; this surprising statement of Sandys[7] is unfounded. It would be farcical for the first διορθωτής of the genuine Homeric text to play the part of the disreputable διασκευασταί, as they were called.[8]

Evidence for Interpolation in Homer (1925) 48 ff.; on μεταγράφειν see below, p. 118, n. 1. For terminology, which is anything but consistent in antiquity, consult J. Baar, *Index zu den Ilias-Scholien* (1961).

[1] In this case I follow E. Schwartz, *Adversaria* (1908) 6, who was the first to do justice to Zenodotus; see also Bolling, loc. cit. 32 f., R. Merkelbach, *Gnom.* 23 (1951) 376. 4.

[2] See above, p. 112 on ἄγνοια.

[3] *Hibeh Papyri* 1 (see above, p. 109, n. 7) pp. 75 and 87.

[4] See above, pp. 111 f.

[5] Pasquali, *Storia* 228 f.

[6] G. Jachmann loc. cit. 174 f.

[7] 1³ 120 without any reference; it seems to repeat a sentence of H. Düntzer, *De Zenod. stud. Hom.* (1848) 157, 'versus . . . quosdam, quos ipse finxit, inseruit', followed by a few very poor arguments, which have been ably refuted by N. Wecklein, 'Über Zusätze und Auslassung von Versen im Homerischen Texte', *Sitz. Ber. Bayer. Akad.*, Philos.-philol. Kl. Jg. 1918, 7. Abh. S. 72 f.

[8] See K. Lehrs, *De Aristarchi stud. Hom.*³ 329 f.

In the discussion of the many problems connected with the text and explanation of *A* 5 Zenodotus' glossary was mentioned.[1] Although our material has much increased since F. A. Wolf's days, his assertion (Prolegomena, p. ccxv) that there is no sign of a scholarly commentary written by Zenodotus still stands. The few instances of epic vocables said to have been explained by Zenodotus may occasionally come from the lecture-notes of his pupils, otherwise they must come from the Γλῶσσαι, of which not only the title is attested, but also the alphabetical arrangement;[2] in scope his glossary was more limited than the Ἄτακτα of his master Philitas,[3] as the few quotations refer to epic and perhaps lyric poets only, but its contents may have been easier to look up because of its new order. It was a model for the future; so was the invention of the ὀβελός as a critical sign, which we also came across in dealing with the proem of the *Iliad*.[4] The appearance of this first σημεῖον, which was followed by many others, should not be regarded just as the introduction of a useful technical device. This was the first time that an editor had provided the serious reader and scholar with an opportunity of appraising his critical judgement. Zenodotus did not suppress the lines of which he doubted the genuineness, but left them in the context, marking them, however, on the margin with the obelus; he disclosed his own opinion and enabled the reader to check it. The early Ptolemaic papyri with their bewildering quantity of 'plus verses', the πολύστιχοι, revealed more clearly than any previous considerations how urgently necessary it was to distinguish the insertions from the original text.

Much less important is the question whether the division of each of the two Homeric poems into twenty-four books and the use of one of the twenty-four letters of the Ionic alphabet for each book are due to Zenodotus. In the fifth and fourth centuries individual episodes are

---

[1] See above, p. 112.

[2] H. Pusch, 'Quaestiones Zenodoteae', *Dissertationes Philologicae Halenses* xi (1890) 188 ff.; 11 fragments pp. 191 f. Fr. 1 = Schol. MHQR γ 444 Ζηνόδοτος δὲ ἐν ταῖς ἀπὸ τοῦ δ γλώσσαις τίθησι τὴν λέξιν (δαμνίον, not ἀμνίον), cf. Hesych. v. δάμνια (sic)· θύματα, σφάγια; cf. H. Erbse, 'Homerscholien und hellenistische Glossare bei Apollonios Rhodios', *Herm.* 81 (1953) 180.— The treatise preserved with the title Ζηνοδότου Φιλεταίρου Περὶ διαφορᾶς φωνῶν ζῴων, or with similar titles, or anonymously, in many manuscripts has nothing to do with the *Glossary* of Zenodotus of Ephesus, see my note on Call. fr. 725; the misleading remark in Schmid–Stählin, *Gesch. d. griech. Lit.* II 1⁶ (1920) 260. 4 is a relic from W. Christ's first edition (1888) 446. 2.　　　　　　　　　　　　　　　　　　　　　　　　[3] See above, pp. 90 ff.

[4] Περὶ Ἀριστάρχου σημείων Ἰλιάδος fragmentum, *Schol. Il.* ed. Dindorf I (1875) p. 1. 11 τὸν δὲ ὀβελὸν ἔλαβεν ἐκ τῆς Ζηνοδότου διορθώσεως. On the other σημεῖα see below, pp. 178 ff. If it is a fact—as we must assume so far—that Zenodotus and Aristophanes of Byzantium did mark certain lines of the text with critical signs, but did not write any commentary, this is a strong argument against E. G. Turner's new theory (*Chronique d'Égypte* 37 [1962] 149 ff.) that the existence of critical signs to a text always implies the existence of a corresponding commentary.

quoted with special titles: Διομήδους ἀριστεία (Herodotus), σκήπτρου παράδοσις, νεῶν κατάλογος (Thucydides), Λιταί, τειχομαχία (Plato), Ἀλκίνου
ἀπόλογοι (Plato, Aristotle). Lachmann[1] first suggested that Zenodotus
may have been responsible for the division, since Aristophanes of
Byzantium and Aristarchus are excluded, because they regarded ψ 296 as
the end of the *Odyssey* and could therefore not be the authors of the
traditional separation between ψ 372 and ω 1. But it may be safer not to
draw such a conclusion from the highly problematical Scholion ψ 296
about the πέρας or τέλος τῆς 'Οδυσσείας, with which we shall have to deal
at length in the chapter on Aristophanes.[2] Two late ancient passages
ascribe the division to the circle of Aristarchus.[3] The papyri seemed to
confirm this date, as there was at first no clear attestation of a division
into books, marked by an empty space between two lines or by a paragraphus or a coronis, before the first century B.C.[4] But it may just be
possible that the earliest of our *Odyssey* papyri, which marks the line 400 of
Book κ with the letter Δ on the margin, points to the existence of the
usual division at the beginning of the third century B.C., perhaps before
Zenodotus.[5] The question of the division into twenty-four books is not
yet definitively settled, either by evidence or by arguments, as far as
Zenodotus is concerned. Only one fact can be regarded as fairly certain:
some time after Aristarchus the division commonly occurs in the ancient
manuscripts, and this coincides with the acceptance of a more firmly
established Homeric text.

Zenodotus' Homeric studies may have included a treatise on the

---

[1] K. Lachmann, 'Über Zenodots Tagberechnung der Ilias', *Berichte über die Verhandlungen
der Akademie der Wissenschaften* (1846) 30 = *Betrachtungen über Homers Ilias*[3] (1874) 93, 'es ist
sicher falsch, erst ihnen (sc. Aristophanes oder Aristarch) und nicht etwa Zenodot oder
einem früheren die kindische Einteilung beider Werke nach den Buchstaben des Alphabets
zuzuschreiben, da die gereiftere Kritik die Odyssee bei ψ 296 schloß.' This imperious
utterance immediately impressed Düntzer (1848) and many others. Against the sceptics
Wilamowitz, *Hom. Untersuch.* (1884) 369, used the same argument (without mentioning
Lachmann's name), vigorously fighting the cause of Zenodotus; see also *Die Ilias und Homer*
(1916) 32 'ohne Frage Zenodot'. So his authorship became almost an established fact for the
handbooks (Susemihl, Christ–Schmid, Sandys, etc.).

[2] See below, pp. 175 f.

[3] [Plut.] *Vita Hom.* II 4 p. 25. 22 ff. Wil. ποιήσεις δύο, 'Ιλιὰς καὶ 'Οδύσσεια, διῃρημένη
ἑκατέρα εἰς τὸν ἀριθμὸν τῶν στοιχείων, οὐχ ὑπ' αὐτοῦ τοῦ ποιητοῦ, ἀλλ' ὑπὸ τῶν γραμματικῶν
τῶν περὶ Ἀρίσταρχον. Eust. p. 5. 29 (after telling the Peisistratus-legend) γραμματικοὶ ... ὧν
κορυφαῖος ὁ Ἀρίσταρχος καὶ μετ' ἐκεῖνον (sic) Ζηνόδοτος ... κατέτεμον αὐτὸ εἰς πολλὰ ...
ὀνομάσαι τὰς τομὰς τοῖς ὀνόμασι τῶν εἴκοσι τεσσάρων στοιχείων.

[4] Wendel, *Buchbeschreibung* 49, 57; W. Lameere, 'Aperçus de paléographie Homérique',
Les Publications de Scriptorium IV (1960) 44 ff. gives a survey up to 1960.

[5] *P. Sorbonne inv.* 2245 ed. O. Guéraud, *Rev. Ég. Anc.* I (1925) 8 ff. = Pack[2] no. 1081;
I owe the reference to Mrs. West, who re-examined the early Ptolemaic papyri, see
Addenda to p. 109.6.

number of days in the *Iliad*[1] and a *Life* of Homer;[2] as in the case of Antimachus it was perhaps published at the front of his text.[3] Homer's poems were to him the *Iliad* and *Odyssey*; it was of the utmost importance for the whole future that the first of the great scholars followed the lead of Aristotle[4] and accepted the differentiation between these two poems as Homeric and the rest of epic narrative poetry as non-Homeric. In this case the κρίσις had already been made in the fourth century; in other cases, as we shall see, the new κριτικοί had to perform the κρίσις ποιημάτων as their highest and finest task.

Of Zenodotus' edition of Hesiod's *Theogony* only one slight trace is left, his reading Τερμησοῖο instead of Περμησσοῖο;[5] his interpretation of χάος as τὸν κεχυμένον ἀέρα, 'the mist shed around', in accordance with Hesiod (Schol. Hes. *Th.* 116) and in contrast to Bacchylides (v 27 'the expanse of air'), was probably part of his glossary. Aristotle and his school in the course of their literary researches had occasionally dealt with Hesiodic problems: the relative date of Hesiod and Homer, the authenticity of some of his poems, antiquarian questions.[6] But we know of no edition before that of Zenodotus, who was the first to have the collected manuscripts at his disposal, nor can we tell whether his edition contained other Hesiodic texts besides the *Theogony*. Homer was without a rival; next to him Hesiod was a favourite with the great poets of the first half of the third century, especially with Aratus and Callimachus. His name was even a sort of programme for the new poetry like Callimachus' *Aitia*. This is what gave Zenodotus' first critical text of the Boeotian epic poet its contemporary significance.

Two short notes in the Scholia to Pindar's *Olympian odes* point to two variant readings of Zenodotus: II 4 ἀκροθίνια instead of ἀκρόθινα, and VI 55 where the word he read instead of βεβρεγμένος is missing (Byzantine scholars supplied it). In our Scholia to Pind. *O.* III 29 χρυσόκερων ἔλαφον θήλειαν a parallel from Anacreon is quoted (fr. 63 Page) νεβρὸν . . . ὅστ' ἐν

---

[1] See above, p. 116, n. 1, Lachmann.

[2] In the long list of writers on Homer's *Life* in Tatian *ad Graecos* c. 31 (p. 31. 24 Schwartz) which starts from Theagenes (see above, p. 11) Zenodotus is after the Peripatetics the first of the γραμματικοί (see also Call. fr. 452).

[3] See above, p. 94.   [4] See above, pp. 73 f.

[5] Schol. Hes. *Th.* 5 (Flach) ἐν δὲ ταῖς Ζηνοδοτείοις γράφεται Τερμησοῖο (*sic*); cf. Hes.*Th.* ed. F. Jacoby (1930), pp. 46 f. and 74 f. and Call. fr. 2 a, 20 (Add. II) and fr. 696. Τὸ ἐν ταῖς (not τοῖς) Ζηνοδοτείοις compare Apollon. Dysc. *pron.* p. 110. 12 Schn. ἐν ταῖς Ζηνοδοτείοις διορθώσεαι sc. Ὁμέρι; but as it is unlikely in the case of Homer that Zenodotus produced more than one edition (see A. Ludwich, *Aristarch* 1 5, and Apollon. Dysc., vol. III (1910), Index p. 288 s.v. Zenodotus), it is still less likely in the case of Hesiod.

[6] See Hes. *Th.* ed. Jacoby, Praef. pp. 45 f. with references to the testimonia; see also J. Schwartz, *Pseudo-Hesiodea* (1960) 614 (cf. 610), who wrongly speaks of a commentary of Zenodotus on the *Theogony*, and F. Wehrli, *Die Schule des Aristoteles* 10 (1959) 134 s.v. Hesiod.

ὕλη κεροέσσης ὑπολειφθεὶς ὑπὸ μητρός, with the remark: Ζηνόδοτος δὲ μετεποίησεν[1] 'ἐροέσσης'; the unnatural implication[2] of a doe having horns was removed by deleting one letter. Aristophanes of Byzantium strongly objected to the conjecture (ἀντιλέγει κατὰ κράτος Ael. *h.a.* VII 39). In the great papyrus *P.Oxy.* 841 which contains substantial fragments of ten *Paeans* with scholia between the columns, the editors[3] recognized in the abbreviations Ζ̄ or Ζη the name of Zenodotus of Ephesus; as far as the Scholia can be deciphered, it is only to variant readings that these letters were six times added, just as in six other cases the abbreviations of the names of Aristophanes and Aristarchus indicated variants due to them. Two more such marginal notes have quite recently come to light in *P.Oxy.* 2442 with new fragments of the *Paeans*;[4] Ζη again introduces a variant reading in one case; in the other the papyrus is broken after the two letters. We realize from this how many references to the earliest textual criticism[5] must have perished on the long way from these ancient copies to our medieval manuscripts; and we need no longer doubt that Zenodotus made the first critical edition of Pindar's text, and possibly of Anacreon, as he did of Homer and of Hesiod. Perhaps he did not mind that ἀκροθίνια spoiled the responsion or that ὕλη ἐροέσσης produced an intolerable hiatus;[6] there seems to have been no real expert in the metre and prosody of early lyric poetry before Aristophanes of Byzantium, Zenodotus' true successor, whose editions far surpassed his. But between

---

[1] μεταποιεῖν = μεταγράφειν is a common term for proposing a conjectural reading; cf. above, p. 113, n. 7.

[2] One had better not compare the omission of *P* 134–6 in Zenodotus' text, as H. Fränkel, *Die homerischen Gleichnisse* (1921) 119 and *GGA* 1926, 240 f., did; cf. Pasquali *Storia*, 229. The same lines were missing in the edition of Chios, as the Schol. A says; so Zenodotus probably followed his copies, and only the Scholia (Aristonicus?) say that he deleted these lines because of a difficulty of natural history. But as in all the other cases, this is no more than a guess, as the Schol. honestly confess: ἴσως, φασὶν ἔνιοι, . . . μήποτε κτλ.

[3] *P.Oxy.* v (1908) ed. Grenfell and Hunt, pp. 15, 92 (to *pae.* IV 58), for re-examination of the papyrus see the editions of Pindar by Turyn (1948) and Snell (1953 and 1964). See also J. Irigoin, 'Histoire du texte de Pindare', *Études et Commentaires* XIII (1952) 32 f. Zénodote, 77 ff. Les Papyrus.

[4] *P.Oxy.* XXVI (1961) ed. E. Lobel, no. 2440, fr. 1 and 2442, fr. 14, pp. 12 and 42 with the commentary on ζη: 'I am doubtful of its interpretation as Zenodotus. I should say it always means ζήτει, ζητεῖται or some other part of this verb.' ζη can certainly mean ζήτει, etc. (cf. e.g. *P.Oxy.* 2430, fr. 79 marg. of ll. 1, 4, 6 and *P.Oxy.* 2429, fr. 1, col. II 21), but as far as my knowledge goes, it is never set in front of a simple variant reading. It usually introduces a question about the subject-matter: διὰ τί or πότερον . . . ἤ, often followed by a λύσις. And in this papyrus similar abbreviations of the names of other grammarians are added to other variants. Therefore I am pretty sure that Grenfell and Hunt gave the correct interpretation.

[5] Pind. *Pae.* VI 55 κελαινεφεῖ; the editors supplied κ]ελα[ινεφέϊ as Zenodotus' reading; but this does not seem a true alternative, and I should venture to suggest μ]ελα[ινεφεῖ or μ]ελα[ννεφεῖ, cf. above, p. 91, n. 6.

[6] The plural ὕλης (ὕλαις Ael. loc. cit.) would be against the grammatical usage of ὕλη, see *Herm.* 87 (1959) 3 f.

them a generation of illustrious poets and scholars had worked incessantly for the recovery and understanding of their literary heritage.

Zenodotus' two collaborators, who dealt with the scenic poets, were mentioned above in connexion with the scholarly work of the library and problems of chronology. Alexander the Aetolian and Lycophron the Chalcidian are always counted as two members of the brilliant group of seven tragedians, the Pleiad,[1] who outshone the numerous tragic poets of the age. Once only in the later history of classical scholarship was the Alexandrian name, Πλειάς, intentionally revived and applied again to a circle of poets and scholars by the French poet Ronsard, the pupil of Dorat, in 1563, after Budé had called the newly founded Collège royal a new Μουσεῖον.[2] Alexander as ποιητής wrote epic, elegiacs, epigrams, and mimes, besides his plays, of which only one title is preserved;[3] as γραμματικός he concerned himself with tragedies and satyr-plays. Of Lycophron, the ποιητὴς τραγῳδιῶν, Suidas enumerates twenty titles,[4] and Tzetzes in his introduction to the *Alexandra* is undecided between the figures 64 and 46; the subjects were partly mythical, partly historical. He seems to have written a unique piece in his satyr-play *Menedemus*, in which he amusingly described the modest living and high thinking of that Eretrian philosopher; Lycophron, himself a native of the island of Euboea, apparently had met him there, before Menedemus was forced to leave Eretria in the year 273 B.C.[5] As a γραμματικός Lycophron specialized in comedy. His *Menedemus* shows his acquaintance with the Old Attic comedy, and his treatise Περὶ κωμῳδίας[6] in at least nine books seems to

---

[1] Strab. xiv 675 ποιητὴς δὲ τραγῳδίας ἄριστος τῶν τῆς Πλειάδος καταριθμουμένων is our earliest and best testimony for the term Pleiad; some names of the poets belonging to the group, varie, cf. F. Schramm, *Tragicorum Graecorum hellenisticae . . . aetatis fragmenta*, Diss. Münster (1929) 4–6; a survey of all the Hellenistic tragedians in *RE* vi A (1937) 1969–79 by K. Ziegler.

[2] See 'Dichter und Philologen im französischen Humanismus', *Antike und Abendland* vii (1958) 79.

[3] I. U. Powell, *Collect. Alexandr.* (1925) 121–30; F. Schramm loc. cit. 40–42 testimonia; see also below, nn. 5, 6.

[4] F. Schramm loc. cit. 25–40.

[5] *Syll.*[3] 406. 7 note: The Eretrian Menedemus appears in the list of the ἱερομνήμονες in Delphi in the year 274/3 B.C., but no longer in 273/2 B.C., when his adversary Aeschylus took his place, *Syll.*[3] 416. 3. This is the only evidence for the date of Menedemus' banishment from Eretria. If it is reliable (see K. v. Fritz, *RE* xv [1931] 790), Lycophron must have met him there before 273 B.C.; but when this meeting took place and when Lycophron left his native island of Euboea for Alexandria we cannot tell. It is not known whether Lycophron stayed with Menedemus and Aratus at the court of Antigonus Gonatas in Pella. Wilamowitz, *HD* i 166, by mistake refers to *Commentariorum in Aratum rel.* ed. E. Maass (1898) 148; in Theon's *Life* of Aratus, which quotes an otherwise unknown writing of Antigonus Gonatas himself to or on Hieronymus of Cardia (ὁ Ἀντίγονος ἐν τοῖς περὶ † Ἱερώνυμον *FGrHist* 154 T 9), Alexander Aetolus is mentioned together with Aratus, Antagoras, and Persaeus, but neither Lycophron nor Menedemus.

[6] C. Strecker, *De Lycophrone, Euphronio, Eratosthene comicorum interpretibus*, Diss. Greifswald

have been based on knowledge of Cratinus, Eupolis, and Aristophanes. It tried to explain the rare words so frequently used in comedy, thus continuing the glossographic work of Philitas[1] in a new field. Quite naturally Lycophron's bold enterprise was heavily attacked by his better-equipped successors, especially by Eratosthenes; they probably picked up his worst blunders (for instance on Aristoph. *Av.* 14 or *Vesp.* 239), and the whole work may not have been as bad as these examples. Like his contemporary, Zenodotus, who was no doubt a much greater scholar, he had to suffer the fate of an explorer of a new literary province. As a connoisseur of the comic poets, he made a recension of the text too, if the word διορθοῦν in the *Prolegomena* has to be accepted.

Certainly a text must have been available when Euphronius in the following generation composed a commentary on individual plays of Aristophanes.[2]

There is a passionate dispute about the genuineness of an iambic poem unanimously ascribed to Lycophron by the ancient tradition,[3] the *Alexandra*, in which Cassandra's prophecies of the future sufferings of Trojans and Greeks are related in 1,474 trimeters. The language of this poem is full of rare and strange vocables, especially epic and tragic glosses; comic ones would hardly fit the sombre subject. This penchant for glosses is characteristic also of the treatise Περὶ κωμῳδίας, and the inclination to enigmatical obscurity would be in harmony with a tendency we observed in the *Technopaegnia* of the early third century B.C. I am therefore disposed, after examining Lycophron's scholarly work, to accept the traditional date of *Alexandra* as correct, a conclusion I reached independently when some time ago I had to consider the relation of the poem to Callimachus.[4]

Another poet of the same generation, Aratus from the Cilician Soloi, never associated with the scholar poets at Alexandria, but after his formative years in Ephesus (?) and Athens stayed at the court of Antigonus Gonatas in Macedonia and for a few years also in Syria at the court of Antiochus.[5] His first teacher was Menecrates of Ephesus, a grammarian as well as a poet in the Hesiodic manner on agriculture and bee-

---

(1884) 2–6 and 23–78; W. G. Rutherford, 'Annotation' 417; cf. K. Ziegler, *RE* XIII (1927) 2323 ff.

[1] See above, p. 90.
[2] See below, p. 161.
[3] *Schol. Lyc.* 1226, however, made a conjecture about a second Lycophron.
[4] Callimachus II (1953) XLIII; a full bibliography of the discussion is given by A. Momigliano, *Secondo contributo alla storia degli studi classici* (Roma 1960) 437. 22. Cf. *Riv. stor. ital.* 71 (1959) 551 f.
[5] See above, p. 107 and p. 119, n. 5.

keeping;[1] in Athens he was imbued with philosophy, particularly Stoic doctrines, and became the friend of Antigonus. He then celebrated the king's marriage to Antiochus' half-sister Phila (276 B.C.) in one or two hymns at Pella, where he met Alexander Aetolus and possibly Timon. Antigonus is said to have encouraged him to put Eudoxus' star catalogue into verse; the result was the epic *Phaenomena*, the most successful of his many poems, highly appreciated even in the literary circles of Alexandria, not to speak of its surprising and age-long popularity as a practical schoolbook on astronomy. A scientific subject was here treated with Stoic religious and philosophic feeling in a style derived from Hesiod. Aratus had learned these things in Ephesus and Athens, but the polished simple form was his own and could not have earned any better praise than the epithet λεπτόν, 'subtle', bestowed on it by Callimachus.[2] Intimate knowledge of the Homeric language is obvious in every line. We have referred to the anecdote that he asked Timon for the best text of Homer he could get and was told to use the 'old copies', not the 'corrected' ones.[3] The tradition in the different versions of the *Life* of Aratus that he produced a critical edition of the *Odyssey* is fairly reliable;[4] in Syria later on he was induced by Antiochus to 'correct the *Iliad*, as it was corrupted by many'. When and why he went to Syria we do not know. It is no more than a modern assumption that he fled from Pella to Antioch when Pyrrhus invaded Macedonia in 274–272 B.C., and turned to editing Homer; but he may have gone there later and for a longer time before Antiochus I

---

[1] Suid. v. Ἄρατος . . . ἀκουστὴς δὲ ἐγένετο γραμματικοῦ μὲν τοῦ Ἐφεσίου Μενεκράτους, φιλοσόφου δὲ Τίμωνος καὶ Μενεδήμου . . . σύγχρονος . . . Ἀλεξάνδρῳ τῷ Αἰτωλῷ; on Menecrates' poems see *Poet. Philos. Gr.* ed. Diels, pp. 171 f., cf. E. Maass, *Aratea* (1892) 328 f.

[2] See also below, p. 136.

[3] See above, p. 98. Timon helped Alexander Aetolus and Homerus of Byzantium with plots (μῦθοι) for their tragedies, see F. Schramm *Tragicorum . . . hellenisticae . . . aetatis fragmenta* (1929) 16 f., 61.

[4] Theo Alex., *Vita Arati* p. 148. 14 Maass (*Commentariorum in Aratum reliquiae*, 1898) διώρθωσε δὲ καὶ τὴν Ὀδύσσειαν—cf. ibid. the Latin version with its addition: didicit (dicit *cod. K*: didicit *cett. codd.*: *fort.* dirigit *Pf.* coll. *Isagog.* III p. 140. 16 et 17 dirigere = διορθοῦν et directio = διόρθωσις) quidem et Odysseam, et Gecraustius inquit . . . et Iliadem (Heliadam *codd.*) scripsisse seu Homerum dirigere; vitiatum enim illum a compluribus . . . Dositheus autem Pelusinus . . . venire inquit et apud Antiochum Seleucium.' *Vita Arati* in Achill. comment. fragm. p. 78. 7 Maass καὶ τὴν Ὀδύσσειαν δὲ διώρθωσε καὶ καλεῖταί τις διόρθωσις οὕτως Ἀράτειος ὡς Ἀρισταρχειος καὶ Ἀριστοφάνειος. τινὲς δὲ αὐτὸν εἰς Συρίαν ἐληλυθέναι φασὶ καὶ γεγονέναι παρ' Ἀντιόχῳ καὶ ἀξιῶσθαι ὑπ' αὐτοῦ ὥστε τὴν Ἰλιάδα διορθώσασθαι, διὰ τὸ ὑπὸ πολλῶν λελυμάνθαι and ibid. p. 78. 32 ἔγραψε δὲ καὶ ἄλλα ποιήματα † περί τε Ὁμήρου καὶ Ἰλιάδος† οὐ μόνον τὰ Φαινόμενα. E. Maass, 'Aratea', *Philologische Untersuchungen* 12 (1892) 243 ff., and J. Martin, 'Histoire du texte des Phénomènes d'Aratos', *Études et Commentaires* 22 (1956) 151 ff., treated these confused and corrupted texts. The sources, on the other hand, Dositheus of Pelusium and Carystius of Pergamum(?), are quite reliable. No one who is at all acquainted with Theon's commentaries on the great Hellenistic poets will believe in the reconstruction of his edition of Aratus attempted by Martin pp. 195 ff.

died in 262 B.C. The existence of a library in the capital is attested for the reign of Antiochus the Great (224/3–188/7 B.C.), who installed the poet Euphorion of Chalcis as his librarian.[1] So Aratus could probably have found in Antioch the necessary books for his scholarly work at an earlier date. Even if this was in the seventies, Zenodotus' edition may well have been finished before 274 B.C., and if there is any sense in the Timon story, ἀντίγραφα διωρθωμένα must have been in existence when he answered Aratus' question. Aratus, himself a prominent writer who took part in the revival of poetry, was also eager to work for the preservation of the masterpieces of the past; this is a particularly striking example of the general historical process that we tried to describe in the preceding chapter.

There is no reference in our Homeric Scholia to the διόρθωσις Ἀράτειος, as it is expressly called in a *Life* of Aratus; but readings of another epic poet, the Cretan Rhianus who published an edition of Homer, are frequently quoted.[2] In his poems, however, he seems to be dependent on Callimachus;[3] this apparently agrees with the ancient biographical tradition, which calls him a contemporary (σύγχρονος) of Eratosthenes.[4] Therefore we had better place him with the younger generation of poets and scholars,[5] not with Zenodotus and Aratus.

---

[1] Suid. v. Εὐφορίων . . . ἦλθε πρὸς Ἀντίοχον τὸν Μέγαν . . . καὶ προέστη ὑπ' αὐτοῦ τῆς ἐκεῖ δημοσίας βιβλιοθήκης; cf. below, p. 150.

[2] List of Rhianus' readings J. La Roche, *Die Homerische Textkritik im Altertum* (1866) 45 ff., and W. Aly, *RE* I A (1920) 788 f.; cf. C. Mayhoff, *De Rhiani Cretensis studiis Homericis* 1870.

[3] Callimachus II, p. XLIII on Rhianus; F. Jacoby, *FGrHist* III a (1943) 89 ff. (commentary on no. 265) and III B p. 754 (Addenda), strongly pleads for an earlier date. But even if in a single case, *Hy.* II 47 ff., Callimachus took over an erotic motif from Rhianus, it would not affect the issue, as this poem in my opinion was written at the beginning of the second half of the third century; passages of the *Hecale* and of the *Aitia* were certainly imitated by Rhianus, see *Hecal.* fr. 266. If Rhianus is the author of the new epic fragment *P.Oxy.* XXX (1964) 2522 A, B according to Lobel's 'reasonable hypothesis', it is even possible that a line of Callimachus' second hymn was his model (l. 17~Call. *hy.* II 15?).

[4] *FGrHist* 265 T 1.

[5] See below, pp. 148 f.

III

CALLIMACHUS AND THE GENERATION OF HIS PUPILS

THERE was no distinguished textual critic in the generation after Zenodotus; only Aristophanes of Byzantium[1] at the end of the third century
was his equal if not his superior in this field. The outstanding representatives of scholarship between Zenodotus and Aristophanes were two men
from Cyrene, Callimachus and Eratosthenes.

After Alexander's death Ptolemy I ruled over the old Dorian colony of
Cyrene as the western part of his Egyptian kingdom (perhaps 322
B.C.); then his stepson Magas[2] was given a kind of independent regency
(about 300 B.C.?), and there was a time of considerable trouble between
Egypt and Cyrene in the seventies. But at length the only daughter of
Magas and Apame, Berenice,[3] was betrothed to the son of Ptolemy II,
and on their marriage and accession in 247/6 B.C. Cyrene was finally
united with Egypt. Although we cannot fix a precise date for the arrival
of the two Cyreneans in Alexandria, there is no doubt that it was after
the Ionians had started the 'new movement'.[4] For literary men were
attracted, not all at once—but in the course of several generations—by the
splendour of the new capital and the patronage of its kings. Callimachus'[5]
Encomion on Sosibius (fr. 384) may have been one of his earliest elegiac

[1] See above, p. 118, and below, pp. 171 ff.

[2] F. Chamoux, 'Le Roi Magas', *Revue historique* 216 (1956) 18 ff.; cf. below, p. 124, n. 4.

[3] It worried Niebuhr, *Kleine historische und philologische Schriften* 1 (1828) 229. 40, and still
confused Geyer, *RE* xiv (1930) 296. 60 ff. s.v. 'Magas', that Iustin. xxvi 3. 3 (and Hygin.
astr. 11 24) called Berenice's mother Apame, but Arsinoe. This mistake can now be
traced back to Call. fr. 110. 45, where Berenice is addressed and mount Athos is called
βουπόρος Ἀρσινόης μητρὸς σέο; the Scholion to this line correctly explains: κατὰ τιμὴν εἶπεν,
ἐπεὶ θυγάτηρ Ἀπάμας καὶ Μάγα. As a matter of fact, Ptolemy III and his wife, the θεοὶ Εὐεργέται, were officially honoured as the children of the θεοὶ Ἀδελφοί (see my note on Call. fr.
110. 45). The expression φίλη τεκέεσσι in the concluding lines of the *Lock of Berenice* (Call. fr.
110. 94 a, and Addenda in vol. 11 p. 116) left out by Catullus, must refer to Arsinoe, the 'diva
Venus' of ll. 89 f., 'dear to her children', Ptolemy and Berenice. It is understandable that
late ancient writers took Arsinoe as the real mother of Berenice. It is less excusable to trans-
late φίλη τεκέεσσι straightway with 'lieb den Eltern', as we read in the Artemis-*Bibliothek der
alten Welt*, 'Die Dichtungen des Kallimachos' (1955) 291.

[4] See above, pp. 93 and 95.

[5] See Callimachus vol. 11, pp. xxxviii ff. 'Quaestiones chronologicae selectae'; see also H.
Herter, *RE* Suppl. v (1931) 386 ff.

poems, written under Ptolemy I in Alexandria; the only well-attested facts are that he celebrated the marriage of Ptolemy II to his sister Arsinoe (between 278 and 273, perhaps 276/5 B.C.) by an epic, and the apotheosis of the queen (shortly after July 270 B.C.) by a lyric poem. This was apparently in the prime of his life; towards its end he composed the *Lock of Berenice* (246/5 B.C.) in honour of the Cyrenean princess recently married to Ptolemy III. It was this king[1] who sent for the other native of Cyrene, Eratosthenes, called a 'pupil' of Callimachus, to be librarian and probably tutor to his son.[2] Both the Cyreneans, very different from each other in age and spirit, seem to have been peculiar favourites of the young royal pair.

There is a complete unity of the creative poet and the reflective scholar in Callimachus.[3] We found this combination first in Philitas. Between him and Callimachus, however, Zenodotus had made a contribution of a new kind to scholarship, and institutions for its promotion had been founded by the kings and especially favoured by a king who was the pupil of Philitas and Zenodotus; so the younger generation started from a better position and was enabled to reach a higher degree of that unity than the older one. There is every reason to believe that Callimachus began to write poetry in his early years in Cyrene. We read on Cyrenean coins of the end of the fourth and the beginning of the third century the same names of members of a noble family as in one of his epigrams[4] in which he mourned their misfortunes. He was apparently still in his mother country when, as he tells us himself, he first put a writing tablet on his knees, and the Lycian Apollo addressed him as 'poet' and 'dear friend' and advised him on the art of poetry.[5] A few lines later he implies that he is one of those 'on whom the Muses have not looked askance in their childhood'.[6] In the proem to his greatest poetical achievement, the four books of the *Aitia*, he pictures himself transferred in dream from 'Libya' to Mount Helicon 'when his beard was just sprouting';[7] and 'Libya'—supposing that the anonymous epigram quotes

---

[1] Suid. v. Ἐρατοσθένης = Call. II test. 15.

[2] Wilamowitz, 'Ein Weihgeschenk des Eratosthenes', *NGG*, Phil.-hist. Kl. 1894. 31 = *Kleine Schriften* II (1941) 65; *Der Glaube der Hellenen* II (1932) 318. 1. See also above, p. 98.

[3] Strab. XVII 838 Καλλίμαχος . . . ποιητὴς ἅμα καὶ περὶ γραμματικὴν ἐσπουδακώς = Call. test. 16; see also below, p. 136.

[4] Call. *Ep.* 20 with my notes. F. Chamoux, 'Epigramme de Cyrène en l'honneur du roi Magas', *BCH* 82 (1958) 587. 3, listed the poems which he regards as 'Cyrenean' and promised to deal with them in another article. The new epigram found in Apollonia has no particular Callimachean flavour.

[5] Call. fr. 1. 21 f., see above, p. 95.   [6] Call. fr. 1. 37 παῖδας.

[7] Schol. Flor. 18 to Call. fr. 2 ἀρτιγένειος; epigr. adesp. *AP* VII 42 ὄνειαρ . . . μιν ἐκ Λιβύης ἀναείρας εἰς Ἑλικῶνα (see notes on fr. 2).

him exactly—can mean Cyrene more easily than Alexandria. When and why he left Cyrene for Alexandria[1] we do not know; we are only told that he started modestly as a schoolmaster in a suburb of the Egyptian capital called Eleusis.[2] This may have been under Ptolemy I;[3] since in the seventies, during the reign of Ptolemy II and his sister Arsinoe, Callimachus already moved in the court circle, celebrating royalty in the two poems we have mentioned, and he was probably still a 'young man' of the court when he was given a responsible commission in the royal library.[4] This swift career seems to have been due entirely to the extraordinary gifts of a masterful personality.

Callimachus' poems, in spite of their novelty, were informed by an exact and wide knowledge of the earlier poetry from which he drew his models. Practising his craft and reflecting on it went together. This reflection quite naturally extended to the literature of the past, to all the various forms of metre and language, and to the recondite sources of its subject-matter. Only the most passionate study could result in exquisite poetical workmanship, and only boundless curiosity could open the untrodden ways (fr. 1. 28) to new fields of learning. Ironically the poet hints at the danger of 'much knowledge' (ἡ πολυϊδρείη χαλεπὸν κακόν) in certain cases; on the other hand, the mere pleasure of listening and learning is to him the least perishable of pleasures in human life.[5]

Two points should be kept in mind. If his verse very often sounds like charming word-play, the poet is never tired of reminding us that everything he is going to tell is true because it is well attested (ἀμάρτυρον οὐδὲν ἀείδω);[6] the Muses, who once taught Hesiod and now answer Callimachus' questions, always utter the truth. In another case he refers to a local writer by name (fr. 75. 54) as his reliable source. In speaking of 'recondite sources', 'reliable source', we apply this word, which originally means the fountain of a stream or a river, figuratively to literature. In the beautiful finale of Callimachus' hymn to Apollo (*hy.* II 108–12) the god contrasts the filthy water of a great river with the clear droplets the bees

---

[1] A visit to Athens and an apprenticeship with Praxiphanes must be dismissed as modern inventions, see above, p. 95, n. 4.

[2] Suid. v. Καλλίμαχος = Call. test. 1. 8; his fifth Iambus (fr. 195) deals with a γραμματοδιδάσκαλος who taught children ἄλφα βῆτα.

[3] See above, p. 123, on the elegiac poem *Sosibius*.

[4] νεανίσκος τῆς αὐλῆς Tzetz. *Proleg.* Mb p. 31. 13 Kaib. = Call. test. 14 c. 17, cf. Ma 1, p. 25. 3 K. = Call. test. 14 b. 14 νεανίαι ἦσαν Καλλίμαχος (sscr. γρ. σώστρατος cod. A) καὶ Ἐρατοσθένης. Whatever these expressions mean, they can hardly refer to a man beyond his twenties.

[5] πολυϊδρείη fr. 75. 8; Strab. IX 438 πολυΐστωρ . . . καὶ πάντα τὸν βίον . . . ‘οὔατα μυθεῖσθαι βουλομέν[οις ἀνέχων]’ = fr. 178. 30; fr. 282 ἀκουή | εἰδυλίς.

[6] Call. fr. 612; cf. test. 79 πολυΐστορος ἀνδρὸς καὶ ἀξιοπίστου.

carry to Demeter from the pure and undefiled fountain-head.[1] In these metaphorical lines spoken by Apollo the poet condemns the lengthy traditional poem with its conventional formulae, but praises brevity and novelty in verse.[2] This meaning is quite obvious. But there seems to be implied another piece of advice, hardly recognized by modern interpreters of the hymn: poets should draw from the original pure source, not from its polluted derivatives. Callimachus was, as far as I can see, the first to use this image in a literary sense.[3] This demand of the scholar poet applies equally to poetry and to scholarship. It became a favourite image in the age of humanism and a fundamental concept of scholarship in the modern world.

If we consider Callimachus' general attitude, occasionally revealed in some lines of his poems, the remarkable feat of scholarship that he achieved in the library is perhaps not quite incomprehensible. His task was to find a system for arranging the texts of all the writers collected for the first time in the royal library (or libraries). When we glanced at the prehistory and early history of script and book in Greece, we observed the oriental background and commented cautiously on the relations between the orient and Greece.[4] Now in Alexandria a Greek library was founded on a grand scale;[5] and this reminds us of the enormous Babylonian and Assyrian libraries of old. It is natural to inquire whether there may have been direct influence, since the door of the east had been opened by Alexander much wider than before, and recent research[6] has at least put this question more urgently; but the answer so far is not very definite. The layout of the papyrus-rolls in the Alexandrian library seems to have resembled that of the clay tablets in the oriental libraries in one or perhaps two significant points. The title of a work was regularly placed at the end of the roll and of the tablet[7] (in contrast for instance to the practice in the Egyptian papyri), and in 'catalogues' not only this title, but also the 'incipit' was cited. On tablets and rolls the number of lines was occasionally counted, and these 'stichometrical' figures were put at the end and sometimes as running figures in the margins; they

---

[1] See Excursus. [2] Cf. below, p. 137.

[3] $\pi\eta\gamma\dot\eta = \dot a\rho\chi\dot\eta$ in Pind., Plat., etc., is totally different; the Callimachean metaphor has also nothing to do with the so-called 'source-research' that seeks to find out what was not invented by the author but taken over from an earlier 'source', see for instance 'Les sources de Plotin', *Entretiens sur l'antiquité classique* v (1960) and esp. the discussion by R. Harder, 'Quelle und Tradition', pp. 325 ff.

[4] Above, pp. 17 ff. [5] On the Lyceum see above, pp. 66 f.

[6] See Zuntz's and Wendel's publications, p. 7, n. 9, above.

[7] Cf. above, p. 18; Wendel, loc. cit. 24 ff., 76, and *passim*; 'Incipit', 29 ff.; stichometry, 34 ff., 44; on titulature see R. P. Oliver, 'The First Medicean MS of Tacitus and the Titulature of Ancient Books', *TAPA* 82 (1951) 232 ff., with examples from the papyri.

appear again in library-catalogues. The earliest example of title and number of lines placed at the end of a roll turned up in a recent publication of Menander's *Sicyonius*; the date of the papyrus seems to be the last third of the third century B.C., very near to Callimachus' lifetime. Even a personal remark of the scribe in verse is added, and these notes altogether may be properly called a 'colophon'.[1] There is very scanty evidence for libraries in the Ionic and Attic periods; but the same technical devices as in the east, or similar ones, may have been used in Greek private houses or in philosophical schools.

Whatever may have been achieved before the third century B.C., Callimachus had no real model for his immense undertaking. Though his task was probably not so much to create as to develop an appropriate method, he did it so successfully that his 'lists', called Πίνακες, were generally acknowledged as a model for the future. Besides the *Pinakes*, he assembled a variety of learned material helpful for the understanding of the ancient texts and invaluable for the writing of poetry in the new style; in these books he resumed the labours of the younger Sophists and the Peripatos with a new purpose.

For the Πίνακες Tzetzes is again our authority; after giving the number of books[2] in the two libraries he goes on to say: ὧν τοὺς πίνακας ὕστερον Καλλίμαχος ἀπεγράψατο. This sentence is slightly enlarged in another later version: ὡς (?) ὁ Καλλίμαχος νεανίσκος ὢν τῆς αὐλῆς ὑστέρως μετὰ τὴν ἀνόρθωσιν τοὺς πίνακας αὐτῶν ἀπεγράψατο; then a reference to Eratosthenes follows[3] and finally the remark: ἀλλὰ τὰ Καλλιμάχου καὶ τοῦ Ἐρατοσθένους μετὰ βραχύν τινα χρόνον ἐγένετο τῆς συναγωγῆς τῶν βίβλων, ὡς ἔφην, καὶ διορθώσεως κἂν ἐπ᾽ αὐτοῦ τοῦ Πτολεμαίου τοῦ Φιλαδέλφου. Obviously it is the sequence of events that is stressed in both versions of the *Prolegomena*: ὕστερον—ὑστέρως μετὰ τ. ἀ.—μετὰ βραχύν τινα χρόνον. Therefore the change of ὑστέρως to ἱστορεῖ ὅς, proposed by Dziatzko and accepted by most modern editors, is not justified.[4] This

---

[1] Menand. *Sicyonius* edd. A. Blanchard et A. Bataille, *Recherches de Papyrologie* III (1964) 161: Pap. Sorb. 2272, col. XXI, pl. XIII. Colophon, although a Greek word, is not an ancient term, but a modern one (not before the eighteenth century?) for the device at the end of early printed books, 'containing the title, the printer's name and the date and place of printing 1774', see *The Shorter Oxford English Dictionary*, s.v. colophon. The word is frequently applied to mere titles at the end of a roll, as if synonymous with 'subscription'; I think it had better be reserved for the cases in which more personal remarks of the scribe were added (as with the printer in modern times); there is no occurrence so far of the name of a scribe in Greek antiquity.

[2] Cf. above, p. 101, where the full text of the version Pb is quoted (cf. Ma p. 25. 2 K.).

[3] See below, p. 153, n. 5.

[4] Call. test. 14 c. I kept ὑστέρως with reference to the parallel ὕστερον in 14 a. Cantarella who reprinted Tzetz. and all the other testimonia (above, p. 100, n. 1), p. 59. 14 did not even mention the manuscript reading in his app. crit.

conjecture would enormously enhance the authority of Tzetzes' report, as it makes Callimachus himself the ultimate source of at least a part of the *Prolegomena*. The unfortunate Italian humanist[1] had no scruples about producing the following 'translation' on the margin of his Plautine codex: 'sicuti refert Callimacus aulicus regius bibliothecarius qui etiam singulis voluminibus titulos inscripsit.' *Hinc illae lacrimae*. Here we have Callimachus not only quoted as a literary authority, but also elevated to the official rank of court-librarian; there is no evidence that he held this position except this slip of the 'translator', and there is not even room for him in the well-known series of librarians.[2]

Tzetzes apparently had in mind a sort of catalogue of books extant in the library. Hesychius–Suidas' biographical article Καλλίμαχος, once probably the introduction to an edition of Callimachus' collected poems (of which therefore very few titles were mentioned in the biography) points to a comprehensive 'bibliography': Πίνακες τῶν ἐν πάσῃ παιδείᾳ διαλαμψάντων καὶ ὧν συνέγραψαν, ἐν βιβλίοις κ΄ καὶ ρ΄, 'Tables of all those who were eminent in any kind of literature and of their writings in 120 books'.[3] The previous generation had done some quite respectable scholarly work in the library at least on the foremost poets,[4] without waiting for catalogues and bibliographies, and this may have been very helpful now in the completion of the *Pinakes*. It is Suidas' description—as we should expect from his much better sources—not Tzetzes' that is correct; this is confirmed by the fragments[5] still preserved. The distinction between a mere library catalogue and a critical inventory of Greek literature is sometimes obscured in modern literature on Callimachus' great work; it was certainly based on his knowledge of the books available in the library, but he also had regard to works only mentioned in earlier literature and to questions of authenticity.[6]

The entire body of Greek literature, the πᾶσα παιδεία, was divided into several classes: only three are attested by verbal quotations: ῥητορικά (fr. 430–2, cf. 443–8), νόμοι (fr. 433), παντοδαπὰ συγγράμματα (fr. 434/5). From references to epic (fr. 452/3), lyric (fr. 441, 450), tragic (fr. 449?, 451), comic poets (fr. 439/40), to philosophers (fr. 438?, 442), historians

[1] Cf. above, p. 101.   [2] See below, p. 142.
[3] Suid. v. Καλλίμαχος = Call. test. 1; translation by A. W. Mair.
[4] See above, p. 106; Tzetzes *Prolegomena to Comedy* and other sources mention poetry only, and this was no doubt the starting-point, but some work on the prose writers cannot be excluded.
[5] Fr. 429–53 and Addenda; conclusions and references after fr. 453, p. 349. Next to the monograph of Schmidt, *Pinakes*, Wendel, *Buchbeschreibung* 69 ff., and O. Regenbogen, *RE* xx (1950) v. *Πίναξ* 1420–6, are to be consulted. P. Moraux, *Les listes anciennes des ouvrages d'Aristote*, 1951, 221 ff. For the only new fragment see below, p. 130, n. 5.
[6] See fr. 442, 445, 446, 449; on fr. 456 see below, p. 132, n. 6.

(fr. 437), and medical writers (fr. 429?) registered in the *Pinakes* we may conclude that seven further classes existed; there were probably many more and a number of subdivisions. It is now fairly certain that the individual authors of every class were arranged in alphabetical order; each name was accompanied by a few biographical details, and later writers were sometimes disappointed by what they considered deficiencies (fr. 447). Less conscientious, even sensational, the vast biographical work of Hermippus of Smyrna,[1] who is called 'peripateticus' as well as Καλλιμάχειος, may be regarded as a more popular supplement to the esoteric *Pinakes*. But we may doubt if his master Callimachus liked it; he had confined himself to the reliable evidence for the lives and works of literary men. The list of their writings which followed the biography cannot always have been arranged in the same way, but the alphabetical system seems to have prevailed. The little we know of some minor epics and all we know of the dramatic poems leads to this assumption, if indeed the order in the lists of later antiquity is derived from the *Pinakes*.[2] The best example is the famous κατάλογος τῶν Αἰσχύλου δραμάτων which was once obviously an appendix to the life of the poet and still presents to us the titles of seventy-three plays, tragedies, and satyr-plays, in strictly alphabetical order.[3] For Euripides there were only fragments of two inscriptional catalogues,[4] until recently published papyri brought very welcome new evidence for titles of his plays arranged in order of the initial letter. In the most important of these papyri,[5] which gives summaries of the plots, the title is followed by the formula οὗ (ἧς, ὧν) ἀρχή and the citation of the first line. This 'incipit' had been introduced by Callimachus in his *Pinakes*, for instance: ἐπικὸν δὲ τὸ ποίημα, οὗ ἡ ἀρχή, followed by the opening verse of the poem (fr. 436).[6] A mere title might have been ambiguous, particularly in the case of prose writings; the 'incipit' made the identification easier. A list similar to that of Aeschylus' plays is preserved in two manuscripts of Aristophanes, where brief details of his life are followed by an alphabetical catalogue of his comedies.[7] Menander

---

[1] F. Leo, *Die griechisch-römische Biographie nach ihrer literarischen Form* (1901) 130 f.; on Hermippus ibid. 124 ff. On Hermippus see also Moraux loc. cit. 221 ff. and below, p. 150.

[2] On Callimachus' special *chronological* table of the dramatic poets see below, p. 132.

[3] Aesch. ed. Wilamowitz, ed. mai. (1914) 7 f.; ed. G. Murray, ed. II (1955) 375. The catalogue is preserved in two codices, M and V.

[4] *IG* xiv 1152 and *IG* ii/iii² 2363. 38 ff.

[5] *P.Oxy.* 2455 in *Oxyrhynchus Papyri* xxvii ed. E. G. Turner and others (1962), see also 2456, 2457, and 2462 (Menander); they are all assigned to the second century A.D. See below, p. 195, n. 4.

[6] Cf. fr. 443, 444, 449; see also Wendel, *Buchbeschreibung*, pp. 32–34 and n. 198, and below, p. 130.

[7] A critical edition based on a new collation of the Milan and Vatican codices by R. Cantarella, *Aristof. Com.* I (1949) no. 231, pp. 142 ff.

may have found a place in the *Pinakes*, like Alexis (fr. 439) and Diphilus (fr. 440); for the beginning of an alphabetical list of his plays (titles only) is preserved in a papyrus.[1]

Cataloguing the lyric poetry (τὰ μελικά) must have presented thorny problems. Callimachus divided the great triadic poems (which we usually call 'choral', although we often cannot tell whether they were actually sung by a choir)[2] into special groups (εἴδη). Simonides' songs of victory, for instance, were called ἐπίνικοι and subdivided according to the type of contest (foot-race, pentathlon, etc.);[3] for we know that Callimachus (fr. 441)[4] had described a part of the *Epinicia* as ἐπίνικοι δρομέσι, 'for runners'. Pindar's *Epinicia* must also have been divided into several groups, but in a different way, according to the place of the contests (Olympia, Nemea, etc.); otherwise it would not have been possible to say that Callimachus (fr. 450) placed the second Pythian ode, as it was later named although it actually celebrated a local victory of Hieron, among the Nemean odes. Finally Bacchylides' dithyrambs seem to have been separated from his paeans; for Callimachus was blamed for having entered among the paeans a poem which Aristarchus declared to be a dithyramb and entitled *Cassandra*.[5] We know these classifications from references to the editions of lyric texts, begun by Aristophanes of Byzantium, and from later grammatical sources;[6] but it is easily forgotten that some fundamental terms and formulae were, if not coined, at least first attested in the Callimachean *Pinakes*. Although we can recognize certain groups of choral songs, we still cannot guess how the individual poems were arranged. No doubt they were registered somehow,[7] as the references to Pindar's second Pythian ode and Bacchylides' *Cassandra* demonstrate. Because the dithyrambs and probably the νόμοι had titles like the plays, they could easily have been listed in alphabetical order. But what about all the others, especially the monostrophic poems of Sappho, Alcaeus, Anacreon? They had no titles; and therefore the only way to register them, it seems, was according to the 'incipit',[8] a method still applied in modern indexes of lyric poems of an author or of an anthology.

---

[1] *P.Oxy.* 2462 (cf. 2456 Euripides), see above, p. 129, n. 5.

[2] See Excursus.

[3] *PMG* 506–17 Page, partly in *AL* ɪɪ², Simonid. fr. 14–23 Diehl. On the arrangement in Aristophanes' edition see below, p. 183.

[4] Cf. E. Lobel on *P.Oxy.* xxv (1959) 2431, fr. 1.

[5] *P.Oxy.* xxiii ed. E. Lobel (1956) 2368. 16; Bacchyl. 23 ed. B. Snell⁸ (1961) 73 and 50*; cf. below, p. 222.

[6] H. Färber, *Die Lyrik in der Kunsttheorie der Antike*, 1936; A. E. Harvey, 'The Classification of Greek Lyric Poetry', *Cl. Qu.* N.S. v (1955) 157 ff.

[7] Schmidt p. 77 was quite right against Regenbogen's doubts col. 1421.

[8] See above, p. 129.

Callimachus lavished his efforts also upon the classification of the prose writers; the different classes, as far as we can make out their names, have been noted above.[1] In principle the arrangement followed the same lines as in the poetical section; but the difficulties were greater than in the *Pinakes* of the poets, as the case of Prodicus shows; Callimachus listed him with the orators (quite correctly, I should say),[2] but others objected that he belonged to the philosophers (fr. 431). The names of writers in every class were given in the usual alphabetical order (fr. 435). The works of each author may have been subdivided into several groups, such as public and private speeches; subdivision was unavoidable in the case of πολυείδεια (fr. 449; 429?). Individual speeches that had titles, for instance Περὶ Ἁλοννήσου (fr. 443), Περὶ τῶν συμμοριῶν (fr. 432) of Demosthenes, or Περὶ Φερενίκου (fr. 448) of Lysias, could be listed alphabetically, though the 'incipit' was usually added (fr. 443, 444). But in cases where there was no title, or where the authorship of speeches (fr. 444–7) or whole books (fr. 437) was a matter of dispute, we have no clue to the arrangement. It seems to be over-optimistic to see in the famous complete list of Theophrastus' writings (Diog. L. v 42–50) a sort of enlarged copy of Callimachus' *Pinakes*;[3] the very complicated tradition does not recommend this simple solution. Neither can we trace the list of Aristotle's writings (Diog. L. v 22–27) back to Callimachus as the ultimate source.[4] As regards the philosophers in the *Pinakes* our knowledge is deplorably poor.[5] Our information is much more precise on the 'Miscellanea' (παντοδαπὰ συγγράμματα fr. 434–5); under this heading a number of writings were registered that did not fit into the main categories of literature. For instance, Athenaeus in his *Deipnosophists*, being particularly concerned with books about 'dinners', has preserved an excerpt with the name of the author of one (a well-known Athenian parasite), the title, the opening words and the number of lines[6] (fr. 434), and another excerpt containing an alphabetical list of four writers on pastry cooking (fr. 435). The intention was clearly to omit nothing from this inventory of the πᾶσα παιδεία, not even books on cookery.

Besides the general *Pinakes* two special ones are known that differ totally from the main work in being one chronological, one linguistic.

[1] See above, p. 128.
[2] See above, pp. 39 ff.
[3] Against the optimism of Schmidt, *Pinakes* 86, see O. Regenbogen, *RE* Suppl. vii (1940) 1363 ff. and xx (1950) 1422 and 1441 ff.
[4] P. Moraux, *Les listes anciennes des ouvrages d'Aristote* (1951) 233, and Düring, *Aristotle* 67 f., agree with this negative statement; their own theories differ from each other.
[5] On Democritus see below, p. 132.
[6] On stichometrics see above, pp. 126 f., and Schmidt, *Pinakes* 69 f.

Both titles are extant only in Suidas' article.[1] The first is Πίναξ καὶ
ἀναγραφὴ τῶν κατὰ χρόνους καὶ ἀπ' ἀρχῆς γενομένων διδασκάλων 'Table
and register of the dramatic poets in chronological order and from the
beginning'. This Pinax must have been based on Aristotle's διδασκαλίαι[2]
taken from the documents in the archon's archives. Alexander Aetolus
and Lycophron had busied themselves with the tragic and comic texts
in the Alexandrian library in the early third century;[3] in its second half
Eratosthenes and Aristophanes devoted major works to the Attic drama.
Between them Callimachus compiled his record, the great scale of which
we can still guess from fragments of three inscriptions found in Rome,
where they had probably occupied a wall in a great library.[4] Körte's
suggestion that the inscriptions are a more or less exact apographon of
the Callimachean Pinax has been universally accepted. The parts preserved enumerate the Dionysiac and Lenaian victories of comic poets
from 440 to 352 B.C.; but if the title given by Suidas is correct the Pinax
extended back to the ἀρχή, that is, to the introduction of comedy into
each of the two festivals, the City Dionysia in 486 B.C. and the Lenaia in
442 B.C. The second special Pinax was apparently a list of glosses, and it
is not surprising to find Callimachus following Philitas and Zenodotus[5]
as glossographer; what surprises is the wording in Suidas: Πίναξ τῶν
Δημοκράτους γλωσσῶν καὶ συνταγμάτων(?).[6] Whatever is meant by
συντάγματα (probably 'writings'),[7] its connexion with γλῶσσαι is strange,
as 'a list of writings' should belong to the great general *Pinakes*. It is, of
course, easy to change the proper name to Δημοκρίτου. Democritus was
a bold innovator in the language of philosophy, but it can hardly be said
that his own language is distinguished by obsolete words. We must also
remember[8] that he wrote something himself on Homer's language and his
glosses, although only the title remains, as in the case of Callimachus'
Democritean Pinax.[9]

---

[1] Call. II test. 1, cf. above, p. 128; fr. 454–6 Call. 1 pp. 349 f. Regenbogen, Πίναξ,
RE xx (1950) 1423. 38 tried to change the odd sequence of words. It is worth while to stress
again the correct view of the young Nietzsche, see note on fr. 456 and cf. above, p. 50, n. 4.

[2] See above, p. 81, on Aristotle's work in the archives and on the term διδάσκαλος.

[3] See above, pp. 105 f.

[4] *IG* xiv 1098 a, 1097, 1098 (A. Wilhelm, *Urkunden dramatischer Aufführungen in Athen* [1906]
195 ff., 255); for further references see my note on Call. fr. 456; the texts are now reprinted
with notes by A. Pickard-Cambridge, *The Dramatic Festivals of Athens* (Oxford 1953) 121–3, cf.
p. 72.   [5] See above, pp. 90 and 115.

[6] Call. II test. 1 and 1 p. 350 after fr. 456 (where the reading of the manuscripts is omitted;
see also Corrigenda II p. 122). *Vors.* 68 A 32 the conjecture of Demetrius Chalkondylas (1499)
Δημοκρίτου is printed without any reference to Δημοκράτους in the codices; but D.-Kr. mention the frequent form -κρατους for -κριτου in the notes to B 35, 160, 161, 178.

[7] Cf. Apollon. Dysc. *Pron.* 65. 17 Schn. and *Synt.* 78. 4 Uhl. συντάγματα 'prose books'.

[8] See above, pp. 42 f. Democritus' language and his books on literature.

[9] Callimachus' critical acumen should no longer be credited with having unmasked the

We have taken pains to call attention to many dry and sometimes baffling titles. Inconspicuous as the individual headings may look, the impression of the whole is overwhelming. To amass hundreds of thousands of rolls in the library would have been of little use without a sensible classification that enabled the prospective reader to find the books he needed. For the first time in history the *Pinakes* of Callimachus made the greatest treasures of literature accessible by dividing poetry and prose books into appropriate classes and by listing the authors in alphabetical order. Only the most passionate desire to save the complete literary heritage of the past from oblivion and to make it a permanent and fruitful possession for all ages could have provided strength and patience for this immense effort. Querulous critics of the scholar poets', Philitas, Callimachus, and their followers in ancient and modern times, may carp at the excessive learning of their poetry and at the amateurish deficiencies of their scholarship. But they should not undervalue the fervent devotion to learning that sprang from the enthusiasm of a great poet.

No doubt the 120 books of the *Pinakes* gave plenty of scope for additions and corrections; even our short quotations have revealed this again and again. Aristophanes of Byzantium published a whole book Πρὸς τοὺς Καλλιμάχου πίνακας.[1] Πρός is ambiguous and often means 'against' in titles, but there is not the slightest reason to assume that Aristophanes ever wrote 'Against Callimachus' *Pinakes*'; his book was meant to be a supplement, which certainly was very welcome about fifty years afterwards, and he made use of Callimachus' chronological tables of the Attic dramatists[2] for the summaries of plays in his editions. This was the immediate effect; but everyone who needed biographical[3] material, who undertook editions of texts, who wrote on any literary subject had to consult the great work; it has never been superseded by a better one. The anonymous Πίνακες[4] of the rival library in Pergamum, very rarely quoted, once for a comic poet and twice for orators, did not compare

Democritean forgeries of Bolos (Suid. s.v. *Βῶλος Δημοκρίτειος*); this strange fellow lived towards the end of the third century B.C. or even later, as the best expert on pseudo-scientific ancient literature finally found out, Max Wellmann, 'Marcellus von Side', *Philol. Suppl.* XXVII 2 (1934) 1 ff., with further references; see also *Vors.* II⁵ 68 B 300 and A. J. Festugière, *La Révélation d'Hermès Trismégiste* I (1950) 196 ff., 222 ff. and Add. 432. F. Schmidt, *Pinakes* 97 f., and Rehm–Vogel, *Exakte Wissenschaften*⁴ (1933) 57 and 63, relied on earlier publications of Wellmann.

[1] See my notes after Call. fr. 453, and below on Praxiphanes p. 135 and on Polemon, p. 248, n. 1.

[2] Call. fr. 456.

[3] See above, p. 129.

[4] Schmidt, *Pinakes*, p. 28 fr. 3 ἐν τοῖς Περγαμηνοῖς πίναξι (fr. 4 has to be cancelled); cf. ibid p. 104 and the whole chapter V on the after-effect of the *Pinakes* 99 ff. See also Regenbogen, *Pinax* col. 1424 ff.

in importance with the Alexandrian *Pinakes* of Callimachus upon which they were probably modelled.

A number of titles, some of them found only in Suidas' article, and some short quotations give an idea of the variety of learned books published under Callimachus' name;[1] in preparing them he may have been assisted by friends and pupils. A throng of students was drawn to Alexandria by the new longing for unlimited knowledge[2] and the fact that incomparably richer material was now offered there than ever before in Athens or elsewhere. The Sophists had had epideictic-oratorical aims in their treatment of literary, especially poetical, subjects, and the great Attic philosophers and their schools had had their philosophical purposes. Now for the first time we find wide literary knowledge being acquired for the sake of the literary tradition itself, that is, for the works to be written in the present age and for the preservation and understanding of the works written in past ages. This is the new separate[3] discipline of scholarship.

The books of Callimachus the scholar (γραμματικός) are often regarded as mechanical compilations of antiquities. As a matter of fact they are not restricted at all to antiquarian matter; we can apply our old scheme to them, though perhaps in a different sequence, briefly reviewing his books on antiquities, on language, and on literary criticism, and finally considering how far he may be regarded as an interpreter of earlier Greek poetry.

The Νόμιμα βαρβαρικά were an antiquarian collection of 'Non-Greek Customs', possibly supplementing Aristotle's book with the same title.[4] A general book Περὶ ἀγώνων probably belongs to the same group, since some of the Sophists and Aristotle and his school[5] frequently compiled material 'On games'. The forty-four excerpts in Antigonus of Carystus, *Hist. mirab.* 129–73, from Callimachus' Παράδοξα[6] show him as a writer on marvels; his keen curiosity for 'Incredibilities' led him to make this *Collection of marvels in all the earth according to localities*[7] from historical, geographical, and antiquarian sources. There is no earlier example of

[1] Fr. 403–28, 457–9, 461–6, 693; fr. 403 ff. are arranged according to the alphabetical order of the titles.

[2] See above, pp. 125 ff.

[3] See above, p. 3.

[4] Call. fr. 405 with notes; on Aristotle see above, p. 83.

[5] Call. fr. 403; on Hippias the Sophist see above, pp. 5 ff., on Aristotle pp. 79 ff., on Duris, the Peripatetic historian, and others see notes to fr. 401.

[6] Thomas Stanley was the first to discover these substantial excerpts, not Bentley, see Call. II, p. XLV. 1 and Addenda p. 122.

[7] Θαυμάτων τῶν εἰς ἅπασαν τὴν γῆν κατὰ τόπους ὄντων συναγωγή is the title in Suidas' table; see fr. 407, 1–XLIV, 408–11.

paradoxography as a distinct literary genre. Like Philitas and Zenodotus he was not scientifically minded, as this work reveals better than any other; there is no recognizable intercourse between science and scholarship in Alexandria before Eratosthenes.

From a book entitled Ἐθνικαὶ ὀνομασίαι,[1] that is, *Local nomenclature*, special names for fishes in different cities (Chalcedon, Thurii, Athens) are quoted; as there was a chapter on fishes, the arrangement of the whole must have been by subjects. Though unproven, it is not impossible that the titles Περὶ ἀνέμων (fr. 404), Περὶ ὀρνέων (fr. 414–28), Μηνῶν προσηγορίαι κατὰ ἔθνος καὶ πόλεις (p. 339, *Local Month-names*) are only the sub-titles of other chapters in the same comprehensive Onomastikon. This vocabulary was certainly not arranged in alphabetical order like Zenodotus' *Glossai*.[2] The relation of names to things was a philosophical problem, discussed at length in Plato's *Cratylus* and also by Aristotle.[3] But Callimachus listed and disposed all the names he could find for the purely literary reasons which we have just stated; it was the first vocabulary of its kind, as far as we know, and was eagerly used by Aristophanes of Byzantium and later generations. It can hardly be decided whether works entitled Κτίσεις νήσων καὶ πόλεων καὶ μετονομασίαι (p. 339) and Περὶ τῶν ἐν τῇ οἰκουμένῃ ποταμῶν (fr. 457–9) belong to the books on antiquities or to the books on language; 'changes of name' rather point to the second group. There remain a few headings and fragments for which we are completely at a loss to find a place, or even to understand the titles.[4] But the important fact is that we are able to find traces of nearly all the learned collections of Callimachus in his poems:[5] fair-sounding names of rivers and islands, of winds and nymphs and birds were picked out of them to embellish the verses, and a number of fine local stories was found in them and saved from oblivion.

One book has been left out of this cursory survey, Callimachus' *Against Praxiphanes*, Πρὸς Πραξιφάνην (fr. 460); we mentioned it earlier, when we were pointing out non-Aristotelian features in the whole new movement in Alexandria.[6] The only fragment quoted from this book is clear evidence

---

[1] Call. fr. 406; in the notes I should have referred also to C. Wendel, 'Onomastikon', *RE* XVIII (1939) 508.

[2] See above, p. 115.

[3] On Plato *Cratylus* see above, pp. 59 ff., on Aristotle pp. 76 and 79. Democritus' so-called Ὀνομαστικά or Gorgias' Ὀνομαστικόν (p. 45, n. 6) are of dubious authenticity.

[4] Περὶ λογάδων (fr. 412), Μουσεῖον (Call. I p. 339, see above, p. 50, on Alcidamas), Περὶ νυμφῶν (fr. 413), Ὑπομνήματα (fr. 461–4; on ὑπόμνημα see above, p. 29), two prose fragments without title (fr. 465/6).

[5] See my short notes to fr. 403–66 and to fr. 43 and 580 on κτίσεις.

[6] See above, pp. 95 f. with n. 4 and p. 125, n. 1.

of literary criticism in so far as it asserts the high poetical qualities of the work of his contemporary Aratus:[1] μέμνηται γοῦν αὐτοῦ (sc. Arati) καὶ Καλλίμαχος ὡς πρεσβυτέρου οὐ μόνον ἐν τοῖς Ἐπιγράμμασιν (*Ep.* 27), ἀλλὰ καὶ ἐν τοῖς Πρὸς Πραξιφάνην, πάνυ ἐπαινῶν αὐτὸν ὡς πολυμαθῆ καὶ ἄριστον ποιητήν. As we know of no other similar book by Callimachus, the polemics against the Peripatetic Praxiphanes may have included both his judgement on Plato's incompetence as a literary critic[2] (the more so as Praxiphanes' Περὶ ποιητῶν[3] was a dialogue between Plato and Isocrates), and also his famous maxim: τὸ μέγα βιβλίον ἴσον τῷ μεγάλῳ κακῷ. Whatever βιβλίον[4] here means, μέγα κακόν, a 'great evil', is a sort of old formula (*O* 134, ι 423), and μέγας with reference to literature is always vituperative; we may compare the filthy μέγας ῥόος in contrast to the pure ὀλίγη λιβάς (*hy.* II 108),[5] or the μεγάλη γυνή of a poem contrasted with subtle small-scale ones, κατὰ λεπτόν (fr. 1. 12). As in the case of Aratus the statement in the prose book has its exact parallel in an epigram, so also there are obvious parallels in the poems to the two other passages tentatively ascribed to the same prose writing. Plato was deemed an incompetent critic, as we have just seen; the reason was that he appreciated the poetry of Antimachus, whose *Lyde* Callimachus condemned in an epigram (fr. 398) as 'a fat and not lucid book'. The general disapproval of the μέγα βιβλίον uttered in the prose maxim is a common topic in Callimachus' poems and is the particular theme of his introductory elegy to the *Aitia* against his adversaries, whom he calls 'Telchines'.[6]

A list of these adversaries compiled by a learned scholiast[7] includes the name of Praxiphanes the Mytilenean; this is invaluable evidence for the opposition between the poet and a leading Peripatetic and shows that the ambiguous Πρός in the title means '*against* Praxiphanes'. There is no tradition that Praxiphanes had personally attacked Callimachus in his writings. The learned collections and also the *Pinakes* may give the impression of being rather Aristotelian in subject-matter, despite their new purpose;[8] but in literary criticism Aristotle's theory and Callimachus' views are plainly incompatible.[9] As the one relevant prose book is almost lost, we have to rely mainly on the poems. Again and again, charmingly as well as firmly, he put forward his clear and consistent opinions. He is never pedantic, but rather humorous and ironical or even of a lively

---

[1] Cf. above, pp. 120 f.   [2] See above, p. 94.
[3] Praxiphan. fr. 2 Brink = fr. 11 Wehrli.
[4] On its various meanings see Wendel, *Buchbeschreibung* 56 ff.
[5] Cf. above, p. 126.
[6] Call. fr. 1.
[7] Schol. Florentina to fr. 1, l. 7, p. 3.   [8] See above, p. 134.
[9] Cf. above, p. 88.

aggressive spirit. Aristotle, we remember, in the severest of styles demanded organic unity of every artistic work: ἕν, ὅλον, τέλος, μέγεθος were the decisive terms.[1] All parts must have a definite relation to the whole work, which itself is distinguished by completeness and magnitude. The *Iliad* and *Odyssey*, but not the other epics, are living organisms of this kind; they and the masterpieces of Attic tragedy alone fulfil these requirements. If it were possible for any further poetical works to be produced at all,[2] they must somehow conform to this standard prescribed by Aristotle. Now Callimachus regarded Homer with the same devotion and affection as Aristotle had done,[3] in contrast to everything 'cyclic' (*Ep.* 28), which lacked organic unity, but abounded in traditional formulae. For that very reason he esteemed Homer inimitable, even unapproachable. It would be a vain ambition to vie with him and the other great poets of the past; if poetry lived on, it was bound to follow principles quite different from those inferred by Aristotle from the ancient poems (τὰ ἀρχαῖα). For years poetical criticism had been in the hands of Sophists and theorizing philosophers; the time had come for a return to its originators, the practising poets.

The new poetical school of Callimachus and his followers was ostentatiously anti-Aristotelian. Rejecting unity, completeness, and magnitude, it consciously aimed at a discontinuous form (fr. 1. 3 οὐχ ἓν ἄεισμα διηνεκές) in a more or less loose series of pieces of a few lines (fr. 1. 9 ὀλιγόστιχος). The proper quality of a poem was to be λεπτόν 'subtle'.[4] It has been rightly noticed that this key term and a few other ones had already occurred in Aristophanes' comedies, especially in the critical passages of the *Frogs*: τέχνη / [κρίνετε] . . . τὴν σοφίην (Call. fr. 1. 17 f.) is almost a verbal quotation.[5] But the truth of this observation was overlaid by two hypotheses: namely that Aristophanes borrowed his phrases from a Sophistic source, probably Gorgias, and that Callimachus used a rhetorical source on the *genera dicendi*. No proof of these hypotheses has yet been produced;[6] they remain a strange but typical example of the

---

[1] See above, p. 74. [2] Aristot. *Poet.* ch. 23 f., esp. p. 1459 b 22.
[3] Also the *Margites* is Homeric to him as to Aristotle, see fr. 397.
[4] E. Reitzenstein, 'Zur Stiltheorie des Kallimachos', *Festschrift für R. Reitzenstein* (1931) 25–40 on λεπτός, ibid. p. 29. 2 M. Pohlenz on Aristoph. *Ran.* 828, 876, 956, 1108, 1111. A great deal of the evidence in Aristophanes had already been better collected and interpreted by J. D. Denniston, 'Technical Terms in Aristophanes', *Cl. Qu.* 21 (1927) 119 f.; see also Aristoph. fr. nov. 33 a Demiańczuk (= Satyr. *vit. Eurip.* p. 3. 20 von Arnim, *Suppl. Eur.*) τὰ λ[επ]τὰ ῥήματ᾽ [ἐξεσ]μήχετο.
[5] Therefore one can risk putting Housman's supplement into the text; Aristoph. *Ran.* 766, 779, 785.
[6] On Aristophanes see above, pp. 47 f.; on Callimachus' supposed rhetorical model see E. Reitzenstein (above, n. 4) 37 ff.

modern quest for hidden sources. The natural assumption is that the
Hellenistic poets derived their critical terminology directly from the
poets of the fifth century, whom they knew so well. Substantial parts of
Callimachus' *Iambi* are indebted to Attic comedy; there is no need to
invent intermediate handbooks. The meaning of the word λεπτός underwent a characteristic change; while it was once used disapprovingly of
over-refinement of spirit or diction, for instance, that of Euripides in
contrast to the vigour that Aeschylus achieved through the magnitude
(μέγεθος) of his words, the Alexandrians, Callimachus, Hedylus, Leo-
nidas, employed it as a term of the highest praise to describe the style they
were eager to achieve in their poems. We find another significant epithet
in the Praxiphanes pamphlet, where Aratus was praised as a poet of the
highest rank: πολυμαθής. 'Much learning'[1] was in archaic times a reproach against those who had no true wisdom; but this word also came
to have the opposite connotation in the Hellenistic age; unlimited
knowledge of subject-matter and language was now deemed an indispensable requisite for the new poetry called σοφίη (Call. fr. 1. 18).

Looking back on Callimachus' own πολυμαθίη amassed in his prose
works, we may ask whether they can be assigned to a particular epoch of
his life. When the epilogue of the *Aitia* came to light, the first editor[2] saw
in the concluding line Callimachus' 'formal farewell to poetry' and
a declaration 'that he will now devote himself to prose'; indeed his
appointment at the Alexandrian library was regarded as the point in his
career at which he turned from poetry to prose. But αὐτὰρ ἐγὼ Μουσέων
πεζὸν [ἔ]πειμι νομόν indicates the *Musa pedestris* of the *Iambi* which followed the *Aitia* in the final edition arranged by the poet himself;[3] the
pentameter gives no answer to this or any other question of chronology.

When we divided Callimachus' prose works into three groups, on
antiquities, on language, and on literary criticism, we asked whether
there was not a fourth one on interpretation. As far as we know, he never
edited a text or wrote a commentary; the few fragments of his Ὑπομνήματα[4] seem to indicate a collection of mythological, linguistic, and
geographical material. But in many passages of his poems he discloses his

---

[1] πολυμαθίη Heraclit. *Vors.* 22 B 40; cf. Plat. *Leg.* 811 AB, 819 A against πολυμαθία and
Phaedr. 275 A against the πολυγνώμονες. On Hippias as πολυμαθής see p. 52, n. 5.

[2] *The Oxyrhynchus Papyri* VII (1910) ed. A. S. Hunt, p. 18 on Fol. 2 verso of *P.Oxy.* 1011,
l. 89.

[3] On text and interpretation see Call. fr. 112. 9 and the discussion in *Philol.* 87 (1932) 226 f.
and Call. II p. XXXVI; the correct reading πεζὸν, not πεζὸς (confirmed by E. Lobel's revision
of the papyrus) and interpretation were found by R. Herzog, *Berl. Philol. Wochenschr.* 1911,
p. 29. Various opinions are registered by H. Herter, Bursian 255 (1937) 144 f.

[4] Above, p. 135, n. 4.

acquaintance with the *Iliad* and *Odyssey* and occasionally allows us to guess not only what text he chose but also how he understood its meaning. In this sense only he may with reserve be called an 'interpreter' of Homer.[1]

First of all we should like to know how far Callimachus used Zenodotus' new critical edition of Homer and how far he relied on pre-critical texts, τὰ ἀρχαῖα ἀντίγραφα, such as Timon recommended to Aratus.[2] Several Callimachean readings of the Homeric text seem to agree with those known to us only as Zenodotean. The beautiful Naxian girl, Cydippe, took part in 'the dance of sleeping Ariede, Ἀριήδης / [ἐς χ]ορὸν εὐδούσης, Callimachus tells us (fr. 67. 13); in the famous Homeric passage to which he alludes, χορόν . . . οἷον . . . Δαίδαλος ἤσκησεν . . . Ἀριάδνῃ (Σ 592), only Zenodotus read Ἀριήδῃ. This certainly is a most remarkable coincidence; but as Zenodotus constituted his text on earlier manuscripts[3] that he found reliable, the same sources may have been accessible to Callimachus. Although it is possible or even very probable that he followed Zenodotus, the coincidence in this and about ten similar cases[4] is not conclusive proof. At least one example proves that Callimachus also consulted other texts older than the Zenodotean edition: only the 'city-editions'[5] had the unique variant reading νήσων ἔπι θηλυτεράων (Φ 454 and X 45), from which he transferred the epithet to another noun, θηλύτατον πεδίον (fr. 548), 'the most fertile plain'.[6] By connecting θηλύτατον with πεδίον Callimachus gave his 'interpretation' of the Homeric phrase: it does not mean 'island where females reign', like Lemnos and Imbros, but 'island that is εὔγειος', with good soil, fertile. It is possible that he consulted the elementary explanatory notes that must have accompanied the Homeric text for a long time[7] and finally became a substantial part of our so-called D-Scholia, in which they were mixed up with more learned grammatical comments. When he took over τοῖος from H 231 in

---

[1] F. de Ian, *De Callimacho Homeri interprete*, Diss. Strassburg 1893; H. Erbse, 'Homerscholien und hellenistische Glossare bei Apollonios Rhodios', *Herm.* 81 (1953) 163 ff., esp. 173 ff. on Callimachus; see also Call. II p. 133 Index s.v. 'Homerus'.

[2] See above, p. 98.

[3] See above, pp. 111 ff. Zenodotus had athetized, but not left out, the whole description of Achilles' shield (Σ 483–617).

[4] I collected in the note to fr. 12. 6 (see also Addenda) the passages where Callimachus' Homeric text agrees with Zenodotus and other editions mentioned in our Scholia; see now Erbse's critical remarks, *Herm.* 81, 179.

[5] αἱ ἀπὸ τῶν πόλεων ἐκδόσεις, cf. above, pp. 94, 110.

[6] See Schol. AT on Φ 454 and X 45 and my notes on Call. fr. 548 with further references to this favourite adjective in fr. 384. 27 and 110. 53.

[7] See above, p. 15 (Aristophanes), Erbse, *Herm.* 81, 170, 178. 2; perhaps the ὑπόμνημα on the Orphic *Theogony* in the new Dervéni papyrus (of the fourth century B.C.? above, p. 103, n. 1) is a specimen of such a pre-Alexandrian 'commentary'.

the sense of ἀγαθός (fr. 627), his interpretation possibly was in accordance
with Aeschylus, certainly with the glossographers;[1] when he called
a messenger ἀπούατος (fr. 315), he was induced by whatever source not
to read ἀπ᾽ οὔατος in Σ 272, but a compound meaning 'bringing the
tidings'. These may be rather odd examples of Homeric epithets; but
there are more common epic words too that have been puzzling in all
ages.[2] We can still distinguish how Callimachus understood some of these
adjectives (οὖλος, πηγός, ἀμαλή, ἤνοψ), nouns (δείελον), or verbs (ἀτέει), or
controversial etymologies of proper names[3] (Ἀκακήσιος, Γλαυκώπιον).

We started from the fact that the creative epic poets were their own
interpreters and that the rhapsodes continued the self-interpretation of the
poets.[4] The Sophists can be regarded as the heirs of the rhapsodes in so
far as they tried to explain poetry for their new purpose, and the great
Attic philosophers and their schools completed this development. Now
once again poets became active in this field; there were no commentaries
produced in the first generations of the Hellenistic age, but these poets
were the immediate forerunners of the writers of continuous interpretations (ὑπομνήματα). It is from Callimachus and his pupils that a line runs
to the true ἑρμηνεία τῶν ποιητῶν by the Alexandrian γραμματικοί of the
following generations. In contrast to them, Crates and his pupils in
Pergamum renewed in a way the ancient allegorical method[5] and forced
their own philosophical, particularly Stoic, views upon the Homeric and
other poems. But the not infrequent quotations from Callimachean verses
in our Scholia to Homer show how helpful they were for the other, the
scholarly way of interpreting old epic poetry.

The most gifted poet among the many people who were styled Callimachus' 'pupils',[6] Apollonius Rhodius, also truly deserves a place in this
decisive period of early Greek scholarship.[7] We have to deal here with the
few fragments of his scholarly work and with the *Argonautica*,[8] in so far as
this great epic poem reveals the scholar.

---

[1] See my note on fr. 627, but also Lehrs, *Aristarch*[3] p. 37, Wackernagel, *Kleine Schriften* I
(1953) 728, 730; on the γλωσσογράφοι see above, p. 79. The best codex of the b-Schol.
(C = Laur. 32. 3) reads τοῖον ἀεί (Erbse, *Byz. Zeitschr.* 50 [1957] 133).
[2] See M. Leumann, *Homerische Wörter* (1950) 213 f.
[3] Fr. 634, *hy.* III 90, fr. 502, 277. 2; fr. 238. 20; fr. 633; *hy.* III 143, fr. 238. 11.
[4] See above, p. 3 and p. 6.
[5] See above, pp. 10 ff., and below, pp. 237 ff.
[6] See Call. test. 11 a–19 a (μαθητής, γνώριμος, Καλλιμάχειος).
[7] Sandys I[3] 114, 116, 122 mentions only the general literary position of Apollonius.
[8] Editions of Merkel and Mooney see below, p. 147, n. 1; Scholia in Ap. Rh. vetera rec.
C. Wendel, Berlin 1935. Apollonii Rhodii *Argonautica* recogn. brevique adn. crit. instruxit H.
Fränkel, *OCT* 1961. Herter's critical bibliographical report up to the year 1955 in Bursian
vol. 285.

There are strange contradictions in the tradition of Apollonius' life and work. He was Zenodotus' successor as head of the library; but to Zenodotus' edition of the Homeric text he had so many objections that he put them down in a book Πρὸς Ζηνόδοτον. As librarian he was also tutor to the crown prince, who became Ptolemy III Euergetes (in 247/6 B.C.), but it is very likely that this royal pupil, married to the Cyrenean princess Berenice, appointed the Cyrenean Eratosthenes,[1] and that his former tutor then went to Rhodes. The first βίος[2] says in one paragraph that Apollonius started to write poetry late in his life (ὀψὲ δὲ ἐπὶ τὸ ποιεῖν ποιήματα ἐτράπετο); and in the next paragraph it reports a rumour that while still in his adolescence he gave the first recitation of the *Argonautica* and met with a hostile reception (λέγεται ἔτι ἔφηβον ὄντα ἐπιδείξασθαι τὰ Ἀργοναυτικὰ καὶ κατεγνῶσθαι); because of this failure, the story goes on, he left his native Alexandria for Rhodes and lived there as a highly esteemed citizen and as a successful poet and teacher (as γραμματικός, no doubt). The Scholia to *Argonautica* Book I declare in six cases that the variant readings which they quote originate from a προέκδοσις, 'a previous edition';[3] so they presume two 'editions' of the poem by the author himself. Apollonius was a faithful follower of Callimachus, as many individual passages of the *Argonautica* prove; in principle, however, he was opposed to certain of his master's new doctrines, as we shall see. This master abused him, according to an ancient biographical tradition,[4] in a poem entitled *Ibis*, full of 'dirt and poison'. It is easy to combine this literary attack with the failure of his recitation and the emigration. The second βίος concludes with the statement that some people tell (τινὲς δέ φασιν) of his rehabilitation in his native city Alexandria and his reconciliation with his hostile teacher, at least in the grave. But the first βίος ends with all his honours in Rhodes.

This is a labyrinth of self-contradictory statements, and no thread of Ariadne leads out of the darkness. But discussion will throw some light on one or two points important for our special purpose. The sentence about Apollonius' rehabilitation that is introduced at the end of the second βίος with the cautious words τινὲς δέ φασιν contains the phrase καὶ τῶν βιβλιοθηκῶν τοῦ Μουσείου ἀξιωθῆναι; this phrase has caused

---

[1] See above, p. 124.

[2] Scholia in Ap. Rh. ed. Wendel pp. 1. 8 ff.; cf. Call. II test. 11 a and 11 b.

[3] See G. W. Mooney, The *Argonautica* of Ap. Rh. (1912) Appendix I pp. 403 ff., and Herter, Bursian 285, 230 ff.

[4] Suid. v. Καλλίμαχος = Call. II test. 1. 13 Ἴβις (ἔστι δὲ ποίημα . . . εἴς τινα †Ἴβιν, γενόμενον ἐχθρὸν τοῦ Καλλιμάχου. ἦν δὲ οὗτος Ἀπολλώνιος ὁ γράψας τὰ Ἀργοναυτικά); Epigr. adesp. = test 23. 8 σκώπτω δ' ἐπαραῖς ἴβιν Ἀπολλώνιον; Schol. Ov. *Ib*. 447 (prob. fifteenth century A.D.) De Callimacho . . . qui scripsit in Apollonium Rhodium.

considerable trouble, because it was universally interpreted as meaning that Apollonius was reappointed to his former librarianship, and this can hardly be reconciled with the other tradition about the sequence of librarians. But this interpretation was wrong, for Eusebius in his *Historia ecclesiastica* and his *Praeparatio evangelica*[1] used exactly the same expression, τῶν κατὰ τὴν Ἀλεξάνδρειαν βιβλιοθηκῶν ἠξιώθη, not about a librarian, but about authors and books 'having been deemed worthy of the Alexandrian libraries'. Consequently there is no ancient tradition at all that Apollonius was twice librarian; if he was head of the Museum library only once, the proper place available for him is between Zenodotus and Eratosthenes.[2] Indeed the whole story of 'the return of the native' has to be rejected. The other dubious story introduced by λέγεται that the young poet, not yet twenty years of age, after the ill success of his first public recitation withdrew in shame to Rhodes, is incompatible with his librarianship after Zenodotus, which we have accepted; so this story too has to be dismissed.

The second point is the meaning of προέκδοσις.[3] It is the usual assumption that the word ἔκδοσις involves formal publication; but this is not necessary. When an author has arranged a text of his own or of another writer, it can be called an ἔκδοσις, editio, edition, whether it is subsequently published or not,[4] in both ancient and modern languages. The serious γραμματικοί in their ὑπομνήματα on the *Argonautica*, not the rather unreliable biographers, repeatedly quote variant readings of a text called the προέκδοσις; the obvious conclusion is that the people who issued the *Argonautica* had two differing texts of which one was believed to be a preliminary and the other consequently the final or vulgate text of the poem. Everything else can only be speculation. Such a definite reference to a preliminary edition is rare; it confirms the interpretation of ἔκδοσις in special cases where it is often misunderstood, and it is welcome evidence for a possible process of book publication, which may encourage us to postulate a similar process in certain cases, when there is no trace in our tradition.

Discussion of librarianships and editions belongs only to the external and technical side of scholarship. But Apollonius' relation to Callimachus[5]

[1] See Excursus.
[2] The sequence is correct in *P.Oxy.* 1241, wrong in Suidas s.v. Ἀπολλώνιος, see Call. II test. 12 and 13; see also below, p. 154, n. 2.
[3] H. Fränkel in the preface of his edition p. vi and in 'Einleitung zur kritischen Ausgabe der *Argonautika* des Apollonios', *Abh. d. Akad. d. Wiss. Göttingen*, Phil.-hist. Klasse III Folge, Nr. 55 (1964) 7–11.   [4] See above, pp. 71 and 94.
[5] E. Eichgrün, *Kallimachos und Apollonios Rhodios*, Diss. Berlin 1961 (279 S.), restates the evidence and discusses all the problems in a sensible way.

also involves questions of principle. The venerable members of the
Museum were, from the beginning, not a very peaceful community;
Callimachus alludes to quarrels in three of his *Iambi*,[1] in the often-quoted
reply given to his adversaries in the introduction to the *Aitia*, at the end
of his *Hymn to Apollo*,[2] and in *Epigram* 21. But there is no ancient reference
at all to Apollonius as the principal enemy except in the case of the *Ibis*,
where it is apparently derived from the biographical tradition.[3] In addition to this we have a late epigram hitting at Callimachus,[4] the writer
of which is called Ἀπολλώνιος γραμματικός in the heading of the Palatine
Anthology, but Ῥόδιος only by the lemmatist of the other epigrams; in
Planudes and Eustathius it is anonymous. This is extremely poor evidence.
Apollonius' views on poetical aims and criticism can be reconstructed
only from the *Argonautica*; no theoretical or polemical utterances of his
in prose or verse are known to us.[5] The true difference between him and
Callimachus was that Apollonius adhered more closely to tradition; the
day of the long heroic epic poem was not yet over for him. He dared to
write a poem which was διηνεκές and formed a ἕν; it had unity and continuity from Jason's and his companions' departure to their return,
telling the complete voyage of the Argo in four books. Each book, of some
1,400–1,700 lines, was about the length of a tragedy. In that respect
Apollonius' work conformed to Aristotle's demands,[6] but ran counter
to fundamental doctrines of Callimachus; he did not attempt the same
scrupulous precision and discipline of language and metre, and he could
never have attained that Callimachean subtlety and graciousness combined with nervous virility. At that crucial time of Greek cultural history
Apollonius' attitude could not help to rescue poetry from the dangerous
situation in which it lay,[7] but might aggravate the danger. This at
least was the view of the Callimachean circle. Yet even if we stress this decisive point, it is very hard to believe that Apollonius' heretical mode of

---

[1] Call. fr. 191, 194, 203.

[2] From the days of Salvagnius (ed. Ov. *Ib.* 1633) and Isaac Vossius (Catull. 1684 p. 342)
people have believed that Callimachus in *hy.* II 105 ff. attacked Ap. Rh. I expressed my
doubts *Herm.* 63 (1928) 341 = *Ausgew. Schriften* (1960) 132; see also H. Erbse, *Herm.* 83
(1955) 424 ff.

[3] See above, p. 141, n. 4.

[4] Call. test. 25 = *AP* XI 275; all the details of the tradition and modern discussion in M.
Gabathuler, *Hellenistische Epigramme auf Dichter* (Diss. Basel 1937) 64 f.

[5] G. W. Mooney, The *Argonautica* of Ap. Rh. (1912), quotes with a certain pomposity
the saying Ἀνάγνωσις τροφὴ λέξεως as characteristic of our Apollonius; but the rhetor
Theo *progymn.* (*Rhet. Gr.* II 61. 28 Spengel) who quoted it with the remark ὡς τῶν πρεσβυτέρων
τις ἔφη, Ἀπολλώνιος δοκεῖ μοι ὁ Ῥόδιος, did not mean the poet, but the rhetor, who was born
in Alabanda and lived as a teacher of rhetoric in Rhodes from the second to the first century
B.C., see W. Schmid, *RE* II 140. 64 ff.

[6] Aristot. *Poet.* 1459 b 19 ff.   [7] See above, pp. 87 f.

thinking and writing could have had such fateful consequences for his
life. There seems to be no parallel in the history of scholarship. We may
think of the infuriated Poggio, who almost hired an assassin to murder
Lorenzo Valla because he had found some very malicious critical notes
of a pupil of Valla's in the margin of his collected letters; but on second
thoughts he contented himself with the weapon of a violent invective,
which led to a spirited literary duel without doing any harm to the rest of
Valla's life. As to Apollonius, we must honestly confess that we are at
a loss to discover what checked his career in Alexandria; fiction is no
substitute for evidence.

The few fragments[1] of Apollonius' minor poems on various cities, their
local legends and their foundations (κτίσεις fr. 4–12), abound, like the
Argonautica, in antiquarian and geographical rarities; they may have
been intended as a revival of the hexametric Ktisis-poetry of earlier ages,
almost completely lost to us.[2] Apollonius also wrote on Homer and on
several other poets.[3] Hesiodic questions (ἀπορήματα) had troubled Aristotle and his school; in Alexandria Zenodotus had started to publish
a critical text,[4] and nearly all the grammarians followed suit. In a work
of at least three books, of which the title is not quoted, Apollonius maintained the Hesiodic origin of the Ἀσπίς; it was perhaps in the same work
that he athetized the Ὀρνιθομαντεία and suspected that something was
missing in the speech of the Muses in the *Theogony* (after l. 26).[5]

Athenaeus[6] says that Ἀπολλώνιος ὁ Ῥόδιος ἐν τῷ Περὶ Ἀρχιλόχου by
referring to a Laconian custom satisfactorily interpreted the much-
disputed phrase ἀχνυμένη σκυτάλη as meaning 'grievous message'; so he
apparently published a monograph on Archilochus. Archilochus, the
Ionian poet of the middle of the seventh century B.C., was of an eruptive
mind and revolutionized the whole realm of Greek poetry; he is properly
ranked next to the great epic poets, as is implied even in Socrates'
ironical question to the rhapsode Ion: πότερον περὶ Ὁμήρου μόνον δεινὸς
εἶ ἢ καὶ περὶ Ἡσιόδου καὶ Ἀρχιλόχου; (Plat. *Io* 531 A). As Archilochus

---

[1] *Collectanea Alexandrina* ed. I. U. Powell (1925) 4–8; cf. H. Herter, Bursian 285 (1955)
409 f., with short references to the fragments of the prose-books.

[2] From the ἀρχαιολογία τῶν Σαμίων of Semonides Amorg. to the Ἰωνικά of Panyassis;
cf. F. Jacoby, *Cl. Qu.* 41 (1947) 4 f. = *Abhandlungen zur griechischen Geschichtschreibung* (1956)
149; on lost epic κτίσεις as sources of Pindar see P. Von der Mühll, *Mus. Helv.* 20 (1963) 201 f.
See also above, Callimachus on κτίσεις p. 135.

[3] J. Michaelis, *De Apollon. Rhod. fragmentis* (Diss. Halle 1875) 16–56.

[4] See above, p. 117.

[5] Hes. *Th.* ed. Jacoby p. 46. 3. The reference to Schol. Hes. *Op.* 58 has to be deleted; οἱ
περὶ Ἀπολλώνιον does not mean the Rhodian, but Ap. Dyscolus, see *de pron.* p. 112. 23 Schn.;
cf. also J. Schwartz, *Pseudo-Hesiodea* (1960) 614 f.

[6] Athen. x 451 D = fr. xxii Michaelis.

introduced new rhythmical elements into recitative poetry, the 'unlike measures' of iambics and trochees, and founded a special style of music for their recitation, the writers on music[1] took a particular interest in his work and concluded that his innovations followed those of Terpander, who had still kept to the dactylic rhythm. Of Aristotle's book no more than the title is preserved in the lists: Ἀπορήματα Ἀρχιλόχου Εὐριπίδου Χοιρίλου ἐν βιβλίοις γ̄[2] after the Ἀπορήματα Ἡσιόδου. Plato's and Aristotle's pupil, Heraclides Ponticus, published two books Περὶ Ἀρχιλόχου καὶ Ὁμήρου, listed by Diogenes Laertius together with two books Περὶ τῆς Ὁμήρου καὶ Ἡσιόδου ἡλικίας.[3] A Ptolemaic papyrus, dated about 270–240 B.C., which is precisely the time of Apollonius Rhodius, recently presented us with a small fragment in which three iambic trimeters of Archilochus are quoted after their obvious epic models without further comment.[4] It is highly improbable that this simple list preserves a part of Heraclides' work, as the first editor suggested, for the remains of his other books on literature suggest that he was mainly interested in the life and chronology of the poets[5] and in the subject-matter of their poems. As the few extant lines are of gnomic character, they may be parts of a gnomologium; its aim may have been educational, not only in a moral but also in a rhetorical sense, in so far as it presents examples of the art of μεταφράζειν.[6] The papyrus is a welcome example of Archilochus' popularity in the third century, but has hardly anything to do with scholarship. Such gnomological anthologies would suit the educational and rhetorical aims of the Sophists, and they may have started to arrange them.

---

[1] Glauc. Rheg. fr. 2, *FHG* II 23 ap. [Plut.] *de mus.* 4 Περὶ τῶν ἀρχαίων ποιητῶν καὶ μουσικῶν; see above, p. 53, n. 8.

[2] On the Ἀπορήματα Ὁμηρικά see above, p. 69; cf. P. Moraux, *Les listes anciennes* (1951) 114 ff.

[3] Diog. L. v 87 = Heracl. Pont. fr. 176–8 F. Wehrli, *Schule des Aristoteles* 7 (1953) 54 and 122 f.; cf. above, p. 70.

[4] *The Hibeh Papyri* II (1955) ed. E. G. Turner, no. 173, reprinted by F. Lasserre, *Archiloque* (Paris 1958, Les Belles Lettres) pp. 19 f., and by M. Treu, *Archilochus* (München 1959) 6 and 174 ff. Accepting that in l. 10 the Homeric hexameter E 130 [μή τι σύ γ'] ἀθανάτοισι θεο[ῖς ἀντικρὺ μάχεσθαι is correctly supplied, I assumed a tmesis in the corresponding trimeter of Archilochus in l. 12 and tentatively supplied κούδε̣ὶς δ' ἔπειτα σὺν θεοῖ[σιν ἥντετο]; συνήντετο in hostile sense Φ 34, cf. P 134 and Pind. *O.* II 39; or σὺν θεοῖ[σ' ἐμίσγετο]; cf. συμμίσγω in hostile sense Hdt. I 127, etc.; also fr. 94. 2 ἐπ' ... ἔργα ... ὁρᾷς has to be understood as ἐφορᾷς 'thou watchest over' (not 'thou lookest at the deeds'), the Ζεὺς Ἐπόψιος being addressed by the wronged fox. The tmesis is surprisingly frequent in Archilochus, fr. 3. 1 D.³; 7. 3 and 6, 68. 2, 112. 2, etc.

[5] See Heraclid. Pont. fr. 157–80 with Wehrli's commentary. Cf. also below, p. 191, on parallel passages from Menander and his models.

[6] The *editio princeps* refers to a similar gnomologium used by Clem. Al. *Strom.* VI 5. 10–7. 4, vol. II pp. 425 f. Stählin; such comparisons of Homer and Archilochus are quoted also in rhetorical school books; see Theo *progymn.* *Rhet. Gr.* II 62. 24 ff. Ὅμηρον μεταφράζων ... ὁ Ἀρχίλοχος. On 'Gnomic anthologies, their history and use' see the very instructive article by J. Barns, *Cl. Qu.* 44 (1950) 132 ff. and 45 (1951) 1 ff.

In the first half of the third century B.C. Theocritus composed an enthusiastic epigram (no. 21) for a statue of Archilochus; the aristocratic Callimachus (fr. 380, 544), on the other hand, could not restrain his deep aversion to the 'winestricken' man and the 'venom' of his verse, which earlier aristocrats, Pindar and Critias, had equally resented. But no one could seriously diminish the μύριον κλέος of the Parian poet, who was still immensely popular when Apollonius published the first[1] scholarly writing on him of which we know. Among the various publications on Archilochus by the preceding generations there was no new critical edition of the text, no commentary. Apollonius, in starting to interpret Archilochus' powerful and original language, was the forerunner of the future editors and ὑπομνηματισταί of the Iambographi in Alexandria. Περὶ Ἀρχιλόχου was an important link with the Peripatetics, who perhaps inaugurated that branch of literature Περὶ τοῦ δεῖνα[2] which anticipated and later accompanied complete commentaries on individual authors; in this connexion also Apollonius seems to have followed a more traditional line than Zenodotus and Callimachus.

In his appreciation of Antimachus Apollonius was equally at variance with Callimachus. It has long been obvious how freely he borrowed from Antimachus in his *Argonautica*;[3] now we find in one of his scholarly books a hexametric line of Antimachus quoted because of the word πιπώ (the woodpecker), which he then explained. But the assumption that there was a whole book Περὶ Ἀντιμάχου is based merely on a supplement of the first editor of the Berlin papyrus which can hardly be maintained.[4]

When we turn to Apollonius as an interpreter of Homer our position is better than in the case of Callimachus,[5] in which we could take our clues only from his poems. Not only did the *Argonautica* as a mythological narrative epic quite naturally take up more Homeric words, phrases, and passages[6] than Callimachus' *hymns*, *Aitia*, and *Hecale*; but Apollonius also

---

[1] At least, as long as we do not know when and what the Cyrenean grammarian Lysanias wrote περὶ Ἰαμβοποιῶν, of which Athen. XIV 620 C quotes from the first book; cf. ibid. VII 304 B; in Suid. v. Ἐρατοσθένης one of Eratosthenes' teachers is probably the same Lysanias.

[2] This genre was, so to speak, discovered by F. Leo in his review of Didymus Περὶ Δημοσθένους, *NGG* 1904 p. 257 = *Ausgewählte kleine Schriften* II (1960) 390 ff.

[3] Antimachus ed. B. Wyss pp. XLVIII f.

[4] *Berl. Klass. Texte* III (1905) Pap. 8439. 5 ff. bearb. von H. Schöne, cf. Powell, *Coll. Alex.* p. 250, and Antim. fr. 158 Wyss; but the revision of the papyrus by F. Della Corte, *Riv. fil. class.* 64 (1936) 395 ff., showed that Schöne's supplement [ἐν τῷ περὶ Ἀ]ντιμάχου cannot be maintained, see also Herter, Bursian 285 p. 410. Cf. above, p. 94.   [5] See above, pp. 139 f.

[6] Gertrud Marxer, *Die Sprache des Apollonius Rhodius in ihren Beziehungen zu Homer*, Diss. Zürich 1935; it is to be regretted that this useful thesis compared Apollonius only with Homer, without regard to the considerable literature in the intervening period; so Apollonius is often credited with making innovations to the Homeric language when he was simply using other poets as his source.

treated problems of wording and interpretation in his monograph *Against Zenodotus*. No doubt, therefore, he knew Zenodotus' edition; but painstaking recent research[1] has proved that he did not always accept Zenodotus' text, as had been generally assumed. He followed older pre-critical texts with elementary explanations to a greater extent than Callimachus did. This is quite convincing; for it agrees with what we called Apollonius' more 'conservative' general attitude. We shall not discuss any of the details of the *Argonautica* where the use of the κοιναὶ ἐκδόσεις of the *Iliad* and *Odyssey* and their short commentaries is implied, but only two examples where his readings of the Homeric text are cited in the Scholia, probably from his monograph Πρὸς Ζηνόδοτον.[2] Looking again at the problematical lines of the proem of the *Iliad*, we remember how Zenodotus dealt with Α 4–5;[3] now we see that Apollonius in Α 3 read πολλὰς δ' ἰφθίμους κεφαλὰς Ἄϊδι προΐαψεν, not ἰφθίμους ψυχάς.[4] There is no objection to the epic phrase itself, which occurs in Λ 55 πολλὰς ἰφθίμους κεφαλὰς Ἄϊδι προϊάψειν and in [Hesiod][5] *Catal.* fr. 96. 80 Rz.[3] π]ολλὰς Ἀΐδη κεφαλὰς ἀπὸ χαλκὸν ἰάψειν, where the 'heads' mean the whole person. But κεφαλάς is not acceptable in Α 3 if it is followed in Α 4–5 by αὐτοὺς δὲ ἑλώρια θῆκε κύνεσσιν / οἰωνοῖσί τε δαῖτα; αὐτούς can only be said in contrast to ψυχάς, 'he sent their ghosts [or shades] to Hades, but made them [that is their bodies] a prey to the beasts'. When Apollonius preferred the variant reading κεφαλάς, he must have left out lines 4–5, the genuineness

---

[1] H. Erbse, *Herm.* 81. 163 ff. He refuted the arguments of R. Merkel, Apollonii *Argonautica* (1854) Prolegomena pp. lxxi ff.; see also G. W. Mooney, The *Argonautica* of Ap. Rh. (1912), who gives a well balanced judgement on the relation of Apollonius to Zenodotus. For the extensive modern literature on Apollonius' language cf. H. Herter, Bursian 285, pp. 315 ff. When Erbse (loc. cit. 167) supposes that Apollonius 'sich gegen die zahlreichen Gewaltmaßnahmen seines dichtenden Zeitgenossen [i.e. Zenodotus] wandte', I part company with him.

[2] The title is given only in Schol. A Ν 657, but we can assume that this book is the source of the other quotations.

[3] Cf. above, pp. 111 ff.

[4] Schol. BT Α 3 Ἀπ. ὁ Ῥόδιος κεφαλὰς γράφει; Schol. A ibid. κακῶς τινες μεταγράφουσι ... κεφαλάς; Schol. A Λ 55 οὐκ ἐνδέχεται (sc. κεφαλάς), ἐπιφερομένου τοῦ 'αὐτοὺς δὲ ἑλώρια' (Α 3–4); Schol. AT Η 330; cf. Eust. 830. 4, 1421. 42. Perhaps too little attention has been paid to ἰφθίμους as epithet to ψυχάς. There is no difficulty in calling the κεφαλάς of the heroes ἰφθίμους, which is always used to mean 'strong, vigorous, stately'; its etymology from ἶφι is very much doubted by modern linguists (see Frisk, *Griech. etym. Wörterb.* s.v.), but not by ancient grammarians (see, e.g., Apollon. Soph. p. 93. 18 ἰσχυροψύχους or Eust. p. 16. 12 ad Α 3). How can the ψυχαί, the 'ghosts' of the dead heroes which are like shades or like a dream, be called ἴφθιμοι? No parallel seems to exist anywhere. I suspect that we have to assume a so-called 'enallagē'; the ἥρωες are ἴφθιμοι (cf. Λ 290 ἰφθίμων Δαναῶν), but the adjective is 'assimilated' to ψυχάς (Λ 55 ἰφθίμους κεφαλὰς Ἄ. πρ. has no genitive ἡρώων). This assimilation, not infrequent in lyric and tragic poetry—see my article in *Corolla Linguistica*, Festschrift F. Sommer (1955) 179 f.—is very rare in Homer. But cf. ξ 197 ἐμὰ κήδεα θυμοῦ and in general F. Sommer in *Sybaris*, Festschrift H. Krahe (1958) 158.

[5] R. Merkelbach, 'Die Hesiodfragmente auf Papyrus', *APF* 16 (1958) H 80, p. 53.

of which Zenodotus had already suspected. Zenodotus probably knew copies in which the two lines were omitted and therefore marked them in his own edition with the obelus, choosing the reading ψυχάς[1] in line 3 and δαῖτα in line 5; Apollonius decided for κεφαλάς in line 3 and condemned lines 4 and 5. He may well have been misled[2] by one of the old κοιναὶ ἐκδόσεις which were disregarded by all the following generations of grammarians. Of course only the statement that Apollonius[3] read κεφαλάς can be accepted as evidence, and our further conjecture that he omitted lines 4–5 must be regarded with due reserve. But there is a striking parallel in Λ 97–98, where Apollonius[4] read at the end of line 97 ἐγκέφαλόνδε instead of ἐγκέφαλος δέ and 'athetized' line 98 which is incompatible with his reading. That is the extent of the evidence; but we may speculate that Apollonius there again, as in the proem of the first book, found in one of the old copies of the *Iliad* in the library a rare variant, which Zenodotus perhaps did not know and the later grammarians did not like, and which somebody therefore registered in a ὑπόμνημα as Apollonian. Apollonius' quite reasonable text in Λ 97, δι' αὐτῆς ἦλθε (sc. δόρυ) καὶ ὀστέου ἐγκέφαλόνδε, has not been confirmed so far by any papyrus,[5] and we cannot compare his text of the whole passage with the vulgate. The significance of his own and his master's Homeric studies lies in the fact that they were the first serious interpreters and thus stimulated the research of the later commentators.

Another poet, the Cretan Rhianus, should perhaps be given a place beside Apollonius, although we cannot be certain that he ever joined the circle of the great Alexandrians;[6] he wrote one lengthy mythological epic poem in four books[7] on Heracles, Ἡράκλεια, and a few other epics on local legends and tribal history: Θεσσαλικά, Ἀχαϊκά, Ἠλιακά, Μεσσηνιακά. In subject-matter the first three of these may be compared with

---

[1] Cf. H 330 and Schol. AT, Eust.

[2] 'Misled' because the proem really becomes κόλον, see p. 112, n. 1.

[3] τινές in Schol. A (see above, p. 147, n. 4) probably does not mean anyone else.

[4] Schol. A Λ 97.

[5] G. Jachmann, 'Vom frühalexandrinischen Homertext', *NGG* 1949, 176 f., 191 f., went wrong in his interpretation of and supplements to P.Lit. Lond. No. 251 (p. 210 Milne 1927); I was sure of this before the objections of K. Reinhardt, *Die Ilias und ihr Dichter* (Göttingen 1961) 522 ff. were published (see also Hölscher's notes, p. 527). But Jachmann, without being dogmatic, has shown Apollonius not as emendator but as critical preserver of variant readings, otherwise lost, see also above on Zenodotus, pp. 113 f. and below, p. 149, n. 4 on Rhianus; this is the permanent value of his paper.

[6] See above, p. 122.

[7] Jacoby follows *Et. M.* p. 153. 4 v. Ἀσέληνα . . . ἐν τῶι ιδ Ἡρακλείας (*FGrHist* 65 F 48) and changes Suid. v. Ῥιανός . . . Ἡρακλειάδα . . . ἐν βιβλίοις ⟨ι⟩δ (ibid. T 1);the blotted figure in *P.Oxy.* 2463. 7 Ῥιανὸς δ' ἐν [τῆι]/. τῆς Ἡρακλείας was 'possibly ι but probably γ' (J. Rea, *P.Oxy.* vol. xxvii, 1962, p. 108).

Apollonius' minor epics on the foundation-stories of various cities, as his *Heraclea* may be considered a parallel to the *Argonautica*. The *Messeniaca* seems to have treated the history of the Messenian wars in a more Iliadic style, laying the accent on stories of revolt and emigration drawn from unfamiliar sources.[1] His language is simpler and his verse is smoother than those of Apollonius, and the influence of Callimachus can hardly be discounted. This remarkable ἐποποιός also produced an edition of the *Iliad* and *Odyssey*, and more than forty of his readings are mentioned in our Homeric Scholia,[2] curiously enough twice as many from the *Odyssey* as from the *Iliad*. He preserved the evidently correct but rare epithet Τρώων εὐηφενέων Ψ 81[3] (εὐηγενέων vulg.) only recently attested by a papyrus and by an inscription and therefore accepted by some editors (cf. Λ 427). They might also have noted Rhianus' description of Ate (fr. 1. 17 f. Pow.), modelled on the famous Iliadic passage in Τ 91 ff.; with its help the corrupt text of our Homeric manuscripts can be emended.[4] Homer: Ἄτη . . . τῇ μέν θ' ἁπαλοὶ πόδες· οὐ γὰρ ἐπ' οὔδει / πίλναται, ἀλλ' ἄρα †ἥ γε κατ' ἀνδρῶν κράατα βαίνει; Rhianus: ἡ δ' Ἄτη ἁπαλοῖσι μετατρωχῶσα πόδεσσιν / ἄκρησ' ἐν κεφαλῇσιν· so his copy of the *Iliad* had the correct text ἀλλ' ἄκρ(α) ἥ γε κατ' ἀνδρῶν κράατα without the hiatus 'illicitus'[5] disfiguring the line. Rhianus and Apollonius did not invent such readings; they selected them from the copies they were able to inspect. In the same way their poems were distinguished not by creative invention, but by the conscious choice of words and style and by delicate allusions.

We may conclude that in the generations, after Philitas and his immediate followers had started the 'new movement', even the more conservative poets were to be found in the ranks of the scholars. But in the second half of the third century B.C. this unity began to dissolve.

[1] See F. Kiechle, *Messenische Studien* (1959) 82 ff., 123 f.

[2] See above, p. 122.

[3] Schol. Au. ἐν τῇ 'Ριανοῦ καὶ Ἀριστοφάνους εὐηφενέων . . . ὡς Κλέαρχος ἐν ταῖς Γλώτταις (Clearch fr. 111 fals. Wehrli, *Schule d. Aristot.* III [1948] 84 prob. Clitarchus); εὐηφενέοντα or εὐηφενέ' ὄντα Epic. adesp. *P.Oxy.* 1794. 13 = Powell, *Coll. Alex.* p. 79 and nom. propr. Εὐηφένης *IG* XII 8. 376. 14.

[4] G. Kaibel, *Herm.* 28 (1893) 59; approved by E. Schwartz, 'Homerica', *Antidoron*, Festschrift für J. Wackernagel (1923) 71. 1, and in his edition of the *Iliad* (München, Bremer Presse 1923); Rhianus' text of the *Odyssey* is several times accepted by E. Schwartz, *Die Odyssee* (1924) 301 ff. 'Textkritische Bemerkungen'. I agree with Jachmann, 'Vom frühalexandrinischen Homertext' (1949) 207. 1, that these special readings are not conjectures of Rhianus, but part of a better paradosis.

[5] See Leaf in his commentary ad loc. who tries to excuse the hiatus. The difficulty of Rhianus' reading, not considered by Kaibel, Schwartz, and Jachmann, lies in the fact that Z 257 ἄκρης πόλιος is the only other instance in which the syllable ἀκρ is not in the 'longum' of the dactyl. For ἄκρα . . . κράατα cf. [Hom.] *hy. Ap.* 33 and for the position cf. Υ 227 ἄκρον ἐπ' ἀνθερίκων καρπόν. See Addenda.

On the one side there is the epic poet Euphorion[1] of Chalcis in Euboea, appointed later in life (about 220 B.C.) librarian at Antioch in Syria;[2] he apparently had no direct connexion with Alexandria and the Ptolemies. He was a chilly virtuoso whose style in studied obscurity of subject, composition, and language is much the same as that of his fellow countryman Lycophron. He used the treasures of earlier poetry, to which access had been made easy by new editions, glossaries, and occasional explanations, and he was equally well versed in Callimachean stylistic devices, which he often perverted.[3] Cicero (*Tusc.* III 19. 45) disapprovingly called the circle of the Roman *poetae novi* 'cantores Euphorionis', and it is always surprising to observe how far the influence of his poetical mannerism reached in Greek and Roman literature.[4] His limited scholarly activity was confined to the collecting of antiquarian material; there is no indication that he ever edited or interpreted texts, except perhaps his own poems.[5]

On the other side are three younger pupils of Callimachus, who are mainly known, even though two of them occasionally composed poems,[6] as writers of learned prose works: Hermippus of Smyrna, Istros, and Philostephanus, Istros possibly, Philostephanus certainly born at Cyrene, as their master and their contemporary Eratosthenes. Hermippus' biographical work[7] has already been mentioned as a continuation of the biographical parts of Callimachus' Πίνακες;[8] written in a more novelistic vein, it became with all its anecdotes a source of doubtful reliability for Diogenes Laertius and for Plutarch. That Hermippus could be called Περιπατητικός as well as Καλλιμάχειος suggests that this term had no longer any philosophical flavour but could be used of any writer on

---

[1] A. Meineke, *Analecta Alexandrina* (1843) 3–168; F. Scheidweiler, *Euphorionis fragmenta*, Diss. Bonn 1908. Powell, *Coll. Alex.* (above, p. 144, n. 1) 29–58. For papyrus-fragments published after 1925 see D. L. Page, *Greek Lit. Papyri* I (1942) no. 121, pp. 488–98, and Pack² no. 371–4; *PSI* XIV (1957) no. 1390 ed. V. Bartoletti, *P.Oxy.* XXX (1964) 2525–8 ed. E. Lobel.

[2] Cf. above, p. 122, n. 1.   [3] See Call. II p. 131 f. v. Euphorio.

[4] The enthusiasm of B. A. van Groningen, 'La Poésie verbale Grecque', *Mededeelingen d. kon. Nederl. Akad. van Wetensch. Afd. Letterk.* N.R. 16. 4 (Amsterdam 1953) 189–217, will, I am afraid, not convert many readers to acknowledge Euphorion as the perfect representative of 'Poésie verbale' in the Hellenistic age. Even one of his modern admirers seems to be affected by this mannerism of style, P. Treves, *Euforione e la storia ellenistica* (1955), who enlarges the few biographical and historical data by his personal inventions; I can do no better than refer to the detailed review by P. M. Fraser, *Gnom.* 28 (1956) 578–86.

[5] Fr. 48–58 and perhaps fr. 148–52 Scheidweiler; cf. F. Skutsch, *RE* VI (1909) 1189 f.—It is highly improbable that he was the Euphorion who wrote a λέξις Ἱπποκράτους in six books (fr. 51, 52 Scheidw.). In *P.Oxy.* 2528 Euphorion apparently is the interpreter of his own poems. I am not aware of any ancient parallel, but in modern times from the late Renaissance to Romanticism it was not unusual that a learned poet commented on his own work, see W. Rehm, *Späte Studien* (1964) 7 ff.

[6] Cf. Suidas v. Ἴστρος . . . ἔγραψε δὲ πολλὰ καὶ καταλογάδην καὶ ποιητικῶς; Philosteph. fr. fr. 17 comes from a poem, cf. fr. 14.

[7] *FHG* III 35–54.   [8] See above, p. 129, with references.

literature and antiquities, in particular the biographer. Istros[1] is not
described as a γραμματικός, but as ὁ Καλλιμάχειος συγγραφεύς, which
means that he brought together historical material by making excerpts
from the earlier literature in the library. His work on Athens, Ἀττικά, or
more fully Συναγωγὴ τῶν Ἀτθίδων, was the focal point of his various collectanea, which included also Ἠλιακά, Ἀργολικά, and Ἄτακτα. To judge
from the fragments, his interest was limited to the early, 'mythical'
period, though it extended from myths to cults and to epic and lyric
poetry.[2] The third of the company, Philostephanus,[3] was a geographer in
the same sense as Istros was a historian; his antiquarian material was
arranged according to countries and cities: Περὶ τῶν ἐν Ἀσίᾳ πόλεων,
'Islands' (Sicily, Thasus, Cyprus), and 'Rivers'. As a true Callimachean
he reported aetiologies, paradoxa, rare customs, and cults of the various
localities. All three had Peripatetic inclinations; but working in Alexandria they were among the first to profit by Callimachus' exhaustive
library catalogues and were able to supplement certain parts of his learned
work in their different spheres of biography, history, and geography.

A contemporary of these Callimacheans was Satyrus from Callatis,
termed Περιπατητικός in the same vague sense as Hermippus; he may
be just mentioned here, as he belongs to the same category of writers.
Since a substantial fragment of his *Life* of Euripides,[4] cast in dialogue
form like Aristotle's Περὶ ποιητῶν, was recovered, modern readers have
sometimes been surprised and disappointed that Satyrus made his inferences about the life and character of his hero from passages in the
poet's own tragedies and in the comedies of Aristophanes. But if we
realize how even Aristarchus used arbitrarily selected lines of Alcman's
poems as a biographical source,[5] we must have mercy on Satyrus. When
documentary evidence was at hand, he used it; for instance, he looked up
and quoted ψηφίσματα for details of cult and constitutional history in his
local treatise 'On the Demes of Alexandria', probably written under the
reign of Ptolemy V and Cleopatra I between 193 and 180 B.C.[6]

---

[1] *FGrHist* 334 T 6; cf. T 1 and 4; the introduction III b (supplement) vol. I (1954) 618–27
gives invaluable information on this genre of literature as a whole.

[2] F 58 (Homer), F 56 (μελοποιοί).

[3] *FHG* III 28–34 (incomplete); F. Gisinger, *RE* xx (1941) 104–18; cf. above, p. 134, n. 7,
Callimachus' Παράδοξα arranged κατὰ τόπους.

[4] *P.Oxy.* IX (1911) 1176, reprinted in *Supplementum Euripideum*, ed. H. v. Arnim (1913) 1 ff.;
cf. F. Leo, *NGG* 1912, 273 ff. = *Ausgewählte kleine Schriften* II (1960) 365 ff., A. Dihle, 'Studien
zur griechischen Biographie', *Abh. Gött. Akad. d. Wiss.*, Phil.-hist. Kl. III no. 37 (1956) 104 ff.

[5] See below, p. 220.

[6] *P.Oxy.* XXVII (1962) 2465, with the commentary of E. G. Turner. Cf. F. Jacoby *FGrHist*
631 (vol. III C, 1958, pp. 180 f.); the date given there in the annotation to the only old fragment (222–205 B.C.) must probably be altered on account of the new papyrus.

IV

SCIENCE AND SCHOLARSHIP: ERATOSTHENES

SCHOLARSHIP grew up in Alexandria as a creation of the new age, but science descended by a long tradition from the Ionian and Attic past. Strato ὁ φυσικός[1] under Ptolemy I and others were the links between the Athenian school of Aristotle and the Alexandrian Museum; an efflorescence of mathematics and the natural sciences was the result. The ranging curiosity of the scholar poets had extended occasionally to scientific matters; they were fond of all sorts of marvels, θαυμάσια.[2] The Greek spirit had always been struck by the wonders of nature; the poet of our *Odyssey* depicted how even the messenger of the gods, Hermes, stood and wondered at the sight of the incredible beauty of Calypso's island. The scholar poets, however, were not only collectors of geographical, ethnographical, and zoological paradoxa, they also displayed some exact scientific knowledge. Writers on medicine were included in the *Pinakes* of Callimachus (fr. 429), and he and Apollonius showed themselves familiar with medical technicalities.[3] Perhaps Aratus too dealt with Ἰατρικά;[4] he certainly must have made a careful study of astronomy before transforming Eudoxus' learned star catalogue into the fluent epic lines of his *Phaenomena*.[5]

But there is an essential difference between all of these and Eratosthenes. He seems to have been the first scholar and poet who was primarily and truly a scientist; for his poetry was, if we compare it with the bewildering width and variety of his other works, no more than a small πάρεργον, though one not without grace and simplicity.[6] So far scholarship had been the domain of poets and their pupils. But in the middle of the third century B.C. the union of poetry and scholarship split up;[7] learning was advancing, poetry in retreat. We can hardly avoid asking

---

[1] See above, p. 92.   [2] See above, pp. 134 f.
[3] Erbse, *Herm.* 81, 186 ff., esp. 190. 2; see also H. Oppermann, 'Herophilos bei Kallimachos', *Herm.* 60 (1925) 14 ff.
[4] E. Maass, *Aratea* (1892) 223 ff.   [5] See above, p. 121.
[6] Auct. Περὶ ὕψους XXXIII 5 called Eratosthenes' *Erigone* διὰ πάντων ἀμώμητον ποιημάτιον.
[7] See above, pp. 149 f.

whether the scientific spirit or method now began to influence scholarship and its future development.

Eratosthenes, born in Cyrene, was said, like so many others, to have been a 'pupil' of the Cyrenean Callimachus.[1] But the difficulties of verifying the scanty biographical data and reconstructing the contents of his books are nearly unsurmountable. Nothing is left to us but hundreds of scattered scraps; and there is not even a reliable modern collection of his fragments. But who is courageous enough to measure himself even as editor against the universality of Eratosthenes, philosopher, mathematician, astronomer, chronographer, geographer, grammarian, and poet? F. A. Wolf's extremely learned pupil G. Bernhardy had the courage in his early youth to put together all the *Eratosthenica* he was able to find out, and to publish them in 1822. But no one has tried since, and after a century and a half an attempt at a *complete* new critical edition would be worthwhile indeed.[2] According to the biographical tradition preserved in Suidas' article, his teachers in Cyrene were Lysanias[3] the grammarian and Callimachus the poet, and in Athens the Stoic philosopher Ariston of Chios[4] and Arcesilaus, the Platonist; called from Athens to Alexandria by Ptolemy III (after 246 B.C.), he lived there until the reign of Ptolemy V (205/4–181/0 B.C.). Born in the 126th Olympiad (276/3 B.C.), he died at the age of eighty. This account seems quite consistent enough; but actually there are a few troublesome inconsistencies. Callimachus had left his native city a long time before Eratosthenes was born; when Eratosthenes was called to Alexandria, Callimachus had nearly reached the end of his life. So we have either to take the statement that Eratosthenes was his μαθητής in a more general, not in a personal way, or to 'interpolate' a sojourn of the young Eratosthenes in Alexandria between Cyrene and Athens for which there is no evidence.[5] But the crucial point

[1] Call. II, test. 15 and 16; the best collection and discussion of the testimonia is in *FGrHist* 241 (1929–30), followed by an edition of the historical fragments; cf. G. Knaack, *RE* VI (1907) 358 ff. A masterly picture of the personality as a whole is given in the essay of E. Schwartz, 'Eratosthenes' in *Charakterköpfe aus der antiken Literatur* II. Reihe, first published in 1909 and often reprinted.

[2] The fragments of works on particular subjects have been collected: H. Berger, *Die geographischen Fragmente des Eratosthenes*, 1880; K. Strecker, *De Lycophr., Euphron., Eratosth. comicorum interpretibus* (1884) 22–78; Powell, *Collectan. Alex.* 58–68 poetical fragments; historical fragments with an appendix of various other important fragments *FGrHist* 241.

[3] See above, p. 146, n. 1, on his book Περὶ ἰαμβοποιῶν. In our Scholia on the *Iliad* he is three times quoted, in Schol. B *I* 378 before Aristophanes and Aristarchus.

[4] Cf. *FGrHist* 241 F 17; M. Pohlenz, *Die Stoa* (1948) I 27 f., II 16 f.

[5] The disordered account in Tzetz. *Proleg.* p. 25. 8, in which, together with Alex. Aet. and Lycophr., Callimachus and Eratosthenes are mentioned—νεανίαι ἦσαν Καλλίμαχος καὶ Ἐρατοσθένης—(see above, p. 127), cannot be regarded as evidence. Furthermore, Eratosthenes' very lively dialogue entitled 'Arsinoe' (Athen. VII 276 A = *FGrHist* 241 F 16) should not have been used as an argument by Susemihl I 410. 6; no doubt it refers to Arsinoe III, the

is this: according to a Stoic source of Strabo's[1] Eratosthenes encountered the reproach that he, τοῦ Ζήνωνος τοῦ Κιτιέως γνώριμος Ἀθήνησι, 'an acquaintance of Zeno in Athens', mentioned none of Zeno's successors, but only his opponents from different points of view, Ariston and Arcesilaus. If γνώριμος is correct in a literal sense and Eratosthenes was acquainted with or a pupil of Zeno, who died in 262/1 B.C., he must have been born ten or even twenty years earlier than 276 B.C. In this case, if the date of his birth is about 296 B.C., the tradition that Eratosthenes was an old man of eighty under Ptolemy V (after 205/4 B.C.) has to be rejected, and yet his birth would still not be early enough for him to have become Callimachus' pupil in Cyrene. These chronological contradictions cannot be ignored.[2] But Strabo, a Stoic 'convert', was always ready to quote censorious hits at Eratosthenes, whom he regarded as a sort of heretic; considering the whole context, therefore, I should not place too much reliance on the isolated remark about the ungrateful Ζήνωνος γνώριμος[3] and reject the vulgate tradition.

Perhaps new evidence will turn up one day to throw some light on these problems, as a papyrus did in the case of his librarianship. The sequence of the librarians in Alexandria was disarranged in the biographical tradition where Eratosthenes was said to have been succeeded by Apollonius and then by Aristophanes;[4] but one of the lists in the so-called *Chrestomathy*, *P.Oxy.* 1241,[5] restored the correct order: Eratosthenes succeeded Apollonius[6] and was followed by Aristophanes. In this list Apollonius and later Aristarchus are expressly called διδάσκαλοι[7] of the royal princes; this position is attested also for the first librarian, Zenodotus, who taught (ἐπαίδευσεν)[8] the children of Ptolemy I, and before him for the poet Philitas.[9] So it is reasonable to assume a similar tutorship for the two other heads of the library, Eratosthenes and Aristophanes.

wife of Philopator, the founder of Dionysiac festivals like the Lagynophoria, not to Arsinoe II Philadelphos.

[1] Strab. 1 15 = *FGrHist* 241 T 10.
[2] Wilamowitz was the first to notice the problem, see Susemihl 1 410. 4; the most vigorous champion of the early date was F. Jacoby *FGrHist* II D pp. 704 f.
[3] I gladly refer to the greatest specialist of this branch of tradition, M. Pohlenz, *Stoa* II 16 'Strabos Angabe 1 15, er sei Zenons Schüler gewesen, ist nicht buchstäblich zu nehmen'; cf. also G. A. Keller, *Eratosthenes und die alexandrinische Sterndichtung* (Diss. Zürich 1946) 134 ff. Beilage zur Chronologie.
[4] Suid. v. Ἀπολλώνιος (= Call. II test. 12) and v. Ἀριστοφάνης (= test. 17); on the confusion in Tzetz. see above, p. 153, n. 5.
[5] Col. II 5 f. τοῦτον (sc. Ap. Rh.) διεδέξατο Ἐρατοσθένης. μεθ' ὃν Ἀριστοφάνης (= Call. II test. 13).
[6] On the probable date see above, p. 142.
[7] On the terms διδάσκαλος, καθηγητής, τροφεύς, τιθηνός see E. Eichgrün, *Kallimachos und Apollonios* (1961) 181 ff. Exkurs I: Prinzenerzieher.
[8] See above, p. 92, n. 5.   [9] See above, p. 92, n. 3.

Eratosthenes placed at the end of a letter to his king on the duplication of the cube an epigram[1] of which the closing distichs reveal his devotion to the royal family: εὐαίων Πτολεμαῖε, πατὴρ ὅτι παιδὶ συνηβῶν / πάνθ' ὅσα καὶ Μούσαις καὶ βασιλεῦσι φίλα / αὐτὸς ἐδωρήσω· ὁ δ' ἐς ὕστερον, οὐράνιε Ζεῦ, / καὶ σκήπτρων ἐκ σῆς ἀντιάσειε χερός. / καὶ τὰ μὲν ὡς τελέοιτο· λέγοι δέ τις ἄνθεμα λεύσσων / τοῦ Κυρηναίου τοῦτ' 'Ερατοσθένεος. Ptolemy is addressed by Eratosthenes as εὐαίων; Callimachus had similarly addressed the queen as εὐαίων . . . Βερενίκα (*Ep.* 51. 3) and put οὐράνιε Ζεῦ at the end of a hexameter (*Ep.* 52. 3). In the line πάνθ' ὅσα καὶ Μούσαις καὶ βασιλεῦσι φίλα the allusion to a famous passage of Hesiod (*Th.* 80 ff.), the favourite poet of the Callimachean circle, is quite obvious. If the later voluptuous and even criminal life of the crown prince as Ptolemy IV Philopator (221–204 B.C.)[2] did no particular credit to Eratosthenes' tutoring, one cannot deny that all the things beloved by the Muses were beloved by the king, who reorganized the Μουσεῖα on Mount Helicon, wrote a tragedy Ἄδωνις,[3] built a temple to Homer in Alexandria, and was a patron of scientists and scholars in the Alexandrian museum. In any case, the lines of the epigram about the young Ptolemy support the assumption that Eratosthenes was his διδάσκαλος. That he passed on to his royal pupil a true love of Homer is only natural in one whose Cyrenean teacher was probably a Homeric scholar and who spent a long life in the capital of Homeric studies.

The whole epigram shows a rare combination of the mathematician[4] and the poet. It is significant that the greatest mathematical genius of antiquity, Archimedes, about ten years his senior, did Eratosthenes the honour of dedicating to him the one book in which he explained his *Method*,[5] of which he never spoke elsewhere; the introduction addressed

[1] Eutoc. comment. in libr. Archimed. de sphaera et cylindro, Archimedes *Opera* ed. J. L. Heiberg, vol. III² (1915) 96 = Powell, *Collect. Alex.* p. 66. The genuineness of Eratosthenes' epigram has been proved by Wilamowitz, 'Ein Weihgeschenk des Eratosthenes', *GGN* 1894, 23 ff. = *Kleine Schriften* II (1941) 56 ff. He strongly protested against Powell's note 'dubium', *Glaube der Hellenen* II (1932) 318. 1 and maintained his earlier conjecture of the year 1894, loc. cit. p. 31 that Eratosthenes was Philopator's tutor: 'Jetzt wird es kein Kenner der Geschichte mehr bezweifeln.' F. Jacoby, however, doubted it, see *FGrHist* II D (1930) 705. 10 ff.

[2] H. Volkmann *RE* XXIII (1959) 1678–91 with further references.

[3] Schol. Aristoph. *Thesm.* 1059 = Nauck, *TGF*² p. 824; F. Schramm, *Tragicorum Graec. hellenisticae aetatis fragm.* (1929) 83 f.

[4] On the mathematical problem of 'The duplication of the cube' see B. L. Van der Waerden, *Science Awakening* (Groningen 1954) 159–165.

[5] Περὶ τῶν μηχανικῶν θεωρημάτων πρὸς 'Ερατοσθένην ἔφοδος, discovered in 1906 by J. L. Heiberg in a palimpsest of the tenth century and first published in *Herm.* 42 (1907) 235 ff.; cf. Archim. *Opera* ed. Heiberg II² (1913) 425 ff.; T. L. Heath, *The Method of Archimedes*, Cambridge 1912. A probable date, *ca.* 238 B.C., Eichgrün, *Kallimachos und Apollonios* (1961), Exkurs II, p. 220.

to Eratosthenes is full of admiration and of a slight humour. There is even a poem in twenty-two distichs which Archimedes is said to have composed and dedicated to Eratosthenes, his only writing in verse, called the *Cattle problem*;[1] its formal quality is far below the faultless and gracious lines of the Eratosthenic epigram. It is not quite certain that the ingenious Sicilian mathematician, about whose life and sayings countless stories circulated throughout the Mediterranean world, ever came to Alexandria to use its library, as we might have expected; but intercourse with his Alexandrian colleague did tempt him to intrude into the sphere of the Homeric scholars and to state in poetical form a preposterous mathematical problem, the number of the cattle of Helios in the *Odyssey*, divided into four herds of different colours. In the first half of the third century B.C. we hear of no contact between science, represented above all by Euclid's *Elementa*, and scholarship. That a lively exchange seems to have started in the forties, was mainly due to Eratosthenes. It is also in this period, after the succession of Euergetes and Berenice to the throne, that we first learn of Callimachus' relations with the mathematician and astronomer Conon. Conon was highly praised by Archimedes in the preface to his *Spirals* and by other scientists, but his name survives because he had named a constellation Βερενίκης Πλόκαμος in honour of the young queen and this astronomical discovery inspired Callimachus to write one of his most delicate elegiac poems, the *Lock of Berenice*,[2] which was translated by Catullus into Latin.

It would be hard to find a comprehensive term for Eratosthenes' manifold spheres of learned activity, if he had not coined one for himself: φιλόλογος.[3] Because of his universality of knowledge Eratosthenes has been compared with Aristotle; but in Aristotle every special branch was subordinated to the general principle of his own teleological philosophy.[4] Eratosthenes, not interested as it seems in the philosophical school of his native country, the Cyrenean hedonism of Aristippus, found his teachers

---

[1] Archimed. *Op.* II² (1913) 527 ff.; see R. C. Archibald, *Americ. Math. Monthly* 25 (1918) 411–14 with bibliography and Van der Waerden, *Science Awakening* (1954) 208; more bibliographical references in A. Lesky, *Gesch. d. griech. Lit.* (1963²) 844.

[2] Call. fr. 110 and Addenda in vol. II.

[3] Herodiani *scripta tria* ed. K. Lehrs (1848) 379–401 'De vocabulis φιλόλογος, γραμματικός, κριτικός'; Sandys I³ 4–11; cf. also the articles in *RE* s.vv. Grammatik, col. 1808 ff., Kritikos, Philologos, and A. Böckh, *Enzyklopädie und Methodologie der philologischen Wissenschaften²* (1886) 12 ff. on φιλόλογος and γραμματικός. Gabriel R. F. M. Nuchelmans, *Studien über φιλόλογος, φιλολογία, φιλολογεῖν*, Diss. Nijmegen 1950. H. Kuch, 'Φιλόλογος. Untersuchung eines Wortes von seinem ersten Auftreten in der Tradition bis zur ersten überlieferten lexikalischen Festlegung', *Schriften der Sektion für Altertumswissenschaft* 48, Deutsche Akademie der Wissenschaften zu Berlin (1965) 30 ff. on Eratosthenes; but see below, p. 158, n. 9.

[4] See above, pp. 79, 84.

in philosophy in Athens which in the Hellenistic world still remained the centre of philosophical studies.[1] In Athens it was not the Aristotelian Peripatos that attracted him, but the Academy, revivified by Arcesilaus, and a new branch of the Stoa, represented by Zeno's unfaithful pupil Ariston of Chios.[2] But the influence of Stoic moralism is confined to a few, probably early, writings. That of Platonic cosmological concepts, especially of the *Timaeus*, is much more evident not only in his *Platonicus*, but also in his mathematical and geographical works and even in his poems.[3] All this, however, did not make him a φιλόσοφος in principle, like Aristotle or later Posidonius.

Strabo, speaking of the famous Coans, applied the word κριτικός[4] to Philitas, the scholar. But Philicus of Corcyra, who led the Dionysiac τεχνῖται in the famous procession of 275/4 B.C., addressed in the proem to his *Hymn to Demeter* not the κριτικοί, but the γραμματικοί; they were the scholars, especially the metrical experts whom he proudly presented with his invention of a whole poem in stichic choriambic hexameters.[5] This precious testimony[6] of the early third century B.C. confirms that the later biographical tradition in which Zenodotus and the scholars of his and the following generations were called γραμματικοί is correct. We are not told, however, by any of them who chose this particular name and thus gave it a new meaning (hitherto the elementary teacher in writing and reading had been the only γραμματικός or γραμματιστής). It was unavoidable that one day the question (ζήτημα) should be raised who was the first γραμματικός in the new sense. The Scholia to the Γραμματικὴ τέχνη of Dionysius Thrax,[7] trying to give a definition of the title, say: τὸ πρότερον δὲ κριτικὴ ἐλέγετο, καὶ οἱ ταύτην μετιόντες κριτικοί· Ἀντίδωρος δέ τις Κυμαῖος συγγραψάμενος "λέξιν" ἐπέγραψεν "Ἀντιδώρου γραμματικοῦ λέξις", καὶ ἐκ τούτου ἤ ποτε κριτικὴ γραμματικὴ λέλεκται καὶ γραμματικοὶ οἱ ταύτην μετιόντες. The date of this otherwise unknown Antidorus of Kyme, whose name is disfigured in some of the manuscripts, may be the

---

[1] W. W. Tarn, *Hellenistic Civilisation* 325 ff.
[2] See above, p. 153.
[3] Suid. v. Ἐρατοσθένης ... δεύτερον ἢ νέον Πλάτωνα; cf. A. Schmekel, *Die positive Philosophie in ihrer geschichtlichen Entwicklung* I (1938) 60–86; W. W. Tarn, *AJP* 60 (1939) 53; F. Solmsen, 'Eratosthenes as Platonist and Poet', *TAPA* 73 (1942) 192 ff., cf. ibid. 78 (1947) 252 ff.
[4] κριτικός above, p. 89, κρίσις p. 117, κρίνειν in Callimachus p. 137, and below, p. 159.
[5] Hephaest. 9 (Π. χοριαμβικοῦ) 4 Philic. fr. 1 B, *AL* II² fasc. 6 (1942) 158 καινογράφου συνθέσεως τῆς Φιλίκου, γραμματικοί, δῶρα φέρω πρὸς ὑμᾶς; new fragments of *ca.* 60 lines of the hymn in *PSI* XII (1951) 1282, pp. 140 ff. ed. C. Gallavotti (first publ. in 1927).
[6] As it was omitted by Lehrs, Herodiani *Scripta tria* (1848), it found no place in the extensive modern discussion on γραμματικός, as far as I can see.
[7] Schol. Dionys. Thr., *Gr. Gr.* III ed. Hilgard p. 3. 24, cf. p. 7. 24; ibid. p. 448. 6 φασὶ δὲ Ἀντίδωρον τὸν Κυμαῖον πρῶτον ἐπιγεγραφέναι αὐτὸν γραμματικόν, σύγγραμμά τι γράψαντα Περὶ Ὁμήρου καὶ Ἡσιόδου.

beginning of the third century B.C.[1] But this answer was not undisputed, as we learn from the excerpt of a catalogue of 'first inventors' in Clement of Alexandria[2] in which, together with Antidorus, two rivals are listed: Eratosthenes, 'because he published two books inscribed Γραμματικά', and Praxiphanes[3] 'according to the usage of the present day the first to be called γραμματικός'. The literary work of Praxiphanes is here regarded as foreshadowing the work of the Alexandrian γραμματικοί; his name appears also in the Scholia[4] to Dionysius Thrax in a remarkable historical construction which draws a line from Theagenes in the sixth century B.C.[5] as the beginning of γραμματική to its τέλος, its culmination, in the literary work of the Peripatetics Praxiphanes and Aristotle.[6] Though we find no solution to the ζήτημα, there are at least traces of a learned inquiry. Its author may well have been Asclepiades of Myrlea (second/first century B.C.), possibly a pupil of Dionysius Thrax, who in a work of no less than eleven books dealt with γραμματική in general as a τέχνη and with the individual γραμματικοί; it is a reasonable assumption that he was the ultimate source of the Scholia to Dionysius and through them even of later Byzantine excerptors like Tzetzes.[7]

Eratosthenes did not regard himself as a γραμματικός, but claimed the new title of φιλόλογος, as Suetonius[8] informs us: 'Philologi adpellationem adsumpsisse videtur (sc. L. Ateius) quia, sic ut Eratosthenes qui primus hoc cognomen sibi vindicavit, multiplici variaque doctrina censebatur.' Apollodorus of Athens, who was so near to Eratosthenes as chronographer and geographer, became the only other great Alexandrian scholar to be called φιλόλογος by Ps.-Scymnus in the next generation. This was very appropriate; the same epithet was less appropriately applied to an antiquarian, Demetrius of Scepsis, by Diogenes Laertius (φιλόλογος ἄκρως).[9]

---

[1] B. A. Müller, *RE* Suppl. III (1918) 121 ff., demonstrates that we can no longer put Antidorus into the fifth century B.C.

[2] Clem. Al. *Strom.* I 16, 79. 3 (II p. 51. 17 ff.). In the passage γραμματικός, ὡς νῦν ὀνομάζομεν, πρῶτος Πραξιφάνης the νῦν, of course, refers to the time of Clement's Hellenistic source, possibly Asclepiades of Myrlea.

[3] See above, pp. 135 f., test. 8 Brink = fr. 10 Wehrli.

[4] Schol. Vat. p. 164. 22 Hilg. and Schol. Lond. p. 448. 13.

[5] See above, p. 11.

[6] Cf. Dio Chrys. *or.* 36, above, p. 67.

[7] G. Kaibel, *Die Prolegomena Περὶ κωμῳδίας, AGGW* N.F. II 4 (1898) 27 ff.; this convincing reconstruction should not have been so often overlooked. On Asclepiades see also below, pp. 162 f. and 273.

[8] Sueton. 'De grammaticis et rhetoribus' c. 10 in Sueton. praeter Caesarum libros *reliquiae* coll. G. Brugnoli I² (1963) 14.

[9] See below, p. 253, on Apollodorus and p. 250, n. 1 on Demetrius. Both these testimonia, not unimportant for our purpose, are missing in all the monographs on φιλόλογος, listed above, p. 156, n. 3.

The Sophists had a predilection for compounds with φιλο-,[1] and it may
be due to them that we find φιλόλογος first in Plato (five times from the
Laches to the *Laws*) and once in a comedy of Alexis in the later fourth
century;[2] it means a man fond of talk, dispute, dialectic in a wide
and rather vague or ironical sense. But when Eratosthenes used it, or
when the new Diegesis[3] to the first *Iambus* of Callimachus says that
Hipponax coming from the dead calls τοὺς φιλολόγους εἰς τὸ Παρμενίωνος
καλούμενον Σαραπίδειον, the compound refers (according to Suetonius) to
persons who are familiar with various branches of knowledge or even with
the whole of the λόγος. Members of the Museum were in fact scientists as
well as scholars.[4] It is, however, not likely that Callimachus himself used
the word φιλόλογος in his choliambic trimeters, and thus anticipated
Eratosthenes' nomenclature;[5] the diegetes agrees with Strabo XVII 794
τῶν μετεχόντων τοῦ Μουσείου φιλολόγων ἀνδρῶν, while Ath. I 22 D calls
them φιλοσόφους and so do inscriptions and papyri of Roman times.
Their Pergamene rivals refused to be known as φιλόλογοι and γραμματικοί and reverted to the earlier term κριτικοί.[6] The conclusion to be
drawn from this survey is obvious. Not only was the time before Aristotle
noticeably free from technicalities in the literary field, but throughout the
Hellenistic age also, though there was more interest in classification,
terminology remained rather vague and fluid.[7] We must be anxious to
understand it, but we cannot use it as a guide when we try to reconstruct
the historical process.

Eratosthenes' books on literary subjects represent only a modest part
of his many-sided φιλολογία. His most voluminous work in the grammatical field was the twelve or more books Περὶ τῆς ἀρχαίας κωμῳδίας.[8]

---

[1] See *Vors.* III 454 ff., especially Gorgias; on φιλο- compounds from Homer to Pindar see
W. Burkert, *Herm.* 88 (1960) 172 ff.

[2] Plat. *Lach.* 188 c, *Rep.* IX 582 E, *Theaet.* 161 A, cf. 146 A φιλολογία, *Phaedr.* 236 E, *Leg.*
641 E φιλόλογος καὶ πολύλογος; Alexis fr. 284 K. (in Ath. II 39 B after Alexis fr. 283) ὅτι οἶνος
φιλολόγους πάντας ποιεῖ τοὺς πλεῖον πίνοντας αὐτόν, trimetros rest. Meineke, alii.

[3] *Dieg.* VI 2 ff. to Call. fr. 191. 9 ff.; see my note on VI 3 about variant readings and parallels
and see above, p. 102, n. 1, about the Serapeum.

[4] See above, p. 97.

[5] Suid. v. Μυρώ, Βυζαντία, ποιήτρια . . . Ὁμήρου τοῦ τραγικοῦ μήτηρ (θυγάτηρ codd.), γυνὴ
δὲ Ἀνδρομάχου τοῦ ἐπικληθέντος φιλολόγου; this Andromachus, the father of a member of the
tragic Pleiad, must have lived at the beginning of the third century B.C. If he was given the
surname φιλόλογος to distinguish him from other Andromachi (we do not know when and
by whom), he has no strong claim to priority against Eratosthenes.

[6] Κράτης . . . ὁ κριτικός, etc. see below, p. 238; cf. E. Schwartz, 'Philologen und Philo-
sophen im Altertum', *Festschrift für P. Hensel* (1923) 72 ff. = *Gesammelte Schriften* I (1938) 88 ff.

[7] See the general remarks of A. Wifstrand in Nilsson, *Griech. Religion* II (1950) 671. 1.

[8] In this form the title is quoted four times. Strecker's useful collection of the fragments of
Lycophron, Euphronius, and Eratosthenes, (see above, p. 119, n. 6) should be used with great
caution, as the author is very generous in assigning anonymous glosses to these three

Lycophron[1] had started to revise the text of the comic poets and to add a glossographic treatise, and Alexander Aetolus had dealt with tragedies and satyr-plays. Callimachus,[2] of course, included all the tragic and comic poets in his general alphabetical Πίνακες and his special chronological Πίναξ of the dramatists. But we know of no successor to Alexander Aetolus before Aristophanes of Byzantium at the end of the century; on the other hand, Lycophron's work was immediately continued by Euphronius, Dionysiades, and Eratosthenes. There again chronology is problematical. If we may rightly infer from the very confused and lacunose biographical article in Suidas v. Ἀριστοφάνης[3] that Aristophanes of Byzantium was Euphronius' pupil, and if the source of the Byzantine commentary of Georgius Choeroboscus on Hephaestio's metrical handbook[4] correctly places him with the tragic Pleiad[5] under Ptolemy II, we may tentatively put Euphronius between Lycophron and Eratosthenes. The other member of this exclusive circle of poets, Dionysiades of Mallos[6] is said by Suidas to have been the author of a work Χαρακτῆρες ἢ Φιλο-κώμῳδοι, 'in which he describes (ἀπαγγέλλει) the characters of the poets'; whatever is meant by the unique Φιλοκώμῳδοι,[7] this looks like the first effort to distinguish the style of the Attic comic poets and may have been the source of later treatises such as those of Platonius Περὶ διαφορᾶς κω-μῳδιῶν and especially Περὶ διαφορᾶς χαρακτήρων[8] (that is, in Cratinus', Eupolis', and Aristophanes' comedies). The fact that it was *poets* who began the scholarly work on Old Attic Comedy fits in quite well with our general picture of the first half of the third century B.C.; it does seem a little odd that all three of them were tragedians, but it is just possible that Machon, the famous producer of comedies in Alexandria and infamous poet of obscene anecdotes (χρεῖαι) in iambic verse, also wrote a book on the parts of the comedy.[9]

Welcome new evidence for Euphronius was supplied by a new

grammarians; Bk. XI is quoted in fr. 25, and probably Bk. XII in fr. 47. A new fragment of this work may be the proverb Ἐρατοσθένης· 'Μὴ ἄνω τῆς πτέρνης' in Cod. Laur. LVIII 24, publ. by L. Cohn, *Zu den Paroemiographen* (1887) 25, 41.

[1] See above, pp. 119 f.   [2] See above, pp. 129 f. and 131 f.

[3] See A. Adler's references ad loc.

[4] Hephaest. ed. M. Consbruch (1906) 236. 14 Διονυσιάδην καὶ Εὐφρόνιον τῇ Πλειάδι συν-τάττουσιν (ibid. 236. 5 ἐπὶ τῶν χρόνων Πτολεμαίου τοῦ Φιλαδέλφου), in the same commentary pp. 241. 11 ff. Εὐφρόνιος ὁ γραμματικὸς ἐπὶ τῶν Πτολεμαίων ἐν Ἀλεξανδρείᾳ is a poet of Priapea (cf. Strab. VIII 382) and one of Aristarchus' teachers—a gross mistake.

[5] On the Pleiad see above, p. 119, n. 1.

[6] See above, n. 4; Suid. v. Διονυσιάδης . . . τραγικός; A. Körte, 'Komödie', *RE* XI (1922) 1208. 50 ff.

[7] Φιλοκώμῳδός coni. Meineke *FCG* I (1839) 12 in his priceless 'Historia critica comicorum Graecorum'.   [8] *CGF* I 6; cf. Kaibel's note on p. 3.

[9] Athen. VI 241 F τῶν κατὰ κωμῳδίαν μερῶν, cf. Körte, *RE* XI 1209. 5 and below, p. 189.

lexicographical source:[1] Εὐφρόνιος ὁ γραμματικὸς ἐν Ὑπομνήματι Πλού-
του Ἀριστοφάνους. We have already noted that a series of poets from
Philitas to Apollonius contributed to the exegesis of early epic, lyric,
dramatic poetry;[2] but this is the first attestation of a ὑπόμνημα, a commentary, written by a member of the tragic Pleiad.[3] Aristophanes' latest
comedy (388 B.C.), fabulous and moralistic and ironical, seems to have
been the favourite of posterity from the early Hellenistic to the latest
Byzantine times and again in the Italian Renaissance, when it was the
first to be translated into Latin and made known to the Western world.
From the only two quotations that we had before Εὐφρόνιος ἐν τοῖς ὑπομνήμασιν,[4] of which the one on Lasus of Hermione and the κύκλιοι χοροί
was particularly important, 'Hypomnemata' could easily be understood
as a loose series of notes like those of Lycophron and Eratosthenes.[5] But
now we see that probably Commentaries on individual plays are meant;[6]
it would be rash to assume that Euphronius wrote a continuous commentary on all the Aristophanic comedies.

Eratosthenes' interest was perhaps stimulated by performances of
comedies and by Peripatetic, Academic, and Atthidographic books on
comedy that he had seen in Athens; later in Alexandria the treasures of
the library were at his disposal including the new writings on this subject
just mentioned (although it must be noted that so far no references of his
to Euphronius have been attested). We cannot tell either whether he
propounded a special theory on the origin of comedy despite an apparent allusion in his elegiac poem *Erigone*.[7] The only comic poets
Eratosthenes quoted by name are Aristophanes, Cratinus, Eupolis, Pherecrates, the foremost representatives of Old Comedy. In our scanty fragments glosses are elucidated (κύτταρον, σισύρα, μολγός, φελλός κτλ.), the
name of his native Cyrene turns up in remarks on dialects, the long ā in
εὐκλεία is discussed in a grammatical note, and so is a special form of the
dual (if this does not belong to a writing on Homer). No doubt he had
more interest in the comic language than his immediate predecessors; and
he seems even to have noted pseudo-Attic forms as signs of spurious plays.

---

[1] Lexicon Messanense (a part of Orus' Orthography, see R. Reitzenstein, *Geschichte der griechischen Etymologika* (1897) 289 ff.) ed. H. Rabe, *Rh.M.* 47 (1892) 411: Aristoph. *Pl.* 138, 1115 ψῶστον . . . ἐκτείνουσι τὸ ᾱ . . . γράφεται σὺν τῷ ῑ.   [2] See above, pp. 140, 146.

[3] For the first *Plutos*, produced twenty years earlier, the only quotation with ἐν Πλούτῳ πρώτῳ expressly added seems to go back to Euphronius fr. 64 Str. = Schol. (v) Aristoph. *Ran.* 1093.

[4] Schol. (v) Aristoph. *Av.* 1403 = 77 Str. and Athen. xi 495 c = fr. 107 Str.

[5] So in *RE* vi (1907) 1221. 10 ff. by L. Cohn.

[6] His name most frequently occurs in the Scholia to the *Birds* and to the *Wasps*; on *Plut.* and *Ran.* see above n. 3 and in general *The Scholia on the Aves of Aristophanes* ed. J. W. White (1914) xvii.   [7] See below, p. 169.

His knowledge of the διδασκαλίαι as well as of the copies in the library led him to inquire into questions of the performances of tragedies and comedies, for instance whether there was a second performance of Aristophanes' *Eirene* or even a second play with the same name and whether another version of Aeschylus' *Persai* was produced in Sicily for Hieron.[1] Furthermore we owe to Eratosthenes' wide literary horizon a few important critical comments on lyrics. He assigned to Lamprocles[2] a popular ancient hymn addressed to Athena, to which Aristophanes and Phrynichus had alluded in comedies, and he[3] recognized that Archilochus' famous "τήνελλα καλλίνικε"[4] was not the beginning of an epinicion but the refrain of a hymn to Heracles; Callimachus also had rightly called it a νικαῖον ἐφύμνιον (fr. 384. 39).

Attic comedy and Hellenistic poetry liked to play with the technical terms of the craftsman, especially the carpenter. Eratosthenes collected and explained them under the title Ἀρχιτεκτονικός[5] 'Master-builder'; the few fragments that survive deal with the parts of the carriage, the boat, and the plough. Another book with the title Σκευογραφικός,[6] of which no fragments are preserved, may have expounded in a similar way the words for domestic utensils. There remain the two books which he is said to have 'published after entitling them Γραμματικά',[7] a rather unusual and non-committal title, the only parallel to which is perhaps the Γραμματικά of Asclepiades of Myrlea.[8] From this work may come the general definition, Ἐρατοσθένης ἔφη ὅτι γραμματική ἐστιν ἕξις παντελὴς ἐν γράμμασι, γράμματα καλῶν τὰ συγγράμματα,[9] and some grammatical fragments which hardly fit into any of the other known books.[10]

[1] Arg. Aristoph. *Pax* II and Schol. Aristoph. *Ran.* 1028.
[2] *PMG* fr. 735 Page = *AL* II² p. 152 Diehl with many references to which Chamaeleo fr. 28–29 with Wehrli's commentary (*Schule des Aristoteles* 9, 1957) has to be added; see esp. Wilamowitz, *Textgeschichte der griechischen Lyriker* 84 f. Call. *hy.* v 43 is also an allusion to the same archaic hymn.
[3] Schol. Pind. *O.* IX I k; cf. Schol. Aristoph. *Av.* 1764 = fr. 136 Str. = *FGrHist* 241 F 44; Wilamowitz, *Griech. Verskunst* 286. 4.   [4] Archil. fr. 120 D.³ = fr. 298 Lasserre.
[5] Erat. fr. 39, 60, 17 Strecker; there is no reason to regard it as a part of the work on comedy.
[6] Poll. x 1, who was very much disappointed when he finally got a copy.
[7] See above, p. 158, n. 2.
[8] Suid. v. Ὀρφεύς, Κροτωνιάτης ἐποποιός, ὃν Πεισιστράτῳ συνεῖναι τῷ τυράννῳ Ἀσκληπιάδης ἐν τῷ ϛʹ βιβλίῳ τῶν Γραμματικῶν; if this is the correct general title of the large work, it was divided into two parts, a systematic Περὶ γραμματικῆς (Sext. Emp. *Adv. math.* I 252, vol. III p. 62. 22 Mau) and a biographical Περὶ γραμματικῶν (*Comment. in Arat. reliqu.* ed. E. Maass, p. 76. 5); on Asclepiades see above, p. 158, and on his Γραμματικά H. Usener, *Kleine Schriften* II (1913) 309. 125.
[9] Schol. Dionys. Thr., *Gr. Gr.* III p. 160. 10. The Scholiast emphasizes the same use of γράμματα for συγγράμματα by Call. *Ep.* 6 and 23; cf. the passage of Asclepiades in Sext. Emp., just quoted.
[10] See G. Knaack *RE* VI 384 f. and below, p. 180, on accents.

Eratosthenes was primarily a scientist as we stated at the beginning. In his writings on Old Comedy and related subjects there is naturally no evidence of this. But in his fundamental books on chronology and geography we can clearly see the scientist in him, especially the mathematician and astronomer, informing the work of the scholar. It is this that distinguishes them from the previous attempts of Sophists, philosophers, and historians.

Eratosthenes fully deserves to be honoured as the founder of critical chronology in antiquity.[1] (It is, of course, no accident that the revival of these studies at the end of the sixteenth and the beginning of the seventeenth century A.D. by J. J. Scaliger coincided with the founding of modern science in the later Renaissance.) The most reliable authentic documents on which Eratosthenes could base the dates of historical events were the lists of the winners in the Olympic games; since Hippias had started to reconstruct the ᾿Ολυμπιονικῶν ἀναγραφή and Aristotle and others like Timaeus had followed him,[2] Eratosthenes was able to build upon these earlier efforts in his own register of ᾿Ολυμπιονῖκαι,[3] a work of at least two books. In his greater work, the Χρονογραφίαι,[4] he first expounded the principles of scientific chronology and then worked out a complete chronological table[5] on the foundation of the Olympic lists. The first known ᾿Ολυμπιονίκης was Koroibos of Elis in the year 776/5 B.C. (according to our era) and this was fixed as the first year of the first ᾿Ολυμπιάς. The fact that Eratosthenes made this choice was decisive for the dating by Olympiads in later antiquity and even beyond it.

But there were historical events before the first Olympiad, and for dating them he had to use one of the local systems; it is now generally accepted that this was not Ctesias' Assyrian list, but the list of the Spartan kings preserved in Eusebius' Χρονικά.[6] The beginning of this list takes us back to the year 1104/3 B.C., which is that of the ῾Ηρακλειδῶν κάθοδος; the Ionic migration was put sixty years later, and the taking of Troy, Τροίας ἅλωσις, eighty years earlier, 1184/3 B.C. The period between this earliest date and the latest, that of Alexander's death (324/3 B.C.), was divided into ten epochs.[7] At this point the modern scientist may be inclined to moderate his appreciation of Eratosthenes' merits, noticing with

---

[1] Van der Waerden, *Science awakening* (1954) 228 ff.
[2] See above, pp. 51 and 80 f.; on Timaeus see *FGrHist* 566 T 1, 10; F 125–8.
[3] *FGrHist* 241 F 4–8.   [4] *FGrHist* 241 F 1–3.
[5] On 'Zeittafeln' see Regenbogen, Πίναξ *RE* xx 1462. 60 ff.
[6] E. Schwartz, 'Die Königslisten des Eratosthenes und Kastor', *AGGW* 40 (1894/5) 60 ff.; the excerpt from Diodorus in Euseb. *Chron.* 1 221. 31 ff. See also W. Kubitschek, 'Königsverzeichnisse', *RE* xi (1922) 1015 ff.
[7] *FGrHist* 241 F 1.

regret 'that, in connection with the Trojan war, he could not avoid deviating from his principle' of eliminating 'all unverifiable legends'.[1] For the Greek mind, however, the siege and taking of Troy was no legend, but a momentous fact of history for which any chronological system must provide a date. Homer too, as the poet of the *Iliad*, in which he trans-mitted and gave form to the heroic deeds of the great war, and of the post-war poem, the *Odyssey*, was a historical person to every Greek; from the sixth century onwards innumerable conjectures were made about this date and its relation to Hesiod's.[2] In the historical part of his *Geography* where he dealt seriously with Homeric problems, Eratosthenes[3] fixed Homer's floruit a hundred years after the Trojan war, but before the Ionic migration, and put Hesiod later than Homer. The lives and works of post-epic writers he could date according to Olympiads,[4] thus applying a systematic approach to literary chronology in place of the earlier rather arbitrary efforts. About a century later Apollodorus of Athens built his *Χρονικά*[5] on the foundations laid by Eratosthenes, although with some alterations; this more popular work superseded the esoteric *Χρονο-γραφίαι*, and this is the reason why so very little of them is left to us. It is fairly well attested and not incredible in itself that Eratosthenes as astronomer and mathematician wrote also on an intricate problem of the calendar, the eight-year-cycle, *Περὶ τῆς Ὀκταετηρίδος*;[6] in this book he is said to have discussed, quite characteristically for him, the genuineness of a work of Eudoxus on the same subject and the position of an Isis-festival in the calendar.

His greatest achievement, his geography,[7]—the compound *γεωγραφία* was possibly coined by him—runs parallel in some respects to his work in chronology. The book *Περὶ τῆς ἀναμετρήσεως τῆς γῆς*[8] 'On the measure-ment of the earth', as a sort of *πίναξ*, corresponds to the Olympic lists, with the help of which he had determined the sequence of historical dates; here using all his mathematical and astronomical training and

---

[1] Van der Waerden, *Science awakening* 230.
[2] See above, pp. 11, 43, etc.
[3] F 9 and Jacoby's commentary.
[4] F 7. 10–13; Empedocles, Pherecydes of Syros, Pythagoras, Hippocrates.
[5] See below, p. 255.
[6] Gemin. *Isag.* 8. 24 p. 110 Manitius and *Commentariorum in Arat. rel.* ed. E. Maass (1898) 47. 23; since the text is restored by E. Maass, 'Aratea', *Philol. Untersuchungen* 12 (1892) 14 f., there is no longer any reason for the scepticism mistakenly expressed by Christ–Schmid, *Griech. Lit.* II 1⁶ (1920) 249 f.
[7] Collections of fragments see above, p. 153, n. 2; cf. H. Berger, *Geschichte der wissenschaft-lichen Erdkunde der Griechen*² (1903) 384 ff., A. Rehm–K. Vogel, *Exakte Wissenschaften*⁴ (1933) 42 ff., and especially F. Gisinger's comprehensive article 'Geographie', *RE* Suppl. 4 (1924) 521–685; on *γεωγραφία* 523 f., on Eratosthenes 604–14.
[8] Heron, 'Dioptr.' c. 35, *Opera* III (1903) ed. H. Schöne, p. 302. 16.

Eratosthenes

with the help of new instruments, he tried to determine the distance of localities from each other, their latitude and longitude, and even the perimeter of the earth. As in the chronology he cautiously and conscientiously adapted, corrected, and supplemented the researches of his predecessors Eudoxus and Dicaearchus. Although the results could only be approximate, modern scientists are always amazed how near he came to the truth.[1]

His main work, roughly corresponding to the Χρονογραφίαι in the other field, was the Γεωγραφικά in three books.[2] The first of these reveals how well he had used the library[3] and made himself familiar with the complete earlier history of geography. The second book is based on his own special research recorded in 'On measurement', and the third on the new maps he had sketched himself. He concluded his systematic work with a descriptive section in which he defined the characteristics of individual countries, and for this he drew heavily on the results of the exploration that had continued from Alexander's time to his own. The Γεωγραφικά met with no lack either of admiration or of severe criticism, the latter especially at the hand of Hipparchus, writing from the astronomical point of view in the middle of the second century B.C., and of Polybius as an adversary of mathematical geography; but unlike the Χρονογραφίαι it was not absorbed by any later work. Eratosthenes' most distinguished successor in the geographical field corresponding to Apollodorus in the chronological, was Posidonius, in the first half of the first century B.C.; but though he arranged his work Περὶ Ὠκεανοῦ καὶ τῶν κατ' αὐτόν[4] after the example of the Γεωγραφικά,[5] he was a Stoic philosopher and physicist of some originality, not an eclectic writer from whose excerpts possible models and sources could be reconstructed. Strabo, on the other hand, at the end of the first century B.C., incorporated extracts from Eratosthenes and Posidonius into the first two books of his Γεωγραφικά; it is to him that we owe our entire knowledge of Eratosthenes' Homeric geography and

[1] F. Gisinger loc. cit. 605 f.
[2] Strab. 1 29, 11 init., xv 688; Schol. Ap. Rh. iv 284, 310 *passim*, v. Index p. 333 give this apparently correct form of the title; occasionally less reliable quotations are Γεωγραφούμενα, Γεωγραφία, Ὑπομνήματα, see Bernhardy, *Eratosthenica* 26 f.; H. Berger, *Erdkunde der Griechen*[2] 387. 2.
[3] Hipparch., quoted by Strab. 11 69 Ἐρατοσθένης ... ἐντετυχηκὼς ὑπομνήμασι πολλοῖς ὧν εὐπόρει βιβλιοθήκην ἔχων τηλικαύτην ἡλίκην αὐτὸς Ἵππαρχός φησι; cf. H. Berger, *Die geographischen Fragmente des Hipparch* (1869) 96. 'The geographical fragments of Hipparchus' ed. D. R. Dicks, *Univ. of London Class. Studies* 1 (1959) 123.
[4] *FGrHist* 87 F 74-105.
[5] K. Reinhardt, 'Poseidonios', *RE* xxii (1953) 664; cf. 624 ff. 'Gesamtcharakteristik, Stil'. On this most extraordinary *retractatio* of the complex Posidonian problem (278 cols.) see *Jahrbuch der Bayer. Akademie der Wissenschaften* 1959, p. 149.

of his general remarks on literary criticism.[1] Strabo's not uncritical compilation is typical of the Augustan age which, no longer productive itself, preserved in its collections some priceless treasures of Hellenistic scholarship and science.

Eratosthenes opened his review of earlier writers on geography with Homer, a natural parallel to the position assigned to him and to the Trojan war in the Χρονογραφίαι. But though he regarded that expedition as the earliest known event in Greek history, he by no means accepted the poet either as a historian, or as a geographer. To the scientific rationalistic mind of Eratosthenes the unrealities in Homeric geography were obvious. He did not blame the poet; the fault was in the interpreters who made the fundamental mistake of identifying epic localities with certain places in the Mediterranean and supposing that Homer made it his business to teach people geography or anything else such as theology, ethics, or military tactics. Homer's geographical passages, for instance the wanderings of Odysseus,[2] were to be regarded as purely imaginary; the aim of the poet was there and elsewhere not to instruct but to give pleasure.

What no scholar had dared to say the scientist was consistent and fearless enough not only to state in Homer's case, but to apply to poetry in general: ποιητὴν γὰρ ἔφη πάντα στοχάζεσθαι ψυχαγωγίας, οὐ διδασκαλίας (Strab. 115).[3] In contrast to διδασκαλία, 'instruction', ψυχαγωγία can only mean 'entertainment'. Eratosthenes' categorical statement that every poet aimed at it was a highly provocative declaration. Strabo, of course, when he had quoted it, immediately contradicted it with his own opinion which he may have derived from earlier Stoics like Posidonius. But even in Eratosthenes' own time or shortly afterwards[4] Neoptolemus of Parium had corrected his predecessor, consciously it seems, as he used the rather uncommon expression ψυχαγωγία in the same connexion and in the same sense: καὶ πρὸς ἀρε[τὴν δεῖν τ]ῷ τελείῳ ποιη[τῇ μετὰ τ]ῆς ψυχαγω[γί]α[ς τοῦ τοὺς] ἀκούοντ[ας] ὠ[φελεῖ]ν καὶ χρησι[μο]λ[ογεῖ]ν καὶ τὸν Ὅμη[ρον τ]έρπειν [τε καὶ ὠφελεῖν] τὸ [πλεῖ]ον.[5] This was the compromise, a very

---

[1] On Strabo's attitude to Eratosthenes see above, p. 154, on Eratosthenes and Homer cf. above, pp. 163 f.

[2] Cf. K. Lehrs, *De Aristarchi studiis Homericis* (1882, 3rd ed.) 240 ff.

[3] Cf. 16 and 25 = Erat. *Geogr. Fragm.* pp. 36 f. with Berger's notes. About a century after Eratosthenes Agatharchides (*GGM* p. 117. 16) changing διδασκαλίας into ἀληθείας said: ὅτι πᾶς ποιητὴς ψυχαγωγίας (sc. μᾶλλον) ἢ ἀληθείας στοχαστός.

[4] Neoptolemus is quoted by Aristophanes of Byzantium, Eust. p. 1817. 19–22 (on ρ 219 μολοβρός); there is no reason to remove this clear testimony by changing φησί into φασί, as Nauck, *Aristoph. Byz. fragm.* p. 119. 70 tried to do. Neoptolemus is correctly characterized and dated by C. O. Brink, *Horace on Poetry* (1963) 43 ff., see esp. 45. 2.

[5] Philodem. Περὶ ποιημάτων V ed. C. Jensen (1923) col. XIII 8–15 p. 33, cf. pp. 108 f., 123, 152 f.; see Brink 55.

effective one, that finally led to Horace's famous formula: Hor. *A.P.* 333 'et prodesse volunt et delectare poetae . . . simul et iucunda et idonea dicere vitae', and ll. 99 ff. 'poemata . . . quocumque volent animum auditoris agunto', a translation of ψυχαγωγεῖν. The reaction against Eratosthenes was quite natural in view of the general Greek belief that all men had *learned* 'from Homer since the beginning',[1] and given the innate ethical and educational tendency in Greek poetry from epic times onwards. In Attic comedy, especially in Aristophanes' *Frogs*, the problem of the moral leadership of the poets and the usefulness (ὠφέλεια) and the danger of their teaching (διδάσκειν) was openly debated.[2] Plato, for various reasons, was inclined to deny poetry real seriousness and usefulness and to take it as 'play' effecting only 'pleasure' (παιδιά, ἡδονή).[3] As a Platonist Eratosthenes could feel himself in agreement with this theory of ἡδονή. His arguments, however, were quite different, since they were those of the scientist who refused to take the geographical ideas and descriptions of the epic poet literally.[4] Still less was he prepared to assume 'hidden meanings' as his Stoic predecessors and contemporaries did,[5] in revival of the ancient practice of allegorical interpretation.[6]

Eratosthenes was successful in so far as the greatest Alexandrian scholars of the following generations considered his opinions with an open mind, although they did not fully accept his radical doctrine; and this seems to be the only point where we have to acknowledge the influence of science on scholarship, an important but very limited influence.[7] On the other hand, learned men and eager amateurs of all ages have ignored Eratosthenes' sober arguments and tried indefatigably to find places exactly corresponding to the indication in the poems, not only historical places like Ithaca or Pylos or the cities in the 'catalogue of ships', but also the localities of Odysseus' wanderings—which are quite a different matter. In the first case the epics became as it were textbooks of geography, in spite of well-grounded protests;[8] in the second case absurdities beyond measure were suggested, by which Odysseus emerged as an explorer of the

---

[1] See above, p. 9.   [2] See above, p. 48.

[3] See above, pp. 58 and 75, on Plato and Aristotle.

[4] Erat. *Geogr. Fragmente* 22 ff. and H. Berger, *Erdkunde der Griechen*[2] 386 ff.

[5] References to the fragments of Zeno, Cleanthes, Chrysippus relative to allegory Pohlenz, *Stoa* II 55.

[6] See above, pp. 10 f.

[7] This is the answer to our question on p. 153; Wilamowitz, *Hom. Untersuchungen* (1884) 385 'die exakten Wissenschaften haben auf die alexandrinische Philologie den bedeutendsten Einfluß ausgeübt', this general assertion is supported only by a vague reference to Eratosthenes. See also the general remarks on the relation of science (incl. medicine) to scholarship by H. J. Mette, *Parateresis* (1952) 63 f.

[8] G. Jachmann, *Der homerische Schiffskatalog* (1958) 10.

arctic zone or, if you please, as a traveller through Africa, or Calypso,
her name derived from teutonic 'hel', was placed in Heligoland. As
a matter of fact, the epic poets display a remarkable indifference towards
both time and space in their narratives. This is not the place to follow up
these difficulties of interpretation on which Eratosthenes had touched;
but in this connexion we may be allowed to cite his well-known quip:[1]
τότε ἂν εὑρεῖν τινα λέγει ποῦ ᾿Οδυσσεὺς πεπλάνηται, ὅταν εὕρῃ τὸν σκυτέα
τὸν συρράψαντα τὸν τῶν ἀνέμων ἀσκόν. That ἀπόφασις, of which Polybius
strongly disapproved, is a good example of Eratosthenes' ironical style,
and with so very few complete sentences preserved we probably have to
regret the loss of other shrewd witticisms.

We have seen how Eratosthenes' inquiries ranged over the whole of the
earth's surface and into the periods of mankind's past; he is also said to
have given a picture of the sky by producing the first complete Greek
catalogue of the constellations. The title and contents of the so-called
Καταστερισμοί[2] are hotly disputed,[3] but it is at least probable that our
manuscripts preserve an epitome and later adaptation of Eratosthenes'
original monograph. It apparently contained not very much astronomy
but a large collection of mythical or popular stories about the origin of
the constellations. Because of its contribution to this important part of
Greek mythography the *Catasterismi* remained a useful textbook for
centuries and underwent considerable alterations in the course of time.
But there is no reason to doubt that the Alexandrian scientist was the
original author;[4] we have realized again and again how easily he moved
from science to literature in various branches of learning, and his own
poems attest his peculiar interest in the heavenly bodies and the beautiful
star-myths.

The mathematician was recognizable in a formally perfect epigram
addressed to his king.[5] The epic poem *Hermes*[6] drew old mythical tales
about the birth and precocious cleverness of the god from the Homeric

---

[1] Fr. 1 A 16 Berger p. 36 = Strab. 1 24 (Eust. p. 1645. 64 on κ 19).

[2] This title is a conjecture of John Fell in his *editio princeps*, Oxford 1672.

[3] G. Knaack *RE* vi 378 ff. gives a concise critical report of this dispute; Keller, *Eratosthenes*
(1946) (above, p. 154, n. 3) 18–28 re-examined the modern literature in detail; cf. Solmsen,
TAPA 73 (1942) 204 f. The reconstructions of C. Robert, *Eratosthenis catasterismorum reliquiae*
(1878, reprinted 1963) and especially A. Rehm, *Herm.* 34 (1899) 251–79 are still fundamental.
J. Martin, *Histoire du texte des Phénomènes d'Aratos* (1956, above, p. 121, n. 4) 58 ff. 'Le Problème
des Catastérismes' published (p. 99) from the codex Scorialensis Σ III 3 a new reference to
Eratosthenes, in which the star of the Virgin is identified with Erigone, the daughter of
Icarius.

[4] I confess I am still sceptical—*pace* Solmsen—about the supposition that Eratosthenes in
the *Catasterismi*, as a faithful Platonist, saw human souls in the stars.

[5] Above, p. 155.   [6] Fr. 1–16 Powell; cf. above, p. 157.

hymn to Hermes and combined them in a unique way with the cosmology of Plato's *Timaeus* and Eratosthenes' own geography; when the god ascended to the heavenly spheres of the planets, where he became one of them himself, he perceived not only their harmony and their identity with the ἁρμονία of his own lyre but also the five zones into which the earth was divided according to Eratosthenes' geographical theory.

In his elegiac poem *Erigone*[1] a local Attic legend of the village Icaria, in which he may have alluded to a post-Aristotelian Hellenistic theory of the origin of tragedy and comedy,[2] ends with a catasterismus of the peasant Icarius, his daughter Erigone and their dog Maira. In contrast to the *Hermes*, there are no traces of science visible in our fragments of the elegy, which have a strongly Callimachean[3] flavour. How far was Eratosthenes' poetical practice in harmony with his literary theory?[4] Did he intend not to teach anything but simply to 'faire plaisir'? The eighteen hexameters on the 'zones', nearly half of them spondaici, sound rather didactic, and in Callimachus' σοφίη pleasure and truth were united.[5] The very few extant lines of Eratosthenes' poems do not enable us to give a satisfactory answer. He may not have been consistent throughout his long life, and there is not the slightest possibility of fixing the

---

[1] Fr. 22–27 Powell; cf. Erat. *carm. reliquiae* ed. E. Hiller (1872) 94–114 and E. Maass, *Analecta Erat.* (1883) 56–138. See also *Kallimachos-Studien* (1922) 102–12 and F. Solmsen, *TAPA* 78 (1947) 254 ff. It came as a total surprise to discover that the διὰ πάντων ἀμώμητον ποιημάτιον was a bulky Greco-Egyptian conglomerate of every detail that every Greek and Latin writer after Eratosthenes ever mentions about this story. Detailed reconstructions of Greek poems, based on supposed imitators, mythographers, lexicographers, etc., have invariably been discredited as soon as substantial parts of these poems have turned up in papyri. This warning was not heeded by R. Merkelbach, although he is so well acquainted with literary papyri ('Die Erigone des Eratosthenes', *Miscellanea di Studi Alessandrini in memoria di A. Rostagni*, 1963, pp. 469–526).

[2] Fr. 22 Powell; see above, p. 161. I regard it as probable that Eratosthenes' hexameter Ἰκαριοῖ, τόθι πρῶτα περὶ τράγον ὠρχήσαντο refers to the origin of tragedy, because the line Eratosthenes–Neoptolemus–Horace seems to be the same as in the general theory of poetry above, pp. 166 f. The readings of the manuscripts of Hygin. *de astr.* II 4 in Hiller's edition of the *Erigone* p. 106; he correctly took εικαριοι as the locative Ἰκαριοῖ (Steph. Byz. v. Ἰκαρία; cf. also Κίκυννα∼Κικυννοῖ Lys. *or.* 17. 5, 8) followed by τόθι as relative. The same text is given by Powell, but Maass, Diehl (*AL* II² fasc. 6, 1942, p. 85, fr. 5), Pickard-Cambridge, Solmsen, Merkelbach, et al. print Ἰκάριοι with or without a reference to Ἰκαριοῖ. But Ἰκάριοι is the δημοτικόν of the island of Ἰκάρα; the inhabitants of the Attic village of Ἰκαρία are always called Ἰκαριεῖς (see Steph. Byz. and the inscriptions). To Ἰκαριοῖ τόθι πρῶτα compare now Call. fr. 229. 10 ἐν ὕλῃ τόθι πρῶτον ὤφθης and to ὠρχήσαντο at the end of the hexameter Call. fr. 177. 27 (ὀρχήσασθαι Hec. fr. 326); Hiller had referred to Call. *hy.* II 52 and III 240 περὶ πρύλιν ὠρχήσαντο, where in III 241 πρῶτα followed the verb.—For the Icarian dance around the goat and the derivation of tragedy and comedy from this ritual dance see the testimonia collected and discussed by A. W. Pickard-Cambridge, *Dithyramb, Tragedy and Comedy* (1927) 97 ff., 2nd ed. (1962) 69 ff. and by K. Ziegler, *RE* VI A (1937) 'Tragoedia' 1924 ff.; the best collection of the texts is given by K. Meuli, *Mus. Helv.* 12 (1955) 226 f., who is, I am afraid, much too confident about the supposed theory of Eratosthenes.

[3] See *Kallimachos-Studien* 102 ff. and Callimachus II, Index s.v. Eratosthenes.

[4] See above, pp. 166 ff.   [5] See above, pp. 125 and 137 f.

chronology of individual poems and their relation to the prose-writings. This short survey confirms the impression that his poetry was only a parergon, though a characteristic one which links him with the scholar poets from Philitas to Callimachus.

The lack of material surviving from his books in his own pointed style has already been deplored.[1] The anecdotes about him preserved in the biographical tradition are a poor substitute. But as they are repeated everywhere, sometimes with a wrong emphasis, they should not be entirely ignored here. If we remember[2] that Philitas was ridiculed, that Timon sneered at the fellows of the Museum, and that much mockery of the φιλόλογοι is contained in Callimachus' *Iambi*, we can hardly doubt the origin of Eratosthenes' nicknames. It was a clever hit to call him Βῆτα[3] implying that he was in a great diversity of fields the second best, but not the first in any special branch of learning; another nickname Πένταθλος 'the five-sports athlete' points in the same direction. But why should one take seriously the malicious gossip of a learned society? It should never be allowed to do any harm to the memory of one of the greatest scholars of all times. The complexity and interrelation of Eratosthenes' numerous writings calls strongly for a new *complete* collection of his fragments.

History rarely repeats itself. But we shall find in modern times a sequence of three stages analogous, on a grand scale, to that in the third century B.C. First came the revival of scholarship in the Italian Renaissance during the fourteenth and fifteenth centuries A.D., led by great poets from Petrarch to Politian. Then an encyclopedic expansion followed in France and in the Netherlands in the sixteenth and seventeenth centuries, in which science played its part; 'philologia' acquired once more the Eratosthenian meaning, and Salmasius was expressly praised as the Eratosthenes[4] of his time. But finally, when Bentley's genius appeared, creative concentration on textual and literary criticism won the day, as it had when Aristophanes of Byzantium came after Eratosthenes in about 200 B.C.

---

[1] See above, p. 168.
[2] See above, pp. 41 f., 91, 98.
[3] Marcian. 'Epit. Peripl. Menipp.' 2 (*GGM* I p. 565. 26) *Ἐ. ὃν Βῆτα ἐκάλεσαν οἱ τοῦ Μουσείου προστάντες.* Suid. v. *Ἐρατοσθένης . . . βῆτα* (βήματα codd., em. Meursius) *ἐπεκλήθη . . . ἄλλοι Πένταθλον ἐκάλεσαν;* πένταλος depreciatingly used in [Plat.] *amat.* 135 E ff.
[4] T. P. Blount, *Censura celebriorum autorum* (1690) 719.

V

ALEXANDRIAN SCHOLARSHIP AT ITS HEIGHT: ARISTOPHANES OF BYZANTIUM

In the biographical literature Aristophanes of Byzantium is described as the pupil of Zenodotus, Callimachus, and Eratosthenes, that is, of all the leading scholars of the three generations of the third century B.C.; he is said to have studied also with Dionysius Iambus, Euphronius, and Machon. If this perhaps is not literally true in every case,[1] it is still perfectly true in the sense that he inherited the scholarly tradition of a whole century. Standing on the threshold of the second century, he dominated it completely; for his own work was continued by his great pupil Aristarchus and the Aristarchean 'school', Apollodorus of Athens and Dionysius Thrax. So scholarship in Alexandria was able to face the dangers of the internal crisis of 146/5 B.C., and to stand up to the growing rivalry of Pergamum, and the city remained, in spite of many setbacks, the centre of studies until the very end of antiquity.

With the reign of Ptolemy IV Philopator (221–204 B.C.) and Ptolemy V Epiphanes (204–180 B.C.) a gradual political, social, and economic decline began in Egypt.[2] But scholarship was not involved in this; on the contrary, it now displayed its utmost power and reached its highest level, a historical fact that should serve as a warning against the modern sociologists' tendency to exaggerate the influence of the 'social' factor on science and scholarship. For it was precisely the end of the third century that saw the rise of 'pure' scholarship, no longer united with poetry, but an autonomous selfconscious discipline whose representatives claimed the distinctive title of γραμματικοί.

Aristophanes'[3] father Apelles, a commander of mercenaries (ἡγούμενος

---

[1] See the general remark on p. 98.

[2] See the relevant chapters in the books quoted above, p. 87, n. 2, and *RE* XXIII (1959) H. Volkmann, 'Die Dynastie der Ptolemaier in Ägypten' 1600–1762, esp. 1678 ff.

[3] Aristophanis Byzantii *Fragmenta* coll. et dispos. A. Nauck (1848, reprinted 1963); it was extraordinarily fortunate that one of the great scholars of the last century made this comprehensive collection; cf. Susemihl I 428–48; L. Cohn, *RE* II (1895) 994–1005.

στρατιωτῶν), seems to have gone from Byzantium to Alexandria when Aristophanes was still a boy. As a παῖς he is said to have listened to Zenodotus, and as a νέος to Callimachus; at the age of sixty-two he was installed as head of the royal library; and he died when he was seventy-seven years old.[1] We may accept these dates with reserve, but the rest of the biographical article is hopelessly confused. It is usually assumed that Aristophanes became librarian when Eratosthenes died, between 196 and 193 B.C.,[2] and that he was born therefore between 258 and 255 B.C. and died about 180 B.C. But it is nowhere attested that Eratosthenes remained in office until his death at eighty. If he retired earlier and Aristophanes succeeded him about or before the year 200 B.C., the chronology breaks down and the possibility of his having been Zenodotus' pupil grows stronger. Two events in Aristophanes' life are recorded in our sources; when he planned for some reason[3] to flee to king Eumenes II of Pergamum, he was imprisoned for a time; this must have happened after 197 B.C., the first year of Eumenes' reign, and would be reconcilable with the traditional dates. In this story the name of Alexandria's future rival, Pergamum, appears for the first time in the history of scholarship and this is the point relevant to our purpose. The other story may have grown out of one of the jokes made by the fellows of the Museum of which we have already had several examples, though none so absurd. The respectable scholar, so it runs, fell in love with a flower girl in Alexandria and his rival was an elephant.[4] There were various tales of elephants being attracted by the scent of flowers[5] and making love to girls binding and selling wreaths, and Aristophanes himself might have included one in his

---

[1] Suid. v. Ἀριστοφάνης, Βυζάντιος· γραμματικός ... μαθητὴς Καλλιμάχου καὶ Ζηνοδότου· ἀλλὰ τοῦ μὲν νέος, τοῦ δὲ παῖς ἤκουσε ... καὶ προέστη τῆς τοῦ βασιλέως βιβλιοθήκης ... ἔτος ἄγων ξβ' ... τελευτᾷ, ἔτη βεβιωκὼς οζ' (see A. Adler's note ad loc.).

[2] We do not accept the much earlier date that has been conjectured, see above, pp. 153 f. A. Rostagni, 'I Bibliotecari Alessandrini', *Scritti minori* II 1 (1956) 185 ff., tried in vain to place Apollonius the Eidographos between Eratosthenes and Aristophanes against the sequence attested by *P.Oxy.* x (1914) 1241, col. II 6 ff. By a curious slip in Wilamowitz's report about the newly discovered papyrus, *Neue Jahrbücher* 33 (1914) 246 (= *Kl. Schr.* I 412; cf. Pindaros 108) the Eidographos appears after Eratosthenes, not after Aristophanes, as the papyrus and the editors assisted by Wilamowitz correctly stated. See below, p. 210; cf. also the discussion by H. Herter, *Rh.M.* 91 (1942) 317 ff.

[3] Suid. (above, n. 1) διασκευασθεὶς δὲ ὡς βουλευόμενος (Codd. A V, βουλόμενος cett.) πρὸς Εὐμένη φυγεῖν, ἐφυλάχθη κτλ.; this text is hardly sound, and perhaps we should read διασκεφθείς 'observed as planning to fly, he was imprisoned'. But it is just a modern embellishment that 'Eumenes tried to steal Ptolemy's librarian' (so for instance Kenyon, *Books and Readers*, p. 89).

[4] Plin. *n.h.* VIII 13, Plut. *de soll. an.* 972 D, Aelian. *n.a.* I 38, probably from a common source; see F. Jacoby *FGrHist* 275 Juba von Mauretanien (vol. III A, Kommentar, 1943, p. 319 and on F 54).

[5] Aelian. *n.a.* VII 43, XIII 8.

comprehensive book 'On animals' (Περὶ ζῴων),[1] but it is hard to detect any wit in the idea of scholar and elephant being ἀντερασταί.[2]

Aristophanes' compilation Περὶ ζῴων based on Aristotle, Theophrastus, and the paradoxographers is the only contribution he is known to have made to that particular Peripatetic and Alexandrine tradition of natural history and paradoxography which we have distinguished from genuine science.[3] But if he is correctly listed in one of Aratus' biographies with many other writers on *Phaenomena*,[4] this work would belong to the same category; there is no reason to assume that it was a poem. He was neither a scientist nor a poet; he was the perfect scholar.

The scheme under which we classified[5] the occasional scholarly efforts of pre-Hellenistic times can now be applied to the fully developed scholarship of Aristophanes; we shall survey his immense output under the same four heads: texts, language, literary criticism, and antiquities.

Three men began the διόρθωσις of epic, lyric, and dramatic poetry at the beginning of the third century B.C.; but it was Aristophanes alone who towards its end made the fundamental recensions of the texts in all these fields.

Zenodotus' pre-eminence as the first διορθωτής of the epic poems was not seriously challenged in his own day.[6] Can we tell how far Aristophanes and his pupils made a fresh start? Zenodotus had been a pioneer; his successors were in a different position, as they could always compare the new manuscripts coming into the library with his revised text. Timon's sarcastic hit[7] at a 'revised' text of Homer where the παλαιὰ γραφή had been altered shows a characteristic attitude of the Greek spirit; distrust of a hypothetical 'genuine' text, and an inclination to save the 'old text' hallowed by tradition. Aristophanes apparently shared this attitude. Reluctant to delete lines[8] or to put conjectures into the text, he and his

---

[1] Aristoph. 'Hist. an. epitome', ed. S. P. Lambros, *Suppl. Aristotelicum* I 1 (1885); cf. L. de Stefani, *Studi it. di fil. class.* 20 (1913) 189 ff. The authentically Aristophanic part of the late Byzantine excerpts contains no version of the elephant-tale; II 119 p. 64 L. is taken from Aelian *n.a.* VII 43.

[2] The anecdote should certainly not have been treated as one of the *Griechische Märchen von dankbaren Tieren* by A. Marx (1889) 93 f.—It would hardly be an improvement to assume that the elephant-story had its origin in Ἐλέφας as proper name (*IG* v 1, no. 699), or surname (Polyb. XVIII 24. 2), or nickname of a human rival and was then transferred to the animal.

[3] See above, p. 152; his arrangement seems to have been a model for the many later writers on the same subject, see M. Wellmann, *Herm.* 51 (1916) 63 f.

[4] *Comment. in Arat. rel.* ed. E. Maass 79. 6, cf. E. Maass, *Aratea* (1892) 151.

[5] See above, p. 67; cf. also p. 134.   [6] Cf. above, pp. 118 and 123.

[7] See above, pp. 98 and 122.

[8] Zenodotus had omitted Λ 78–83 and M 175–81, probably for internal reasons (see above, p. 114), but Aristophanes kept these passages in his text, obelizing them as not genuine.

pupils preferred to express their opinions by signs in the margin; Aristarchus resorted to separate commentaries or monographs. Zenodotus may have been by no means as bold and arbitrary in his textual criticism as many believe, but Aristophanes and Aristarchus became more conservative still.

In Aristophanes' case it is easier to assess the technical improvements in his editions, of which we have special information,[1] than to reconstruct his actual text, for which we have to rely on occasional remarks in the late Scholia.[2] These are sparse, because from the next generation onwards the Homeric work of his pupil Aristarchus was regarded as the authority on Homer and the agreement or disagreement with his master was not often expressly stated by himself or registered by Aristonicus and Didymus. Similarly we may recall that the success of Apollodorus' Χρονικά made it almost impossible to reconstruct the chronography of Eratosthenes.[3] Even when readings had been originally marked as Aristophanic,[4] some of the later compilers of our Scholia left his name out, keeping only those of Zenodotus or Rhianus (Schol. T *B* 53, *H* 443, *O* 33), although others preserved it (Schol. A to these lines); vice versa, at *Σ* 10 Schol. T has the name, but Schol. A omits it. The hypomnema to Book 21 of the *Iliad*, preserved in *P.Oxy.* 221 of the second century A.D. agrees with the medieval manuscripts of our Scholia in giving the readings in lines 1 and 249 under the name of Aristophanes; but it also contains the words παρὰ Ἀριστοφάνει to the variant reading in line 217 πελάσας for γ' ἐλάσας which are no longer extant in the manuscripts. So in assessing the nature of Aristophanes' edition we must be conscious that our knowledge of it depends on mere chance.

Some of his well-attested readings, rejected by Aristarchus, sound very sensible and plausible. In Zeus' teasing speech to Hera at the beginning of Book 4 of the *Iliad* Aristophanes wrote (*Δ* 17) εἰ δ' αὔτως τόδε πᾶσι φίλον καὶ ἡδὺ γένοιτο 'if this [the second alternative, namely to make peace] would equally please all [the gods]'; the adverb αὔτως (explained by ὁμοίως in Schol. T ad loc.) is exactly what we should expect[5] in this

---

[1] See below, p. 178.

[2] The number of Aristophanic readings in each of the 24 books of the *Iliad* is given by T. W. Allen, Hom. *Il.* 1 (1931) 202; it is about a fifth of the Zenodotean and a tenth of the Aristarchean readings, ibid. 199–201.

[3] See above, p. 164.

[4] A list of all the readings, complete for its time, was compiled by A. Nauck; the text has to be checked against such new editions as are available, and the list supplemented from the papyri.

[5] Aristarchus' αὖ πως (Schol. A) would express uncertainty, and οὕτως in a few manuscripts is a frequent false reading for αὔτως. Cf. Hes. *Th.* 402 αὔτως πάντεσσι, Theocr. XXII 78 αὔτως . . . πάντας.

context before πᾶσι and it can even help to restore a corrupt and sorely tried line of the *Odyssey*.[1]

As the most striking example of Aristophanes' 'acuteness' modern critics frequently emphasize his assumption that line 296 of Book 23 was the 'limit' of the *Odyssey*. The reunion of Odysseus and Penelope, ψ 296 οἱ μὲν ἔπειτα / ἀσπάσιοι λέκτροιο παλαιοῦ θεσμὸν ἵκοντο, is commented on in the Scholia: Ἀριστοφάνης δὲ καὶ Ἀρίσταρχος πέρας[2] τῆς Ὀδυσσείας τοῦτο ποιοῦνται, 'Aristophanes and Aristarchus took that line as the limit of the Odyssey.' Eustathius correctly paraphrased this by περατοῦσι τὴν Ὀδύσσειαν and added, to make it perfectly clear, that 'they considered the following part, up to the end of the Odyssey as spurious' ἕως τέλους τοῦ βίβλου (sc. τῆς Ὀδυσσείας) νοθεύοντες. After stating a series of objections to this view he finally suggested that perhaps the two ancient grammarians had said that this was the end not of the *Odyssey* as a book, but that of its main action. This suggestion reveals the embarrassment of Eustathius,[3] who clearly felt that the simple wording of the Scholion did not admit such an evasion; nevertheless, it has been repeatedly approved in recent times.[4] Aristophanes only inserted marginal sigla,[5] then Aristarchus in his ὑπομνήματα interpreted his predecessor's σημεῖα and may also have published some comments from his 'lectures'; but excerpts from Aristarchus' commentary still had a long way to go before reaching the rather poor medieval Scholia on the *Odyssey*. There is no parallel[6] to this note on ψ 296. We may ask many questions: did Aristophanes mark the

---

[1] θ 167 οὕτως (codd.) οὐ πάντεσσι θεοὶ χαρίεντα διδοῦσιν: read αὔτως 'not equally do the gods give gracious gifts to all men'.

[2] Schol. MV Vind.; τοῦτο τέλος τ.᾿Ο. φησὶν Ἀρίσταρχος καὶ Ἀριστοφάνης (Schol. HMQ); Eust. p. 1948. 49 κατὰ τὴν τῶν παλαιῶν ἱστορίαν Ἀρίσταρχος καὶ Ἀριστοφάνης, οἱ κορυφαῖοι τῶν τότε γραμματικῶν, εἰς τὸ . . . "ἀσπάσιοι—ἵκοντο" περατοῦσιν τὴν Ὀδύσσειαν, τὰ ἐφεξῆς ἕως τέλους τοῦ βιβλίου νοθεύοντες. οἱ δὲ τοιοῦτοι πολλὰ τῶν καιριωτάτων περικόπτουσιν . . . εἴποι δ᾿ ἂν οὖν τις ὅτι Ἀρίσταρχος καὶ Ἀριστοφάνης οἱ ῥηθέντες οὐ τὸ βιβλίον τῆς Ὀδυσσείας, ἀλλὰ ἴσως τὰ καίρια ταύτης ἐνταῦθα συντετελέσθαι φασίν. Cf. Eust. p. 1393. 57 (on α 88 ff.) αὐτὴ (sc. ἡ μνηστηροφονία) γάρ ἐστι τὸ σκοπιμώτατον τέλος τῆς ποιήσεως ταύτης. A grammarian Euclides (L. Cohn, *RE* VI 1003. 27) in Schol. BT *A* 5 ὅπερ ἐστὶ τέλος τῆς Ἰλιάδος seems to have used τέλος in the same sense of σκοπός as Eust., but Aristoph. and Aristarch. by saying πέρας meant the 'limit'.

[3] It sounds to me like Eustathius' own arguing; but Wilamowitz, *Die Heimkehr des Odysseus* (1927) 72 f. supposed that he had 'vollständigere Scholien' as his source.

[4] See especially E. Bethe, 'Odyssee-Probleme' I. τέλος τῆς Ὀδυσσείας, *Herm.* 63 (1928) 81–85.

[5] See above, pp. 173 f.

[6] The conventional form in the rare case of longer passages was: Ζηνόδοτος ἠθέτηκεν ἀπὸ τούτου τοῦ στίχου τὰ λοιπά Schol. *A Σ* 483–608 (shield of Achilles). Aristarchus athetized only a few lines of the ὁπλοποιία. Schol. ψ 310–43 ἠθέτησεν Ἀρίσταρχος τοὺς τρεῖς καὶ τριάκοντα (οὐ καλῶς QV, καλῶς Vind. 133) Schol. MV ω 1–204 Ἀρίσταρχος ἀθετεῖ τὴν Νέκυιαν, with arguments and counter-arguments. Thus although he accepted Aristophanes' view of ψ 296 as the 'limit' of the poem, he continued to obelize individual passages of the following part; it was therefore not 'athetized' as a whole.

line with one of his symbols?[1] If so, did Aristarchus correctly interpret it
as τέλος or πέρας? Does our Scholion preserve his interpretation? Given
all the hazards of the tradition we can only hope that the answer will be
in the affirmative; there is no chance of proving it.

But why did Aristophanes raise the problem at all? It has been suggested[2] that Apollonius Rhodius, in the last line of his *Argonautica* (IV 1781
ἀσπασίως ἀκτὰς Παγασηΐδας εἰσαπέβητε) was already deliberately alluding
to ψ 296, in order to demonstrate to his learned audience his belief that
Homer had concluded the *Odyssey* at this point.[3] But there is no re-
semblance at all between the two lines beyond the three syllables at the
beginning.[4] So obscure an allusion would have been intelligible only if
the notion that this line was the 'limit' of the Homeric poem was already
familiar to the connoisseurs of his generation, either from copies of the
Odyssey ending there or from the discussions of Homeric scholars. The
text of the *Argonautica* by no means proves that Apollonius held this
notion and that Aristophanes was influenced by him. It is not impossible,
though unlikely, that Aristophanes came across good copies of the
Odyssey ending at ψ 296, copies which so strongly impressed him that he
marked this line as the πέρας of the poem in his own edition. Could he
have believed that a sentence starting with οἱ μὲν ἔπειτα brought a great
epic poem to a satisfactory close? We should suppose that it was followed by at least one adversative sentence with αὐτάρ or δέ, which had to
be deleted when the longer version preserved in all our manuscripts,
αὐτὰρ Τηλέμαχος κτλ., was added.[5] But whether Aristophanes had documentary evidence or not, his assumption of the 'limit' at that place
must have corresponded with his own feelings. Did he perhaps feel the
difference between the poetical quality of the preceding part and that of
the following 600 lines? Without doubt a change does take place here.
The poetical power gripping the mind of the listener throughout Books

---

[1] He could have put a lectional sign like the κορωνίς after ψ 296 marking the end. For the
coronis see the lists and drawings by W. Lameere, *Les publications de Scriptorium* IV (1960)
190–204. On the symbols introduced by Aristophanes see below, p. 179. The codex Harleianus
(H, saec. XIII) added after ἴκοντο a colon and a paragraphos (:—).

[2] It was first put forward by L. Adam, *Die aristotelische Theorie vom Epos nach ihrer Entwicklung
bei Griechen und Römern* (1889) 92, but hardly noticed, until Eduard Meyer, *Herm.* 29 (1894)
478 f., championed it, see H. Herter, Bursian 285. 400, with bibliography; I agree with
D. L. Page, *The Homeric Odyssey* (1955) 130, n. 1.

[3] On Ap. Rh. as epic poet and Homeric scholar see above, pp. 146 ff.

[4] Ap. Rh. five times began a hexameter with ἀσπασίως and he may have had ψ 296 in
mind when he wrote II 728 ἀσπασίως . . . ὅρμον ἵκοντο; the Homeric model for IV 1781 might
have been ψ 238 ἀσπάσιοι δ᾽ ἐπέβαν γαίης.

[5] This might be a possible solution of the grammatical difficulties discussed by P. Friedlaender, *Herm.* 64 (1929) 376. See also above, p. 116, on the traditional division into twenty-
four books.

21 to 23, in which the contest of the bow, the killing of the suitors, and the reunion of Odysseus and Penelope are told, suddenly crumbles away. In a rapid sequence of short scenes, lacking vigour of language, every motif, every action is quickly, even impatiently, brought to a happy end. We cannot know whether Aristophanes' mind was really struck by the inferiority of the whole complex as unworthy of the great poet of the Return and the Vengeance. But we can say that the hint given in our Scholia under his name had enormous effect; it has been unanimously welcomed by modern critics of every denomination, unitarians and analysts alike.[1] As Zenodotus had done in the proem of the *Iliad*,[2] so in the finale of the *Odyssey*[3] Aristophanes posed a crucial problem which has been a subject for continuous dispute up to the present day.[4]

The scholar poets of the third century were remarkably fond of Hesiod, as we have observed, and their interest stimulated the activity of the grammarians. As Aristophanes is said to have put a critical σημεῖον at Hes. *Th.* 68,[5] he must have followed Zenodotus[6] in editing Hesiod. We saw how he raised a special problem of authenticity in the Homeric *Odyssey*; similarly in Hesiod he continued the discussion of the Pseudo-Hesiodea, which had apparently been started by Apollonius Rhodius.[7] Aristophanes denied the Hesiodic origin of the Χίρωνος Ὑποθῆκαι[8] and doubted that of the *Shield of Heracles*, which Apollonius had maintained. The 'Shield of Achilles' in the eighteenth book of our *Iliad*, which Zenodotus had athetized[9] was the model for this later poem; according to the hypothesis of the *Scutum* the first fifty-six lines on Heracles' mother

---

[1] They have used it, of course, in quite different ways.

[2] See above, pp. 111 ff.

[3] On Aristophanes Byz. and the *Odyssey* see also below, p. 191.

[4] If we carefully consider the style as well as the purpose of the whole finale, we are strongly reminded of the style and aim of the first book. The quality of the poetry is essentially the same: it lacks vigour of language and power of intuition, it displays an anxious accumulation of motifs, carried out more quietly in the first book for the exposition, but more quickly in the concluding book. This is not an addition to an already finished poem, a 'continuation' or 'epilogue', but the work of the poet who finally built up our *Odyssey* and by his intentional references from Book 24 to Book 1 constructed something like an arch over the whole vast composition for which he had used a number of older powerful epic poems. Even the most scrupulous re-examination by Page 101–36 (see above, p. 176, n. 2) has not convinced me that ψ 297 ff. is 'a later appendix, loosely attached to a poem already substantially complete'; in his notes he refers to earlier literature. Page's view is shared by G. S. Kirk, *The Songs of Homer* (1962) 248 ff. As regards the relation of ω to α I agree in general with P. Von der Mühll, 'Odyssee', *RE* Suppl. VII (1940) 764 ff. On Homeric εἰδωλοποιία see Excursus.

[5] Schol. Hes. *Th.* 68 ἐπεσημήνατο; Schol. Hes. *Th.* 126 is hopelessly corrupt and we had better wait for a new edition.

[6] See above, p. 117.   [7] See above, p. 144.

[8] Quintil. I 1, 15 (= Hes. test. 57 Jacoby) nam is primus (sc. Aristoph. Byz.) Ὑποθήκας . . . negavit esse huius poetae; cf. Schol. Pind. *P.* VI 22.

[9] See above, p. 175, n. 6.

Alcmene were identical with a part of the fourth book of the Κατάλογος (γυναικῶν)[1] and 'therefore Aristophanes suspected' its non-Hesiodic provenance.[2] This shows that he gave reasons for his suspicion; perhaps he did so in his supplement to the *Pinakes* of Callimachus.[3] Yet, despite his doubts, the *Scutum* remained with the *Theogony* and *Erga* in every ancient text of Hesiod,[4] just as the end of our *Odyssey* also survived his verdict.

We have no information about Aristophanes' views on orthography or methods of marking variant readings in the margin, but we have several times referred to the use of critical signs as an integral part of Aristophanes' extensive editorial work. Since the presence of such signs in a few very early papyri is not proven,[5] we may fairly see in Zenodotus the originator of the first critical symbol, the obelus, which meant more than the introduction of a mere technical device. Aristophanes then seems to have improved the whole editorial technique[6] by increasing the number of critical σημεῖα.[7] By the ἀστερίσκος he marked the lines repeated from another place in which they appeared to be more appropriate (Schol. γ 71–73 = ι 253–5),[8] by the σίγμα and ἀντίσιγμα (ↄ) two consecutive lines having the same contents and being therefore interchangeable (ε 247 ff., with Schol. cf. Schol. Aristoph. *Ran.* 153).[9] The choice and critical decision he left to the reader or future editor, following the example of Zenodotus.[10]

Lectional signs, one might say, are not in the strict sense the business of the scholar, but of the scribe and corrector; punctuation and accentuation therefore are part of the general history of the script. But as we paid some attention to the early development of the script, to books and to libraries, we may now say a few words about the growing importance of

---

[1] *P.Oxy.* XXIII (1956) 2355 (= Hes. fr. P Merkelbach), in which *Scut.* 1–5 are preceded by the ends of six other hexameters, may belong to this part of the fourth book; see Lobel's introduction.

[2] Argum. Hes. *Scut.* 1 (= Hes. test. 52 Jac.) τῆς Ἀσπίδος ἡ ἀρχὴ ἐν τῷ τετάρτῳ Καταλόγῳ φέρεται μέχρι στίχων ν̄ καὶ ς̄. διὸ καὶ ὑπώπτευκεν Ἀριστοφάνης ὡς οὐκ οὖσαν αὐτὴν Ἡσιόδου, ἀλλ' ἑτέρου τινὸς τὴν Ὁμηρικὴν ἀσπίδα μιμήσασθαι προαιρουμένου. Hes. *Scut.* ed. C. F. Russo (1950) 67, cf. 36; J. Schwartz, *Ps.-Hesiodeia* (1960) 458.

[3] See above, p. 133; cf. Nauck 247 f.

[4] Hes. *Th.* ed. F. Jacoby, Proleg. pp. 48 f.

[5] Jachmann, 'Vom frühalexandrinischen Homertext', *NGG* 1949, 223 is inclined to believe in a sort of pre-Alexandrian σημείωσις.

[6] See above, pp. 115, 173 f. and p. 176, n. 1.   [7] Nauck 16–18.

[8] *Anecd. Parisin.* Schol. Il. 1 p. xlvii 29 Aristophanes, etc. (text confused).

[9] Aristarchus used ἀντίσιγμα and στιγμή in such cases, see below, p. 218.

[10] The κεραύνιον is mentioned only once in the Homeric Scholia, when Penelope drew gifts from the suitors, παρέλκετο Schol. σ 282 ἀντὶ τοῦ ἐφέλκετο· εὐτελὲς τοῦτο, διὸ καὶ κεραύνιον παρέθηκεν Ἀριστοφάνης. This might mean that he condemned this line or the whole passage because of its εὐτέλεια, its 'meanness' (?); cf. Isid. *Etym.* I 21. 21 ceraunium . . . quotiens multi versus improbantur', and *Anecd. Roman.* Schol. Il. 1 p. xliii 27 Dind. (rather vague).

punctuation for critical texts and about the writing of accents. We must be careful to separate these two things, which are unfortunately mixed up in our only literary source on this subject, chapter 20 of Ps.-Arcadius' epitome of Herodian's Καθολικὴ Προσῳδία. This chapter bears the title Περὶ τῆς τῶν τόνων εὑρέσεως κτλ. only in one Paris manuscript, Par. gr. 2102,[1] which was written by a disreputable forger of the sixteenth century, Jacobus Diassorinus. He put together bits of treatises on the subject in Theodosius and in the Scholia to Dionysius Thrax, adding the misleading title Περὶ . . . εὑρέσεως κτλ. and some other sentences of his own, as the comparison of other manuscripts of Ps.-Arcadius' epitome shows. Thus he makes Aristophanes of Byzantium appear as the 'inventor' of Greek punctuation.[2] But in fact, some sort of punctuation was indispensable for the Greek *scriptio continua* from the beginning; the hexametric verse graffito of about 700 B.C., found in Ischia, is at the moment the earliest[3] inscription known to me which bears signs of punctuation. The earliest literary papyri at our disposal, from the second half of the fourth century B.C., are sometimes furnished with signs and symbols of punctuation; the Timotheus papyrus,[4] for instance, has a birdlike drawing (coronis?), and others have the paragraphos, a short stroke below the first letters of the line in which the end of the sentence will occur. Isocrates had already used the form παραγραφή.[5] Aristotle stated the dilemma whether one should punctuate (διαστίξαι)[6] the opening sentence of Heraclitus after ἐόντος or after ἀεί; he also referred to the παράγραφος.[7] Aristophanes, far

---

[1] This manuscript was known to Montfaucon, *Palaeographia Graeca* (1708) 31, and its text was first published as Ἀρκαδίου Περὶ τόνων e cod. Paris. primum ed. E. H. Barker, 1820 (repr. by Nauck, Aristoph. Byz. 72 ff.); K. E. A. Schmidt, *Beiträge zur Geschichte der Grammatik des Griechischen und Lateinischen* (1859, pp. 571–601 'Die Erfindungen des Aristophanes v. B. und das Buch des Arkadios'), [Arcad.] 'Ἐπιτομὴ τῆς καθολικῆς προσῳδίας Ἡρωδιανοῦ rec. M. Schmidt (1860) was based on more and better manuscripts (reprinted by A. Lentz, Herodian. *rell.* I 1867 xxxviii ff., who denied its derivation from Herodian). L. Cohn proved that Par. 2102 was written by Jacobus Diassorinus, *Philol. Abhandlungen f. Martin Hertz* (1888) 141 ff. A 'critical' text of chapter 20 is printed by Laum (below, p. 180, n. 4) who unfortunately mixed up the text of Par. gr. 2603 with the forgery of Diassorinus in 2102. See also the following note.

[2] The few relevant sentences on punctuation from the two Paris manuscripts were separately printed by W. Lameere, *Les publications de Scriptorium* IV (1960) 91, who added an exhaustive bibliography. Cf. the still useful thesis by G. Fluck, *De Graecorum interpunctionibus* (Greifswald 1908) esp. pp. 4 ff. on Aristophanes.

[3] See above, p. 24, n. 4; references to chronological and technical details of punctuation are given by Miss Jeffery p. 50.

[4] See above, p. 103, n. 2; cf. W. Schubart, *Einführung in die Papyruskunde* (1918) 60; *Das Buch bei den Griechen und Römern*, 80 f. and 181; *Griechische Palaeographie* (1925) 173.

[5] Isocr. *or.* xv 59.

[6] *Rhet.* III 5 p. 1407 b 18 = *Vors.* 22 A 4. But so far no instance of a στιγμή in the earliest papyri is known.

[7] *Rhet.* III 8 p. 1409 a 21; on the παράγραφος as metrical sign see below, p. 186.

from 'inventing' punctuation, continued a long tradition. No reference to Zenodotus is preserved, and there is only one testimony left in our Homeric Scholia (Schol. HQ *v* 96), in which Aristophanes is blamed for a wrong στιγμή in α 72. This is sufficient to prove that he did punctuate the text; perhaps he used no more than two different stops, the τελεία στιγμή and the ὑποστιγμή, as Dionysius Thrax[1] did two generations later. The more elaborate system finally developed in the Hadrianic age by Nicanor should not be dated back to Aristophanes.

If we now turn to the question of accents in our papyri, we see that none were written in the early Ptolemaic papyri; Aristotle and his pupils apparently read their texts without them. In the first century B.C. prosodic signs were occasionally inserted,[2] and slowly they became more frequent in the time of the empire. Aristophanes is the first grammarian whose accentuation is quoted (Schol. (*P*) η 317 Ἀριστοφάνης περισπᾷ τὸ εἰδῇς).[3] So in that respect the otherwise untrustworthy literary tradition in Ps.-Arcadius seems to be confirmed. Laum in his controversial book on the history of Greek accentuation,[4] in which he re-examined and compared the evidence of the Homer-papyri[5] and the theories of the grammarians, made it perfectly clear that as far as accents are concerned nothing leads back into the time before Aristophanes.

There is an isolated remark of Eratosthenes quoted in the chapter 'De Accentibus' by Sergius, *Explanationes in Artem Donati*: he is said to have explained the pronunciation of the circumflex 'ex parte priore acuta in gravem posteriorem (sc. flecti putavit)',[6] while others gave different explanations. But this paragraph, like the whole chapter, deals with the question of the *spoken* accents, which probably had been discussed in musical, rhetorical, and metrical books for a long time. Granted that the reading 'Eratosthenes' is correct, the passage still does not show that he anticipated Aristophanes in devising and using *written* signs in the

---

[1] See below, p. 269.

[2] Schubart, *Das Buch* 81 ff. and 181.

[3] See also the following note Laum 116 ff. giving a few more uncertain references.

[4] B. Laum, 'Das alexandrinische Akzentuationssystem', *Studien zur Geschichte und Kultur des Altertums*, 4. Erg. Bd. (published 1928, but written before 1914) 99–124 and 452. 1; cf. E. Schwyzer, *Griech. Grammatik* (1939) 371 ff. and especially H. Erbse, 'Beiträge zur Überlieferung der Iliasscholien', *Zetemata* 24 (1960) 371–406.

[5] For accents in lyric texts see J. Gießler, *Prosodische Zeichen in den antiken Handschriften griechischer Lyriker*, Diss. Gießen 1923.

[6] *G.L.* ed. H. Keil IV (1864) 530. 24; the author of this treatise is called Sergius (or Seregius) in the manuscripts, not Servius, see Keil, Praef. pp. xlix and liv. The doctrine seems to be derived through Varro ('Reliquorum de grammatica librorum fragmenta' no. 84 in Varr. *De lingua Lat.* rec. Goetz–Schoell, 1910, p. 215. 23) from Tyrannio, see C. Wendel, 'Tyrannion', *RE* VII A (1948) 1816 and 1818. As far as I can see, the Eratosthenes fragment is mentioned only by Knaack, *RE* VI 385 as a possible part of the Γραμματικά (cf. above, p. 162).

editions of texts. This is the only aspect of accents, as a help to the reader πρὸς διαστολὴν τῆς ἀμφιβόλου λέξεως, that concerns us in this chapter. In this case we are indeed entitled to regard Aristophanes as the first to accentuate the Homeric and other texts. But he was not the first to punctuate them, and this distinction should not be disregarded any longer.[1]

Momentous as Aristophanes' achievement in Homeric studies was, his edition of lyric poetry[2] (including the lyrical parts of the drama) was an epoch-making event. When we say 'lyrics' we mean language and metre; although they presumably understood the symbols or script by which the classical melopoeia was expressed and handed down from the Ionic and Attic ages to the third century, the grammarians who spent so much labour on saving literature and language did nothing for the 'music', but let it perish.[3] In the histories of ancient music this in-difference of the scholars is not duly recorded as far as I can see; they can hardly be quite without blame for the total loss of the musical notation. We should not forget, however, that in the course of the fourth century the original unity of words and music was breaking down and that certain groups of Sophists and philosophers cared only for the language when they treated the old poetry;[4] it may be regrettable, but it is under-standable, that the Alexandrian grammarians followed their lead.

Zenodotus took the first steps in editing Pindar and Anacreon and perhaps others, and one of his conjectures in Anacreon's text provoked a sharp rejoinder from Aristophanes.[5] Callimachus in his *Pinakes* took pains to classify the various lyric poems, a preparatory work invaluable for every future editor and critic, especially for Aristophanes. Erato-sthenes agreed with Chamaeleo in ascribing an archaic hymn to a certain author and a lyric poem of Archilochus to a special class.[6] Apollonius Rhodius seems to have devoted a book to Archilochus in which he gave a new explanation of the ἀχνυμένη σκυτάλη;[7] on the same phrase—which occurred in an epodic, not in a lyric poem—Aristophanes wrote a whole treatise.[8] This seems to have contained polemics against Dicaearchus

---

[1] Even Laum and Schwyzer are incorrect in this point.
[2] Nauck pp. 60–62.
[3] See Isobel Henderson, 'Ancient Greek Music', *New Oxford History of Music* 1 (1957) 336 ff.
[4] See above, p. 53 on Hippias and p. 76 on Aristotle; see furthermore Aristoxenus fr. 92, Wehrli, *Die Schule des Aristoteles* 2 (1945), Heraclid. Pont. fr. 157, ibid. 7 (1953), Chamaeleo fr. 28/29, ibid. 9 (1957).
[5] See above, pp. 117 f.   [6] See above, p. 162.
[7] See above, p. 144.
[8] Nauck p. 274 Ἀριστοφάνης ὁ γραμματικὸς ἐν τῷ Περὶ τῆς ἀχνυμένης σκυτάλης συγγράμματι.

about the meaning of a word in the lyric text of Alcaeus.¹ Aristophanes, we see, had the benefit of several predecessors in the lyric field; but it was he, through his more extensive and much more penetrating labour, who dominated the future.

In modern times all non-epic and non-dramatic poetry is usually called lyric. But the ancient theorists and editors distinguished between elegiac and iambic poems on the one hand, and melic poems on the other. The stichic or distichic poems in dactylic or iambic rhythms, falling into well demarcated recurrent 'lines', were regarded as special kinds of ἔπη, recited poetry like the hexametric epic poems and hymns, and their makers were termed ἐλεγειοποιοί and ἰαμβοποιοί.² Although there were sometimes instrumental preludes and interludes, the delivery of elegy and iambus was declamatory or perhaps melodramatic, as opposed to singing with obligatory instrumental accompaniment. Verse that was sung to music and very often also to dancing and was composed of elements of varying rhythm and length was called μελική or λυρική ποίησις. It may seem surprising, in view of the statement that the grammarians concentrated on the text and allowed the music to perish, that this firm distinction was based on the relation of text and music. The metrical form, however, remained and was the feature which chiefly distinguished the lyric text from all the rest. A lyric poem was a μέλος in early Greek literature, the poet a μελοποιός, a maker of songs,³ or μελικός (sc. ποιητής), and the whole genre μελικὴ ποίησις; and these remained the normal terms in later disquisitions about poetical theory and the classification of poetry.⁴ But in references to editions of texts and in lists of the 'makers' the authors are called λυρικοί; Περὶ λυρικῶν ποιητῶν was the title Didymus gave to the book he wrote under Augustus, based on the research of the entire Hellenistic age. The foremost poets were always spoken of as the ἐννέα λυρικοί, and from the first century B.C. onwards their work began to be termed λυρικὴ ποίησις, that is, 'poetry sung to the lyre' (as the lyre had once been the most important of the accompanying instruments). Latin writers occasionally used 'melicus', as Cicero does when he borrows from Greek theoretical literature, but 'lyricus' became the usual Latin term in Augustan times and later. Horace hopes to be included among the 'lyrici vates' (not the 'melici'); Ovid always says 'lyricus',

---

¹ Dicaearch. fr. 99 Wehrli, *Schule des Aristoteles* I (1944). On Alcaeus fr. 359 L.–P. = fr. 103 D. see below, p. 185.

² Cf. Lysanias (Eratosthenes' teacher?) Περὶ ἰαμβοποιῶν above, p. 153, n. 3.

³ Aristoph. *Ran.* 1250, Plat. *Ion* 533 E al., Heraclid. Pont. fr. 157, Wehrli, *Die Schule des Aristoteles* 7 (1953), [Aristot.] *Probl.* 920 a 11.

⁴ H. Färber, *Die Lyrik in der Kunsttheorie der Antike* (1936) 7 ff. 'Der Name der Lyrik'; on the nine poets see below, pp. 205 f.

and so do Quintilian, Pliny, and Seneca. Even in the Latin theorists 'melicus' was displaced by 'lyricus', and the derivations from it became more and more purely musical terms. The modern use of the term 'lyric', from which we started in this paragraph, comes from Latin literature since Quintilian as well as Ovid and Horace were favourite reading in the Italian Renaissance.

On the basis of this survey I venture to suggest that Aristophanes' influence was decisive for the change of terminology. Both Istros,[1] the Callimachean, and the poet Euphorion,[2] who were a few years senior to him, gave their books the title Περὶ μελοποιῶν; after his editions no such title seems to occur. But indeed the whole classification of lyric poems was determined by the needs of the editor, not by any older tradition of poetical theory or artistic practice. The *Indexes* of Callimachus were the only work on which Aristophanes could have built; they at least pointed the way to the arrangements of poets and poems in several classes and subdivisions.[3] There never was a general system; authors were given individual treatment according to the contents or the form of their poems.

Pindar[4] is the only great lyric poet of whose works four complete books (the *Epinicia*) were preserved and commented on in later ancient and medieval times. Of the lost poems a great number of quotations and recently discovered papyrus fragments are now available to us,[5] and many references in the biographical tradition and in the Scholia supplement our knowledge. One of our most precious testimonies tells us that in Aristophanes' arrangement Ἄριστον μὲν ὕδωρ headed the *Epinicia* (προτέτακται ὑπὸ Ἀριστοφάνους τοῦ συντάξαντος τὰ Πινδαρικά).[6] The word συντάττειν confirms that he was not the first collector of the Pindaric poems, but that he put them into proper order. Something similar may have been said in the recently published *Life of Pindar*, if we are justified in supplying: δ]ιῄρηται δὲ αὐτ[ο]ῦ τ[ὰ ποιήματα ὑπ' Ἀριστοφάν]ους εἰς βιβλία ιζ̄. The songs of victory were divided into four books according to the four places of the national games, Olympia, Delphi, Isthmus, and Nemea, a principle taken over from Callimachus,[7] though not applied to Simonides and Bacchylides. The ἐπίνικοι were the concluding group of seventeen

---

[1] *FGrHist* 334 F 56, a biographical anecdote about Phrynis.
[2] Euphor. fr. 58 Scheidweiler, about the mythical inventors of the σῦριγξ.
[3] See above, p. 130; on a modern mistake of a 'Platonic' classification see Excursus on p. 74. Names of choral songs occur in Plat. *Leg.* 700 CD (above p. 75, n. 1).
[4] Cf. J. Irigoin, *Histoire du texte de Pindare* (1952) 35–50 'L'édition d'Aristophane de Byzance'.
[5] Pind. ed. B. Snell II³ (1964).
[6] Schol. Pind. I (1903) *Ol.* ed. Drachmann p. 7.   [7] Above, p. 130.

books: γέγραφε δὲ βιβλία ἑπτακαίδεκα· ὕμνους, παιᾶνας, διθυράμβων β´, προσοδίων β´, παρθενίων β´, φέρεται δὲ καὶ γ´ ὃ ἐπιγράφεται κεχωρισμένων (-μένον Snell) παρθενίων, ὑπορχημάτων β´, ἐγκώμια, θρήνους, ἐπινίκων δ´.[1] It is obvious that the songs in the first six books belong to the religious sphere and those in the concluding six books to the secular; doubts are possible about the five books of ὑπορχήματα and παρθένια in the middle.[2] The scheme as a whole roughly corresponds to the division of μελικὴ ποίησις into poems εἰς θεούς and εἰς ἀνθρώπους, followed by a third mixed group; this kind of arrangement is best preserved in the *Chrestomathy* of Proclus[3] and is probably taken over from Didymus' book Περὶ λυρικῶν ποιητῶν. It is hard to believe that it does not somehow depend on Aristophanes' classification of the Pindaric poems. Wilamowitz[4] once conjectured that Apollonius ὁ εἰδογράφος was the successful author of this scheme. Apollonius of Alexandria, the so-called Classifier,[5] became the holder of the librarianship after Aristophanes (with whom he agreed against Callimachus and others about the character and place of Pindar's second Pythian ode). But what the ambiguous word εἶδος really means in this case is unmistakably settled by a unique passage of the *Etymologica*:[6] Apollonius attributed the lyric poems to their '*musical*' classes, Dorian, Phrygian, Lydian, and so on. This evidence pointing to the εἴδη διὰ πασῶν or ἁρμονίαι flatly refutes the assumption that he devised a literary classification based on the difference of contents; so far the probability remains that Aristophanes was its creator.

Very few references to Aristophanes' text of the lyric poets are left to us; for, as in the case of Homer, his plain text with critical signs was superseded by Aristarchus' commentary. A few remarks on prosody are attested as Aristophanic, but none about dialect or orthography. We do

[1] Schol. Pind. 1 p. 3. 6 (Vita Ambrosiana), cf. p. 6. 3 (Vita Thomana) and Suid. v. Πίνδαρος. *P.Oxy.* XXVI (1961) no. 2438, II 35 ff. with E. Lobel's supplements and commentary.

[2] Part of the sequence is different in *P.Oxy.* 2438 (late second or third century A.D.); but a supplement ὕμ]ρων between ἐγκώμια and ὑπορχήματα is very unlikely.

[3] Procl. in Phot. *Bibl.* 319 b 33 ff. Bekker.

[4] Wilamowitz, *Pindaros* (1922) 108; unfortunately the conjecture was accepted by H. Färber, *Die Lyrik in der Kunsttheorie der Antike* (1936) 19.

[5] On the papyrus-list of the librarians see above, p. 172, n. 2; Schol. Pind. *P.* II inscr. (II p. 31 Drachmann) ἔνιοι Πυθικήν, ὡς Ἀπολλώνιος ὁ εἰδογράφος.

[6] Et. gen. B = Et. M. p. 295. 52 v. εἰδογράφος· Ἀπολλών⟨ιος⟩ εἰδογράφος, ἐπειδὴ εὐφυὴς ὢν ἐν τῇ βιβλιοθήκῃ τὰ εἴδη τοῖς εἴδεσιν ἐπένειμεν. τὰς γὰρ δοκούσας τῶν ᾠδῶν (? Sylburg: εἰδῶν codd.) Δώριον μέλος ἔχειν ἐπὶ τὸ αὐτὸ συνῆγε, καὶ Φρυγίας καὶ Λυδίας, μιξολυδιστὶ καὶ ἰαστί. On the διὰ πασῶν εἴδη see *Musici Scriptores Graeci* ed. C. von Ian (1895) 308 f. and *passim*. A. Böckh made the perfectly correct statement: 'Apollonius . . . carmina secundum genera harmoniae, Dorium, Phrygium etc. . . . distinxit et consociavit.' Pindari *Opera* II 1 (1819) xxxi. We shall not ask how the εἰδογράφος was able to make this distinction, if musical notation was already lost, see above, p. 181.

not even know how many of the lyric poets Aristophanes edited. Pindar was certainly one of them; to the single quotation in the Scholia to the Epinicia[1] can now be added three of his variant readings in the marginal notes of the great papyrus of the *Paeans* (*P.Oxy.* 841) II 75 (ἐν δὲ, not ἐν δὲ), VI 89 (ὅσσα, not ὅσα), and VI 181 (unintelligible). To Alcman's great *Parthenion* the Louvre papyrus notes on the margin opposite col. I, 32 (= *PMG* p. 6 Page) Aristophanes' reading Ἄϊδας (not Ἄϊδας); it is likely that at col. III, 27 (= *PMG* p. 6) Ἀρι[to the reading ναῦι (instead of ναῦϊ) means Aristophanes, not Aristarchus, since it is proposed like the other Aristophanic variants, for prosodic reasons. The quotation of the lines 64 ff. of the Parthenion[2] for the meaning of ἀμύνασθαι may belong to his Λέξεις; *P.Oxy.* 2390, fr. 50. 7, begins with the name Ἀριστοφαν[, but it is uncertain whether this fragment belongs to a commentary on Alcman, as the other forty-nine fragments apparently do. We know by chance that Aristophanes defended a traditional reading in Anacreon against Zenodotus' conjecture;[3] but Aelian's phrase ἀντιλέγει κατὰ κράτος, points rather to an article on κερόεις–ἐρόεις in the Λέξεις, or even to a passage on the 'horned doe' in Περὶ ζῴων, than to an edition of Anacreon's text. On the other hand, in Hephaestio's metrical handbook[4] the strophe of Anacreon's first poem is said to be divided into eight cola κατὰ τὴν νῦν ἔκδοσιν, that is, according to the edition of Aristarchus; but it could be divided in another way, εἴς τε τριάδα καὶ πεντάδα. Th. Bergk[5] convincingly argued that the phrase 'present edition' implies the existence of an earlier edition with differing κῶλα, which could only be that of Aristophanes; and in fact in the chapter on the metrical σημεῖα Hephaestio[6] contrasted τὴν Ἀριστοφάνειον ἔκδοσιν of Alcaeus with τὴν νῦν τὴν Ἀριστάρχειον. So it is very likely that there was an Aristophanic edition of Anacreon and certain that there was one of Alcaeus; there is a reference to a reading in the latter (χέλυς instead of λέπας) in his treatise on the ἀχνυμένη σκυτάλη.[7]

Aristophanes' lyric texts were distinguished from all the previous ones by a prominent new feature; they were not written in continuous lines like prose, but divided into shorter metrical κῶλα. We do not know anything about pre-Aristophanic division of lyric poetry into cola. But poets of the time of Philitas and especially of Callimachus' circle used 'members' of old lyric strophes for new recitative poems κατὰ στίχον;[8] this

---

[1] See below, p. 187. [2] Schol. L *E* 266 (Eust. 546. 29) = Nauck p. 213, fr. inc. sed. 61.
[3] See above, pp. 117 and 181.
[4] Hephaest. ed. M. Consbruch (1906) 68. 18 ff. [5] Anacr. ed. Th. Bergk (1835) 26.
[6] Hephaest. 74. 12. [7] See above, p. 182, n. 1.
[8] Cf. P. Maas, *Greek Metre*, translated by H. Lloyd-Jones (1962) § 15; on Callimachus' lyric metres see Call. II p. 135 Index: 'metrica' and the metrical notes to fr. 201 and 202.

implies a certain consciousness of individual cola in the text of early lyric and dramatic poetry. It is not unlikely that in this field also the poets paved the way for the scholars, as so often in the third century B.C. Aristophanes also observed the repetition of given sequences of these metrical units and marked the beginning of the corresponding parts by a παράγραφος.[1] The word στροφή, a stanza, used for these corresponding parts, was probably a traditional musical term. Sappho, Alcaeus, and Anacreon composed 'monostrophic' songs in which the same stanza, built up from a fixed number of κῶλα, was repeated as often as the poet liked; the end of the last stanza was marked by a κορωνίς. But Aristophanes used the ἀστερίσκος instead of the κορωνίς in those cases where a poem in a different metre followed; this is especially noticeable in his edition of Alcaeus.[2] The second principal form of song is 'triadic': a strophe, often very complicated, and a corresponding ἀντίστροφος is followed by a third part different in metre and length from the two corresponding parts, an ἐπῳδός. The triad may be repeated, as in Pindar and already, on a much smaller scale, as I believe, in Alcman's Parthenion.[3] The ends of the two corresponding strophes are marked by paragraphi and the end of each epodos by the coronis, for which the asteriscus is substituted at the conclusion of the poem. Hephaestio's handbook is in general agreement with the practice of the papyri.[4] The *Persae* of Timotheus[5] and the so-called *Scolia* of Elephantine[6] are still written like prose, as they belong to the fourth and early third centuries. But the Alcman papyrus of the first century B.C. (*P.Oxy.* 2387) shows the text divided into short κῶλα and each triadic structure subdivided by two paragraphi and a coronis; the often-quoted great papyrus of Pindar's *Paeans* (*P.Oxy.* 841) is a splendid example of the editorial technique introduced by Aristophanes, and so to a lesser degree are the Bacchylides papyri. There is of course no pedantic consistency in the papyri[7] and the ἀστερίσκος became relatively rare in the course of time; but the concluding epode of *Paean* v was denoted by coronis and obelus and the commencement of *Paean* vi by a 'separate sign' which must be acknowledged as an asteriscus.[8]

---

[1] Cf. above, p. 179.
[2] Hephaest. p. 74. 11 ff. ἐπὶ δὲ τοῦ Ἀλκαίου ἰδίως κατὰ μὲν τὴν Ἀριστοφάνειον ἔκδοσιν ἀστερίσκος ἐπὶ ἑτερομετρίας ἐτίθετο μόνης.
[3] E. Lobel, *P.Oxy.* xxiv (1957) 8 regards them as monostrophic compositions.
[4] Hephaest. p. 74. 1 ff.   [5] Cf. above, p. 179.
[6] See W. Schubart, *Einführung in die Papyruskunde* (1918) 59 (Zur metrischen Gliederung) and *Das Buch* 86 and 181 f. with many references, and especially the facsimiles in *Papyri Graecae Berolinenses* (1911) pl. 1 and 3.
[7] Cf. Snell, Bacchyl. praefat. p. 13+.
[8] See *P.Oxy.* v p. 14; Pind. ed. Snell II³ (1964) p. 24 and ibid. p. 56 = *P.Oxy.* 2441 (*Pae.* xiv/xv); cf. the asteriscus in Bacchyl. after c. vi and c. vii.

When Aristophanes tried to determine the metrically corresponding parts, he detected in Pindar *O.* II 27 between φιλεῖ δέ μιν Παλλὰς αἰεί and καὶ Ζεὺς πατήρ the bold interpolation of the words φιλέοντι Μοῖσαι, which were without responsion in the other stanzas: Schol. (A) τὸ κῶλον τοῦτο ἀθετεῖ Ἀριστοφάνης· περιττεύειν γὰρ αὐτό φησιν πρὸς ⟨τὰς⟩ ἀντιστρόφους.[1] He condemned this obvious interpolation by an obelus in the margin, but it remained[2] in the text of the Byzantine manuscripts, until the conscientious metrician Demetrius Triclinius omitted it in the early fourteenth century.[3] Only once in our metrical scholia on Pindar did the responsion remain unnoticed, namely in *O.* XIV, and once three corresponding stanzas were assumed without recognizing the triadic structure, *O.* V; these very rare mistakes must have already been made by Aristophanes and faithfully preserved by his successors.

Aristophanes was always regarded in later antiquity as the originator of κωλίζειν; when Dionysius of Halicarnassus contrasts the κῶλα of lyric poets (Pindar, Simonides) with those of artistic prose, he says: κῶλα δέ με δέξαι λέγειν οὐχ οἷς Ἀριστοφάνης ἢ τῶν ἄλλων τις μετρικῶν διεκόσμησε τὰς ᾠδάς, ἀλλ' οἷς . . . ῥητόρων παῖδες τὰς περιόδους διαιροῦσι and τὰ Σιμωνίδεια ταῦτα· γέγραπται δὲ κατὰ τὰς διαστολὰς οὐχ ὧν Ἀριστοφάνης ἢ ἄλλος τις κατεσκεύασε κώλων, ἀλλ' ὧν ὁ πεζὸς λόγος ἀπαιτεῖ.[4] His colometry was copied through late antiquity and through the Byzantine age with occasional modifications, especially by Triclinius.

It underwent a fundamental change only when A. Böckh[5] discovered that the stanza is built up from a number of metrical περίοδοι of which the ends are marked by a 'pause' and that the periods usually consist of several cola or sometimes of one colon only. The occurrence of a pause means that in corresponding syllables of the stanzas a full word-end is strictly observed and hiatus and syllaba anceps are permitted. No such external distinctive mark exists for the 'members' of the period, the κῶλα; metrical analysis is needed to find out their elements and length.

For the understanding of Aristophanes' colometry Hephaestio's handbook[6] can still be helpful, as it is in the case of the σημεῖα; a colon is

---

[1] In Schol. BEQ the name of the grammarian is left out as so often in the Homeric Scholia; cf. above, p. 174.
[2] Cf. the general remarks, above, p. 173. [3] Irigoin, *Histoire du texte* 346.
[4] Dionys. Hal., *de comp. verb.* 22, p. 102. 1 ff. and 26, p. 140. 18 ff. Us.–Rad.
[5] 'De metris Pindari libri tres' in Pindari *Opera* I 2 (1811) 1–340.
[6] Hephaest. p. 63. 2 Consbr. (Περὶ ποιημάτων I 1) τὸ δὲ ἔλαττον ὂν τριῶν συζυγιῶν . . . καλεῖται κῶλον; cf. F. Leo, 'Die beiden metrischen Systeme des Altertums', *Herm.* 24 (1889) 292. 1; Irigoin, *Histoire du texte* 45 ff. and especially 'Les Scholies métriques de Pindare', *Bibliothèque de l'École des Hautes Études* 310 (1958) 17–34 'La colométrie Alexandrine'. The description of the metrical schemes of every colon in our Scholia to Pindar is based on

defined as a metrical unit 'containing fewer than three dipodies (συζυγίαι) without catalexis'. The practice of the papyri generally is in conformity with this theory. The Louvre papyrus of Alcman's *Parthenion* (fr. 1 Page = fr. 1 D.[2]) shows the stanza written in fourteen cola; in this very simple and lucid structure each colon contains only one rhythmical element, trochees or enhoplia or dactyls, which are all known to us from Archilochus. No other division is practicable; modern colometry can only state that cola 1–10 actually are ten periods, separated by word-end and hiatus or syllaba anceps, while the two cola 11–12 are parts of one period, and so are the cola 13–14.[1] Most of Bacchylides' stanzas also have a relatively simple structure; so the colometry of the British Museum and other papyri can be kept with only minor changes in our editions.[2] A typical instance when correction is needed is neglect of the hiatus in the papyrus Bacchyl. c. x 15–16 Νίκας ἕκατι ἄνθεσιν and at the same place twice in the second triad, 33 ff. and 43 ff., where the correct end of a period can be restored with certainty. In Pindar's complex and extensive stanzas the modern editor has to alter the ancient or Byzantine cola more often;[3] on the other hand, there are nearly always sufficient criteria for the distinction of periods, as the triads are so often repeated. In the strophic lyrics of the drama, where usually only one antistrophos responds to one strophe, external marks of the end of the period are often lacking.[4]

This lengthy section on Aristophanes' edition of the lyric poets has ranged over a wide space of time; it was no exaggeration to call his innovations in this field 'epoch-making'. We turn now to his work on dramatic poetry. Its dialogue was, as far as we can guess, always written in separate 'lines', in στίχοι of equal length, usually trimeters or sometimes tetrameters, like the hexametric lines of the epics; but no one before Aristophanes seems to have divided the choral passages into metrical

a compilation of the second century A.D.; a critical text of the ancient metrical Scholia is printed by Irigoin pp. 131–77.

[1] Lines 12 (the second trochaic dimeter) and 14 (the second dactylic dimeter) should be indented; by this simple arrangement the reader is able to recognize at once the intentions of the editor and to get a clear picture of the metrical structure. It is hard to understand why this opportunity is so frequently missed by editors.

[2] A firmly established ancient tradition of colometry is now proved by the almost complete agreement of the two papyri of Bacchyl. c. 17; see Snell, praef. pp. 15+ f., 35+ f., text p. 57, and on colometry in general p. 31+.

[3] Böckh did not break up his periods into cola in his big Quarto edition of 1811, but the following editors (except A. Turyn 1948) tried to do so; they are naturally often at variance with each other and with the Byzantine manuscripts of the *Epinicia*. On the colometry of the papyri and the unavoidable adjustments see Snell, Pind. ii³ pp. 17, 26, 73, 88.

[4] On Pindar's periodic technique and on the difficulties in respect of the choral passages of the drama see P. Maas, *Greek Metre* (1962) § 66.

units of varying length and movement. The question is how far his colometry is preserved in our manuscripts.

If we look first at Attic Comedy, we find that in the foremost codex of the Aristophanic comedies, the Venetus, the *Clouds* is followed by the subscription: κεκώλισται ἐκ τῶν Ἡλιοδώρου.[1] Heliodorus, a metrist in the middle of the first century A.D., maintained the principles of the Alexandrian tradition as his younger contemporary Hephaestio did;[2] but he had various ἀντίγραφα of the comedies at his disposal, applied a developed system of colometrical signs[3] and accompanied his ἔκδοσις of the text with a running metrical commentary. As a result, it is almost impossible to reconstruct the details of Aristophanes' colometry in the text of the scenic poets as we could with that of Pindar; and this must be taken as characteristic of the situation in general. There was a continuous and lively scholarly activity/in the field of drama throughout the later centuries which has obscured/its beginnings in Alexandria.

We have described how the previous generations of scholars tried to cope with the difficulties of language and subject in Attic comedy.[4] Aristophanes of Byzantium was doubtless influenced by the work of his teachers Euphronius and Eratosthenes on old comedy, and it is specifically attested that he was an eager pupil of the comic writer Machon,[5] from whom he learned 'the parts of comedy' in his youth. The Scholia to Aristophanes' comedies, like those to Homer and Pindar, preserve a few references to Aristophanes of Byzantium;[6] they are just sufficient to reveal the main lines of his textual criticism. He emended (μεταγράψας)[7] a corrupt proper name in *Thesm.* 162 (Ἀλκαῖος for Ἀχαιός); he marked consecutive interchangeable lines by the same σημεῖα as in his edition of the *Odyssey* (*Ran.* 152 ff.);[8] he felt that after *Av.* 1342 something is missing

---

[1] Cf. the subscription after the *Peace*: κεκώλισται πρὸς τὰ Ἡλιοδώρου. P. Boudreaux, *Le Texte d'Aristophane et ses commentateurs* (1919) 179; cf. 138 ff. on Heliodorus, pp. 25–47 on Aristophanes of Byzantium and esp. on his colometry 35 ff. For a balanced review of this rare book (written in 1914) see P. Geißler, *Gnom.* 2 (1926) 213 ff.

[2] F. Leo, *Herm.* 24 (1889) 284.

[3] O. Hense, *RE* VIII (1913) 31 f.; the διπλῆ was introduced to mark antistrophic responsion and lyric lines were separated from the dialogue by εἴσθεσις 'indenting'; the ἀστερίσκος was no longer used.

[4] Cf. above, pp. 119 f., 159–162.

[5] See Athen. XIV 664 A ὁ γραμματικὸς Ἀριστοφάνης ἐσπούδασε συσχολάσαι αὐτῷ νέος ὤν and VI 241 F διδάσκαλος γενόμενος τῶν κατὰ κωμῳδίαν μερῶν Ἀριστοφάνους τοῦ γραμματικοῦ. See Machon, 'The Fragments' ed. by A. S. F. Gow, *Cambridge Classical Texts and Commentaries* I (1965) 6 f.

[6] Nauck pp. 63–66.

[7] In this case I am not inclined to regard μεταγράψας as an error of the Scholiasts on Aristoph. *Thesm.* 162 and to assume a better manuscript as source of Aristophanes' correct reading, as Pasquali, *Storia* 199, did.

[8] See above, p. 178; cf. H. Erbse, *Gnom.* 28 (1956) 275.

(διάλειμμα), though the awkward stopgap (πλήρωμα) attributed to him by the Scholia can hardly be his manufacture.[1] Unfortunately his name never occurs in the Scholia when they are explaining the distribution of speakers, although we might expect that as a master of editorial technique he would have paid particular attention to marking the change of speakers in the dialogue of scenic poetry. In ancient papyri and medieval manuscripts it is usually indicated by paragraphus and double point, later also by abbreviated names, perhaps in accordance with a pre-Alexandrian tradition.[2] None of the great grammarians, however, seems to have attached much weight to these indications and this is the cause of a rather irritating instability in all our manuscripts.

We saw no reason to assume that Aristophanes wrote any ὑπομνήματα on epic or lyric poetry; he did not produce any commentary on the scenic poets either; a few explanations of comic or tragic expressions attributed to him may be part of his Λέξεις[3] or preserved in the ὑπομνήματα of his pupil Callistratus.[4] But he certainly wrote introductions to individual plays, perhaps to all of them, his famous ὑποθέσεις, which we shall be discussing in connexion with his work on tragedy.[5]

Apart from his editing the Aristophanic plays, it is a plausible guess, no more, that he published the text of other representatives of Old Comedy, Cratinus, and Eupolis, as Lycophron had tried to do before him,[6] but nobody has supposed that he made an edition of his beloved Menander.

That he admired Menander is well attested. Though not one of the scholar poets, he was nevertheless inspired by his boundless enthusiasm for him to compose a few comic trimeters in his honour,[7] and a later epigram affirms that he placed him second only to Homer.[8] A probably Peripatetic theory had defined comedy as 'imitation of life';[9] alluding to

---

[1] Cf. M. Haupt, *Opuscula* III 2 (1876) 524, and Coulon in his edition (1928) ad loc. One may furthermore compare the short remarks in Schol. *Nub.* 958, *Thesm.* 917, *Ran.* 1206.

[2] J. C. B. Lowe, 'The Manuscript Evidence for Changes of Speaker in Aristophanes', *University of London Institute of Classical Studies Bulletin* no. 9 (1962).

[3] Cf. above, p. 185, and below, pp. 197 ff.

[4] R. Schmidt, *Commentatio de Callistrato Aristophaneo* in Nauck's Aristoph. Byz. (1848) 307 ff.; cf. Boudreaux, *Le texte d'Aristophane* 48–51; A. Gudeman, *RE* x (1919) 1738–48.

[5] See below, pp. 191 ff. [6] See above, pp. 107, 119.

[7] Syrian. *comment. in Hermog.* II 23. 6 Rabe = Men. test. 32 Körte: "ὦ Μένανδρε καὶ βίε, πότερος ἄρ' ὑμῶν πότερον ἀπεμιμήσατο;"

[8] *IG* xiv 1183 c = Men. test. 61 c Körte δεύτ]ερα ἔταξε . . . μετ' ἐκεῖνον (sc. Homerum).

[9] Cic. ap. Donat. *de com.* v 1 comoediam esse . . . imitationem vitae (p. 22. 19 Wessner = Kaibel, *CGF* I p. 67, l. 147; the attribution to *de rep.* iv 11 Ziegler is questionable). A Greek Peripatetic source was suspected by Wilamowitz, *Einleitung in die Tragödie* 56. 13; cf. also A. Rostagni, *Scritti minori* I (1955) 230 and 339. 5. In the debate about Cicero's source and its author a literal testimony has been overlooked which may be of some help for further research. Schol. A Heph. p. 115. 13 Consbr. παρὰ τοῖς κωμικοῖς . . . τὸν γὰρ βίον οὗτοι μιμούμενοι.

this and also ingeniously reversing it, Aristophanes asked 'whether the comic poet Menander imitated life or life imitated Menander's comedy'. Homer's *Odyssey* had been called 'a fair mirror of life' by Alcidamas in the fourth century B.C.;[1] did Aristophanes put Homer and Menander in the same class because of their poetry being so near to βίος? The quotations in our Scholia suggest that Aristophanes and his pupil Callistratus had a particular interest in the *Odyssey*.[2] Whatever is meant by βίος (hardly the social life of the epoch), we get a glimpse here of one of Aristophanes' general views on poetry, and we can appreciate his clear and correct discernment of the most accomplished poet among the various post-classical writers. As regards his φιλία of Menander, Porphyry in his Φιλόλογος ἀκρόασις attests[3] that Aristophanes, drawing up a list of parallel passages from Menander and his models, 'gently' (ἠρέμα) proved him to have borrowed from others. We know of no earlier book on what is less gently called plagiarism;[4] but we may recall what we said about the pre-Aristophanic Hibeh papyrus with a list of Archilochean lines and their Homeric models,[5] and we may think of a typical story told by Vitruvius (*De architect.* VII praef. 5 ff.) : how Aristophanes by his amazing memory immediately detected the 'furta' (κλοπαί) of the contestants in a public literary competition and proved their plagiarism afterwards by unrolling innumerable volumes in the library.

Now, however, the papyrus Bodmer of the late third century A.D., which contains the almost complete *Dyscolus* of Menander,[6] strongly suggests that Aristophanes did in fact publish a text of the comic poet so near to his own lifetime. The text of the *Dyscolus* is preceded by a versified summary of the plot, which is ascribed to Aristophanes the grammarian, like the metrical summaries in our manuscripts of the Aristophanic comedies and of all the tragedians; this hypothesis is accompanied by the διδασκαλία, which informs us about the festival, the archon, the victory, the principal actor, and an alternative title, and by a list of dramatis personae. We shall not credit Aristophanes personally with the bad and

---

[1] See above, p. 51.

[2] See above, pp. 175 f.

[3] Long excerpts in Euseb. *Praep. ev.* x 3, on Menander § 12, 1 p. 563. 20 ff. Mras (= test. 51 Körte, where the necessary reference to Porphyry is missing) Ἀριστοφάνης ὁ γραμματικὸς ἐν ταῖς παραλλήλοις αὐτοῦ τε καὶ ἀφ' ὧν ἔκλεψεν ἐκλογαῖς.

[4] K. Ziegler, 'Plagiat', *RE* xx (1950) 1956–97; on Aristoph. Byz. col. 1979; cf. E. Stemplinger, *Das Plagiat in der griechischen Literatur* (1912) 7 f.

[5] Above, p. 145; Vitruv. praef. ad VII 4 ff.

[6] Papyrus Bodmer IV: Ménandre, *Le Dyscolos*, ed. V. Martin, 1958. This *editio princeps* was followed by numerous editions all over the world; in the OCT Lloyd-Jones gave a much improved recension of the *Dyscolus*, 1960. A running commentary was added in the edition of E. W. Handley, The *Dyskolos* of Menander, London 1965.

corrupt lines of the iambic ὑπόθεσις,[1] and we may doubt whether he put together the list of characters, but the learned didascalia in prose displays his style,[2] and even the description of the plot may be in substance his work, as is usual in the many hypotheses to comedies and tragedies. Whether or how he managed to treat the total of more than a hundred Menandrean comedies in the same way as is implied by the *Dyscolus* papyrus,[3] we had better not ask.

In contrast to comedy, tragedy seems to have been neglected by the scholars of the third century. Apart from Tzetzes' reference to Alexander Aetolus' διόρθωσις,[4] we have no information at all; other members of the Πλειάς imitated the tragic poems, but preferred comedy in their learned work. The official Athenian copy of the three great tragedians made at the instigation of Aristotle's friend Lycurgus had been secured for the Alexandrian library, if we can trust Galen's story,[5] during Eratosthenes' librarianship and was therefore at Aristophanes' disposal from the beginning of his career. In our medieval manuscript tradition the only traces of his editing are in the Scholia to Euripides—a few, probably three, of his variant readings[6] and two references to his critical σημεῖα. The papyri bear witness to his text of Sophocles. On the margin of the great roll of the *Ichneutai*[7] his name is four times added to variants, and probably also in the papyri of two other plays, the *Trachiniai* and *Theseus*;[8] exactly the same sort of marginal notes occur in the papyrus of Pindar's *Paeans*.[9] Of his work on Aeschylus' text there is still no evidence.

We come now to speak of Aristophanes' so-called hypotheses.[10] Wilamowitz was perfectly right to stress their importance.[11] They are indeed the most substantial remains of Aristophanes' editions of the tragedies and in a lesser degree of the comedies. But fresh discoveries and recent researches into the old and new evidence have altered and clarified the picture.

---

[1] I emended a few blunders of the scribe; see the Oxford text p. 3 and the *Tusculum-Bücherei* by M. Treu who edited the Greek text with German translation and short commentary (München 1960) p. 6. In l. 10 I prefer ⟨γ⟩έρων to the many published proposals I happen to know, although we should expect an article.

[2] Cf. below, p. 193.

[3] H. Erbse, 'Überlieferungsgeschichte der klassischen und hellenistischen Literatur' in *Geschichte der Textüberlieferung* I (1961) 223, drew from the publication of the *Dyscolus* the same conclusion, but no one else, as far as I can see. See Addenda.

[4] See above, pp. 105 f.; cf. p. 160.

[5] See above, p. 82.

[6] Nauck, pp. 62 f.; cf. Schol. Eur. ed. E. Schwartz II p. 380 Index: Aristophanes grammaticus. Schwartz's text has always to be consulted.

[7] *P.Oxy.* IX (1912) 1174, col. III 20, VI 5. 8, IX 6(?); see also Hunt p. 31.

[8] *P.Oxy.* XV (1922) 1805, Soph. *Tra.* 744; *P.Oxy.* XXVII (1962) 2452 fr. 2. 16, Soph. *Theseus*, see Turner's note p. 3.

[9] See above, p. 185.   [10] See above, p. 190.

[11] *Einleitung in die Tragödie* pp. 145 f.; cf. 133. 19.

The word ὑπόθεσις has various meanings; it may have been used in
Peripatetic circles for the plots of plays: Δικαιάρχου τινὰς ὑποθέσεις τῶν
Εὐριπίδου καὶ Σοφοκλέους μύθων.[1] The summaries prefixed to the plays in
our manuscripts also refer several times to this pupil of Aristotle; he seems
to have dealt with the contents of tragedies and comedies and with questions of scenic poetry in writings on festivals with poetical competitions,
of which one was entitled Περὶ Διονυσιακῶν ἀγώνων.[2] Aristophanes made
use of this Peripatetic source of about 300 B.C., as the fragments prove.
On the other hand, his aim was not to produce learned collections in the
'rich' style of Dicaearchus ('Peripatetici magni et copiosi'), but to write
simple and correct introductions to the text of individual plays; and the
obvious basis of these was, as is attested, Callimachus' chronological
Pinax of the dramatic poets.[3] The making of the hypotheses is thus typical
of the interrelation between the Peripatetic tradition and Alexandrian
scholarship. As Aristotle's and his pupil's didascalic works and Callimachus' *Pinakes* are lost, it is only through Aristophanes' hypotheses that
a great deal of priceless information has reached us.

If we exclude for the present the late Byzantine elaborations, there are
two groups of introductions, both labelled ὑποθέσεις, extant in papyri
and medieval manuscripts.[4] Of the one group only a few are explicitly
attributed to Aristophanes; but there is a large number of anonymous
hypotheses built on the same formal plan. They treated the subject-
matter of the play (ἃ ὑπόκειται τῷ δράματι) very briefly, touching on the
treatment of the same theme by other dramatists; then they mentioned
the scene, and the identity of the chorus and of the prologist; finally they
gave the date of the first performance, the titles of the other plays produced
simultaneously by the author, the names of the competitors with the

[1] Sext. Emp. *Adv. Math.* III 3 = Dicaearch. fr. 78 Wehrli.

[2] F. Wehrli, *Die Schule des Aristoteles* I (1944) Dikaiarchos, fr. 73–89, esp. fr. 79–84, title
fr. 75; cf. fr. 63 from the *Βίος Ἑλλάδος*. On his style Cic. *de off.* II 5. 16 = fr. 24 W.

[3] See above, pp. 132 and 133; *Et. gen.* B v. πίναξ . . . πίνακας . . . οἷς ἐντυχὼν ὁ γραμματικὸς
ἐποιήσατο τὰς ὑποθέσεις τῶν δραμάτων, see my notes on Call. fr. 456.

[4] As regards Aristophanes' ὑποθέσεις Nauck's otherwise sound scepticism was exaggerated
(pp. 252–63): he reluctantly admitted the authority of three of them as possible: Aesch.
Eum., Soph. *Ant.*, Eur. *Med.*, but refused to acknowledge Eur. *Or.*, *Phoen.*, *Bacch.* and [Eur.]
Rhes. (pp. 256 ff.). The way for their understanding was prepared by F. G. Schneidewin, 'De
hypothesibus tragoediarum Graecarum Aristophani Byzantio vindicandis', *Abhandlungen der
K. Gesellschaft der Wissenschaften zu Göttingen*, Hist.-phil. Kl. VI (1856) 3–38. Th. O. H.
Achelis, 'De Aristophanis Byz. argumentis fabularum', *Philol.* 72 (1913) 414 ff. and 518 ff.
and 73 (1914–16) 122 ff., provided a very useful collection and discussion of all the material
known at that time; G. Zuntz, *The Political Plays of Euripides* (1955) 129–52 'on the tragic
Hypotheseis', with bibliography p. 130. 3 made the best critical inquiry into the main types
of the tragic, esp. Euripidean, hypotheses. Compare also the commentators of the Oxford
Euripides, esp. of *Med.*, *Alc.*, *Hipp.* Too little attention had been paid to the Aeschylean
hypotheses, see below, p. 194. On the hypotheses to comedies see below, p. 196.

result of the competition, occasionally the number the play had in the chronological register of the author's works, and a critical judgement. If a ὑπόθεσις contains some of these items in a simple, condensed style its Aristophanic origin is at least highly probable; he meant them to be a necessary help for the scholarly reader.[1] Modern research has naturally concentrated on the rich material preserved in our tradition of Euripides; as far as we can reconstruct Aristophanes' edition, we cannot recognize any difference between his prefaces to the plays which now have no scholia, the so-called nine 'alphabetic' plays, and those to the ten 'selected' plays with ample commentaries.

Recently discovered hypotheses have provided important new evidence for Aeschylus. The sequence of the plays in his Theban tetralogy, previously much debated, was established when the didascalian part of the hypothesis to the *Septem*, missing in the minor manuscripts, was published from the codex Mediceus; its complete and exact wording has been confirmed as ancient by a papyrus[2] of the second century A.D. Another fragment of the same papyrus surprisingly revealed that Sophocles was Aeschylus' competitor when he performed the *Danaides* tetralogy, and so made the conclusion inevitable that the *Supplices* were performed after 468 B.C., not in the early fifth century B.C.;[3] no hypothesis is preserved in the codex unicus Mediceus. A hypothesis which, with good reason, is believed to be that of Aeschylus' Sicilian festival play Αἰτναῖαι (or Αἶτναι)[4] brought unexpected news not about the date, but about the place represented in the play. This play, whatever its title, to which the preface belongs, was divided into five μέρη, 'acts', and for each of them a change of scene was mentioned; the fifth scene seems to have been the same quarter of Syracuse in which the theatre was situated and the plays were performed, namely the Temenites. In these examples we catch a glimpse of the many data once supplied to the reader by Aristophanes, but often lost in the slow process of epitomizing through the centuries.

The arguments of the second group are of a quite different type, but

---

[1] Wilamowitz, *Einleitung* 139 (cf. 145), called Aristophanes 'Gesamtausgaben der Klassiker . . . in erster Linie ein buchhändlerisches Unternehmen'; he repeated this assertion in later books and succeeded in persuading others (see E. Schwartz, *Ethik der Griechen*, 1951, p. 136). But I have never found any proof for this enterprise of an Alexandrian book-trading.

[2] *P.Oxy.* xx (1952) 2256, fr. 2 = Fragmente des Aischylos, hg. von H. J. Mette (1959) fr. 169.

[3] *P.Oxy.* 2256, fr. 3 = fr. 122 Mette; it is to be regretted that G. Murray in his much-improved second edition of Aeschylus (*OCT* 1955) desperately tried to stick to the early date, p. vi and p. 2. See now H. Lloyd-Jones, *L'Antiquité Classique* 33 (1964) 356 ff.

[4] *P.Oxy.* xx (1952) 2257, fr. 1, with E. Lobel's commentary = fr. 26 Mette. I cannot think of any better supplement in l. 13 than [ἐν τῷ Τεμενί]τῃ which I once proposed to Lobel. On the play itself see E. Fraenkel, *Eranos* 52 (1954) 61–75.

bear the same name, ὑπόθεσις, not only in the medieval manuscripts, but also in the ancient papyri. This easily leads to confusion. In this group ὑπόθεσις means a description of the contents of a play without any details of erudition; a complete, but relatively short summary in a clear and rather dry style is the rule.[1] Διήγησις would be a more appropriate term; it is used for the summaries of Callimachus' poems in the Milan papyrus[2] and for a summary of a part of the *Odyssey*. Hypotheses of this sort were even cast into verse and honoured by the great name of Aristophanes.[3] Two papyri have preserved parts of a collection of ὑποθέσεις[4] to the complete works of Euripides in alphabetical order according to the first letter of the title. The title is followed by the formula οὗ ἀρχή and the first line of the play; then ἡ δ' ὑπόθεσις introduces the summary of the plot. The alphabetical order and the whole form of the 'incipit' are derived from the Callimachean *Pinakes*.[5] So even in books which were certainly destined for the general reader, we find traces of Alexandrian scholarship, and that is why they are mentioned here. It is hardly possible to fix the age which produced these collected summaries of epic[6] and scenic poetry, probably for a developed book-trade; but if the *Tabulae Iliacae*[7] reproduced them on stone in the time of Augustus, it must have been the later Hellenistic age. When afterwards each popular hypothesis from the collection was transferred to its individual play, it was often placed side by side with another one derived from Aristophanes' scholarly work. Later still Byzantine scholars and schoolmasters of the thirteenth and fourteenth

---

[1] Wilamowitz, followed by others, repeatedly compared the *Tales from Shakespeare* by Charles and Mary Lamb (first publ. 1807); but these 'Tales', far from giving only a skeleton story, retell the plots of the tragedies and comedies in lively and gracious prose and have taken their place as an English classic.

[2] *P.Med.* 18 (publ. 1934), v. Call. vol. II, p. XII, XXVIII with bibliography; cf. also Διήγησις εἰς τὰς καθ' Ὅμηρον πλάνας τοῦ Ὀδυσσέως, *Mythographi Graeci* ed. Westermann (1843) 329.

[3] See above, p. 191.

[4] *PSI* XII (1951) 1286, first published by C. Gallavotti, *Riv. fil. cl.* N.S. XI (1933) 177 ff.; *P.Oxy.* XXVII (1962) 2455 (cf. above, p. 129, n. 5); cf. E. G. Turner, L'érudition alexandrine et les papyrus', *Chronique d'Égypte* 37 (1962) 136 f., on this papyrus. 'Un Argument sur papyrus de la Médée d'Euripide' published by M. Papathomopoulos in *Recherches de la Papyrologie* III (1964) 37–47 (with a list of dramatic hypotheses on papyrus) clearly belongs to this type, though the number 2 (*B*) points to a different arrangement, in which possibly *Medea* took the second place in a selection.—See also R. A. Coles and J. W. B. Barns, 'Fragments of dramatic hypotheses from Oxyrhynchus', *Cl. Qu.* N.S. XV (1965) 52 ff., with references to smaller papyrus fragments which may be parts of larger or even complete collections. The new fragment of Eur. *Phoen.* finally published in *P.Oxy.* XXXI (1966) as no. 2544 is treated by W. S. Barrett, 'The epitome of Eur. *Phoen.*: ancient and medieval versions', ibid. 58 ff. who identified three fragments of the hypothesis of the *Phoen.* in *P.Oxy.* 2455 and showed that Moschopulos's version of the hypothesis is fairly close to the version in the papyrus.

[5] See above, pp. 129 f.

[6] Pack[2] no. 1185, prose summary of *Il.* VI (third century B.C.), 1190, 1208.

[7] O. Jahn–A. Michaelis, *Griechische Bilderchroniken* (1873) 79 ff., esp. 86 f.

centuries A.D. felt the need to add for their pupils much more extensive prefaces, which are preserved as a third group in many manuscripts of the scenic poets.[1]

The hypotheses to comedies run parallel to those to tragedies;[2] they have a similar structure, and nine out of eleven introductions to Aristophanes' comedies preserved in our manuscripts contain διδασκαλίαι. There is good reason to trace them back to Aristophanes of Byzantium although his name appears only once in a title, and although Symmachus[3] may have recast them when he wrote his commentary at the beginning of the second century A.D., just as Heliodorus rehandled the colometry. Beside these short scholarly prefaces we find a second, more popular, kind of hypothesis in prose and verse. The arrangement in the *Dyscolus* papyrus shows a close affinity, which we have already used to support the view that a text of Menander should be added to the previously known editions of Aristophanes.[4] The papyri[5] have also yielded an alphabetical collection of summaries of Menandrean comedies; but unlike those of Euripides' tragedies, they follow the 'incipit' with didascalic information, and the account of the plot with a critical appreciation of the play. Nowhere else is the influence of Aristophanes so constant as in the variations of his ὑποθέσεις to the tragic and comic plays.

All the scholars of the third century devoted their critical labours to the poetry of the past—quite naturally, as they were the pupils of poets and mostly poets themselves. It has been argued that Aristophanes also produced an edition of Plato. But Diogenes Laertius,[6] after speaking about the arrangement of Plato's dialogues in tetralogies, then gives us only the dry remark: ἔνιοι δέ, ὧν ἐστι καὶ Ἀριστοφάνης ὁ γραμματικός, εἰς τριλογίας ἕλκουσι τοὺς διαλόγους, and adds the list of fifteen dialogues grouped into trilogies; perhaps ἕλκουσι, 'they drag', implies a notion of force in this arrangement of Plato's philosophic work. A list of the νόθοι concludes the chapter. The most probable interpretation of the passage is that some scholars, including Aristophanes in his supplement to the *Pinakes*,[7]

---

[1] On Moschopulos see above, p. 195, n. 4.

[2] See above, pp. 192 f.; cf. P. Boudreaux, *Le Texte d'Aristophane* (1919) 31–35.

[3] A. Koerte, *RE* XI (1921) 1211 f.; cf. the hypothesis to Cratinus' Διονυσαλέξανδρος *P.Oxy.* IV (1904) 663 = *Suppl. Comicum* ed. I. Demiańczuk (1912) 31 ff.

[4] See above, pp. 191 f.

[5] *P.Oxy.* X (1914) 1235 = Menander ed. A. Koerte I (1938) 146 ff. They may be identical with the Περιοχαὶ τῶν Μενάνδρου δραμάτων of a certain Σέλλιος or Σίλλιος, see Koerte p. lxiv. See also *Cl. Qu.* N.S. XV (1965) 55 ff. a new fragment published in *P.Oxy.* XXXI (1966) as no. 2534, possibly from the hypothesis of Menander Αὐτὸν τιμωρούμενος.

[6] Diog. L. III 61 f.

[7] So very sensibly Nauck p. 250, fr. VI; Pasquali, *Storia* 264; Erbse in *Geschichte der Textüberlieferung* (1961) 221.

criticized the tetralogies of an edition, perhaps of the Academy, and put forward the case for trilogies. Nothing in this sentence points to an edition made in Alexandria.[1] On the other hand, a later chapter deals with critical σημεῖα in what was possibly an Alexandrian edition; but this system of σημείωσις is totally different from that of Aristophanes.[2] So, on our present evidence, there is no reason to regard Aristophanes as the first to have included a prose author in the series of his editions.

His great lexicographical work, the Λέξεις,[3] ranged over all fields of literature, prose as well as poetry; there are references to Herodotus, Thucydides, Xenophon, Isocrates, Demosthenes. We have already mentioned it several times when the question arose whether certain exegetical notes to epic, lyric, and dramatic expressions originated from a commentary or from the *Lexeis*, and we decided in each case that it was unnecessary to assume the existence of a commentary. As in his editions, Aristophanes had the labours of the whole third century at his disposal; he was the true successor both of Zenodotus as a glossographer and of Callimachus as a compiler of various onomastica arranged according to subjects or localities.[4] But in this case we ought to look much further back in order to get the right perspective for his historical position.

From the very beginning poetry had itself paved the way to its understanding;[5] it was part of the poetical technique in the epic age to elucidate difficult and ambiguous expressions by exegetical or etymological

---

[1] Wilamowitz, *Antigonos von Karystos* (1881) 286 'Ar. hätte keinen so zuverlässigen Text konstituieren können'; but *Platon* II (1919) 324 correctly 'an eine Ausgabe (sc. by Aristoph. Byz.) ist nicht zu denken'. On Jachmann, *Der Platontext* (1942) 334, see above, p. 65, n. 4. On the various attempts at arranging Plato's writings from the fourth to the first centuries B.C. see A.-H. Chroust, 'The Organization of the Corpus Platonicum in Antiquity', *Herm.* 93 (1965) 34 ff.

[2] Diog. L. III 65 f. A small, but very interesting Florentine papyrus of the second century A.D. is perhaps a part of the source of Diog. L.; the arrangement of the text is better and the critical signs themselves, missing in our manuscripts, are inserted. See V. Bartoletti in 'Mélanges Eugène Tisserant' I, *Studi e Testi* 231 (1964) 25–30.

[3] In Nauck's book of the year 1848 the whole of the fragments fills 274 pages, out of which 165 are dedicated to the Λέξεις, that is three-fifths of the space. But in a codex Athous (now cod. Par. suppl. Gr. 1164, 13th/14th century) E. Miller discovered more substantial excerpts from different sections of the Λέξεις, published in *Mélanges de littérature grecque* (1868) 427–34; their importance was immediately recognized by Nauck, *Bulletin de l'Acad. de St. Pétersbourg* 1869, 344 ff. = *Mélanges Gréco-Romains* III (1874) 166 ff.; in connexion with other excerpts from a Florentine codex they were treated by A. Fresenius, *De Λέξεων Aristophanearum et Suetoniarum excerptis Byzantinis* (1875) and by L. Cohn, 'De Aristoph. Byz. et Suetonio Eustathi auctoribus' *Jahrbücher für class. Philologie*, Suppl. Bd. 12 (1881) 283 ff.; see also above, p. 171, n. 3, and Latte, 'Glossographika', *Philol.* 80 (1925) 164 ff. On Eustathius' excerpts from the Λέξεις H. Erbse, 'Untersuchungen zu den attizistischen Lexika', *Abhandlungen der Deutschen Akademie d. Wiss. zu Berlin*, Phil.-hist. Kl., Jg. 1949, Nr. 2 (1950) 5 and *passim*.

[4] See above, pp. 115 and 134 f.; also Callimachus' poems were one of his sources, see the notes on Call. fr. 224, 487, 543, 587.

[5] See above, p. 3.

additions. There was hardly any following age in which the Greek mind was not attracted by this problem of explaining λέξεις. Their origin and their changes, the differentiation of kindred words, the comparison between Greek dialects or between Greek and foreign words were discussed by the Sophists, by Democritus, and by the great Attic philosophers.[1] In the new era the poets revived these studies with fervour, not only Philitas and Simias, but also Callimachus and Apollonius;[2] they composed scholarly works themselves or stimulated scholars like Zenodotus, Eratosthenes, or Neoptolemus to enter this vast field of research. Whatever had been undertaken piecemeal here and there in the course of time, was all now united into one great enterprise, the Λέξεις of Aristophanes.[3] A collection of γλῶσσαι was usually limited to obsolete and obscure terms; but under the neutral title Λέξεις every word which was peculiar in form or significance and therefore in need of explanation could be listed, whether it was out of date or still in use. The fragments quoted from Aristophanes' lexicographical work allow us to estimate its wide range, its systematic arrangement in sections, and the method of exegesis. It was, above all, this method which became the model for later Greek and Roman antiquity. Viewing the past and the future, we can clearly recognize Aristophanes' central position.[4]

The first thing a lexicographer needs is a reliable text based on the best manuscripts; in this respect Aristophanes had the advantage over all his predecessors, as his own editions of the Greek poets from Homer to Menander were within his reach. It was, of course, a mutual benefit: the lexicographer's detailed research into the proper form and meaning of a word at a given time and in a special dialect helped the διορθωτής to take his choice between variant readings of the manuscripts of his text.

As regards method the most interesting section of the Λέξεις was entitled Περὶ τῶν ὑποπτευομένων μὴ εἰρῆσθαι τοῖς παλαιοῖς, 'words supposed to be unknown to the ancients', a fact first learned from the Athos manuscript discovered by Miller.[5] In that manuscript the first item of this first chapter is σάννας, explained as ὁ μωρός, 'the fool'. It was well known

[1] See above, pp. 39–42, 43, 62–64, 78 f.
[2] See above, pp. 90 f., 115, 135, 139 f., 148.
[3] Περὶ λέξεων in the 'Fragmentum Parisinum', first published by Boissonade in 1819, repr. by Nauck pp. 79 ff.
[4] It has been convincingly argued that Aristophanes was a main source of the *Antiatticista* (K. Latte, *Herm.* 50 (1915) 374. 379, 2. 384 f., 392) and also of Helladius, *Chrestomath.* (K. Strecker, *Herm.* 26 (1891) 276 f.).
[5] Miller, *Mélanges* 427 f., Cohn, *Jahrbücher f. class. Philologie*, Suppl. Bd. 12 (1881) 288–98. Cf. Wilamowitz, *Einleitung* 163. 88, who regards it together with the so-called Ἀττικαὶ λέξεις as criticism of pseudo-Attic forgeries of the third century, but our fragments do not point in that direction.

from a large excerpt in Eustathius that Aristophanes had dealt with this rare word, its various forms and derivations as well as its possible meanings. But Nauck and everyone else went wrong in the quite natural assumption that it was classed as one of the many expressions of blasphemy.[1] Before the discovery of Miller's codex it was impossible to guess the existence of a chapter which treated λέξεις under the chronological, not to say historical aspect. Two classes of words were distinguished: those λέξεις said to be used by the παλαιοί and those said to have been unknown to them, the καινότεραι λέξεις.[2] Aristophanes probably discussed the opinions of earlier scholars and confirmed or rejected them. If—to return to our example—σάννας had been regarded as a word of later origin, we can conclude with some probability from Eustathius' excerpt that Aristophanes referred to its use in Old Comedy by Cratinus.[3] There is even a slight chance that he went further back to the sixth century B.C. and quoted an epodic poem of Hipponax,[4] who addressed someone with the nickname ὦ Σάνν', which implied his 'foolish' character; the fragmentary very learned commentary on this poem in a papyrus of the second century B.C. contains the name of Aristophanes[5] besides those of his older contemporary Hermippus and of his younger one Polemo. Though it is still impossible to say to what line or word that fragment of the commentary belongs, there can be little doubt the reference is made to Aristophanes the grammarian, not the comic poet. At the very least the text confirms his view that the word σάννας was known to the παλαιοί.

In the same first section of the Λέξεις we find the strange verbal forms ἐφεύγοσαν καὶ ἐλέγοσαν· ἀντὶ τοῦ ἔφευγον καὶ ἔλεγον.[6] Eustathius has preserved a longer excerpt with references: παραδίδωσι δὲ (Ἀριστοφάνης) καὶ ὅτι τὸ "ἐσχάζοσαν" παρὰ Λυκόφρονι (21) καὶ παρ' ἄλλοις τὸ "ἐλέγοσαν" καὶ τὸ "οἱ δὲ πλησίον γενομένων ⟨ἐ⟩φεύγοσαν" φωνῆς Χαλκιδέων ἴδιά εἰσιν. The main point seems to be that there was no literary authority amongst the παλαιοί for the ending in -οσαν, as Aristophanes correctly observed; but he found it in one of the new poets and perhaps[7] conjectured that this poet,

---

[1] There was no section Περὶ βλασφημιῶν in Aristoph. Λέξεις, see below, p. 201, n. 6.

[2] παλαιοί are, if the few fragments are not misleading, pre-Alexandrian writers; Eust. p. 279. 38, περὶ καινοτέρων λέξεων and p. 1761. 24 καινοφώνους λέξεις seems to refer to post-Attic authors. [3] Cratin. fr. 337 K.

[4] *P.Oxy.* XVIII (1941) 2176, fr. 1. 1 = Hipponax ed. O. Masson (1962) fr. 118. 1 with commentary.

[5] *P.Oxy.* 2176, fr. 8. 21; see Masson pp. 86 and 162. 1.

[6] Miller, *Mélanges* p. 428. 1, cf. Eust. p. 1761. 30 (cf. 1759. 35); Tzetz. in Lyc. 21 and 253. Nauck p. 204, Fresenius p. 115.

[7] Nauck p. 204 'fortasse'; he believed there was one pre-Alexandrian example, Eur. *Hec.* 574, where Choer. II 64. 25 Hilg., in discussing the endings in -οσαν, read δ' ἐπληροῦσαν

Lycophron[1] of Chalcis, borrowed it from the dialect of his native country, and that others followed him. I doubt if this was meant to be a critical hit at Lycophron.[2] We know Aristophanes had a peculiar interest in dialects; but when he took -οσαν in the praeteritum of the verbs in -ω as a Chacidian local dialectal form, he made a mistake.[3] It was a quite common ending in the κοινή throughout the late ancient and Byzantine times from the third century B.C. onwards,[4] and therefore certainly a καινόφωνος λέξις. In both these very different examples, σάννας and ἐσχάζοσαν, we see Aristophanes trying to solve the same problem: the chronological distinction between ancient and modern usage, and possibly the local origin of the latter. This was priceless preparatory work for the study of the development of the Greek language.[5]

The following chapters had the character of ὀνομαστικά,[6] that is, of vocabularies arranged according to subjects. The most copious of them, entitled ᾿Ονόματα ἡλικιῶν or Περὶ ὀνομασίας ἡλικιῶν,[7] denoted the different times of life of men and women, of animals living in herds, and of wild beasts. Even in our rather poor excerpts an intimate knowledge of the poetical language and of all the dialects is displayed. As in the case of σάννας and ἐσχάζοσαν, many more literal quotations or references are preserved in Eustathius and in other writers and onomastica than in the Athos manuscript. One of its extracts about the young of wild animals, for instance, gives various names of deer and adds only the short remark: τὰ δὲ νέα τούτων, ὄβρια καὶ ὀβρίκαλα.[8] But the longer excerpts[9] mention

---

(δὲ πληροῦσιν Eur. codd.). From Nauck our grammars and the critical apparatus of the Eur. editions took it over; but this vulgarism is not a *varia lectio*, but a bad conjecture of late antiquity trying to 'correct' the *inconcinnitas temporum* in the Euripidean line.

[1] On Lycophron see above, pp. 119 f. If we consider all the excerpts of Eustathius from Aristophanes which far exceed the short extracts in the Athos manuscript, there is not the slightest probability that he interpolated just this one reference to Lycophron, as P. Maas, *Gnom.* 3 (1927) 320, suspected.

[2] Wilamowitz (who had always taken Nauck's conjecture as a proven fact) *Hell. Dicht.* II (1924) 147. 1 'dem Lycophron zum Tort'.

[3] On similar mistakes see Latte, 'Glossographika', *Philol.* 80 (1925) 174.

[4] E. Mayser, *Grammatik der griechischen Papyri aus der Ptolemäerzeit* I 2² (1938) 83 f., with bibliography.

[5] See below, pp. 201 f.　　　　　　　　　　　　　　　　[6] See above, p. 197.

[7] Miller, *Mélanges* 428–31; Fresenius 82–89 and 116–22; Cohn 298–311.

[8] Miller, *Mélanges* p. 431. 9; Fresenius p. 26.

[9] Ael. *n.a.* VII 47, Phot. *lex.* II 2, 10 Nab., Eust. 1395. 46 ff. and 1625. 47: ὄβρια (Eur. fr. 616) and ὀβρίκαλα (Aesch. *Ag.* 143); Hesych. v. 'ὀβρικάλοις'; Poll. v 15 πάντων τῶν ἀγρίων τέκνα ὀβρίκαλα οἱ ποιηταὶ καλοῦσι καὶ ὀβρικά (*sic* the common ancestor of codd. SF, written before the twelfth century A.D.). Is ὀβρικά a slight corruption of ὄβριχα? H. Frisk, *Griech. etymol. Wörterbuch*, fasc. 14 (1963) 345, is inclined to take ὀβρίχοισι in *P.Oxy.* 2161. 809 as dat. plur. neut. and refers to similar formations; perhaps the surprising form in the *Dictyulci* papyrus was not new after all, but only hidden in a variant reading of Pollux, who depends on Aristophanes, as Cohn p. 311 had pointed out.

more names of animals and refer for these two forms to Aeschylus' *Agamemnon* (ὀβρίκαλα) and *Dictyulci* and to Euripides' *Peliades* (probably ὄβρια); in the *Dictyulci* an Oxyrhynchus papyrus has brought a third form to light, ὀβρίχοισι.[1] This shows how difficult it is to reconstruct Aristophanes' original wording, as special forms of ὀνομασίαι dropped out rather early; on the other hand, this example and many others prove that additions in Eustathius are by no means his interpolations, but derived from Aristophanes. The same is true of the next chapters, 'On terms of relationship', Περὶ συγγενικῶν ὀνομάτων, and 'On terms of civic life', Περὶ πολιτικῶν ὀνομάτων.[2] Every effort was made not only to distinguish the usage in epic, lyric, and dramatic poetry, and in the local dialects, but to point out changes of form and meaning and even to trace words to their origin.

Aristophanes seems to have actually initiated the methodical scholarly treatment of the πάθη and ἔτυμα of words; it is true that the term πάθη τῆς λέξεως for the modifications in form of words had been used by Aristotle, but Varro expressly refers to their treatment by Aristophanes,[3] and the forms ὄβρια, ὄβριχα, ὀβρίκαλα, quoted above, are as good an example as Varro's 'in turdo turdario et turdelice'. The ancient game of ἐτυμολογεῖν, that is, analysing a word and finding its origin, was sparingly and soberly played by him,[4] in contrast to his Stoic contemporaries, of whom Chrysippus was the first to write several books entitled Περὶ ἐτυμολογικῶν.[5]

The excerpts from the Λέξεις in the Athos manuscript and in Eustathius stop after the συγγενικά and πολιτικὰ ὀνόματα. Four more sections were added by conjecture in Nauck's edition; but the author of one of them, Περὶ βλασφημιῶν, turned out to be Suetonius.[6] For the other three chapters the editor had gathered fragments from various sources and arranged them according to subject-matter or locality, under the titles Περὶ προσφωνήσεων ('Forms of salutation'),[7] Ἀττικαὶ λέξεις, and Λακωνικαὶ γλῶσσαι.[8] Aristophanes certainly spoke of some προσφωνήσεις like ἄππα, πάππα, μάμμα, etc., but there is no evidence for a whole chapter of

[1] *P.Oxy.* xviii (1941) 2161 Aesch. *Dictyulc.* 809 ὑστρίχων ὀβρίχοισ[ι] = fr. 474. 809 Mette.
[2] Miller, *Mélanges* 431. 13–432. 22 and 432. 23–434 without separate headings; the heading Πολιτικὰ ὀνόματα was proposed by Fresenius pp. 12 f. and pp. 123–7.
[3] Varro, *L.L.* vi 2; Nauck p. 269.
[4] Nauck pp. 268 f.; cf. R. Schröter, 'Studien zur varronischen Etymologie', *Akademie der Wissenschaften und Literatur in Mainz*, Abh. der geistes- u. sozialwissenschaftl. Kl. Jg. 1959, Nr. 12, 53 ff., esp. 60–63.
[5] *SVF* ii p. 9. 13, 14; cf. fr. 146, p. 44. 42; cf. below, p. 241.
[6] Nauck's chapter pp. 163–80 has to be cancelled, see Miller, *Mélanges* 413–26 Suétone.
[7] Nauck pp. 151–62; cf. Cohn 321 ff.
[8] Nauck pp. 181–90; cf. Cohn pp. 288. 6 and 322 ff.

the Λέξεις with this special title and contents; on the other hand, of the few dialectal quotations we have, four are labelled ἐν Ἀττικαῖς λέξεσιν and perhaps five ἐν Λακωνικαῖς γλώσσαις. Of whatever larger work they may be subdivisions, they bear witness again not only to Aristophanes' knowledge of dialectal forms in literature, but also to his special interest in the spoken language of his own day.[1] Though books of his teacher Dionysius Iambus Περὶ διαλέκτων and of Sosibius Laco 'On Lacedaemonian cults' with a collection of Laconic glosses may have given some kind of impulse and help,[2] it seems to have been as the fruit of his own observations that he recorded the sound of Laconic words, as for instance ἄδδα for Ionic ἄζη.[3] Aristophanes was, as far as we know at present, the first who, besides his immense reading, listened to the vernacular and so went beyond the sphere of mere bookishness.[4]

The multifarious studies that went into the building of this rich lexical treasure-house must have been accompanied by theoretical inquiries of which Aristophanes may have talked more fully to his pupils. We are only once told of his reflection upon a formal grammatical problem. He[5] discovered recurrent patterns in the Greek declension (κλίσις) and stated general rules of regular inflexion; this principle of 'regularity' was called ἀναλογία. Beyond this short statement no clear and reliable information can be elicited from our sources, Varro and Donatian–Charisius;[6] but the door was opened for endless speculation. It cannot be proved that Aristophanes coined the grammatical term ἀναλογία or wrote a

---

[1] Eust. pp. 877. 49 ff. in a long excerpt in which Aristophanes first says that in Homer μῆλα can mean also the αἶγες, and then goes on: "καὶ ἡμεῖς δέ", φησί (sc. Ἀριστοφάνης), "μηλωτὴν καλοῦμεν καὶ τὴν αἰγείαν δοράν"; cf. ibid. pp. 1828. 56 ff. (Nauck pp. 197–9); see also above, p. 200.

[2] On Dionysius see above, p. 171; cf. L. Weber, *Quaest. Lacon.*, Diss. Göttingen (1887) 55–64 who gives a list of Sosibius' glosses, perhaps first half of the third century B.C.

[3] Nauck p. 189, fr. 33; cf. F. Bechtel, *Griech. Dialekte* II (1923) 323.

[4] On this delicate problem see J. Wackernagel, *Berl. philol. Wochenschr.* (1896) 1399 = *Kleine Schriften* I (1953) 538, and Wilamowitz, *Geschichte der griechischen Sprache* (1928) 36 f.

[5] Nauck 264–71. Varro, *L.L.* x 68 'tertium genus (sc. analogiae) . . . in quo et res et voces similiter proportione dicuntur ut bonus malus, boni mali, de quorum analogia et Aristophanes et alii scripserunt'; cf. ibid. IX 12 'Aristophanes improbandus, qui potius in quibusdam veritatem quam consuetudinem secutus?'—Charisius, *Ars grammatica* (ed. C. Barwick, 1925) p. 149. 26 'huic (sc. analogiae) Aristophanes quinque rationes dedit vel, ut alii putant, sex; primo ut eiusdem sint generis . . . dein casus, tum exitus, quarto numeri syllabarum, item soni. sextum Aristarchus, discipulus eius, illud addidit ne unquam simplicia compositis aptemus'; cf. Donatiani fragm. *GL* VI 276. 5 ff.

[6] H. Dahlmann, 'Varro und die hellenistische Sprachtheorie', *Problemata* 5 (1932) 52 ff. H. J. Mette, *Parateresis* (1952) 11 ff., who included a critical text of Varro *L.L.* VII 109–x 84. D. Fehling, 'Varro und die grammatische Lehre von der Analogie und der Flexion', *Glotta* 35 (1956) 214 ff., 36 (1957) 48 ff. with bibliography p. 48. 1, 2, to which has to be added A. Dihle, 'Analogie und Attizismus', *Herm.* 85 (1957) 170 ff.; a postscript pp. 203 ff. modifies Fehling's overstatements about Varro's incompetence, confusions, and inventions. *Entretiens sur l'antiquité classique* IX (1962) 'Varron', see F. Collart, 'Analogie et anomalie', pp. 117–40.

monograph Περὶ ἀναλογίας,[1] and it is unbelievable that he intended to refute Chrysippus' three or four books Περὶ τῆς κατὰ τὰς λέξεις ἀνωμαλίας.[2] Chrysippus of Soloi, who had declined a call to Alexandria and died as an Athenian citizen and head of the Stoic school between 208 and 204 B.C., developed as part of his formal logic the theory that words are not in harmony with things they express and called it ἀνωμαλία; it is illogical if a plural signifies a singular subject (as the plural Θῆβαι for one city), a masculine form a feminine idea, and so on. He was thus renewing under a new aspect an old philosophical dispute upon the relation of words to things well known to us from Plato's and Aristotle's writings.[3] Aristophanes, on the other hand, never entered the arena where the philosophers were fighting; he confined himself in this case, as in others, to a scholarly problem of grammar. The term 'grammar',[4] so far consciously avoided, can now indeed be used; we can see that as part of scholarship in general a separate discipline was being built up which reached its height in the second generation after Aristophanes, in the τέχνη γραμματική of Dionysius Thrax, the pupil of Aristarchus. We are in the dark about the way the rules of inflexion were shaped in the meantime.[5] The concept of analogy was apparently extended by Aristarchus to the interpretation of texts. Then in the fields of grammar and exegesis a dispute must have arisen between analogists and anomalists, which is known to us from Latin sources only; Aristophanes had nothing to do with it.[6] If we take a broad view of his lexical and of his formal linguistic studies, it becomes clear that they were auxiliary to his editorial work.

Aristophanes' editions were confined to a certain number of poets and even the references in the *Lexeis* rarely go beyond a limited group of poets and prose writers. This cannot have happened by chance. A sort of sifting of the whole literature, as stored in the library and registered in

---

[1] It is hardly derived from the mathematical and philosophical term ἀναλογία (= proportion) used by Eratosthenes, the Platonist, in his *Platonicus*, see above, p. 137.

[2] *SVF* II p. 6. 10; cf. ibid. Chrysipp. fr. 151, p. 45. 23 and 26; cf. Barwick, *Stoische Sprachlehre* 53 ff.

[3] See above, pp. 59 ff. (Plato), 75 ff. (Aristotle).

[4] Sext. Emp. *adv. math.* I 44 ed. Mau, vol. III, p. 12. 17 ff. (perhaps from Asclepiades of Myrlea) γραμματικὴ τοίνυν λέγεται . . . ἡ ἐντελὴς καὶ τοῖς περὶ Κράτητα τὸν Μαλλώτην Ἀριστοφάνην τε καὶ Ἀρίσταρχον ἐκπονηθεῖσα.

[5] To Aristophanes' five rules Aristarchus added a sixth negative one (above, p. 202, n. 5).

[6] L. Lersch, *Die Sprachphilosophie der Alten, dargestellt an dem Streite über Analogie und Anomalie der Sprache* (Bonn 1838), actually based the whole history of ancient philosophy of language on this dispute opened by Aristophanes. It is still worth while to read Nauck's ironical devastating criticism (p. 270) written more than a century before Fehling *Glotta* 35 (1956) and 36 (1957) who now rejects the possibility of reconstructing the quarrel from the Latin sources, particularly from Varro. His paper is a typical example of the reaction against the excesses of source-research, but not wholly successful.

Callimachus' *Pinakes*, must have taken place. In this process Aristophanes played a decisive part, if Quintilian (x 1. 54) was right in saying: 'Apollonius in ordinem a grammaticis datum non venit, quia Aristarchus atque Aristophanes, poetarum iudices,[1] neminem sui temporis in numerum redegerunt.' About a century earlier Cicero had written in the same sense to Atticus (xvi 11. 2): 'cui ut Aristophani Archilochi iambus[2] sic epistola longissima quaeque optima videtur.' These Latin texts,[3] of which the Greek sources are unknown, clearly state that some authors were received in and others excluded from an *ordo* established by literary criticism (κρίσις, *iudicium*). The tendency to select the best writers for various reasons is a very old one;[4] the passionate debate about pre-eminence among the Attic tragedians, still going on in Aristophanes' *Frogs*, must have been settled by the middle or second half of the fourth century B.C. when Heraclides Ponticus wrote Περὶ τῶν τριῶν τραγῳδοποιῶν.[5] The same number is implied by Aristophanes in the Hypothesis to Euripides' *Medea*, παρ' οὐδετέρῳ κεῖται ἡ μυθοποιία, which can only mean 'neither in Aeschylus nor in Sophocles', and it remained authoritative for the later ages. It is in the hypotheses to tragedies and comedies that we still find precious traces of his individual judgements on poems and poets.[6]

Three iambographers were received into the ranks by Aristarchus, and Archilochus[7] was acknowledged as the best both by him and by Aristophanes. There is no further evidence for the judgement of the two Alexandrian grammarians. As the foremost ('praecipui', ἀξιόλογοι) of the many early comic poets Quintilian (x 1. 66) enumerates the three whose names Horace had used to build up the harmonious first line of his fourth satire, 'Eupolis atque Cratinus Aristophanesque poetae / atque alii quorum comoedia prisca virorumst'. This famous triad reappeared quite often in literature on Old Comedy, but was not exclusively accepted; Eratosthenes and Aristophanes regarded Pherecrates, for instance, as its equal.[8] In the field of epic poetry Homer as the author of *Iliad* and *Odyssey* and Hesiod as the author of *Theogony* and *Erga* always occupied the first

---

[1] Cf. Quintil. 1 4. 3 'quo (sc. iudicio) . . . ita severe sunt usi veteres grammatici ut . . . auctores in ordinem redegerint, alios omnino exemerint numero.'
[2] Quintilian x 1. 59 'ex tribus receptis Aristarchi iudicio scriptoribus iamborum ad ἕξιν maxime pertinebit unus Archilochus.'
[3] Nauck pp. 67 and 249; L. Radermacher, 'Kanon', *RE* x (1919) 1873 ff. on Quintil. and Dionys. Hal. and their common source.
[4] See above, pp. 43 ff. (cf. p. 14, n. 4), 73 ff., 135 f.; on κρίσις p. 117.
[5] Fr. 179 Wehrli, *Die Schule des Aristoteles* 7 (1953) with commentary p. 123.
[6] A. Trendelenburg, *Grammaticorum Graecorum de arte tragica iudiciorum reliquiae* (Bonn 1867) 23 ff.
[7] Cf. above, pp. 144 ff.
[8] See *CGF* 1 pp. 3. 3, 58. 165, 81 ad test. 10 Kaibel; on Eratosthenes see above, p. 161.

places which Aristotle and his school, followed by Zenodotus and his pupils,[1] had assigned to them; but the common source of Dionysius of Halicarnassus and Quintilian (x 1. 53 ff.) and of later lists seems to have given four or five names of pre-Hellenistic epic poets.[2]

The number of the nine lyric poets was firmly established. As the iambic poets were led by Archilochus, and the epic by Homer, so of the lyric poets Pindar was always the first, 'novem lyricorum longe . . . princeps', as we find in the anonymous Hellenistic epigram,[3] perhaps composed about a century after Aristophanes, which is our earliest testimony for the Nine: Pindar, Bacchylides, Sappho, Anacreon, Stesichorus, Simonides, Ibycus, Alcaeus, and Alcman. This relatively large number, compared with the small circle of the epic, iambic, and scenic poets, is puzzling. It may lead, and has indeed led, to the conclusion that the Nine were all the lyric poets whose works had survived from the pre-Hellenistic era and were stored in the Alexandrian library. Even if that were correct in this one case, it would be rash to extend it to all the other groups of poets we have just surveyed, and to deny[4] the existence of selective lists alongside the complete *Pinakes*. Aristophanes' most effective work was, as we have seen, that on the lyric poets. Though his name is not expressly mentioned in the poor evidence, we may conjecture that his edition comprised the nine poets and that therefore this number became authoritative in the same way as his terminology, classification, and colometry.[5] The order might differ, but the actual names were the same in all the Hellenistic epigrams and prose lists until the latest Byzantine times. Moreover, a fair number of names and small fragments of other early lyric poets is known to us.[6] Writers about history and theory of music in the fourth century B.C., such as Aristoxenus and Heraclides Ponticus, quote them very freely, but they occur also in the metrists and encyclopedists. There was even an addition made to the Nine—we cannot tell at what time—a Boeotian poetess, δεκάτη Κόριννα; of her poems,

---

[1] See above, p. 117.

[2] Regenbogen, 'Pinax', *RE* xx 1455 ff.

[3] *A.P.* ix 184. The evidence is assembled by H. Färber, *Die Lyrik in der Kunsttheorie der Antike* (1936) II 22 ff.; cf. I 25 f.

[4] Wilamowitz, 'Die Textgeschichte der griechischen Lyriker', *AGGW*, N.F. IV 3 (1900) 63–71 Der Alexandrinische Kanon; unstinted approval was expressed by D. L. Page, 'Corinna'. The Society for the Promotion of Hellenic Studies *Supplementary Paper* No. 6 (1953) 68 ff. Well-founded objections were raised by Radermacher *RE* x 1873 ff., Regenbogen *RE* xx 1455 ff. and especially by J. Stroux, who was wrong only in so far as he brought in Plato's concept of ὀρθότης (see above, p. 75, n. 1); see also Färber, loc. cit. and W. Döring, 'Zur pädagogischen Problematik des Begriffes des Klassischen', *Göttinger Studien zur Pädagogik* 24 (1934) 20 ff., who gives a sensible survey of the problem with bibliography although from his own pedagogical point of view.

[5] See above, pp. 182 ff.

[6] *PMG* p. 360: 'Poetae melici minores'.

novel in language and style, some fragments have turned up on papyri. It is very hard to believe that the works of all these people were lost temporarily or for ever by the third and second centuries B.C. when the critical editions were made and the lists arranged. It is much more natural to suppose that by the severe judgement of the great grammarians they were regarded as minor poets—which they actually were—and not admitted to the higher ranks.

If therefore the existence of selective lists cannot be denied in the case of the lyric poets, it is still less deniable for the other groups. This assumption is in full agreement with an unprejudiced interpretation of the passages from Quintilian Books 1 and 10 quoted above, in which he called the great grammarians 'poetarum iudices'. If we consider the origin and development of scholarship in Alexandria and Aristophanes' personal activity in particular, it is not surprising that in this field also the poets were the first to be treated. But lists of the foremost orators, historians, and philosophers followed in the course of time; though only the list of the orators could rival that of the poets in significance, and besides Alexandria other places like Pergamum, Rhodes, Athens, and Rome began to play their parts.[1]

The Greek expression for selecting authors and registering their names in the selective list was ἐγκρίνειν; they were then called ἐγκριθέντες. At least, we have direct evidence of this only for the orators,[2] but it must also have been applied to the poets. For when Horace concluded the first ode of the first book with the flourish, 'quodsi me lyricis vatibus inseres...', he was surely alluding to this term and cherishing the hope that Maecenas would ἐγκρίνειν him to the group of the 'novem lyrici'. Quintilian's term, 'ordo', transferred from the terms of social ranks into the literary sphere, was not favoured by later authors. But in Cicero[3] we find a distinction of 'classes', as when he assigned some Stoic philosophers, in

---

[1] Every section has its special problems of chronology and locality. In the late Byzantine lists the confusion of indexes and selective lists makes reconstruction almost impossible; H. Usener could not succeed in his bold and acute attempt: Dion. Hal. *De imitatione* (1889) 110 ff. Most of the evidence is assembled by O. Kroehnert, *Canonesne poetarum, scriptorum, artificum per antiquitatem fuerunt?* Diss. Königsberg 1897.—J. Cousin, *Études sur Quintilien* 1 (1936) 546 ff. esp. 565–72, discusses Quintilian's sources and the origin and codification of the lists at great length; he stresses the activity of Pergamum in the second century B.C. as far as the orators are concerned. But see A. E. Douglas, *Mnemosyne* IV 9 (1956) 30 ff. and below, p. 208, n. 2; cf. also below, p. 242.

[2] Suid. v. Δείναρχος . . . ῥήτωρ τῶν μετὰ Δημοσθένους ἐγκριθέντων εἷς; ibid. v. Πυθέας . . . οὐκ ⟨ἐν⟩εκρίθη (recte suppl. Toup) μετὰ τῶν λοιπῶν ῥητόρων ὡς θρασὺς καὶ διεσπασμένος; Phot. *bibl.* 20 b 25 Αἰσχίνην . . . καὶ Φρύνιχος . . . εἰς τοὺς ἀρίστους ἐγκρίνει, κανόνα μετά γε τοὺς πρώτους Ἀττικοῦ λόγου τοὺς ἐκείνου ἀποφαινόμενος λόγους.—Diodor. IX fr. 6 ἐκκρίνειν = 'numero eximere'.

[3] Cic. *Acad.* II 73 'qui mihi cum illo collati quintae classis videntur'.

comparison with Democritus, to the fifth class; and it became the Roman way to call the ἐγκριθέντες 'classici', which means writers of the *first* class, 'primae classis' in the political and military language. We shall, later on, hear more about this term, familiar to us through its adoption by the scholars of the Renaissance.

The complete repertories were called πίνακες (indexes); but there was no corresponding Greek or Latin word for the selective lists. In the year A.D. 1768 the term 'canon' was coined for them by David Ruhnken,[1] when he wrote: 'Ex magna oratorum copia tamquam in canonem decem dumtaxat rettulerunt' (sc. Aristarchus et Aristophanes Byzantius). Then Ruhnken dropped the cautious 'tamquam' and went on calling all the selective lists 'canones'. His coinage met with worldwide and lasting success, as the term was found to be so convenient; one has the impression that most people who use it believe that this usage is of Greek origin. But κανών[2] was never used in this sense, nor would this have been possible. From its frequent use in ethics κανών always retained the meaning of rule or model. Aristophanes' grammatical observations about analogy in declension could be called κανόνες, rules, or a certain author and his style could be described as κανών, a model or exemplar.[3] So it was not by the ancient, but it could have been by the Biblical, tradition that the catachrestic use of canon was suggested to Ruhnken. Though the Biblical canon does not mean a list of writers, it does mean a list of books of the Bible accepted by the Christian church as genuine and inspired;[4] and this usage was and is current in all the modern languages. The word 'canon' has been intentionally avoided in this chapter on Aristophanes; nevertheless, everyone is at liberty to speak of the Alexandrian canon of the nine lyric poets or the ten orators, since the expression is sanctioned by its age and convenience, and will, I am afraid, never disappear. But if one calls such lists 'canons', one should be aware that this is not the proper significance of the Greek κανών but a modern catachresis that originated in the eighteenth century.

---

[1] D. Ruhnken, 'Historia critica oratorum Graecorum' in his edition of Rutilius Lupus 1768 and often reprinted: *Opuscula* I² (1823) 386.

[2] H. Oppel, '*Κανών*. Zur Bedeutungsgeschichte des Wortes und seiner lateinischen Entsprechungen (regula–norma)' *Philologus*, Suppl. XXX 4 (1937) *passim*; on Ruhnken see p. 47. Cf. the review by K. v. Fritz, *AJP* 60 (1939) 112 ff.

[3] See above, p. 202 (declension) and p. 206, n. 2 (Aeschines' λόγοι as κανών).

[4] Euseb. *hist. eccl.* VI 25. 3 τὸν ἐκκλησιαστικὸν φυλάττων κανόνα, μόνα τέσσαρα εἰδέναι εὐαγγέλια μαρτύρεται (sc. Origen) seems to be the earliest evidence of the word for the canon of scripture; Oppel *Κανών* 70 f. and others refer to a passage of Athanasius, written about A.D. 350, at least twenty-five years after Euseb. *hist. eccl.*, Athanas. 'de decr. Nic. syn.' 18 (*Werke*, hg. von der Preuß. Akad. d. Wiss. II 1, 1935, p. 15. 20) μὴ ὂν ἐκ τοῦ κανόνος (sc. Hermas).

The ἐγκριθέντες became the πραττόμενοι;[1] they were 'treated', that is, commented on by the grammarians, and the vast activity of Aristarchus in the next generation was dedicated to this 'treating' of the ἐγκριθέντες. Their writings or at least a great number of them were copied again and again to be read in schools and by the educated public;[2] so they were saved for eternity, while the ἐκκριθέντες were left to perish. It is difficult enough to establish the fact of ἐγκρίνειν and the contents of the lists; much as we should like to know Aristophanes' own criteria, the attempt to reconstruct them from the late sources would be quite chimerical. If he ever published such lists, the additions to Callimachus' *Pinakes* would have been an appropriate place.

A short final word about the few titles and fragments of Aristophanes' monographs;[3] they were supplementary to his great literary works and seldom merely antiquarian. We have seen that it is very doubtful whether he wrote a book Περὶ αἰγίδος about Athena's shield (which would have belonged to his Homeric studies), or a separate grammatical work on analogy. His treatise on the phrase Ἀχνυμένη σκυτάλη in an epode of Archilochus has been referred to in connexion with his treatment of lyric poetry, and 'The Parallels to Menander and other writers' regarded as part of his work on the comic poets.[4] We have not yet mentioned two rather antiquarian collections Περὶ προσώπων,[5] 'On masks', and Περὶ τῶν Ἀθήνησιν ἑταιρίδων, 'On Athenian courtesans',[6] a continuation of his labours devoted to Attic Comedy. Two further monographs were in the Peripatetic tradition. Aristotle had regarded the proverbs as survivals of early wisdom[7] and encouraged his pupils to collect them. But Aristophanes, while not disregarding the popular origin of the παροιμίαι, seems to have been interested in their complete and proper wording and their different meanings, and to have searched for them in the literary texts, especially of the comic poets.[8] Under this aspect he arranged the first scholarly collection of Μετρικαὶ παροιμίαι in two books and of Ἄμετροι

[1] Schol. Dionys. Thr. p. 21. 17 Hilg. λυρικοὶ οἱ καὶ πραττόμενοι ἐννέα; cf. Schol. Nic. *Th.* 11, Suid. v. Ἀριστοφάνης (com.) . . . δράματα δ᾽ αὐτοῦ μδʹ. ἅπερ δὲ πεπράχαμεν Ἀριστοφάνους δράματα ταῦτα Ἀχαρνεῖς κτλ.

[2] See Marrou 161 ff., who has too much confidence in Cousin's arguments (above, p. 206, n. 1).

[3] Nauck, pp. 264–83.

[4] See above, pp. 181 f., 191.

[5] The only fragment deals with the comic character Μαίσων, *CGF* 1 p. 76 Kaibel; Poll. IV 133–54 is supposed to have derived some material from Aristophanes, see C. Robert, 25. *Hallisches Winckelmannsprogr.* (1911) 60 ff.

[6] Aristoph. Byz., *FGrHist* 347 F 1, cf. T 1 with references to four other writers on the same subject.

[7] See above, pp. 83 f.

[8] Cf. Eratosth. above, p. 139, n. 8.

παροιμίαι in four books;[1] it was a great enterprise that well befitted the writer on Λέξεις and on comedy. Aristophanes' two books Περὶ ζῴων, based on Peripatetic sources of natural history and paradoxography, which we lightly touched on at the beginning of this chapter,[2] remained, as we see, an isolated compilation.

If we now look back over all Aristophanes' accomplishments, two outstanding features catch our eye: an impressive series of 'firsts' in many fields, and the central position held by his other works in a long historical development.

[1] Nauck pp. 235–42; fr. 9 is to be cancelled (see Excursus to p. 177) and fr. 13 belongs to the Λέξεις.—O. Crusius, *Analecta ad paroemiographos Graecos* (1883) 75 ff., discovered a series of proverbs in the Athos MS. (Miller, *Mélanges* 349 ff.) as excerpts from Aristophanes; cf. K. Rupprecht, 'Paroemiographi', *RE* xviii (1949) 1742 ff.; this important article confirms Crusius' discovery and makes further additions.
[2] See above, p. 173.

VI

ARISTARCHUS: THE ART OF INTERPRETATION

ARISTOPHANES exerted his influence not only by his unremitting productiveness, but also through his followers. The earliest of his personal pupils seems to have been Callistratus,[1] who perhaps made his teacher's oral interpretations, in part at any rate, known to a wider public and tried to refute atheteses of his schoolfellow Aristarchus; but as late as the first century B.C. Artemidorus, the collector of the bucolic poems, and Diodorus of Tarsus were styled Ἀριστοφάνειοι. The greatest figure among them was Aristarchus.

He was a native of the island of Samothrace (φύσει or ἄνωθεν Σαμοθρᾴξ), but became a citizen of Alexandria (Ἀλεξανδρεὺς θέσει), where he lived under Ptolemy VI Philometor (180–145 B.C.);[2] no precise dates are given in the biographical tradition. If Aristarchus reached the age of seventy-two, as Suidas says,[3] and if it is correctly conjectured that he died about 144 B.C., he was born about 216 B.C. When the post of librarian became vacant before or after Aristophanes' death in 180 B.C., Apollonius ὁ εἰδογράφος[4] succeeded, and it was only after him that Aristarchus was appointed, the fifth head of the library after Zenodotus.[5] Like most or perhaps all of his predecessors, Aristarchus also had to act as tutor in the royal family, first to Philometor's younger brother, later

---

[1] See above, p. 190, n. 4.

[2] Suid. v. Ἀρίσταρχος... ἐπὶ Πτολεμαίου τοῦ Φιλομήτορος; P.Oxy. 1241 II 15 Φιλοπάτορος is one of the many clerical errors of the papyrus. On the Ptolemies VI to IX often referred to in this chapter see H. Volkmann, RE XXIII (1959) 1702–43, whose article 'Ptolemaios' is based on the careful studies of W. Otto and H. Bengtson. On Aristarchus' life and writings L. Cohn, RE II (1896) 862–73, is still useful.

[3] Suid. v. Ἀρίσταρχος... τελευτᾷ δ' ἐν Κύπρῳ... ἔτη δ' αὐτοῦ τῆς ζωῆς οβ'; but in γέγονε δὲ κατὰ τὴν ρνε' Ὀλυμπιάδα (156–152 B.C.) the figure must be corrupt as he was at that time in his sixties.

[4] See above, p. 172, n. 2.

[5] Tzetz. Proleg. Ma pp. 25. 9 ff. Kaib. πρότερος δὲ ἦν Ζηνόδοτος, ε' ἢ δ' μετ' αὐτὸν Ἀρίσταρχος, cf. Schol. Plaut. (above, p. 100, n. 2) produced nonsense, as usual, 'Aristarchus autem quattuor annis minor fuerit... Zenodoto', etc.—If one Apollonius were counted, Aristarchus would be the fourth from Zenodotus, if two Apollonii, the fifth; the second alternative is correct.

Euergetes II,[1] then to the king's eldest son Eupator, who was born in 163 and died as king of Cyprus in 150 B.C., finally to the younger son, born probably in 162/1 B.C., who succeeded his father in 145 as Ptolemy VII Neos Philopator[2] and was murdered in the following year on the wedding day of his widowed mother and his father's younger brother. The latter usurped the throne as Ptolemy VIII and styled himself Euergetes II, but was called Κακεργέτης[3] by the Alexandrians and Φύσκων 'pot-belly'[4] by his learned enemies, no doubt in allusion to the nickname given by Alcaeus[5] to the hated tyrant Pittacus. All the friends of his murdered nephew, the 'fautores pueri', were persecuted, including Aristarchus although he had been the usurper's own tutor; he escaped to Cyprus where he is assumed to have died shortly afterwards.[6] The two sons he left were, unlike their father, of feeble mind.

There were hardly any anecdotes or jokes current about Aristarchus' life and habits, except perhaps Callistratus' indignant remark that he was negligent in appearance, ἐπὶ τῷ μὴ εὐρύθμως ἀμπέχεσθαι.[7] The reason might be a lack of humour in the fellows of the Museum at that time or the absence of any eccentricity in the simple and serious behaviour of the hard-working man himself. According to Suidas[8] he had as many as forty pupils. Only one poet was a member of this large and, as we shall see, illustrious learned circle, Moschus of Syracuse, best known as the writer of the graceful epic poem *Europa*.[9] Not the slightest vestige exists of any verse composed by Aristarchus himself. If he had been asked why he, who found fault even with Homer, did not try his hand at writing poems, he might have said in reply: 'ea re poemata non facio quia cuiusmodi volo non possum, cuiusmodi possum nolo.' This saying, anonymously quoted in the *Rhetorica ad Herennium*, is attributed to Aristarchus by the scholiasts to

---

[1] Athen. II 71 B Πτολεμαῖος ὁ Εὐργέτης ... εἰς ὢν τῶν Ἀριστάρχου μαθητῶν = FGrHist 234 T 1.

[2] *P.Oxy.* XIX (1948) 2222. 1 f. provided the solution that he has to be counted as king (see C. H. Roberts, ad loc.); therefore Euergetes II was correctly described as the eighth Ptolemy: *Script. Hist. Aug.* Caracalla 6.

[3] Andron *FGrHist* 246 F 1; cf. Posidon. *FGrHist* 87 F 6.

[4] Strab. XVII 795, Plut. *Coriolan.* 11.

[5] Alc. fr. 129. 21 L.–P. (φυσγων pap.) and 429 (φύσκων).

[6] Iustin. XXXVIII 8. 2 'fautores pueri'; cf. Andron *FGrHist* 246 οὐκ ὀλίγους φυγαδεύσας, Suid. v. Ἀρίσταρχος. It is surprising that he chose Cyprus, which was firmly in Ptolemy's hand, as asylum. Rostagni's suggestion that Aristarchus went together with the king to Cyprus in 131/30 B.C. is not acceptable, *Scritti minori* II 1, pp. 211 f. [7] Athen. I 21 C.

[8] Suid. v. Ἀρίσταρχος ... μαθηταὶ δὲ αὐτοῦ γραμματικοὶ περὶ τοὺς μ' ἐγένοντο ... παῖδας ... ἄμφω εὐήθεις.

[9] Suid. v. Μόσχος, Συρακούσιος. γραμματικός, Ἀριστάρχου γνώριμος (on γνώριμος cf. p. 154) ... ὁ δεύτερος ποιητὴς μετὰ Θεόκριτον κτλ.; his poems including the fragments in *Bucolici Graeci* rec. A. S. F. Gow (1952) 132 ff.; W. Bühler, 'Die Europa des Moschos', *Hermes*, Einzelschriften 13 (1960).

Horace who saw an allusion to it in a line of the Letter to Augustus.[1] Even if not authentic, it is well invented.

Aristarchus' best pupils and many other scholars of the younger generation fled to various places not under Egyptian rule, Rhodes, Pergamum, Athens. From this *secessio doctorum* the first crisis ensued in the history of scholarship. That the chief-librarianship fell to an obscure military officer, called Cydas, ἐκ τῶν λογχοφόρων,[2] speaks for itself.

Ptolemy VIII, dissolute and violent, was a repellent figure, but he was not unintelligent and not uninterested in learning, as the fragments of the twenty-four books of his *Memoirs* on a strange variety of subjects disclose and as Plutarch asserts (φιλομαθεῖν δοκοῦντι). As Aristarchus' disciple, he even ventured to conjecture λειμῶνες μαλακοὶ σίου (for ἴου) ἠδὲ σελίνου (ε 72) because the water-parsnip, not the violet, seemed to suit Calypso's watery meadows.[3] Under him and his successors the institutions were carried on, the Museum and the two libraries;[4] papyrus-documents and inscriptions give some names of later privileged members and administrators.[5]

Turning from Aristarchus' place in the troubled history of the second century B.C. to his literary work, we immediately realize that he filled a gap left by his predecessors; they had, with very few exceptions,[6] abstained from writing commentaries on the texts they edited. No doubt they had explained them to their personal pupils; but we cannot judge how far the listeners wrote these lectures down and used them for their own publications, as no reference is preserved,[7] though a monograph of Apollonius Rhodius, for instance, foreshadowed the ὑπομνήματα.[8] Aristarchus was ready to work out running commentaries with great courage

---

[1] *Rhet. ad Herenn.* IV 28. 39; Porphyrio ad Hor. *epist.* II 1. 257 si, quantum cuperem, possem quoque'; cf. Schol. Pseudacr. ad loc. 'iuxta Aristarchum'.

[2] *P.Oxy.* 1241 II 16. M. Launey, 'Recherches sur les armées hellénistiques', *Bibliothèque des Écoles françaises d'Athènes et de Rome* 169 (1949/50) 273 and 1163, lists Cydas because of his name as Cretan, unfortunately accepting Rostagni's date; see also other λογχοφόροι pp. 316, 565 and πρῶτοι φίλοι καὶ χιλίαρχοι λογχοφόροι p. 1279 (Index). There seems to be no clear definition of the military rank of this group and of its relation to the royal court.

[3] Ptolem. Euerg. II: *FGrHist* 234 F 11 = Eustathius' epitome of Athen. II 61 C and repeated in his commentary on ε 72 p. 1524. 52 (cf. l. 40 σίου . . . ὡς καὶ πολλοῖς ἀρέσκει τῶν παλαιῶν).

[4] Cf. Müller-Graupa, 'Museion', *RE* XVI (1933) 815 f., and Schmidt, *Pinakes* 15, on the libraries.

[5] On the four γραμματικοί, said to have lived under Ptolemy IX see below, p. 254.

[6] See above, pp. 140, 146 (?), 161, 175; we disregard in this connexion colloquial explanations in schools, preserved in the vulgate scholia.

[7] Cf. above, p. 108; on lectures of scholars and copies made by pupils see H. Diels in 'Didymos Kommentar zu Demosthenes' bearb. von H. Diels u. W. Schubart, *Berliner Klassikertexte* I (1904) xxx ff., and G. Zuntz, *Byzantion* XIV (1939) 560 ff.

[8] On the word ὑπόμνημα see above, p. 29.

and success. Λέγεται δὲ γράψαι ὑπὲρ ω' βιβλία ὑπομνημάτων μόνων, we read
in Suidas, who mentions no other writings by him. The sentence can
hardly mean, as F. A. Wolf[1] supposed, that Aristarchus wrote nothing
but commentaries; this would probably have been ω' βιβλία ὑπομνημάτων
μόνα, not μόνων. The Greek words, as they stand, say that he wrote more
than 800 books of commentaries alone (that is, if one only counts the
commentaries), leaving it open what other books there might have been
not included in this figure—about which one certainly feels a little
uneasy.[2] Even if the commentary on Homer had forty-eight books, if
every commentary on an individual play was regarded as a separate unit
and so on, it would still be difficult to account for 800 ὑπομνήματα.

In the traditional line, at least from Apollonius Rhodius on, Aristarchus wrote a number of monographs called συγγράμματα, as distinguished from the continuous ὑπομνήματα by Didymus, who thought
them of more value than the latter.[3] They were mostly polemics: Πρὸς
Φιλίταν[4] (Schol. A A 524, B 111), Πρὸς Κωμανόν (A 97, B 798, Ω 110),
Πρὸς τὸ Ξένωνος παράδοξον (M 435) (that is against Xenon's assumption
that two poets had composed Iliad and Odyssey); two of them dealt with
specific questions of subject-matter: Περὶ 'Ιλιάδος καὶ 'Οδυσσείας (I 349)
and Περὶ τοῦ ναυστάθμου (K 53, M 258, O 449, cf. Λ 166, 807). These
συγγράμματα were also interpretations, though in a form different from
that of the ὑπομνήματα, and F. A. Wolf could easily have regarded συγγράμματα and ὑπομνήματα together as 'commentarios'. So when he said
that Aristarchus wrote nothing but commentaries, 'nihil aliud' can only
mean 'no separate editions of the Homeric text' (like those of Zenodotus,
Aristophanes, and some others). Wolf's simple sentence implies an interpretation which is still questionable today.

By a unique stroke of good fortune large excerpts from Aristarchus'
ὑπομνήματα are preserved in a Venetian codex of the Iliad with text and
copious marginal and interlinear scholia,[5] the most precious parts of

---

[1] F. A. Wolf, Prolegomena ad Homerum (1795) ccxxix 'dicitur A. . . . conscripsisse . . . si
Suidam recte intelligo, nihil aliud quam Commentarios'; cf. ibid. n. 8 and p. ccxliv n. 30.
[2] In Suidas' life of Callimachus precisely the same conventional figure appears for his
whole output: Call. II, test. 1. 6 βιβλία ὑπὲρ τὰ ὀκτακόσια. On the inconsistency in the relation
of the cases of μόνος to the respective nouns see Kühner–Gerth, Grammatik der griech. Sprache
II 1 'Satzlehre' (1898) 275. 3.
[3] Schol. A B 111 εἰ . . . συγγράμματα τῶν ὑπομνημάτων προτάττομεν.
[4] Cf. above, p. 91.
[5] Codex Venet. Marc. 454 (A); cf. H. Erbse, 'Beiträge zur Überlieferung der Iliasscholien',
Zetemata 24 (1960) esp. 78 ff. and 123 ff. Erbse is preparing a new edition of all the Scholia
on the Iliad; meanwhile we have to use the editions of Schol. A and B by Dindorf and of
T by E. Maass, and to consult the facsimile of cod. Ven. A in Codices Graeci et Latini photo-
graphice depicti VI ed. D. Comparetti (Leiden 1901).

which are based on the labours of four men, Didymus, Aristonicus, Herodian, and Nicanor, who had made excerpts from Hellenistic sources in the time of Augustus and of the early Roman empire. To two of them we owe substantial passages of authentic Aristarchean material: to Didymus Περὶ τῆς Ἀριστάρχείου διορθώσεως and to Aristonicus Περὶ σημείων ('Ἰλιάδος καὶ 'Οδυσσείας).[1]

It was the special interest of the French in manuscripts and palaeography awakened by Montfaucon that led J.-B. de Villoison in 1781 to the discovery of the two foremost manuscripts of the *Iliad* in Venice, which he published in 1788; and this discovery made possible the modern reconstructions of Aristarchus' Homeric studies. F. A. Wolf acknowledged the 'insigne meritum Villoisonii' when he made the first attempt at a history of the Homeric text. His chapter on its treatment by the Alexandrian grammarians, especially by Aristarchus, became a model for future writers on the history of any ancient text; it is therefore of lasting value. But this, of course, was not the part of Wolf's *Prolegomena ad Homerum* (1795) which stirred the emotions of the whole literary world. In tracing the history of the transmission of the Homeric text from the Hellenistic age back to the age of the epic poets for the first time, he had to raise the question of the origin of the epic poems, of their unity and genuineness. Wolf opened the eyes of his contemporaries and of posterity to the unique *historical* position of the Homeric poetry. One should always keep in mind his starting-point from the wealth of new material in the Venetian codex and the new spirit of bold historical inquiry, even if one sees him taking the wrong way in individual arguments and conclusions.

After the general prelude in Wolf's *Prolegomena* the foundation for special Aristarchean studies was laid in 1833 by the monograph of K. Lehrs, *De Aristarchi studiis Homericis*. It was Lehrs, not Wolf, who discovered the importance of the subscriptions which give the names of the 'four men'; no wonder that he overestimated the value of codex A and neglected the scholia in the other manuscripts. They were all (A B D L V) printed together in I. Bekker's edition of 1825, and unfortunately arranged in one continuous text; Lehrs's reconstruction of Aristarchus' work was handicapped by being based on this sometimes delusive text. His

---

[1] Didymi Fragmenta coll. M. Schmidt (1854, reprinted 1964) 112 ff.; A. Ludwich, *Aristarchs homerische Textkritik nach den Fragmenten des Didymos* 1 (1884) 11 (1885). Aristonicus, Περὶ σημείων 'Ἰλιάδος reliquiae, ed. L. Friedlaender (1853) 39 ff., Περὶ σημείων 'Οδυσσείας, ed. O. Carnuth (1869). M. Van der Valk, *Researches on the Text and Scholia of the Iliad*, part 1 (1963) 536 ff. 'The critics transmitting the text and views of Aristarchus' (cf. H. Erbse, *Gnom.* 36 [1964] 549 ff., esp. 555).

interpretations of the relevant passages in the Scholia and in the whole grammatical literature were nevertheless penetrating; they were augmented and corrected in two later editions, and his pupils continued research in this field.[1] One of the first things Lehrs did was to object to Wolf's assertion that Aristarchus had produced ὑπομνήματα only,[2] and to his refusal to believe that there had been more than one edition of them by Aristarchus himself.[3] Lehrs concluded that Didymus had had at his disposal two Aristarchean editions of the Homeric text preceded by two editions of the commentary; and this conclusion met with universal approval until it was challenged by Erbse.[4] He took great pains to reinterpret the references to Aristarchus' writings as ἐκδόσεις, διορθώσεις, ὑπομνήματα in our Scholia and to extricate the proper meaning of these terms as used by Didymus. These investigations led to the following conclusion: Aristarchus did write ὑπομνήματα, with many references to the previous recensions, but probably only once;[5] they contained, of course, lemmata from the Homeric text and ample textual criticism besides the main exegetical part. On the other hand, he did not make new separate editions of the text, but accepted the 'vulgate' text (the κοιναὶ ἐκδόσεις) for general use. All this would fit very nicely into our picture of Homeric scholarship in the third and second centuries B.C. Towards the middle of the second century the imperative demand was not for editing the text anew, but for explaining it in its entirety; the absence of a more or less authoritative text arranged by the γραμματικώτατος would make it easier to understand why the textual criticism of the Alexandrian grammarians had relatively little influence on the Homeric text itself, as it is preserved in papyri and manuscripts.[6] It looks to me as if by a sort of unconscious counter-revolution Wolf has now been put back on the throne from which Lehrs had driven him; the details and still more the arguments differ, but the two essential points are the same: there was no separate edition of the text, but just a commentary in only one edition by Aristarchus himself.

[1] Second edition 1865, third edition 1882; see especially above, p. 214, n. 1 Ludwich on Didymus, Friedlaender on Aristonicus, Lentz on Herodian.

[2] Lehrs *Ar.*[3] 22 was unjust in believing that Wolf did 'not remember' the monographs; he actually mentioned them *Proleg.* ccxliv n. 30 as ὑπομνήματα.

[3] Wolf p. ccxxxvii and Lehrs *Ar.*[3] 23 ff.

[4] H. Erbse, 'Über Aristarchs Iliasausgaben', *Herm.* 87 (1959) 275–303 (see also above, p. 213, n. 5); but J. A. Davison, 'Homeric Criticism' in *A Companion to Homer* (1963) 224, correctly speaks of Aristarchus' commentary as having been prepared to accompany his text.

[5] Ammonius may have supplemented his master's ὑπομνήματα in a sort of second edition (ἐπέκδοσις).

[6] See above, p. 109, n. 7, the reference to *The Hibeh Pap.* 1, in which pp. 70 ff. the problem of the vulgate post-Aristarchean text also is discussed.

The meaning of the words ἔκδοσις and διόρθωσις and the rather vague use of grammatical terms in general has caused us some difficulty already.[1] When Schol. A on *A* 522 μή σε νοήσῃ comments οὐχὶ "μή σε", ἀλλὰ "μή τι" αἱ Ἀριστάρχου καὶ αἱ ἄλλαι σχεδὸν πᾶσαι διορθώσεις, it is very hard to suppose that anything was meant but 'the recensions of Aristarchus and nearly all the other ones'. It is almost impossible not to supply ἐκδόσεις or διορθώσεις in the traditional sense of (critical) editions in Schol. A *Γ* 126 καὶ αἱ Ἀριστάρχου καὶ ἡ Ζηνοδότου καὶ ἡ Ἀριστοφάνους "πορφυρέην" εἶχον, οὐ "μαρμαρέην"; for Zenodotus and Aristophanes were authors of editions, and only διορθώσεις by Aristarchus could be put on a par with them, not commentaries. In the phrase κἂν ταῖς διορθώσεσι καὶ ἐν τοῖς ὑπομνήμασι (Schol. A *B* 192) the recensions of the text and the commentaries stand side by side neatly distinguished; so the reference must be to two different works.[2] On the other hand, I cannot detect in Didymus' fragments any unmistakable evidence for the use of the term ἔκδοσις as 'interpretation'. It may be that Apollonius Dyscolus meant 'exposition, treatise' by ἔκδοσις,[3] and in Christian literature it seems to have been actually used in the sense of 'interpretation',[4] but this does not prove that Didymus applied it to Aristarchus' commentary. It is also difficult to suppose that the sum of the lemmata in the ὑπομνήματα represented Aristarchus' recension of the Homeric text, as it ought to have done if he left no separate edition.

On the question of the number of Aristarchus' recensions and commentaries, we find that Didymus usually speaks of two recensions, and quotes the divergent readings, or simply notes διχῶς. But Ammonius, Aristarchus' personal pupil and 'his successor in the school' (διαδεξά-μενος τὴν σχολήν), wrote Περὶ τοῦ μὴ γεγονέναι πλείονας ἐκδόσεις τῆς Ἀρισταρχείου διορθώσεως.[5] On the natural interpretation, this heading means that in the opinion of Ammonius there was only *one* edition, not more, and no context of the Scholion suggests otherwise.[6] Yet Ammonius

---

[1] See above, pp. 71, 94, 110; I cannot accept that the term διόρθωσις is correctly applied in the case of Antimachus and Aristotle, as Erbse loc. cit. p. 289 does. On 'terminology' and its dangers see above, p. 159.

[2] Schol. A *B* 355 οὕτως Ἀρίσταρχος διὰ τοῦ ε̄ (that is, περ not παρ) καὶ τὰ ὑπομνήματα is convincingly emended into κατὰ τὰ ὑπομνήματα (= in commentariis) by Erbse p. 284.

[3] Apollon. Dysc., *Synt.* ed. G. Uhlig (1910) p. 513 Index s.v. ἔκδοσις and *Fragmenta* ed. R. Schneider (1910) p. 195 Index s.v. ἔκδοσις; I think one could argue against Uhlig's explanation of ἔκδοσις on pp. 1 f. of his edition of the *Syntax*.

[4] *A Patristic Greek Lexicon* ed. Lampe fasc. 2 (1962) s.v. ἔκδοσις 2. 'interpretation' and ἐκδίδωμι 2. 'interpret.'

[5] Schol. A *K* 397–9.

[6] Lehrs, *De Aristarchi stud. Hom.*³ 24, took πλείονας here as πλείονας τῶν δύο (because of the constant references to two editions by Didymus); but by this insertion of τῶν δύο he exerted a hardly legitimate strain on the simple text. Recent scholars followed Lehrs (see above,

is also said to have written Περὶ τῆς ἐπεκδοθείσης διορθώσεως,[1] perhaps in the same treatise. If he was not contradicting himself, the 're-issued recension' must have been a revised text drawn up not by Aristarchus himself, but by a pupil like Ammonius from material left by the master.

As to the ὑπομνήματα, a commentary based on Aristophanes' text, and therefore written earlier than Aristarchus' own recension, is implied by Schol. A B 133 ἐν τοῖς κατ᾿ Ἀριστοφάνην[2] ὑπομνήμασιν. But one of the most learned extracts in Schol. A B 111 suggests the existence of more than one commentary when it quotes what Didymus had found ἔν τινι τῶν ἠκριβωμένων ὑπομνημάτων of Aristarchus; this commentary 'made accurate' appears to be the one which is called 'closely revised' in Schol. H 130: ἐν τοῖς ἐξητασμένοις[3] Ἀριστάρχου. So it is a reasonable assumption that the earlier commentary was regarded as less accurate, and that it was followed by a revised one after Aristarchus had finished his recension of the text. The sequence seems to have been: Aristarchus' first ὑπομνήματα based on Aristophanes' text, Aristarchus' διόρθωσις, his second ὑπομνήματα using his own text, the revised recension made by others.

Whether Didymus was able to work on copies of these *original* διορθώσεις and ὑπομνήματα of Aristarchus and of his monographs, the συγγράμματα, is an insoluble problem. F. A. Wolf's doubts have been repeated[4] and expressed even more strongly, but no proof has been forthcoming. Didymus was confronted with several books of Aristarchus, as we have seen, and it is understandable that he was sometimes embarrassed and doubtful about what Aristarchus' Homeric text had been and how he had interpreted it; but he never complains that he had no access to copies of the originals and had to put up with revisions or with defective ἀντίγραφα. It is hardly correct to regard Didymus' writing Περὶ τῆς Ἀρισταρχείου διορθώσεως as an effort to reconstruct the original διόρθωσις no longer available; its title and its fragments assign it to that special

---

p. 215) with the exception of Monro, Homer's *Odyssey* II (1901), Appendix p. 441. See now Erbse's article above, p. 215, n. 4.

[1] Schol. A T 365; cf. above, p. 215, n. 5.

[2] Compendium in A; but κατ᾿ Ἀριστοφάνους is very unlikely in the context. Nauck, Aristoph. Byz. p. 23 'commentarios ex Aristophanis ore exceptos', misunderstood the text.

[3] ἐν ταῖς ἐξητασμέναις A, corr. Lehrs.

[4] See Ludwich, *Aristarchs Hom. Textkritik* 38 ff.; cf. Wilamowitz, *Homerische Untersuchungen* 297 f. They both make the fire of the year 47 B.C. responsible for the loss of the originals. This is always a very convenient kind of argument; but what actually happened was that warehouses near the harbour in which grain and books were stored were destroyed by fire, see Dio Cass. XLII 38 τάς τε ἀποθήκας καὶ τοῦ σίτου καὶ τῶν βίβλων . . . καυθῆναι (cf. Schmidt, *Pinakes*, test. 32 a–e pp. 13 f.). W. Schubart, *Das Buch bei den Griechen und Römern* (2. Aufl. 1921) 47, correctly stated against the *communis opinio*: 'Der viel beredete Brand . . . hat der Bibliothek wenig geschadet.' Anyhow, the losses would have been made good in time for Didymus by the donation of Mark Antony; but see below, p. 236.

branch of Περί-literature of which the earliest known representative in Alexandria was Apollonius Rhodius.[1] Didymus also composed Ὑπομνή-ματα Ἰλιάδος καὶ Ὀδυσσείας;[2] and Περὶ τῆς Ἀρισταρχείου διορθώσεως may have been related to them in the same way as his book Περὶ λυρικῶν ποιητῶν was to his ὑπομνήματα on a number of lyric poets. Running commentaries had to follow the text of the author line by line, while the Περί-literature was at liberty to select aspects and problems of text, language, and subject; it seems that Didymus made a sensible selection. Supposing that he and his younger contemporary Aristonicus had the benefit of copies of the originals, we should still like to know how far they were faithful and intelligent excerptors and compilers. This delicate subject can be discussed only later on when we come to speak about the so-called principle of Aristarchus' scholarship.

The marginal sigla in Aristarchus' ἐκδόσεις were the link to his ὑπομνήματα. He used the σημεῖα introduced by Zenodotus and Aristophanes[3] with a few alterations and supplements: disagreements with Zenodotus he marked by the διπλῆ περιεστιγμένη, his own notable observations against other editions and explanations by the simple διπλῆ; in the frequent cases of repetitions of lines in Homer, he added the ὀβελός to the ἀστερίσκος when the repeated lines seemed to be out of place; when the order of lines was disturbed, he put instead of Aristophanes' σίγμα and ἀντίσιγμα the ἀντίσιγμα and στιγμή; a simple dot indicated that he suspected the spuriousness of a line which he was reluctant to obelize. The exposition of these critical signs was no longer left to oral tradition or to guesswork; Aristarchus himself provided it now in a specific part of his ὑπομνήματα, preserved in the excerpts of Aristonicus.[4] As long as papyrus volumes were used so that text and commentary had to be written on separate rolls, the symbols marked the lines of the critical text and were repeated with the lemmata in the roll of the commentary, though short notes were occasionally jotted down in the margins and between the columns of the text. The situation changed only when the codex was introduced and its margins provided space for notes.

So far we have considered only two of the four men mentioned in codex Venetus A. Of the other two the subscriptions to most of the books of the *Iliad* say: τινὰ δὲ καὶ ἐκ τῆς Ἰλιακῆς προσῳδίας Ἡρωδιανοῦ καὶ ἐκ

---

[1] See above, p. 146 and esp. n. 2, on the 'discovery' of Leo; he refers p. 393 to Didymus Περὶ τῆς Ἀρισταρχείου διορθώσεως.

[2] M. Schmidt, Didym. Fragm. pp. 179–211.   [3] See above, p. 178; cf. p. 175.

[4] See above, p. 214; some are better preserved in Suidas than in cod. Ven. A (cf. Erbse, *Beiträge* 174 ff.).

τῶν Νικάνορος Περὶ στιγμῆς (sc. παράκειται). Both lived about 200 years after Didymus, Nicanor under Hadrian, and Herodian under Marcus Aurelius.[1] While not dealing exclusively with the accentuation and punctuation of Aristarchus, they referred to him as their authority more often than to other grammarians. Aristophanes[2] had apparently been the first to introduce accents into the texts of the poets he edited; the novelty in Aristarchus' editions was that he was able in his commentaries to give the specific reasons for his accentuation.[3] Our evidence is limited to Homer, and we may doubt whether even there Aristarchus went far beyond the διαστολὴ τῆς ἀμφιβόλου λέξεως. The same probably applies to his punctuation. There was no change of practice between his teacher Aristophanes and his pupil Dionysius Thrax, both using only two stops;[4] but Aristarchus could justify his punctuation, whenever necessary, in his ὑπομνήματα.

Compared with the uncommonly rich tradition in the corpora of the Homeric Scholia, to which Eustathius (so often quoted above) has to be added, the papyri have yielded little new material. The earliest substantial fragment of a ὑπόμνημα on B 751–827,[5] written about the middle of the first century B.C. probably before Didymus and Aristonicus, provides a significant example of the prefixing of the Aristarchean critical signs to the lemmata. It includes some signs as well as explanations not recorded in the medieval codex Venetus A; that is what we should have expected in the usual process of eclecticism. In two other fragments of commentaries to be dated to the second century A.D.,[6] the time of Nicanor and Herodian, the Aristarchean strain seems to be smaller, but more miscellaneous learned material is accumulated.

Aristarchus was certainly entitled to be called ὁ Ὁμηρικός;[7] but it would be unjust to disregard the merits of his work on other texts. For he also interpreted non-Homeric epics, lyrics, and drama, and was the first

---

[1] Herodiani *Reliquiae* ed. A. Lentz II 1 (1868) 24–165 Περὶ Ὁμηρικῆς προσῳδίας; cf. 1, pp. lxxiv ff.—Nicanor, Περὶ Ἰλιακῆς στιγμῆς ed. L. Friedlaender 1850; Περὶ Ὀδυσσειακῆς στιγμῆς ed. O. Carnuth 1875; cf. C. Wendel, *RE* XVII (1936) 274 ff.

[2] See above, pp. 180 f.

[3] Lehrs, *Ar.*[3] pp. 247–300 'de accentibus'. Laum (above, p. 180, n. 4) tried in vain to refute Lehrs's arguments and to deny that Aristarchus showed any interest in accentuation. Erbse, strongly criticizing Laum's many mistakes in the interpretation of the Homeric Scholia, deferred judgement on Aristarchus' treatment of prosodic problems. A new inquiry could indeed be helpful; meanwhile I see no reason for disagreeing with Lehrs.

[4] See above, pp. 179 f.

[5] *P.Oxy.* VIII (1911) 1086 (= *P. Lit. Lond.* 176) with A. Hunt's introduction and notes.

[6] *Papa. Hawara* (Pack² no. 616) and *P.Oxy.* II 221; O. Müller, *Über den Papyruskommentar zum Φ der Ilias* (Diss. München 1913), successfully identified lemmata and joined small scraps; I cannot find his merits anywhere acknowledged.

[7] Schol. cod. Vindob. Γ 125 (Bekker p. 102).

to comment on a prose author. In Hesiodic criticism Aristarchus vigorously
continued the work of the third century.[1] He athetized the proem of the
Erga which was missing in a copy found by Praxiphanes,[2] and the σημεῖα
by which Hesiodic lines were marked were explained by Aristonicus who
wrote on the sigla in Homer. Specimens of Aristarchus' interpretation of
the *Theogony* and *Erga* are preserved by our Scholia;[3] and as he, unlike his
predecessors, did not write Γλῶσσαι or Λέξεις, they must be remains of
Ὑπομνήματα. He distinguished the catalogue style of the Hesiodic poems
from Homer's epic narrative style, and when he came across passages of
a Ἡσιόδειος χαρακτήρ in *Iliad* and *Odyssey*, he condemned them as un-
Homeric.[4] The existence of his Ἀρχιλόχεια Ὑπομνήματα, which is expressly
attested, is important evidence for the transition from monographs Περὶ
Ἀρχιλόχου to a running commentary.[5] It may be at least suggested that the
reference in the Scholia to Pindar, περὶ δὲ τῆς σκυτάλης καὶ ἐν τοῖς Ἀρχιλόχου ὑπομνήμασιν εἴρηται (without the name of a grammarian), is to this
commentary of Aristarchus, since no other Ἀρχιλόχεια ὑπομνήματα are
known;[6] it might even derive from a reference by Aristarchus himself in
his commentary on Pindar to another of his own books.

It was Aristophanes of Byzantium who in his critical editions of the
lyric texts had provided the fundamental terminology, classification,
colometry, and metrical analysis for all later ancient times.[7] Not much is
known about Aristarchus' alterations, adjustments, or variant readings.
But in a commentary on Alcman, written in the second half of the first
century A.D.,[8] Aristarchus' note of the Colaxaean and Ibinean horses in
the Louvre Parthenion is quoted verbatim, and the passage that immediately follows may be Aristarchean too, in which it is inferred (in
opposition to Sosibius Laco, but apparently in conformity with Aristotle)
from the name of the Ibeni as a people of Lydia that the poet himself was

---

[1] See above, p. 144.
[2] Proleg. Ac in Hes. *Op.* p. 2. 8 Pertusi (Schol. vet. in Hes. *Op.* 1955) = test. 47 a in Hes.
Th. ed. F. Jacoby, pp. 124 f.; Praxiphan. fr. 5 Brink; cf. F. Leo, 'Hesiodea', *Index Scholarum*,
Gottingae 1894 = *Ausgew. Kleine Schriften* II (1960) 343 ff., esp. 346, 354.
[3] Suid. v. Ἀριστόνικος . . . ἔγραψε Περὶ τῶν σημείων τῶν ἐν τῇ Θεογονίᾳ Ἡσιόδου; Schol.
Hes. *Th.* 79, *Op.* 97; cf. Rzach, *RE* VIII 1226.
[4] Schol. A Σ 39, Ω 614, Schol. HQ o 74; cf. Lehrs³ p. 337.
[5] Clem. Al. *Strom.* I 117. 2, II p. 73. 25 Stählin = Archiloque ed. F. Lasserre (1958) test.
2 d, p. civ; cf. above, pp. 146 and 217 f. on Περὶ τοῦ δεῖνα.
[6] Schol. Pind. *O.* VI 154 a. When Didymus or Aristonicus cite anonymous ὑπομνήματα in
our Scholia to Homer, they always mean Aristarchus, see Ludwich, *Arist. Hom. Textkritik*
I 25 f.
[7] See above, pp. 181 ff.
[8] *P.Oxy.* XXIV ed. E. Lobel (1957) 2389 fr. 6, col. I 7 = *PMG* ed. Page (1962) p. 7 Schol.
B 7 on Alcm. fr. 1. 59; on Sosibius see above, p. 202, on Aristotle *P.Oxy.* 2389, fr. 9, col. I 12,
on Crates in this case agreeing with Aristarchus see below, p. 242.

a Lydian. That there was an Aristarchean ὑπόμνημα on Alcman, there-fore, can no longer be doubted, and it may be worth noting that Aristoni-cus,[1] who treated of Aristarchus' critical signs on Homer and Hesiod, also concerned himself with Alcman's poems. One of his textual variants was noted on the margin of the Louvre papyrus.[2] Ἐκδόσεις of Alcaeus and Anacreon are mentioned in Hephaestio's metrical handbook, and in Athenaeus Aristarchus appears as an interpreter of a passage in an Anacreontic poem (ἐξηγούμενος τὸ χωρίον).[3]

But it is only from the Scholia to Pindar's *Epinicia* in our medieval manuscripts and from the marginal notes in the great papyrus of the *Paeans* that we gain fuller information.[4] Though Aristarchus' name turns up about seventy times altogether, and we can be sure that a number of excerpts under Didymus' name are Aristarchean in substance, there is no reference either to an ἔκδοσις or to a ὑπόμνημα. If anyone says that all the examples of his verbal criticism were part of a commentary,[5] he cannot be refuted; on the other hand, a defender of the theory of 'commentary only' will not be able to prove that Aristarchus did not produce a new recension of Pindar's text. It was difficult enough to reach a decision in the case of Homer where the tradition is a hundred times richer; with regard to Pindar we can only state the possibility that Aristarchus re-tained the text established shortly before by his master Aristophanes, and occasionally marked his disagreement. As a matter of fact, the Aristo-phanean text of Pindar continued to enjoy a degree of authority that no text of Homer ever achieved. Callistratus had probably been the first to comment on some of the Pindaric poems, and historians like Timaeus or Peripatetics like Chamaeleo could offer helpful material.[6] But to com-pose a complete commentary on the whole of Pindar's poetry was still a highly ambitious undertaking. Aristarchus, though familiar with vocabulary and to a lesser degree with metre, had not at his command the full knowledge of the historical background and the acquaintance with local history that was indispensable for the interpretation of Pindar. It has been easy for ancient and modern critics to carp at his obvious

---

[1] *P.Oxy.* xxiv 2387, fr. 1 marg. with Lobel's commentary.
[2] Alcm. Schol. A on fr. 1. 38 p. 6 Page.
[3] On Alc. see above, p. 185, n. 6, on Anacr. n. 4 and Athen. xv 671 F; on ἐξηγούμενος see below, pp. 222 f.
[4] Schol. Pind. ed. Drachmann, vol. III pp. 313 f. v. Ἀρίσταρχος and v. Δίδυμος and *P.Oxy.* v p. 322 v. Ἀρίσταρχος.
[5] J. Irigoin, *Histoire du texte de Pindare* 51 ff.
[6] R. Schmidt, *Commentatio de Callistrato Aristophaneo* pone Aristoph. Byz. Fragm. ed. Nauck (1848) p. 323; Timaeus 566 *FGrHist* III B (1955) Kommentar b (Noten) p. 313, n. 29; Chamael. fr. 31 f. Περὶ Πινδάρου, Wehrli, *Schule des Aristot.* 9 (1957) 56 and 82.

deficiencies;[1] but there is more reason to respect the courageous efforts of the great Homeric scholar in a quite different field.

A commentary on Bacchylides' *Dithyrambs* preserved in a papyrus of the second century A.D. states that Aristarchus, in disagreement with Callimachus,[2] assigned the *Cassandra* to this group. But the author of the commentary, possibly Didymus ἐν ὑπομνήματι Βακχυλίδου ἐπινίκων,[3] does not give the title of the book concerned; so it may have been a casual remark. Aristarchus'[4] name, but no more, occurs also in a very large but fragmentary papyrus of the first or early second century A.D. dealing with Alcman, Stesichorus, Sappho, and Alcaeus. It is certainly not a ὑπό-μνημα in the proper sense of a 'commentary', as it is labelled in the *editio princeps*; I am pretty confident that it should be regarded as a fresh specimen of that earlier literary form Περὶ τοῦ δεῖνα[5] which continued to be used besides the developed ὑπόμνημα. The interweaving of biographical material and problems with the interpretation of selected passages of texts, often starting from long lemmata, is typical of this form; typical also are the references to Peripatetic authorities in the first place (Aristotle, Dicaearchus, and especially Chamaeleo) and then to Alexandrian grammarians, of whose names only Ἀρίσταρχος is legible (probably in two places). So our knowledge of Aristarchus' work on lyric poetry is being slowly improved by the trickle of fresh papyrus finds.[6]

This cannot be said of his work on dramatic poetry. For Aeschylus we have still to rely on Schol. Theocr. x 18 e. Ἀρίσταρχος[7] ἐν ὑπομνήσει Λυκούργου Αἰσχύλου[8] (with reference to the μάντις καλαμαία in the satyr-play *Lycurgus*). The explanation of a few Sophoclean expressions is attributed to Aristarchus. The δερμηστής was usually supposed to be a 'worm eating skin or leather'; but Ἀρίσταρχος τὸ Σοφόκλειον (*Niobe* fr. 449 P.) ἐξηγούμενος took it to mean a 'snake'.[9] The word ἐξηγεῖσθαι

---

[1] Cf. Irigoin loc. cit. 54 ff.   [2] See above, p. 130.

[3] Bacchyl.[8] ed. Snell, test. 10 p. 122.

[4] *P.Oxy.* xxix ed. D. Page (1963) 2506, fr. 6a 6 and fr. 79. 7 (?); preface p. v 'an ancient commentary on Greek Lyric Poets'.

[5] See above, esp. pp. 217 f. with the reference to F. Leo.

[6] The label Σιμωνιδείων ὑπ(όμνημα) *P.Oxy.* xxv (1959) 2433 of the second century A.D. hardly means a commentary on Simonides' poems by one of the grammarians (Aristarch., Didym., etc.), but a popular exposition of his famous 'Sayings'.

[7] This is the reading of codd. UEA; Ἀ. ἐν ὑπομνήματι Λυκούργου codd. GPT; but our best manuscript, Ambrosianus K reads Ἀριστοφάνης instead of Ἀρίσταρχος and omits the following words. We have to accept the longer version; see also C. Wendel, 'Überlieferung und Entstehung der Theokrit-Scholien', *AGGW*, Phil.-hist. Kl. N.F. XVII 2 (1921) 145, and compare p. 151.

[8] *TGF* p. 40 N.² = fr. 100 Mette, from the Λυκοῦργος Σατυρικός; cf. Mette, *Der verlorene Aischylos* (1963) 141.

[9] Harpocr. p. 55. 2 Bekker, Hesych., Suid. s.v., al.; cf. Didym. *Fragm.* ed. M. Schmidt p. 21.

itself and in isolation does not suggest the writing of a commentary;[1]
it is used properly of individual interpretations. But it can mean the
interpretation of a particular passage or word in the course of a commentary,[2] and as Aristarchus' interpretations of passages from no less
than three plays—ἐλαιοῦται (*Troilus* fr. 624 P.), κρέας (*Chryses* fr. 728 P.),
λυκοκτόνου θεοῦ (*El.* 6)—are cited by lexicographers and scholiasts, we
may reasonably infer that he did write a commentary on Sophocles.[3]
It would be more hazardous to draw the same conclusion from the only
reference to Ion's *Omphale*; Aristarchus is said to have explained the
μάγαδις as a sort of flute, but this could have been just a reference to the
special sense of μάγαδις in Ion's iambic line (τὸ ἰαμβεῖον ἐξηγούμενος)[4]
inserted for contrast in one of his commentaries on lyric poets where
μάγαδις occurs as a stringed instrument. There is also one quotation in
our copious Scholia to Euripides; in the passage on the night-watches in
the Ps.-Euripidean *Rhesus* 539 ff. Aristarchus is said to have disagreed
with other (anonymous) grammarians, in taking Coroebus as the leader
of the Paeones.[5] This hardly justifies the conclusion that he wrote a complete commentary on Euripides, as Priam's belated ally and Cassandra's
unhappy suitor, Coroebus, was a heroic figure in an epic poem of the
νεώτεροι to whose works Aristarchus often referred in his ὑπομνήματα on
the epics. There are, however, parts of the Scholia to Euripides that were
almost identical with Aristarchean explanations in the Homeric Scholia;
but they may be borrowings from there by Didymus, not self-quotations
of Aristarchus.[6] Yet one of the grammarians of the second century B.C.
must have laid the foundation for all the later comments on Euripides'
tragedies; and though this could have been one of his pupils or his coeval
Callistratus, Aristarchus himself is still the likeliest candidate. It is bitter

---

[1] The most notable mistake of this kind was made by those who inferred from Sext. Emp.,
Adv. math. VII 93 ὁ Ποσειδώνιος τὸν Πλάτωνος Τίμαιον ἐξηγούμενος that Posidonius wrote
a whole 'commentary' on the *Timaeus*; this and all its consequences were completely refuted
by K. Reinhardt, *Poseidonios* (1921) 416 ff. and *RE* XXII (1953) 569. The evidence referred
to in the two following notes confirms his interpretation of ἐξηγούμενος.

[2] See Schol. A B 111 (Didym.) κἂν ταῖς Λιταῖς ἐξηγούμενος "αὐτὰρ ἔπειτ' Αἴας" (*I* 169)
. . . ἔν τινι τῶν ἠκριβωμένων ὑπομνημάτων γράφει ταῦτα, sc. Ἀρίσταρχος; cf. above,
p. 221.

[3] In the Scholia to Pindar (above, p. 221, n. 4) the individual ἐξηγήσεις of Aristarchus
were part of his ὑπόμνημα (cf. e.g. Schol. Pind. *O.* II 102 b al.).

[4] Io fr. 23 N.² = fr. 66 Blumenthal (1939) with an impossible conjecture.

[5] Schol. [Eur.] *Rhes.* 539 f. οἱ μὲν τοὺς Κίλικας καὶ τοὺς Μυσοὺς τοὺς αὐτοὺς ἤκουσαν·
Ἀρίσταρχος δὲ Κόροιβον Παιόνων ἡγεμόνα καὶ τὴν φυλακὴν ποτὲ μὲν ἀπὸ τοῦ ἡγεμόνος, ποτὲ δὲ
ἀπὸ τῶν ὑπηκόων (on the text see the app. crit. of E. Schwartz) ; A. seems not to have taken part
in the astronomical debate, cf. Wilamowitz, *De Rhesi Scholiis* (1877) = *Kl. Schr.* I (1935) 10,
Einleitung i. d. Trag. (1889) 155. 69.

[6] W. Elsperger, 'Reste und Spuren antiker Kritik gegen Euripides', *Philol.* Suppl. Bd. XI 1
(1908) 98 ff., gives no more than some hints at possibly Aristarchean passages.

to have to confess our ignorance, the more so as Aristarchus had the
reputation of having been able 'to recite the whole of tragedy by heart';
at least his pupil Dionysius Thrax, who combined a talent for painting
with a knowledge of grammar, depicted him with the tragic Muse on his
breast διὰ τὸ ἀποστηθίζειν αὐτὸν πᾶσαν τὴν τραγῳδίαν.[1]

It can hardly be a caprice of Fortune that our sources tell us more
about Aristarchus' study of comedy. From the early third century onwards
it was not tragedy, but Attic comedy and particularly Aristophanes, that
interested the Alexandrian grammarians; even ὑπομνήματα on a few
plays by Euphronius and by Callistratus are attested[2] as having been
written before those of Aristarchus. He himself commented on eight
Aristophanic comedies at least, perhaps on all of them and not only on
the eleven plays which have survived entire with Scholia in our medieval
manuscripts. Again, as in the case of Pindar,[3] the question whether he
worked out a new recension[4] of the text cannot be definitely answered;
readings divergent from the edition of Aristophanes of Byzantium or
references to obelized lines, preserved in our Scholia under Aristarchus'
name, may only have been drawn from his commentary. This commentary suffered the same fate as that on Pindar; it was censured again
and again because of its occasional inadequacy in the treatment of historical and antiquarian matter. Nevertheless throughout later ancient
and Byzantine times it provided a firm basis for unceasing efforts to
master the difficulties of the Aristophanic text.

The founders of scholarship in Alexandria were poets and they had
concentrated quite naturally on the poetry of the past. But someone had
to turn to the prose writers—though it was learnt only from a papyrus
published at the beginning of the twentieth century[5] that this was
Aristarchus. He, having no poetical ambitions himself, was the first to
comment on Herodotus, who perhaps appealed to him as Ὁμηρικώτατος.[6]
It is just good luck that in this papyrus-fragment the end of Herodotus'
first book is preserved with the subscription Ἀριστάρχου / Ἡροδότου / ᾱ /
ὑπόμνημα. As chapters 193–4 are followed by chapter 215, the scribe
must have used a defective copy or an arbitrary excerpt of Aristarchus'

---

[1] Schol. Dionys. Thr. ed. Hilgard, *Gr. Gr.* III 160. 32 (from there *Et. gen.* B = *Et. M.* p. 277.
54); cf. Eust. p. 974. 10 τῶν τις παλαιῶν γραμματικῶν ἐκστηθίζειν τὰ τραγικά.

[2] See above, p. 190, n. 4.   [3] Above, p. 221.

[4] Boudreaux, *Le texte d'Aristophane* (1919) 52–55, denied its existence; the 26 (or perhaps
28) verbatim quotations from Aristarchus are collected by Rutherford, 'Annotation' 423–26.

[5] *Pap. Amherst* II (1901) ed. Grenfell and Hunt, no. 12 (third century A.D. from Hermu-
polis); reprinted with bibliography by A. H. R. E. Paap, *De Herodoti reliquiis in papyris et
membranis Aegyptiis servatis.* Diss. Utrecht (1948) 37 ff.

[6] W. Bühler, *Beiträge zur Erklärung der Schrift vom Erhabenen* (1964) 93 f. on Π. ὕψ. 13. 2–3.

commentary. To the lemma ἄνιπποι (Herod. 1 215. 1) Aristarchus noted with his explanation and approval the variant ἄμιπποι,[1] which is missing in the manuscripts of Herodotus' *Histories*, just as so many of Aristarchus' readings are absent from the manuscript text of Homer. It is characteristic of the Homeric scholar that he should immediately compare the horse-riding of the Massagetae with the use of the chariot by the Greek heroes. In the next paragraph also there is a parallel from poetry: Herodotus' sentence, 'iron and silver they use not at all', is compared with Sophocles' Ποιμένες (fr. 500 P.).[2] It is remarkable to find Aristarchus' ὑπόμνημα, though abbreviated, still copied with the original title four centuries later; as there is a *varia lectio* introduced and discussed in the course of the commentary, we see again that no separate critical edition of the text can be inferred from occasional quotations of variant readings.[3] It could not be very surprising if Aristarchus had also written the first commentary on Thucydides, because it cannot be doubted any longer that Didymus was able to use earlier scholarly Alexandrian work;[4] but there is as yet no reason to assume that he did the same for Xenophon and for the Attic orators. However, from the evidence we have one fact emerges clearly and becomes understandable: the ὑπομνήματα on prose writers were bound to follow the patterns of those on the poets, Homer above all.

Having surveyed the extent of Aristarchus' efforts as editor and interpreter (it hardly needs saying that it did not go beyond the 'selected authors')[5] we come now to describe the tendency of his interpretation. Explaining a literary work was to him at least as worth while an endeavour as the editing of the text, if not more worth while.

It has become a common conviction that Aristarchus expressed a firm principle himself. From the end of the last century up to the present day nearly every book on Alexandrian scholarship, when it gets to Aristarchus, fastens upon him the general maxim that 'each author is his own

---

[1] W. Crönert in his new edition of Passow's *Wörterbuch d. griech. Sprache* (1913) 375 gives the best collection of the evidence for ἄμιππος; cf. H. Erbse, *Untersuchungen zu den attizistischen Lexika* (1950) 159. But only the gloss in Bekker's first rhetorical lexicon, *AG* 1 205. 5 has a clear affinity with Aristarchus' discussion of ἄνιππος and ἄμιππος; cf. Pasquali, *Storia* 314.

[2] No reason why Aristarchus quoted Sophocles is preserved; as the date of the *Poimenes* is now fairly well established in the year 464/3 B.C. (above, p. 21), the Sophoclean line cannot be used as fresh evidence for Sophocles' dependence on Herodotus, as Paap 49 would like.

[3] Cf. above, p. 221; F. Jacoby, 'Herodotos', *RE* Suppl. 2 (1913) 515, means that it is 'very likely' that Aristarchus also made an edition of the text; but the papyrus is no basis for this hypothesis.

[4] See O. Luschnat, '*Die Thukydidesscholien*', *Philol.* 98 (1954) 22 ff.; he is only wrong in identifying ἐξηγήσεις and ὑπομνήματα, see above, p. 223. Cf. also R. Stark, *Annales Universitatis Saraviensis*, Serie Philosophie 8 (1959) 41 f. and 47, 9–11.

[5] Cf. above, p. 208.

best interpreter'; other versions say 'Homer' instead of 'each author' or put it down in Greek "Ὅμηρον ἐξ Ὁμήρου σαφηνίζειν;[1] usually no reference is given.[2] As a matter of fact, there is no real evidence that Aristarchus ever uttered such a sentence. The all too famous τόπος has its origin in the following words of Porphyry:[3] ἀξιῶν δὲ ἐγὼ (sc. Porphyrius) "Ὅμηρον ἐξ Ὁμήρου σαφηνίζειν αὐτὸν ἐξηγούμενον ἑαυτὸν ὑπεδείκνυον, ποτὲ μὲν παρακειμένως, ἄλλοτε δ' ἐν ἄλλοις; a long series of Homeric passages follows in which the poet 'immediately', παρακειμένως, interprets himself.[4] It was as a young philosopher, an Athenian pupil of the φιλόλογος and κριτικός Cassius Longinus, that Porphyry wrote his learned and sober Ὁμηρικὰ ζητήματα;[5] later, in his Roman days after A.D. 263 under the spell of Plotinus, though he never lost his love of Homer, he approached him as a Neoplatonic allegorist and treated for instance the *Cave of nymphs* in the *Odyssey* (ν 102–12) as an allegory of the universe, in a monograph which, in sharp contrast to his earlier studies, no longer explains the poet 'out of himself'. There is no hint that Porphyry had Aristarchus in mind either in the eleventh *Homeric Question* just quoted or in his dedicatory letter to Anatolius where he said: ἐμοῦ δεικνύναι πειρωμένου ὡς αὐτὸς μὲν ἑαυτὸν τὰ πολλὰ "Ὅμηρος ἐξηγεῖται;[6] in this second passage he was simply restating his personal endeavour as an interpreter of Homer without repeating the formula with σαφηνίζειν. Yet the sense of his formula does not disagree with Aristarchus' opinion; one may compare the unique Scholion D on E 385: Ἀρίσταρχος ἀξιοῖ τὰ φραζόμενα ὑπὸ τοῦ ποιητοῦ μυθικώτερον ἐκδέχεσθαι κατὰ τὴν ποιητικὴν

[1] W. Christ, *Geschichte der griech. Lit.* (1889) 453 'in der Exegese ging er ... von dem Grundsatz aus, daß man jeden Autor zunächst aus sich selbst erklären müsse' (repeated verbatim in the later editions by W. Schmid). L. Cohn (see above, p. 210, n. 2) *RE* II (1896) 868. 62 (Aristarch) 'war der Ansicht, daß Homer nur aus sich selbst erklärt werden müsse'. Sandys I (1903) 131 A. 'insisted that each author was his own best interpreter', repeated in the 2nd and 3rd editions. E. Heitsch, *Antike und Abendland* IX (1960) 21 'Die von A. für die methodische Erklärung aufgestellte Maxime lautet: "Ὅμηρον ἐξ Ὁμήρου σαφηνίζειν.' H. Erbse in *Geschichte der Textüberlieferung* I (1961) 225 'Homer aus Homer zu erklären, lautet Aristarchs berühmter Leitsatz.' See also my own festival speech *Philologia Perennis* (1961) 8 'A. vertrat die unanfechtbare Maxime ... Homer möglichst aus sich selber zu erklären.'
[2] The exception is A. Gudeman, *Grundriss der Geschichte der klass. Philologie* (1907) 40. 1 'Sein kritisches Verfahren ... kann mit den Worten des Porphyrius bezeichnet werden' (Schrader p. 297 and p. 281, see the following notes); he found 'denselben Grundsatz' expressed in Schol. D on E 385 (see below, p. 227). A. Roemer, *Philol.* 70 (1911) 178, was less cautious 'die beiden Sätze (des Porphyrius) sind gewiß Aristarchischer Provenienz'. He regularly described the σαφηνίζειν sentence as Aristarchean in other papers and books, without references.
[3] Porphyr. *Qu. Hom.* (1880) p. 297. 16 Schrader with the important footnote: 'Aristarchum hac in re Porphyrio praeiisse Aristonicus Z 194. 201 docet.'
[4] On 'self-interpretations' in Homer see above, pp. 3 f.
[5] J. Bidez, *Vie de Porphyre* (1913) 31 ff.
[6] p. 281. 3 Schrader; cf. p. 344.

ἐξουσίαν, μηδὲν ἔξω τῶν φραζομένων ὑπὸ τοῦ ποιητοῦ περιεργαζομένους, where interpreters of the myth of Otus and Ephialtes are admonished to take it as a legendary tale according to poetic licence, not wasting their time on anything not said by the poet.[1] Furthermore, as the etymology of Ἀλήϊον πεδίον (Z 201) from ἀλᾶσθαι, given by Porphyry in the eleventh *Homeric Question*, essentially corresponds to that in Aristonicus' excerpt from Aristarchus Schol. A Z 201, ἀπὸ τῆς γενομένης ἐν αὐτῷ τοῦ Βελλερο-φόντου πλάνης,[2] it is very likely that Porphyry also preserved Aristarchus' interpretation of this line. All this might seem to support the guess that Aristarchus could have given the maxim of σαφηνίζειν τὸν ποιητήν somewhere; but could he really? Scholars are not inclined to pronounce general principles, but philosophers are, and Porphyry was always, even in his early grammatical studies, of a philosophical bent. The conclusion is twofold: that the formula Ὅμηρον ἐξ Ὁμήρου σαφηνίζειν[3] was coined by Porphyry and should not be taken as an authentic remark of Aristarchus, though it is not against his spirit; and that one must be a little cautious about attributing a winged word to a special author.

Aristarchus' main object was to discover the Homeric usage; for the explication of words and facts he collected all the parallels in the *Iliad* and *Odyssey*, treating any without parallels as ἅπαξ λεγόμενα of the poet. But when he encountered something which seemed not to fit at all into the pattern of the Homeric language or the Homeric life, he termed it κυκλικώτερον in contrast to Ὁμηρικώτερον, the genuinely Homeric. He went far beyond the earlier glossographic, lexicographic, and antiquarian studies[4] and criticized their deficiencies, having a wider view over the whole epic period.

We earlier discussed at some length[5] the text of the proem of the *Iliad* and mentioned that Aristarchus rejected Zenodotus' reading in line A 5 οἰωνοῖσί τε δαῖτα, because he was not able to find a parallel in Homer for δαίς meaning 'animal food', and because the derivation of the word itself (from δατεῖσθαι 'distribute among themselves') seemed to justify its use only for the meals of civilized human beings. So Aristarchus put the non-committal οἰωνοῖσί τε πᾶσι in his text and achieved a complete triumph

---

[1] Eust. ad loc. p. 561. 29 Ἀρίσταρχος ἠξίου . . . μηδέν τι τῶν παρὰ τῇ ποιήσει μυθικῶν περιεργάζεσθαι ἀλληγορικῶς ἔξω τῶν φραζομένων, probably 'interpolated' ἀλληγορικῶς; according to Schol. D Aristarchus' sentence was more general, not particularly against allegory.

[2] See esp. Schrader's note on p. 298. 17–20.

[3] In our Scholia, as far as they represent the Alexandrian tradition, the rare word σαφηνί-ζειν is not used for the activity of the interpreter; but if the poet makes something clear, it is said ὁ ποιητὴς σαφηνίζει. In the philosophical and rhetorical literature of the Roman empire it is a quite common expression, see for instance Clem. Al. vol. IV 699 St.

[4] See above, p. 197.   [5] See above, p. 112.

in so far as δαῖτα disappeared from all the manuscripts of the *Iliad* and survived only in a quotation by Athenaeus. Even if one is convinced that δαῖτα not πᾶσι is the original reading, and the one known to all the tragedians, this example aptly illustrates the processes of thought behind Aristarchus' decisions. In innumerable other cases there has never been any doubt that the result of his acute observations was correct: he chose the right variants, he detected in the explanations of glosses errors that had been traditional for centuries, he much improved the distinction of synonyms, following the earlier efforts of Prodicus and Aristotle, and, continuing the research of Aristophanes of Byzantium, he saw how many more words, often quite common ones, had changed their meaning in the interval between the epic age or even the Attic and his own time. As Aristarchus pointed out the use of some 'Attic' forms and words in the epic language,[1] it has become one of the commonplaces of modern literature on Homer that Aristarchus for this reason regarded him as an Athenian by birth.[2] If one looks for proof of this assumption in the Scholia, one finds nothing more substantial than one διπλῆ on N 197[3] which according to Aristonicus, draws, attention to the dual Αἴαντε μεμάοτε; the scholiast adds a sentence that its use has some reference to the mother country (of the poet?), as it is peculiar to the Athenians. This rather implies that the Athenian birth was known from other sources and is only confirmed by the use of the dual. Certainly, the long list of birth-places in the popular βίοι of Homer includes the statement that he was an Athenian according to Aristarchus and Dionysius Thrax.[4] In his commentary on Archilochus,[5] that is, in the serious grammatical literature, Aristarchus dated Homer to the time of the Ionian migration; these Ionian colonizers came, as a widely accepted ancient version says, from Athens. So it is not improbable[6] that Aristarchus was referring here not only to the time, but also to the home of Homer, namely Athens. In one of the βίοι the two things are actually combined.[7]

In the course of his tireless exegetical work Aristarchus also discovered

---

[1] See, e.g., J. Wackernagel, *Sprachliche Untersuchungen zu Homer* (1916) 156.

[2] Wilamowitz, *Hom. Unters.* 258 f., *Il. und Hom.* 9, 507.

[3] Schol. A N 197 (ἡ διπλῆ) ὅτι συνεχῶς κέχρηται τοῖς δυϊκοῖς· ἡ δὲ ἀναφορὰ πρὸς τὰ περὶ τῆς πατρίδος· Ἀθηναίων γὰρ ἴδιον. G. W. Nitzsch, *De historia Homeri*, Fasc. posterior (1837) 89, was reluctant to draw strict consequences from this dubious sentence, but correctly referred to the connexion of Homer's life with Ionian migration in the biographical tradition; cf. Aristonic. ed. L. Friedlaender p. 15. 2 and Jacoby below, n. 6.

[4] Homeri *Opera* ed. T. W. Allen, v (1911) p. 247. 8 = *Vitae Hom. et Hes.* ed. Wilamowitz (1916) p. 29. 9; cf. Allen p. 244. 13 = Wil. p. 25. 8.   [5] See above, p. 220, n. 5.

[6] Cf. F. Jacoby, *FGrHist* III Suppl. (A Commentary on the ancient historians of Athens) I 577, II 474 f.

[7] Allen, Homeri *Opera* v p. 244. 18 (and 13) = Wil. *Vitae Homeri* p. 25. 13 (and 8).

a few general grammatical and metrical rules. We are told that he added
a sixth rule of inflexion to the five stated by Aristophanes[1] and recognized eight parts of speech.[2] He obviously observed that ending a word
with the 'fourth trochee' of the hexameter is avoided, since he at *I* 394
instead of the vulgate reading γυναῖκα / γαμέσσεται suggested reading
γυναῖκά γε / μάσσεται,[3] though he did not alter the text.

The concept of grammatical analogy is first attested for Aristophanes
in the limited sphere of declension; it seems to have become a sort of
guiding principle of Aristarchus' interpretation and to have involved him
in heated disputes with an opposition that defended anomaly. But he
was no pedant in his search for parallels. Unlike any of his predecessors,
Aristarchus, by surveying the epic usage in its entirety, was able to pick
out those words which occurred only once in Homer; Aristonicus preserved the Aristarchean sentence in Schol. A *Γ* 54 πολλὰ δέ ἐστιν ἅπαξ
λεγόμενα παρὰ τῷ ποιητῇ.[4] Dealing with the problems of these many
singularities was an integral part of his interpretation, as we can recognize not only from the Scholia, but also from the lexicon of Apollonius
Sophista, who used Aristonicus and perhaps earlier writings of the
Aristarchean tradition.

We must observe the distinction between the ἅπαξ λεγόμενα acknowledged as Homeric and the expressions or passages marked with the
obelus as οὐχ Ὁμηρικῶς or κυκλικῶς for various reasons. Even when one
disagrees with Aristarchus' decisions, one must appreciate his sober
arguments based on carefully collected evidence; as they are preserved in
excerpts from his own commentaries, we are much better informed about
him than about his predecessors. He was reluctant to alter the παράδοσις,
that is the agreement of most manuscripts, by conjectures or by omission
of lines. His caution is criticized as excessive in the (Didymus-) Schol. A *I*
222 ἄμεινον οὖν εἶχεν ἄν, φησὶν ὁ Ἀρίσταρχος, ⟨εἰ⟩ (add. Bekker) ἐγέγραπτο
. . . ἀλλ' ὅμως ὑπὸ περιττῆς εὐλαβείας οὐδὲν μετέθηκεν, ἐν πολλαῖς οὕτως
εὑρὼν φερομένην τὴν γραφήν. Aristarchus marked repeated lines with the
asteriscus; when, as often happened, he found them not only empty, but
inappropriate in certain places, especially in speeches, he added obeli to

---

[1] See above, pp. 202 f.

[2] Quint. *Inst.* I 4. 20 octo partes (ὄνομα, ῥῆμα, μετοχή, ἀντωνυμία, ἄρθρον, ἐπίρρημα, πρόθεσις,
σύνδεσμος). This list is different from the parts of diction distinguished by Aristotle, see above,
pp. 76–78; on the Stoics and on Dionysius Thrax see below, p. 269.

[3] *I* 394 Πηλεύς θήν μοι ἔπειτα γυναῖκα γαμέσσεται αὐτός in all the ancient (Schol. T ad loc.)
and medieval manuscripts; γυναῖκά γε μάσσεται Aristarch. Schol. A intermarg. ad loc. Both
readings are objectionable, see P. Maas, *Greek Metre* § 87.

[4] F. Martinazzoli, *Hapax Legomenon*, pt. I 1 (1953), pt. I 2 (1957) 'Lexicon Homericum di
Apollonio Sofista'; cf. H. Erbse, *Gnom.* 27 (1955) 52 ff. and 31 (1959) 216 ff.

the asterisci. He did so, for example, in Hera's speech (*B* 160–2 and 164)[1] ὅτι οἰκειότερον ἐν τῷ τῆς Ἀθηνᾶς λόγῳ ἑξῆς εἰσι τεταγμένοι (176–8 and 180), νῦν δὲ κυκλικώτερον[2] λέγονται (Aristonic. Schol. A *B* 160). But he disagreed with Zenodotus' omission of the whole speech, judging it to be Ὁμηρικῶς ἔχοντα, provided that the few lines just referred to were athetized, since they were suitable in Athena's admonition of Odysseus to go round to the individual Greek heroes, but not in Hera's address to Athena.

The use of the term κυκλικώτερον or κυκλικῶς,[3] reflects the distinction first drawn by Aristotle between the great poet of the *Iliad* and *Odyssey* and the makers of the other early epics, the κυκλικοί.[4] Originally this word referred to the subject of the poems, especially to the Trojan cycle from the causes of the war to the death of Odysseus, the latest homecomer; but after Aristotle, compared with the two selected poems of Homer, everything 'cyclic' was regarded as inferior, which meant at least conventional, and often trivial. In that respect Zenodotus,[5] Callimachus,[6] and all the Alexandrian poets and scholars—so often in opposition to the Peripatos—accepted the Aristotelian doctrine. Callimachus' angry pronunciamento, ἐχθαίρω τὸ ποίημα τὸ κυκλικόν (*Ep.* 28), was widely acclaimed and frequently repeated; there is also an obvious allusion to it by Horace in his famous lines *A.P.* 132 'non circa vilem patulumque moraberis orbem' and 136 'ut scriptor cyclicus olim'.

On the other hand, if the *Iliad* and *Odyssey* were to be esteemed as creations of perfect workmanship by one poet,[7] not a few difficulties and discrepancies presented themselves to the scrutinizing scholarly mind. It was relatively easy to recognize and to remove lines missing in some of the manuscripts as post-Homeric insertions. But there were many lines or even passages in all the manuscripts which seemed hardly reconcilable with the idea of perfection and unity, and had therefore to be carefully

---

[1] Zenodotus had a different text in *B* 156 followed by *B* 169, completely omitting Hera's speech. Since that time ancient and modern critics have never stopped discussing the whole passage, see P. Von der Mühll, *Krit. Hypomnema zur Ilias* (1952) 40.

[2] I read κυμικωτερ(ον) in the facsimile of cod. Ven. A p. 27ʳ last line, which is, I should think, a slightly corrupt κυκλικώτερον. Villoison's κοινότερον was accepted by Dindorf; Bekker read (?) κωμικώτερον, Lehrs conjectured ἀνοικειότερον (Herodiani *scripta tria*, Epimetrum, 1848, p. 459), followed by Friedlaender, Aristonic. p. 62.

[3] Aristarchus in Schol. A (Aristonicus) *O* 610 said of five lines κυκλικῶς ταυτολογεῖται and athetized them while Zenodotus had left them out. Cf. Schol. A *Z* 325 κυκλικῶς κατακέχρηται, *I* 222 κυκλικώτερον; Schol. T *Ω* 628 κυκλικῶς (Wilamowitz: ἰδίως cod.); Schol. BEP η 115 οὐ κυκλικῶς . . . ἀλλ' . . . τὸ ἰδίωμα with the annotation of the editors.

[4] See above, pp. 73 f.   [5] Above, p. 117.   [6] Above, p. 137.

[7] Aristarchus rejected the view of the separators (χωρίζοντες) who assumed two poets for *Iliad* and *Odyssey*, as a 'paradox' (see above, p. 213). He gave references from the *Iliad* to the *Odyssey*; cf. Schol. *Δ* 354, *Λ* 147, etc.

considered and, if necessary, marked as un-Homeric or, in special cases, as 'cyclic'. The only solution was not to delete them, but to mark them as spurious, as 'interpolations' (τὸ ἀθετεῖν); athetesis, invented by his predecessors, was practised by Aristarchus with the utmost skill[1] and continued to be practised by his followers in the field of Homeric criticism through two millennia.

No change in method was possible until a new concept of history dawned in the eighteenth century and oral, popular poetry was discovered as the product of an early age, essentially different from the later ones. Aristarchus had been able to distinguish certain traces of the Homeric language from the Attic and Hellenistic usage and to pick out differences in civilization; but the new concept demanded an attempt to understand the specific character of epic poetry as a whole, its origin, development, and final form. Many passages that had startled the Alexandrian and later scholars were no longer deemed interpolations but were acknowledged as signs of different strata in the structure of the great poems. F. A. Wolf, starting from the newly discovered Venetian Scholia,[2] tried to give proofs for the new historical research step by step, in contrast to the vague generalities of the Homeric enthusiasts; he at least paved the way for the analytical efforts of the following generations of scholars who were eager to unveil the mysteries of epic stratification.

It is quite natural that the negative aspect of Aristarchus' Homeric criticism prevails in this chapter; our sources[3] say almost nothing in praise of the positive values he admired and loved in the greatest of all poets. Like Eratosthenes he saw in Homer an imaginative and creative poet whose aim was to give pleasure, not to instruct.[4] The scattered aesthetic and rhetorical terms that have come down to us do not suggest that Aristarchus followed the principles of a theory of poetics. Occasional phrases like διὰ παντός (Schol. A Θ 562, Λ 217 κτλ.), οἰκονομικῶς (Ψ 616, Schol. μ 103, ν 356), ἕνεκα τῆς ἀντικαταστάσεως ('balance'? Ο 212) call

---

[1] Cf. his commentary on ψ 296 as the τέλος of the *Odyssey*, where he agrees with Aristophanes, above, p. 175. Perhaps his most striking athetesis is that of Ω 25–30, the worst patchwork in our Homeric text.

[2] See above, pp. 213 f.

[3] Didymus had hardly an opportunity of mentioning aesthetic judgements of Aristarchus, but Aristonicus had. The exegetical Scholia in b T contain little Aristarchean material. W. Bachmann, 'Die ästhetischen Anschauungen Aristarchs in der Exegese und Kritik der Homerischen Gedichte', Beilage zum *Jahresbericht des Alten Gymnasiums Nürnberg* i (1901/2) ii (1903/4) gives a partly useful collection of evidence. Less helpful is Atkins, *Literary Criticism* i (1934) 188 ff.; on the art of composition see also R. Griesinger, *Die ästhetischen Anschauungen der alten Homererklärer*, Diss. Tübingen (1907) 9 ff.

[4] See above, pp. 166 f.

attention to the art of composition in the epic narrative; other phrases emphasize the harmony between the speech and the character of an epic hero, ἐν ἤθει λέγεται (A 117 κτλ.). Stylistic observations explain the specific function of metaphors (πρὸς ἔμφασιν B 670) or of similes (Ξ 16, Σ 207 ἐμφατικῶς, I 14 εἰς αὔξησιν) or of 'not mentioning a thing' (κατὰ τὸ σιωπώμενον Z 337, Π 432 κτλ.). In contrast to appreciations of this sort, censorious epithets ἀπρεπές, εὐτελές, περισσόν, crop up again and again; but his deep affection is always present even if it remains in the background. He quite honestly accepted, as many of his interpretations confirm, the Aristotelian and Callimachean distinction between Homeric superiority and cyclic insufficiency and he used critical signs and words to make it clear in the interests of true poetry.

Aristarchus achieved supreme authority as critic and interpreter. In the second half of the second century B.C. Panaetius, born in Rhodes and then the leading figure amongst the Stoics in Athens and Rome, so admired the ease with which Aristarchus divined the sense of the difficult ancient poetry that he called him a 'seer': μάντιν . . . διὰ τὸ ῥᾳδίως καταμαντεύεσθαι τῆς τῶν ποιημάτων διανοίας.[1] In the first century B.C. Cicero and Horace attest that his name was almost proverbial[2] as that of the serious and sincere critic. Indeed the legend of his infallibility had its dangers in the uncritical days of later antiquity, and he would hardly have approved of those naïve admirers who followed him blindly even against their better knowledge.[3]

After Villoison's discovery of the Venetian codices and Lehrs's studies based on it Aristarchus' authority rose again to an overwhelming height; in the year 1848 Nauck protested against what he called 'Aristarchomania'.[4] If the image of the grammarian reconstructed from the commentary of the four men in the Venetian codex A appeared in the eyes of the modern Aristarcheans to be disfigured by some impurities, the

---

[1] Athen. xiv 634 c = Panaet. Rhod. *Fragmenta* ed. M. Van Straaten (1962) fr. 93. Bentley alluded to this saying in the preface to his Horace (1711) xx 'opus . . . est, ut de Aristarcho olim praedicabant, divinandi quadam peritia et μαντικῇ.'

[2] Cic. *ad Att.* I 14. 3 'quarum (orationum) tu Aristarchus es' (cf. *in Pison.* 73 more jokingly, *fam.* III 11. 5, IX 10. 1). Hor. *A.P.* 450 'fiet Aristarchus'.

[3] The remarks on Aristarchus' accentuation at the end of Schol. A B 316 πτερύγος (against the κανών the Schol. adds πειθόμεθα αὐτῷ ὡς πάνυ ἀρίστῳ γραμματικῷ) and Δ 235 ψευδέσσι (μᾶλλον πειστέον Ἀριστάρχῳ ἢ τῷ Ἑρμαππίᾳ, εἰ καὶ δοκεῖ ἀληθεύειν) are, of course, not part of the genuine excerpts from Herodian's προσῳδία, but later additions (see Herodian. 1 p. lxxix n. Lentz, cf. Lehrs³ 297). One is reminded of an amusingly simple sentence of Boccaccio in his very learned compilation *De montium, sylvarum, fontium . . . nominibus* (printed after 'Περὶ γενεαλογίας deorum' in ed. Basil. 1532, p. 503) 'ut mallem potius eorum autoritati quam oculis credere meis', when what he read in the beloved books of the ancients did not agree with what he saw with his own eyes.

[4] Aristoph. Byz. Fragm. p. 56, n. 75. He seems to have coined 'Aristarchomania'.

stupid excerptors, first Didymus,[1] then Aristonicus[2] were blamed for having misunderstood the original. On the other side there were the anti-Aristarcheans who did not highly respect either his textual criticism or his exegetical work.[3] One thing is quite certain: on the eternal Homeric battlefield Aristarchus remains an outstanding controversial figure. We have tried here only to put him and his predecessors into their proper historical place.

At the beginning of this chapter we described the crisis of the year 145/4 B.C., which broke the living chain of eminent personalities that had stretched from Philitas and Zenodotus to Aristarchus. They were, as we have seen, connected by personal links, as the younger scholars were the pupils of the previous generations; but there were no διαδοχαί, as in the philosophical schools with their particular δόξαι. The great Alexandrians were united, not by doctrine, but by the common love of letters, and every one of them was an independent individuality. We shall find only *one* parallel in the Italian Renaissance of the fourteenth and fifteenth centuries A.D.: the living chain of freely associated masters and disciples through five generations from Petrarch to Politian, whose common love and labour restored scholarship from dangerous decline to life and dignity.

---

[1] A. Roemer relentlessly attacked Didymus in his numerous books and articles, see especially *Aristarchs Athetesen in der Homerkritik* (1912); bibliography in A. Roemer and E. Belzner, 'Die Homerexegese Aristarchs in ihren Grundzügen', *Studien zur Geschichte und Kultur des Altertums* 13 (1924) 267.

[2] M. Van der Valk, *Researches on the Text and Scholia of the Iliad* 1 (1963) 553 ff. tried to discredit Aristonicus.

[3] Van der Valk in this and in his earlier book on the *Odyssey* takes a very poor view of the Alexandrian grammarians, particularly of Aristarchus. See Addenda to p. 105.1.

VII

PERGAMUM: SCHOLARSHIP AND PHILOSOPHY
A NEW ANTIQUARIANISM

GREEK scholarship in Alexandria suffered heavy losses, as we have seen, in the first great crisis of its history; nevertheless it was able to continue its existence[1] until Egypt, after a thousand years of Greek civilization, finally returned to the orient. In the course of the second century B.C., when the political and economic power of the Ptolemies declined, other places in the Aegean world grew mightier and rose to importance as seats of learning also, Pergamum above all.[2]

Even if we take into account all the energy, ambition, and skill of the family of the Attalids, it still seems a miraculous feat that Pergamum was brought into such prominence by them for a century and a half. Philetaerus,[3] the son of Attalus, governor of the hill fortress of Pergamum, having in 282 B.C. betrayed and deserted Lysimachus, at that time lord of Macedonia, Thrace, and Asia Minor, left a more or less independent principality to his nephews Eumenes and Attalus and their heirs. They consolidated and enlarged it into a kingdom, defeating the violent Celtic invaders and with Rome's help in 190 B.C. even the Seleucids; they made their capital a new centre of cultural life,[4] and in its magnificent setting the arts, philosophy, science, and scholarship flourished until the country was 'legally' inherited by Rome in 133 B.C.

But no Pergamene literary monument could equal the splendour of the colossal marble altar erected to Zeus Soter by Eumenes II to commemorate his final victory over the barbarians. There were no poets at any time in Pergamum comparable to those in Alexandria, nor can Pergamene scholarship in its origin and development be compared with that of Alexandria.

---

[1] Cf. also above, p. 171.
[2] See the references to the history of the Hellenistic age above, p. 87, n. 2.
[3] Strab. XIII 623 f.
[4] *Altertümer von Pergamon*, by A. Conze and others, vol. I–X (1885–1937). H. Kähler, *Der große Fries von Pergamon* (1948), see esp. Pt. III 'Der große Fries und die Geschichte Pergamons', pp. 131 ff., the date of the altar 142 f., the question of allegory 149.

The Attalids had first invited distinguished members of the Peripatos, Lacydes, and Lycon, who politely refused to emigrate to the new Hellespontic kingdom. Aristophanes of Byzantium, although for an unknown reason he had seriously considered fleeing to Eumenes II, was prevented from leaving Egypt.[1] But this enterprising king (197–158 B.C.) finally succeeded in attracting a Stoic philosopher from the south of Asia Minor to his capital, Crates from Mallos in Cilicia.[2] It was not the intention of the kings to set up a sort of Pergamene school in opposition to the Alexandrians; it just happened that earlier invitations were declined, and then the Stoics came. The 'Stoics' mean Crates and a few personal pupils; one should not speak of a 'school' of Pergamum at all, as is so often done.[3] There was no sequence of teachers and disciples like that in Alexandria, where we saw five generations following one another. Quite independently, as it seems, a new kind of antiquarian research was started in Pergamum towards the end of the third century B.C. under the reign of Eumenes' predecessor, Attalus I (241–197 B.C.) and continued throughout the second century.

Books are the indispensable tools of scholars; the Ptolemies,[4] stimulated by the scholar poets, had collected and stored hundreds of thousands of papyrus rolls in Alexandria, and appointed the leading scholars in succession as librarians. In Pergamum only Eumenes II is attested as founder of the library (Strabo XIII 624).[5] This seems to be confirmed by the excavations. For according to a dedicatory inscription it was Eumenes II who added to the great temple of Athena on the Acropolis the dignified building that housed his library.[6] Crates may have helped his king in organizing and administering the library; this is suggested by the fact that he is said[7] to have played a part in devising a finer method of preparing sheepskin for writing material and advising its export to Rome.

[1] See above, p. 172. Wendel, *Buchbeschreibung* 60 ff., tried in vain to prove that Aristophanes' pupil Callistratus moved to Pergamum and there wrote against Aristarchus.

[2] Sueton. *De grammaticis et rhetoribus* 2 (p. 4. 4 Brugnoli 1963) 'Crates . . . missus ad senatum ab Attalo rege . . . sub ipsam Ennii mortem' (169 B.C.); Attalus (II) became king in 159/8 B.C., and cannot have sent off Crates to Rome in 168 B.C., it was Eumenes II. The same confusion of Attalus and Eumenes in Lyd. *de mens.* 1 28 who depends on Sueton. Varro correctly mentions Eumenes; Sandys I³ 111 (who overlooked Lydus' testimony) by a further confusion understood Eumenes I (263–241 B.C.).

[3] Sandys I³ 163. 'The school of Pergamum' contrasted with 'the school of Alexandria'.

[4] See above, pp. 98 ff.

[5] Schmidt, *Pinakes* test. 45–54, p. 16, on the Pergamene library, p. 28 on the Pergamene Πίνακες; cf. pp. 43 f. See also Kenyon, *Books and Readers* 68 ff., and Wendel, *Buchbeschreibung* 90, and *Handbuch der Bibliothekswissenschaft* III 1² (1955) 82 ff.

[6] *Altertümer von Pergamon* II and *RE* XIX (1937) 1258 f.

[7] Lydus, *De mensibus* ed. R. Wuensch (1898) 1 28 = Mette, *Sphairopoiia* (1936) 105, test. 7; the often-quoted sentence in F. Boissonade, *Anecd. Graec.* 1 (1829) 420 goes back to Lydus, see Wuensch p. xxxi.

The use of this particular material made the name of Pergamum immortal: Lydus ʿΡωμαῖοι τὰ μέμβρανα Περγαμηνὰ καλοῦσιν, Suidas Περγαμηναί· αἱ μεμβρᾶναι; parchment, parchemin, Pergament. It became a common legend in ancient times that parchment was 'invented' in Pergamum when Ptolemy V, the coeval of Eumenes II, stopped the export of papyrus.[1] But in fact, writing on leather rolls was quite common in the Near East in early times and was adopted by the Greeks on the west coast of Asia Minor[2] before the fifth century B.C. Since the excavations of Dura-Europos on the upper Euphrates brought to light[3] a document of the year 195/4 B.C. which was written on perfectly manufactured parchment, we are no longer entitled to say that the Pergamenes were the first to produce it in the finest quality. But they do seem to have produced it in a larger quantity, probably because the import of papyrus for the scriptoria of the expanding library became too expensive, and they may have been the first to export it to the west, as we have just heard. Whether there really was for some time an Egyptian embargo on papyrus remains an open question. Parchment, in any case, had a glorious future, especially when the form of the codex came slowly to supplant that of the roll.[4]

The literary treasures had to be catalogued; we referred to the Περγαμηνοὶ πίνακες when we dealt with their great Alexandrian model.[5] Only one librarian is known by name, the Stoic Athenodorus of Tarsus,[6] who went to Rome in 70 B.C. Figures of books in the libraries are to be regarded with due scepticism. Plutarch in his *Life of Mark Antony* took from a source hostile to Antony and Cleopatra the story that she was presented by the last of her lovers with 200,000 volumes from the Pergamene libraries;[7] modern scholars usually assume that it was the losses of the Alexandrian Museum library, caused by the fire in the harbour in

---

[1] Varro (de bibliothecis?, see Dahlmann *RE* Suppl. VI 1221) in Plin. *n.h.* XIII 70 'mox aemulatione circa bibliothecas regum Ptolemaei et Eumenis, supprimente chartas Ptolemaeo idem Varro membranas Pergami tradit repertas'; cf. also Lydus.

[2] See above, p. 19.

[3] F. Cumont, *Fouilles de Doura-Europos* 1922–23, Textes (1926) 281–5, Parchment Document no. 1.

[4] C. H. Roberts, 'The Codex', *Proc. Brit. Acad.* 40 (1954) 169 ff.; terminology 'membrana', 'membranae', etc. p. 174.—See also F. Wieacker, 'Textstufen klassischer Juristen', *Abh. Akad. d. Wiss. Göttingen*, Phil.-hist. Kl., 3. Folge, Nr. 45 (1960) 93 ff., esp. 99.

[5] See above, p. 133.

[6] H. v. Arnim, *RE* II (1896) 2045, Athenodorus no. 18.

[7] Plut. *Anton.* 58 Καλουίσιος . . . καὶ ταῦτα τῶν εἰς Κλεοπάτραν ἐγκλημάτων Ἀντωνίῳ προὔφερε· χαρίσασθαι μὲν αὐτῇ τὰς ἐκ Περγάμου βιβλιοθήκας, ἐν αἷς εἴκοσι μυριάδες βιβλίων ἁπλῶν ἦσαν; cf. ibid. 59 ἀλλὰ τούτων μὲν ἐδόκει τὰ πλεῖστα καταψεύδεσθαι Καλουίσιος. On Calvisius see F. Münzer, *RE* III (1899) 1411 f.; perhaps Clunius is to be read. Plut. *Anton.* 58 should not be quoted without the reservation made at the beginning of ch. 59.

47 B.C., that were made good by this donation (about or after 41 B.C.).[1] Plutarch himself doubted the reliability of his source (Calvisius?), and there is no confirmation anywhere else that a transfer of the whole library took place. It is hard to imagine how, for instance, the most distinguished native of Pergamum in the second century A.D., Galen, could have written a number of his immensely learned works in that city, to which he twice returned from abroad, if it had been robbed of its library; the same may be said of Galen's older contemporary and fellow citizen Telephus, a prolific writer on grammatical subjects.[2]

Alexandria was partly Pergamum's model, partly its rival, and we have already had to make some comparisons. In scholarship, we saw, Crates was the dominating figure in Pergamum; in contrast to the Alexandrian scholar poets he and his pupils approached the literary heritage as philosophers, and in particular as orthodox Stoics.[3] This difference in general approach did not prevent the younger Pergamenes profiting from the advances that Alexandrian scholarship had made in the course of a century or more.

Orthodox Stoics were necessarily allegorists in their interpretation of poetry. Allegorism was not new. There is genuine allegory in the *Iliad* itself, the Λιταί-passage *I* 502 ff.[4] Early interpreters of Homer in the sixth century B.C. claimed to have discovered hidden meanings in many other passages, particularly when they tried to justify Homer against his detractors.[5] In the fifth and fourth centuries Anaxagoras' pupil Metrodorus from Lampsacus seems to have been a true allegorist, but not Democritus or any of the Sophists. Plato and Aristotle rejected allegorism, and so consequently did the Academy as well as the Peripatos. There is, however, now evidence that in the fourth century members of the Orphic sect composed an allegorical commentary on Orpheus' *Cosmogony* to which Euripides, Aristophanes, and Plato alluded; this was a highly appropriate text for an allegorical treatment,[6] combined with that 'etymology' which tried to find the 'true' meanings of words, and with the explanation of glosses. Though more elementary, it is in the line of Metrodorus.

But the world-wide spread of allegorism was due to its acceptance by the Stoic school. Leading Stoic philosophers (though not all of them) took up the old threads and connected them with their own basic

---

[1] See above, p. 217, n. 4. [2] Cf. Wendel, *RE* v A (1934) 369.
[3] Cf. above, p. 140. [4] See above, p. 5.
[5] See above Pt. I, chapters I–III *passim*.
[6] See Kapsomenos, Ἀρχ. Δελτ. 19. 22 (above, p. 103, n. 1); see also below, p. 239.

doctrines.[1] As the λόγος (reason) is the fundamental principle of everything, it must manifest itself in poetry also, though hidden behind the veil
of mythical and legendary tales and pure fiction. Zeno[2] and Cleanthes
initiated this new 'method', and Chrysippus of Soloi perfected it; 'Chrysippus[3] ... vult Orphei, Musaei, Hesiodi Homerique fabellas accommodare
ad ea quae ipse ... de deis immortalibus dixerat, ut etiam veterrimi
poetae ... Stoici fuisse videantur.' In that way they secured the support
of Homer and the other great poets of the past for their own philosophy.
Crates, whose own teacher is still unknown, was born in Cilicia like
Chrysippus; he agreed in principle with him, but his aim was different.
Stoic philosophy was no longer in need of corroboration or illustration
by the early poets; on the contrary, Crates could now use the philosophy
to give a complete new interpretation of the true meaning of the Homeric
poems. He may have been unconscious of doing violence to poetry; certainly a great many future scholars down to the present day have been
induced by his example to apply philosophical doctrines in various forms
to the explanation of poetic and prosaic literature.

Crates is said by Suidas to have been a contemporary of Aristarchus
under the reign of Ptolemy Philometor, which roughly coincided with
the reign of Eumenes II in Pergamum.[4] In conscious opposition to the
Alexandrian γραμματικοί the Στωϊκὸς φιλόσοφος revived the title of κριτικός,[5] using it, of course, in the wide philosophical sense we have just
tried to explain. But unfortunately there is no list of writings anywhere,
and the quotations we have very rarely mention the title of a book.
Suidas' biographical article correctly terms him Ὁμηρικός, but stops
short after a corrupt reference to one book on Homer.

It is generally assumed that Crates composed a 'commentary' on the
two Homeric poems. The actual references are: Κράτη[ς δ' ἐν . Δ]ιορθωτι-
κῶν ... φησίν on a reading in Φ 363;[6] Κράτης ἐν τοῖς Διορθωτικοῖς on the
proem of the so-called *Iliad* of Apellicon,[7] Κράτης ἐν τοῖς Περὶ διορθώσεως

[1] Pohlenz, *Stoa* I 97 and references II 55.
[2] See above, p. 154, on chronology.
[3] Cic. *de nat. deor.* I 41 = *SVF* II p. 316, Chrys. fr. 1077.
[4] H. J. Mette, *Sphairopoiia. Untersuchungen zur Kosmologie des Krates von Pergamon* (1936)
103–10, test. 1–18. Test. 1 = Suid. s.v. Κράτης Τιμοκράτους Μαλλώτης; W. Kroll, *RE* xi
(1922) 1634–41; Pohlenz, *Stoa* I 182 f. and II 92.
[5] See above, p. 157, n. 4 and p. 159, n. 6; cf. esp. Sext. Emp. *adv. math.* I 79. 248.
[6] *P.Oxy.* II (1899) 221. col. XVII 30, Scholia on Φ, ed. Grenfell and Hunt, p. 74; between ἐν
and Δ]ιορθ. one letter seems to be missing, the number of the book. Crates is quoted also col.
XIV 9 on Φ 282. The same title Schol. AT Ξ 255 Καλλίστρατος (Καλλίμαχος T) ἐν τοῖς Διορθωτικοῖς, probably identical with his σύγγραμμα Περὶ 'Ιλιάδος (Schol. A B I 11. 131. 435), and
Schol. (HP) η 80 Χαῖρις ... ἐν Διορθωτικοῖς, apparently not a ὑπόμνημα; cf. also Schol. A
P 607 Δίδυμος ἐν τοῖς Διορθωτικοῖς and Ω 557 Δ. ἐν πρώτῳ Διορθωτικῶν.
[7] An excerpt in Osann's *Anecd. Roman.* after the 'Vita Romana' and the section on the

on the meaning of a gloss in μ 89.[1] We should not be misled by the doubtful remark in all our manuscripts of Suidas at the end of his article on
Crates: συνέταξε †δὲ ὄρθωσιν† 'Ιλιάδος καὶ 'Οδυσσείαις βιβλία θ καὶ ἄλλα;
this is all too easily changed into διόρθωσιν (and into ἐν βιβλίοις) and then
used for the conclusion that Crates made a critical recension of the text.[2]
The three quotations in grammatical literature do not point either to an
ἔκδοσις or to a ὑπόμνημα, but to a writing on the Homeric text in the
style of the traditional Περί-literature.[3] Only one other title is twice
quoted: Κράτης ἐν β τῶν 'Ομηρικῶν on the Oceanus in Φ 195 f. (εἶπε δὲ
τῷ γ̄ ibid.)[4] and Κράτης ἐν δευτέρῳ 'Ομηρικῶν on a reading in Ο 193, in
which the poet tells of the division of the world into three parts, each
with its divine ruler.[5] As Διορθωτικά and 'Ομηρικά can hardly be the
same, it is most likely that Crates composed two monographs in more
than one book each, the former perhaps in nine books (βιβλία θ?). In the
Διορθωτικά textual criticism may have predominated, in the 'Ομηρικά
(sc. ζητήματα, προβλήματα?) cosmological and geographical problems
with allegorical explanations; but the quotations rather suggest a free
mixture in the two monographs. We should perhaps compare the Orphic
commentary of the fourth century B.C. with this similar combination of
allegorical and lexical comments on a much higher level in Crates. It
is just possible that he wrote more books on related subjects than the two
of which the titles are known.[6]

The Ἀριστάρχειοι, Didymus and Aristonicus, did not pay much atten-
tion to Crates' heretical views; our main sources of the fragments,[7]
therefore, are not the Scholia in the Venetus A, but the exegetical
Scholia in the other manuscripts of the *Iliad* B (Ven. 453), T (Townleianus
Brit. Mus. Burnley 86), Gen. (Genav. 44), and the related Scholia in
P.Oxy. 221, together with Scholia in a few manuscripts of the *Odyssey*

σημεῖα (see below, p. 240, n. 1) refers to special proems of the *Iliad*, see T. W. Allen, Hom. *Il.*
II (1931) p. 1 to *A* 1; *Vitae Homeri* p. 32. 20 Wil., who printed by mistake Κρ. ἐν διορθωτικαῖς.

[1] Schol. HM μ 89; on διόρθωσις see above, p. 216.
[2] Suid. v. Κράτης (above, p. 238, n. 4). The editio Basileensis printed διόρθωσιν; βιβλία
cod. G, βιβλίοις cett. codd.
[3] See above, p. 218.
[4] Schol. Gen. Φ 195 = fr. 32a Mette; if εἶπε τῷ γ̄ means τῶν 'Ομηρικῶν, the work had at
least three books.
[5] Schol. A Ο 193.
[6] See E. Maass, 'Aratea', *Philolog. Untersuchungen* 12 (1892) 170 ff.; I cannot accept his
conclusions.
[7] We have no complete collection of fragments; K. Wachsmuth, *De Cratete Mallota* (1860),
is antiquated; the carefully edited texts in Mette, *Sphairopoiia* (1936) 112–298, continued in
Mette, *Parateresis*, Untersuchungen zur Sprachtheorie des Krates von Pergamon (1952)
65–185 with bibliography and Quellenindex, are very helpful; but Mette emphasizes in his
introduction p. VI. 5 that his 'texts' are not a collection of fragments, but are confined to the
problems discussed in the two books and designed only to help the reader.

(HM), and particularly Eustathius, who was able to excerpt Scholia lost to us. These sources are supplemented by the monographs on allegory, Ps.-Heraclitus ἀλληγορίαι and Ps.-Plutarch on Homer. The rivalry between Aristarchus and Crates in readings of the text and in the method of interpretation is visible everywhere, but it is not at all certain which wrote earlier; if it were better attested that the sign of διπλῆ περιεστιγμένη was used πρὸς τὰς γραφὰς ... Κράτητος by Aristarchus (?),[1] the priority of Crates' Διορθωτικά over Aristarchus' second ἔκδοσις would be established.

Examples of Crates' readings can be found in the lines quoted above from his two Homeric monographs; the most conspicuous instance of his exposition of a whole episode is his allegorical interpretation of Σ 483–608, the making by Hephaestus of the shield of Achilles. The Aristonicus Scholion on Σ 483[2] tells us that Zenodotus athetized the whole passage; why he did so is anybody's guess, as in the case of all his other atheteses and conjectures.[3] He apparently found some fault with the very detailed description of Hephaestus' masterpiece, as having no parallel in Homeric poetry, and obelizing it was the only course available to him.[4] From that day onwards the 'Shield' has been a matter of dispute in all ages; Wilamowitz, for instance, admired Zenodotus' boldness and acuteness. Crates, far from suspecting the description as an interpolation, found another solution, the same that he applied to the shield of Agamemnon Λ 32–40: Homer, in depicting ten parts of a shield, meant something else, namely the ten circles of the sky.[5] The uniqueness of the 125 lines is justified in his opinion, in that they express the fundamental cosmic knowledge and wisdom of the poet behind the veil of words which only the interpreting philosopher is able to remove. The sentence in Schol. Arat. *Ph.* 26 δημιουργῷ γὰρ τῷ Ἡφαίστῳ χρησάμενος τῆς Ἀχιλλέως ἀσπίδος ⟨ταύτ⟩ην ὑπέθετο κόσμου μίμημα can be confidently attributed to Crates, as it is identical with that on Agamemnon's shield in Schol. T Λ 40 ταύτην δὲ ὁ Κράτης μίμημα τοῦ κόσμου φησὶν εἶναι. The sober-minded Alexandrian grammarians had no use for fancies of that sort; it is understandable, however, that Crates impressed and even influenced later Stoic philosophers when they had to deal with Homer. Posidonius

---

[1] *Anecd. Roman.* (see above, p. 178, n. 10) p. XLIII 15 Dind. Ἀριστάρχεια σημεῖα . . . ἡ περιεστιγμένη διπλῆ πρὸς τὰς Ζηνοδοτείους γραφὰς (above, p. 218) καὶ Κράτητος καὶ αὐτοῦ Ἀριστάρχου κτλ.; cf. ibid. p. XLV 15 *Anecd. Ven.*; Mette, *Sphairop.* test. 18 a, b, see also Wachsmuth. The priority of Crates seems to be implied by Varro *L.L.* VIII 68 (= Crat. fr. 64a p. 100. 31 Mette) 'sic enim respondere voluit Aristarchus Crateti.'
[2] See above, p. 175, n. 6.
[3] See above, pp. 108 ff.
[4] Cf. above, p. 231; he did not question the few lines dealing with Agamemnon's shield.
[5] Mette, *Sphairopoiia* 36 ff. on Σ 468 ff., 30 ff. on Λ 32 ff.; fr. 23 a–i pp. 172–88.

became a 'moderate Cratetean'[1] and believed he had discovered in Homer the knowledge of the tide of the Ocean by which he felt his own theories confirmed; this was his aim as it had been that of his predecessors from Zeno to Chrysippus, while Crates as a scholar made it his prime endeavour to explain Homer.

What we know of Crates' etymologies[2] suggests that they are part of his Homeric exegesis. In the second century B.C. etymology was not yet an essential branch of grammar.[3] Chrysippus had been the Stoic specialist Περὶ ἐτυμολογικῶν,[4] but his influence on Crates seems to have been negligible except in the explication of the names of gods, as for instance Ζεύς (fr. 2 and 3 Mette) and ῞Ηιε Φοῖβε (fr. 55). As a ῾Ομηρικός Crates sides in this field more with the Alexandrian grammarians than with Chrysippus, which is not so surprising if we compare his attitude to several other problems of language.

A few references to epic, lyric, and dramatic poetry show that he interested himself in various non-Homeric problems; but no title of a ὑπόμνημα or a monograph is quoted anywhere, and modern efforts to attribute the fragments to books with invented titles have been unsuccessful.[5]

As a Stoic cosmologist, Crates was bound to criticize Hesiod's account of Γῆ and Οὐρανός (Schol. Hes. *Th.* 126 = fr. 47 Mette). His interest in the Hesiodic poems, however, went much further; he rejected a line about the godlike Cyclopes (Hes. *Th.* 142) and was bold enough to substitute an alternative one, possibly of his own manufacture.[6] He athetized not only the proem of the *Erga*, as Praxiphanes and Aristarchus had done, but also that of the *Theogony*.[7] Of the post-classical poetry Aratus' astronomical *Phaenomena* attracted his attention, though the relevant fragments belong to his writings on Homer.[8] He was again on the side of Aristarchus and also of Aristotle in the puzzling controversy about Alcman's birthplace[9] since according to Suidas he believed him

---

[1] K. Reinhardt, 'Posidonius' *RE* xxii 667 ff., esp. 668. 24 ff.; he had reconstructed Crates' allegorical comment on the shield of Achilles and Eustathius' (cf. esp. pp. 1154. 35 ff.) intermediate source in his dissertation *De Graecorum theologia capita duo* (1910) 59 ff. 'De Cratete Mallota'.

[2] R. Schröter, *Studien zur Varronischen Etymologie* (1959) 64 ff.

[3] Cf. R. Reitzenstein, 'Etymologika', *RE* vi (1909) 810.

[4] See above, p. 201, n. 5.

[5] Wachsmuth, *De Crat. Mall.* 55 ff.; critical objections by E. Maass, *Aratea* 167 ff., 213. 4; sensible Kroll, *RE* xi 1635.

[6] Jacoby ad loc.; I refused to believe that epic lines were fabricated by Zenodotus, but should not think it impossible in Crates.

[7] See above, p. 220, on the *Erga*; on the *Theogony* see Jacoby test. 47 b (Vita Chisiana) p. 125. [8] See Maass, *Aratea* 33 ff., 165 ff.

[9] D. L. Page, Alcman *Partheneion* (1951) 167 ff.

to have been a Lydian from Sardis; a newly discovered commentary on
Alcman has proved beyond doubt that this view was derived from
passages in the poems[1] while the opposition seems to have based its
assumption of Alcman's Laconian origin on local patriotism. Interested
as Crates naturally was in the astronomical passage of the *Rhesus*,[2] he
criticized Euripides' ignorance of astronomy, excusing it, however, on
the ground that the play was an early one of the young poet; it is at least
probable that for this statement he had consulted the διδασκαλίαι, which
were accessible in the introductions of Aristophanes of Byzantium. Like
the Peripatetics and the Alexandrians he did not question the authenticity
of the play, as 'some' (ἔνιοι) did in ancient and many in modern times.[3]
Crates is said to have dealt with the 'parts of comedy' (κατὰ Κράτητα . . .
μέρη κωμῳδίας),[4] and his pupil Herodicus listed the Κωμῳδούμενοι,[5] like
Ammonius, but there is no reason to conjecture that the Pergamenes[6] distinguished two periods of Attic comedy (ἀρχαία and νέα) on stylistic–
rhetorical grounds, in contrast to the usual Hellenistic division into three
periods (ἀρχαία, μέση, νέα).

Even this short survey of scanty evidence gives the impression that
Crates was a serious scholar capable of displaying solid learning who did
not disregard the results of previous research, even though it was the
work of scholars who were his opponents in principle. If this is kept in
mind, the honesty and sincerity of his sometimes bewildering method of
allegorical interpretation can hardly be doubted.

All the pre-Hellenistic poets whose names occur in Crates' fragments
had their place in the Alexandrian selective lists which he certainly knew.
If the Pergamenes had their own lists of ἐγκριθέντες[7] as they had general
indexes, these lists, at least of the poets, cannot have differed much from
the Alexandrian ones, though there may have been in Pergamum a
keener interest in the orators. Whether Crates was concerned in ἐγκρίνειν
himself, we do not know; but we do know that he who proudly claimed
to be a κριτικός, not a simple[8] γραμματικός, practised the κρίσις ποιημάτων.

---

[1] *P.Oxy.* 2389 (1957) fr. 9 I 11; cf. fr. 6 I 6 ff. On Aristarchus see above, p. 220.
[2] Schol. [Eur.] *Rhes.* 539 f., cf. above, p. 223, n. 5; on Aristoph. Byz. and Dicaearch.
see p. 193.
[3] See E. Fraenkel's detailed review of W. Ritchie, 'The Authenticity of the *Rhesus* of
Euripides' (1964) in *Gnom.* 37 (1965) 228–41.
[4] Tzetz. *Proleg.* p. 21. 68 Kaibel.   [5] Athen. 586 A, 591 C.
[6] G. Kaibel, *Herm.* 24 (1889) 56 ff., cf. Susemihl 1 426. 88; but see the objections by
A. Körte, 'Komödie', *RE* XI (1921) 1256 f., esp. 1257. 48 ff.
[7] See above, p. 206.
[8] Sext. Emp. *adv. math.* I 79 = Crat. fr. 17 Mette τὸν μὲν κριτικὸν πάσης, φησί, δεῖ λογικῆς
ἐπιστήμης ἔμπειρον εἶναι, τὸν δὲ γραμματικὸν ἁπλῶς γλωσσῶν ἐξηγητικῶν καὶ προσῳδίας
ἀποδοτικὸν καὶ τῶν τούτων παραπλησίων εἰδήμονα; cf. ibid. I 248 = fr. 18 M.

As the readings and explanations of the last editor of the Philodemus-papyrus Περὶ ποιημάτων were apparently confirmed by a careful re-examination,[1] it is not unlikely that Crates was guided by Chrysippus' theory of φωνή, and claimed to recognize the value of a poem from the sound of its words, from euphony, by the mere act of hearing (ἀκοή).

A sordid epigram attacking Euphorion[2] which is anonymous in Planudes bears in *AP* XI 218 the name Κράτητος. The two spiteful distichs are rather pointless if not written in or near Euphorion's lifetime. It was not a good idea[3] to ascribe this accumulation of obscene implications to the scholar from Mallos, who could hardly have started to write before Euphorion's death (about 200 B.C.); we should also expect that this Crates would have put his own theory into practice and striven for euphony which is totally absent from the epigram. There have been many Κράτητες,[4] and among them even an epigrammatist (Diog. L. IV 23); one can definitely acquit the Mallotes of perpetrating this sort of poetry. There is no evidence that he or any of his pupils wrote verse.

Allegorism was, we saw, an essential part of Stoic philosophical thought, particularly as developed by Chrysippus;[5] then Crates applied it to his new exposition of Homeric poetry. There is a noticeable parallel in the field of language. Chrysippus, in the wake of Zeno and Cleanthes, had expounded a theory of language within the wider scheme of his formal logic;[6] in the next generation Crates adopted his concept of linguistic anomaly and, like all the adherents of the Stoic school, accepted certain grammatical rules. We took pains earlier to find out how some of the Ionian poets foreshadowed patterns of declension and etymology,[7] and to consider how far the Sophists and Democritus, Plato and Aristotle were devoted to linguistic studies. But it was among the Stoics that

---

[1] Chr. Jensen, Philodemos *Über die Gedichte*, v. Buch (1923) 146 ff. 'Zur Poetik des Krates von Pergamon'; the reading of col. XXI 25, pp. 48 f. = fr. 86 Mette p. 182. I is decisive, cf. 59 f. See now F. Sbordone, 'Filodemo e la teoria dell' eufonia', *Rendiconti della Accademia di Archeologia, Lettere e Belle Arti*, N.S. XXX (Napoli 1955) 25–51.

[2] See above, p. 150.

[3] A. Meineke, *Analecta Alexandrina* (1843) 7 f., 30 ff. Meineke's authority never lost its influence in spite of occasional objections, see M. Gabathuler, *Hellenistische Epigramme auf Dichter* (1937) 94, 172 and A. S. F. Gow, *The Greek Anthology* II (1965) 222 f. On the epigrammatist Crates see Geffcken, *RE* XI 1625.

[4] Another of these Κράτητες is the author of a work on Attic dialect frequently quoted by Athenaeus; it is almost certainly the Athenian who also wrote Περὶ τῶν Ἀθήνησι θυσιῶν, not the Pergamene grammarian. Mette's arguments (*Parateresis* 48 ff.) for his authorship are not convincing. All the fragments are now collected and commented on by F. Jacoby *FGrHist* 362 'Krates von Athen' (vol. III B 1950–5).

[5] See p. 238.

[6] See p. 203 about the relation of words to things; language was to him, of course, φύσει, not θέσει, cf. above, p. 63.

[7] See above, pp. 12 ff.

a definite place was accorded to these studies in their system of philosophy; grammatical rules and terms were now strictly fixed and the preliminary efforts of centuries completed.

Only a few examples[1] can be given, mainly to show the relation of the Stoic to earlier classifications and terms. Four parts of speech (μέρη τοῦ λόγου) were taken over from Aristotle:[2] ὄνομα, ῥῆμα, ἄρθρον, σύνδεσμος. But in the first part a new subdivision was made (by Chrysippus?) between the ὄνομα as 'proper name' (later κύριον ὄνομα) and the προσηγορικόν, 'the appellative'. The term πτῶσις, formerly applied to various changes of word-forms and derivations,[3] was confined to ὄνομα and ἄρθρον and to their four 'cases', one ὀρθή and three πλάγιαι. This is particularly noteworthy as the three πλάγιαι πτώσεις are already present in Anacreon's Cleobulus poem and all four in Archilochus' Leophilus-Iambus.[4] The rhetorician Cleochares who in the first half of the third century B.C. surprisingly played with five cases of a proper name, including the vocative (Δημόσθενες), may have been acquainted with a theoretical order of that time unknown to us;[5] what we find in early Ionic poetry of the seventh and sixth centuries B.C. was obviously only a playing at will on the changing forms of the same words.

As regards the nomenclature of the individual πτώσεις, which all of us still learn in school, the name of the αἰτιατικὴ πτῶσις, 'accusativus', always caused uneasiness and is still under discussion. The difficulty has been to reconcile the usage of this case with the natural derivation of the word αἰτιατική from αἰτιᾶσθαι, 'accuse', ('in accusandi' sc. casu, Varro, *L.L.* VIII 66), or from αἴτιον, 'cause'; so the proposal was made[6] that the name should be understood as derived from αἰτιατόν 'the effect' (Aristot. *An. post.* 98 a 36, al.), and this was accepted with unanimous applause as correct for the case that denotes the effect of an action. But quite recently it has been argued with great subtlety[7] that there is at least a possibility of maintaining the origin of the term from αἰτιᾶσθαι via the construction of the accusative with the infinitive and the accusative in *oratio obliqua* to which Aristotle referred repeatedly in Περὶ σοφιστικῶν ἐλέγχων.

---

[1] Cf. Steinthal I 271 ff., J. Wackernagel, *Vorlesungen über Syntax* I 14 ff., R. H. Robins, *Ancient and Mediaeval Grammatical Theory* (1951) 25 ff., Barwick, *Stoische Sprachlehre, passim*, and above all M. Pohlenz, 'Begründung der abendländischen Sprachlehre durch die Stoa', *GGN* 1939 = *Kleine Schriften* I (1965) 39 ff., and *Die Stoa* (1948/9) I 37 ff., II 21 ff.

[2] Above, pp. 76 f.   [3] See, pp. 77 f.

[4] See p. 13, n. 1 on πτῶσις.

[5] See p. 14, n. 1.

[6] F. A. Trendelenburg, *Acta Societatis Graecae Lipsiensis* I (1836) 123; cf. Wackernagel, *Vorlesungen über Syntax* I 19, Sandys I³ 147, Wilamowitz, *Griech. Lesebuch*, Erläuterungen, 2. Halbbd. 245 (on Dionys. Thr. in Textbd. II 384. 21).

[7] E. Kapp, 'Casus accusativus', *Festschrift B. Snell* (1956) 17–21.

In the traditional division of nouns into three genders the name of the third gender had changed once already (from σκεῦος to μεταξύ) ;[1] it now became οὐδέτερον 'neuter', that is, neither masculine nor feminine.

There was no clear statement before Aristotle that the different forms of the ῥῆμα, the verb, express different temporal relations; the Stoics, with a delicate sense of language, fixed six χρόνοι 'tenses', four ὡρισμένοι (present, imperfect, perfect, pluperfect) and two ἀόριστοι (future and aorist).

Many details of the development remain obscure to us; but the final standardization and codification of the τέχνη γραμματική is extant, not in a book of a Stoic philosopher, but in the handbook of an Ἀριστάρχειος, Dionysius Thrax.[2] We mentioned earlier the dispute[3] between the Stoic anomalists to whom Crates belonged and the so-called Alexandrian analogists, a dispute so often stressed in later Latin[4] and modern literature. It should not be overemphasized; for there was always a lively interplay between the opposite camps, which led to a sort of reconciliation in Dionysius' book. The most remarkable point of contact was this: although Aristophanes' main approach was to deduce a few general rules of inflexion from his discovery of analogous patterns in the declension,[5] he also observed with an open mind the variety of forms in the spoken language, the συνήθεια. It was just this observation of irregularity in which Crates excelled. Sextus Empiricus termed it τὴν κατὰ τὴν κοινὴν τῶν πολλῶν συνήθειαν παρατήρησιν ;[6] this term, so often used by the school of medical empiricists, has not yet turned up in the quotations of Crates himself or of his pupils, but it characterizes his procedure. It may even be that this empirical observation itself and its name were due to a new influence of science on scholarship.[7]

The Pergamene scholars of the next generation who are known to have been Crates' own pupils[8] were not of very high standing. But the leading Stoic philosopher Panaetius is also attested as his μαθητής. While others of the so-called Κρατήτειοι continued to fight the Alexandrians to some extent, Panaetius fully appreciated the greatness of Aristarchus as an interpreter[9]—as, on the other hand, Aristarchus' school willingly acknowledged the superiority of the Pergamenes in the field of grammar.[10]

---

[1] See above, p. 77.   [2] Below, Chapter 8.   [3] See p. 203.
[4] Gell. *N.A.* II 25. 4 'duo Graeci grammatici illustres Aristarchus et Crates summa ope ille ἀναλογίαν, hic ἀνωμαλίαν defensitavit' (= Crat. fr. 64 b p. 138. 12 Mette).
[5] See above, pp. 202 f.; cf. p. 229.
[6] Sext. Emp. *adv. math.* 1 179 (= Crat. fr. 64 e p. 140. 33 Mette).
[7] K. Deichgräber, *Die griechische Empirikerschule* (1930) 378 παρατηρεῖν; Mette, *Parateresis passim*, but see the critical objections of R. Schröter, *Gnom.* 27 (1955) 328 ff.
[8] Kroll, *RE* XI (1922) 1640. 57 ff.   [9] See above, p. 232.   [10] See below, p. 270.

However, Crates' most far-reaching influence derived from his mission to Rome in 168 B.C. Rome's contact with Greek culture had begun four or five centuries before that mission, and the Hellenization of its literature was intensified in the second half of the third century B.C. by translations of Greek poetry into Latin. Rome had its own scholar poets before Crates' visit. This visit was unexpectedly prolonged when he broke his leg in a defective cloaca on the Palatine hill, and he used the time of his recovery for giving lectures to a Roman audience; the effect on the Romans was, as Suetonius[1] tells, 'ut carmina diligentius retractarent ac legendo commentandoque etiam ceteris nota facerent'. It was not a bad omen that the first personal approach to the Romans happened to be that of a Stoic scholar; for Stoicism always appealed to the Roman spirit.[2] The best example is Panaetius' intimacy with the younger Scipio and his friends in the following generation.

Compared with the Stoa other schools of philosophy in the later Hellenistic age were of secondary importance in scholarship as well as in other respects.[3] When, for instance, twelve years after Crates an Athenian delegation in which Carneades represented the Academy and Critolaus the Peripatos arrived in Rome, we hear nothing of their scholarly activity or influence. Not until the first century B.C. did Academy and Peripatos begin to edit and explain the writings of their own founders, and to continue in some way the work of Aristophanes and Aristarchus as editors and interpreters.

This chapter on Pergamum must conclude with a glance at a side-line of scholarship. There were now a number of antiquarian writers[4] who made their compilations not from literary sources or from the narratives of visitors from abroad, but from autopsy. Callimachus, for his part, had insisted on the fact that he had never traversed the sea[5] but collected his immense learning at home in Alexandria; and his disciples followed his example. But now we find travellers who described places they had personally inspected and all their treasures. The earliest in Pergamum may have been Antigonus of Carystus, whom Attalus I (241–197 B.C.) called to his court; if the identification of at least three bearers of this

[1] Sueton. *De grammaticis et rhetoribus* c. 2, see above, p. 235, n. 2.

[2] M. Pohlenz, *Die Stoa* I 257 ff. 'Die Stoa in Rom'.

[3] The meagre testimonia are collected by M. Gigante, 'Poesia e critica letteraria nell' Accademia antica', *Miscellanea di Studi Alessandrini in memoria di A. Rostagni* (1963) 234 ff., C. O. Brink, 'Peripatos', *RE*, Suppl. Bd. VII (1940) 937 ff.; Ph. de Lacy, 'The Epicurean Analysis of Language', *AJP* 60 (1939) 85 ff.

[4] On the terms ἀρχαιολογία and 'antiquitates' see above, p. 51.

[5] Call. fr. 178. 27 ff. and vol. II p. xxxix.

name is correct,[1] he must have been a unique figure. He examined works of art with the keen eyes of the artist—he was a sculptor himself—and depicted them in his writings; it was Antigonus who noticed that the famous statue of Nemesis in Rhamnus ἔχει ἐν τῇ χειρὶ μηλέας κλάδον· ἐξ οὗ
... πτύχιόν τι μικρὸν ἐξηρτῆσθαι τὴν ἐπιγραφὴν ἔχον "Ἀγοράκριτος Πάριος ἐποίησεν."[2] Elsewhere we find him copying Παράδοξα verbatim from Callimachus in the traditional way.[3] But again, as a biographer, he rejected the literary approach of Hermippus and Satyrus[4] and the like and gave first-hand character sketches of his contemporaries, especially of the philosophers he had met in Athens and in other cities.

Compared with this picturesque, versatile personality of the later third century, Polemo,[5] a native of Ilium and therefore a subject of the Attalids, was very much a specialist, an immensely learned antiquary, ὁ κληθεὶς Περιηγητής (Suid.). The geographical periegesis is as old as the Γῆς περίοδος 'the journey round the world' of Hecataeus of Miletus in the early fifth century B.C.; but the 'antiquarian' periegesis,[6] not concerned with geography, but with antiquities and in particular with monuments, is a new feature of the Hellenistic age. It was gratefully used in the second half of the second century A.D. by Pausanias[7] who combined what he had seen with what he had read in his Ἑλλάδος Περιήγησις, the only periegesis completely preserved. Polemo was honoured in 177/6 B.C.[8] by being made a πρόξενος in Delphi, probably in recognition of his book Περὶ τῶν ἐν Δελφοῖς θησαυρῶν (fr. 27 Pr.); for similar reasons he was given the

---

[1] Wilamowitz, *Antigonos von Karystos* (1881). H. Usener happily appreciated the dedication of this book, see *Usener und Wilamowitz*, Ein Briefwechsel 1870–1905 (1934), Nr. 12–14. H. Diels, *DLZ* III (1882) 604 f., approved of its bold hypotheses. To E. Rohde, *Lit. Zentralbl.* (1882) 56 ff. = *Kl. Schriften* I 356 ff., the 'style' was repellent and the self-confidence of the young genius was irritating. In the background there was, besides the old controversy between Wilamowitz and Nietzsche, Rohde's own quite different conception of the Hellenistic age. The bitterness of his final verdict 'Originalität des Humbugs', is understandable, but nevertheless unjust.—There is still a certain doubt about some of the identifications, as no one has re-examined all the arguments of Wilamowitz.

[2] Zenob. vulg. v 82; the lexicographers, Phot., etc., omitted the reference to Antigonus.

[3] See above, p. 134.

[4] See above, p. 151.

[5] Polemonis Periegetae *Fragmenta* coll. L. Preller, 1838 (reprinted 1964); cf. the review of O. Jahn, *Jahrbücher für wissenschaftliche Kritik* 2 (1840) 585–605. K. Deichgräber, *RE* XXI (1952), 1288 ff.

[6] The distinction is drawn by F. Jacoby on 369 *FGrHist* (vol. III B [1955], pp. 132 ff.) Kommentar I and II, pp. 90 f.; but I prefer the expression 'antiquarian periegesis' to his 'historical periegesis' (cf. Polemo, ed. Preller, p. 155). A useful survey is given by H. Bischoff, *RE* XIX (1937) 725 ff.; cf. E. Pernice, 'Handbuch der Archäologie' = *Handbuch der Altertumswissenschaft* VI 1 (1939) 240 ff. 'Periegeten und Periegesen'.

[7] G. Pasquali, 'Die schriftstellerische Form des Pausanias', *Herm.* 48 (1913) 161 ff.

[8] *SIG*³ 585. 114 Πολέμων Μιλησίου Ἰλιεύς: Suid. s.v. puts him under Ptolemy V (204–180 B.C.) as a contemporary of Aristophanes of Byzantium, but adds καὶ διήκουσε καὶ τοῦ Ῥοδίου Παναιτίου.

citizenship of Athens and other cities. The Delphian inscription is the best evidence for the date of his life and shows that he was a contemporary of Aristophanes and Aristarchus. His Ἐπιστολὴ πρὸς Ἄτταλον (fr. 70, 72 Pr.) may have been addressed to king Attalus I (241–197 B.C.).

About thirty titles of Polemo's writings are known; one of them in at least six books improved on the description of works of art given by Antigonus of Carystus and Adaeus,[1] and he is known to have stated in it that the old Attic pronunciation was Ἀζηνιεῖς, Ἐρχιεῖς, Ἁλιεῖς with rough breathing.[2] A new fragment in the papyrus commentary on Hipponax to which we referred above[3] is welcome as additional evidence for the attention that he paid to questions of language: he is quoted for the explanation of σαννάδες as 'wild goats', a dialectal gloss peculiar probably to the Cretans.[4] Polemo's sources were the inscriptions. They had not been neglected by the historians from early times onwards; but it is uncertain how far even Craterus,[5] when he made his ψηφισμάτων συναγωγή about 300 B.C., used the archives and how far he worked at the stones. We do know, however, that Polemo went about copying inscriptions from the στῆλαι himself and was nicknamed στηλοκόπας by Crates' pupil Herodicus.[6] He had no true peer, until Cyriac of Ancona in the fifteenth century A.D. began once more to search out and record the remains of ancient monuments and inscriptions.

Polemo visited Asia Minor, the Aegean, the mother country, the western Magna Graecia, and Sicily; but his studies quite naturally centred on Athens. Four of his writings were devoted to its antiquities, one of them in four books to the votive offerings on the Acropolis (fr. 1–5 Pr.); we can add as a fifth item to this group his attack on Eratosthenes Περὶ τῆς Ἀθήνησιν Ἐρατοσθένους ἐπιδημίας (fr. 47–52 Pr., also abbreviated τὰ πρὸς Ἐρατοσθένην). Polemo, a much more acute and trained observer of the monuments than the great scientist and 'philologus', found him so often

---

[1] Πρὸς Ἀδαῖον καὶ Ἀντίγονον fr. 56–69 Pr., cf. pp. 193 f. Even if the text of the fragments is not expressly polemical, it is most likely that πρός means 'against', as it certainly does in some other comparable titles Πρὸς Τίμαιον (fr. 39 ff.), Πρὸς Ἐρατοσθένην (fr. 48 f.) and others. On πρός see above, p. 133, n. 1.

[2] Phot. Berol. pp. 38. 11 ff. Reitzenstein; Polem. fr. 65 Pr. from Suid. who copied Photius. On the aspiration see K. Meisterhans, *Grammatik der attischen Inschriften*[3] (1900) 86.

[3] See above, p. 199; *P.Oxy.* XVIII (1948) 2176, col. 1 6; it is overlooked in Deichgräber's article on Polemo, *RE* XXI (1952), where a reference to *P.Oxy.* 1611, 101–11 also is missing.

[4] Latte's reading and supplement Κρ[ῆτ]ας *Philol.* 97 (1948) 40 is compatible with the traces of ink and with the space.

[5] 342 *FGrHist.*

[6] Fr. 78 Pr. with an extensive commentary; but no one can tell what Herodicus exactly meant by his joke ('tablet-tapper' Sandys, 'tablet-glutton' L–S, etc.); Pasquali, *Herm.* 48, 177, understands the compound by analogy with λιθοκόπος as 'Steinhauer', which is not convincing at all.

at fault that he could not refrain from expressing the half humorous, half malicious doubt whether Eratosthenes had ever stayed at Athens;[1] at least three of the five certain fragments seem to allude to Eratosthenes' twelve books Περὶ τῆς ἀρχαίας κωμῳδίας.[2] Attic comedy had been a favourite subject of Alexandrian, though not of Pergamene scholarship. Polemo was able to draw on the work of the Alexandrians and to profit at the same time from his personal knowledge of the local monuments, festivals, and customs. In the same way his Sicilian visit furthered his acquaintance with Epicharmus and Doric comedy, as is revealed by his work in twelve books Πρὸς Τίμαιον (fr. 39–46 Pr.). Here he also traced the origin of parody to Hipponax, apparently in connexion with the study of early comedy (fr. 45); everywhere, we see, he freely indulged in excursuses.

Although an indefatigable traveller through the whole Greek world (not beyond it) Polemo did not lack a sense of local patriotism; Suidas opens the list of his writings with ἔγραψε Περιήγησιν ᾿Ιλίου ἐν βιβλίοις γ΄. No quotations from these three books survive, but it is possible to assign to them two fragments, one on the cult of Apollo in Σμίνθος, τόπος τῆς Τρῳάδος (fr. 31 Pr.), and another on the stone still shown to visitors in Ilium (fr. 32 Pr.), on which Palamedes was supposed to have played chess, the game invented by him in the dreary years of the Trojan war. This implies that Polemo identified his native place as the site of Homeric Troy and the battlefield of the *Iliad*. But there is not the slightest hint in the quotations and testimonia that he ever discussed this delicate problem. His name is not mentioned in the extensive treatment of it by his fellow countryman Demetrius of Scepsis,[3] although earlier writers are lavishly quoted, and no polemics between the two περιηγηταί on Homeric topography[4] are attested.

Demetrius' exposition of the Τρωϊκὸς διάκοσμος, 'The marshalling of the Trojan forces',[5] must have been written in the middle of the second century B.C., after Crates, whom he attacked (fr. 68 Gaede), and before Apollodorus, who had the book at hand for his Νεῶν κατάλογος.[6] He

---

[1] *FGrHist* 241 T 10; on Eratosthenes in Athens see above, pp. 153 f.

[2] See above, pp. 159 ff.

[3] R. Gaede, *Demetrii Scepsii quae supersunt*, Diss. Greifswald 1880; E. Schwartz, *RE* IV (1901) 2807 ff. = *Griechische Geschichtsschreiber* (1957) 106 ff.

[4] Sandys I³ 155 f. unfortunately gives the impression that Polemo and Demetrius forestalled the modern champions of this topic; Hellanicus 'of Miletus' is a slip of the pen.

[5] Strab. XIII 609 ἐκ δὲ τῆς Σκήψεως καὶ ὁ Δημήτριός ἐστιν, οὗ μεμνήμεθα πολλάκις, ὁ τὸν Τρωϊκὸν διάκοσμον ἐξηγησάμενος γραμματικός, κατὰ τὸν αὐτὸν χρόνον γεγονὼς Κράτητι καὶ ᾿Αριστάρχῳ.

[6] Strab. VIII 339 παρ᾽ οὗ (sc. Demetr. Sceps.) μεταφέρει τὰ πλεῖστα (sc. Apollodor.).

lived as a rich independent country squire[1]—an exceptional case for
a scholar—in his small home-town, which claimed to have been founded
by Scamandrius, son of Hector, and the only compliment he paid to the
Pergamene court was his quotation from a pamphlet of King Attalus I
(already dead) of the famous passage about the Καλὴ Πεύκη, the giant
pine tree, a landmark of the Troad.[2] In contrast to Polemo, Demetrius
confined himself to the topography and antiquities of his native country
and published the results of his researches in the form of an interpretation[3] of sixty-two lines of the second book of the *Iliad* (B 816–77), the
catalogue of the Trojans; in not writing a monograph Περὶ τοῦ Τρωϊκοῦ
διακόσμου,[4] he was following in principle the model of the Alexandrian,
especially the Aristarchean, ὑπόμνημα, but he inflated it to the monstrous
extent of thirty books.[5] All the information about peoples and places,
dialect glosses·and rare literary forms—but without Stoic allegories or
the like—he arranged according to the sequence of the Homeric lines.[6]

Demetrius reproached Hellanicus[7] with partiality for the inhabitants
of Ilium (χαριζόμενος τοῖς Ἰλιεῦσι) because he had supported in his
Τρωϊκά (about 400 B.C.) what was apparently the local opinion that the
modern and the Homeric town were the same. He in his turn, because he
rejected this opinion, was reproached by Schliemann with envying
Ilium's fame.[8] Yet Demetrius in fact called to witness τὴν Ἀλεξανδρίνην
Ἑστίαιαν who had written Περὶ τῆς Ὁμήρου Ἰλιάδος, . . . πυνθανομένην εἰ
περὶ τὴν νῦν πόλιν ὁ πόλεμος συνέστη,[9] though he did not say whether the
learned Alexandrian lady was the first to ask this question. In any case,
there is no trace of 'jealousy' in Demetrius' fragments; he took great pains
to argue his point, as he always did. He argued the case in good faith for
a hill some six miles further to the south on the other bank of the river
Scamander near Bunárbashi, and many modern experts from the end of
the eighteenth century onwards accepted his view. But the results of the
excavations from Schliemann's golden days up to the present time have

----

[1] Diog. L. v 84 πλούσιος καὶ εὐγενὴς ἄνθρωπος καὶ φιλόλογος ἄκρως.
[2] Strab. XIII 603 excerpting Demetrius; cf. W. Leaf, *Strabo and the Troad* (1923) XXVII ff.
and 204 f.
[3] ἐξηγησάμενος above, p. 249, n. 5, ἐξήγησιν below, n. 5.
[4] Strabo who still used the original (cf. Leaf, loc. cit.) never quoted Περὶ τοῦ Τρ. δ., but
always ἐν τῷ πρώτῳ (δευτέρῳ, etc.) τοῦ Τρ. δ.; Hestiaea's book was a monograph Περὶ τῆς
Ὁμήρου Ἰλιάδος.
[5] Strab. XIII 603 ἀνδρὶ ἐμπείρῳ καὶ ἐντοπίῳ φροντίσαντί τε τοσοῦτον περὶ τούτων ὥστε
τριάκοντα βίβλους συγγράψαι στίχων ἐξήγησιν μικρῷ πλειόνων ἑξήκοντα τοῦ καταλόγου τῶν
Τρώων.   [6] Gaede (above, p. 249, n. 3) 16.
[7] *FGrHist* 4 T 22 and F 25ᵇ (cf. F 31).
[8] H. Schliemann, *Trojanische Altertümer* (1874) Einleitung p. xl, cf. R. Jebb, *JHS* 2 (1881)
36 f.   [9] Strab. XIII 598 (= fr. 26 Gaede).

told against Demetrius. The final statement of C. W. Blegen was:[1] 'If there ever was a Troy (and who can really doubt it?), it must have stood on the hill at Hissarlik', and that means the region of Ilium.

The wide scope of original antiquarian research in Pergamum roused sincere enthusiasm in the nineteenth century[2] when a so-called realism felt the 'narrowness' of critical and grammatical scholarship and looked for all the manifestations of the spirit of the ancient world. Demetrius was justly praised, in so far as his realistic exegesis furthered the understanding of a special part of the *Iliad*. But in a case like his the poetry itself may get lost from sight behind the mountains of learned stuff heaped upon it. Five generations in Alexandria had been working to restore and to explain the literary creations of the past for their own sake. If the poems were to become merely sources for historical or topographical research, the objective of classical scholarship would be almost lost. This danger is for the first time apparent in the new Pergamene antiquarianism.

[1] 'The Principal Homeric Sites' in *A Companion to Homer* (1963) 385; this masterly survey is based on his own monumental work *Troy* 1–4 (1950–8) and gives references to Schliemann, Dörpfeld, Leaf, Page.

[2] See above, Preller, E. Schwartz, and the surprising hymn on Demetrius by Jebb, reprinted by Sandys 1³ 155.

VIII

THE EPIGONI: FROM ARISTARCHUS' PUPILS TO DIDYMUS

I T is a striking coincidence that scholarship was represented in the same generation at different places by Aristarchus, Crates of Mallos, and Demetrius of Scepsis; but only Aristarchus' school produced any great young scholars of distinction, Apollodorus of Athens and Dionysius Thrax.

The violence of Ptolemy VIII forced master and disciples, together with many others, to leave Alexandria;[1] this 'first crisis in the history of scholarship', as we have called it, led not to its extinction, but to its dissemination and renewal in other parts of the Greek world and finally in Rome. The only report of this crisis is preserved in an excerpt drawn by Athenaeus from the Χρονικά of Andron of Alexandria, who seems to have quoted Menecles of Barca,[2] possibly a contemporary of the crisis and himself an emigrant. This report, slightly confused in Athenaeus, needs and deserves more careful interpretation than it has received so far. In Pericles' Funeral Speech Thucydides (II 41. 1) glorified Athens: τὴν πᾶσαν πόλιν τῆς Ἑλλάδος παίδευσιν εἶναι, and Isocrates[3] loved to repeat this theme in many variations. The two Hellenistic historians[4] of the late second or early first century B.C. apparently had those famous words in mind when they made the even prouder claim that the Alexandrians εἰσιν οἱ παιδεύσαντες, πάντας τοὺς Ἕλληνας καὶ τοὺς βαρβάρους, only not all the Greeks as the Athenians had done, but Greeks and non-Greeks, the whole world.[5] After a period of decline (ἐκλειπούσης ἤδη τῆς ἐγκυκλίου παιδείας), the passage goes on, a revival took place, paradoxically as the consequence of the tyranny of Ptolemy VIII: ἐγένετο οὖν ἀνανέωσις πάλιν παιδείας ἁπάσης κατὰ τὸν ἕβδομον [6] . . . Πτολεμαῖον . . . καλούμενον Κακεργέτην. οὗτος γὰρ . . . οὐκ ὀλίγους . . . φυγαδεύσας . . . ἐποίησε πλήρεις τάς τε

---

[1] See above, p. 212.

[2] *FGrHist* 246 F 1 Andron, 270 F 9 Menekles; Athen. IV 184 BC.

[3] Isocr. *or.* 15 Περὶ ἀντιδόσεως 293 ff., etc.; see above, pp. 50 f.

[4] The following quotations are parts of the fragments just referred to.

[5] J. Jüthner, 'Hellenen und Barbaren', *Das Erbe der Alten*, N.F. VIII (1923) 7 and *passim*; it is out of the question that καὶ τοὺς βαρβάρους should mean in this context the Romans, as E. Schwartz, *RE* I 2160. (1899) 35, and F. Jacoby, *FGrHist* IIIa (1943) p. 223, are inclined to assume.

[6] About the differing figures see above, p. 211.

νήσους καὶ πόλεις ἀνδρῶν γραμματικῶν, φιλοσόφων, γεωμετρῶν, μουσικῶν, ζωγράφων, παιδοτριβῶν τε καὶ ἰατρῶν καὶ ἄλλων πολλῶν τεχνιτῶν, οἳ διὰ τὸ πένεσθαι διδάσκοντες ἃ ἠπίσταντο πολλοὺς κατεσκεύασαν ἄνδρας ἐλλογίμους. The παιδεία of Alexandria, with the qualification ἐγκύκλιος, was thus not identical with the lofty ideal of Greek culture in Thucydides and Isocrates, but meant hardly more than 'general education',[1] a syllabus of various subjects. That there are seven groups of men listed here who practised and taught them may be accidental, especially as the list ends with the words 'and of many other τεχνῖται'; but we ought to note that the list is headed by the γραμματικοί, and that 'grammar' remained the first of the three literary arts when the conventional sequence of the seven liberal arts was formulated.[2] From Alexandria the exiled and penniless γραμματικοί spread their τέχνη over the islands and the cities and stimulated intellectual life—among them Aristarchus' two prominent pupils: Apollodorus fled from Alexandria probably to Pergamum, and possibly returned later on to his native city Athens, Dionysius Thrax moved to the island of Rhodes, and both vigorously continued their scholarly work.

If this course of events was of considerable value to the places concerned, it also benefited Apollodorus[3] to have lived in all the three great cultural centres of his time, the old one as well as the two new ones. All that we know for certain of the facts and dates of his career is given by an anonymous Hellenistic geographer (about 100 B.C.), traditionally called Scymnus since the days of Lucas Holstein (1630) and Isaac Vossius (1639); in a long passage of the proem of Ps.-Scymnus' Περιήγησις,[4] written in comic trimeters, an unnamed φιλόλογος is described, born in Athens and a pupil there of a great teacher, the Stoic Diogenes of Babylon (who went on a mission to Rome in 155 and died about 151 B.C.), then collaborator with Aristarchus in Alexandria 'for a long time', and author of an iambic Chronicle of the 1,040 years from the fall of Troy (1184/3 B.C.) to the year in which the work was dedicated to King Attalus II Philadelphus of Pergamum (144/3 B.C.). Thomas Gale in 1675 rightly identified this φιλόλογος as Apollodorus of Athens.[5] If Apollodorus

---

[1] E. Norden, *Die antike Kunstprosa* II (1898) 670 f., Marrou see below, n. 2.

[2] See above, pp. 52 f. on Hippias the Sophist and cf. Marrou 176 f., 406 f. The important Hellenistic evidence, probably from the time of Dionysius Thrax, was not registered by F. Marx (p. 52, n. 8) and therefore neglected in the later literature on the artes. The ἰατροί and ζωγράφοι appear also in other lists.

[3] *FGrHist* (1929) 244 T 1–20, F 1–356, with commentary; cf. *RE* I 2 (1894) 855–75 by R. Münzel (life) and E. Schwartz (writings; reprinted in *Griech. Geschichtschreiber* 1957 pp. 253 ff.).

[4] *GGM* I 196 f., ll. 16–48 = T 2 Jac.; Diogenes Babyl. *SVF* III 210 ff.

[5] Th. Gale, *Historiae poeticae scriptores antiqui* (1675) 43 ff.

belonged to Diogenes' school in the early fifties, he was probably born about 180 B.C. As he dedicated the Chronicle to Attalus just a year after the catastrophe in Alexandria, we can assume that this dedication was either an attempt to support a request for refuge in Pergamum or an expression of thanks for his reception there. Not only was Pergamum, after Alexandria, the best place for a scholar, but Attalus, and his brother Eumenes before him, had been the greatest royal benefactors of Apollodorus' native city, Athens.

There is hardly anything to add to Ps.-Scymnus' information from other sources. The biographical tradition in Suidas[1] which makes Apollodorus a pupil of Panaetius is obviously wrong, since Panaetius was his coeval and had been a member of Diogenes' school himself. But it is suggested by Stratocles' excerpt in the papyrus 'Index Stoicorum', though not in the passage about Panaetius' pupils, that the γραμματικός and the Stoic φιλόσοφος were acquainted. Indeed the usual modern assumption that Apollodorus returned from Pergamum to Athens (after 133 B.C.?) is based on the supplement to the damaged line ὁ δὲ Πα[ναί]τιος καὶ τὸν γραμμ[ατικὸν Ἀ]πολλόδωρον ἀπ[εδέχετο,[2] which might mean that Panaetius, having finally returned from Rome (about 135 B.C.) and become head of the Stoic school in Athens (about 130 B.C.), 'welcomed him'. If Apollodorus added to the first three books of his Χρονικά, which ended (like Polybius' Ἱστορίαι) in 144/3 B.C., a fourth book reaching down to 120/19 B.C. or even to 110/09 B.C., as fragments 56 and 219 suggest, he may well have done so in Athens in the last decade of his life. There is no help to be gained from the 'Chrestomathy' which listed the γραμματικοί between famous painters and warriors; after the compiler had ended the catalogue of the heads of the Alexandrian library with the name of a military officer Cydas,[3] he made the further remark that 'under Ptolemy IX (116–80 B.C.) the grammarians Ammonius, Zeno[dotus], Diocles, and Apollodorus flourished (ἤκμασαν)'.[4] It may be that he meant the two well-known pupils of Aristarchus, Ammonius and Apollodorus of Athens, but if so he made a slip with his 'ninth' as he had done twice before with figures and names of kings; it may also be that he put together the names of persons belonging to a later generation who are unknown to us.

We owe to Ps.-Scymnus not only the reliable biographical material,

---

[1] *FGrHist* 244 T 1 = Panaet. fr. 148 van Straaten; even of Polemo who belonged to the generation of Aristophanes of Byzantium it is said that he διήκουσε καὶ τοῦ Ῥοδίου Παναιτίου = Panaet. fr. 7. Conjectures are quite useless; someone, writing on Panaetius, had produced wrong synchronisms.

[2] *Ind. Stoic. Hercul.* col. LXIX ed. A. Traversa (1952) 90 = Panaet. fr. 149.

[3] See above, p. 212.

[4] *P.Oxy.* 1241, col. II 17 ff.; on Ammonius see above, p. 216.

but also a sketch of the contents of the Χρονικά[1] (ll. 25–32) and an explanation of the uncommon use of a metrical form (33–44) instead of prose; as he was an admiring and faithful reader of the original, from which he even transferred a whole line with very slight changes (l. 21∼ Apollod. F 58. 3), we can take his words as authentic. He repeated Apollodorus' own argument that the comic trimeter was chosen for mnemonic purposes.[2] It must have been an unexpected novelty[3] for his contemporaries that an Aristarchean scholar should strive for popularity and therefore risk writing an immensely learned book in a 'poetic' form intended to be an aid to the memory. Apollodorus displayed a remarkable faculty for putting all the proper names and figures into verse and he may have enjoyed doing it. But his Chronicle has nothing in common either with the genuine poems of the great scholar poets or with the didactic poetry of Aratus and his followers. As a sound and accurate versified epitome of historical events in chronological order, it appealed to a wider reading public, and its greatest (but not wholly desirable) success was that it supplanted the fundamental work on critical chronology, the Χρονογραφίαι of Eratosthenes.[4]

Apollodorus had, of course, to base his Χρονικά on Eratosthenes' work, but he made some penetrating alterations: being no scientist, he dropped the section on the principles of scientific chronology, exactly as his contemporary Polybius had dropped the mathematical part of Eratosthenes' geography. While Eratosthenes' latest date was that of Alexander's death in 324/3 B.C., Apollodorus included the time after Alexander, probably until the end of his own life in about 110/09 B.C.[5] He accepted

---

[1] F. Jacoby, 'Apollodors Chronik', *Philologische Untersuchungen* 16 (1902); parts of this book (416 pp.) are still indispensable in spite of the enlarged and revised edition of the fragments in *FGrHist* 244.

[2] T 2. 35 μέτρῳ ... τῷ κωμικῷ ... εὐμνημόνευτον; this iambic form is hardly to be compared with the dactylic Καρνεονῖκαι of Hellanicus Ath. XIV 635 E = 4 *FGrHist* 85a.

[3] Suid. = T 1 ἦρξε δὲ πρῶτος τῶν καλουμένων τραγιάμβων, a sentence in which only 'τραγ'-ιάμβων is a mistake. The ἰαμβεῖον was called by Aristotle *Poet.* 1449 a 24 μάλιστα λεκτικὸν τῶν μέτρων, etc. Cf. F. Jacoby, 'Apollodors Chronik' 60–74 on the 'didactic iambus' of Apollodorus and his imitators; if anyone should inquire again into the metrical technique of those versifications, he will have to consider also the new Menander, see J. W. White, *The Verse of Greek Comedy* (1912) 58 ff., and E. W. Handley, *The Dyscolos of Menander* (1965) 56 ff.

[4] See above, pp. 163 ff.; cf. Jacoby, 'Apollodors Chronik' 39–59 on Apollodorus' method; see also E. Schwartz and H. Diels, who had initiated the research in this field by his article 'Chronologische Untersuchungen über Apollodors Chronika', *Rh.M.* 31 (1876) 1 ff.

[5] The metrical fragments (52–59) relating events after 144/3 do not betray any difference in style and technique. There is at least no cogent argument for attributing the fourth book of the Χρονικά to a clever continuator, though it is beyond our means to distinguish a perfect imitation from the original in this sort of literature. F 58. 2 γιγνώσκεις addresses the general reader as in Hermesianax fr. 7. 49 and 73 Powell, not a special person.

Eratosthenes'[1] earliest date, the fall of Troy in 1184/3 B.C. (F 63), but in dating Homer 240 years later in 944/3 B.C. he followed Ephorus, not Eratosthenes, who had assumed an interval of a hundred years.[2] The length of early epochs in Greek history was calculated by γενεαί, that is, generations of kings or other leading persons; and both Eratosthenes and Apollodorus had to operate within this system. The trouble was that the duration of the γενεά was not precisely established, but only approximately viewed as a period of 30 or 33⅓ years, the third of a century, or even longer. A further trouble was that the dates of birth and death of individuals were often unknown; but the date of the most important events and deeds in their lives was known, and Apollodorus assumed that they usually happened at the culminating age of forty, called in medical language the ἀκμή. It cannot yet be proved whether this term was transferred to chronography by Apollodorus himself or by later chronographers. Using the number 40,[3] he was in an old popular tradition, of which the earliest literary witness is Hesiod, *Op.* 441, where a man in full vigour is called τεσσαρακονταετὴς αἰζηός, which was expressly understood by the grammarians (and why not by Apollodorus?) as ἀκμάζων.[4] I do not believe the immediate source of an omnivorous reader like Apollodorus can be traced;[5] but the lasting effect of his experiment is still recognizable in Suidas' biographical articles, where the puzzling word γέγονε nearly always refers to the date of the Apollodorean ἀκμή ('floruit'), not that of birth.[6]

Apollodorus' second innovation was that he tried to render his dates more accurate by basing them on the lists of the archons.[7] The archon's name, which could be more easily put into verse than figures of Olympiads, had been used for dating in the διδασκαλίαι from Aristotle's time onwards,[8] and Demetrius of Phaleron[9] had published an extensive Ἀρχόντων ἀναγραφή which now not only the author of the chronicle, but also the reader could consult. Frequent synchronisms were added as a convenient

---

[1] See above, p. 163.

[2] Aristarchus dated Homer to the time of Ionian migration, 1044/3, see also p. 228.

[3] On this and other figures see the well-documented and graceful paper of F. Boll, 'Die Lebensalter', *Neue Jahrbücher für das klassische Altertum* 31 (1913) 103. 2 (= *Kleine Schriften* 1950, p. 172. 5).

[4] Hesych. (Cyrill.) v. αἰζήϊος· ἀκμάζων, cf. *Et. Gud.* 42.16 Stef. with many parallels.

[5] A possible source for the choice of the number 40 may have been Aristoxenus on Pythagoras (see fr. 16 Wehrli) and Apollod. F 339.

[6] See the famous paper of E. Rohde, 'Γέγονε in den Biographica des Suidas', *Rh.M.* 33 (1878) 161 ff. = *Kleine Schriften* I (1901) 114–84.

[7] Jacoby, 'Apollodors Chronik' 57 ff.

[8] See above, p. 81, cf. pp. 132 (Callimachus), 193 (Aristoph. Byz.).

[9] *FGrHist* 228 F 1–3. 10; cf. Apollod. 244 F 31 (ἐπὶ Καλλίου), 34 (ἐπὶ Ἀφεψίωνος and ἐπὶ Καλλιάδου).

help in many cases, as for instance that of the ἀκμή of Pythagoras with the tyranny of Polycrates.

Ps.-Scymnus in his summary of the Χρονικά enumerates πόλεων ἁλώσεις, ἐκτοπισμοὺς στρατοπέδων (l. 26) κτλ., and φυγάς, στρατείας, καταλύσεις τυραννίδων (l. 31). The fragments themselves are probably unrepresentative in so far as they deal relatively little with politics and history, but very much with philosophy and poetry. This is, of course, due to the mainly grammatical character of the sources from which we derive our quotations of Apollodorus; but it may still betray a certain predilection of the disciple of Diogenes and Aristarchus for literature. If we consider only one literary example, three lines on Menander, we see that between the biographical dates the total number of his plays is given as 105: Κηφισιεὺς ὤν, ἐκ ⟨δὲ⟩ Διοπείθους πατρός, | πρὸς τοῖσιν ἑκατὸν πέντε γράψας δράματα | ἐξέλιπε πεντήκοντα καὶ δυεῖν ἐτῶν.[1] 'ex istis tamen centum et quinque omnibus solis eum octo vicisse idem Apollodorus eodem in libro scribit.' The figure πέντε (others counted 109 or 108) is guaranteed for the text of the Χρονικά by the metre, while figures in prose texts are exposed to corruption. The information on the plays in which Apollodorus was especially interested was certainly drawn from the διδασκαλίαι in the revised Πίνακες and in the Ὑποθέσεις of Aristophanes of Byzantium; Apollodorus had only to cast the figures into his not inelegant trimeters.

The iambic Χρονικά became a standard authority as continuations, imitations, and even forgeries prove. One obvious forgery was a geographical guide-book, also in comic trimeters and under Apollodorus' name[2] written in the first century B.C. Among the continuations one on oriental history, written in prose at the end of the first century B.C., was frequently quoted by Christian writers from Clement and Eusebius to Syncellus. But unfortunately for our knowledge of Apollodorus' work was superseded in Augustan times by a more practical textbook, the Χρονικά of Castor of Rhodes.[3]

Apollodorus published two other great works and a few minor ones; there is no evidence for the dates of their origin or publication. Even the Chronicle was the product of a γραμματικός, as we have seen; in these other works we find him concentrating entirely on the interpretation of Greek poetry. The monograph Περὶ τοῦ τῶν νεῶν καταλόγου was a scholarly

---

[1] Gell. *N.A.* XVII 4. 5 = F 43 with commentary; on the problematical number of the comedies see A. Körte *RE* xv (1931) 713 f.—As the line before Κηφισιεύς is unknown, it is difficult to supply the missing short syllable before Διοπείθους; I should prefer δέ to Casaubon's τε.

[2] F 313–30, cf. T 16.

[3] *FGrHist* 250; cf. E. Schwartz, 'Die Königslisten des Eratosthenes', *AGGW* 40 (1894/5) 93 ff. on Castor's pseudochronology.

treatment of Homeric geography, and that Περὶ θεῶν dealt with Homeric religion.

Aristarchus' intention in his monograph Περὶ τοῦ ναυστάθμου had been to reconstruct the whole order of the Greek ships on the roadstead from all the relevant passages in the *Iliad*;[1] he had already here and there in his commentary tried to discover how the poet had located the several heroes and their men on the shore. Demetrius of Scepsis, the great local specialist, had given a minute account of the Trojan allies in Asia Minor in his Τρωϊκὸς διάκοσμος.[2] These studies may have had some influence on Apollodorus; he certainly knew Demetrius well.[3] In Apollodorus' opinion the poet of the Catalogue of Ships in the second book of the *Iliad* had given a description of heroic Greece, and it was the duty of the interpreter to explain all the names of places and tribes and heroes to the reader.[4] We can be sure that he would not have spent so much labour on his twelve books, if he had not believed in the Homeric authorship of the Catalogue. As a matter of fact, none of the grammarians suspected it as a passage of 'Hesiodic character' or 'cyclic' origin; they were content to athetize some individual lines as in other parts of the poem. So Apollodorus did not have to face the question whether there had been interpolation from a later source, or whether there was a pre-Homeric tradition preserved in the Greek Catalogue. It was modern Homeric criticism that suggested those possibilities which are still being explored not without bitter feuds and personal invectives.[5] To Apollodorus the Catalogue was a genuine part of Homer's work, and he used all the knowledge of post-Homeric geography available to him in order to identify the names recorded there.

He again followed the lead of Eratosthenes' genius; the descriptive—but not the scientific—parts of Eratosthenes' Γεωγραφικά, which began with Homer, were his model and the main source for his twelve books Περὶ τοῦ τῶν νεῶν καταλόγου.[6] The relation is similar to that which we noted between the chronological works of the two scholars. The most substantial extracts from Apollodorus are preserved by Strabo, especially

---

[1] See above, p. 213; cf. Lehrs[3] 221 ff.

[2] See above, pp. 249 ff.

[3] T 14 οὐχ ὁμολογεῖ τοῖς ὑπὸ τοῦ Σκηψίου Δημητρίου λεγομένοις (cf. F 157 d, 181).

[4] F 154–207; cf. T 12–15.

[5] See G. Jachmann, *Der homerische Schiffskatalog*, 1958, and D. L. Page, *History and the Homeric Iliad* (1959) 118 ff. and notes pp. 155 ff., with ample references to the quarrelling parties. I am inclined to agree with Eduard Meyer, *Geschichte des Altertums* II 1[2] (1928) 294 n., where the conclusion of T. W. Allen's monograph (*The Homeric Catalogue of Ships*, 1921, p. 168) 'the Catalogue appears ... the oldest Greek verse we possess', is frankly condemned as 'Unfug'; it becomes, nevertheless, fashionable from time to time.

[6] T 13 τὰ πλεῖστα μετενέγκας παρὰ τοῦ Ἐρατοσθένους; cf. above, pp. 165 f.

in Books VII–X of his great geographical compilation[1]—just as in other parts (I/II and XIII) he is our principal source for Eratosthenes and Demetrius. But Strabo did not often attribute his extracts to Apollodorus by name so that a minute analysis[2] of whole chapters will be necessary before the Apollodorean extracts can be distinguished from those of other writers like Ephorus, Artemidorus, and Demetrius. When Strabo did introduce a verbatim quotation with the title of the work, he used the formula ἐν τοῖς (τῷ) Περὶ (τοῦ) νεῶν καταλόγου;[3] and we can conclude from this that Apollodorus did not write a running commentary, a ὑπόμνημα, on B 494 ff. line by line, but treated the sections of the Catalogue more loosely, in the style of the Περί-literature.[4]

His immense learning and wide range of vision over the epic period enabled Apollodorus to form a coherent picture of Homer's Greece and of the changes that took place after him; his object was to determine the poet's geographical views, as Aristarchus had tried to discover the Homeric usage of words and facts. Like Eratosthenes,[5] he was far from imputing to the poet any intention of 'teaching', and with both Eratosthenes and Aristarchus he ignored the Stoic assumption of 'hidden' meanings which had led Crates astray and not only in the field of geography. But, as far as we can judge from our fragments, Apollodorus, as a true Aristarchean in every respect, did not bother to set forth his principles in a systematic introduction, though he may have given an occasional hint in an excursus.[6] For instance, in a digression on the *Odyssey*,[7] he bitterly criticized Callimachus for having identified the island of Calypso with Γαῦδος, an islet near Malta, and the Phaeacian Scheria with Corcyra. Callimachus, as a poet pretending (μεταποιούμενος) to be a γραμματικός, could not be forgiven when he sinned against the fundamental distinction between the historical places in the Catalogue and the imaginary localities of Odysseus' wanderings (παρὰ τὸν ἐξωκεανισμὸν τῶν τόπων), a distinction accepted by Apollodorus from Eratosthenes.

An interpreter of an epic text with hundreds of proper names was bound to explain the form and meaning of the names themselves, not

---

[1] See the table in *FGrHist* II *Kommentar* pp. 776 f.

[2] Is it too much to hope that this analysis, begun by Niese nearly a century ago and meanwhile advanced by others, will be completed one day? See B. Niese, 'Apollodors Commentar zum Schiffskatalog', *Rh.M.* 32 (1877) 267–307; E. Schwartz *RE* I 2866 ff., F. Jacoby in his commentary pp. 776 ff.

[3] Steph. Byz., less exact than Strabo in several respects, but still very valuable, said only ἐν τῷ Νεῶν καταλόγῳ; see G. Neumann, *Fragmente von Apollodors Kommentar zum homerischen Schiffskatalog im Lexikon des Stephanos von Byzanz*, Diss. Göttingen 1953 (in typescript).

[4] See above, p. 213, with further references.　　　　　　　　　　[5] Cf. above, pp. 166 f.

[6] I agree with Jacoby in his commentary, p. 779, 20 ff. against E. Schwartz 2864.

[7] F 157 (a) and (d); Call. fr. 13 and 470.

only their geographical significance. We have noticed the repeated attempts of the Greeks from epic times onwards to find the ἔτυμα of proper
names. For a long time these amounted to little more than a playing with
similarities of sound; later the question was very seriously discussed in
Plato's *Cratylus*.[1] The philosophical treatment of etymology[2] was continued by the Stoics, who, in contrast to Plato, came to the conclusion that
an analysis of language could open the way to the knowledge of things.
It may well have been under the Stoic influence of his master, Diogenes
of Babylon, that Apollodorus became the first grammarian in Alexandria
to write a monograph[3] on etymologies; there is, however, not the slightest
evidence in the fragments that he accepted the extravagant linguistic
doctrines of the Stoics.[4] On the contrary, he seems to have followed the
lead given by Aristophanes of Byzantium who had set the example of
a more modest treatment of ἔτυμα in his comprehensive Λέξεις,[5] which
were intended as an aid to the interpretation of poetry. We might expect
that Apollodorus would have tried to find certain criteria to put his
studies on a firmer basis. It is not easy to recognize them clearly as long
as Περὶ τοῦ νεῶν καταλόγου is not completely reconstructed; but we can
learn something by looking from the Catalogue to the other great work,
Περὶ θεῶν, in which the etymologies of names of gods and places are
numerous. (The fragments of the monograph Περὶ ἐτυμολογιῶν give no
examples of proper names, but only of nouns.)

Apollodorus usually disapproved of the derivations of local names from
names of heroes or from events of the heroic age. Attica (*Il. B* 546 ff.),
so he explained, is also called Ἀκτή, not from the Attic hero Ἀκταῖος,
but because it stretches along the sea (F 185); its name, that is, is taken
ἀπὸ τῆς τοῦ τόπου φύσεως (F 188 on *B* 532 Βῆσσα), as he asserts in another
passage.[6] The question is only whether he was quite consistent in the
application of his criteria. Have we to alter the text of Stephanus of
Byzantium because it lets Apollodorus (F 192) derive the name of the
islands called Ἐχῖναι or Ἐχινάδες (*B* 625) ἀπὸ Ἐχίνου μάντεως, that is,
from a ἥρως ἐπώνυμος? Or must we blame Strabo for a careless excerpt
from Apollodorus when he first reports (ΙΧ 436) that Πάγασαι owes its

---

[1] See above, pp. 4 f., and 61 f.

[2] Chrysippus Περὶ ἐτυμολογιῶν, *SVF* ιι 9. 13, 14 and ibid. 44. 42; cf. Diogen. Bab., *SVF*
ιιι 213. 5 ff. λέξις. The formation ἐτυμολογία is not attested before Chrysippus.

[3] The dispute between E. Schwartz, who denied any Stoic influence, and his philostoic
opponents should be settled by this suggestion.

[4] F 222–5 two books Ἐτυμολογούμενα or Περὶ ἐτυμολογιῶν; several of the grammatical
quotations without title of a book (F 226–84) contain etymologies.

[5] See above, p. 201.

[6] Cf. G. Neumann's Dissertation (above, p. 259, n. 3) 16 ff.

name to its many πηγαί, not to the ναυπηγία[1] of the ship *Argo*, but immediately afterwards explains Ἀφέται as the ἀφετήριον τῶν Ἀργοναυτῶν, using here not a topographical etymology, but a mythological one of the kind rejected in other cases?[2] We should never forget that Apollodorus was an interpreter of early poetry, not a linguistic doctrinaire.

In discussing the Catalogue of Ships we started from general questions of Homeric geography and ended with the explanation of local names. Turning to the twenty-four books entitled Περὶ θεῶν,[3] we are justified in beginning with the names of Homeric gods and their etymologies; this seems to have been Apollodorus' own starting-point, as the substantial fragments on Apollo (F 95 ff.) show. The treatment of the individual names will finally lead to general statements of his views on Homeric religion and of his own religious attitude. The question whether this work of Apollodorus was influenced by Stoic doctrines has naturally been raised again and again, and differently answered. The idea of planning a complete monograph on all the Homeric gods with the stress on the etymology of their names may have been suggested by certain writings of Stoic philosophers on the same subject, but that by no means implies that Apollodorus was affected by or agreed with their theories. The quotations generally prove that he did not; an occasional similarity of treatment was unavoidable and unimportant. Here again[4] we probably come nearest to the truth by adopting a middle position in which Stoic influence is not denied, but strictly limited.

If some people have been surprised that Apollodorus excluded non-Greek gods from his voluminous work, this is because they were not aware that this too was essentially a work on Homer. As in the Catalogue, he used his knowledge of post-Homeric literature in order to explain the Homeric usage more clearly, though he could not altogether suppress the mistrust of the νεώτεροι, appropriate to a pupil of Aristarchus. The Homeric epithets and ἐπικλήσεις as well as the proper names themselves could reveal the qualities and deeds of the gods. So Apollodorus was

---

[1] Cf. notes on Call. fr. 18. 12 f.

[2] Even Jacoby, who put his conjecture into the text of F 192, seems not to have been absolutely certain of Apollodorus' consistency: 'daß in der Namenerklärung die mythologischen Ableitungen *stark oder ganz* (italics are mine) abgelehnt werden', Commentary on F 154 ff., p. 778. 34.

[3] T 9–11, F 88–153, cf. 352–6 (number of books F 103). On Περὶ θεῶν see the special studies of Münzel (below, p. 262, n. 3 and p. 263, n. 1); cf. also E. Schwartz, *RE* 1 2872, Reinhardt, *Graec. theol.* 83 ff., who reject the assumption of Stoic influence; Jacoby in his commentary on the fragments, pp. 753 ff., is very cautious. Stoic elements were acknowledged or even stressed by Barwick, *Stoische Sprachlehre* 61 and especially by Pohlenz, *Stoa* 1 182 and 11 92 with many references.

[4] Cf. above, p. 260, n. 3.

anxious to derive epithets of gods not 'from holy places', οὐκ ἀπὸ τῶν ἱερῶν τόπων[1] ... ἀπὸ δὲ τῶν ψυχικῶν ἐνεργειῶν ἢ ... συμβεβηκότων περὶ τὸ σῶμα. He seems to have applied his own criterion more consistently than in the *Catalogue of Ships* at least, if the source of the famous passage about the Κούρητες in Strabo x 466 is Posidonius, not Apollodorus.[2] Even Apollo, according to him, is called Δήλιος not because he was born and worshipped in the island of Δῆλος, but because he makes all things 'visible', δῆλα (F 95. 32). This etymology is one of the many in Macrobius (*sat.* 1 17. 32) which Usener's pupil R. Münzel assigned to Apollodorus by conjecture;[3] the conjecture was confirmed beyond any doubt by the Geneva Scholia to the *Iliad*, and the number of attested fragments on Apollo in Books 13 and 14 of Περὶ θεῶν increased considerably (F 95-99). What have been hitherto the most important fragments on Athena[4] are contained in the discussion of the etymology and meaning of γλαυκῶπις, where Apollodorus tells us that it is not to be connected with the place Γλαυκώπιον on the Acropolis, as apparently it had been by Callimachus,[5] but that it is derived from the γλαύσσειν of her eyes. We may now have a substantial addition to these scanty remains in two columns of an anonymous papyrus[6] conjectured by R. Merkelbach to be a part of Περὶ θεῶν.[7] The writer strongly criticizes the use of δολιχάορος as an epithet of Pallas Athena in two poems of the νεώτεροι on the ground that it is against the Homeric usage of ἄορ, which means sword, not spear; but, he continues, she sprang (ἐξανέπαλτο) swaying (παλλομένη) the spear from the head of Zeus which Hephaestus had opened by a blow of his axe.[8] Everything here seems to point to Apollodorus as the author: the impressive display of learning, the polemics against the wrong usage of a word in post-Homeric poetry, above all, the etymology, which is exactly in his style. Merkelbach's arguments may be supplemented by another. There is a slight coincidence of the new papyrus with a passage in Philodemus Περὶ εὐσεβείας about Zeus' head being split by the axe of Hephaestus for

---

[1] F 353. 11 and 354. 2, 7.

[2] K. Reinhardt, 'Poseidonios über Ursprung und Entartung', *Orient und Antike* 6 (1928) 34 ff.

[3] *De Apollodori Περὶ θεῶν libris* (Diss. Bonn 1883) 14 ff.

[4] F 353. 11 and 354. 2, 7; cf. F 105, 147.

[5] Cf. Call. fr. 237. 11.

[6] *P.Oxy.* xx (1952) 2260 (early second century A.D.) ed. E. Lobel.

[7] *APF* 16 (1956) 115 ff. It is impossible to decide whether the two columns are part of Apollodorus' original or part of a very learned commentary in which Περὶ θεῶν was excerpted. The paragraphus, the blank space, and the ἔκθεσις are used not only in ὑπομνήματα, but in all sorts of prose books, see for instance Schubart, *Das Buch*[2] (1921) 86.

[8] For the etymology of Παλλὰς ἀπὸ τοῦ πάλματος ample evidence is given from the *Phoronis* (new fr.), Stesichorus (fr. 56 Page), Ibycus (fr. 17 P.), Euripides (fr. 1009ª Snell, Supplementum ad Nauck *TGF*, 1964, p. 19), Philitas (fr. 23 Pow.), Callimachus (fr. 37).

the birth of Pallas; and that this is derived from Apollodorus was cautiously and convincingly argued a long time ago by R. Münzel.[1] Philodemus must have known Apollodorus' work: his Περὶ εὐσεβείας is the only source of our knowledge of the number of books into which Περὶ θεῶν was divided and of the statement that Apollodorus 'was fighting (μάχεται) against the συνοικειοῦντες'—Stoic philosophers, who were always ready to propose absurd identifications of different gods, as for instance of Asclepius and Apollo (F 116). So reference to Philodemus may help us to attribute the new papyrus on Pallas Athena to its proper author.

Two conclusions can perhaps be stated as a result of our observations. In Apollodorus' geography the local names expressed the nature of the place (τὴν τοῦ τόπου φύσιν); in his theology the analysis of the names revealed the nature of the divine being. An allusion to this doctrine seems to be preserved in the remark of Moschopulos that a single name signified the δύναμις as well as the god τὴν δύναμιν ἐνεργοῦντα.[2] But we look in vain for any confession by Apollodorus himself of his attitude to religion, although it is hard to believe that he would have undertaken a theological work of the highest scholarly intensity if he had not possessed a genuine religious feeling.

In all the books so far reviewed, on chronology, Homeric geography, and theology, we have seen the mind of the γραμματικός at work. A new purely grammatical title turned up not long ago in a Milan papyrus[3] which contains the subscription without the text: Ἀπολλοδώρου γραμματικοῦ Ἀθηναίου Ζητήματα γραμματικὰ εἰς τὴν Ξ τῆς Ἰλιάδος. This is a curious title,[4] referring to a curious fact; for the Peripatetic fashion of presenting Homeric problems in the form of ζητήματα and λύσεις[5] did not find much favour with the Alexandrian scholars. I wonder if it will be possible to distinguish clearly any ζητήματα from Γλῶσσαι (F 221), Λέξεις (F 240?), Ἐτυμολογούμενα (F 222-25) among the unspecified 'grammatical' fragments (F 232-84),[6] but it may be worth trying.

---

[1] *Quaestiones mythographicae* (Berlin 1883) 18 ff. dedicated to Usener.

[2] Moschop. Schol. in Hes. *Op.* p. 36. 23 ff. Gaisf.; cf. Reinhardt, *De Graec. theol.* 109 f., Wilamowitz, *Glaube d. Hell.* II 418. It is unlikely that Aristophanes of Byzantium anticipated the recognition of the Homeric εἰδωλοποιία, see Excursus to p. 177, n. 4.

[3] *PRIMI* I (1937) no. 19 ed. A. Vogliano, taking no account of *FGrHist* 244 (1929/30), esp. of F 275 and 240.

[4] I am not aware of any exact parallel; Porphyry who used Apollod. Π. θεῶν frequently in his Ὁμηρικὰ ζητήματα wrote Γραμματικὰς ἀπορίας (Suid. s.v. at the end of the list of writings; cf. Bidez, *Vie de Porphyre* 71⁺).

[5] See above, pp. 69 f. with references.

[6] Schol. Nic. *Al.* 393 (of which we have no critical edition so far) refers for the gloss στρόμβος in the same book Ξ of the *Iliad*, l. 413, to Apollod. ἐν τοῖς Ὁμήρου (F 275); one would expect either ἐν τοῖς ⟨περὶ⟩ Ὁμήρου or ἐν τοῖς Ὁμηρ(ικοῖς) sc. ζητήμασι (?), cf. Crates' Ὁμηρικά above, pp. 239.

Apollodorus followed the old Alexandrian tradition also in making comedy his second field of study after Homer; like Aristophanes of Byzantium and others¹ he produced a monograph on the Athenian courtesans, chiefly based on Attic comedy (T 17 and F 208–12). But his main efforts were devoted to the so-called Doric comedy, the δράματα of Epicharmus and the μῖμοι of Sophron (T 18 and F 213–18); in that field his predecessor, as we noticed, was a Pergamene scholar, Polemo.² The evidence for the character of Apollodorus' work is ambiguous. The explanation of a Sicilian gloss is quoted from the sixth book of Περὶ Ἐπιχάρμου (F 213), and there are five attestations (F 214–18) of the title of a work on Sophron, Περὶ Σώφρονος, which was in at least four books. This points to monographs with interpretations in the Περί-style. On the other hand, Porphyry³ says that Apollodorus had collected and arranged Epicharmus' writings in ten books not chronologically, but according to subjects, as Andronicus had done with Aristotle and Theophrastus; and by this he must have meant that there was an edition arranged by Apollodorus. Can it be true that as well as writing a monograph Περὶ Ἐπιχάρμου Apollodorus also published the complete text of the plays? Of course, Andronicus' edition of Aristotle and Theophrastus is not undisputed,⁴ but Porphyry apparently used one under that name for his many philosophical writings. He was also well acquainted with several works of Apollodorus, and not likely to be misled by errors of an intermediate source. Therefore it is difficult to discount his plain testimony, as Jacoby⁵ would like to do. A new papyrus⁶ containing a fragment of a catalogue of Epicharmus' plays in iambic trimeters, of which Apollodorus is the only candidate for authorship, provides no solution; but it is at least more probable that these iambics—which remind us of the iambic Χρονικά— introduced a text of the plays⁷ than a monograph on the poet. The titles of six mythical plays can be read on the papyrus fragment, but not any

---

¹ See above, p. 208, n. 6.   ² See above, p. 249.
³ Porphyr. *Vit. Plot.* 24 = T 18 τὰ βιβλία (sc. Plotini) οὐ κατὰ χρόνους ἐᾶσαι φύρδην ἐκδεδομένα ἐδικαίωσα, μιμησάμενος δ᾽ Ἀπολλόδωρον τὸν Ἀθηναῖον καὶ τὸν Ἀνδρόνικον τὸν Περιπατητικόν, ὧν ὁ μὲν Ἐπίχαρμον τὸν κωμῳδιογράφον εἰς δέκα τόμους φέρων συνήγαγεν, ὁ δὲ τὰ Ἀριστοτέλους καὶ Θεοφράστου εἰς πραγματείας διεῖλε, τὰς οἰκείας ὑποθέσεις εἰς ταὐτὸν συναγαγών. Cf. Bidez, *Vie de Porphyre* 118 ff.
⁴ Cf. O. Regenbogen, 'Theophrastos', *RE* Suppl. VII (1940) 1376. 60 ff.; Düring, *Aristotle* 412 ff.
⁵ Commentary p. 795 with many references.
⁶ *P.Oxy.* XXV (1959) 2426 ed. E. Lobel; cf. B. Gentili, *Gnom.* 33 (1961) 332 ff.
⁷ There is not only the iambic list of Callimachean poems introducing the text of the hymns in a few manuscripts, referred to by Lobel and published a long time before Reitzenstein by H. Hagen, *Catalogus codd. Bernens.* (1875) 520 = Call. II p. XCVIII test. 23, but there are other very late summaries of books in iambic trimeters, collected in *Anth. Pal.* vol. III ed. E. Cougny (1890) pp. 327–9 (see Call. II p. LV).

allegorical or realistic ones; this would be in harmony with Porphyry's statement that Apollodorus had arranged Epicharmus' δράματα according to subjects. And if *Medea* was counted as a genuine work of Epicharmus, not of Dinolochus,[1] the editor presumably had to say something about the disputed authorship of this and other plays and the problem of the Ψευδεπιχάρμεια, which had already been raised by Aristoxenus.[2] But all that may have been part of his monograph Περὶ Ἐπιχάρμου; and this book was perhaps the source of later ὑπομνήματα of which we have a welcome example in the papyrus commentary on Epicharmus' Ὀδυσσεὺς αὐτόμολος.[3]

Plato was very fond of Sophron's μῖμοι,[4] which he got to know in Syracuse and brought to Athens; there is even an allusion in the *Republic*[5] to their division into ἀνδρεῖοι (for instance 'The Tunnyfisher') and γυναικεῖοι (for instance 'The Sempstresses'). These scenes of everyday life became in some details a model for Theocritus and Herondas,[6] and now, in the wake of poets, Apollodorus tried in his Περὶ Σώφρονος to give a grammatical explanation of the rare Syracusan dialectal words and forms. There is no suggestion of his having made an edition of Sophron; if we can rely on Porphyry, we must say that Epicharmus' δράματα were the only text Apollodorus edited.

The historical position of Apollodorus can now be defined. The five generations from Philitas and Zenodotus to Aristarchus formed, as we have said,[7] a living chain; each of the leading personalities took over the best from his master, and made a decisive step further, opening a new prospect for scholarship. Apollodorus' research did not lack intensity and originality, but its effect was to sum up and to supplement in a grand style the creative work of the previous generations. It seems therefore out of proportion to put him on a par with Eratosthenes and Aristophanes of Byzantium or to conjecture that in certain cases he inspired Aristarchus, not Aristarchus him.[8] Apollodorus is to be regarded as the first

---

[1] *CGF* I p. 149 Kaib., Dinoloch. fr. 4 = fr. 3 Olivieri.

[2] *CGF* I p. 133 Kaib., cf. p. 90; A. Olivieri, *Frammenti della commedia Greca e del mimo nella Sicilia* I² (1946) pp. 108 ff.; cf. Aristoxen. fr. 45, Wehrli, *Schule des Aristot.* 2 (1945).

[3] *P.Oxy.* xxv (1959) 2429.

[4] *CGF* I pp. 152 ff. Kaib.; Olivieri, *Frammenti* II² (1947) pp. 59 ff. A. Körte, *RE* III A (1927) 1100 ff.

[5] Plat. *Rep.* 451 c; cf. Duris, *FGrHist* 76 F 72.

[6] Theocritus ed. Gow II (1950), Commentary pp. 33 ff. and 265 f. on the relation of Theocr. mimic poems to Sophron, with due reserve. O. Crusius, *Untersuchungen zu den Mimiamben des Herondas* (1892) 187–9.   [7] See above, p. 233.

[8] E. Schwartz, *RE* I 2875; his enthusiastic and authoritative judgement made a great impression, for instance on Ferguson, *Hellenistic Athens* 340. As far as our evidence goes, there is no reason to reverse the relation of Apollodorus who was after all the younger man to Aristarchus; Strab. I 31 = Apollod. F 157e speaks strictly against it.

and foremost of the 'epigoni', towering high above the compilers of the following centuries. The case of Aristarchus' other most devoted pupil, Dionysius Thrax, is paradoxical in one respect. No book of any Hellenistic scholar is still extant—they have to be reconstructed from fragments and testimonia—with the one exception of the Τέχνη γραμματική that goes under the name of Dionysius Thrax. Yet in later antiquity and in recent times critics have tried to deprive Dionysius of the authorship and to assign the book to an anonymous compiler of a later date.

Dionysius,[1] like Apollonius 'Rhodius', was one of the few scholars who were natives of Alexandria; he was surnamed Θρᾷξ because his father Τήρης bore a name that was believed to be Thracian. His formative years in Aristarchus' school must have ended in 144/3 B.C., when the political upheaval drove him from Alexandria to Rhodes:[2] we know that his grateful Rhodian pupils collected the means for his reconstruction of Nestor's cup in silver. If the elder Tyrannion,[3] who later distinguished himself in Rome, was a member of the audience to which Dionysius lectured, this must have been about 90 B.C. It is possible also that the founder of classical scholarship in Rome, L. Aelius Stilo, who accompanied Q. Metellus Numidicus in the year 100 B.C. into his voluntary exile at Rhodes, was decisively influenced by Dionysius' instruction.[4] The island of Rhodes had been a home of philosophy and rhetoric for a long time. The Peripatetic tradition had flourished there since the days of Aristotle's pupil Eudemus, and Praxiphanes,[5] though an immigrant, was counted as one of the famous Rhodians. The Stoa was represented by the illustrious names of Panaetius, a native Rhodian, in the second and of Posidonius in the first century B.C. Schools of rhetoric were established by an Apollonius 'Rhodius' (not the poet) who came from Alabanda about 120 B.C. and later by Molon, from whom Cicero learned to control his

---

[1] Suid. v. Διονύσιος Ἀλεξανδρεύς, Θρᾷξ δὲ ἀπὸ τοῦ πατρὸς Τήρου κληθείς . . . Ἀριστάρχου μαθητής, γραμματικός. Part of the text of the article is confused. For biographical dates and bibliographical references see L. Cohn, RE v (1905) 977–83. There is no collection of testimonia and fragments more recent than that of M. Schmidt, Philol. 7 (1852) 360 ff., esp. 369 ff.; see also below, p. 271, n. 5.

[2] See above, p. 211. Cf. Strab. xiv 655 on Rhodian philosophers and scholars, Athen. xi 489 A on Nestor's cup (Λ 632 ff.); cf. below, p. 273 Tyrannion. On the relation of the famous Mycenaean Dove cup to the Homeric description of Nestor's cup see H. L. Lorimer, Homer and the Monuments (1950) 328 ff.

[3] Suid. v. Τυραννίων . . . γεγονὼς ἐπὶ Πομπηΐου τοῦ μεγάλου καὶ πρότερον (ca. 70 B.C.) . . . διήκουσε καὶ Διονυσίου τοῦ Θρᾳκὸς ἐν Ῥόδῳ . . . διαπρεπὴς δὲ γενόμενος ἐν Ῥώμῃ. . . . Cf. below, pp. 272 f.

[4] Rhet. ad Herenn. ed. F. Marx (1894) p. 139, F. Leo, Geschichte der Röm. Lit. i (1913) 362. G. Funaioli, 'Lineamenti d'una storia della filologia attraverso i secoli', Studi di letteratura antica i (1948) 204.   [5] See above, p. 135.

voice in the delivery of his speeches and so to restore his health.[1] With
Dionysius' arrival the intellectual exchange between east and west on
Rhodian soil was extended to scholarship. As the Romans did not like
to go to Alexandria, his enforced *secessio* to Rhodes was a stroke of good
fortune, bringing the best of Alexandrian scholarship to Rome as a
counterbalance to the earlier influence of doctrines from Pergamum.[2]

Dionysius was first of all an interpreter of Homer. He followed
Aristarchus in regarding him as an Athenian;[3] but from Didymus' and
Aristonicus' excerpts in the Scholia it is evident how often he contradicted
his master in detail, when referring to his readings, critical σημεῖα, and
explanations.[4] We learn from Suidas that besides γραμματικά his numerous
writings included ὑπομνήματα (running commentaries) and συνταγματικά
(treatises).[5] A book of polemics against Crates' Homeric interpretations,
Πρὸς Κράτητα[6] (Schol. A *I* 464), and another Περὶ ποσοτήτων (Schol.
A *B* 111) probably belong to this group of treatises. His Μελέται (Schol.
χ 9) may have been a collection of Homeric 'Exercises' or of rhetorical
'Declamations'.[7] The fact that he explained a gloss in Hesiod (φερέοικος
as κοχλία)[8] and the description of him in a passage, possibly from Varro,
on the three usual accents, as 'lyricorum poetarum longe studiosissimus'[9]
need not imply that he wrote monographs or commentaries on post-
Homeric epic and lyric poetry; more probably the reference in both cases
is to his linguistic and prosodic studies. However that may be, these other
writings were considerable both in quantity and in critical quality and
do not deserve to be totally overshadowed by the *cause célèbre* of the Τέχνη
γραμματική.[10]

This slim book of no more than fifty printed pages in Immanuel

---

[1] F. Klingner, 'Ciceros Rede für den Schauspieler Roscius', *Sitz. Ber. Bayer. Akad.*, Phil.-hist. Klasse 1953. 4 = *Studien zur griechischen und römischen Literatur* (1964) 548 ff.

[2] See above, p. 246.

[3] See above, p. 228.

[4] Cohn, *RE* v 978 f., gives a list of the quotations with references to Ludwich and Lehrs.

[5] Cohn, *RE* v 977. 62, is inclined to conjecture συγγράμματα; but as σύνταγμα means a 'treatise' in the grammatical terminology (see Apollonius Dyscolus *pron.* p. 65. 17 Schn., *synt.* 56. 5 Bekker–Uhlig), so does συνταγματικά in the commentaries on Aristotle, see L–S s.v.

[6] Parmeniscus, a school-fellow of Dionysius, wrote at about the same time a book of the same title, cf. C. Wendel, *RE* xviii (1949) 1570 ff.

[7] Possibly in *P. Würzburg* 2, col. 116 ff., as restored by F. Della Corte (below, p. 270, n. 2).

[8] Schol. Procl. in Hes. *Op.* 571.

[9] [Sergius] in Donat., *GL* iv 529. 17 = Varro, fr. 84 Goetz–Schoell p. 214. 4; cf. Dionys. Thr. p. 7. 1 Uhlig.

[10] M. Fuhrmann, *Das systematische Lehrbuch* (1960) 29 ff. (with bibliography), 145 ff., 152 ff., and 192 (Addenda); V. di Benedetto, 'Dionisio Trace e la techne a lui attributa', *Annali della Scuola Normale Superiore di Pisa*, Ser. II, vol. 27 (1958) 169–210, vol. 28 (1959) 87–118.

Bekker's *Anecdota Graeca*[1] stands at the end of a long series of studies of language from the Sophists to the philosophers and scholars; it summed up in a concise form the results of the past and became a school-book in the future, suffering the corruptions and alterations unavoidable in this sort of literature. The brief and abrupt sentences in a staccato style called forth copious explanatory notes through the centuries; indeed these so-called *Scholia*, collected from various Byzantine manuscripts, fill more than 300 pages in Bekker and nearly 600 in Hilgard's large critical edition.[2] The lengthy Byzantine notes include some precious relics of ancient learning, in some of which even the problem of the origin of the *Techne* is raised.

The *Techne* itself starts with a definition: Γραμματική ἐστιν ἐμπειρία τῶν παρὰ ποιηταῖς τε καὶ συγγραφεῦσιν ὡς ἐπὶ τὸ πολὺ λεγομένων.[3] 'Grammar is the empirical knowledge of what is for the most part being said by poets and prose writers.' This definition is in the best Alexandrian tradition, as everyone will appreciate who has followed us on our way from the early third to the first century B.C.; it suits the pupil of Aristarchus perfectly, and we hardly need the confirmation of its genuineness by Varro and Sextus Empiricus.[4] All the terms of the sentence were discussed in the Scholia; distinguishing between a lower (μικρά) grammar confined to the knowledge of writing and reading and a higher one (μεγάλη), they produced a formula for the latter which precisely corresponds to the practice of the Alexandrian scholars: μεγάλην δὲ γραμματικὴν λέγουσι τὴν καταγιγνομένην περὶ τὴν ἐμπειρίαν τῶν ποιητῶν;[5] indeed we can see from Cicero *de or.* I 187, where the first item in a system of *ars grammatica* is 'pertractatio poetarum', that this definition goes back to the first century B.C. The prose writers are not excluded in Dionysius' introductory sentence; but he put them second because they had not been treated by any scholar before Aristarchus.

The sentence immediately following the definition distinguishes six parts[6] of γραμματική. The first is the ἀνάγνωσις, reading aloud with

---

[1] Ed. princ. in I. A. Fabricius, *Bibliotheca Graeca* VII (1715) 26–34.

[2] Dionys. Thr. *Ars grammatica*, ed. G. Uhlig, *Gr. Gr.* I 1 (1883); Scholia in Dionys. Thr. A. gr., ed. A. Hilgard, *Gr. Gr.* I 3 (1901), both volumes reprinted 1965; cf. Cohn, *RE* v 982 on the importance of the Scholia for the history of grammatical studies.

[3] Dionys. Thr. p. 5. 1 f. Uhl. with all the variants in manuscripts, translations, and ancient quotations; ὡς om. *PSI* I 18. 13, see below, p. 270, n. 2.

[4] Varro fr. 107 Goetz–Schoell p. 227, Sext. Emp. *adv. math.* I 58 D. Thr. ἐν τοῖς Παραγγέλμασί φησι 'γραμματικὴ ... ἐμπειρία ὡς ἐπὶ τὸ πλεῖστον τῶν ... λεγομένων' (cf. 63, 72, 80 f.); see also di Benedetto on the variants of the text. Παραγγέλματα seems to have been the title in Sextus' copy.

[5] Schol. in Dionys. Thr. p. 114. 28 Hilg. (Prolegom. Schol. Vat.).

[6] Rutherford 'Annotation' 97–455 dealt thoroughly with all the six parts.

attention to the correct modulation of the voice, a very important part that involves the whole problem of the relation of the written letters to the spoken words. The other parts are: the ἐξήγησις, the explanation of the poetical tropes; the exposition of obsolete words (γλῶσσαι) and subject-matter (ἱστορίαι); the finding of etymologies; the setting out of analogy, ἀναλογίας[1] ἐκλογισμός; and the noblest of all, the κρίσις ποιημάτων, 'literary criticism'.[2] Of these six parts only the first, on reading, accents,[3] and punctuation is elaborated in paragraphs two to four of the *Techne*, and anybody expecting an elaboration of the rest will be disappointed.

The dislocation between paragraphs four and six is obvious. A short paragraph (5) is squeezed in, mentioning ῥαψῳδία as a feature of the Homeric poems and giving its two popular etymologies from ῥάπτειν and ῥάβδος; it now looks rather out of place, but perhaps it was not quite so inappropriate in the original, given that Dionysius' main interest was in Homer and that the rhapsodes were the first 'interpreters' of epic poems.[4] From paragraph six onwards there is again a coherent series of chapters right through to the end; they contain, as we should say, a simple system of technical grammar. Beginning with the letters of the alphabet (στοιχεῖα) and their division into vowels, diphthongs, and consonants (6), they go on to the syllables, long, short, anceps (7–10), and finally to the eight parts of speech (11), which are elaborated one after another (12–20). We meet again here all our old acquaintances encountered at different stages of our long journey from the fifth to the second century B.C. and now united in an apparently happy company.

The members of this company are: the noun with its three genders (the third bearing the Stoic name οὐδέτερον) and its five case-inflexions including the vocative; the appellative (προσηγορία) regarded as a species (εἶδος) of the ὄνομα, not as a separate part of speech; the verb with its tenses; the participle, as μετοχή sharing formal and functional characteristics of noun and verb; the ἄρθρον, meaning article and relative pronoun; the pronoun, used in place of the noun; the preposition (πρόθεσις), placed before other parts of speech; the adverb (ἐπίρρημα); the σύνδεσμος, now merely 'conjunction', limited to the function of connecting other parts of speech.

A glance back at all the passages, in which we have analysed the study of language from Protagoras to the Stoics[5] will reveal clearly what the

---

[1] See above, pp. 202 f. and 229.
[2] See above, p. 157; di Benedetto 179. 4 by mistake translated 'textual criticism', which would be διόρθωσις and is not mentioned in the *Techne*.
[3] The passage is possibly quoted by Varro, see above, p. 267, n. 9.
[4] See above, p. 5. [5] See especially pp. 37 f., 59 ff., 76 ff., 203, 229, 273 ff.

author of the *Techne* accepted from his various predecessors, what he rejected, what he added or slightly changed. It is unnecessary to repeat all the details, but one general fact should be emphasized: the Stoic influence is stronger in this technical part of the grammar than in the earlier paragraphs. This leads back to the crucial question whether Dionysius actually was the author of the *Techne*, as the tradition claims, and whether its arrangement, as represented in all our manuscripts, was the author's original one.

It is understandable that the purely Stoic elements in the book, for instance the case-inflexions of the noun and the tenses of the verb, should have raised a doubt whether its author could have been the Aristarchean Dionysius. But what it proves is the superiority of the Stoic systematization and the eventual acknowledgement of this by the Alexandrian school; the grammatical section (Περὶ τῆς φωνῆς τέχνης)[1] of the logic of Diogenes of Babylon, who taught Apollodorus in Athens, seems to have been particularly effective. It cannot be regarded as a decisive objection to Dionysius' authorship. The papyri seem at first sight to provide stronger arguments. The few papyri from the first to the third and fourth centuries A.D. that contain fragments of technical grammar differ to some extent from the *Techne*, and it is only when we reach the fifth century that we find one containing the beginning of the *Techne* itself.[2] But these are arguments *e silentio*, and it is not safe to draw conclusions from them. It has happened so often that the missing evidence, upon which papyrologists or archaeologists had built far-reaching historical hypotheses, has suddenly come to light and shown the most subtle arguments and inferences to have been delusive.[3]

Dionysius, as we saw, produced a number of notes and linguistic studies, and later grammarians, especially Apollonius Dyscolus, preserved

---

[1] See above, p. 253, and esp. K. Barwick, *Remmius Palaemon* (1922) 99 ff.

[2] *PSI* I (1912) ed. G. Vitelli, no. 18; Pack² no. 344 and 345 Dionys. Thr., no. 2138–76 Grammar. V. di Benedetto 185–96 scrupulously re-examined the papyri, seeking their support for his dating of the *Techne*. P. Lond. (inv. no.) 126 should no longer be quoted as a fifth-century codex; Kenyon's dating in the ed. princ. (1891) has been corrected by H. J. M. Milne, *Catalogue of the Lit. Papyri in the Brit. Mus.* (1927) p. 150, now *P. Lit. Lond.* 182, third/fourth century A.D. *P. Würzburg* 2, second century A.D. (U. Wilcken, 'Mitteilungen aus der Würzburger Papyrussammlung', *Abh. d. Preuss. Akad. d. Wiss.*, Phil.-hist. Kl. Jg. 1933, Nr. 6 (1934) 22 ff.) has apparently escaped di Benedetto's attention; if the Dionysius col. 1 14 were D. Thrax and what follows a verbatim reference to the *Techne*, as F. Della Corte, *Riv. fil. class.* 64 (1936) 406 ff. suggests (with the help of bold supplements), the origin of the *Techne* could not be attributed to the later centuries of the empire.

[3] A unique papyrus-codex of the sixth century A.D. published in 1952 refuted the assumption that large marginal commentaries around the text could not have been written before the time of Photius, see Call. vol. II, p. XXVII 3; one small lamp found in a proto-geometric grave in 1955 put an end to the debate about the non-existence of lamps in the epic age, see *Ausgewählte Schriften*, p. 3. 5.

a few fragments of these dealing with grammatical questions. The Scholia on the *Techne*[1] report that τινές—it was a bad habit of grammarians to say 'some' instead of quoting the name of the source—τινές had found in these works three small items which contradicted the corresponding passages in the *Techne* and had therefore concluded that this book could not have been a genuine work of the pupil of Aristarchus (μὴ γνήσιον εἶναι). But the discrepancies are by no means fundamental, and Dionysius may well have changed his mind[2] about minor controversial points. If in one work he had treated appellatives and proper names as two different parts of speech in the Stoic sense,[3] he might have returned to Aristarchus' standpoint in the *Techne*, where προσηγορία is a subdivision (εἶδος) of ὄνομα; if elsewhere he had followed the Stoics in making no distinction between ἄρθρον and ἀντωνυμία, he could still have listed them in the *Techne* as two of the eight parts of speech, which was apparently how Aristarchus had treated them. In the third instance, the definition of the verb quoted by Apollonius Dyscolus from some book of Dionysius, the wording differs from that in the *Techne*, but the meaning (ῥῆμα as κατηγόρημα, that is 'predicate') is compatible with it.

These variants were picked out from the Scholia in 1822 shortly after Bekker's publication of them by K. W. Göttling, who as a young professor in the University of Jena was one of Goethe's advisers in classics; he tried with great eloquence to persuade his readers that the so-called *Ars grammatica* of Dionysius was a Byzantine compilation.[4] The controversy thus provoked was silenced in favour of Dionysius by Moritz Schmidt,[5] the strange and learned editor of Didymus' fragments and of Hesychius in five volumes, and by Uhlig, the editor of the *Techne*. In fact, classical scholars and linguists[6] of the late nineteenth and the twentieth centuries hardly recognized the existence of a problem, until in 1958 di Benedetto brought it into the foreground again. But we have already considered his main points without finding in them any completely decisive objection to Dionysius' authorship. If he did not write the *Techne* about 100 B.C., the part played by scholars in the systematization of grammar a century later

---

[1] Schol. Dionys. Thr. pp. 124. 7–14 and 161. 2–8 Hilg. (Prolegom. Schol. Vat.), Apollon. Dysc. vol. III Fragm. ed. R. Schneider (1910) 71. 27 ff.

[2] Compare for instance the self-contradiction of the grammarian Philoxenus in Et. Or., s.v. μοχλός (C. Wendel, *RE* xx, 1941, col. 200. 15).

[3] See above, p. 244.

[4] Theodos. Alex. *Grammatica* ed. C. G. Goettling (1822), praef. pp. v ff.

[5] M. Schmidt, 'Dionys der Thraker', *Philol.* 8 (1853) 231 ff., 510 ff.; pp. 231 f. a bibliography of the controversy.

[6] Only a small selection of references is given: Steinthal, Wilamowitz, Rutherford, G. Murray, Robbins, Barwick, Pohlenz, Marrou, Schwyzer.

must have been greater than we believed;[1] but this is not a very plausible supposition, because our tradition offers no evidence for it.

The arrangement of the *Techne* in our manuscripts, however, cannot be original, as we noticed when we analysed the sequence of the paragraphs. We cannot guess what happened; something seems to have been lost after paragraph four, and perhaps a meddlesome redactor tried to combine as much of the original as he could still get hold of. We must hope that a friendly papyrus will disclose the *fata libelli* one day. But even in its damaged condition the structure of the *Techne* is not unlike that of the typical textbooks (εἰσαγωγαί) of the Hellenistic age; and the comparative analysis of them recently undertaken[2] is very welcome for our purpose.

If I am right, technical grammar is the latest achievement of Hellenistic scholarship. It would have come much earlier, if Aristotle had been the father of philology, as many believe he was; but the scholar poets who actually created it turned to the ἑρμηνεία τῶν ποιητῶν and regarded the study of language as no more than the handmaid of textual criticism and interpretation. Very late, and under the influence of Stoic doctrines, an Alexandrian scholar constructed from observation (ἐμπειρία) of the language of poets and prose writers a 'system of γραμματική' that is a τέχνη.[3] The lateness of its appearance, often regarded with surprise, is in harmony with the line of development we have traced from the third to the first century B.C.

With Dionysius Thrax and his school in Rhodes we have entered the first century B.C. The name of Didymus in Augustus' reign will mark the terminus of our wanderings through the Hellenistic age. But between the two, there is at least a triad of scholars which has a right to be briefly mentioned.

Two came from Asia Minor, Tyrannion from Amisus in Pontus, and Asclepiades from Myrlea in Bithynia. Tyrannion, having been a member of Dionysius' school,[4] returned to his native city as a teacher; made prisoner during the second Mithridatic war he was taken to Italy in 71 B.C. and lived in Rome from about 67 B.C. onwards. Like his fellow captive, the poet Parthenius,[5] he found great patrons and friends: Caesar, Cicero,

[1] See di Benedetto 118.

[2] See Fuhrmann, *Das systematische Lehrbuch* (1960); cf. D. Fehling, *Gnom.* 34 (1962) 113 ff., esp. 116.

[3] On ἐμπειρία and τέχνη see above, pp. 57 f., 64 f., 75.

[4] See above, p. 266, n. 3; cf. C. Wendel, *RE* VII A (1948) 1811–19. Testimonia with interpretations and many references in *GRF* Prolegomena pp. xv f. no. 26; ibid. p. xvii no. 27 Asclepiades, pp. xx f. no. 39 Philoxenus.

[5] Cf. 'A Fragment of Parthenios' Arete', *Cl. Qu.* 37 (1943) 30 f. = *Ausgewählte Schriften* (1960) 144.

Atticus. In Suidas' article the titles of his books are hopelessly mixed up with those of a younger Tyrannion; but we can distinguish at least two groups, one on Homeric subjects and one on problems of technical grammar. His object was to improve on his teacher's Homeric and grammatical writings. Asclepiades[1] may have spent some of his early years in Alexandria, though this is doubtful, but he certainly went to Rome and even to Spain. His interests were the same as Tyrannion's; but there is no evidence that he was a pupil of Dionysius, and his Homeric monographs, in which, like Dionysius, he reinterpreted Nestor's cup (Λ 352 ff.) and the passage on the Pleiads, contained polemics against the Alexandrians as well as against the Pergamenes. Asclepiades' collection of biographies Περὶ γραμματικῶν was perhaps the source of the story about Peisistratus in Cicero *de oratore*.[2] His systematic treatise Περὶ γραμματικῆς[3] and Tyrannion's definition of γραμματική[4] both intentionally differed from Dionysius' *Techne*, a fact which shows how controversial this field had become.

A very peculiar and unexpected task awaited Tyrannion in Rome, that of dealing with Theophrastus' library, which included a substantial part of Aristotle's manuscripts. Strabo,[5] who prided himself on having attended Tyrannion's lectures in Rome (some time after 44 B.C., perhaps about 30 B.C.), gives a rather unsatisfactory report of the fortunes of this unique Peripatetic library. It was transferred from Athens to Rome by Sulla in 84 B.C., but apparently in disorder and neglect. Tyrannion, φιλαριστοτέλης ὤν, 'had a hand in dealing' (διεχειρίσατο) with the library, 'having made friends with the librarian' (θεραπεύσας τὸν ἐπὶ τῆς βιβλιοθήκης). Plutarch, in his life of Sulla, is hardly more precise: λέγεται . . . ἐνσκευάσασθαι τὰ πολλά, 'he is said to have put ready most things', but he adds the information that from Tyrannion (παρ' αὐτοῦ) the work of final arrangement and publication was passed on to a specialist, the Peripatetic philosopher Andronicus of Rhodes.[6]

The third of these scholars, Philoxenus,[7] was born in Alexandria and came from there to Rome. The Alexandrian school had lived on in a modest way after the great 'secessio'; Aristarchus' pupil Ammonius[8]

---

[1] G. Wentzel, *RE* II (1896) 1628 ff.; B. A. Müller, *De Asclepiade Myrleano*, Diss. Leipzig 1903; A. Adler, 'Die Kommentare des Asklepiades v. M.', *Herm.* 49 (1914) 39 ff.

[2] See p. 6, n. 3.   [3] See above, pp. 158 and 162.   [4] Sext. Emp. *adv. math.* 1 72 f.

[5] Strab. XIII 608 f.; Plut. *Vita Sullae* 26. On Aristotle's library see above, p. 67. All the relevant evidence is collected and commented on by Düring, *Aristotle* 337 f. and 412 ff.

[6] Cf. above, p. 264, on Porphyry's testimony.

[7] C. Wendel, *RE* XX (1941) 194 ff.; R. Reitzenstein, *Geschichte der griech. Etymologika* (1897) 180 ff., 338 ff. is still important.

[8] On Ammonius see above, pp. 216 and 254; *OGI* 172 Ὀνάσανδρος ἱερεὺς . . . τεταγμένος [ἐπὶ τῆς ἐν Ἀ]λεξανδρείᾳ μεγάλης βιβλιοθήκης.

was its head in the second half of the second century B.C., and an inscription gives us the name of a librarian appointed by Ptolemy IX at about 100 B.C. Varro's relation to Philoxenus makes it fairly certain that he belonged to the first half of the first century B.C. He wrote on Homeric subjects, but these are far surpassed by the variety and originality of his linguistic studies. Among his treatises on dialects was one new feature: Περὶ τῆς Ῥωμαίων διαλέκτου.[1] But clearly he regarded Latin as a species of Greek dialect, and he did not initiate a comparative study of two different languages, as it is sometimes said. His technical grammar centred on the verbs, especially the ῥήματα μονοσύλλαβα from which he derived other forms of verbs and even of nouns. The monosyllables as the ἀρχαί, the prototypes, had a particular value, he believed, for the recognition of the ἔτυμα and were also the criteria for the correct use of the Greek language (ἑλληνισμός). These are old problems, already met in a series of philosophical debates ranging from Plato's Cratylus[2] to the Stoics, but the emphasis has shifted. The peculiar merit of this generation was to keep discussion going among the Greek scholars and at the same time to strengthen Rome's philhellenism in this field.[3] It is only a modern legend, however frequently retold, that the Romans brought destruction upon Greek science and scholarship. But there was, as we have seen, a general inner decline of the Greek spirit, quite natural in the world of rival small kingdoms and cities and of the decaying Ptolemaic régime. Scholarship gained new life in Rome, and even in Egypt the growing interest of Caesar, Mark Antony, and Augustus, and the lively exchange between Alexandria and Rome[4] had an encouraging effect on scholars.

It is uncertain whether Didymus, born and grown up in Alexandria,[5] ever settled down in Rome; Alexandria, where the libraries were but slightly damaged, is more likely to have been the scene of all his amazing feats of learning. In spite of them—or perhaps because of them—his reputation has never been very high. The fellows of the Museum,

---

[1] GRF 443–6; the Tyrannion who treated the same subject was the younger one after Philoxenus.

[2] See above, pp. 60 ff., on the ἀρχαί.

[3] Cf. above, p. 246. This will be the subject of another volume, which will also deal with Didymus' (younger) contemporaries Tryphon, Theon, etc., in connexion with scholars of the following generation.

[4] Strab. XIV 674 f.

[5] Suid. v. Δίδυμος. L. Cohn, RE v (1905) 445 ff. Didymi . . . Fragmenta coll. M. Schmidt (1854, repr. 1964); on the Didymus-fragments in the Scholia on Homer sorted out by A. Ludwich, Aristarchs hom. Textkritik and on Van der Valk, Researches see above, p. 214, n. 1. Research was very much stimulated by the publication of the Berlin papyrus Διδύμου Περὶ Δημοσθένους (see above, p. 212, n. 7 and p. 218, n. 1 on Leo's review); bibliography in Pack[2] no. 339 with references to other papyri containing short quotations of Didymus. See also M. Lossau, 'Untersuchungen zur antiken Demosthenesexegese', Palingenesia 11 (1964) passim.

inclined to mockery in the golden days of the earlier Ptolemies,[1] but not in the times of disturbance, seem to have recovered their sense of humour; at any rate we find them once again coining malicious nicknames. The title Χαλκέντερος, 'of brazen guts', stuck to Didymus for ever; βιβλιολάθας characterized him as one who had produced so many books that he could not remember what he had written. The fantastic figure of 3,500 or 4,000 books is probably derived from the same source; it was known, like the name βιβλιολάθας, in the first century A.D.[2]

What was the driving force behind Didymus' productivity, which obviously differed from that of the other Hellenistic scholars? Before we answer this question, we must try to state the verifiable facts of his life and work.

The dates of his lifetime and the age he reached are not precisely known, as Suidas puts his ἀκμή rather vaguely 'under Antony and Cicero' and says that his life 'extended until Augustus', synchronizing Didymus with king Juba of Mauretania, the historian;[3] so we cannot say more than that he worked in the second half of the first century B.C. and at the beginning of the first century A.D. The younger Heraclides Ponticus and Apion, the grammarian, were his pupils and assistants—indeed the number of his assistants must have been considerable.

It is impossible to give here a complete survey of Didymus' innumerable publications,[4] and it is also unnecessary because a few examples can show the tendency and value of his whole work. Homer had been the chief subject of Hellenistic scholarship throughout two and a half centuries; and Didymus' first achievement was to sum up all these Homeric studies. We shall not repeat what has been said in the chapter on Aristarchus,[5] but one statement should be emphasized again. Didymus' Περὶ τῆς Ἀρισταρχείου διορθώσεως belonged, as the title shows, to the Περί-literature. It gave excerpts from Aristarchus' critical editions of Homer and from the corresponding passages in his commentaries and monographs, with Didymus' own opinion occasionally added. It was not, as is so often asserted, a reconstruction of Aristarchus' critical edition, supposedly lost in the meantime. Its primary importance lies in the verbatim excerpts, and its weakest points are Didymus' own comments. He reported, for instance, the agreement of the readings of Zenodotus, Aristophanes, and

---

[1] See above, p. 170.
[2] Quintil. *inst.* I 8. 20; Demetr. Troezen. in Athen. IV 139 C; cf. Sen. *ep.* 88. 37.
[3] *FGrHist* 275 T 1, cf. T 13 (*ca.* 50 B.C.–A.D. 23 Jacoby). Cf. E. Rohde, *Kleine Schriften* I 177. 1, who understands ἐπὶ Ἀντωνίου as the year 43; if Didymus flourished then, he was born in 83.
[4] The section in Wilamowitz, *Einleitung in die Tragödie* 157–68, on Didymus is still very valuable, as it covers a wide field, not only tragedy.
[5] See above, pp. 215 ff.; also the text of the Schol. Γ 126 and A 522 is quoted.

Aristarchus (Γ 126), or the agreement of Aristarchus with 'nearly all the other editions' (Δ 522), and he noted their disagreement, for instance at K 306, where the vulgate text of our manuscripts reads οἵ κεν ἀριστεύωσι: οὕτως Ἀρίσταρχος "οἵ κεν ἄριστοι ἔωσι"· ὁ δὲ Ζηνόδοτος "αὐτοὺς οἳ φορέουσιν ἀμύμονα Πηλείωνα". Ἀριστοφάνης "καλοὺς οἳ φορέουσι" (Schol. AT). He was a careful preserver of variants, whether through collation of all the editions or by taking some over from the latest edition. In his ὑπομνήματα, running commentaries on the *Iliad* and *Odyssey*, he collected exegetical, especially mythographical,[1] material from many sources, and also precious items of information like that about the opinions of Aristophanes and Aristarchus on the τέλος of the *Odyssey*.[2]

Like his predecessors in Alexandria,[3] Didymus dedicated his most strenuous labours, after his books on Homer, to Attic comedy, gathering various readings and explanations of the comic poets, especially Aristophanes,[4] from the earlier editions, commentaries, and monographs. His most valuable contribution was in the collection of a vast amount of literary, historical, biographical, and prosopographical[5] material; for this non-linguistic matter had been inadequately treated by Aristarchus.[6] There is no evidence that he made a new recension of the text. Although his name is quoted sixty-seven times in the Scholia of Aristophanes, the usual expression ἐν ὑπομνήμασι is not added. So it is only a conjecture[7] that he chose to publish his material in the form of ὑπομνήματα, but an almost certain conjecture, as it is hardly imaginable that the quotations could have come from a series of monographs. Aristophanes of Byzantium had made the striking emendation[8] Ἀλκαῖος for Ἀχαιός (Ar. *Thesm.* 162) in his fundamental recension of the text; Didymus, however, tried to defend the manuscript tradition by arguments which were justly called 'silly' (λελήρηται) by a later commentator in our Scholia. This example is characteristic of Didymus' lack of common sense—and also of the conservative narrow-mindedness of compilers in general.

Didymus' commentaries on Homer, Pindar, and the tragedians have the same limitations; but it would be very unfair to dwell on these[9] and

---

[1] C. Wendel, 'Mythographie', *RE* xvi (1935) 1358–61.   [2] See above, pp. 175 ff.

[3] See above, pp. 159 ff. and 224.

[4] Cf. P. Boudreaux, *Le texte d'Aristophane* 91–137 on Didymus.

[5] Ammonius' κωμῳδούμενοι were a convenient source, not yet at the disposal of Aristarchus.

[6] See above, p. 224.

[7] Athen. II 67 D Δίδυμος δ᾽ ἐξηγούμενος τὸ ἰαμβεῖον (Aristoph. *Pl.* 720) must not mean a commentary on the *Plutos*, as is generally supposed; cf. above on ἐξηγεῖσθαι pp. 222 f.

[8] See above, p. 189.

[9] A. Roemer not only did this, but made Didymus the scapegoat for everything which he regarded as mistaken in the Scholia; cf. above, p. 233, n. 1.

let them obscure his genuine merits. For the exposition of Pindar's *Epinicia*,[1] as with Aristophanes' comedies, he made excerpts from earlier comments, but he also scanned the historians, especially those on Sicily, and even the antiquarian Polemo, and thus supplied what Aristarchus had left unexplained. Didymus' ὑπομνήματα included the *Paeans* and the *Hymns* and probably many more of the seventeen books into which Aristophanes of Byzantium had divided the Pindaric poems.[2] Of his ὑπόμνημα Βακχυλίδου ἐπινίκων[3] only the title survives. The classification of the various genres, with all its subdivision and definition was the subject of his monograph Περὶ λυρικῶν ποιητῶν.

We cannot be certain whether Didymus wrote on Aeschylus.[4] His favourite tragedian was Sophocles, and an analysis of the exceptionally learned Scholia on Sophocles' *Oedipus Coloneus* can give some idea of his ὑπόμνημα, even if the wording is hardly his own. His name is quoted three times (Schol. *OC* 155, 237, 763), and the references to the earlier ὑπομνηματισάμενοι (Schol. *OC* 388, 390, 681) are in his style,[5] though he probably added to them something of his own on Attic antiquities, mythography, and history. While he collected facts and judgements favourable to Sophocles, in his commentaries on plays of Euripides he combined the critical voices of the past with his own criticism.[6] His name occurs eighteen times in the Scholia on six plays, but we cannot yet say how many plays altogether he commented on. The διάφορα ἀντίγραφα cited in the subscription of the Scholia on *Medea* included a copy of Didymus from which extracts were made. These ἀντίγραφα were, of course, ὑπομνήματα; no clear reference has yet been found to an ἔκδοσις or διόρθωσις by Didymus of any lyric or dramatic poet.[7]

His work stopped at the point beyond which he had no predecessors to draw on. So he had to confine himself mainly to the exegesis of the poets. With the possible exception of the great historians,[8] the only prose writers on whom there were commentaries at his disposal for excerpting and compiling were the orators, especially Demosthenes. This is strange,

---

[1] See Irigoin, *Histoire du texte de Pindare* 67–75.

[2] See above, p. 183.   [3] See above, p. 222.

[4] W. Schmid, *Gesch. d. griech. Lit.* ii (1934) 305, is much too confident in his arguing; by a slip of the pen, a commentary on Aeschylus is attributed by him to Aristophanes of Byzantium.

[5] Scholia in Sophoclis *Oedipum Coloneum*, rec. V. de Marco (1952); in praef. pp. xxii f. the exaggerations of J. Richter, *W.St.* 33 (1911) 37 ff., are reduced to their proper limits.

[6] See Elsperger, 'Antike Kritik gegen Euripides', *Philol.* Suppl. xi 1 (1908) 108 ff., 114 ff. and Index p. 167.—Cf. Eur. *Hipp.* ed. W. S. Barrett (1964) p. 48.

[7] G. Zuntz, *An Inquiry into the Transmission of the Plays of Euripides* (1965) 253 f., believes in an edition of 'the text which Didymus issued for those students of his voluminous commentaries who cared to have the wording preferred by him at their elbows'.

[8] See above, pp. 224 f.

seeing that they had traditionally been studied in the schools of rhetoric, and not by the γραμματικοί. Yet some titles and some fragments of Didymus' comments on the Attic orators[1] were known even before the great Berlin papyrus gave us a substantial part of the original of *Διδύμου Περὶ Δημοσθένους*.[2] In this monograph, composed of irregular lemmata from *Philippica* IX–XII followed by explanatory notes, Didymus often refers to ἔνιοι or τινές or οἱ ὑπομνηματίσαντες with whom he did, or did not agree. The *Πίνακες* of Callimachus[3] had contained a section on the orators, and he had also raised various questions of authorship; later, in the time of Aristophanes of Byzantium selective lists[4] of the foremost orators had been arranged. Didymus' references reveal the important fact that, besides these, there were exegetical writings on Demosthenes in existence before his time; careful investigations have shown it to be likely that they belonged to the late second or the early first century B.C. and treated questions of chronology, history, and language.[5] So, just in this one branch of prose literature, he had ample material to exploit.[6]

Otherwise he could draw only on the interpreters of poetry. Thus his lexical writings[7] are best represented by his *Λέξις κωμική* and his *Λέξις τραγική*. In the long series of glossographical, lexicographical, and onomatological collections the *Λέξεις* of Aristophanes of Byzantium had been the highlights, ranging over wide fields of literature. Didymus, in making his excerpts from this material and from exegetical works, confined himself to the usage of the comic and tragic poets. But his work on the language of the tragedians amounted to at least twenty-eight books, of which the arrangement is still unknown;[8] it must have been an immense storehouse in which the treasures of earlier research were piled up, waiting for the future. A few titles and fragments of other specialized lexical and grammatical writings[9] are ascribed to Didymus; but in some of these cases the reference may be to younger grammarians of the same name.[10]

---

[1] Didym. fragm. pp. 310–17 Schm.

[2] See above, p. 212, n. 7; the characteristic form of *Περὶ Δημοσθένους* was recognized by F. Leo in his often quoted review of the *editio princeps*.

[3] See above, pp. 128 ff.   [4] See above, p. 206.

[5] Lossau, *Palingenesia* II (1964) 66 ff. 'Die frühalexandrinische Demosthenesexegese (vor Didymos)'; on σύγγραμμα, ὑπόμνημα, etc., see p. 213.

[6] The usual assumption that his studies of the orators were more original than the other ones (Cohn *RE* v 458. 35 ff.) has not been confirmed.

[7] Didym. fragm. pp. 15–111 Schm.

[8] Hesychius in the dedicatory epistle of his lexicon speaks of 'alphabetical order' (κατὰ στοιχεῖον), but Harpocrat. s.v. ξηραλοιφᾶν (Didym. p. 84 Schm. fr. 1) and Macrob. *Sat.* v 18. 9, 11 f. are hardly reconcilable with this statement.

[9] Didym. fragm. pp. 15–27 and 335–55 Schm.

[10] Cohn, *RE* v 465 f. and 471 f.

There is finally a group of monographs.[1] That on the classification of the lyric poets has already been mentioned, and we shall refer to only two others here. Περὶ παροιμιῶν[2] augmented the collection of proverbs compiled by Aristophanes of Byzantium; it owed most of its material to Attic comedy. A miscellaneous work, called Συμποσιακά (or Συμμεικτά), was an accumulation of what had not found a place elsewhere; but even here there were some trifles of genuine learning on Homer, Sappho, and Anacreon.

The scholar poets and their successors in the third and second centuries B.C. had been moved by their love of letters and by their own work as writers to preserve the literary heritage of the epic, Ionic, and Attic ages;[3] they firmly believed in its eternal greatness. Didymus in his turn was moved by the love of learning to preserve the scholarly heritage of the Hellenistic age; he had a sincere admiration for the greatness of scholars and a firm belief in their authority, although he was not totally devoid of critical judgement. He also knew that editions, commentaries, and monographs ought not to be treated as sacrosanct monuments of literature. Their substance had to be preserved, not their form; the careful compilation of intelligently chosen excerpts gave them the best chance of survival in a declining civilization that wished for short cuts to knowledge.

We earlier postponed the answer to the question whether the driving force behind Didymus' fantastic activity can be recognized; the answer, now that we have found it, defines his relation to the whole of Hellenistic scholarship and his historical position at the end of the age. We can say with some confidence that Didymus was enabled to become the most efficient servant of an ancient intellectual community, because a decent order had been re-established in the whole Mediterranean world by Augustus' peace.

[1] Didym. fragm. pp. 356–400 Schm.
[2] See O. Crusius, *Analecta ad paroemiographos Graecos* (1883) 48 ff., 92 ff. and K. Rupprecht, *RE* xviii (1949) 1747 ff.
[3] See above, pp. 87 f., cf. p. 3.

EXCURSUSES

Excursus to p. 37

Plat. *Phaedr.* 267 c (= *Vors.* 80 A 26 = *Art. script.* B III 4 Raderm.) Πρωταγό-
ρεια δέ . . . οὐκ ἦν μέντοι τοιαῦτ' ἄττα;—ὀρθοέπειά γέ τις . . . καὶ ἄλλα πολλὰ
καὶ καλά. This probably was Protagoras' own expression, but certainly not the
title of a book, as τις shows. On Democritus see above, p. 42. For the later use
of the term in rhetorical writings see Radermacher, *ad loc.* Themistius, *or.* 23
p. 350. 19 Dind., tried to make it clearer by adding καὶ ὀρθορρημοσύνη—. In
Plat. *Crat.* 391 B (= *Vors.* 80 A 24 = *Art. script.* B III 9) Socrates says διδάξαι
σε τὴν ὀρθότητα περὶ τῶν τοιούτων ('about such questions of language') ἥν
ἔμαθεν παρὰ Πρωταγόρου. Hermogenes replies that it would be absurd to
accept single doctrines, if one rejects the 'Truth' of Protagoras entirely: εἰ τὴν
Ἀλήθειαν τὴν Πρωταγόρου ὅλως οὐκ ἀποδέχομαι. So Protagoras possibly treated
such problems in this book. But one should not take τὴν ὀρθότητα περὶ τῶν
τοιούτων simply as περὶ ὀνομάτων ὀρθότητα (as Diels–Kranz seem to do; for
similar misinterpretations of τῶν τοιούτων = τούτων in Aristotle see M. Pohlenz,
Herm. 84 [1956] 61) and assume that this was the Protagorean expression. As
far as we have any evidence, it is more characteristic of the so-called Heraclitean Cratylus, whom Plato introduced as the principal person of his dialogue
(*Cratyl.* 383 A = *Vors.* 65 A 5 Κρατύλος φησὶν ὅδε . . . ὀνόματος ὀρθότητα εἶναι
. ἑκάστῳ τῶν ὄντων φύσει πεφυκυῖαν κτλ.; cf. 397 A), and again in a different
way of Prodicus (see p. 40); we should also hesitate to attribute the 'etymological' arguments for the 'correctness' of Homeric names in the discussion
between Socrates and Hermogenes (*Cratyl.* 391 A–393 B) to Protagoras, as they
are connected with the question of φύσις and νόμος (see above *Cratyl.* 383 A);
see p. 39, n. 3 and p. 53.

Hermeias (fifth century A.D.) in Plat. *Phaedr.* 267 CD p. 239. 14 Couvreur =
Art. script. B III 5 explained ὀρθοέπεια as κυριολεξία; this neoplatonic explanation is not supported by any other tradition, and there is no reason for
accepting it, especially when we compare his explanations of Polus' and Licymnius' 'doctrines' which immediately precede that of Protagoras. For the obvious
mistakes see Radermacher, *Art. script.* B XIV 10 and B XVI 2: Hermeias ascribed
the distinction of κύρια, ἐπίθετα, etc., to Licymnius whom he called the teacher
instead of the pupil of Polus, and he went on to attribute to Protagoras, who
belongs to the older generation, the precept to use the κύρια, not the other
species of ὀνόματα. Even Wilamowitz seems to have been misled by Hermeias
in his otherwise important note to Eur. *Herc. F.* 56 ὀρθῶς φίλος, when he says
that 'Protagoras by ὀρθοέπεια meant τὸ τοῖς κυρίοις ὀνόμασιν χρῆσθαι'. H.
Koller, 'Die Anfänge der griechischen Grammatik', *Glotta* 37 (1958) 5–40,
reconstructs a theory of Protagoras' ὀρθόεπεια on the basis of κυριολεξία, but he

Excursuses 281

rejects Hermeias' own explanation of κύρια as 'literal' in contrast to 'figurative'
and imposes a different meaning upon it: 'words in common usage', 'current
words' in contrast to poetical, artistic, obsolete, ornamental words. The whole
article is based on the same writer's book *Die Mimesis in der Antike* (Bern 1954).
If the foundations laid in the book on μίμησις are not solid enough, as I am
convinced they are not (see also W. J. Verdenius, *Mnemosyne* ser. IV, vol. 10
[1957] 254–8 and H. Herter, *DLZ* 1959, 402 ff.), almost everything breaks
down that is said in this article about the beginnings of Greek grammar.
[*Addendum.* D. Fehling, 'Zwei Untersuchungen zur griech. Sprachphilosophie' 1. 'Protagoras und die ὀρθοέπεια', *Rh.M.* 108 (1965) 212–17, came at
least partly to similar conclusions. 2. 'Φύσις und θέσις' 218–29: I can just refer
to his polemics against oversimplifications in late ancient and modern times
without taking sides. Cf. p. 202, n. 6.]

Excursus to p. 46

Plut. *Qu. conviv.* VII 10 p. 715 E καὶ τὸν Αἰσχύλον ἱστοροῦσι τὰς τραγῳδίας
ἐμπίνοντα ποιεῖν, καὶ οὐχ, ὡς Γοργίας εἶπεν, ἐν τῶν δραμάτων αὐτοῦ "μεστὸν
(μέγιστον cod.: em. Reiske) Ἄρεως" εἶναι, τοὺς "Ἑπτ' ἐπὶ Θήβας, ἀλλὰ πάντα
Διονύσου (Aesch. *trag.* ed. Wilamowitz 1914, p. 78; cf. ibid. pp. 14 f. test. 43).
These polemics against Gorgias stressing the point that *all* the plays of Aeschylus are 'full of Dionysus' are derived from a Peripatetic source, probably
Chamaeleo Περὶ Αἰσχύλου, see fr. 40 a and b, F. Wehrli, *Die Schule des
Aristoteles* 9 (1957) 61 and commentary 85 f. The first to notice the identity of
the quotation from Gorgias in Plutarch with the wording in the *Frogs* is said to
have been Th. Stanley (who edited Aeschylus in 1663); so Van Leeuwen in his
commentary (1896) to Aristoph. *Ran.* loc. cit., but I was unable to verify this
statement in one of Stanley's editions.—Another reference which is so far
missing should be added to our collections of Gorgias' fragments: Philodem.
Herculan. Volum. coll. altera (1873) T. VIII, p. 15 (Pap. no. 1578) τοῦ Αἰσχύλου
δ[. . .] Ἄρεως ἔλεγε. Its relation to Aristoph. *Ran.* 1021 was recognized by
I. Kemke, Philod. *de mus.* (1884) III fr. 16, p. 27; Th. Gomperz, *Zu Philodems
Büchern von der Musik* (Wien 1885) 15, also referred it to Gorgias and proposed
supplements; independently, a similar supplement was proposed by E. Scheel,
De Gorgianae disciplinae vestigiis (Diss. Rostock 1890) 25. 1.

Excursus to p. 60

Theo Smyrn., *Expositio rerum mathem.* ed. E. Hiller (1878) 49 ff. (Latin translation in Chalcid. *Comment. in Plat. Tim.* c. 44, ed. J. H. Waszink, *Plato Latinus*
IV, Leiden 1962, p. 92); Erich Frank, *Plato und die sogenannten Pythagoreer* (1923)
167 ff., believed he had discovered a pre-Platonic atomistic system of the
'music' in this passage and gave a detailed interpretation of some Democritean
fragments; but he has not convinced me either that Adrastus is dependent on

an early atomist source or that one is able to get *so* much out of the scanty
titles and quotations, listed by Diels under the heading Μουσικά (above,
p. 42). There is nothing beyond the ordinary Platonic–Peripatetic tradition to
be found in Adrastus' few sentences. H. Koller, 'Stoicheion', *Glotta* 34 (1955)
161 ff., accepted Frank's dating of the Adrastus-passage in Theo Smyrn., but
instead of an atomist source he invented a pre-Platonic musical system in
which στοιχεῖον was used for the 'reihenbildende Töne'; he himself admitted,
however, that there is no clear evidence for στοιχεῖον as a musical term in the
sense of 'scale'; see also the short refutation of Koller's arguments by W. Burkert, 'Στοιχεῖον', *Philol.* 103 (1959) 177 f.

Excursus to p. 70

The λύσεις to this question (Schol. A *A* 50) are inserted by Schrader into
Porphyr. *Quaest. Hom. in Il.* p. 4; but there is no evidence for this (see also
Schrader's own note on l. 6). The first solution quoted by the Schol. is a rare
and interesting one: καὶ οἱ μὲν ῥητορικῶς λύοντές φασιν, ὅτι φιλάνθρωπον ὂν τὸ
θεῖον . . . πρότερον ἀπὸ τοιούτων ζῴων ἤρξατο μετάνοιαν τοῖς ἁμαρτήσασι διδούς.
This Schol. p. 13. 18 Dind. is written on the outer margin in two columns;
cf. on the inner margin p. 14. 11 Dind. φιλάνθρωπος ὢν ὁ θεὸς πρῶτον . . . τὰ
ἄλογα ζῷα ἀναιρεῖ, ἵνα διὰ τούτων εἰς δέος ἀγαγὼν τοὺς Ἕλληνας ἐπὶ τὸ εὐσεβεῖν
παρασκευάσῃ (nothing about μετάνοια). If I had known this passage earlier,
I should have been glad to quote it as a very welcome piece of new evidence
for my interpretation of Callimachus fr. 114, where I said: 'The main point
. . . left out by the later paraphrases . . . is expressed in the concluding distichon of Apollo's answer: the god is intentionally slow in practising retribu-
tion in order that there should be even a chance of μετανοεῖν for the evildoer—
that is, of changing his mind' ('The image of the Delian Apollo and Apolline
ethics', *The Journal of the Warburg and Courtauld Institutes* 25 [1952] 30 f. =
Ausgewählte Schriften [1960] 69). This is exactly what the anonymous λυτικός
says: 'The god as φιλάνθρωπος started his revenge first with the animals,
granting repentance to the human evildoers μετάνοιαν τοῖς ἁμαρτήσασι διδούς.'
He has preserved what the other paraphrases left out.—On λυτικοί in general
see A. Gudemann, 'Λύσεις', *RE* XIII (1927) 2511 ff., esp. 2517. 30 ῥητορικῶς
λύοντες.

Excursus to p. 74

Plat. *Leg.* 764 DE. This is the *only* passage where the words μονῳδία and χορῳδία
are applied to lyrical songs and opposed to one another. Modern scholars
generally refer to it, when they deal with the classification of lyric poetry into
'monody and choral song'; so for instance C. M. Bowra, *Greek Lyric Poetry*
2nd ed. (1961) 4. But this is a traditional mistake. Plato was actually speaking
of the training of solo-singers and chorus-singers in the course of a discussion of

musical education. The two terms are not used either by him or by any other ancient writer for theoretical classification; χορῳδία does not occur elsewhere at all and μονῳδία is strictly applied to the song of a single actor in tragedy. On the 'catachrestic' use of the word μονῳδός for the single reciter of a whole tragic iambus, like Lycophron in the *Alexandra*, see Tzetz. in Lyc. p. 4. 15 Scheer (cf. Bekker, *AG* iii 1461 n.). The distinction into monodic and choral lyric is a modern one and may well be used for the purpose of literary history. On the other hand, it is quite inappropriate to invent Greek titles 'μονῳδίαι' and 'χορῳδίαι' (*sic*) for an edition of the texts, as E. Diehl unfortunately did in his *Anthologia Lyrica* fasc. 4 (2nd ed. 1935) and 5 (2nd ed. 1942); for it gives the wrong impression that they were terms of the ancient grammarians. On ancient classifications see below, pp. 130 and 183 ff.

Excursus to p. 98

When I read the London Paper on *Hellenistic Poetry* in 1954, I knew only of two passages in G. Flaubert's letters on the 'Tour d'ivoire' (*Œuvres complètes. Correspondance*, Nouvelle édit. augmentée, ii. Série Paris 1926, p. 396. 24. April 1852 to Louise Colet: 'Il faut . . . monter dans sa tour d'ivoire et là, comme une bayadère dans ses parfums, rester seuls dans nos rêves' and ibid. iii (1927) p. 54. 22. Nov. 1852; 'montons au plus haut de notre tour d'ivoire, sur la dernière marche, le plus près du ciel'). I was rash enough to say that Flaubert had 'invented the ivory tower as a refuge for nineteenth-century littérateurs' (*JHS* 75 [1955] 73 = *Ausgewählte Schriften* 158). But later I was startled by my own rashness and began to make further inquiries with the help of Hugo Friedrich, who referred me also to E. R. Curtius, *Kritische Essays zur europäischen Literatur* (Bern 1950) 382. No doubt Sainte-Beuve, the greatest French critic and a minor poet, was the first to use the phrase for the seclusion of an unworldly poet, namely Alfred de Vigny, in a poem of 1837 (Pensées d'août, 1837, in *Poésies complètes* ii nouv. éd. 1863 p. 231, A. M. Villemain [epistula Horatiana]): 'La poésie en France . . . Lamartine, Hugo . . . et Vigny plus secret, / Comme en sa tour d'ivoire, avant midi, rentrait.' A very bold turn was given herewith to the famous image in *Song of Songs* 7. 5 ὁ τράχηλός σου ὡς πύργος ἐλεφάντινος (Sulamith), transferred to the Blessed Virgin in the *Lauretan Litany*: 'Turris eburnea.' It would have saved a lot of trouble, if I had looked up in time the *Shorter Oxford English Dictionary*, s.v. ivory, where the reference to Sainte-Beuve and A. de Vigny is given (the French dictionaries I had consulted did not help). But who made this ivory tower so popular again that it became a stock phrase in the daily papers in England and Germany? Henry James started to write a novel *The Ivory Tower* before the First World War, but broke it off in August 1914; the unfinished book was published in London 1917, but 'no mention is made of the symbolic object itself' (see Preface, p. vi). T. S. Eliot in his introduction to Paul Valéry, Essays, *Collected Works*, ed. J. Mathews, vol. vii (1958) xix speaks of 'a new conception of the poet. . . . The tower of ivory has been fitted up as a laboratory . . . a solitary laboratory.'

Excursus to p. 126

Call. *hy.* II 110 ff. *Δηοῖ δ' οὐκ ἀπὸ παντὸς ὕδωρ φορέουσι μέλισσαι, | ἀλλ' ἥτις καθαρή τε καὶ ἀχράαντος ἀνέρπει | πίδακος ἐξ ἱερῆς ὀλίγη λιβὰς ἄκρον ἄωτον*. When Anna Fabri edited Callimachus in 1675, her learned father referred her to Schol. Theocr. xv 94 *τὰς ἱερείας* (*ἑταίρας* codd.: em. T. Faber) *αὐτῆς* (sc. *τῆς Κόρης*) *καὶ τῆς Δήμητρος μελίσσας λέγεσθαι*. From that day on the *μέλισσαι* were taken to mean 'priestesses' who carry water to a temple of Demeter to wash the holy image; see especially G. Pasquali, *Quaestiones Callimacheae* (1913) 86–92; cf. also *P.Oxy.* xv (1922) 1802 col. II 29 = Apollod. *Π. θεῶν* 244 *FGrHist* 89, where Parian *θεσμοφοριάζουσαι γυναῖκες* are called *μέλισσαι* and an anonymous hymn to Demeter (Page, *Greek Lit. Pap.* p. 408) v. 2 *δεῦτε μέλισσαι*. In my edition (1953) I quoted Hesych. *μέλισσαι· αἱ τῆς Δήμητρος μυστίδες*. I have to recant it now with some regret. *Μέλισσαι* simply are bees doing what Aristotle said in *h.an.* VIII 1 p. 596 b 18 *ὕδωρ δ' ἥδιστα εἰς ἑαυτὰς λαμβάνουσιν, ὅπου ἂν καθαρὸν ἀναπηδᾷ* (more references *RE* III 453. 29 ff.); see also Virg. *georg.* IV 54 f. 'flumina libant / summa leves' (sc. apes), where 'summa' coincides with *ἄκρον ἄωτον*. If Virgil had these lines of the hymn in mind (cf. F. Klingner, *Virgils Georgica*, 1963, pp. 166 f.), he certainly understood *μέλισσαι* not as priestesses, but as bees. There is no reason to assume that Hesychius' gloss goes back to a commentary on Callimachus. See Schol. Theocr. xv 94 with Wendel's notes. We may be pleased to get rid of the priestesses and to restore the poetical simplicity of the passage; on the other hand, we have to confess that we are not able to see why the bees offer their tiny drops of water to Demeter. (On Demeter and bees see Olck, *RE* III 448. 58 ff.) But there are very many allusions in Callimachus' poems of which we do not yet grasp the meaning. One rather rash suggestion may be worth consideration. Callimachus refers to Philitas' *Demeter* more often than we could guess from the old fragments (fr. 5–8 Kuchenmüller): the *ὄμπνια θεσμοφόρος* Call. fr. 1. 10 is the Demeter of Philitas and the much discussed gloss *ἄεμμα* for *τόξον hy.* II 33 is taken from the poem, as the new Scholia disclosed (Call. II p. 47). The *μέλισσαι* as *βουγενεῖς* occur in a hexameter of Philit. fr. 18 K., possibly imitated by Call. fr. 383. 4 (see my note ad loc.), but we do not know the context of the line; some scholars suspected it may belong to the *Demeter*. So it is possible that the connexion of the bees with Demeter at the end of the second *hymn* is a reminiscence of Philitas' *Demeter* which was present to his mind when he wrote the hymn and the polemics against the Telchines.

Excursus to p. 142

The text has been misunderstood by Meineke, Wilamowitz, and by Wendel, who printed the conjectures of his predecessors in his apparatus; see also his 'Die Überlieferung der Scholien zu Apoll. Rh.', *AGGW* III 1 (1932) 113; cf. H. Herter, *Rh.M.* 91 (1942) 313 and *Bursians Jahresbericht* 285 (1955) 227 ff.; P.

Händel, *Herm.* 90 (1962) 431; Lesky (above, p. 88, n. 3) 666. They all understand τῶν βιβλιοθηκῶν τοῦ Μουσείου ἀξιωθῆναι as a reference to his librarianship; but the same phrase is used by Euseb. *Hist. eccl.* III 9. 2 βιβλιοθήκης ἀξιωθῆναι or *Praep. ev.* VIII 1. 8 τῶν κατὰ τὴν Ἀλεξάνδρειαν βιβλιοθηκῶν ἠξιώθη in the sense of τῆς ἐν βιβλιοθήκαις ἀναθέσεως . . . καταξιωθῆναι (*Hist. eccl.* II 18. 8); see also above (p. 100) Aristeae *epist.* 9 ἄξια καὶ τῆς . . . βιβλιοθήκης. After his first failure and his exile to Rhodes, Apollonius returned, 'as some said', to Alexandria and recited his *Argonautica* with the highest success, so that he was deemed worthy of the libraries of the Museum and was buried beside Callimachus himself. It simply is a legendary story of his complete rehabilitation in his native city and of the final reconciliation with his adversary in the grave. This dubious passage at the end of the second *vita* cannot be compared with the serious tradition in *P.Oxy.* 1241; the story of the 'return of the native' may be due to a confusion with the later Apollonius, the Eidographer and librarian after Aristophanes of Byzantium; but as the *vita* does not say anything about such an appointment of Ap. Rh. at the library, it becomes still more doubtful whether it is necessary to assume such a confusion.

Excursus to p. 177. 4

Attentive readers of Wilamowitz's posthumous work on Greek religion may be startled by a remark on Aristophanes of Byzantium in the important paragraph on 'personifications' (Wilamowitz, *Der Glaube der Hellenen* I (1931) 26, repeated II (1932) 417). Aristophanes is there praised for having dealt sensibly with the Homeric εἰδωλοποιία, because he said that the poet had formed mythical images of certain deities bearing the same names as human πάθη and πράγματα, like ἔρως, ἔρις, φόβος, and so on. Wilamowitz refers to Porphyry on the *Iliad* (p. 42 Schrader) as evidence. But in fact Eustathius was the only one to attribute the first appearance of the theory of the δαίμονες εἰδωλοποιούμενοι μυθικῶς to a monograph of Aristophanes, Περὶ Αἰγίδος (Eust. p. 603. 28 on *E* 738). In our Homeric Scholia B on *B* 787 no author is quoted, in that on *E* 741 Aristotle (cf. Schol. BHQ λ 634; doubtful Schol. A *Λ* 4). Nauck's suspicion that the reference to Aristophanes in Eustathius is an error was reinforced by Schrader with stronger arguments. (Nauck pp. 271–3; Porphyr. *Quaest. Hom. ad Il.* ed. H. Schrader [1880] 44 f.; independently L. Cohn, *Jahrbb. f. class. Phil.* Suppl. 12 [see p. 197, n. 3] 287. 4 came to the same conclusion as Schrader, and Jacoby *FGrHist* II [1930] 754. 36 on Apollodor. Περὶ θεῶν was right in following them. Cf. Aristot. Pseudepigr. ed. V. Rose [1863] 162 f.) On Schrader's questionable reconstruction of Porphyry and on the possible relation of Porphyry to Aristotle see above, p. 70, n. 7. A parallel is the wrong attribution of the explanation of the proverb Κερκυραίων μάστιξ to Aristophanes Byz. in Schol. (V, Ald.) Aristoph. *Av.* 1463; Zenob. Ath. III 14 (Miller, *Mélanges* p. 370) confirmed with the reference to Ἀριστοτέλης . . . ἐν τῇ Κερκυραίων Πολιτείᾳ the less exact and therefore rejected statement of Zenob.

Par. IV 49 (cf. Aristot. fr. 513 R.). Another parallel may be Erotian. *Voc.
Hippocr.* s.v. πικερίῳ p. 73. 13 Nachmanson, who following Rose, Aristot. fr.
636, reads Ἀριστοτέλης ἐν τοῖς Ὑπομνήμασιν for Ἀριστοφάνης in the manuscripts.
So it is quite uncertain whether there was a σύγγραμμα of Aristophanes on the
Aegis and whether he ever dealt with this or any other fundamental problem
of Greek religion; on evidence for εἰδωλοποιία see also K. Reinhardt, *De
Graecorum theologia* (Diss. Berlin 1910) 107 ff. and add Plut. *adv. Colot.* 11
p. 1113 A οἱ ποιηταὶ . . . ἀνειδωλοποιοῦντες . . . (Σ 535), Schol. AD *I* 502
ἀνειδωλοποιεῖ τὰς Λιτὰς ὡς δαίμονάς τινας (cf. Schol. Eur. *Or.* 256).

ADDENDA

p. 36. 3 'Antisthenis Fragmenta', coll. Fernanda Decleva Caizzi, *Testi e documenti per lo studio dell'Antichità* 13 (1966), based in part on an unpublished thesis by Jean Humblé, *Antisthenes' Fragmenten* (Gent, 1932).

p. 42. 3 Cf. below, p. 243. 1 Addenda.

p. 43, l. 19 G. M. A. Grube, *The Greek and Roman Critics* 1965. This is a welcome study by an expert in ancient rhetoric; just because it is written from a different point of view, it may be useful to compare some of its chapters with our passages on literary criticism (cf. pp. 47, 204, etc.).

p. 52. 1 B. Snell, *Philol.* 96 (1944) 170 ff. = *Gesammelte Schriften* (1966) 119 ff.

p. 53. 3 The scanty and ambiguous tradition is carefully re-examined by G. A. Privitera, 'Laso di Ermione nella cultura ateniese e nella tradizione storiografica', *Filologia e Critica*, 1 (1965).

p. 54. 2 On *P.Oxy.* 1083, fr. 1 as part of a Sophoclean satyr-play see *WSt* 79 (1966) 63 ff.

p. 70. 5 *Add* Duris *FGrHist* 76 F 30 Προβλήματα Ὁμηρικά (in *Schol. Gen.* Φ 499).

p. 82, l. 4 *from bottom read* Attic annalists *instead of* Attic historians.

p. 93. 4 'the very few exceptions', scil. made by Plato in regard to poets.

p. 105. 1 The manuscript of this book was in its final form before I was able to see the second volume of M. Van der Valk, *Researches on the Text and Scholia of the Iliad* (1964); for references to the first volume see pp. 214. 1, 233. 2, 3, 274. 5. It is now impossible to do justice to an honest and diligent author whose painstaking researches cover part of the same ground as some of the following chapters, especially those on Zenodotus and Aristarchus. This is the more regrettable as Mr. Van der Valk often expresses different or even opposite views on the critical work of the Alexandrians. But his opinion that 'the Alexandrian critics had no correct idea of the significance of a diplomatic text', which is now openly expressed (pp. 565 f.), was the unspoken assumption behind his *Textual Criticism of the Odyssey* (1949) and the first volume of his *Researches on the Text and Scholia of the Iliad* (1963), and must unfortunately be regarded as a preconceived idea, not as a result of historical inquiries. The new volume was nobly reviewed by H. Erbse, *Gnom.* 37 (1965) 532 ff. See now also A. Lesky, 'Homeros', *RE*, Suppl. XI (1967), Sonderausgabe 151. 38 ff.

p. 109. 6 A new edition of 'The Ptolemaic Papyri of Homer' by Stephanie West has just been published in *Papyrologica Coloniensia* iii (1967); cf. p. 116. 5.

p. 128. 6 Callimachus' *Pinakes* are expressly attested as the source in all these cases; but I ought to have referred to some other anonymous passages on the authenticity of which the *Pinakes* or Aristophanes' supplement are the most likely sources. In the catalogue of Aeschylus' plays (below, p. 129) Αἰτναῖαι γνήσιοι as well as Αἰτναῖαι νόθοι are registered. According to the *Vita Sophoclis* Aristophanes gave a total of 130 plays, τούτων δὲ νενόθευται ιζ' (ζ' coni. Bergk in order to make the figure equal to Suidas' figure of 123 genuine Sophoclean plays). Aristophanes probably made this statement in his supplement to Callimachus' *Pinakes* (Nauck p. 249), cf. below, p. 192. 8 Addenda. In the same work he may have doubted the Hesiodic origin of the *Shield of Heracles* (see below, p. 178). Cf. also Arg. [Eur.] *Rhes.* ἔνιοι νόθον ὑπενόησαν . . .· ἐν μέντοι ταῖς διδασκαλίαις ὡς γνήσιον ἀναγέγραπται. The notes οὐ σῴζεται or οὐ σῴζονται against the titles of plays of which the text did not reach the 'haven of safety' in Alexandria are probably taken over from the *Pinakes* into Aristophanes' hypotheses: see Arg. Eur. *Med.* to the satyr-play Θερισταί or Arg. Aristophan. *Ach.* to Cratinus' Χειμαζόμενοι (cf. Arg. II Aristophan. *Pax*).

p. 133, l. 19 Ammon. *De adfin. vocab. differentia* ed. K. Nickau (1966) § 202 εὐθὺς καὶ εὐθὺ καὶ εὐθέως διαφέρουσιν cum adnot. p. 53. 11: 'Eren. Phil. *Epitome* καὶ Ἀριστοφάνης (nomen Aristophanis etiam in Symeonis *Synagoge* exstat, ubi ὁ γρ. — Ἀντιφάνους omissa sunt) ὁ γραμματικὸς ἐν τῷ *Πρὸς τοὺς Πίνακας Καλλιμάχου περὶ Ἀντιφάνους* διαστέλλει τὴν λέξιν (Sym.: τάξιν Eren.).' If Erennius Philo's *Epitome* had not preserved the title of Aristophanes' book, the new fragment would most probably have been attributed to a part of the *Λέξεις*, as σάννας was ascribed to a treatise on blasphemy before Miller's discovery of the codex Athous (see below, pp. 198 f.). The comic poets were registered in Callimachus' *Pinakes* (see above, pp. 129 f.); did Aristophanes' supplement contain chapters on individual poets (*Περὶ Ἀντιφάνους*)? Cf. p. 178, l. 3. The editor of Ammonius has promised (p. 182) to publish a paper on the new Aristophanes fragment in *Rh.M.*, vol. 110.

p. 133. 1 See also above, p. 128. 6, and Addenda.

p. 143. 2 Dionysius Salvagnius, Ov. *Ib.* Comment. (first published 1633), Proleg. pp. 12 f.

p. 143. 5 Apollon. Rh. *Argonautica* ed. G. M. Mooney (1912) reprinted 1964.

p. 149. 5 The suggestion of R. Führer, ἀλλ' ἤ γ' ἄκρα κατ' ἀνδρῶν κράατα, would avoid this difficulty; it would avoid also the elided form ἄκρ' which never occurs in Homer.

p. 150, l. 19 P. Von der Mühll, 'Antiker Historismus in Plutarchs Biographie des Solon', *Klio* 35 (1942) 89 ff., seems to go a little too far in his task of restoring Hermippus' reputation as the biographer of Solon against Leo's grim censure (see above, p. 129. 1; cf. also above, pp. 82 f. about Aristotle on Solon).

p. 151, l. 12 'Rivers'. There is possibly a new reference in a 'Commentary on Choral Lyric', *P.Oxy.* XXXII (1967) 2637 fr. 10, 3 Φιλοστ [ἔφανος ἐν τῷ Περὶ τῶν παραδόξων πο]ταμῶν, as E. Lobel suggested; cf. Athen. VIII 331 D = Philostephan. fr. 20 M.

p. 151. 1 A short reference to Philochorus (*FGrHist* 328), who belongs to the generation before Istros and was one of his principal sources, dropped out by mistake; he was the most learned of all the Attic annalists, and his voluminous works (list of titles Jacoby, loc. cit., p. 242) include writings on archaic and classic poetry (ibid. pp. 232 f.). But to Jacoby's assertion that he was '*the first scholar among the Atthidographers*' (ibid. p. 227 his italics), we must at least reply that antiquarian research is not quite true scholarship as we have defined it in this book (see p. 3 and *passim*).

p. 157, l. 9 *from bottom*. In the Hippocratic *Epidem.* iv. 37 (vol. v, p. 180. 1 Littré) written towards the end of the fifth century B.C. γραμματικός means a teacher of the rudiments.

p. 178, l. 4 Cf. above, p. 128. 6 Addenda.

p. 192. 3 R. Cantarella, 'Il nuovo Menandro', *Rendiconti dell'Istit. Lombard.*, *Classe di Lettere* 93 (1959) 82, and F. Stoessl, *Menander Dyskolos, Kommentar* (1965) 14, even assume that the existence of Aristophanes' edition is proved. Stoessl pays particular attention to the distribution of parts (*passim*, see index, p. 267), and so does Handley (above, p. 191. 6) 44 ff.

p. 192. 8 For Aristophanes on the authenticity of a number of Sophoclean plays see above, p. 128. 6 Addenda.

p. 195. 4 'The dramatic hypotheses from Oxyrhynchus' (of Menandrean plays?) first published by Coles and Barns 1965, are now *P.Oxy.* xxxi (1966) 2534.

p. 197. 3 E. Miller, *Mélanges* 427–34 reprinted in *Lexica Graeca Minora*, selegit K. Latte, disposuit et praefatus est H. Erbse (1965) 273–82 Aristophane de Byzance.

p. 206. 1 J. Cousin, *Études sur Quintilien*, reprinted Amsterdam 1967.

p. 206. 2 Iambl. *Vit. Pythag.* 18. 80 speaking of the *selecti*, says that Pythagoras τοὺς ἐγκριθέντας ὑφ' ἑαυτοῦ διῄρηκε χωρίς . . . ; Plat. in *Rep.* and *Leg.* uses ἐγκρίνειν and ἀποκρίνειν also about literature, cf., e.g., *Rep.* 377 C τοὺς δ' ἐγκριθέντας, sc. μύθους. The grammarians may have borrowed the expression from a philosophical source.

p. 213, l. 16 The name of the Naucratite grammarian (Schol. Gen. Φ 363) Κωμανός is differently spelt and accentuated in our manuscripts; see also my note on Call. fr. 495 and P. M. Fraser, *Cl. Rev.* 67 (1953) 43. It is uncertain whether P. Yale inv. 446 (Pack² no. 2138) can be attributed to him.

p. 215. 4 Erbse repeated the result of his paper on 'Aristarchs Iliasausgaben' in his contribution to *Geschichte der Textüberlieferung* i (1961) 224 f. G. Zuntz contradicted him, successfully I think, in his review *Gnom.* 35 (1963) 3.

p. 215. 6 A good example to illustrate the relation between early Homeric papyri and the critical Alexandrian editions and the so-called vulgate text is Pap. Hamburg 153; see *Griechische Papyri der Hamburger Staats- und Universitätsbibliothek* (1954) 98 with Merkelbach's commentary.

p. 219. 1 Nicanor (1850 and 1875) reprinted 1967.

p. 219. 5 The papyrus *P.Oxy.* 1086 of the first century B.C. is further proof that Alexandrian critics continued to use paraphrases (τὸ ἑξῆς on B 819) for their exegesis, as the vulgate commentators had done in schools for generations (cf. Rutherford, 'Annotation' 336 ff. with further references). As his predecessors had not produced commentaries, it is very likely that Aristarchus set the fashion (see also Call. ii p. lxxviii on paraphrases of ancient scholiasts).

p. 229, l. 10 *from bottom*. The early Ptolemaic Pap. Hib. ii (1955), ed. Turner 193 (*c.* 250 B.C.) preserved in *Z* 4 the reading which Aristarchus, once he had found it, received into his text (Schol. ABT); previously in his ὑπομνήματα he had adopted another reading mentioned with a third variant in the Scholia (see A. Ludwich, *Aristarchs hom. Textkr.* i. 262 f.). He carefully considered the documentary evidence, attested by the early papyrus (cf. above, p. 114, on similar cases in Zenodotus), and in this case his final choice became also the reading of the medieval manuscripts.

p. 230. 7 J. W. Kohl, *De chorizontibus*, Diss. Gießen 1917, contains 'chorizontum fragmenta' with notes on the text; a second part on the general problems was promised but never published.

p. 234. 4 Cf. also Esther V. Hansen 'The Attalids of Pergamon', *Cornell Studies in Classical Philology* 19 (1947) 353–94 Attalid patronage of learning.

p. 242. 1 *P.Oxy* 2389, fr. 9 = *PMG* Alcm. fr. 13 p. 33; ib. fr. 6 = *PMG* Alcm. fr. 1, Schol. B p. 7.

p. 243. 1 If the headings of some writings of Democritus on Μουσικά are correctly registered by Diog. L., he seems to have dealt with euphony in Περὶ καλλοσύνης ἐπέων and in Περὶ εὐφώνων καὶ δυσφώνων γραμμάτων (*Vors.* 68 B 18 a, b). See above p. 42. 3 and cf. Licymn. *Art. script.* B XVI 3 κάλλος δὲ ὀνόματος κτλ.

pp. 246. 5 and 247. 3 Callimachus was fond of describing works of archaic art, but derived his knowledge from literary sources only, see fr. 114 with Add. II (Delian Apollo), fr. 100 (Samian Hera), fr. 197 (Hermes of Ainos).

p. 248. 3 *P.Oxy.* xxxi (1966) 2535; col. ii. 12 φησι Πο[λέμων, proposed by Turner as an alternative to other supplements; Polemo, who wrote about the Athenian acropolis and about epigrams, may be quoted in this commentary on the epigram which is said to have been cut on the bronze quadriga near the Propylaeon on the acropolis (I owe the reference to this possible but uncertain supplement to M. Treu).

p. 252. 2 F. Kühnert, 'Allgemeinbildung und Fachbildung in der Antike', Deutsche Akademie der Wissenschaften zu Berlin, *Schriften der Sektion für Altertumswissenschaft* 30 (1961) 31 f. took note of Menecles.

pp. 272 f. I ought to have mentioned that in a commentary on Alcman, *P.Oxy.* 2390, fr. 2 col. II 5 = *PMG* Alcm. fr. 5 p. 22 a special reading of Tyrannion is referred to: Θέων[καὶ Τ]υραννίων ἀναγιγνώσκου[σι χρυσῶ κατὰ γενικήν; it probably means χρυσῶ πέλας (not the dative χρυσῷ πέλας), and may have been quoted by Theon in one of his many commentaries from a grammatical writing of Tyrannion, who wrote no commentaries, as far as we know.

GENERAL INDEX

* indicates a specially extensive reference

Academy, Plato's school: 65, 97.
— revivified by Arcesilaus: 157.
— delegation to Rome: 246.
— and Peripatos explaining the writings of their own founders: 246.
'Academy Edition' of Plato: 66.
Accadian, see glossaries.
accentuation: 178; cf. Aristophanes Byz.
— in papyri: 180.
— Aristarchus' accentuation: 219.
Adaeus: 248.
Adrastus of Aphrodisias: 60 and Excursus.
adverb, see ἐπίρρημα.
Aeschylus, catalogue of plays: 128.6 Addenda, 129.
— 'slices from the great banquet of Homer': 44.
— *Septem*: 'μεστὸν Ἄρεως' (Gorgias): 46.
— *Supplices* performed after 468 B.C.: 194.
— etymologies, *Ag.* 1485 ff.: 4; *Supplices* 584: 5.
— writing *Eum.* 273–5: 26; *Prom.* 470 f., 788 f.: 26; fr. 530 M. (*Aitnaiai*?): 26.3.
— hypotheses (*Septem, Supplices, Aitnaiai*): 194.
— no evidence for Aristophanes' work on the text: 192.
— Ἀρίσταρχος ἐν ὑπομνήσει Λυκούργου Αἰσχύλου: 222.
— no evidence for Didymus' commentary: 277.
Agatharchides, on poetry: 166.4.
Agathon, and the Sophists: 55.
Alcaeus, one of the nine lyric poets: 205.
— monostrophic songs: 186.
— edition of Aristophanes Byz.: 185.
— edition of Aristarchus: 221.
— v.l. λέπας: χέλυς: 181 f., 185.
— allegory: 5.
— in *P.Oxy.* 2506: 222.
Alcidamas: *50 f., 191.
Alcman, one of the nine lyric poets: 205.
— a Lydian: 220 f., 241.
— *Parthenion* (fr. 1 Page), colometry: 188.
— in *P.Oxy.* 2505: 222.
Alexander Aetolus, one of the tragic Pleiad: 119.
— revised the text of tragedies and satyrplays: 105 ff., 132, 160, 192.
Alexander the Great, φιλόμηρος, text of the *Iliad*: 71.

— empire: 87.
— and Ptolemy I: 95 f.
Alexandria, capital of the Ptolemies: 92 f.
— Satyrus' *On the Demes of Alexandria*: 151.
— birthplace of Apollonius Rhodius, Dionysius Thrax, Philoxenus, and Didymus: 141, 266, 273 f.
— climax of a new cultural movement: 95.
— attracted students: 134.
— scholarship at its height: 171 ff.
— five generations of scholars from Philitas and Zenodotus to Aristarchus: 233, 265.
— ἐγκύκλιος παιδεία: 253.
— and Athens: 99.
— and Cyrene: 123.
— and Pergamum: 237.
— and Rome: 274.
— exiled Alexandrian scholars in other cities: 253.
allegorical interpretation:
— physical, Schol. Υ 67: 10; cf. Pherecydes, Theagenes.
— not used by Sophists: 35; cf. Metrodorus, Antisthenes.
— rejected by Plato, Aristotle, Eratosthenes, Apollodorus: 10, 237, 259.
— not practised by Alexandrian scholars, but by the Stoics, Crates and his pupils, in Pergamum: 140, 167, 237.
— practised by Orphics: 237.
— practised by Neoplatonists: 226; cf. Porphyry.
allegory, Ι 502 ff. Λιταί: 5, 237; cf. Archilochus, Alcaeus.
alphabet, Phoenician origin: 20 ff.
— definitive Greek alphabetical system: 23, 103.
Ammonius, pupil and successor of Aristarchus: 216 f., 254 (?), 273 f.
— treatise(s) on Aristarchus: 216 f.; cf. 215.5.
— Κωμῳδούμενοι: 242.
Anacreon, celebrated by Critias: 54.
— one of the nine lyric poets: 205.
— edition of Zenodotus (?): 118; of Aristophanes Byz. (?): 185; of Aristarchus with interpretations: 221.
— in Didymus' Συμποσιακά: 279.
— fr. 14 Page: 12, 14, 244.
— fr. 63: 117 f.
analogy, cf. anomaly.

Aristonicus (*cont.*):
— disregarded Crates' views: 239.
Aristophanes Com., alphabetical catalogue of his comedies: 129.
— plays edited by Aristophanes Byz. with those of Cratinus and Eupolis: 190.
— one of the selected authors: 204.
— 9 ὑποθέσεις contain διδασκαλίαι: 196.
— commentary of Euphronius on individual plays: 120.
— Aristarchus commented on eight comedies: 224.
— commentary of Didymus: 276.
— dramatic criticism, topic of Old Comedy: 47.
— adopted more topics from contemporary discussions than the phrase of Gorgias on Aeschylus: 48.
— 'Ομήρου γλῶτται (fr. 222 K.): 15, 79.
— *Frogs*, on pre-eminence among the Attic tragedians: 204.
— — problem of the moral leadership of the poets, usefulness and danger of their teaching: 167.
— — passages on criticism taken up by Hellenistic poets (Callimachus, etc.): 137.
Aristophanes of Byzantium: *172 ff.
— succeeded Apollonius Rhodius as librarian: 154.
— use of critical σημεῖα: 178, cf. 173 f.
— use of lectional signs (punctuation and accentuation): 178; cf. 180.
— ψ 296 the 'limit' of the *Odyssey*: 175.
— Aristarchus in his commentary on ψ 296 agreed: 231.1.
— editions of lyric texts: 130.
— objected to Zenodotus' conjecture in Anacreon: 118.
— edition of Pindar; put Pindaric poems into proper order: 183.
— his influence decisive for the terminology of lyric poetry: 183.
— colometry: 187 f.
— work on dramatic poetry: 188 ff.
— successor of Alexander Aetolus in dealing with tragedies and satyr-plays: 160.
— published text of Cratinus, Eupolis, and Aristophanes: 190.
— Aristoph. *Thesm.* 162 coni. Ἀλκαῖος for Ἀχαιός: 189, 276.
— hypotheses of tragedies and comedies: 192 ff.
— edition of Plato (?): 196 f.
— Λέξεις: 197 ff.
— — used Callimachus' comprehensive vocabularies: 135.
— discovered recurrent patterns in the Greek declension (κλίσις): 202 f.

— interest in the spoken language of his own day: 202, 245.
— Πρὸς τοὺς Καλλιμάχου πίνακας: 133; *see also* Addenda (new fragment).
— arranged selective lists of authors: 204 ff.; cf. 278.
— monograph about Athena's shield (?): 208, 285.
— monograph on analogy (?): 208.
— on Homeric εἰδωλοποιία (?): 285.
Aristotle: *65 ff.
— Neoplatonic lives of: 71.
— and Alexander the Great: 96.
— library: 99.
— school: 65.
— attachment to Apollinism: 80.
— manuscripts of, in Theophrastus' library: 273.
— Andronicus' edition arranged according to subjects: 264.
— lists of his writings: 66, 131.
— *Dialogues*: 66.
— Πραγματεῖαι, *Memoranda and Collections*: 66.
— not the founder of scholarship, father of philology, etc.: 67, 272.
— the new poetical school of Callimachus and his followers ostentatiously anti-Aristotelian: 137.
— and Apollonius Rhodius: 143.
— and Eratosthenes: 156.
— and Aristophanes Byz., Περὶ ζῴων: 173.
— is to be read instead of Aristophanes Byz.: 285 f.
— *Iliad* and *Odyssey* as living organisms, works of Homer; first place as epics: 137, 204 f.
— the non-Homeric ('cyclic') epics: 73, 230.
— defender of Homer: 69.
— *Homeric Problems*: 67.
— quotations of Homer: 109.
— Ἀπορήματα Ἀρχιλόχου: 145.
— on Alcman's birthplace: 220, 241.
— Διδασκαλίαι: 81, 132.
— *Poetics*: 75.
— — ch. 20: 76.
— relation of words to things: 75 ff.
— πάθη τῆς λέξεως, modification in form of words: 201.
— four parts of speech: 76 f., 244.
— synonyms: 78.
— writings on politics, Πολιτικά, Πολιτεῖαι: 82.
— antiquarian studies: 83.
— proverbs: 83, 208.
Aristoxenus, quoted minor lyric poets: 205.
— on Ψευδεπιχάρμεια: 265.
Arsinoe II: 92, 100, 123.3, 124.

Callimachus (*cont.*):
— Homeric text (of Zenodotus and others) used in his poems: 139 f.
— lyric cola: 185.
— describing works of archaic art in his poems: 246.5 Addenda.
— *Aetia*, Apollo Delius (fr. 114): 282.
—— aims of poetry: 137 f.
—— *see also* 'Homeric text used in his poems'.
— *Lock of Berenice* (fr. 110): 123 f.
— *Encomion on Sosibius* (fr. 384): 123.
— *Ibis*: 141.
— Πίνακες: 127 ff.
—— alphabetical order: 129; cf. 195.
—— classification of lyric poems: 181.
—— tragic and comic poets: 160.
—— orators: 278.
—— writers on medicine: 152.
—— 'Miscellanea': 131.
—— questions of authenticity: 128.6 and Addenda.
—— two special Pinakes: 131 f., 193.
— books of the scholar besides the Πίνακες: 134.
— the first Onomasticon (?): 135, 197.
— study of language: 198.
— *Against Praxiphanes*: 135 f.
Callinus of Ephesus: 43.
Callisthenes: 71, 80.
Callistratus, earliest (?) pupil of Aristophanes Byz.: 190 f.
— writer of ὑπομνήματα: 210 f.
— on the *Odyssey*: 191.
— on Pindar: 221.
— on Aristophanes: 224.
canon as term for selective list of authors coined by D. Ruhnken: 207; cf. κανών.
— Biblical: 207.
Carneades: 246.
case: grammatical system of cases, *see* πτῶσις.
Castor of Rhodes: Χρονικά: 257.
Catullus, translation of the *Lock of Berenice*: 156.
Chamaeleo, on lyric poets: 181, 221.6, 222.
— on Aeschylus: 281.
chronology, Greek: 51 (Hippias), 79 (Aristotle), 163 (Eratosthenes), 255 (Apollodorus).
Chrysippus of Soloi, Περὶ ἐτυμολογικῶν: 201, 241.
— Περὶ τῆς κατὰ τὰς λέξεις ἀνωμαλίας: 203, 243.
— allegorism: 238.
Cicero, pupil of the rhetor Molon in Rhodes: 266.
— patron of Tyrannion: 272.

— on selected authors and distinction of 'classes': 204, 206.
— *de or.* 1 187, on *ars grammatica*: 268.
— on Aristarchus' name as proverbial: 232.
classici, writers of the first class: 207; cf. ἐγκριθέντες.
clay tablets, Mesopotamian: 18.
Cleanthes, allegorism: 238.
— theory of language: 243.
Clearchus of Soloi, Παροιμίαι: 84.
Cleochares, order of five cases: 13, 244.
Cleopatra: 236.
Collège Royal, a new Μουσεῖον: 119.
colometry: 187 f.
Colophon, birthplace of Antimachus, Hermesianax, and Phoenix: 93.
colophon: 127.
Comanos, Aristarchus Πρὸς Κωμανόν: 213 and Addenda.
Comedy, Attic, dramatic criticism topic of Old Comedy: 47.
—— first effort to distinguish the style of the comic poets: 160.
—— division into periods: 242.
—— Eratosthenes' special theory on the origin: 161.
—— Eratosthenes' interest in the language: 161.
—— Aristophanes Byz., textual criticism and colometry: 189.
—— commentaries of Euphronius and Callistratus: 224.
—— commentaries of Aristarchus: 224.
—— less studied in Pergamum than in Alexandria: 242, 249.
—— Apollodorus' monograph on courtesans: 264.
—— Didymus' compilation of earlier explanations: 276.
Comedy, Doric, Polemo acquainted with: 249.
—— Apollodorus' edition of Epicharmus and monograph on Sophron: 264.
commentary, *see* ὑπόμνημα.
— marginal commentary around the text: 270.3.
Conon, astronomer, and Archimedes and Callimachus: 156.
Corinna: 205 f.
Cos: 92.
Craterus: 248.
Crates of Athens: 243.4.
Crates of Mallos in Pergamum: 235, *238 ff.
— and the library: 235.
— Διορθωτικά: 238 f.
— ῾Ομηρικά: 239.
— Stoic allegorical interpretation of Homer: 238 ff., 259; cf. 140.

Eudoxus, and Eratosthenes: 164 f.
— star catalogue used by Aratus: 121, 152.
Euenus, and the Sophists: 55.
Eumenes I of Pergamum: 234.
Eumenes II of Pergamum: 172, 235, 238, 254.
euphony, in Plato's *Cratylus*: 64.
— in Crates' aesthetical theory: 243.
— in Democritus (?): 243.1.
Euphorion of Chalcis, epic poet: *150.
— librarian of Antiochus the Great: 122.
— Περὶ μελοποιῶν: 183.
— *cantores Euphorionis*: 150.
— attacked by an epigrammatist Crates: 243.
Euphronius, and Aristophanes Byz.: 160, 171, 189.
— and the tragic Pleiad: 160.
— commentary on Aristophanes' *Plut.* and other commentaries: 161, 224; cf. 120.
Eupolis, name quoted by Eratosthenes: 161.
— edition of text by Aristophanes Byz. (?): 190.
— one of the selected authors: 204.
— fr. 304 'books on sale': 27.
Euripides, Satyrus' *Life* of Euripides: 151.
— library and book-knowledge: 29.
— titles and incipit in the *Pinakes*: 129.
— collection of ὑποθέσεις to the complete works: 195.
— Aristarchus' commentary: 223.
— authenticity of the *Rhesus*: 242.
— astronomical passage *Rhes.* 539 ff.: 223, 242.
— *Ion* 504 f. and *Hec.* 1078 ∼ *A* 5 δαῖτα: 111.
— references to writing, fr. 506 N.²: 26; fr. 382 N.²: 30.
– lines criticized in the *Frogs*, fr. 157 sq. N.²: 40.
— etymology of Παλλάς fr. 1009ᵃ Snell: 262.8.
Euripides (not the tragedian), editor of Homer (?): 72.4.
Eurydice, third wife of Ptolemy I: 96.
Eusebius, *Hist. eccl.* v 8. 11 (Alexandrian library): 98.
— Χρονικά, list of Spartan kings: 163.
— *Hist. eccl.* VI 25. 3 on κανών: 207.4.
Eustathius, on *A* 5 v.l. πᾶσι: δαῖτα: 113.
— on ψ 296 as the end of the *Odyssey*: 175.
— excerpts from Aristophanes' Λέξεις: 199 ff.
— and the Homeric Scholia: 219, 240.
— on εἰδωλοποιία: 285.

Faber, Tanaquil: 284.
Fabri, Anna: 284.

Flaubert, Gustave, on the 'ivory tower': 283.
floruit (ἀκμή): 256; cf. γέγονε.
Fouilles de Delphes III 1, no. 400: 80.5.

Galen, on the official copy of the three tragedians: 82, 192.
— and the Pergamene library: 237.
Glaucon: 35.
glossaries, Greek, *see* γλῶσσαι.
— Sumerian–Accadian: 18.
gnomologium (?): 145.
Göttling, K. W.: 271.
Gorgias the Athenian: 45.6.
Gorgias from Leontini: *45 ff.
— pupils: 49 ff.
— rhetorical training: 45.
— new prose style: 46.
— on tragic art and on poetic art in general; its relation to artistic prose: 47 ff., cf. 281.
grammar, *see also* γραμματική and γραμματικοί.
— no separate branch of grammar in the fourth century: 64, 76.
— as special discipline from Aristophanes Byz. to Dionysius Thrax: 203.
— superiority of Pergamenes: 245.
— remained the first of the three literary arts: 253.
— technical grammar the latest achievement of Hellenistic scholarship: 272.
Grote, George: 7.

Haffter, Heinz: 88.1.
harmonics: 53.
Hecataeus of Miletus: 12, 20, 29, 51.7, 247.
Hedylus: 93.
Heliodorus: 189, 196.
Hellanicus of Lesbos: 30, 250, 255.2.
Hephaestio, metrical handbook in the Alexandrian tradition: 185 ff.
Heraclides Ponticus, *Homeric Solutions*: 70.
— On Homer, Hesiod, and Archilochus: 145.
— Περὶ τῶν τριῶν τραγῳδοποιῶν: 204.
— quoting minor lyric poets: 205.
— sent by Plato to Colophon in order to collect Antimachus' poems: 94.
Heraclides Ponticus (the younger), pupil of Didymus: 275.
Heraclitus, on etymology of names: 12.
— against Homer: 42.
— Cratylus represents ideas of Heraclitus on language: 59.
— on punctuating the opening sentence: 179.
[Heraclitus] *Quaest. Homer.*: 5.4, 240.
Hereas: 6.
Hermeias, explained ὀρθοέπεια as κυριολεξία in his commentary on Plat. *Phaedr.*: 280.

Hermesianax of Colophon: *89.
— list of early poets in an elegy: 52, 89.
— and Philitas: 93.
— and Antimachus' *Lyde*: 94.
Hermippus of Smyrna, Περιπατητικός and Καλλιμάχειος, biographical work: *129, 150 and Addenda, 247.
— on Demetrius of Phaleron: 96.
Herodian, on prosody in Cod. Ven. A of the *Iliad*: 214, 219.
[Herodian], Περὶ σχημάτων, definition and examples of polyptoton: 12 f.
Herodicus, pupil of Crates of Mallos, Κωμῳδούμενοι: 242.
— on Polemo as στηλοκόπας: 248.
Herodotus, and the growth of the book (?): 29.
— observations on language: 41.
— on *Iliad* and *Cypria*: 44.
— references in Aristophanes' Λέξεις: 197.
— first commentary by Aristarchus: 224 f.
Herondas, and Sophron: 265.
— Philitas not in the *Dream*: 90.5.
Hesiod, *Op.* 2 f. 'etymology': 4.
— *Op.* proem, its anaphoras and antitheses: 14.
— his date in relation to Homer's date: 164.
— in selective lists of authors: 204 f.
— Aristotle's *Hesiodic questions*: 144.
— favourite with the great poets of the first half of the third century B.C.: 117.
— Zenodotus' edition of the *Theogony*: 117.
— Apollonius Rhodius on Hes. *Theog.*, Ἀσπίς, and 'Ορνιθομαντεία: 144.
— Aristophanes Byz. edited the *Theogony* (Suppl. to *Pinakes*): 177 f.
— — doubted the Hesiodic origin of Χίρωνος 'Υποθῆκαι and Ἀσπίς: 177 f.
— Hesiodic criticism of Aristarchus: 220.
— proems of *Theogony* and *Erga* athetized by Crates: 241.
— Dionysius Thrax on a gloss in Hesiod: 267.
Hipparchus, criticism of Eratosthenes' Γεωγραφικά: 165.
Hippias of Elis, ἀρχαιολογία 'antiquarian lore': 51, 79, 83.
— register of Olympic winners, basis for Greek chronology: 51, 80, 163.
— polymath, but not the inventor of the seven liberal arts: 52 f.
— language and 'music': 53.
— antithesis νόμος—φύσις: 39.3, 53.
— on early poets and philosophers: 52, 84.
— on 'elements' of words (?): 60 f.
Hippias of Thasos, on Homeric textual questions: 45.
Hippocraticum Corpus, φόβος—ἔλεος and

the somatic symptoms mentioned in sophistic and philosophical literature probably derived from 'Hippocratic' writings: 48.3.
— no evidence for ἐμπειρία—τέχνη as formula in 'Hippocratic' literature: 57.
Hipponax, probably quoted in Aristophanes' Λέξεις: 199.
— explanation of a dialectal gloss by Polemo: 248.
— origin of parody according to Polemo: 249.
historians, in selective lists: 206.
— commentaries on historians: 224, 277.
Hittites, cuneiform tablets with words in Hittite, Sumerian, and Accadian: 18.
Homer, his own interpreter: 3 f.
— Attic text (?): 7, 109 f.
— Peisistratean recension: 6 f., 25.
— official copy for the Panathenaic festivals: 110.
— city-editions: 94, 110, 139.
— historical person for every Greek, his date and life: 11, 43, 117, 164.
— regarded as an Athenian: 228, 267.
— Codex Ven. Marc. 454 (A) of the *Iliad* with Scholia: 213 f., 219.
— Codices Ven. Marc. 453 (B), Townl., Genav., etc., of the *Iliad* with exegetical Scholia: 239.
— Codices HM of the *Odyssey* with Scholia: 239 f.
— correct use of Greek language: 42.
— criticism, starting-point of philosophical criticism: 9.
— — scholarly criticism: 105 ff.
— — textual criticism: 215.
— the poet of most of the narrative poems (sixth century B.C.): 11, 43 f.
— the poet of *Iliad*, *Odyssey*, *Margites* (fourth century B.C.): 73.
— only *Iliad* and *Odyssey* Homeric: 117, 204 f.
— and Aeschylus, *see* Aeschylus.
— and Antisthenes: 36.
— and Gorgias: 46.
— and Alcidamas (*Odyssey βίου κάτοπτρον*): 50 f., 191.
— and Plato: 9, 58.
— and Aristotle: 67–73, 137.
— and Antimachus: 94, 117.
— and Zenodotus: 105 ff.
— division of *Iliad* and *Odyssey* into 24 books: 115 f.
— and Aratus: 121 f.
— and Rhianus: 122, 148 f.
— and Callimachus: 137, 139 f.
— and Apollonius Rhodius: 146–8.
— and Eratosthenes: 164, 166, 168 f.

lyric poetry, arrangement in the *Pinakes*: 130.
— editions from Zenodotus to Aristophanes Byz.: 181 ff.
— terms λυρική and μελική ποίησις, λυρικοί (*lyrici*) and μελοποιοί (*melici*): 182 f.
— division of lyric texts into cola by Aristophanes Byz.: 185 f.
— selective list of the nine lyric poets: 205.
— monostrophic and triadic songs: 186.
— modern distinction into monodic and choral lyric: 283; cf. μονῳδία.
— Didymus' monograph on the classification of the various genres: 277.
Lysandreia, festival in Samos: 93.
Lysanias, teacher of Eratosthenes: 146.1, 153.
Lysimachus, one of the *Diadochi*: 93, 234.

Machon, poet, on the parts of comedy: 160.
— teacher of Aristophanes Byz.: 171, 189.
Macrobius, and Apollodorus: 262.
Magas: 123.
Margites: 73 f.
Massilia: 110.
mathematics, as ἐπιστήμη: 64.
medicine, writers on medicine in Callimachus' *Pinakes*: 152.
Melanchthon: 49.
melicus, see lyric poetry.
Menander, *Dyscolus*: 191, 196.
— *Sicyonius*, colophon: 127.
— in Callimachus' *Pinakes*: 129 f.
— and Aristophanes Byz.: 190 ff., 208.
— total number of plays in Apollodorus' Χρονικά: 257.
Menecles of Barca: 252.
Menecrates of Ephesus, teacher of Aratus: 93, 120.
Menedemus, Eretrian philosopher: 119.
metaphors, in Homer, explained by Aristarchus: 232.
Metellus Numidicus: 266.
metricians: 76.
Metrodorus of Lampsacus, pupil of Anaxagoras: 35, 237.
Mimnermus: 89.
Molon: 266.
Mommsen, Theodor: 98.
monosyllables, as prototypes regarded by Philoxenus: 274.
Moschopulus, Apollodorus' theology: 263.
Moschus of Syracuse, *Europa*: 211.
Musaeus: 27, 52.
Muses, name: 62.
— telling the truth (Hesiod, Callimachus): 125.

Museum, Alexandrian: 96 ff.; cf. Μουσεῖον and libraries.
— free fellowship of masters and disciples: 98, 233.
— scholars and scientists, no philosophers: 97, 159.
— no peaceful community: 97, 143.
Museum, Ashmole's: 97.3.
Museum, British, Greek papyri: 82.
— Assyrian tablets: 18.
music, attribution of lyric poems to their musical classes by Apollonius εἰδογράφος: 184.
— loss of musical notation on Greek lyric poetry: 181.
musicians, Lasus of Hermione, Damon the Athenian: 53.

Nemesis of Rhamnus: 247.
Neoptolemus of Parium, and Eratosthenes: 166.
Nicanor, under Hadrian, on punctuation: 180, 214, 219.
Niceratus, rival of Antimachus: 93.
noun, *see* ὄνομα.

obelus, *see* ὀβελός.
Odysseus, etymologies of the name: 4.
Olympic winners, *see* Hippias of Elis; Ὀλυμπιονικῶν ἀναγραφή: 51; Aristotle: 80; Eratosthenes: 163; Apollodorus: 256.
Onasander, librarian: 273.8.
Onesicritus: 71.
Onomastika, vocabularies arranged according to subjects or localities, Callimachus: 135, 197.
— Aristophanes Byz.: 200.
oral composition, of epic poetry: 25.
oral tradition, of interpretations of Zenodotus: 108.
— — of Aristophanes Byz.: 210.
oral transmission, of epic poetry: 25.
orators, Attic, in Callimachus' *Pinakes*: 128, 131.
— — selective lists in Alexandria: 206 f.
— — keener interest in the orators in Pergamum: 242.
— — exegetical writings by Didymus (and his predecessors?): 277 f.
ordo, of selected authors: 204.
oriental background of Greek culture: 17 ff., 103, 126.
Orpheus, heading the series of the earliest poets: 52, 89.
— allegorical commentary on Orpheus' *Cosmogony*: 103.1, 237, 239.
Orphics, and Aristotle (?): 83.

General Index

307

— and Dionysius Thrax: 267 f.
— and Philoxenus: 274.
vases, Attic red-figured, representations of inscribed rolls: 27.
Ventris, Michael: 21.
Vigny, Alfred de: 283.
Villoison, J.-B. de, discovery of the two foremost manuscripts of the *Iliad* in Venice, 1781: 214.

Wilamowitz-Moellendorff, Ulrich von: *Aristoteles und Athen*: 82.
Wolf, F. A., *Prolegomena ad Homerum*, first attempt at a history of the Homeric text and disclosure of the unique historical position of the Homeric poetry: 214 f.
— — paving the way for future analytical efforts: 231.
words, *see also* anomaly, ὄνομα, ῥῆμα.
— relation of words to things: 59, 63, 76, 243.6.
— as δηλώματα: 60.
— origin of words: 63, 79.
writing, oriental: 18 f.
— Semitic: 22 f.
— Mycenaean: 20 f.
— of epic poets: 25.
— a work of art in archaic Greece: 24.
— references to writing and reading in poetry and art of the fifth century B.C.: 25 ff.

Xenocritus of Cos: 92.2.
Xenon, one of the χωρίζοντες: 213.

Xenophanes: 8 f., 42, 58, 69.
Xenophon: 30 f., 225.

Zeno of Kition, and Eratosthenes (?): 154.
— allegorism: 238, 241.
— theory of language: 243.
Zenodotus of Ephesus: *105 ff.
— pupil of Philitas, tutor to Ptolemy II (and Arsinoe?): 92.
— scholarly co-operation with two poets, Alexander Aetolus and Lycophron: 107.
— first librarian of the Museum, succeeded by Apollonius Rhodius: 105, 141.
— and his followers called γραμματικοί: 157.
— first διορθωτής of epic and lyric poetry: 94, 106, 108, 173.
— — Homeric text based on documentary evidence: 114.
— — atheteses: 114, 177, 240.
— invention of the obelus: 115, 178; *see also* σημεῖα.
— Timon alluding to his edition of Homer (?): 98, 139.
— no commentary or monograph: 108, 115.
— Γλῶσσαι, alphab. arranged: 108, 112, 115.
— text of A 4–5: 111 ff., 147 f.
— edition of Hesiod's *Theogony*: 117.
— — lyric poetry: 117 f.
— and Callimachus: 139.
— and Apollonius Rhodius: 141, 147 f.
— and Aristophan. Byz.: 171 f.
Zenodotus Philetaerus: 115.2.
Zeno[dotus], grammarian under Ptolemy IX: 254.
Zoilus of Amphipolis: 70.

INDEX OF GREEK WORDS

ζήτημα: 69 ff., 263; *see also* λύσεις.

ἡμίφωνα: 61, 76.

θαυμάσια, θαύματα: 134 f., 152.
θεοὶ Ἀδελφοί: 123.3.
θεοὶ Εὐεργέται: 123.3.

ἰαμβοποιοί: 182.
ἱστορίαι: 269.

καθηγητής: 154.7.
καιρός: 33.1, 38.
κανών: 207.
κλίσις, 'declension': 202, 243.
κορωνίς, marginal symbol: 176.1, 179, 186.
κρίσις (ποιημάτων): 117, 204, 242, 269; cf. ἐγκρίνειν.
κριτικός: 89, 157, 159, 238, 242.
κυκλικόν, κυκλικῶς, κυκλικώτερον, 'cyclic' as inferior: 227, 229, 230; cf. νεώτεροι.
κύκλος, epic cycle: 44, 73.
κυριολεξία, neoplatonic explanation of ὀρθοέπεια: 280 f.
κῶλον: 187.

λέξεις, words peculiar in form or significance (in contrast to γλῶσσαι, rare and obsolete words); cf. glossaries.
— Aristophanes Byz. *Λέξεις*: 197 ff.
— Didymus *Λέξις κωμική* and *τραγική*: 278.
λέξις, diction: 76.
λεπτός: 137 f.
λόγος, sentence: 37, 75 f., 78.
— speech: 49, 229.2, 244, 269.
— reason (Stoic): 238.
λυρικὴ ποίησις, *see* lyric poetry.
λύσεις: 70, 282; cf. ζητήματα.
λύχνος: 112, 270.3.

μελαννεφής or μελαινεφής: 91.6.
μελικὴ ποίησις or τὰ μελικά, *see* lyric poetry.
μέμβρανα or μεμβρᾶναι: 236.
μεταγράφειν: 189.
μετάνοια: 282.
τὰ μεταξύ: 77.
μεταχαρακτηρισμός: 30.
μετοχή: 269.
μίμησις: 58.
μονῳδία: 282.
Μουσεῖα on Mount Helicon: 155.
Μουσεῖον, 'shrine of the Muses': 50; cf. Museum.

νεώτεροι: 262; cf. κυκλικόν.
νόθοι and νενόθευται: 128.6 Addenda.
νόμος: 34 f., 39.3, 53, 63, 280; cf. φύσις.
νοῦς: 43; cf. ψυχή.

ξενικά (ὀνόματα): 41, 79.
ὀβελός, first critical symbol: 115, 178.
ὄβρια, ὀβρικά (?), ὄβριχα, ὀβρίκαλα: 200 f.
ὀλιγοστιχίη: 89, 137.
'Ολυμπιονικῶν ἀναγραφή, *see* Olympic winners.
'Ομηρίδαι: 11.
ὄνομα, *see also* ῥῆμα, words.
— ὀνόματα one expression for words in Protagoras, etc.: 59.
— γένη ὀνομάτων: 38.
— ὀνόματα—ῥήματα first distinguished by Plato: 59 f.
— — in Aristotle: 76 ff.
— Stoic distinction between ὄνομα, 'proper name', and προσηγορικόν, 'appellative': 224.
— final definition in the *Τέχνη* of Dionysius Thrax (three genders, five case-inflexions): 269.
ὀρθοέπεια: 37, 42, 53, 280.
ὀρθότης: 39 f., 62, 74 f., 205.4.
οὐ σώζεται: 128.6 Addenda.
οὐδέτερον, 'neuter': 245.

πάθη (τῆς λέξεως): 201.
παιδεία, ἀρχαία: 15.
— ἐγκύκλιος: 253.
παίδευσις, παιδεύω: 50, 252.
παραγραφή, παράγραφος: 179.
παρατήρησις: 245.
πείθειν, πειθώ: 59.
Πένταθλος, nickname of Eratosthenes: 170.
Περγαμηνά (or -ναί): 236.
Πίνακες of Callimachus: 127 ff. and *passim*.
— supplement of Aristophanes Byz.: 133, 178, 257.
— Περγαμηνοί: 133, 236.
πίναξ: 52.
πολυϊδρείη: 125.
πολυμαθής: 138.
πολύπτωτον; cf. πτῶσις.
— noun, pronoun: 12 ff.
πολύστιχοι: 115.
πραττόμενοι: 208.
προέκδοσις: 141 f.
προσηγορικόν: 244.
πτῶσις, poets playing on the various forms of the same word: 12 ff.; cf. πολύπτωτον.
— applied to noun and verb: 76 f.
— confined to noun and article; four cases (one ὀρθή, three πλάγιαι): 244.
— five cases (including the vocative): 269.
πύργος ἐλεφάντινος, *see* Ivory tower.

ῥαψῳδία: 269.
ῥαψῳδός: 12.1; cf. rhapsodes.
ῥῆμα, cf. ὄνομα.

INDEX OF PASSAGES DISCUSSED

OTHER TITLES IN THIS HARDBACK REPRINT PROGRAMME FROM SANDPIPER BOOKS LTD (LONDON) AND POWELLS BOOKS (CHICAGO)

ISBN 0–19–	Author	Title
6286409	ANDERSON George K.	The Literature of the Anglo-Saxons
8228813	BARTLETT & MacKAY	Medieval Frontier Societies
8148348	CAMPBELL J.B.	The Emperor and the Roman Army 31 BC to 235 AD
826643X	CHADWICK Henry	Priscillian of Avila
8219393	COWDREY H.E.J.	The Age of Abbot Desiderius
8148992	DAVIES M.	Sophocles Trachiniae
825301X	DOWNER L.	Leges Henrici Primi
8143109	FRAENKEL Edward	Horace
8201540	GOLDBERG P.J.P.	Women, Work and Life Cycle in a Medieval Economy
8266162	HANSON R.P.C.	Saint Patrick
8224354	HARRISS G.L.	King, Parliament and Public Finance in Medieval England to 1369
8581114	HEATH Sir Thomas	Aristarchus of Samos
8140444	HOLLIS A.S.	Callimachus Hecale
8212968	HOLLISTER C. Warren	Anglo-Saxon Military Institutions
8223129	HURNARD Naomi	The King's Pardon for Homicide – before AD 1307
8140401	HUTCHINSON G.O.	Hellenistic Poetry
8142560	JONES A.H.M.	The Greek City
8218354	JONES Michael	Ducal Brittany 1364–1399
8225253	LE PATOUREL John	The Norman Empire
8212720	LENNARD Reginald	Rural England 1086–1135
8148224	LIEBESCHUETZ J.H.W.G.	Continuity and Change in Roman Religion
8141378	LOBEL Edgar & PAGE Sir Denys	Poetarum Lesbiorum Fragmenta
8152442	MAAS P. & TRYPANIS C.A .	Sancti Romani Melodi Cantica
8223447	McFARLANE K.B.	Lancastrian Kings and Lollard Knights
8226578	McFARLANE K.B.	The Nobility of Later Medieval England
8148100	MEIGGS Russell	Roman Ostia
8142641	MILLER J. Innes	The Spice Trade of the Roman Empire
8147813	MOORHEAD John	Theoderic in Italy
8264259	MOORMAN John	A History of the Franciscan Order
8116020	OWEN A.L.	The Famous Druids
8143427	PFEIFFER R.	History of Classical Scholarship (vol 1)
8142277	PICKARD–CAMBRIDGE A.W.	Dithyramb Tragedy and Comedy
8269765	PLATER & WHITE	Grammar of the Vulgate
8213891	PLUMMER Charles	Lives of Irish Saints (2 vols)
820695X	POWICKE Michael	Military Obligation in Medieval England
8269684	POWICKE Sir Maurice	Stephen Langton
821460X	POWICKE Sir Maurice	The Christian Life in the Middle Ages
8225369	PRAWER Joshua	Crusader Institutions
8225571	PRAWER Joshua	The History of The Jews in the Latin Kingdom of Jerusalem
8143249	RABY F.J.E.	A History of Christian Latin Poetry
8143257	RABY F.J.E.	A History of Secular Latin Poetry in the Middle Ages (2 vols)
8214316	RASHDALL & POWICKE	The Universities of Europe in the Middle Ages (3 vols)
8148380	RICKMAN Geoffrey	The Corn Supply of Ancient Rome
8141076	ROSS Sir David	Aristotle: Metaphysics (2 vols)
8141092	ROSS Sir David	Aristotle: Physics
8264178	RUNCIMAN Sir Steven	The Eastern Schism
814833X	SALMON J.B.	Wealthy Corinth
8171587	SALZMAN L.F.	Building in England Down to 1540
8218362	SAYERS Jane E.	Papal Judges Delegate in the Province of Canterbury 1198–1254
8221657	SCHEIN Sylvia	Fideles Crucis
8148135	SHERWIN WHITE A.N.	The Roman Citizenship
8642040	SOUTER Alexander	A Glossary of Later Latin to 600 AD
8222254	SOUTHERN R.W.	Eadmer Life of St. Anselm
8251408	SQUIBB G.	The High Court of Chivalry
8148259	SYME Sir Ronald	History in Ovid
8143273	SYME Sir Ronald	Tacitus (2 vols)
8200951	THOMPSON Sally	Women Religious
8201745	WALKER Simon	The Lancastrian Affinity 1361–1399
8161115	WELLESZ Egon	A History of Byzantine Music and Hymnography
8140185	WEST M.L.	Greek Metre
8141696	WEST M.L.	Hesiod: Theogony
8148542	WEST M.L.	The Orphic Poems
8140053	WEST M.L.	Hesiod: Works & Days
822799X	WHITBY M. & M.	The History of Theophylact Simocatta
8114877	WOOLF Rosemary	The English Religious Lyric in the Middle Ages
8119224	WRIGHT Joseph	Grammar of the Gothic Language